NATIONAL GEOGRAPHIC

TRAVELER

# australia

NATIONAL
GEOGRAPHIC
TRAVELER

# australia

by Roff Martin Smith

National Geographic
Washington, D.C.

# CONTENTS

TRAVELING WITH
EYES OPEN  6

CHARTING YOUR TRIP  8

**History & Culture**  13
Australia Today  14
Food & Drink  24
The Land  26
History of Australia  32
The Arts  56
Flora & Fauna  66

**Sydney**  73
Introduction & Map  74
Sydney Harbour Walk  82
Feature: Cricket  90
Feature: A Sydney-style
New Year's  98

**New South Wales**  101
Introduction & Map  102
Feature: Bushfires  106
Pacific Highway Drive  118

**Australian Capital Territory**  127
Introduction & Map  128
Feature: Anzac Day  134

**Queensland**  137
Introduction & Map  138
Tropic of Capricorn Drive  150
Feature: National Parks  172

**Northern Territory**  181
Introduction & Map  182
Feature: Aboriginal Art  202

**Western Australia**  211
Introduction & Map  212
Feature: Wildflowers  222
Gibb River Road Drive  238

**South Australia**  249
Introduction & Map  250
Feature: Australian Wines  264
Feature: Festival State  272
Stuart Highway Drive  284

**Victoria**  289
Introduction & Map  290
Feature: Melbourne Cup  297
Melbourne Walks  298
Great Ocean Road Drive  310
Feature: Australian Rules Football  318
Feature: Bushrangers  322

**Tasmania**  329
Introduction & Map  330
Huon Valley Drive  338
Feature: Tasmanian Greens  344
Scenic Loop Drive  348
Feature: Trout Fishing  352

**Travelwise**  355
Hotels & Restaurants  367
Shopping  386      Activities  388

INDEX  390      CREDITS  398

**Pages 2–3: The Red Centre near Alice Springs**
**Opposite: Beach shades near Melbourne**

# TRAVELING WITH EYES OPEN

Alert travelers go with a purpose and leave with a benefit. If you travel responsibly, you can help support wildlife conservation, historic preservation, and cultural enrichment in the places you visit. You can enrich your own travel experience as well.

To be a geo-savvy traveler:

- Recognize that your presence has an impact on the places you visit.

- Spend your time and money in ways that sustain local character. (Besides, it's more interesting that way.)

- Value the destination's natural and cultural heritage.

- Respect the local customs and traditions.

- Express appreciation to local people about things you find interesting and unique to the place: its nature and scenery, music and food, historic villages and buildings.

- Vote with your wallet: Support the people who support the place, patronizing businesses that make an effort to celebrate and protect what's special there. Seek out shops, local restaurants, inns, and tour operators who love their home—who love taking care of it and showing it off. Avoid businesses that detract from the character of the place.

- Enrich yourself, taking home memories and stories to tell, knowing that you have contributed to the preservation and enhancement of the destination.

That is the type of travel now called geotourism, defined as "tourism that sustains or enhances the geographical character of a place—its environment, culture, aesthetics, heritage, and the well-being of its residents." To learn more, visit National Geographic's Center for Sustainable Destinations at *www .nationalgeographic.com/travel/sustainable.*

# australia

## ABOUT THE AUTHORS

Originally a New England Yankee, **Roff Smith** has lived most of his adult life in Australia since arriving down under in 1982. He began work as a journalist for the *Sydney Morning Herald* and later for Melbourne's *Sunday Age*. He joined *Time* magazine in 1993, and as an award-winning senior writer he covered stories around Australia and as far afield as New Guinea, French Polynesia, and Antarctica.

In 1996, Smith set off into the Australian outback on a 10,000-mile bicycle trek. The story of his journey appeared as a three-part series in *National Geographic* magazine and is described in more detail in *Cold Beer and Crocodiles: A Bicycle Journey into Australia*, published in 2000 by National Geographic. *Australia: Journey Through a Timeless Land*, another of his books, was also published by National Geographic. His 2004 *National Geographic* story on Australia's national poet, Banjo Paterson, won a North American Travel Journalist's Association award for best feature. Smith now freelances for a number of international magazines and publications, including *National Geographic*.

**Peter Turner** wrote the updates and sidebars for this edition. Australian by birth, journalist by trade, and wanderer by nature, he has worked as an editor, publisher, and journalist in Australia and for newspapers in Indonesia, Thailand, and Brunei. As a travel writer and photographer specializing in Southeast Asia and the South Pacific, he has contributed to newspapers and magazines worldwide and to more than 20 guidebooks.

# Charting Your Trip

Thousands of miles of glorious coastline and beaches, the world's greatest fringing coral reef, unique and varied wildlife, the rugged outback desert landscapes and lifestyles, sophisticated cities, tropical rain forest, and alpine national parks—the question is not so much what to see, but how much of it can you see.

## How to Visit: If You Only Have a Week

Whether you're staying two days or two months, Australia has plenty to offer. But with a whole continent of diverse attractions to choose from, you may find planning your itinerary difficult. Given the great distances that most visitors travel just to get to Australia, the fatigue that comes with jet lag, and the fact that Australia is as large as the continental United States, it's probably best to visit only a few main destinations if your time is short.

If your trip to Australia is limited to one week, concentrate on Sydney, the awe-inspiring Great Barrier Reef, and the massive monolith of Uluru (Ayers Rock) in the Red Centre. Direct flights (Qantas is the main airline with the most extensive routes; *www .qantas.com.au*) make it possible to do the big three in just seven days.

First port of call for most visitors is **Sydney,** on the country's southeast coast. This lively city with a glorious harbor has fine beaches including famous Bondi, interesting historic areas, and scenic icons like Sydney Harbour Bridge and the Opera House.

After a couple days in Sydney, fly north (about three hours) to **Cairns** and take a day cruise on the **Great Barrier Reef.** The reef is everything you ever imagined—amazing giant corals and colorful fish scattered around tropical islands. If you stay in Cairns or **Port Douglas** (40 miles/64 km up the coast) for another day or two, you can rent a car and visit the ancient rain forests of **Daintree National Park,** head up into the lush mountains at **Kuranda** or the **Atherton Tablelands,** or just lie on the northern beaches, all nearby.

From Cairns, a direct three-hour flight takes you to **Uluru,** where you can take a walking tour around the rock with Aboriginal guides and head to the otherworldly rock formations of nearby **Kata Tjuta** (the Olgas).

### If You Have More Time

You'll need at least two weeks (preferably more) to really explore Australia. If you enjoy long road trips, car rental agencies abound throughout the country, though you'll likely want to fly a few legs to make your travels more manageable. Even so, you may not

**An Australian denizen**

have the time to see every region of Australia—here's an itinerary, looping around the country, from which you can pick and choose what interests you most.

**Sydney & Around:** After visiting Sydney, explore the panoramas and walks of the nearby **Blue Mountains** to the west. You could then drive southwest a few hours to reach **Canberra,** the country's planned, spacious capital, and on south another 100 miles (160 km) or so to the **Snowy Mountains,** for skiing in winter or fine hiking in summer.

But most visitors head north from Sydney along the **Pacific Highway** that skirts past the fine surf beaches on the coast. The lush **Hunter Valley wine district** is about 2.5 hours north of Sydney. Of the beach resorts along this coast, **Byron Bay** is a favorite, but great beaches spread all the way into Queensland.

## NOT TO BE MISSED:

Exploring Sydney, one of the world's great harbor cities **73**

Cruising the incredible Great Barrier Reef **160**

The teeming wetlands of Kakadu National Park **188**

Imposing Uluru, "the Rock" in the heart of the outback **204**

The Barossa Valley and its old-world wineries **267**

Driving the stunning Great Ocean Road **310**

Port Arthur, convict hell-hole turned scenic treasure **340**

### Queensland & the Northern Territories:

The state of Queensland, home to the Great Barrier Reef, is the biggest tourist destination in the country. The coastline is glorious and the weather warm to hot year-round. In the south, the **Gold Coast** is a Miami-style strip of hotels, theme parks, and surf beaches that almost merges with the state capital, **Brisbane** (950 miles/590 km from Sydney). Farther north, the **Sunshine Coast** is mercifully less developed and includes the chic resort of **Noosa Heads.** Nearby **Fraser Island** is an interesting oddity—the world's largest sand island covered in rain forest.

Beyond, the Great Barrier Reef stretches north for 1,300 miles (2,100 km). Cairns/ Port Douglas and the resorts of the **Whitsunday Islands** (300 miles/500 km south of Cairns) are the main bases for exploring the reef, but tours operate from towns all along the coast. The coastal range inland has rain forest, much of it protected by national parks.

## Koalas

**Koalas are one of Australia's most popular tourist attractions, but finding koalas in the wild isn't that easy. Zoos and game parks will be your best option. You can also try evening walks through the bushy fringe suburbs of Sydney, Melbourne, or Brisbane, but your chances of encountering a wild koala are much better on Kangaroo Island, off South Australia, or on Victoria's Phillip Island.**

Many visitors then fly west three hours from Cairns, across interior Queensland's vast cattle stations, to the **Northern Territory** in the middle of the country. **Darwin** (2,500 miles/4,000 km from Sydney) is the tropical capital in the north of the territory and the staging point for trips to **Kakadu National Park.** Wetlands, wildlife, waterfalls, and Aboriginal rock art make this park a must-see.

From Darwin, drive south toward the **Red Centre** for gorges, stunning rock outcrops, and desert landscapes. **Katherine Gorge** in **Nitmiluk National Park,** about 150 miles (240 km) south of Darwin, is a chain of gorges carved out of the sandstone plateau by the river. Another 775 miles (1,250 km) farther south, in the center of the country, **Alice Springs** is a desert oasis and base for exploring the gorges of the **MacDonnell Ranges,** the towering **Kings Canyon,** and, of course, Uluru and Kata Tjuta.

**Western Australia:** Alternately, from Darwin you could head southwest into Western Australia and the **Kimberley,** a little-explored but stunning region. Travel via the gravel **Gibb River Road,** one of the great adventure drives, or take the main highway with a detour to the eerie tiger-striped rock formations of **Purnululu National Park.** Both routes reach **Broome** (1,150 miles / 1,860 km from Darwin), an old pearling town turned beach resort.

Western Australia is huge and mostly desert. The coast road from Broome down to the capital, Perth—a 1,400-mile (2,255 km) jaunt—passes beaches, remote towns, and **Ningaloo Reef,** Australia's other stunning barrier reef, with fantastic diving and snorkeling. Farther south, wild dolphins come to play in the shallows at **Monkey Mia.**

Thriving **Perth** (2,450 miles / 3,950 km from Sydney), in the green southwest of the state, is one of the world's most remote cities. On the city's doorstep lies the historic port of **Fremantle,** and a day's drive south brings you to **Margaret River,** a major wine district on a scenic coast. Nearby are the towering karri forests and the old whaling port of **Albany.** From Perth, the main highway heads east through the gold-mining town of **Kalgoorlie** across the **Nullarbor Plain** to Adelaide, a long (1,675 miles / 2,700 km) but classic outback road trip.

**South Australia & Victoria: Adelaide**—870 miles (1,400 km) from Sydney—the city of churches, is the gracious capital of South Australia, ringed by beaches, hills, and wine districts. The nearby **Barossa Valley,** with its old European-style wineries,

## When to Go

Winter (June–August) is the best time to visit Queensland, the Northern Territory, and Western Australia. The weather is balmy and dry, and tourism is at its peak, so book ahead. Temperatures are colder in the southern latitudes, especially in the Australian Alps and inland, where night temperatures can drop below freezing.

The coastal regions come alive in summer (December–February), when temperatures soar and the days are long and ideal for outdoor activities. Prices rise and beach resorts fill up between Christmas and the end of January, Australia's main holiday break. The northern wet season lasts from around October to March and spreads as far as southeast Queensland and northern New South Wales.

Autumn (March–May) is cooler and pleasant in much of the country, while spring (September–November) is similar if a little wetter in the south.

September–October is the best compromise for a major tour of the country.

Aboriginal guides apply traditional face paint at a homestead near the Katherine River.

is a must. The city is also the starting point for **The Ghan,** the classic trans-outback train, which heads north 950 miles (1,540 km) to Alice Springs The **Stuart Highway** also runs north through the desert, passing **Coober Pedy,** the opal-mining town so hot in summer that residents live underground.

East of South Australia lies Victoria, the smallest and greenest of the mainland states. Gold rush wealth flowed through the elegant capital, **Melbourne,** a garden city of grand Victorian-era architecture 1.5 hours by air from Sydney. Verdant mountains, wineries, beaches, and colonies of penguins are just a day trip away from the city. The big draw in Victoria is the **Great Ocean Road,** a stunning coastal drive, to see the **Twelve Apostles,** great shafts of sandstone carved over millions of years by the sea. Other attractions include the historic goldfields towns and fine national parks such as **Wilsons Promontory.**

**Tasmania:** An overnight ferry or short flight away from Melbourne (or a two-hour flight from Sydney), the island of Tasmania is lush and green, with dense wilderness, superb hiking, and intriguing convict history. The island is easy to tour over a few days on a 600-mile (960 km) loop, taking in historic **Stanley,** the untamed western rivers and wilderness, the colonial capital of **Hobart,** and the old penal settlement of **Port Arthur—** before returning to Sydney for your trip home.

## Currency

The unit of currency is the Australia dollar, comprising 100 cents. It was introduced in 1966 when decimal currency replaced pounds, shillings, and pence. Notes come in $5, $10, $20, $50, and $100 denominations and are made of polymer propylene, a tough, colorful, and difficult-to-forge plastic alternative to the old paper notes. Coins in circulation are the silver-colored 5c, 10c, 20c, and multi-sided 50c pieces, and gold-colored $1 and $2 coins. Confusingly, the $2 coin is smaller than the $1.

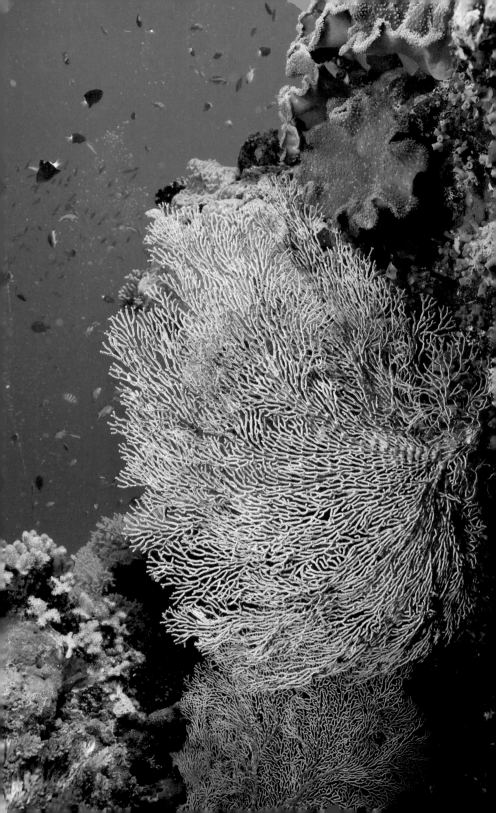

# History & Culture

**Australia Today**   14–23

**Experience: Talkin' Aussie**   19

**Feature: Food & Drink**   24–25

**Experience: Savoring Vegemite**   25

**The Land**   26–31

**Experience: Shopping for Opals**   31

**History of Australia**   32–55

**Experience: Remembering Anzac Day**   50

**The Arts**   56–65

**Flora & Fauna**   66–72

Australia's national flag incorporates the British Union Jack, a visible reminder of the country's heritage. Opposite: Sea fan, Great Barrier Reef

# Australia Today

**Australia has intrigued the rest of the world for more than two centuries, with its fantastic marsupials, noisy and colorful birds, and incredibly vast sweeps of outback landscape. Home to one of the world's oldest human cultures, it is also a geological marvel, famous for the haunting monolith of Uluru, the tropical wetlands of Kakadu, and of course the magnificent Great Barrier Reef.**

Australia is the world's smallest continent and its largest island, a 2.9-million-square-mile (7.5 million sq km) landmass that went walkabout 65 million years ago to peaceful isolation in the South Pacific. Some of the world's most ancient landscapes are found here, dating back more than 3.5 billion years. Living examples of the world's earliest life-forms, stromatolites, can still be found on the rocks along the shore of Hamelin Pool in Western Australia. Primitive cycad palms are found nestled in gorges in the heart of the outback. In 1994, a living specimen of Wollemi pine—an ancient species of tree previously known only through fossils—was found in a dense forest close to Sydney.

Aborigines came here by rafts and little boats from Asian archipelagos more than 50,000 years ago. It was a period known to them as the Dreamtime, a central concept of Aboriginal spirituality. The magical events of that time are celebrated with an elaborate cycle of songs and enshrined in rock paintings and engravings found in thousands of rock shelters and caves throughout the country. The songs and ceremonies provide the basis for Aboriginal law and custom.

> **Thankfully . . . in a world grown small, Australia is still tinged with the romance of distance.**

Fascination has drawn visitors here as tourists for more than 160 years. Charles Darwin remarked on Sydney's high real estate prices when he passed through in 1836. English novelist Anthony Trollope was enamored with the high Victorian architecture in the gold rush town of Ballarat. Mark Twain marveled at Tasmania's paradoxical beauty and its violent, sordid history. The millions of visitors who come through the turnstiles here today come primarily to experience Australia's sunny beach-loving lifestyle: Sydney's Opera House and Bondi Beach, Melbourne's bustling restaurant scene, the theme parks along Queensland's Gold Coast, and Adelaide's festivals and wine country of the Barossa Valley.

Thankfully Australia is far more accessible now than it was in the days of steamers and the Qantas Empire flying boats that made the journey from London to Sydney's Rose Bay in "just" five days. But it is still a marathon journey: about a 15-hour flight nonstop from Los Angeles and 24 hours from London. Jet-lagged travelers step off the plane into another time, another day, and another season. The stars are strange and new, the Australian bush has a bracing, spicy tang, and even in the city a traveler can wake to the raucous screeches of cockatoos. Thankfully, too, in a world grown small, Australia is still tinged with the romance of distance.

**A nation of surfers, Australia boasts several world pros, including top-ranked Taj Burrow.**

## The Real Australia

*In my wild erratic fancy visions come to me of Clancy;*
*Gone a-droving 'down the Cooper' where the western drovers go;*
*As the stock are slowly swinging, Clancy rides behind them singing;*
*For the drover's life has pleasures that the townsfolk never know.*
—From "Clancy of the Overflow" (1889) by Andrew Barton "Banjo" Paterson

Ask any Australian where the real Australia is, and chances are he or she will point you toward a broad immensity of dust and sky, while sketching a verbal portrait of a sun-bronzed stockman with a tattered Akubra hat nudging a mob of sheep along a gum-shaded lane. It's a lovely, picturesque fancy, but the truth of the matter is that the real Australia is a sprawl of terra-cotta roofs in the suburbs. Typical Australians work in offices, pushing bureaucratic pens, as they did even in 1889 when Banjo Paterson wrote his much-loved bush classic, "Clancy of the Overflow."

**The lights of Sydney's glittering skyline reflect in the waters of its famous harbor.**

Ninety percent of Aussies live along the coast, usually within a 30-minute drive of the nearest beach. Aussie children grow up between surf-lifesaving flags, walking sidewalks bright with Lebanese, Chinese, Italian, Greek, and Vietnamese shops, and dodging city traffic. They aspire to a brick veneer home in a comfortable suburb, ideally one with a quarter-acre (0.1 ha) backyard, a Hills Hoist (an ingenious Australian clothesline), and a barbecue. Although real estate is expensive—hideously so in Sydney—Australians have the highest rate of home ownership in the world. Home improvement and gardening shows have long been popular staples of Australian TV, with their cheerfully middle-class do-it-yourself advice, remodeling ideas, and landscaping tips. Cities tend to spread outward rather than upward. Sydney's metropolitan sprawl reaches nearly 80 miles from end to end. There are tough neighborhoods, but few slums. By and large this is a safe country, with a murder rate of 1.9 in 100,000 population—about half that of Switzerland.

**This is an easygoing, generally permissive society, with a belief that everybody ought to have a "fair go" at leading life the way they see fit.**

Australians generally spend their lives close to the neighborhood where they grew up. Although shopping malls, American fast-food chains, and supermarkets are making huge inroads, a lot of shopping in country towns and inner cities is still done the old-fashioned way: People walk along a main street and dip into the butcher's, the baker's, the fishmonger's, and the greengrocer's shops. Or they visit a bustling market, where vendors shout and thrifty shoppers haggle over prices.

This is an easygoing, generally permissive society, with a belief that everybody ought to have a "fair go" at leading life the way they see fit. Despite the presence of more than 160 different nationalities, everyone gets along pretty well. Sydney has a higher percentage of gay people than San Francisco, and its Gay and Lesbian Mardi Gras is the single biggest fete in Australia, attracting crowds of more than 500,000—gay and straight— from around the country and overseas.

Surveys show that three-quarters of Australians believe in God, but on a typical Sunday morning only 20 percent will be in church. Most will be sleeping late, perusing a newspaper, or gearing up to play (or watch) some kind of sport. This is a nation of weekend warriors. Flick on the TV news Saturday or Sunday evening and you'll see a litany of horse-race results, footy or cricket highlights, and sporting news from overseas, often followed by reports of the rescue of a hiker from the bottom of a gorge, a Jet Ski collision, or a fisherman swept off a rock by a "freak" wave of the sort that claimed another life at that very spot the previous week.

Weekends and vacations are the only times most Australians ever actually visit the "bush," the Australian term for countrified landscapes. Even then they are mighty particular where they go. Kakadu, Uluru, the Great Barrier Reef, the Flinders Ranges, and the Snowy Mountains (for skiing) are favorites. Or maybe day trips to the Dandenong Ranges, if one lives in Melbourne, or the Blue Mountains, near Sydney.

Adventurous young Aussies usually head for Europe when they want to do some wandering, but a few go to the gold mines or the remote iron-ore ports on Australia's northwest coast. Adventurous retirees increasingly haul their caravans on a several-month loop around the continent. But by and large, Australians are content to let the bush remain a comfortably distant place, something from the pages of Henry Lawson or Banjo Patterson (see p. 56). Go to a suburban footy match on a rainy winter's day in Melbourne and a lot of the crowd will be wearing Driza-Bones, the traditional stock-man's oilskin. In the parking lot will be gleaming, fully-equipped Land Cruisers with four-wheel-drive, kangaroo (bull) bars, and cellular phones. It's not that Australians don't love the bush; they treasure it deeply—but they prefer to live in the city or suburbs.

## The Outback & Its Stations

When you talk to graziers in the outback and hear their descriptions of bushfires, floods, and droughts, it's easy to understand why most Australians prefer the sub-urbs. The outback landscape is often windswept and hauntingly barren. The nearest town might be 250 miles (400 km) away. The work is tough, dirty, and sometimes hazardous: Wild bulls, rolling tractors, and dirt-bike accidents during livestock mus-ters (Aussie for "round-ups") help make farming the most dangerous occupation in Australia. The workdays are long, frequently stretching from dawn to dusk and beyond. On the other hand, once you've felt the camaraderie and buzz of a woolshed at shearing time, with a team of shearers toiling like demons, family and friends pitching in as roustabouts and sorters while the smallest kids play on the wool bales, it's hard to imagine wanting anything else.

**It's not that Australians don't love the bush; they treasure it deeply —but they prefer to live in the city or suburbs.**

The Australian economy relies on its 130,000 farmers to the tune of about A$20 billion (U.S. $15.5 billion) a year. Australia is the world's second largest exporter of beef and veal behind Brazil, having a national herd of 25 million or so cattle. It is also a major producer of wheat. But traditionally wool is king. Since the first merinos were introduced in 1795, Australia has built up a flock of around 100 million sheep and supplies about 25 percent of the wool used by the world's clothing industry. The Golden Fleece of legend seems a little less remarkable when you consider some of the ultrafine fleeces produced on specialist farms in Victoria and Tasmania. These can literally be worth more than their weight in gold and are used by top-name fashion houses for lightweight suits. Sheep that grow wool this fine (about 11 microns) are cosseted creatures that wear little coats to protect them from burrs and aren't shorn so much as given a haircut.

The rest of the nation's flock is clipped in the spring by roving teams of contract shearers. This is brutally tough and competitive work. Because shearers are paid per fleece, both money and pride rest on getting the highest total possible in a day.

# EXPERIENCE: Talkin' Aussie

Australian English—called Strine, from the clipped pronunciation of "Australian"—is characterized by nasalized vowels, abbreviated words, and the addition of suffixes. Thus "utility" becomes "ute," "tin" becomes "tinnie," and "David" becomes "Davo." Australians also use many words of unique meaning. Common Strine words include:

**agro** – aggressive

**arvo** – afternoon

**barbie** – BBQ

**billabong** – waterhole or cut-off branch of a river

**blowie** – blowfly

**bludger** – work-shy person

**boomer** – large male kangaroo; anything large or successful

**chook** – chicken

**cobber** – see "mate"

**crikey** – exclamation of surprise

**crook** – sick, bad, inferior

**digger** – see "mate"; also, World War I soldier

**drongo** – fool, simpleton

**dunny** – toilet

**fair dinkum** – true, genuine

**galah** – fool; pink and gray parrot

**g'day** – greeting, often accompanied by "mate"

**grog** – alcohol

**hoon** – lout, show-off

**mate** – buddy; general term of familiarity

**milk bar** – convenience store

**no worries** – no problem, good, fine

**ocker** – stereotypical uncultured Australian, redneck (also "yobbo")

**piker** – someone who chickens out or shirks their duty

**ratbag** – rascal, eccentric

**ripper** – great, fantastic

**roo** – kangaroo

**sheila** – woman

**snag** – sausage

**swag** – bed roll used in the outback

**thongs** – flip-flops

**troppo** – mad, as in "gone troppo" (too long in the tropics)

**tucker** – food

**two-up** – traditional coin gambling game

**walkabout** – nomadic wandering, as in "gone walkabout"

**Woop Woop** – remote imaginary place

**yonks** – a long time

A top hand (a "gun shearer" in outback parlance) will regularly shear more than 150 a day, and some do many more. In the 1890s, when shearers used crude scissorlike shears, Big Jackie Howe used to draw crowds to watch him clip 250 a day. In 1892, he sheared a record 321 ewes in a union-prescribed working day of seven hours and forty minutes. This record has never been beaten, at least with hand-powered shears. Modern electric combs have changed things a bit. The world record is held by a New Zealander named Dion King, who sheared 866 lambs in nine hours in 2007.

Anyone who has read or watched *The Thorn Birds* knows that Australian ranches, called stations, can be vast. The world's largest is Anna Creek Cattle Station, owned by the long-established Kidman family, in the South Australian outback. At 7.7 million acres (about 12,030 square miles, 31,000 sq km) it is about the size of Connecticut and Massachusetts combined. The world's biggest sheep property, Commonwealth Hill, also in South Australia, covers just over 4,000 square miles (10,360 sq km) and runs 55,000 sheep. In the vastness of the outback, particularly in the Northern Territory or Western Australia's rugged Kimberley region, a million-acre spread is nothing unusual.

Sometimes the scale can be a little hard for visitors to comprehend. A cattleman who ran 465,000 acres (188,325 ha) in the Great Sandy Desert tells the story of how his immigrant father returned to his home on an island off the coast of Yugoslavia and told relatives how, back in Australia, his son had a ranch bigger than their entire island.

His brother simply shook his head and replied sadly, "We never thought you would come back and lie to us." But in Europe it doesn't take 50 acres (20 ha) to support one cow; out in the Great Sandy Desert, it does.

Station life is unique. A trip to town can mean a daylong trek in a four-wheel-drive vehicle or a gut-churning plane ride bouncing over the thermals rising from the hot outback scrub. Supplies come by road train, monster-size triple-trailer trucks that can be 165 feet (50 m) long and weigh 170 tons. Cattle are mustered by helicopter. Services come by air. Out here, flying priests take the sacrament to stations and outlying Aboriginal communities, and the Royal Flying Doctor Service provides medical care (see sidebar). Station children between the ages of 6 and 11 attend another unique outback institution: the School of the Air. They receive their lessons by hands-free telephone and send in their homework by mail. A couple of times a year, they go into town to meet their teachers and classmates. Older kids go to boarding school.

## Aborigines & Europeans

About 300,000 Aborigines lived in Australia in 1788, when the First Fleet arrived from England and began the uneven contest for control of the continent. Actually, at first it wasn't such a one-way game. The soldiers were starving in this strange new land, and the unwilling convict-settlers were demoralized by being so far from home. The Aborigines were home and feasting on native foods that had sustained them for generations.

Two years after the fleet arrived, an Aboriginal leader named Pemulwuy united some of the local tribes and launched a highly effective guerrilla campaign against the invaders. Colonial authorities posted large rewards for his capture. A convict who grabbed him could get a pardon and passage back to England. Pemulwuy was killed in 1802, his head pickled and sent to England. Pemulwuy's son continued the resistance movement for a few more years until the fragile alliance of tribes broke up.

Because there were so many different, widely scattered tribes—divided by about 400 languages—Aborigines had difficulty putting up a united front against the invaders. The latter

### Flying Doctors

Since 1928, the Royal Flying Doctor Service has tended the sick in remote communities across the outback and on the isolated islands of the Indian Ocean and Great Barrier Reef. From 21 bases around the country, 50 aircraft fly more than 14 million miles per year to tend on-site emergencies, evacuate patients to the hospital, and deliver doctors and nurses to remote clinics. Established by Presbyterian minister Rev. John Flynn, the service relied on radio (now mostly telephone and satellite communications) to advise and attend to medical matters. Until the 1990s, it also linked students in remote areas with teachers via the School of the Air.

A stockman nudges a mob of cattle through the scrub in a timeless scene.

soon gained the upper hand, using rifles against spears. The most appalling instances were in Tasmania, where farmers simply shot Aborigines on sight. In the 1830s, the few who survived were rounded up and shipped off to Flinders Island in Bass Strait.

As settlers with their sheep and cattle pushed deeper into the continent, taking up huge swaths of land, Aborigines were pushed off to ever more remote pockets. Tribes that had nothing in common found themselves scratching a living together on hard-scrabble terrain many days' journey from their ancestral grounds. Ancient traditions and cultures built over 50,000 years crumbled and vanished.

Some Aborigines received food from church missions, others worked on the stations for the new property owners. Although raising animals and riding horses had never been part of their culture, Aborigines quickly became superb stockmen and riders and made it possible for the early stations to prosper. They were generally paid in food and tobacco. By the 1930s, the authorities had settled on a program of assimilation to bring half-caste Aborigines into society. One breathtakingly cruel policy was to rob Aboriginal mothers of their babies and foster them out to white parents. Incredibly, this practice went on until the 1960s. It left a ghastly legacy of broken families and heartbreak, but Aboriginal culture refused to disappear.

The 1960s were a time of radical change all over the world, including even the remotest stretches of the outback. There were sit-ins, a prominent strike by Aborigine stockmen at the Wave Hill Cattle Station in the Northern Territory, and freedom buses traversing Queensland. Aborigines and their supporters set up a tent embassy outside Parliament House in Canberra. A constitutional referendum in 1967 gave Aborigines

Some Aborigines retain their ancestral skills and social structures.

full Australian citizenship and voting rights. An Aboriginal flag was designed that same year. It comprised a red-and-black field with a yellow circle in the center and has come to symbolize the struggle for land rights.

A quarter of a century passed before the next big step was taken in the recognition of Aboriginal rights. In 1992, the Australian High Court issued a landmark ruling that the continent had not, in fact, been *terra nullus* (no-man's-land) when Captain Cook claimed it in 1770, and that the indigenous people had been wrongfully dispossessed. It became known as the Mabo Ruling, after Torres Straits islander Eddie Mabo, who brought the suit against the government, and it meant that Aborigines who could prove continuous contact with their land could claim vacant Crown land.

Later, in 1996, a further landmark High Court ruling, known as the Wik Decision, established that native title could coexist with mining and pastoral leases. The ruling sparked an uproar: Farmers and miners demanded legislation that would protect their rights and investments, and Aborigines insisted that the government obey the rulings of its own High Court. The debate continues, but everyone in Australia realizes that it is no longer possible to ignore the past. The Mabo and Wik rulings have forever changed the relationship between Aborigines and the people who have arrived since 1788, and put the matter of reconciliation near the top of the political agenda.

Politics and High Court rulings notwithstanding, two centuries of "civilization" have been a steep downhill slide for Australia's indigenous people. The mortality and morbidity figures of Aborigines are shocking. Their infant mortality rate is triple that of non-Aboriginal Australians, and, as a killing diet of booze, drug abuse, and fast food takes its toll, their life expectancy is shorter by 15 years. Aborigines suffer from alcoholism, tuberculosis, heart disease, hepatitis, and diabetes at far higher rates than the rest of the population. Their unemployment rate is more than 20 percent, and they are 16 times more likely than the rest of the Australian population to be in prison.

Statistics do not tell the whole story, though. Some Aboriginal communities have preserved their heritage with vibrant arts and music and matchless knowledge of the environment. Many of the strongest communities are also the most remote. Increasingly, these communities are cautiously opening the doors to allow outsiders a glimpse of their ancient culture and to try to build bridges of understanding.

Those bridges, however, suffered a setback in 2007 after the release of a report detailing child sex abuse and chronic alcoholism in remote indigenous communities. The former government ignored the report's recommendations and instead sent in police and troops, a move that outraged Aboriginal communities. The U.N. called the intervention discriminatory, and while the current government promises more consultation, it remains to be seen if any progress will be made beyond rhetoric. ∎

## Boomerangs

**Captain James Cook thought they were wooden swords, and popular myth viewed boomerangs as hunting weapons that somehow magically hit a prey and returned to the thrower. In fact, the returning boomerang was often just a plaything. More effective nonreturning boomerangs were typically used to hunt and cripple fleeing kangaroos and other animals. Boomerang shapes vary widely, and often have one arm longer that the other. They were used for fishing, hunting, fighting, or ceremonial purposes, such as a percussion instrument in dances. Not all were thrown; some were used as weapons in hand-to-hand combat.**

# Food & Drink

There was a time when "Australian cuisine" rated with "Holy War" as one of the English language's great oxymorons. Aussie tucker conjured up visions of Vegemite sandwiches, gristly meat pies, and a stodgy dinner of lamb chops, three watery vegetables, and a bowl of ice cream for dessert. Pizza was regarded as ethnic fare.

Fresh seafood is a staple of Australian cuisine.

Then came the great melting-pot decades of the 1970s and '80s, when immigrants from virtually every country could be found rubbing elbows in jostling city markets. Australians became curious about the herbs, spices, and exotic foods their new neighbors were cooking and found clever ways of adapting them to local fare. Out of this cultural mélange a unique cuisine evolved—a blend of Asian and Mediterranean styles, complemented by some of the world's best wines. These days Australia's top chefs enjoy celebrity status, and the vibrant restaurant and café scene is one of the highlights of a visit down under.

## Asian & Mediterranean Influences

Asia is the dominating influence in this new Australian cuisine, although Australians are doing much more than merely aping Asian styles. With its large Mediterranean population and burgeoning vineyards, Australia has a strong wine culture—something Asia doesn't have. "Consequently we use Asian spices and ingredients in nontraditional ways that really surprise Asian visitors when they come here," says Neil Perry, one of Australia's most famous chefs and owner of Sydney's Rockpool restaurant. "It is very much an Australian style."

It helps, too, that Australia has some of the world's best produce: Sydney's rock oysters, handcrafted cheeses from King Island, olive oil from the Adelaide Hills, venison from Tasmania, corn-fed chickens from Kangaroo Island, and scallops and abalone from Coffin Bay, for example. Australia is a horn of plenty, and it is also largely unpolluted.

## Native Cuisine

In recent years Australia's unique native fare—kangaroo, for instance—has been appearing more frequently on the menu. Once disdained by white Australians as the "bush tucker" that older rural Australians remember eating in the grimmest days of the Depression, kangaroo is now celebrated as a lean and delicate-tasting alternative to beef or lamb at the barbecue. It frequently appears on trendy city menus as well. Although it could be a long time before the Aboriginal delicacies of goanna, Bogong moths, or witchety grubs make regular appearances on the carte du jour, other native foods such as quandong berries, wild bush tomatoes, and wattle seeds are popular enough to be found in supermarkets. They sit beside cardamom, wasabi paste, lemon grass, and tabouli. Australians are settling into their own uniqueness. Anyone for smoked emu prosciutto?

## Dining Out

Australia's restaurant scene is incredibly diverse, from Singaporean-style food stands and Japanese sushi bars to elegant French restaurants and Lebanese takeouts. There are more than 160 nationalities in Australia, and when you walk down some of the crowded "eat streets" you get a sense that every one of them has brought a thriving ethnic cuisine.

Melbourne, Adelaide, and Sydney in particular are famous for their eateries. Lygon Street in Melbourne has Italian restaurants, cafés, and gelaterias, and the inner suburb Richmond is crammed with little hole-in-the-wall Vietnamese eateries. Adelaide has Australia's highest concentration of restaurants, with polyglot Gouger Street alone counting more than 40. Sydney's famed for its seafood, with elegant restaurants at The Rocks and around the harbor, but also has its jumble of Asian, Indian, Italian, Greek, and Lebanese eateries and coffeehouses in inner suburbs such as Newtown, Glebe, and Paddington.

Even the sandwich shops are getting in on the act, serving focaccia sandwiches, Greek salads, and venison meat pies. And what of the traditional Aussie barbecue, with its burned lamb chops, sausages, and potato salad? It is still alive and well and very popular, but now it is just one of hundreds of possibilities.

## EXPERIENCE:
## Savoring Vegemite

Resembling axle grease and with a taste some compare to undiluted beef bouillon, Vegemite is widely regarded as the national food. An Australian icon, despite being manufactured by the U.S. company Kraft, Vegemite is a very popular breakfast spread, usually eaten on buttered toast. Made from brewers yeast, a by-product of the beer industry, it closely resembles the British spread Marmite. Try it at your own peril.

If you give it a try in Australia and find you just can't live without it upon your return home, an order is just a click away at www.aussiecatalog.com, www.about-australic-shop.com, or www.simplyoz.com.

# The Land

With the Pacific Ocean on one side and the Indian Ocean on the other, Australia seems smaller than it actually is. However, at just under 3 million square miles (7.8 million sq km), it is roughly the same size as the continental United States, but with a population of 21 million, barely matching the state of Florida.

## Climate & Terrain

There's a reason for the low head count. With the exception of the fertile crescent along the eastern coast and a green pocket in the southwestern corner, most of this continent is arid and inhospitable scrub, if not outright desert. The ragged northern coasts are fringed with brackish mangrove swamps, inhabited by crocodiles, and lashed by tropical cyclones.

The Northern Territory's haunting sandstone mass of Uluru

Australia is the driest inhabited continent. The tropical north has a wet-dry climate, with winters that are sunny and dry followed by torrid summers, punctuated by monsoon rains and occasional cyclones. Bone-dry central Australia gets scorching heat in the summer and sharp cold winter nights. Most of Australia's rain falls in Tasmania or along the east coast, where rain forests flank the mountains. Perth and Adelaide enjoy a sunny Mediterranean climate. Australia does get snow—dustings have been recorded even in southern Queensland—but only the Snowy Mountains in New South Wales, the Victorian Alps, and the highlands in Tasmania receive regular snowfalls. It is sun that draws most visitors, and the majority enjoy it near the sea. Australia has more than 7,000 named beaches on nearly 37,000 miles (59,533 km) of coastline, and it also has the 1,300-mile-long (2,092 km) Great Barrier Reef.

## How the Land Was Made

Sometime around 65 million years ago, Australia broke away from the vast super-continent called Gondwanaland and began a slow migration to its isolation in the southern Indian and Pacific Oceans. It was an ancient land even then. Some formations along the northwest coast are among the oldest on the planet—well over three billion years old. One series of 3.4-billion-year-old rocks, found near the remote town of Marble Bar, contains stromatolites, primitive blue-green algae that are the oldest known form of life on the planet. Tracks in the red sandstones of Kalbarri National Park, not far off the North West Coastal Highway in Western Australia, mark the first recorded instance of creatures—nightmarish amphibious scorpions 6 feet long (2 m) and aquatic centipedes even longer—stepping onto land about 420 million years ago. A fossil found nearby, of a 6-inch-long (152 mm) cockroach-like animal named *Kalbarria*, is the oldest of its kind by far and could prove to be the ancestor of all insects.

**Around 65 million years ago, Australia broke away . . . and began a slow migration to its isolation in the southern Indian and Pacific Oceans.**

Australia is the flattest continent. Because the landscape is so ancient, wind and rain have had millions of years to erode once-towering mountains to nubs. The most significant mountain range is the Great Dividing Range, which forms a spine along the eastern coastline from Victoria's Grampian Ranges to the rain forest–clad mountains in far northern Queensland. The range contains the highest point on the continent, Mount Kosciuszko (7,317 feet/2,230 m) in New South Wales. West of these mountains, flatness reigns virtually all the way across the continent to the Indian Ocean. Notable exceptions are the Flinders Ranges in South Australia, the craggy mountains of Western Australia's rugged northwest, and those world-famous stony protrusions known as Uluru and Kata Tjuta (aka Ayers Rock and the Olgas, respectively). Although there are occasional fits of seismic activity, most notably a lethal earthquake measuring 5.6 on the Richter scale near the New South Wales town of Newcastle in 1989, the continent is one of the world's most stable landmasses. Geologically speaking, Australia is a finished product.

The largest and only navigable river on the continent is the Murray-Darling, which stretches 1,650 miles (2,655 km) from the Victorian mountains to the coast of South Australia, through four states. It drains one-seventh of the continent's surface and nourishes much of its farmland. Although the outback is harsh and dry, it lies atop the Great Artesian Basin, a huge water source that helps support Australia's millions of sheep and cattle.

## Export Boom

As Australia's manufacturing shifts offshore to labor-cheap Asia and drought and falling world prices hit the farm sector, mining has emerged as the country's economic savior. Even when the global financial crisis of 2008–2009 sent the world into economic meltdown, Australia's growth held, due largely to mining exports to China, Japan, Korea, and India.

Melbourne was once the country's busiest port. Now remote Dampier and Port Hedland take the title, shipping out Western Australia's massive deposits of iron ore and gas, followed by coal ports on the east coast.

Coal is Australia's biggest export, worth U.S. $47 billion a year, followed by iron ore ($30 billion). Gold ($14 billion), gas ($10.5 billion), oil ($9 billion), alumina ($5.5 billion), and aluminum ($4.5 billion) are all major earners. Other important mineral exports are copper, nickel, zinc, lead, manganese, titanium, uranium, and diamonds.

## Mineral Wealth

Fickle geology may have left Australia alone in one of the globe's most isolated corners, and left much of it uninhabitable, but it has more than compensated for these inconveniences by making this land a virtual treasure trove of precious metals, coal, natural gas, diamonds, uranium, and opals.

The fabulous gold rushes in Victoria during the 1850s were the richest Australian strikes in history and changed the face of the country forever. Lured by gold, tens of thousands of prospectors flocked to Australia from all over the world. Some found vast fortunes; most didn't, but often stayed on anyway, establishing families, farms, businesses, and towns. Victoria's gold rushes were followed by rich strikes in Western Australia and Queensland. To this day Australia is one of the world's richest sources of gold, producing nearly 300 tons a year. Much of the gold comes from huge open-cut mines in Western Australia, northern Queensland, and the Northern Territory's remote Tanami Desert. The Super Pit Mine, near the historic Western Australian town of Kalgoorlie, is one of the world's largest mines, producing more than 800,000 ounces (22,676 kg) of gold each year. There are plans to boost that total to more than a million. Tours of the mine are available.

In 1883, at Broken Hill in far western New South Wales, a cowboy stumbled on the world's biggest known lode of silver-lead-zinc, a single chunk of rock containing more than 280 million tons (284 million tonnes) of incredibly rich ore. It spawned Australia's greatest mining companies and is still being mined to this day. The rollicking old mining town, with its gracious two-story pubs and grand Victorian and Italianate

**The Walls of China, a range of wind-sculpted dunes, are a dramatic feature in Mungo National Park, New South Wales.**

architecture, is popular with tourists, artists, and, increasingly, film crews shooting commercials and movies in its clear desert light. Underground mine tours are available, and for claustrophobics who don't wish to go below, there is an excellent mock-up of a mine in town.

Mount Isa, in northwestern Queensland, is another rich deposit of silver, lead, zinc, and copper and has been mined since 1923. Visitors here also have the opportunity to go underground. Untapped as yet is another fabulously rich deposit, known as the Century Zinc deposit. It was discovered about 200 miles (320 km) northwest of Mount Isa.

South Australia made its early fortunes in copper, with rich diggings at Kapunda, at Burra, and around the Yorke Peninsula. More recently, the giant Olympic Dam Mine in the state's desert outback has been found to have such enormous reserves of copper and uranium that mining could continue for hundreds of years. Again, tourists have the opportunity to inspect this mine, if they care to take the detour off the Stuart Highway on the drive from Adelaide to Alice Springs.

Coober Pedy, which is on the Stuart Highway and about eight hours' drive north of Adelaide (528 miles/850 km), accounts for almost 85 percent of the world's opals. Roadside shops sell opals, tours of the diggings can be arranged, and, if you have the time and the inclination to do some digging yourself, a miner's permit is readily obtained.

> **Western Australia is perhaps the world's richest mineralized zone, with vast reserves of gold, nickel, and mineral sands.**

Western Australia is perhaps the world's richest mineralized zone, with vast reserves of gold, nickel, and mineral sands. The iron-rich Pilbara makes Australia one of the largest exporters of iron ore. The Argyle Diamond Mine in the state's remote Kimberley region is the biggest in the world. It produces about 30 million carats a year, more than one-third of the planet's total production, including almost all of its ultrarare pink diamonds, which can fetch a cool million dollars a carat in the trading rooms in Antwerp. Tours of this remote, highly security-conscious operation can be arranged in the town of Kununurra, about 120 miles (192 km) north of the mine.

The seabed off the Western Australian coast is the habitat for countless numbers

Fog rises from the rain forest in Daintree National Park in Queensland.

# EXPERIENCE: Shopping for Opals

Australia's fiery opals are lovely and make wonderful souvenirs, but buying them in Coober Pedy (Australia's opal capital; see pp. 280–281) or city jewelry shops requires care. You need to know what you are looking for.

Opal is made of delicate layers of silica that refract light like a prism and give the stone its distinctive sparkle. Like other gems, opals are valued by their size, the strength and brilliance of their color, and their clarity. Flaws or cracks in a stone detract from its value. The brighter and clearer the stone, the higher the value.

Black and crystal opals are the rarest and most valuable, followed by semiblack opals. Milky opals, although still pretty, are the least valuable because they lack that special dark fire.

Shape is also very important. There are three categories of opal. A "cabochon" is a solid, domed piece of opal that is the most valuable shape. A less valuable "doublet" is a thin wafer of opal against a dark background, while a "triplet" has a quartz lens as well and is the least expensive.

Unless you know opals very well, avoid deals with any kippered old characters you might meet down at the pub, however colorful such a transaction may seem. Stick to reputable dealers, shop around, and ask a lot of questions.

Coober Pedy has plenty of spots to buy opals. In Sydney, try **National Opal Collection** (60 Pitt St., tel (02) 9251 1599), which stocks opal jewelry as well as loose opals, and **Opal Fields** (190 George St., The Rocks, tel (02) 9247 6800), which offers opals for sale and also has a museum of opal fossils and specimens. See Travelwise, p. 385, for more information.

---

of pearl-bearing oysters. The historic pearling port of Broome, now a popular resort, is the hub of a modern pearling industry now worth about A$200 million (U.S. $175 million) a year. Beneath the turquoise waters of the Timor Sea, off Australia's remote northwest coast, are sandstone formations containing billions, possibly trillions, of cubic feet of natural gas.

The craggy mountain ranges of Western Australia's isolated Pilbara region, about 1,000 miles (1,600 km) north of Perth, contain some of the world's largest iron mines, at Mount Newman, Tom Price, and Paraburdoo. They turn out 120 million tons of high-grade iron ore each year. The ore is loaded into the world's longest freight trains, up to a mile (1.6 km) in length, and are hauled almost 300 miles (480 km) to the wharves at Port Hedland and Karratha. As with almost all of Australia's great mining projects, these operations can be visited, although they are too remote for tourists on a time budget.

New South Wales and Queensland have vast seams of coal, not only of high quality but also conveniently close to the coast, helping make Australia the world's largest exporter of coal.

Off the coast of Western Australia, the giant North West Shelf venture accounts for more than 40 percent of the county's oil and gas production. There are zinc, gold, tin, and copper deposits in Tasmania. Some of the world's richest deposits of bauxite (source of aluminum) lie near Weipa on the Gulf of Carpentaria side of Queensland's Cape York Peninsula, only a few miles away from where the first Dutch ship made landfall and whose captain dismissed the continent as barren. ■

# History of Australia

The first Australians arrived at least 50,000 years ago—some say as far back as 120,000 years—coming south from Asia in one of prehistory's great migrations. They came on foot and in small boats, making a series of short hops. Because the sea level was as much as 400 feet (122 m) lower than it is today, it was possible to walk across the Torres Strait from New Guinea to Australia.

Nobody knows why these people came. Restlessness or famine may have driven them; perhaps they were pushed out by stronger tribes to the north. Over thousands of years several more migrations occurred, the last one about 5,000 years ago. At least two types of people made the journey: a very heavily framed people

Aboriginal rock paintings at Obiri Rock in Arnhem Land

anthropologists call "Robust," and a slender race called "Gracile" Today's Aborigines are descendants of the Gracile people.

They scattered themselves widely around the unpeopled continent, which in those days contained such bizarre creatures as giant kangaroos up to 10 feet (3 m) tall and rhinoceros-size wombats. Archaeologists have found 40,000-year-old campsites near Melbourne's Tullamarine Airport, stone tools dating from 45,000 years ago in the Nepean Valley outside Sydney, and skeletal remains 35,000 years old in a cave as far south as Hobart. (In those days it was possible also to walk from today's mainland Australia to Tasmania without getting your feet wet.) At Lake Mungo National Park in far western New South Wales, anthropologists discovered the cremated remains of a woman 35,000 years old, the world's earliest known cremation. Much of what we know about these early Australians comes from

> **The first Australians arrived at least 50,000 years ago . . . coming south from Asia in one of prehistory's great migrations.**

stone tools, campsite remains, and rock art. Some of these sacred sites, burial grounds, and rock-art galleries are off-limits to non-Aborigines, but there are many thousands of rock art murals, particularly in Kakadu and the Cape York Peninsula in the north, that are open to tourists, often with the benefit of an Aboriginal guide.

About 8,000 years ago, the Earth began to warm. As the ice sheets melted, sea levels began to rise, and the broad plains where many generations of Aborigines had camped and hunted became shallow seas—the Gulf of Carpentaria, Torres Strait, and Bass Strait.

Vast galleries of rock art in Kakadu National Park in the Northern Territory and remote locations in the rugged Kimberley appear to tell the story of those days. Desert scenes give way to coastal ones filled with trees. Dancing figures yield to people brandishing spears. Perhaps these scenes represent conflict as lowlanders were pushed by the rising waters onto their high-ground neighbors' territory. When the water stopped rising and Australia assumed its present shape, the Aborigines were locked away on their island, hardly to be disturbed until a hot summer day in 1788 when a fleet of 11 English ships—now known as the First Fleet—sailed into Botany Bay. The first recorded words spoken by an Aboriginal to a white man were *"Warra Warra!"* or "Go away!"

## Early Navigators

Australia's "discovery" by Capt. James Cook in 1770, its stolidly British-to-the-bootstraps past, and the Union Jack on the flag make it easy to overlook

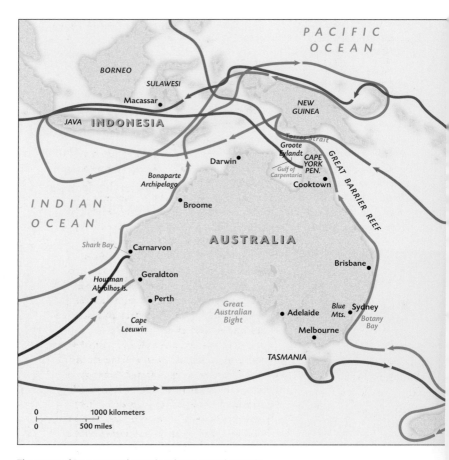

**The routes of European traders and explorers around Australia**

the fact that the English were relative latecomers when it came to exploring the antipodes. Others were here first, although they left behind only scattered artifacts, shipwrecks, and place-names.

Look at a modern map of Australia and you can read which Europeans unveiled the continent. Tasmania, Western Australia's Cape Leeuwin, and Queensland's Groote Island are all Dutch names from the 17th century, when the continent was known as New Holland. The Northern Territory's Bonaparte Archipelago and South Australia's Fleurieu Peninsula were christened by the French. Western Australia's Houtman Abrolhos Islands, the site of early shipwrecks, is a corruption of the Portuguese phrase for "keep your eyes open." Torres Strait, which separates the tip of Queensland's Cape York from Papua New Guinea, is named for the Spaniard Luis Torres, who sailed this narrow stretch of sea in 1607 and somehow missed sighting the continent.

That is the story of this continent's earliest European history: a 3-million-square-mile (7.8 million sq km) landmass in the emptiest quarter of the South Pacific found and

| | | |
|---|---|---|
| ▬▬ | "Duyfken" | 1606 Dutch |
| ▬▬ | Torres | 1607 Spanish |
| ▬▬ | "Eendracht" | 1616 Dutch |
| ▬▬ | "Batavia" | 1629 Dutch |
| ▬▬ | Tasman | 1642 Dutch |
| ▬▬ | Dampier | 1699 British |
| ▬▬ | Cook | 1768-71 British |

FIJI
ISLANDS

NEW
ZEALAND

charted by a series of accidents, chance landings, missed opportunities, and coincidences.

## The Great South Land

People have wondered about Australia for centuries. The ancient Greek geographer Ptolemy speculated about the existence of a great southern land, believing the weight of such a continent was necessary to balance the globe. Early Arab merchants may have pulled into Australian waters in the 13th century when they were spreading the word of Islam through Indonesia. Chinese and Malay ships may also have come here around the same time, fishing for trepang, or sea slugs, a delicacy in the markets of Canton. Fishermen from Macassar, on the Indonesian island of Sulawesi, are known to have come here since the early 16th century, catching boatloads of trepang, which they boiled and then smoked on shore while waiting for the southerly winds that would carry them back home.

Although no records exist to prove it, the Portuguese could well have been the first Europeans to visit Australia, sometime in the late 15th or early 16th century. By 1516, the Portuguese had established a stronghold on the island of Timor, less than 300 miles (480 km) from the Australian coastline. From there they traded throughout the Indonesian archipelago, buying pepper, nutmeg, and sandalwood and spreading the Catholic faith. It seems inconceivable that fortune-seeking Portuguese sea captains did not venture south. They would have known the legends of the Great South Land and heard tales from the Macassar fishermen who had been there. If their curiosity did not bring them, the fickle weather must have done so. For three months a year—generally from January through March—the monsoons blow strongly from the north. Sooner or later a Timor-bound ship would have been blown off course to within sight of the Australian coast. Tantalizing clues include a 15th-century-style brass cannon found near Broome, on the northwest coast of Australia, and the Dieppe Maps.

The Dieppe Maps are believed to have been copied from Portuguese sources in 1536 and suggest that the Portuguese were acquainted with Australia's eastern seaboard. It remains a matter of debate whether the lines on the map were based on exploration or were a lucky coincidence for a cartographer who sketched

> [For Europeans, Australia was] found and charted by a series of accidents, chance landings, . . . and coincidences.

in the mythical Great South Land. The original map and notes were destroyed when a great earthquake struck Lisbon in 1755.

The honor of the first undisputed European sighting of the continent goes to the Dutch. In 1606, Willem Jansz sailed the *Duyfken* (meaning "Dove") from Java, entered the Gulf of Carpentaria, and landed on the western shore of the Cape York Peninsula. Like all employees of the Dutch East India Company, Jansz hoped for ivory, silks, and spices, but found instead shimmering, heat-warped horizons, a parched coast, and "wild, cruel black savages." He left unimpressed, having lost several of his men to the Aborigines. His experience set the pattern for the Dutch contact with Australia: brief landings and hurried departures.

The directors of the Dutch East India Company disapproved of idle exploration. They wanted a clear potential for profit before committing company funds or ships. From early reports, at least, that seemed to rule out the Great South Land, or New Holland as the Dutch had taken to calling it. Nonetheless, this same brusque efficiency was ultimately responsible for their mapping much of the western two-thirds of the coast.

Company navigators had discovered that the quickest way to reach Java was to sail into the Roaring Forties, south of Africa, ride the strong west winds of those latitudes across the Indian Ocean, and then turn north and sail to Indonesia. But storms and powerful westerlies often drove ships too far, too fast, and onto the west Australian coast.

The first of these was Dirk Hartog's ship, the *Eendracht,* which in 1616 landed near Shark Bay, about halfway up the coast. Hartog nailed a pewter plate to a tree to mark the occasion. (The plate was taken as a souvenir by another Dutch seaman, Willem de Vlamingh, who landed in 1697. He, in turn, left a plate of his own that was taken a century later by an errant French explorer.)

Plenty of others followed suit. In 1627 one captain badly overshot his cue to head for Java and found himself sailing near the cliffs flanking the Great Australian Bight, more than 1,000 miles (1,600 km) off course.

Two years later another ship, the *Batavia,* was wrecked off the Houtman Abrolhos

## Captain Cook

Born in Yorkshire of humble origins, James Cook (1728–1779) found his sea legs as a merchant navy apprentice before joining the Royal Navy and rising through the ranks during the Seven Years' War in North America.

In Tahiti, after observing the transit of the planet Venus for the Royal Society in 1769, Cook read his secret Admiralty instructions to search for Terra Australis Incognita. Although he never found the mythical great southern land, he charted New Zealand and Australia's east coast on his epic voyage before returning to England a hero two years later.

Two more Pacific expeditions (1772–1775 and 1776–1779) cemented Cook's place as the greatest British explorer. He was hailed as an enlightened leader, a man of science, and chronicler of Pacific cultures. However, judgment deserted him in 1779, when he tried to abduct the King of Hawaii in a dispute over a stolen dinghy and was stabbed to death.

Popularly hailed as the discoverer of Australia, Cook is honored with monuments and place-names across the country. Cook's Cottage, his parents' home, now lies in Melbourne, where it is a popular tourist attraction.

Islands, near present-day Geraldton, Western Australia. While its captain, François Pelseart, took a few men in an open boat to Java to summon aid, the crew he left behind mutinied and murdered 125 of their shipmates and passengers. They planned to seize any rescue ship and embark on careers as pirates. Instead, Pelseart returned in force, rounded them up, and meted out savage justice. Two of the younger mutineers were spared hanging but were abandoned as castaways, earning them the dubious distinction of being Australia's first convict exiles. Their fate is unknown.

Captain Cook claimed Possession Island, northern Queensland, for Britain in 1770.

The directors of the Dutch East India Company decided to give New Holland another chance, although the only things reported by their captains were cliffs, desolate coasts, and the smoke of Aborigines' campfires. In 1642, they sent Abel Tasman to sail around the continent. He sailed the wild coastline of Tasmania (which he christened Van Diemen's Land, after the Dutch East Indies governor-general, Anthony Van Diemen), discovered the coast of New Zealand, and went on to the Fiji Islands. Tasman's voyage may rank among the great sea adventures of all time, but the directors were unimpressed. They wanted spices, busting markets, gold, or at least a few willing souls to save. In 1644, they sent Tasman back again, but when he returned with more tales of waves crashing on cliffs, scrubby forests, and savages, they had had enough. For the next century Australia was largely left alone by the Dutch, undisturbed except for the occasional East Indies–bound ship driven by storms onto the west coast.

English buccaneer and explorer William Dampier arrived in 1688 and again in 1699, with the notion of using New Holland as a staging-post cum watering-hole for English ships in the Pacific. He landed on the cheerless, treeless, sun-blasted coast of northwest Australia, and like the Dutch before him, went away shaking his head.

Local boys play cricket on the island of Tasmania, near the ruins of notorious Port Arthur prison.

### Voyage of the *Endeavour*

In 1768, the British Admiralty and the Royal Society decided to send an expedition to Tahiti to record the transit of Venus across the face of the sun. As the transit would occur on the morning of June 3, 1769, and wouldn't happen again for another 105 years, this was a once-in-a-lifetime opportunity. A distinguished 41-year-old Royal Navy lieutenant named James Cook (see sidebar p. 36) was selected to captain the ship, a 368-ton (374 tonnes) barque called *Endeavour*. Cook was a proud, stern man with a strong sense of duty and an equally strong sense of fair play, who had advanced on merit alone. Leading the scientific party was 25-year-old Joseph Banks—soon to be Sir Joseph Banks—an extremely wealthy young man, educated at Harrow, Eton, and Oxford and already on his way to becoming the preeminent botanist in England. Onto this crowded ship he brought

his Swedish colleague Daniel Solander, artists Sydney Parkinson and Alexander Buchan, and four assistants. The ship sailed out of Plymouth on August 25, 1768, bound for the southern tip of South America and then across the Pacific. They were to record the transit of Venus, explore the South Pacific, and investigate the fabled great southern continent. In size and scope, the *Endeavour's* expedition was the 18th-century equivalent of a moon shot.

After wrapping up their astronomical business in Tahiti, the expedition spent six months charting the coast of New Zealand. From there they turned toward the unknown east coast of New Holland. On April 19, 1770, they sighted land that is not far from the present-day border of New South Wales and Victoria. After sailing up the coast, they turned into a large bay and dropped anchor. Here they encountered so many new species of plants, ferns, herbs, shrubs, and trees never before seen by European eyes that Cook decided to name the place Botany Bay. They also found rich black soils, lush meadows, and rushing creeks. The *Endeavour* continued up the coast of Australia, running aground on the Great Barrier Reef, but filling in the blank parts of the map. After repairing the *Endeavour* near present-day Cooktown, Cook claimed the eastern half of the continent in the name of George III and called it New South Wales.

## Convict Colony

Despite all Captain Cook's efforts, Australia might still have been left alone had it not been for events taking place on the other side of the planet. Britain's 13 American colonies declared their independence on July 4, 1776, which meant that England could no longer ship convicts to Georgia, Virginia, and the Carolinas. A backlog of prisoners built up at the rate of about a thousand a year. In 1779, Sir Joseph Banks suggested that the Crown consider sending the prison riffraff to colonize Botany Bay. The idea drew a skeptical response. Dispatching shiploads of felons halfway around the world to New South Wales seemed an expensive way to clean out prisons. But French ambitions in the Pacific provided the government in London with a good reason to act. With America gone, England had to focus on its colonies to the east. The age-old enemy France was busily widening its sphere, establishing ports in Madagascar, combing the Indian Ocean,

> **[In 1770, Capt. James Cook] claimed the eastern half of the continent in the name of George III and called it New South Wales.**

and sailing along the coast of Australia. A British colony in Botany Bay could be a useful foothold. The timing was impeccable: Shortly after the First Fleet landed at Botany Bay, two French ships, captained by the Comte de la Perouse, just happened to drop by.

## The First Fleet

What in America was a fine piece of rhetoric to inscribe at the base of the Statue of Liberty was harsh fact down under: This nation was literally settled by huddled masses yearning to breathe free. Who wouldn't be yearning to breathe free after spending eight months chained in a stinking hold of a ship? But along with the relief at taking that first breath of fresh air and blinking in the dazzling Australian sunshine came the terror of the unknown and the grim certainty that life here was going to be rough.

On January 18, 1788, a flotilla of 11 ships, known as the First Fleet, arrived in Botany Bay. It carried 778 convicts—men, women, and children as young as nine—and 250 soldiers and colonial administrators under the command of Capt. Arthur Phillip, who became the first governor of New South Wales.

A quick look around was enough to tell the newcomers that they had no chance of establishing a settlement at Botany Bay. Cook had visited in autumn, when rains had freshened the place up, but this was summer and Botany Bay was anything but green

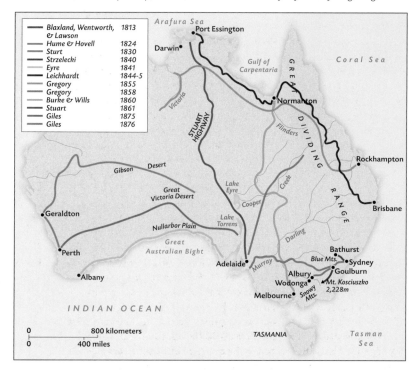

| | |
|---|---|
| Blaxland, Wentworth, & Lawson | 1813 |
| Hume & Hovell | 1824 |
| Sturt | 1830 |
| Strzelecki | 1840 |
| Eyre | 1841 |
| Leichhardt | 1844-5 |
| Gregory | 1855 |
| Gregory | 1858 |
| Burke & Wills | 1860 |
| Stuart | 1861 |
| Giles | 1875 |
| Giles | 1876 |

The routes of Australia's inland explorers slowly filled in the center of the map.

and lush. The creeks were dry, the bay was exposed, and rich meadows described by Cook were just scrub shimmering in blinding white heat. The fleet sailed 12 miles (19 km) north along the coast, between two sandstone heads that Cook had sighted but not entered. In it they discovered "the finest harbour in the world in which a thousand ships of the line may ride with the most perfect security," as Phillip put it to Lord Sydney, for whom he named the new settlement. The date was January 26, known now as Australia Day. Phillip then dispatched a ship to claim Norfolk Island, establishing an English presence and penal colony there.

Times were tough. The little colony was racked with hunger and scurvy. The soil was thin, the seed wheat had gone moldy at sea, the livestock wandered off or died. Many of the prisoners were products of London's slums and knew nothing of farming. Others were too old, ill, or weakened by the voyage to perform much work. A ship had to be sent to Cape Town, the nearest port, for emergency supplies. The Aborigines made their feelings known by spearing Phillip in the shoulder, an act that stunned the governor, who had apparently never considered that the colonists were trespassing.

> **Most [convicts] were petty criminals . . . although the Irish Rebellion of 1798 provided a few genuine political prisoners.**

As time passed and no supplies arrived from England, more and more convicts were shifted to Norfolk Island, where the soil was better and more fish could be caught. In 1791, the Second Fleet arrived and struggling Sydney Town began to gain its feet.

Who were the convicts? Novels such as *For the Term of His Natural Life* by Marcus Clarke (1874), an Australian classic, often portray early convicts as innocent victims who were wrongly convicted, political prisoners, or starving wretches who had stolen a cabbage to feed their children. Most, in fact, were petty criminals who had committed the kinds of crimes that might draw jail time today—or juvenile hall. Theft was the most common charge and most of the convicts were from the English slums—not Ireland, although the Irish Rebellion of 1798 provided a few genuine political prisoners.

About half drew sentences of seven years, although given the distance and cost of returning to England, transportation to Australia generally meant a life term. Skilled, lucky, wealthy, or well-behaved prisoners earned their ticket-of-leave early and were granted farms or were able to set up small businesses. Others did hard time. Floggings, leg irons, and soul-breaking work regimes were routine. Punishments were meted out with breathtaking severity—sometimes up to 300 lashes at a time, enough to leave backbones and shoulder blades exposed. Medical treatment was a dousing with a bucket of saltwater. Hard cases were sent to Norfolk Island, Van Diemen's Land (Tasmania), or Moreton Bay (Brisbane), where conditions were horrific. Weighted down with irons so tight the flesh was rubbed off their bones, working 16-hour days in the rain on short rations, and infested with lice and disease, convicts were known to commit murder simply so they could be hanged and released from misery.

Escape was fairly easy in Australia. The trouble was, there was no place to go. Some convicts headed toward the Blue Mountains, in the misguided belief that China was only a few days' hike beyond the horizon. For the most part, those who managed to get away then starved to death, died of exposure or fell to Aborigines' spears. Some resorted to cannibalism, killing and eating their fellow absconders. Others talked their way onto Nantucket whalers that passed this way, although that was rarely a good bargain. Some Yankee whaling captains were even more brutal than the prison guards.

One woman, Mary Bryant, led an escape party north along the coast in a boat. They reached Indonesia before they were recaptured and taken back to England. Her heroism touched a chord in England. She and her group were pardoned, and she returned to her native Cornwall.

**For generations . . . convict blood was a stain on the family tree. These days it is a point of pride.**

With the exception of South Australia, all of Australia's states were founded on convict labor. Transportation ended in 1868; in all, about 160,000 were sent to Australia. For generations afterward, convict blood was a stain on the family tree. These days it is a point of pride. Having an ancestor on the First Fleet—either convict or guard—has the cachet of being a *Mayflower* descendant in Boston.

### Settlement

Bengal rum was the currency of early Sydney, which by the early 1800s had the reputation of being one of the roughest ports anywhere on the Pacific. Most of the moneymaking enterprises in the colony were controlled by a military mafia known as the Rum Corps, named for the monopoly they held on that vital commodity. Alcoholism was rampant. Many officials were corrupt or incompetent or both, conducting business in a rummy fog. Convicts were effectively slaves, working for an elite group of profiteers and landowners, who kept them pliant with rum or the cat-o'-nine-tails.

In all, New South Wales did not have the kind of atmosphere that would induce decent men and women to migrate there, which was what this embryonic society needed to transform itself from a bawdy penal colony to a prosperous settlement. It needed a governor who knew how to run a tight ship, and the man selected was Capt. William Bligh, whose crew on the *Bounty* had so famously mutinied. He was dispatched to Sydney with a brief to clean up the place. Captain Bligh wasn't the lash-crazed disciplinarian of popular legend, though. He arrived in Sydney sympathetic to the little guys and sided with them against the Rum Corps. But the Rum Corps' members were army men and well entrenched. He was navy and a newcomer. On January 26, 1808, the 20th anniversary of the founding of the colony, Bligh suffered the second mutiny of his career. For the next two years, New South Wales was run by the army. Then a new governor arrived—a reform-minded Scot named Lachlan Macquarie. He broke the power of the

Rum Corps and established the first banks and the colony's own currency. He promoted expeditions across the Blue Mountains and began a series of public works and town planning projects for the fledgling colony. Macquarie even offered a name for the place, telling his masters in London of his plans to explore "the coasts of the Continent of Australia which I hope will be the name given to this country in the future."

## Inland Explorers

In the early 19th century, mapmakers could sketch at least a rough outline of Australia. Matthew Flinders and George Bass had proved in 1799 that Tasmania was an island, not a long Florida-like peninsula, and between 1801 and 1803 they circumnavigated the continent. But what lay inside this 3-million-square-mile (7.8 million sq km) mass was anybody's guess.

"South Brisbane from the North Shore, Moreton Bay, Australia" (1868) by Thomas Baines

Although settlements had been established at Sydney and in Van Diemen's Land, nobody had ventured inland other than a handful of escaped convicts. There were hopes of an inland sea and hints of mineral wealth. One escaped convict stumbled upon a coal outcrop north of Sydney, and by the mid-1790s, the colony was already exporting small cargoes of coal to India. The first major barrier was a range called the Blue Mountains, steep hills about 3,000 feet (915 m) high just west of Sydney. Today this is a vacation area less than two hours from the city, but two centuries ago the mountains were formidable, forest-cloaked obstacles to progress. Several attempts were made to breach them before Gregory Blaxland, William Wentworth, and William Lawson finally succeeded in 1813.

> Today [the Blue Mountains range] is a vacation area . . . but two centuries ago [they] were formidable, forest-cloaked obstacles to progress.

After a route was opened up through the mountains, settlers soon followed, spilling out into the flat, open grazing land beyond. In 1815, the town of Bathurst was founded 130 miles (209 km) west of Sydney, and exploration started in earnest. In 1824, explorers Hamilton Hume and William Hovell probed the Snowy Mountains to the south and chanced upon the Murray River near present-day Albury-Wodonga. The sight of the river flowing west, seemingly into the middle of the continent, rekindled dreams of an inland sea and a fertile heartland. Those hopes were dashed in 1830 when Charles Sturt followed the river more than a 1,000 miles (1,600 km) through the outback to its bitter end, a large brackish lake on South Australia's coastline. In 1840, a Polish count, Paul Edmund de Strzelecki, climbed the continent's highest mountain, the 7,310-foot (2,228 m) peak he named for Polish freedom fighter Gen. Tadeusz Kosciuszko.

**The Desert Center:** Early expeditions sketched in the southeastern corner of the continent, but vast empty reaches still awaited explorers. Edward Eyre was the first of these, crossing the continent east to west through the Nullarbor Plain in 1841. This 800-mile-wide (1,287 km) stretch of scabby earth was a brutal introduction to Australia's interior. Eyre and one of his Aborigine guides, Wylie, survived. They stumbled into Albany, Western Australia, after four months. Less fortunate was Ludwig Leichhardt, a Prussian-born immigrant, who, after crossing 3,000 miles (4,800 km) of outback between Brisbane and what is now Darwin, vanished without a trace while attempting to cross Australia's Red Centre in 1848. In 1855, Augustus Gregory successfully crossed from the Victoria River country in the Northern Territory, around the Gulf of Carpentaria, and south to Brisbane. Three years later, he and his brother Francis trekked across Queensland to learn what had happened to Leichhardt. The German's fate remained a mystery, but the brothers found a passage through the glaring salt lakes and on to Adelaide.

**Burke and Wills:** Australia's most famous and elaborate inland expedition left Melbourne on a midwinter's day in 1860. Robert O'Hara Burke and William John Wills led the expedition, and the government financed it lavishly in the hope that it would discover rich pastoral lands to the north. The goal was the Gulf of

Carpentaria, more than 2,500 miles (4,000 km) away. At a spot called Cooper Creek in the South Australian outback, the party divided. Four of the group remained as a sort of base camp, while Burke and Wills and two associates, John King and Charles Grey, pressed on, traveling light and fast and impatient for glory.

They reached the gulf in February—in the peak of summer heat, when the temperatures may soar to more than 120°F (50°C) and the monsoon rains had soaked the crocodile-infested wetlands. Their progress on the final push to the coast was slow.

They began retracing their footsteps immediately, but the clock was running down. Grey died and the three survivors pressed on, weak and dazed, through the desert, traveling by moonlight, eventually throwing away most of their supplies in a frantic bid to get back to base camp. Burke, Wills, and King arrived seven hours too late. They found a message carved into a giant coolabah tree instructing them to dig for a cache of supplies their colleagues had left on the off chance they returned. They discovered the supplies but lacked the strength to push on to Melbourne. The expedition's two celebrated leaders perished. King was nursed back to health by passing Aborigines. The famous "Dig Tree" still stands and can be seen by expeditions traveling on the Strzecki Track.

**Stuart & Other Explorers:** At around the same time, a tough Scot named John McDouall Stuart was trying to complete his own crossing of the continent. He had traveled north from Adelaide bound for near where Darwin is today, but disease, hostile Aborigines, and unbearable heat had held him back. He finally reached the Arafura Sea on July 24, 1862. Burke and Wills had performed the first south-to-north trek, but Stuart managed the more difficult feat of returning. Even so, he barely survived, staggering back blind and hardly able to stand. His journey marked the apex of inland exploration and resolved the matter of an inland lake: There was none. It also established a route that would be followed fairly closely in 1872 by the telegraph line and later the Stuart Highway, the trucking lifeline between Adelaide and Darwin.

Expeditions struggled through the Western Australian deserts in the 1870s. Ernest Giles explored the Great Victorian Desert in 1875 and the Gibson Desert the following year, the latter named for his partner, Alfred Gibson, who died on the journey. Giles's two expeditions were the last gasps of Australia's heroic age of exploration. By the 1880s, most of the interior had been explored, although some isolated pockets still remained untouched for another 50 years. As recently as the 1930s, clans of desert Aborigines were still leading a traditional lifestyle, as they had for 50,000 years.

### Burke & Wills

Of all the explorers of Australia, Burke and Wills are the most fêted, despite the disastrous end to their expedition. Although Irish-born Robert O'Hara Burke lacked exploration experience, he was chosen as leader, and massive funds backed the expedition. Camels were imported from India and four Indian camel drivers joined the party of 19 men, 26 camels, 23 horses, 6 wagons, and 20 tons (18 tonnes) of supplies, enough for two years.

A crowd of 15,000 gathered in Melbourne on August 20, 1860, to bid farewell to the explorers they expected to bring glory to the colony. When news of the expedition's failure came back (one newspaper called it "one prolonged blunder throughout"), a Commission of Enquiry issued a scathing report but applauded the bravery of Burke and Wills, who were given state funerals.

## Gold

Gold was the single biggest force in Australia's transformation from a clutter of struggling settlements on the rim of the world into one of Britain's most prosperous colonies. The first real gold rush began in May 1851 after a prospector named Edward Hargraves found gold at Ophir, near Bathurst, New South Wales, and bragged about it. Almost overnight a tent city of more than a thousand diggers sprang up in the mud, and thousands more fortune seekers from around Australia quit their jobs and raced for the diggings. The human stampede was so big that employers in Melbourne, alarmed at the sudden loss of workers and envious at New South Wales's sudden prosperity, offered a reward for anybody who succeeded in finding gold close to their city.

They didn't have long to wait. Within weeks gold was discovered at Clunes, and then came the fabulous finds around Ballarat. Gold seemed to be everywhere in Victoria. Before the end of the year, people made enormously rich finds at Castlemaine and Bendigo, and 20,000 prospectors were scouring the hills looking for more. Word quickly spread overseas, and soon Chinese, English, Irish, and Americans were pouring into Australia at a rate of 90,000 a year.

**Eureka Stockade:** Anybody could do it. For the first time in Australia's history, the common man had a shot at serious wealth. There were no big mining companies, just small operators. To try to keep control of events, the authorities imposed a stiff tax of 30 shillings a month ($7.50, a sizeable sum at that time) on prospectors, whether they were successful or not. Resentment at this tax smoldered in the camps and finally boiled over in November 1854 in an uprising at Eureka Stockade, a hastily built fort near the Irish diggings just east of Ballarat. This was the closest thing Australia ever had to outright civil war.

> **Gold was the single biggest force in Australia's transformation . . . into one of Britain's most prosperous colonies.**

Prospectors were already simmering over the murder of one of their number because the authorities had discharged the hotelkeeper whom they believed was responsible. The volatile mix of gold diggers included German and Italian revolutionaries, Irish Republicans, and hot-tempered Americans. At a rally they burned their licenses, proclaimed their defiance of the law, and set up a barricade. They raised a flag—a white Southern Cross on a blue field (notably without the Union Jack). The government responded savagely and on December 3 crushed the rebellion. The 10-minute fight left 6 soldiers and as many as 30 miners dead. A number

"Australian Gold Diggings," circa 1855, by Edwin Stocqueler (1829–circa 1880)

of miners were arrested and charged with high treason. Melbourne juries, however, refused to convict. In the political fallout after the Eureka Stockade fight, miners won many of the rights they had campaigned for: the abolition of the hated licenses and the right to vote and run for office. The following year their leader, Peter Lalor, who had lost an arm in the battle, was elected to Parliament.

To this day the Eureka Stockade flag remains a symbol of defiance to overbearing authority, and a spacious new museum dedicated to the uprising and the early life of Ballarat stands on the site of the battle. The prodigious wealth pouring in from the gold diggings quickly transformed muddy shantytowns into elegant cities, with gardens, wide streets, mansions, and grand public buildings. Victoria's gold rushes were the biggest, but the 1860s and '70s brought finds in New South Wales, at Forbes and Young. Queensland had the white quartz reefs of Gympie, then the rich beds of Charters

Australians waded into history and a hail of bullets at Gallipoli, Turkey, on April 25, 1915.

Towers, Palmer River, and Cape York. Prospectors went on to Pine Creek in the Northern Territory, and by the 1880s, Halls Creek in the Kimberley, the remote northwest. Prospectors scrambled for the Pilbara, then the Murchison field and Western Australia's Southern Cross. The last of the huge gold strikes was at Coolgardie and Kalgoorlie in the 1890s. Most of the sites are marked, and the towns' ornate goldfield-style architecture, which characterized the optimism and wealth, are monuments to these early days.

## Federation

On New Year's Day, 1901, a crowd gathered in Sydney's Centennial Park to witness the birth of a nation: the Commonwealth of Australia. Until then, the continent had been a patchwork of colonies, each of which stubbornly set its own time zone, issued its own postage stamps, and imposed confiscatory customs duties on goods crossing its borders. There was little cooperation, only competition. Colonies could not even agree on which railway gauge to use, a "mental paralysis" that dumbfounded humorist Mark Twain when he swung through this part of the world in 1895.

After years of painstaking diplomacy, with the help of compromises and nudged along by a particularly destructive drought and recession, the colonies agreed to federate in 1901. The new constitution, thrashed out in a second-floor suite in Melbourne's Windsor Hotel, was not exactly a radical piece of legislation. Queen Victoria and her successors would remain head of state, the Crown's local representative would still be a regally appointed governor-general, and Britain's parliamentary style of government would prevail. In fact, the British parliament could still override any legislation passed in the Australian parliament, and for legal matters the final court of appeal would be the Privy Council in London. In essence Mother England's six Australian colonies had simply agreed to cease their sibling rivalry. Edmund Barton, a Sydney lawyer, became the first prime minister. He put aside whatever native New South Wales parochialism he may have harbored and moved to rival Melbourne, which was to be the capital until a neutral city could be agreed upon. The six states (the present states, less the Northern Territory, which was a part of New South Wales) remained powerful, but shared a vision: Australia would be stable, white, prosperous, white, protected by trade tariffs and social welfare legislation—and white. One of the first laws they passed was to restrict Asian immigration, the beginning of the infamous White Australia policy that lasted until the late 1960s. As Australia's second prime minister, Alfred Deakin, put it in a remarkably candid moment: "It is not the bad qualities but the good qualities of these alien races that make them dangerous to us. It is their inexhaustible energy, their power of applying themselves to new tasks, their endurance, and their low standard of living that make them such competitors." And so would-be migrants from Asia had to take a literacy test, in any European language the immigration officer cared to name. Gaelic was a favorite. Not surprisingly, few passed.

Because nobody could agree on which city should be the capital, the fledgling government decided to create one from scratch. In 1909, they settled on a bit of pastureland on the Monaro Tablelands, about 200 miles (320 km) southwest of Sydney. Two years later, the New South Wales government ceded the 9,650-square-mile (25,000 sq km) parcel of land to the federal government. Chicago architect Walter Burley-Griffin was selected to design the city; it would be called Canberra, from an Aboriginal word meaning either "meeting place" or "women's breasts," depending on who is doing the telling.

## World War I & Gallipoli

After a good deal of bureaucratic haggling and compromise, Australia achieved nationhood by a stroke of the royal pen. There had been no death-or-glory freedom fighters, no midnight rides by a Paul Revere, no Bunker Hill battle to forge a unifying national myth in blood. But Australia didn't have long to wait.

On New Year's Day, 1901, a crowd gathered in Sydney's Centennial Park to witness the birth of a nation: the Commonwealth of Australia. Until then, the continent had been a patchwork of colonies.

In August 1914, Britain went to war with Germany, which meant that Australia, as part of the British Empire, was at war also. In a frenzy of patriotism, more than 20,000 Aussies enlisted in the first two months, eager for bold overseas adventure. They got it starting at 4:30 a.m. on April 25, 1915, on a cliff-lined coast in Turkey, near a town called Gallipoli. Winston Churchill, who was then First Lord of the Admiralty, had decided to open a new front by taking the Dardanelles and ordered a multinational force to attack from the sea. The Turks directed withering fire onto the beaches. For the next eight months the allied troops clung onto the exposed beachhead.

Both sides saw desperate fighting and horrific carnage. Although Australians had fought for Britain in the Sudan campaign and in the Boer War, this was the first time

## EXPERIENCE: Remembering Anzac Day

The first Anzac Day march took place a couple of years after World War I ended, and the occasion grew in stature with the passing of the years. The motto for the day is "Lest We Forget." Ceremonies all over the country begin before dawn with a solemn religious service—always well attended despite the cold early hour—that progresses into a parade.

If the word "parade" makes you think of floats and fire trucks on the Fourth of July, think again. There are a few martial bands, but mostly you see row after row of war veterans in Sunday suits and regimental ties, wearing their war medals and marching in step with their battalions. Crowds gather on the sidewalks, waving flags and calling out their thanks. It can be a haunting spectacle. Sometimes the only sound is the rasp of shoe leather

and the clinking of hundreds of campaign medals. Later the gray-haired vets will gather at the local pubs, drink, and remember.

The dawn ceremonies that start off Anzac Day are held at war memorials across the country. Well-known services are at the **Australian War Memorial** in Canberra, the **Shrine** in Melbourne, and the **Cenotaph** in Sydney's Martin Place. The service is generally only for veterans and invited dignitaries, but

in recent years, veterans' families have been encouraged to attend. The same applies to the march, but anyone is welcome to join the spectators who line the streets. Newspapers print march gathering points and routes, and the **Returned Services League** (www.rsl.org.au) is instrumental in organizing marches. Other details can be found on government defense and war veteran websites: www.dva.gov.au, www.awm.gov.au, and www .defence.gov.au.

they had fought as Australians. Australia's national myths were born at Gallipoli, out of courage, mateship, and the understated heroics of men such as Simpson, who with his donkey braved the deadly open ground to retrieve those who had been wounded, until he himself was killed by a sniper. In all, 8,587 men from the Australian and New Zealand Army Corps (ANZAC) were killed. The French, English, Indians, and especially the Turks suffered far greater losses at Gallipoli, something Australians often overlook in their patriotic fervor on Anzac Day (April 25). They also tend to overlook Australia's much greater losses in France, at the Somme (23,000) and Ypres (38,000).

### World War II

World War II marked a turning point in Australia's view of the world. "Without inhibitions of any kind, I make it quite clear that Australia looks to America, free of any pangs as to our traditional links or kinship with the United Kingdom," said John Curtin, Australia's prime minister, after Singapore fell to the Japanese in February 1942. Japanese planes began bombing Darwin that same month and Broome in March.

Australia was faced with the very real possibility of a Japanese invasion. For the United States, Australia offered a last-chance Pacific foothold near Asia. Three months later a combined U.S. and Australian naval force stopped the Japanese fleet in the Battle of the Coral Sea. Australian slouch-hatted infantry soldiers then had to fight a brutal guerrilla war in the Papua New Guinea Highlands to save Australia's colonial outpost at Port Moresby. Its fall would have given the Japanese a springboard into mainland Australia.

Although the Japanese came within 30 miles (48 km) of the town, the Australians fought a gritty hand-to-hand, yard-by-yard campaign and pushed them back to the island's north coast. They were assisted by Papua New Guinea inhabitants, who became known as the Fuzzy Wuzzy Angels. In Thailand, thousands of Australian prisoners of war died of abuse, starvation, and disease while being forced to build the infamous Burma Railway (the railroad of the film *Bridge on the River Kwai*). Others were saved by the

In the 1950s and '60s, more than two million New Australians arrived at steamship terminals.

Started as a service to safeguard swimmers, surf rescue quickly became a sport.

unflagging efforts of "Weary" Dunlop, their fellow prisoner and an army surgeon who became a symbol of Australia's unflinching yet soft-spoken style of heroism.

## New Australians

After World War II, Australia went through enormous changes. When the government launched one of the greatest migration programs of the 20th century, more than two million immigrants poured into the country. According to the census of 1947, about 98 percent of Australians were Anglo-Saxon. Now "New Australians" were coming in from all over war-ravaged Europe—Italy, Germany, Yugoslavia, Greece, and the Baltic countries. As long as they were white, the government would underwrite the cost of their passage. A berth on one of the liners could be had for as little as ten English pounds (A$23 at the current exchange rate).

The newcomers settled in with surprisingly little friction. For one thing, plenty of jobs could be had all around in those prosperous postwar years, so nobody felt cheated. Factories were sprouting up, steel mills and coal mines were busy, and the government was spending big money on major public works such as the Snowy Mountains Hydroelectric Scheme, an enormous project. There were also thousands of new suburban houses to build for this booming population. The country positively oozed good health and high spirits. Bronzed Aussie tennis players won at Wimbledon, and the nation's swimmers were the finest in the world. When the Olympics came to Melbourne in 1956, the home team walked off with 35 medals—an unheard-of success for such a small population.

The age was also an artless one. Australians wince today when they see old newsreel footage and hear the narrator's cheerfully jingoistic, sexist, and racist observations. Blokes were blokes, and the women stayed home. Aborigines were not citizens and could not vote until 1967. For all the influx of other peoples after the war, Australia remained culturally a stodgy pocket of the British Empire.

## Time for Change

It wasn't all sunny isolation. Always obliging to its allies, Canberra signed up for the Korean War and conflicts in Malaya and Borneo. It let Britain use a patch of South Australian desert to test atomic bombs and allowed the United States to set up spy-satellite monitoring posts around the continent. In 1962, Australia followed the U.S. into Vietnam. But as the body bags came back—Australia lost about 500 lives in Vietnam—a vocal antiwar movement sprang up. In Australia, as elsewhere, the late sixties blossomed into a time of liberalization, questioning, and protest. Australia was changing rapidly. A charismatic, bushy-browed giant named Gough Whitlam emerged to lead the Australian Labor Party to victory in 1972 with the slogan "It's time." The time brought health-care reforms, free college education, the formal end of the White Australia policy, widespread new social programs, and increased support for the arts. Like Camelot of the U.S., the Australian version lasted about three years, ending abruptly in November 1973, although with considerably less brutality. Whitlam's administration could not pass through parliament the spending

> After World War II, Australia went through enormous changes. . . . "New Australians" were coming in from all over war-ravaged Europe.

legislation necessary to keep the government running. On November 11, the governor-general, Sir John Kerr, exercised a rarely used and highly controversial prerogative: He sacked the Whitlam government and declared a general election. Conspiracy theorists have dined out on it ever since. Was it a coup d'état? Was the CIA involved? What really happened? The only thing beyond dispute is that four weeks later Whitlam lost the election in a landslide, and Malcolm Fraser, an equally physically towering but very conservative sheep grazier from Victoria, became Australia's next prime minister.

## Pacific Rim & Republic

Alarm clocks rang all over Australia at four o'clock one morning in September 1983, and a sleepy nation got out of bed to watch live TV coverage of a yacht race on the other side of the world. Australians held their collective breath while their yacht, *Australia II,* knifed through the waters of Narragansett Bay in Rhode Island. An American yacht was bobbing somewhere astern. A horn blared. The race was over. Australia had won the America's Cup.

Back in Sydney, people danced in the streets, free beer flowed in the pubs, and Bob Hawke, the new Labor prime minister, crowed on national TV that any boss who didn't give his workers this historic day off was "a bum." For Australians this was more than a great sporting triumph. It was a catharsis, dispelling lingering doubts about whether their remote country, with its tiny, fiercely blue-collar population and convict roots, could make it in the glamour leagues. For many it seemed to kick-start the roaring eighties. A confident, outward-looking Australia strode onto the world stage as a player in its own right, not as England's wild colonial cousin.

It was the time of the global bull market, and Australia dealt itself in with alacrity. The dollar was floated on the world exchange, trade barriers were lowered, and foreign banks were allowed to set up shop in Australia. Meanwhile Australians headed overseas, buying 20th Century Fox, the London *Times,* and the national telephone company in Chile. *Crocodile Dundee,* Foster's lager, and "tossing another shrimp on the barbie" became part of the world's vernacular.

The clock could not be turned back. In 1988, as the country started its third century since colonization, Australians began to ask themselves questions about who they were and where they belonged in the world. After 200 years of being distracted by links to Europe, they suddenly realized they had box seats where it seemed the economic action was going to be in the 21st century—Asia. They began to think of themselves in Asian terms, rather than as a far-flung corner of England.

### Poms

Pom or Pommy is a slang term for British, as in "thrash the Poms," a common cry when British cricket or rugby teams tour. Akin to Limey, it is primarily used as a good-hearted gibe, though many Brits regard Pom as derogatory, reflecting the love-hate relationship between Australians and the British. Because Australia was first settled by exiled convicts and then waves of British migrants, many Australians identified themselves as British subjects well into the 1950s, despite being scorned as uncouth colonials. Broad postwar migration strengthened a divergent national identity, but strong ties, with a hint of resentment, linger. The origins of the word are disputed, though Pom most likely comes from pomegranate, early Australian rhyming slang for immigrant.

Asian countries already devoured the majority of Australia's exports, Asian immigration flourished, and an Australian initiative drove the founding of the Asian-Pacific Economic Cooperation Forum. The Labor government exhorted Australians to look East and promoted multiculturalism to break down the barriers of xenophobia, but out in the broad sunny suburbs of the cities, disquiet grew at this rapid shift in the national identity.

Promising an end to political correctness, the conservative government of John Howard came to power and changed the political landscape over the next decade, taking a harder line against refugees, unions, Aborigines, and welfare. At the same time,

"Tinnies" or "stubbies" of beer quench the thirst at the William Creek hotel, near Oodnadatta.

it turned away from multiculturalism and reaffirmed traditional ties to the U.S. and Britain, even though many Australians questioned why the Union Jack was still on the flag and the English monarch on the currency. Opinion polls suggested the majority of Australians favored a republic, but a 1999 referendum to dump the Queen was defeated when republicans split the vote by bickering over the best model for a republic.

Although the cultural focus swung away from Asia, trade was unstoppable. The China boom drove a resurgent Australian economy into the 21st century, as the country scrambled to dig up and ship out coal, iron ore, and other highly profitable minerals.

Going forward, a prosperous Australia brims with optimism and an independent spirit. A new government with a Mandarin-fluent leader promises a new direction, including confronting some of the ugly truths about the plight of Aborigines. One of Prime Minister Kevin Rudd's first initiatives was to stand before the parliament and issue a national apology for the "grief, suffering and loss" of the Aboriginal people. ■

# The Arts

Anyone who still thinks that Australians are simply sports-mad Philistines should consider that touring art exhibitions regularly attract more than 500,000 visitors. Or they could listen to the squabbling over which painting should really have won the Archibald Prize—Australia's most prestigious art award, given to the best portrait painted within the previous year.

## Literature

Aborigines were the earliest storytellers on the continent, with a rich heritage of Dreamtime tales to draw upon. Their oral tradition was handed down through stories told around campfires. The first Aborigine to have work published was David Unaipon, whose book *Native Legends* came out in 1929. Since then several translations of Dreamtime legends have been published, such as *Joe Nangan's Dreaming: Aboriginal Legends of the Northwest* (1976) and a variety of children's books illustrated by Aboriginal artists. One good source of Aboriginal literature, both modern and ancient, is Magabala Books, an Aboriginal publishing house based in Broome on the remote northwest coast of Western Australia. Paul Marshall's *Raparapa: Stories from the Fitzroy River Drovers* (1995) gives an Aborigine's perspective on life on the remote Kimberley stations. Some of the best books about Aborigines are *The Chant of Jimmie Blacksmith* (1972) by Thomas Kenneally, Bruce Chatwin's offbeat *The Songlines* (1988), and David Malouf's *Remembering Babylon* (1994).

**Aborigines were the earliest storytellers on the continent, with a rich heritage of Dreamtime tales to draw upon.**

White Australia's literature began with the journals of such explorers as Edward Eyre, Charles Sturt, and Ernest Giles. Some are still available in bookshops (look under Australiana) and make a nice read if you're crossing the country on the Indian-Pacific Railway or traveling up to Alice Springs on the Ghan. It wasn't until the latter part of the 19th century that Australian writers began to tackle their bizarre landscapes and convict heritage. Marcus Clarke's *For the Term of His Natural Life* (1874) tells the tale of Rufus Dawes, a wealthy young gentleman wrongfully convicted of murder and sentenced to transportation to Australia. He endures the penal colonies at Port Arthur and Macquarie Harbour but in the end retrieves name and fortune. Gold rushes and bushrangers provided material for Rolf Boldrewood's *Robbery Under Arms* (1888), another Australian classic.

In the 1890s, Australia's strongest national myths were forged by a handful of journalists and poets. Perhaps the best known is the balladeer and humorist Andrew Barton Paterson, who borrowed his pen name "Banjo" from a family racehorse. His ballads and yarns of swagmen, shearers, outlaws, and squatters celebrated a freedom that Australians, and the rest of the world, still like to imagine exists. He is best known for "The Man from Snowy River" (1890), "Clancy of the Overflow" (1889), and the lyrics of Australia's unofficial national anthem, "Waltzing Matilda." Henry Lawson, a dour and

**Aboriginal rock group Yothu Yindi's lead singer, Mandawuy Yunupingu**

much less folksy contemporary of Paterson's, is arguably Australia's finest short-story writer. While he could be as ironically humorous as Banjo, his social commentary goes much deeper. "The Drover's Wife" (1892), about a woman sitting up all night to protect her young children against a snake that has crawled into a crack in the wall of their bush shack, is a haunting story of strength, struggle, and aching loneliness.

Arthur Hoey Davis, writing under the name Steele Rudd, created two of Australia's best loved characters, Dad and Dave, in *On Our Selection* (1899). These two wide-eyed bumpkins went on to greater glory in a radio serial and in novels, plays, and films.

Coupled with C. J. Dennis's verse novel about a city-bred larrikin (mischievous young chap), *The Sentimental Bloke,* it reinforced the already popular image of the good-hearted Aussie battler.

Australia's outback landscapes began to find their way into novels in the 1920s, helped along by English novelist D. H. Lawrence, who published *Kangaroo* in 1923. Fifteen years later came Xavier Herbert's sweeping epic *In Capricornia* (1938), with its vivid and often brutal descriptions of life in the tropical landscapes of Australia's far north. Nobel Prize winner Patrick White used the outback as a backdrop for such major works as *Voss* (1957), a novel about a mad explorer trying to cross a desert, supposedly based on the life of Ludwig Leichhardt.

If you are looking for something evocative but a trifle easier to read, try Nevil Shute's 1950 classic *A Town Like Alice* or Colleen McCullough's *The Thorn Birds* (1979).

Poet, essayist, and songwriter Andrew Barton "Banjo" Paterson (1864–1941)

Among the nonfiction, Robert Hughes's *The Fatal Shore* (1987) is a gripping and deeply thought-out history of Australia's years as a convict colony. Sarah Murgatroyd's lively and engaging *The Dig Tree* (2002) reads like a novel and tells the tale of the ill-fated Burke and Wills expedition in 1860. In the rugged Kimberley, Mary Durack chronicled three generations of her family history in the 1959 outback classic *Kings in Grass Castles* and its 1983 sequel, *Sons in the Saddle.* In 1981, 87-year-old A. B. Facey stepped seemingly out of nowhere with an autobiography that began when he went to work at the age of eight on a farm in the outback and followed his adventures through Gallipoli and his life in Western Australia. *A Fortunate Life* went on to sell more than 600,000 copies—a blockbuster in the tiny Australian market.

Over the past 55 years Australians have shifted their literary gaze from the outback that few of them really know to the cities and suburbs where they live. Ruth Park's *Harp in the South* (1948) and *A Poor Man's Orange* (1949) are set in the inner Sydney slums and have never been out of print. Helen Garner's 1984 novel *Monkey Grip* is about sex and drugs in the inner Melbourne suburb of Carlton during the 1970s. Multiculturalism has become another big theme in modern Australian literature, sparking a major literary scandal in the early 1990s, when a young author who went by the name of Helen

Demidenko won the prestigious Miles Franklin Literary Award for her novel
*The Hand That Signed the Paper* (1994). The novel's unusual and disturbing perspective
on the Holocaust, seen through the eyes of a camp guard, relied heavily on the
author's exploration of painful aspects of her Ukrainian ancestry for its acceptability.
When it turned out that Helen Demidenko was in fact Helen Darville, an imaginative
descendant of English immigrants, Australia's hoodwinked literary establishment was
turned on its ear.

## Theater & Dance

For most of its history, Australia was dismissed as a cultural wasteland by the rest
of the world and even by Australians themselves. This "cultural cringe" was partly
a hangover from colonial days, when sophistication was considered an inverse
ratio of distance from Europe. Certainly Sydney is about as far as you can go from
London's West End theaters or the gilt of the Paris Opéra. Australians who aspired
to careers in theater and opera were obliged to head overseas. Opera singers
Dame Nellie Melba and, much later, Dame Joan Sutherland did just that. So did
pianist Percy Grainger, best known for his 1908 composition "In an English Country
Garden." "Sing 'em muck," Dame Nellie reportedly told a performer heading down
under, "that's all they understand."

If that was ever the case, it isn't anymore. Australia not only has a world-famous
opera house, it also has something to put in it. The Australian Opera Company, the
Australian Ballet, and the Sydney Dance Company—New South Wales's first professional
ballet troupe, founded in 1971—are all based at the Sydney Opera House.

Across the bay from the Opera House, the Aboriginal Islander Dance Theatre has
performances of traditional and modern
Aboriginal dances. Melbourne competes with
Sydney to be the theater capital of Australia,
and Adelaide's Festival Centre is said to have
even better acoustics than Sydney's Opera
House. Adelaide's biennial Festival is huge.

Formed as a training ground for actors,
directors, and set designers, the National Institute for Dramatic Arts (NIDA) has launched
Mel Gibson and other international stars. In
Melbourne's suburb of Carlton, experimental
theaters La Mama and the Pram Factory give
fledgling playwrights an opportunity to stage
their works. Alumni include David Williamson
(1942– ), Australia's most successful playwright.
His credits include *Don's Party*, *The Club*, and the
screenplay for the 1981 film *Gallipoli*.

## Music

Australia's mainstream musical tastes tend
to revolve around American-style light rock,
with major radio stations playing a familiar

### Rock Stars

Australia has contributed enormously
to the global talent pool, from Johnny
O'Keefe in the 1950s ("Real Wild
Child") to superstar rock groups such
as INXS, AC/DC, Silverchair, Men at
Work, the Little River Band, the Bee
Gees, Black Sorrows, and Midnight
Oil. Not everyone looked overseas for
success, however. Cold Chisel, an iconic
band of the 1970s and early '80s, is
scarcely known outside of Australia
but to this day remains arguably the
nation's greatest and most influential
rock group. On the indigenous front,
Aboriginal rock group Yothu Yindi
has successfully incorporated age-old
tribal rhythms and the didgeridoo into
the mainstream, while highlighting
Aboriginal rights issues with songs
such as "Treaty."

blend of Top 40 hits and baby boomers' golden oldies. Government efforts to stem this cultural tide by requiring stations to include at least 20 percent of local music in their programs, for example, have come to little because much of the local sound is indistinguishable from that produced in the United States or Europe.

**Country:** Country music has deep roots in Australia as it does in America. As with rock, it was strongly influenced by American stars in the early years—Aussie performers used to give themselves names like "Tex"—although Australians have always included a healthy dose of outback humor and bush themes in their music.

Tamworth, a modest-size town in rural New South Wales, about 200 miles (322 km) northwest of Sydney, is Australia's version of Nashville. Every January it hosts a popular country music festival at which the coveted Golden Guitar award is given to the year's top performer. One former winner who has gone on to a successful recording career in Nashville is Kasey Chambers, who grew up on Australia's desolate Nullarbor Plain.

Probably the best known Australian country star was Slim Dusty, who died in 2003 at the age of 76, after a lifetime of touring outback towns and Aborigine communities. He wrote hundreds of songs about living in the bush, the most famous being his iconic 1957 hit, "The Pub with No Beer," which the congregation sang at his funeral.

The 2,679-seat concert hall is the heart of the Sydney Opera House.

**Jazz & Classical:** Australia has world-class jazz musicians such as trumpeters James Morrison and Bob Barnard, pianist Graeme Bell, and multi-instrumented Don Burrows. Barry Tuckwell, one of the world's leading virtuosos on the French horn, is an Australian, and Australia's composers include Richard Meale, Peter Sculthorpe, Nigel Butterley, and Anne Boyd. The Australian Broadcasting Corporation maintains six symphony orchestras around the country.

## Cinema

Australia got off to a quick start in the film industry. A cinema opened on Pitt Street, Sydney, in 1896, only a year after the Lumière brothers opened the world's first cinema in Paris. Four years later, in Melbourne, a Salvation Army officer named Joseph Perry produced *Soldiers of the Cross,* which film historians regard as the world's first genuine movie in the sense that it relied on a plot, not just visuals. It premiered at the Melbourne Town Hall in 1901 and was shown in the United States the following year. In 1906, the world's first feature film, *The Story of the Kelly Gang,* was also produced in Melbourne.

Although it lasted only 40 minutes, short by today's standards, it was considerably longer and more involved than the typical ten-minute offerings of the age.

Australia had a thriving film industry throughout the silent film era, and more than 250 movies were produced here. Perhaps the most popular was an adaptation of C. J. Dennis's verse novel, *The Sentimental Bloke*, in 1919. But Hollywood outshone the Australian film industry in the 1930s and helped to establish the American cultural hegemony in movies, pop music, and TV that Australia has never been able to shake.

Cinematic high points during World War II included Charles Chauval's *Forty Thousand Horsemen* (1940), about the charge of the Australian Light Horse at Beersheba in 1917, and the 1942 documentary *Kokoda Front Line!*, which captured the toughness of the New Guinea campaign and earned cameraman Damien Parer an Oscar. It wasn't until 1968, and the establishment of the Australian Film Institute to promote Australian cinema, that local filmmaking began a renaissance that continues to this day. The 1970s saw an emphasis on introspective productions, such as Peter Weir's *Picnic at Hanging Rock* (1975) and *My Brilliant Career* (1979), which launched the international career of actress Judy Davis. In the 1980s, Australian filmmaking became more commercial, with *Gallipoli* (1981), *Breaker Morant* (1980), *The Man from Snowy River* movies, and *Mad Max* (1979) and its sequels. In 1986, Paul Hogan's *Crocodile Dundee* became Australia's first international blockbuster, and it remains the most profitable Australian film ever made.

Over the past few years, Australian filmmakers have relied on Australia's unique brand of offbeat humor, with quirky films like *Strictly Ballroom* (1992); *The Adventures of Priscilla, Queen of the Desert* (1994); *Muriel's Wedding* (1994); *Babe* (1995); and *The Castle* (1997). A moving recent film, *Rabbitproof Fence* (2002) tells the story of three Aboriginal children who find their way home through the bush after being taken from their parents by the authorities. *Japanese Story* (2003), starring Toni Collette, is a skilful romance set in Western Australia's rugged Pilbara region. But the biggest thing to hit Australian cinemas in recent years is Baz Luhrmann's *Australia* (2008). Part social commentary, part western cliché, mostly rousing historical romance, it pitted Nicole Kidman and Hugh Jackman against the stunning backdrop of Western Australia's Kimberley region.

## Aussiewood

Australia is immensely proud of its many actors, directors, cinematographers, and other film technicians who have found success in Hollywood. National pride swells when Nicole Kidman, Russell Crowe, Cate Blanchett, Naomi Watts, Hugh Jackman, Eric Bana, Geoffrey Rush, or Mel Gibson—dubbed the Gumleaf Mafia—shine at the Oscars. Many well-known actors, like Gibson, are graduates of the prestigious National Institute of Dramatic Arts in Sydney, and film schools across the country continue to pump out graduates who eye Hollywood as the main prize.

## Television

The first image on Australian TV was of Brisbane's old convict-built windmill, broadcast to Ipswich, Queensland, in 1934. Regular television broadcasting did not begin until 1956, and color TV reached Australia only in 1974.

From the start, American fare dominated Australian television, with early lineups including *Lassie*, *Father Knows Best*, and *Hopalong Cassidy*. So it remains today. Australian television producers have also tended to borrow heavily from successful American themes. Late-night shows have hosts who shamelessly style themselves after David Letterman, Jay Leno, or Conan O'Brien, and medical dramas bear a striking resemblance to *ER*. The Australian versions of *60 Minutes, Wheel of Fortune,* and *Big Brother,* as well as *Australian Idol,* are straightforward syndications.

**This is a young nation. A 19th-century building rates as "old" here, and 18th-century structures are almost unknown.**

For years Australians were vaguely embarrassed by their own locally conceived television, which seemed amateurish in comparison with slick American productions. No longer. Smartly produced Australian shows are gaining ground, and although American fare still takes up many broadcasting hours, more of the top-rated shows are homegrown. One favorite is *MacLeod's Daughters,* a drama about a trio of beautiful sisters determined to run a sprawling outback cattle station. Filmed in rural South Australia, the program is now shown in more than 60 countries.

Other popular Aussie TV exports include the evergreen children's show *Bananas in Pajamas,* the soap opera *Home & Away,* and *Neighbours,* the show where pop singer Kylie Minogue got her start more than 20 years ago. Australia's best known TV star was the late Steve Irwin, aka the Crocodile Hunter, whose wildlife shows were a hit around the world.

Australians are pretty frank and don't shirk from discussing the mechanics of sex on programs, showing bare breasts, or salting dialogue with a modest number of expletives. Janet Jackson's famous flash of breast at the Super Bowl, which scandalized America, would scarcely have raised an eyebrow in Australia. The episode of *Ellen* that turned America on its ear, when the title character acknowledged she was gay, drew a yawn here. That had already been explored back in the early 1970s with the racy Sydney soap opera *Number 96,* which had an openly gay character. *(Number 96* also featured full-frontal nudity, something American TV is still unlikely to show.)

That said, Australian TV is not one big bawdy cavalcade. Years ago, Channel Nine ran a show called *Australia's Naughtiest Home Videos*—or rather, they started to do so. When the network's proprietor, the late billionaire Kerry Packer, got a glimpse of what was airing on his TV screen, he called the producers and ordered them to take it off the air immediately. Suddenly a rerun of *Cheers* appeared, and the next morning switchboards at talk-back radio stations around the nation lit up with calls congratulating Packer and asking him to be Australia's next prime minister.

**TV Channels:** Australia has three major commercial networks—Seven, Nine, and Ten—and they command the lion's share of the audience. Next in line comes the government-owned Australian Broadcasting Corporation (ABC), affectionately known as "Aunty" in TV's early days. It has a lock on the "quality" end of news and current affairs shows, as well as some of the best locally produced dramas. Foreign fare on the ABC tends to come from Britain. Last in the ratings stakes comes SBS. This station is devoted almost exclusively to foreign-language broadcasts and arts movies and has an audience share of about 4 percent. Its evening news is superb, covering all parts of the globe. All of these networks have expanded with extra channels since the introduction of digital television. There are also two cable networks, and smaller networks in rural centers. Outback Australia has the Aboriginal-run Imparja Network, which shows a mix of popular American, Australian, and British shows.

## Architecture

This is a young nation. A 19th-century building rates as "old" here, and 18th-century structures are almost unknown. A convicted forger named Francis Greenway laid the foundations of Australia's architecture. He arrived in New South Wales in 1814 and was appointed civil architect two years later by Lachlan Macquarie, the high-minded governor who was embarking on an ambitious public works program.

**The balconied streets of Ballarat, Victoria, epitomize classic Australian town architecture.**

Over the next six years, Greenway designed 40 buildings—including the Hyde Park Barracks, St. James Church, and the courthouse in Windsor—often using the honey-colored sandstone from the nearby Hawkesbury Valley. Although his classic Georgian lines were crisp and harmonious, Greenway himself was argumentative and hot tempered; he was dismissed by Governor Brisbane in 1822. (A footnote to history: Greenway's portrait appeared until recently on Australia's ten dollar note, giving him the distinction of being the only forger honored on a nation's currency.)

For the most part Australia's civil architecture through the 19th century simply borrowed Europe's neo-Gothic, Renaissance, and classical styles. The University of Sydney was patterned on Oxford. Melbourne and the goldfield towns of Ballarat and Bendigo used the ornate styles of Victorian England to display their mid-19th-century wealth

Domestic buildings, on the other hand, began to reflect their unique surroundings—after all, Australians had to live in them. In tropical Queensland, settlers elevated their homes and opened them up to allow cooling air to circulate. Verandas appeared all over Australia. So did the classic Aussie pub, with its double-decked veranda and lacy ornamental ironwork. Row houses, embellished with similar ironwork, mushroomed in the inner cities. Out in the suburbs, the bungalow came into its own in the 1920s.

Around this time Australian civil architects began experimenting with their own style. The Sydney Harbour Bridge, completed in 1932, was the country's first quintessentially Australian landmark. It was to have been the world's longest single-arch bridge, but by the time it opened, New York's Bayonne Bridge had beaten it by 2 feet (0.6 m). Sitting opposite its southern pylons, over on Bennelong Point, is that other great Australian architectural marvel, the Sydney Opera House, designed by Danish architect Jørn Utzon in 1955. Other buildings of note include Melbourne's sprawling new Federation Square building, built along the banks of the Yarra River, which houses the National Gallery of Victoria, theaters, and a suite of galleries and museums.

> **The Old Elizabeth Farm**
>
> The oldest building in Australia is Elizabeth Farm, a brick farmhouse built for the MacArthur family in Parramatta, west of Sydney, in 1793. The MacArthur family was responsible for the early development of Australia's wool industry. The house, with its simple lines and wide veranda, is open to visitors (tel (02) 9635 9488, www .sydney.com.au).

The principal designer for the Olympic Games site was Phillip Cox, designer of Darling Harbour, the Sydney Football Stadium, and Yulara Resort near Uluru (Ayers Rock).

## Painting

Australia's first European artists did not know what to make of the prehistoric landscapes that spread before them, so they did what came naturally to 19th-century European minds: They rendered Arcadia, with noble savages and gum tree–lined lanes that look suspiciously like those in English villages.

In the late 1880s, Australian artists began to confront their country's harsh open spaces and blinding sun. A group of Melbourne artists, influenced by French plein-air painters and the Japanese aesthetic movement, took their easels out of their studios and into the sunshine. They went to villages like Box Hill and Heidelberg, now suburbia, where they painted Australian bush scenes, refusing to succumb either to Australia's 100°F (38°C) summer heat or to the Old World notion that landscapes must be lush to be beautiful. They embraced sunburned scrub with nationalist zeal. They became known as the Heidelberg school—after the village in the Yarra Valley, not the German city—although they painted in other areas as well. Tom Roberts, Arthur Streeton, Charles Condor, and Frederick McCubbin were among the school's biggest names. Their works, found in most major art galleries in the country, are some of Australia's masterpieces. Roberts's "Shearing the Rams," which he painted in 1890 at a shearing shed in Brocklesby, New South Wales, is an Australian icon. Equally iconic is Condor's "A Holiday at Mentone," a beach scene at a resort town (now suburb) south of Melbourne that captured Australia's heat probably better than any previous painting.

Landscapes and the bush have continued to be major themes in Australian art. Some of the biggest names are Sidney Nolan (who made a classic series of portraits of the bushranger Ned Kelly), Arthur Boyd, Clifton Pugh, Lloyd Rees, and Fred Williams. Albert Namatjira, an Aboriginal watercolorist who died in poverty in 1959, had one of the surest eyes in capturing the harsh light of the central Australian deserts.

The National Gallery in Canberra houses Australia's largest art collection. Although the building was opened in 1982, the national collection was started in 1968. In the early days, there was a great deal of controversy about some of the purchases—most notably the million-dollar sum paid for American artist Jackson Pollock's "Blue Poles." Lately, Australian artists have been nudging their way into the seven-figure bracket. In 1988, "Nuit de Canicule" by Rupert Bunny, a landscape artist in 1920s Melbourne, brought A$1.25 million dollars (U.S. $965,000) at auction. You won't see it hanging anywhere, however. It was destroyed in a fire. To date, the record for an Australian painting is the A$1.9 million dollars (U.S. $1.47 million) paid in 1996 for Eugene von Guerard's 1856 landscape "View of Geelong."

Who is Australia's best known modern artist? That depends. The cognoscenti in Sydney's art circles will almost invariably point to the late Brett Whiteley, who died of a heroin overdose in 1992. Down in The Rocks neighborhood of Sydney, however, a large gallery sells the splashy works of Ken Done. Decried as kitsch by Australia's "serious" art world, Done is regarded as a living treasure in Japan, where he has been accorded rare honors. Displays of his work there attract the same size of crowd as rock stars do. ■

**The art deco "Australian Beach Pattern" (1940) by Charles Meere**

# Flora & Fauna

**Undisturbed by outside influences for millions of years, Aussie wildlife evolved into the strangest assortment of creatures on the planet. Only Australia has monotremes (egg-laying mammals)—the platypus and echidna. It also has prehistoric landscapes with termite mounds 50 feet tall (15 m), boab trees, and ancient cycad palms, a species that dates back to the time of the dinosaurs.**

Most of Australia's mammals are marsupials, a primitive family of animals that vanished long ago from most other parts of the world. A female marsupial gives birth to an embryo that continues its development in a separate pouch on the mother's belly (or back, depending on the species). As the offspring grows older and larger, it can climb in and out of the pouch, riding piggyback on its mother. Kangaroos

**A boab tree stands solitary in the Kimberley bush near Wyndham, Western Australia.**

are best known for this, and you may see surprisingly large joeys—baby kangaroos—bundling themselves into their mother's pouches for a fast bound across the plains. There are 150 species of marsupials, in a variety of sizes, from tiny kangaroo mice to powerful western gray kangaroos that can be well over 5 feet (1.3 m) tall. Koalas and wombats are also marsupials. As with the animals, the flora here often seems like a variation on a theme, with more than 600 species of eucalyptus and a similar variety of acacias found in the bush.

Australia is also full of surprises. In 1994, a ranger rappelled into a narrow 2,000-foot-deep (600 m) gorge in Wollemi National Park, less than 100 miles (160 km) from downtown Sydney, and discovered an ancient species of pine tree thought to have been extinct for 170 million years. Until that moment it had been known only through fossils.

Only a month later came the discovery of a unique stand of Huon pines, which appears to be more than 10,000 years old, on the jungly flanks of Tasmania's Mount Read.

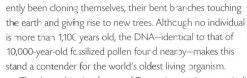

**Undisturbed by outside influences . . . Aussie wildlife evolved into the strangest assortment of creatures on the planet.**

The pines, all male, have apparently been cloning themselves, their bent branches touching the earth and giving rise to new trees. Although no individual is more than 1,100 years old, the DNA—identical to that of 10,000-year-old fossilized pollen found nearby—makes this stand a contender for the world's oldest living organism.

The deep, dripping forests of Tasmania give rise to periodic—but unconfirmed—sightings of the thylacine, a striped, wolf-size, carnivorous marsupial known as the Tasmanian tiger, believed to have been extinct since the 1930s. While this mystery captures the public's imagination, rangers in the central deserts have recently found several supposedly extinct mouse-size marsupials with far less fanfare.

If you travel in the outback up north, you'll see "wanted" posters tacked up on roadhouses and pubs for the night parrot, thought to have been extinct for more than a century. A dead specimen was found by a roadside in Queensland a decade ago. Although large rewards have been posted for (living) proof of another night parrot, the shy bird has proved elusive.

## Kangaroos & Koalas

Although 17 species of mammals are thought to have become extinct since the First Fleet arrived, kangaroos are believed to be more numerous now than 200 years ago, with a population estimated at 50 million, or about three times the number of Australians. This is because graziers have made water so much more plentiful out on the plains. Farmers regard kangaroos as pests, and the government permits a cull of around three million yearly. Many are shot for food (see p. 22). If you want to see them, just take a

Australia's famous red kangaroos can stand 6 feet (1.8 m) tall and weigh up to 145 pounds (66 kg).

drive at dusk out in grazing country beyond the coastal ranges. Carry collision insurance, though, because kangaroos blend in splendidly along the roadside. They look left, look right, and then hop out anyway.

While 'roos might be easy to spot in the wild, koalas are not. In fact, most Australians have never seen a koala in the wild. Estimates of koala numbers vary from 40,000 to 500,000, a far cry from the 1920s, when more than three million koalas were killed for their pelts. They have been protected since 1927, but expanding suburbs have swallowed their habitats. Although tree-planting and koala relocation programs are underway, suburban spread continues. These days, koalas are also plagued by chlamydia infections, blamed partly on stress, which cause infertility and blindness.

Kangaroo Island, off South Australia, gives probably the best chance of seeing a koala in the wild. Look in the forks of blue gums or manna gums—two of their favorite tree species—along the riverbanks. Victoria's Phillip Island is another possibility. Or go to zoos or game parks, such as Cleland in the Adelaide Hills, Healesville near Melbourne, or Eastern Creek Wildlife Park near Sydney. Private game parks used to let visitors cuddle the tubby little creatures, but many discourage that now because it stresses the animals. As former Australian tourism minister John Brown said, "It stinks, it scratches you, and it's covered with fleas." His point was that they are wild animals, not toys.

You are unlikely to see Australia's other special creatures—wombats, Tasmanian devils, echidnas, and platypuses—outside a zoo or game park. It is not that they are endangered or rare, but they are shy, nocturnal creatures and keep to themselves in forests and scrub or quiet little streams.

## Birds

More than 750 species of birds live in Australia, and many of them are found nowhere else. Galahs, brolgas, jabirus, and parrots, bright as rainbows, flit through the bush, and in the summer it's not unusual to see a large gum tree virtually white with sulfur-crested cockatoos, cackling and screeching in the branches. Bird fanciers overseas pay thousands of dollars for a pair of these cockatoos, making smuggling and poaching major problems.

The Aussie birds best known outside the country are the kookaburra and the emu. The hooting laughter of a kookaburra is the sound effect Hollywood uses to evoke monkeys in the jungle. Emus, which can grow to 6 feet (1.8 m) tall and 130 pounds (59 kg), strut the outback and are a haunting sight when silhouetted against a dying sun. Like kangaroos, they also find their way onto the dinner plates of the discerning, but the smoked emu prosciutto served in trendy city bistros will have been farmed, not shot in the wild. The emu is paired with the kangaroo on Australia's national coat of arms

## Killers

Australia is also home to deadly snakes, poisonous spiders, venomous sea life, saltwater crocodiles, and the great white shark. All can kill, although fatalities are rare, newsworthy events. The taipan, the world's most toxic land snake, lives in the remote deserts of northern Australia and carries enough neurotoxin to kill 100,000 mice. The brown snake, death adder, and tiger snake also rate among the world's deadliest and are more common, but you are unlikely to see them. As a rule, snakes are shy. Treat any that you see as potentially poisonous, though, and give them a wide berth. If you happen to be one of the 300 or so people who get bitten each year, stay calm, wrap the wound snugly, and head for the nearest hospital. Don't wash the bite; doctors will need a sample of the venom.

Most of Australia's deadly critters inhabit remote pockets of bush, but the country's most poisonous spider—the funnel web—lives in Sydney's suburbs. A relative of the trapdoor spider, it lurks in rocks and cracks in brick, sometimes around swimming pools, and springs on its prey. Funnel webs are found across southeast Australia, but the most toxic varieties are near Sydney. The redback, cousin to the black widow, is found throughout the country. Antivenoms are available for both.

## In the Water

Northern Australia, north of the Tropic of Capricorn, has some of Australia's loveliest beaches and most inviting turquoise waters. Summers are crushingly hot and muggy, so it is deeply disappointing to see signs forbidding swimming from November through March. There are several very good reasons. Sea wasps, which are a highly toxic box jellyfish with nearly invisible tentacles up to 10 feet (3 m) long, killed about 60 swimmers in the last century. (Diehard surfers usually wear nylon stockings to help protect them from stings.) Bluebottles, another variety of jellyfish, are painful, but not deadly, nuisances. Stonefish lurk in tidal pools, and their spines can kill if stepped upon. The shy blue-ringed octopus, which is actually brown until it gets upset, is found all around Australia. It has a gentle nibble, but its toxin causes respiratory failure within 12 hours. Given all that, the hotel pool starts to look pretty good.

### Giant Lizards

Australia has a good selection of lizards, about 400 species ranging from harmless little skinks that scamper around backyards to the goanna, a monitor lizard that can grow to a powerfully built 7 feet (over 2 m) long. They are astoundingly fast, have large, strong, and razor-sharp claws, and if spooked will scamper up the highest thing they see. Out on the plains, that's likely to be you. The goanna is a much prized delicacy among desert Aborigines. The largest species of goanna is the perenties, second in size only to the Komodo dragon. Perenties are found in the central deserts and should be left alone. For sheer comic-nightmare quality, the frill-necked lizard is hard to top. Looking like an animated gargoyle, it scampers across the desert on its hind legs with a wide frill of leathery skin extended to frighten potential predators.

Farther out along the Queensland coast lies the Great Barrier Reef, at 1,300 miles (2,092 km) long the world's largest living organism. Made of around 300 species of hard reef coral polyps, it grows as successive generations build on their predecessors. Around it live 1,500 species of tropical fish, 4,000 species of shellfish, and 400 species of sponge. There are giant clams, tortoises, whales, black marlins, and dugongs (relatives of the manatee). Exploring it is an otherworldly experience.

The largest shark ever caught with rod and reel, a 2,664-pound (1,208 kg) white pointer, was taken in the waters off Ceduna, South Australia, in 1959. An even larger one was caught more recently near Albany, Western Australia, but was disallowed for record purposes because whale meat was used as bait. Steven Spielberg got his live shark footage for *Jaws* near Port Lincoln, South Australia. This is frightening stuff, but actually these magnificent creatures have been victims of bad press. Honeybees kill three times as many Australians as sharks do. There have only been about 635 known shark attacks in Australia since European settlement, according to the shark-attack file at Sydney's Taronga Park Zoo. Of these about 200 were fatal, a very small number considering the millions of Australians who swim in the ocean every weekend. The last fatal shark attack in Sydney Harbour was in 1937. South Australia put sharks on its protected species list in 1997, and today ecotourists flock to places like Port Lincoln for opportunities to dive, in protective cages, with these amazing animals.

Crocodiles are the other monsters in Australian waters. At the Shire Offices, in the northern Queensland town of Normanton, is a plaster cast of possibly the world's largest crocodile—28 feet 4 inches (8.6 m) long, with the build of a modest-size dinosaur. It was shot in 1957 in the Norman River, which flows past this rough outback town into the Gulf of Carpentaria. Saltwater crocodiles inhabit the estuaries, rivers, and mangrove swamps along the coast of tropical Australia, but they sometimes appear in pools up to 60 miles (96 km) inland. They are extremely sly and dangerous, using a high degree of skill to stalk prey, which includes anything up to and including packhorses, cattle, and sometimes people. It is extremely unwise to swim in these rivers and estuaries. Some victims, sadly, didn't know any better because tourists had taken the Beware of Crocodile signs as souvenirs. To thwart that, copies of the signs are available for sale.

> Laymen tend to divide Australian trees into two broad categories: those that are eucalyptuses and those that are not.

Freshwater crocodiles are also found in the tropics. They are smaller and shy, although on rare occasions they, too, have been known to attack people. They have slightly different snouts than saltwater ones, although this can be rather a fine distinction to try to make if you are swimming in a pond and see a "log" puttering along the bank.

## Trees, Shrubs, & Flowers

Laymen tend to divide Australian trees into two broad categories: those that are eucalyptuses and those that are not. After you have asked a dozen locals to identify scores of different trees and learned that nearly all were some form of eucalyptus—blue gum, manna gum, red gum, snow gum, ghost gum, and so on—it is no surprise that there are about 600 different species of gum, found everywhere from harsh outback desert to mountain snowfields. They range from stunted mallee gums to towering karri trees in southwestern Australia, which at more than 300 feet (91 m) tall are the world's tallest hardwoods. The coolabah tree, under which the jolly swagman camps in the song "Waltzing Matilda," is another form of gum tree.

Australia also has more then 660 species of acacias, commonly known as wattle trees because the early settlers used the supple branches to build wattle-and-daub cottages like the ones they used to make in England. One variety of this flowering tree, known as mulga, dominates large parts of the outback. Another, golden wattle, has become Australia's floral emblem, inspiring the green-and-gold livery of its sports teams. Banksias, named for botanist Joseph Banks, are widely found and have orange, red, or yellow flowers. Casuarinas, or shea-oaks, are nearly as widespread and varied as eucalyptuses, ranging from the desert oaks of central Australia to river shea-oaks along the banks of the Murray River.

**An adventurous diver faces a great white shark at Dangerous Reef, off Australia's southern coast.**

The Huon pine is an ancient and extremely slow-growing species found these days only in Tasmania. Its beautiful, dense, honey-colored wood was used to fashion cabinetry and rot-resistant boats until people realized that it could take a thousand years to replace just one big Huon pine.

The floral emblem of New South Wales is the waratah tree, famed for its flaming red flowers. Up in the floodplains of the remote Kimberley are bizarre boab trees, which look as though they've been planted upside down. Although they do not grow exceptionally high—60 feet (18 m) is a tall one—their bulbous trunks can grow more than 80 feet (24 m) in circumference. The hollowed shell of one near Derby, Western Australia, was used as a jail.

Much of Australia's interior is covered with low grasses and shrubs. Spinifex is ubiquitous north of the Tropic of Capricorn. From a distance these spiny shrubs look downy, but they were the torment of early desert explorers. Their needlelike leaves are capable of easily penetrating blue jeans and scratching your skin. Snakes and lizards love them.

Cattle flourish on the Mitchell grass that covers vast areas of the tropics. During the rainy season, these grasses can grow up to 30 feet (9 m) in a month. In the south, silvery-green saltbush covers much of the open country and supports most of the cattle and sheep in this arid landscape. Thousands of species of wildflowers grow in Australia, and many are found nowhere else on Earth. Western Australia is particularly rich, with more than 7,000 varieties (see pp. 220–223).

## Alien Invaders

Australia's native flora and fauna had the continent to themselves for millions of years, during which they adapted to the changing moods of the land. Then newcomers arrived, and Australia's landscape was changed forever by sheep, cattle, wheat, barley, blackberry vines, carp, cats, and foxes. Crown of Thorns starfish invaded Australia's waters, while in 2004 it was discovered that Argentine ants had set up a vast (and harmless to humans) colony in the soil beneath Melbourne.

Rabbits may be the most destructive of the introduced species (see sidebar below), but they are far from alone. In the past two centuries, settlers have let loose an army of plants, fish, reptiles, and mammals that have wreaked havoc on the environment. Some, such as foxes and trout, were introduced for sport. Others, such as the American cane toad, were brought in to control pests—in this case, insects that ravaged sugarcane—only to became noxious pests themselves (see sidebar p. 180).

The domestic cat is believed to be responsible for endangering many species of native birds and smaller mammals. Some city councils have passed ordinances requiring cats to be neutered and locked up at night, but cat owners are vocal lobbyists. The worst offenders are feral cats—descendants of pets gone wild.

Pigs, horses, and donkeys also run wild in the bush. So do camels, which were brought to Australia for the Burke and Wills expedition in 1860 and later to carry supplies to crews building the railroads and telegraph lines across the deserts. When trains and roads made the camels obsolete, they were simply slapped on the rump and chased into the bush where they have prospered ever since. ■

## The Rabbit Scourge

In 1859, Thomas Austin, a grazier in Victoria, had a dozen rabbits shipped from England to provide a bit of sporting pleasure for him and his guests. The rabbits were turned loose in the scrub, and soon their numbers were far beyond anything hunting could control.

By 1865, hunters had killed more than 20,000 rabbits, but thousands more lived in the bush. By the 1930s, the rabbit population had exploded to an estimated one billion. Their destructive nibbling had stripped bare large areas of land and endangered many native species of grass and wildflowers.

Nothing seemed to work against this scourge until the 1950s, when scientists let loose the myxomatosis virus, which is lethal to rabbits but doesn't infect humans or native Australian species. Rabbit numbers plummeted, but then rebounded as some rabbits developed immunity to the virus.

By the early 1990s, there were an estimated 350 million rabbits hopping around the bush. In 1996, scientists released a new disease, rabbit calicivirus, which wiped out 98 percent of rabbits in parts of the outback but seems to have left other populations untouched.

Australia's oldest, largest, and wealthiest city, with one of the most beautiful harbors in the world

# Sydney

Introduction & Map    74–77

Sydney Harbour    78–87

**Experience: Sydney Harbour Cruises**    79

Sydney Harbor Walk    82–85

Downtown Sydney    88–89

Feature: Cricket    90–91

Darling Harbour    92–93

Bohemian Sydney    94–95

**Experience: Priscilla Tours**    95

Beaches    96–97

Feature: A Sydney-style New Year's    98–99

Zoos & Wildlife Parks    100

Hotels & Restaurants    368–369

Eclectic architecture in The Rocks neighborhood of Sydney

# Sydney

**Flying into Sydney has to be the finest introduction to Australia imaginable. Look out your window and it's all there: the dramatic city skyline, the deep blue of the harbor spread into scores of inlets and bays, and a sprawl of terra-cotta roofs stretching to the horizon. And then you see it: the graceful ironwork of the Harbour Bridge, a perfect miniature from this height, and beside it, the white tiles of the Opera House shimmering like a pearl.**

You've definitely arrived. This is Australia. And it's just as they said it would be. From 1,000 feet, anyway. After you land and begin to make your way through the tangle of grubby and crowded urban streets, craning your neck to look for landmarks such as the 960-foot-tall (293 m) Sydney Tower, you realize that this city can be a little deceptive as well. Some Australians—chiefly staid Victorians from archrival Melbourne, who tend to draw morals from this sort of thing—will say you've learned your first lesson about the shallowness of Sydney's flashy money and California-style glamour.

A Sydneysider, on the other hand, will simply give you directions down to Circular Quay. The view is like a visual mantra—just sitting on an ornamental bench by the Opera House brings back the magic, as you watch the sunlight sparkle on one of the world's great harbors, the ferries coming and going, and the spread of million-dollar bungalows along the North Shore. No matter how many times you've been there before, when you go down to the quay on a sunny afternoon it's like seeing it for the first time all over again. Even the convicts supposedly cheered on their first glimpse of the harbor when the First Fleet sailed in through the Heads in 1788.

## NOT TO BE MISSED:

Cruising the city's azure harbor on a ferry to Manly **78–79**

A climb up the iconic Sydney Harbour Bridge **81**

A walk through the city's historic district, The Rocks **84**

Sydney Opera House, a World Heritage masterpiece **86–87**

Darling Harbour, the rejuvenated waterfront packed with popular tourist attractions **92–93**

People-watching at world-famous Bondi Beach **96–97**

EASTWOOD
Koala Park
NORTH RYDE
RYDE
GLADESVILLE
2
3
30
7
55
NORTH PARRAMATTA
40
45
Parramatta
MILLENNIUM PARK
Homebush Bay
35
Elizabeth Farm
HOMEBUSH
BICENTENNIAL PARK
Featherdale Wildlife Park
Glenbrook
PARRAMATTA
Duck
Sydney Showground
WESTERN MOTORWAY
GRANVILLE
44
4
Sydney Olympic Park
PARRAMATTA ROAD
7
45
HOMEBUSH
55
LIDCOMBE
STRATHFIELD
GUILDFORD
HOMEBUSH WEST
3
0    6 kilometers
0    3 miles
Cabramatta
A          B          C

## The Lure of the Water

Sydney's secret is this dazzling waterfront, with its ornamental palms, gleaming yachts in quiet coves, and 70 beaches. Walk along any of them and you feel like whistling something bold and adventurous. If somebody hasn't made you a vice president, they will any day now. It's this infectious waterborne confidence that lures Australia's smartest and most artistically gifted, the very rich and those who want to be. Their scramble for waterfront footage has bumped real-estate prices to absurd levels, and the shock

Area of map detail

Sydney
Canberra

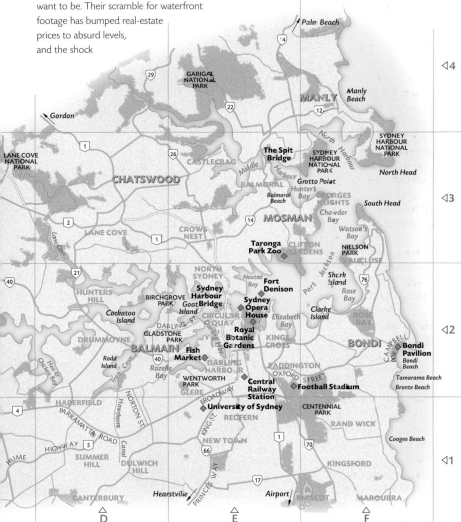

Palm Beach

GARIGAL NATIONAL PARK

Manly Beach

MANLY

Gordon

LANE COVE NATIONAL PARK

CHATSWOOD

CASTLECRAG

The Spit Bridge

SYDNEY HARBOUR NATIONAL PARK

SYDNEY HARBOUR NATIONAL PARK

North Head

Middle Harbour

BALMORAL

Grotto Point

Balmoral Beach

Hunter's Bay

GEORGES HEIGHTS

South Head

LANE COVE

CROWS NEST

MOSMAN

Chowder Bay

Watson's Bay

Taronga Park Zoo

CLIFTON GARDENS

NIELSON PARK

VAUCLUSE

NORTH SYDNEY

Neutral Bay

Fort Denison

Shark Island

Rose Bay

HUNTERS HILL

BIRCHGROVE PARK

Sydney Harbour Bridge

Goat Island

Sydney Opera House

Clarke Island

ROSE BAY

Cockatoo Island

DARLING ST.

CIRCULAR QUAY

Elizabeth Bay

GLADSTONE PARK

Royal Botanic Gardens

KINGS CROSS

BONDI

Bondi Pavilion

DRUMMOYNE

BALMAIN

Fish Market

DARLING HARBOUR

Bondi Beach

Rodd Island

Rozelle Bay

WENTWORTH PARK

PADDINGTON

OXFORD STREET

Tamarama Beach

GLEBE

Central Railway Station

Football Stadium

Bronte Beach

HABERFIELD

BROADWAY

University of Sydney

CENTENNIAL PARK

PARRAMATTA ROAD

REDFERN

RANDWICK

Coogee Beach

HIGHWAY

SUMMER HILL

DULWICH HILL

NEW TOWN

KINGSFORD

HUME

KING ST.

CANTERBURY

Hearstville

PRINCES WAY

Airport

MASCOT

MAROUBRA

D    E    F

The downtown Sydney skyline overlooks Hyde Park.

waves can be felt in the western suburbs, where much of the population lives. A house out there can still cost A$350,000 (U.S. $266,000), but a comparable one along the harbor could range well into eight figures. So most of Sydney's 4.4 million residents reluctantly live away from the water, then crowd the beaches, the Manly ferry, Darling Harbour, and Circular Quay on the weekends.

## City Districts

Sydney sprawls. Despite its relatively small population, it covers almost as large an area as Los Angeles and is seven times larger than Paris. It has more than 400 suburbs, the farthest being about 60 miles (96 km) from the Central Business District, or CBD.

The historic section of the city is known as **The Rocks,** a beautifully restored warren of alleyways and old stone buildings tucked away under the southern approach to the Harbour Bridge.

Pitt Street and George Street are the city's two main thoroughfares. They both begin at

**INSIDER TIP:**

The Fortune of War, at 137 George Street in The Rocks, is Sydney's oldest pub. This tiny but popular watering hole has been in continuous operation since 1828. Catch live music here on weekends.

—HOLLY SHALDERS
*National Geographic contributor*

**Circular Quay** and stretch through the heart of downtown Sydney. Both streets are lined with glittering skyscrapers and department stores, as well as gritty old shops that have somehow managed to survive the scramble for building land. This juxtaposition of styles, old and new, gives Sydney flair. For the past ten years, **North Sydney,** across the harbor, has been sprouting modernistic skyscrapers, and it now looks like an annex of downtown.

Residential suburbs in the North Shore and Sydney's ritzy east, such as **Point Piper, Double Bay,** and **Vaucluse,** rank among the priciest real estate in Australia, with harbor-front mansions running into many millions of dollars. Farther east is **Bondi Beach,** the most famous of the chain of surfing beaches fronting the Pacific Ocean close to the city.

The inner east section has Kings Cross, Paddington, and Darlinghurst. **Kings Cross** is Sydney's red-light district, filled with pulsing nightclubs, fast food, and crime. Oxford Street is the main artery of trendy **Paddington** and **Darlinghurst.** With their brash nightlife, stylish row houses, and great little cafés, this is the place to go if you want to soak up the city's social scene. This is also Sydney's gay center, where the Gay and Lesbian Mardi Gras draws half a million spectators, gay and straight, from Australia and around the world.

To the west is **Darling Harbour,** a pleasant walk from most places in the downtown part of the city. Filled with hugely popular museums and wildlife attractions, Darling Harbour is a great place for families. Or you can ride the monorail that runs along Pitt and Market Streets. Farther out are the inner west suburbs of **Glebe** and **Balmain,** old working-class docklands that have become fashionable. Also at this end of town is the raffishly chic **Newtown,** which was formerly a tough slum but today boasts a funky artistic and intellectual vibe. Neighboring **Redfern** is still tough.

Farther west are **Homebush Bay**—site of the Olympics in 2000—and **Parramatta,** Australia's second oldest city. You can reach these by ferry from Circular Quay, a better option than struggling through miles of stop-start traffic on the Parramatta Road, with its aggressive motorists, garish advertising, and tacky used car lots.

## Asian Culture

Sydney is multicultural, home to more than 160 nationalities. In the past 20 years it has become a strongly Asian city, though you might be disappointed by Chinatown, which is just a token two streets on the Darling Harbour side of the city. To see Sydney's Asian community at its most vibrant, go west to suburbs like **Cabramatta,** with its busy food stands, Asian apothecaries, sidewalks cluttered with signs in Chinese, Vietnamese, and Cambodian, cramped restaurants, and everywhere a fragrance of scorched spices and cooking oil.

### Slip, Slop, Slap

This enduring health campaign slogan delivers the message to "slip on a shirt, slop on sunscreen, and slap on a hat" to avoid skin cancer. Surrounded by wonderful beaches, warm climate, and abundant sunshine, Australians reveled in their sun-bronzed image until health studies showed Australia had one of highest rates of skin cancer in the world. Visitors are also advised to follow the slogan.

## Transportation

For all the urban sprawl and tangle of streets, getting about Sydney is fairly easy. Central Railway Station and bustling Circular Quay are the main transportation hubs in the city, with regular trains, buses, and ferries reaching all parts of the city, into the nearby Blue Mountains, and down the Illawarra Coast. You can also catch water taxis on the harbor, and a monorail links Darling Harbour with the CBD.

## Hiking & Biking

There are nice walks to be had downtown, notably in Hyde Park and the Botanic Gardens. This is not a bicycle-friendly city, but there are spectacularly scenic bicycle lanes over the Harbour Bridge. The safe exception for riders is leafy Centennial Park, near Paddington, where there is a riding track and jogging path through the gardens and past ornamental ponds. ■

# Sydney Harbour

The best way to acquaint yourself with Sydney Harbour is to take a ferry, and the pick of the bunch is the legendary ferry to Manly. Take the slower-moving old-style ferry, rather than the speedy hydrofoil, and savor the sea air on the half-hour trip. The ferry cuts its way east from Circular Quay, around the Opera House and the Botanic Gardens, past glamorous suburbs, and out toward the grand promontories—the Heads—that guard the entrance to the harbor.

An aerial view of Sydney Harbour and the central business district behind Circular Quay

**Sydney**

⚏ Map pp. 74–75 & 83

**Visitor Information**

✉ Corner of Argyle St. & Playfair St., The Rocks; Palm Grove, between Cockle Bay Wharf and Harbourside, Darling Harbour

☎ (02) 9240 8788

✉ Circular Quay Kiosk

☎ (02) 9931 1111

**www.sydneyvisitor centre.com.au**

Manly itself is a breezy seaside suburb on a spit of land between the north shore of the harbor and the open ocean, with a line of Norfolk pines along its esplanade and the sun-splashed Manly Corso humming with life. It is a much more family-oriented place than Sydney's other famous beach, Bondi. The return trip on the ferry is, if anything, even more majestic as you pass Fort Denison and draw up to the city skyline, Opera House, and Harbour Bridge.

The harbor spills into countless bays and coves. **Chowder Bay** (see map p. 75), on the north shore, was where 19th-century Yankee whalers tied up and made their chowder out of local shellfish. **Neutral Bay** was where ships of various nationalities docked. The city's earliest attempts at agriculture were at Farm Cove, now the **Royal Botanic Gardens.**

**Rose Bay** was where the old Empire flying boats used to take off in the 1930s on the nine-day hop to London. Reprise a bit of that golden age travel with a scenic flight on a classic Beaver seaplane, which takes off from this same pretty bay. A variety of packages are available, including an option that takes you a short way up the coast to beautiful Pittwater, offers lunch at the award-winning Jonah's restaurant with its stunning views over the Pacific Ocean, and provides an aerial tour of the harbor as you return (tel (02) 9388 1978, www.seaplanes.com.au).

## Ferry Tours

Water travel is a way of life in this harbor city. There are ferries from Circular Quay to the Olympic grounds at **Homebush Bay**, **Taronga Park Zoo**, **Watson's Bay**—where you can sprawl in a manicured park eating some of Sydney's best fish and chips—and **Darling Harbour** precinct. The Hunter's Hill Ferry gives a nice tour of the hidden northwest arms of the harbor. All of the western ferry rides provide

spectacular photo opportunities of the Opera House and Botanic Gardens, framed by the Sydney Harbour Bridge, as you return to the quay.

Tours operate to some of the harbor's islands. **Fort Denison** was originally a place where poorly behaved convicts were sent to reconsider their conduct—sharks and strong currents proving efficient guards. Tours are also available to **Goat Island,** an old quarantine station and shipyard.

## Walking Tours

Landlubbers who get queasy even at the thought of being on a ship can take some excellent harbor walks, including the mile-long **Hermitage Walking Track** (start from Nielson Park) around the exclusive suburb of Vaucluse and Rose Bay. A longer hike can be had on the **Manly Scenic Walkway,** which goes 6 miles (9.6 km) from Manly Cove to the Spit Bridge (brochures and maps from the Sydney or Manly visitor centers).

### Sydney Harbour
🗺 Map pp. 74–75 & 83

### Manly
🗺 75 F4

**Visitor Information**
✉ Manly Wharf
☎ (02) 9976 1430

**Manly Ferry**
✉ Circular Quay
🕐 30 minutes
💲 $

### Fort Denison Tours
✉ Cadmans Cottage, 110 George St., The Rocks
☎ (02) 9247 5033
🕐 60-minute tours depart No. 6 Jetty, Circular Quay, 2–3 times daily
💲 $

---

# EXPERIENCE: Sydney Harbour Cruises

In addition to the ferries that ply commuters around Sydney, there are several additional ways to get out onto the magnificent harbor:

**Captain Cook** (No. 6 Jetty, Circular Quay, tel (02) 9206 1111, www.captaincook.com.au/sydney) cruise ships offer everything from breakfast and high tea cruises to weekend trips.

**Matilda Cruises** (Pier 26, Aquarium Wharf, Darling Harbour, tel (02) 9206 1111, www.matilda.com.au) operates ferries and catamaran cruises.

**Sydney by Sail** (Australian National Maritime Museum, Darling Harbour, tel (02) 9280 1110, www.sydneysail.com) offers three-hour yachting experiences that teach sailing basics.

**Sydney Harbour Tall Ships** (79 ½ George St., tel 1300 664 410, www.sydneytallships.com.au) features 1850s-style tall ships that depart from The Rocks.

**Sydney Jet** (Cockle Bay Wharf, Darling Harbour, tel (02) 9807 4333, www.sydneyjet.com) combines harbor views with high-speed thrills.

Hinges at the base support the full weight of the bridge and also allow for expansion.

Ventilation shafts for the Harbour Tunnel

# Sydney Harbour Bridge

## The Bridge

Sydney Harbour Bridge is instantly recognizable. This iconic structure is one of Australia's architectural and engineering wonders, and for 30 years it was the tallest structure in Sydney. The bridge was designed by Dorman Long and Co. of England to the specifications of its chief engineer J.J.C. Bradfield. Construction started in 1923, and the bridge was completed during the Depression in 1932.

The bridge has a span of 1,650 feet (503 m), and the top of the arch is 439 feet (134 m) above the water. Originally designed to carry 6,000 cars an hour, it now tops 15,000 at peak times, in eight lanes. It also carries two railroad lines, a pedestrian walkway, and a bicycle track.

## The Bridge Climb

Once a dare taken up by university students, climbing the steel arch of the Sydney Harbour Bridge is now a tourism possibility for those with a good head for heights. **Sydney Harbour Bridge Climb** (Cumberland St., The Rocks, tel (02) 8274 7777, $$$$$, www.bridgeclimb.com) offers guided tours to the top of the arch. Visitors are attached by harnesses to a safety rail, used by maintenance workers, and led by experienced guides to the finest viewing spot in Sydney. There are higher points in the city (MLC Centre is 780 feet/238 m, Sydney Tower 990 feet/302 m), but nothing commands the skyline the way Sydney's "Coathanger" does.

Those who don't care for such drama can cross the bridge on the pedestrian walkway or go to the top of the South Pylon ($) which, at 290 feet (88 m) above the water, gives nearly as spectacular a view.

(continued on p. 86)

# Sydney Harbour Walk

With a distance of just over 4 miles (7 km), this route can be anything from a brisk hour-long walk to an all-day excursion. It can even be satisfactorily jogged because it crosses only one busy street.

Massive Corinthian columns mark the entrance to the Art Gallery of New South Wales.

Start at the **Art Gallery of New South Wales ❶** *(Art Gallery Rd., The Domain, tel (02) 9225 1744, www.artgallery.nsw.gov.au),* which is located in the leafy park known as The Domain. (To get there, you can take the Explorer Bus or walk about 1500 feet/500 m from St. James Railway Station.) This beautiful, colonnaded, sandstone building dates from 1885 and is inscribed with mood-setting names of great Italian artists of the Renaissance, none of whom are actually represented inside. Instead the gallery has a collection of Australian masterpieces and one of the nation's most comprehensive collections of Aboriginal and Torres Strait Islander art.

---

## NOT TO BE MISSED:

**Mrs. Macquarie's Point • Circular Quay • The Rocks • Sydney Harbour Bridge**

---

From the gallery steps, follow the narrow road down through the botanic gardens and toward **Mrs. Macquarie's Point ❷**. This fig-shaded promontory was named in honor of Governor Macquarie's wife, Elizabeth, when the gardens were laid out in 1816. Supposedly she used to sit out here to watch the harbor and wait for the next ship to arrive from

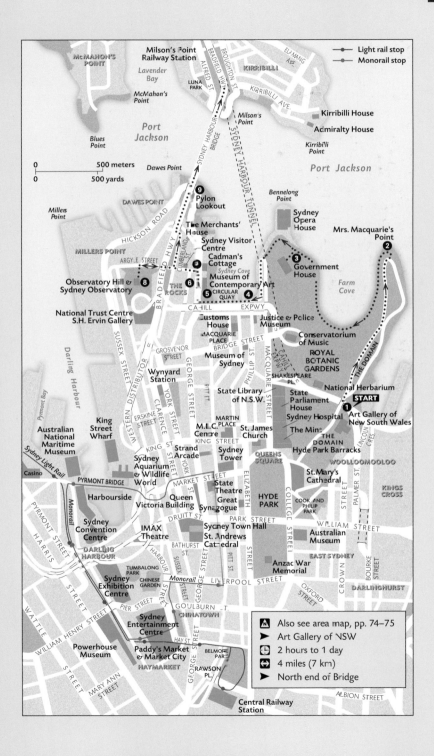

McMAHON'S POINT

Milson's Point Railway Station

KIRRIBILLI

EL AMANG AVE.

● Light rail stop
● Monorail stop

*Lavender Bay*

LUNA PARK

ALFRED ST.

BROUGHTON ST.

BRADFIELD HWY

*McMahon's Point*

KIRRIBILLI AVE.

**Kirribilli House**

*Milson's Point*

**Admiralty House**

*Port Jackson*

*Blues Point*

*Kirribilli Point*

SYDNEY HARBOUR BRIDGE

SYDNEY HARBOUR TUNNEL

*Port Jackson*

*Dawes Point*

0 — 500 meters
0 — 500 yards

*Millers Point*

DAWES POINT

**9 Pylon Lookout**

*Bennelong Point*

**Sydney Opera House**

**Mrs. Macquarie's Point**

**2**

HICKSON ROAD

**The Merchants' House**

**Sydney Visitor Centre**

**3 Government House**

BRADFIELD HWY

CUMBERLAND

**Cadman's Cottage**

*Sydney Cove*

MILLERS POINT

ARGYLE STREET

**7**

**Museum of Contemporary Art**

*Farm Cove*

THE DOMAIN

**Observatory Hill & Sydney Observatory**

**8**

THE ROCKS

**6**

**5** CIRCULAR QUAY

**4**

**National Trust Centre S.H. Ervin Gallery**

CAHILL EXPWY

**Customs House**

**Justice & Police Museum**

**Conservatorium of Music**

SUSSEX STREET

GROSVENOR STREET

MACQUARIE PLACE

BRIDGE STREET

PHILIP ST.

MACQUARIE STREET

CAHILL EXPY

**ROYAL BOTANIC GARDENS**

*Darling Harbour*

**Museum of Sydney**

**National Herbarium**

**Wynyard Station**

GEORGE STREET

PITT ST.

SHAKESPEARE PL.

*Pyrmont Bay*

WESTERN DISTRIBUTOR

ERSKINE STREET

CLARENCE STREET

YORK STREET

**State Library of N.S.W.**

**State Parliament House**

**START 1**

**Art Gallery of New South Wales**

Casino

Sydney Light Rail

PYRMONT BRIDGE

KING ST.

**King Street Wharf**

**M.L.C. Centre**

MARTIN PLACE

KING STREET

**St. James Church**

**Sydney Hospital**

**The Mint**

THE DOMAIN

LINCOLN CRES.

**Australian National Maritime Museum**

**Harbourside**

**Sydney Aquarium & Wildlife World**

**Strand Arcade**

**Sydney Tower**

QUEENS SQUARE

**Hyde Park Barracks**

WOOLLOOMOOLOO

**Queen Victoria Building**

MARKET STREET

**State Theatre**

ELIZABETH STREET

**HYDE PARK**

**St. Mary's Cathedral**

COLLEGE STREET

COOK AND PHILIP PARK

WILLIAM STREET

PALMER ST.

KINGS CROSS

**Great Synagogue**

**Sydney Convention Centre**

**IMAX Theatre**

DRUITT STREET

PARK STREET

**Sydney Town Hall**

**St. Andrews Cathedral**

BATHURST ST.

SUSSEX ST.

HARBOUR ST.

GEORGE ST.

PITT ST.

**Australian Museum**

EAST SYDNEY

BOURKE STREET

DARLINGHURST

DARLING HARBOUR

PYRMONT STREET

HARRIS STREET

**Sydney Exhibition Centre**

TUMBALONG PARK

CHINESE GARDEN

*Monorail*

LIVERPOOL STREET

**Anzac War Memorial**

CROWN STREET

OXFORD STREET

**Sydney Entertainment Centre**

PIER STREET

GOULBURN STREET

CHINATOWN

**Powerhouse Museum**

WILLIAM HENRY STREET

WATTLE STREET

**Paddy's Market & Market City**

HAY ST.

HAYMARKET

GEORGE STREET

BELMORE PARK

RAWSON PL.

⬥ Also see area map, pp. 74–75
▶ Art Gallery of NSW
🕐 2 hours to 1 day
⬌ 4 miles (7 km)
▶ North end of Bridge

MARY ANN STREET

**Central Railway Station**

ALBION STREET

England. The **Royal Botanic Gardens** are a wonderful place for a picnic. In addition to the ornamental trees, duck ponds, sweeping lawns, and flower beds, the gardens have a glassed-in pyramid housing a collection of tropical plants and ferns.

## INSIDER TIP:

**Avoid the tourist traffic and join the office workers for pre-dinner drinks (and fabulous waterfront views) at the Opera Bar, outside the front of the spectacular Opera House.**

—PETER TURNER
*National Geographic author*

From Mrs. Macquarie's chair, you can look straight across Farm Cove to the Opera House. The path hugs the waterfront, but you can take a side trip to **Government House ❸** *(tel (02) 9931 5222, house closed Mon.–Thurs.)*, whose grounds lie within the botanic gardens. This massive two-story home in Gothic Revival style was built in 1843 for the governor of New South Wales, but the republican-minded Labor government gave it to the people in 1996. You can wander freely in the gardens or take a tour of the house, with its Australian masterpieces on the walls, ornate drawing and dining rooms, and stenciled ceilings.

The shoreline path curves around to the **Sydney Opera House** (see pp. 86–87), and from there it follows another inlet (Sydney Cove) a couple hundred yards to **Circular Quay ❹**. This stretch of footpath honors Australia's literary greats, with commemorative plaques set into the paving.

Circular Quay is the point of arrival for thousands of office workers who come daily to the city by ferry. It also attracts visitors taking sightseeing cruises and tour buses or simply

strolling the waterfront. It is probably the liveliest place for people-watching in all of Australia, with its blend of stockbrokers, secretaries, and street sweepers, tourists speaking almost any language imaginable, derelicts, peddlers, hippies, and rural Australians taking a look at "the big smoke." You usually see a gaggle of jugglers, puppeteers, and street musicians, whose talents range from brilliant to embarrassingly awful. Just beyond the quay is the **Museum of Contemporary Art ❺** *(George St., tel (02) 9245 2400)*, in a restored art deco building with a fashionable outdoor café.

The area known as **The Rocks ❻** lies between George Street and the approach road to the bridge. This is Sydney's historic district, a warren of narrow streets and old stone buildings that have been lovingly restored. It is a far cry from the way the place looked in Sydney's Dickensian days, when these alleyways were the most squalid and dangerous in Australia. Here lurked pickpockets, razor gangs, and hard-case thugs. An outbreak of bubonic plague around the turn of the century forced the authorities to step in and demolish some of the rat-infested structures. More were torn down in the 1920s to make way for the approach to the Harbour Bridge. By the 1970s, the government was ready to raze what was left of Sydney's oldest structures and replace them with office blocks. Only a hard-fought campaign by left-wing unions saved the historic quarter. Militant construction workers placed the first of their famous "green bans" on the proposed redevelopment, thereby stopping work. It was a tactic they were to use throughout the 1970s to save numerous heritage buildings around Sydney.

These days, The Rocks is one of Sydney's treasured tourist precincts. It has boutiques, art dealers, cafés, an upscale hotel, and pubs such as the Hero of Waterloo, Sydney's oldest, built in 1844. Also here is the Sunday Market—a popular and relaxed street fair with stalls of food, art, and various bric-a-brac. **Cadman's Cottage ❼**, the oldest house in Sydney (built in 1816), is at 110 George Street (tel (02) 9247 5033). Just along the street, at No. 106, is the Sailor's Home (now Sailor's Thai Restaurant), built in 1864 to provide respectable lodgings for sailors. Upstairs, you can see a sailor's cubicle fitted out as it would have been in the 19th century.

From George Street you can take a short side trip along Argyle Street and then up **Observatory Hill** 8. It is a steep climb, but well worth it for the spectacular—and different—view of the Harbour Bridge, across to North Sydney and down to The Rocks below. Otherwise wind your way through the lanes up to the steps for the Sydney Harbour Bridge walkway on Cumberland Street.

The walk across the bridge to the North Shore is about three-quarters of a mile long (1.2 km), and every step seems to put both Sydney and the bridge's graceful ironwork in a new perspective. A museum inside the massive South Pylon tells the story of the building of the bridge and gives a grand view of the skyline and harbor if you climb to the **Pylon Lookout** 9 at the top. For a really stupendous view, ambitious visitors might like to attempt the Bridge Climb, right over the top of the arch itself (see p. 81).

The walk ends on the north side of the bridge, and the two options for getting back to the city are both beautifully simple. The Milson's Point train station is only a stone's throw from the northern end of the bridge walkway, and from there you can catch a train back across the bridge to Wynyard station. Or you can go the scenic way and walk a couple hundred yards down to the Luna Park or Milson's Point ferry landing then cut across the harbor back to Circular Quay.

At Circular Quay, ferries set out for waterside suburbs and ocean liners still berth.

## Opera House

🅰 75 E2

✉ Bennelong Point

☎ (02) 9250 7111,
reservations
(02) 9250 7777

💲 Tours: $$

**www.sydneyopera
house.com**

# Sydney Opera House

Sydney's Opera House, with its billowing sail roofs and breathtaking harbor setting, is one of the most potent symbols of Australia. The story of its creation is worthy of an opera itself. In fact, the Australian Opera Company recently wrote and staged just such a piece, aptly titled *The Eighth Wonder.*

The saga started in 1955 with a contest to design an opera house for the site of the old tram terminus on Bennelong Point. After looking over 233 entries, the judges selected an innovative design by a Danish architect named Jørn Utzon. His vision for the building, which was to cost around A$7 million (U.S. $3.5 million), resembled sails on the harbor—perfect for a breezy, yachtie-style city like Sydney. (Utzon later said he had actually been inspired by a sequence of orange segments.)

Construction began in 1959, and the trouble started almost immediately. Controversy over the radical design, as well as technical

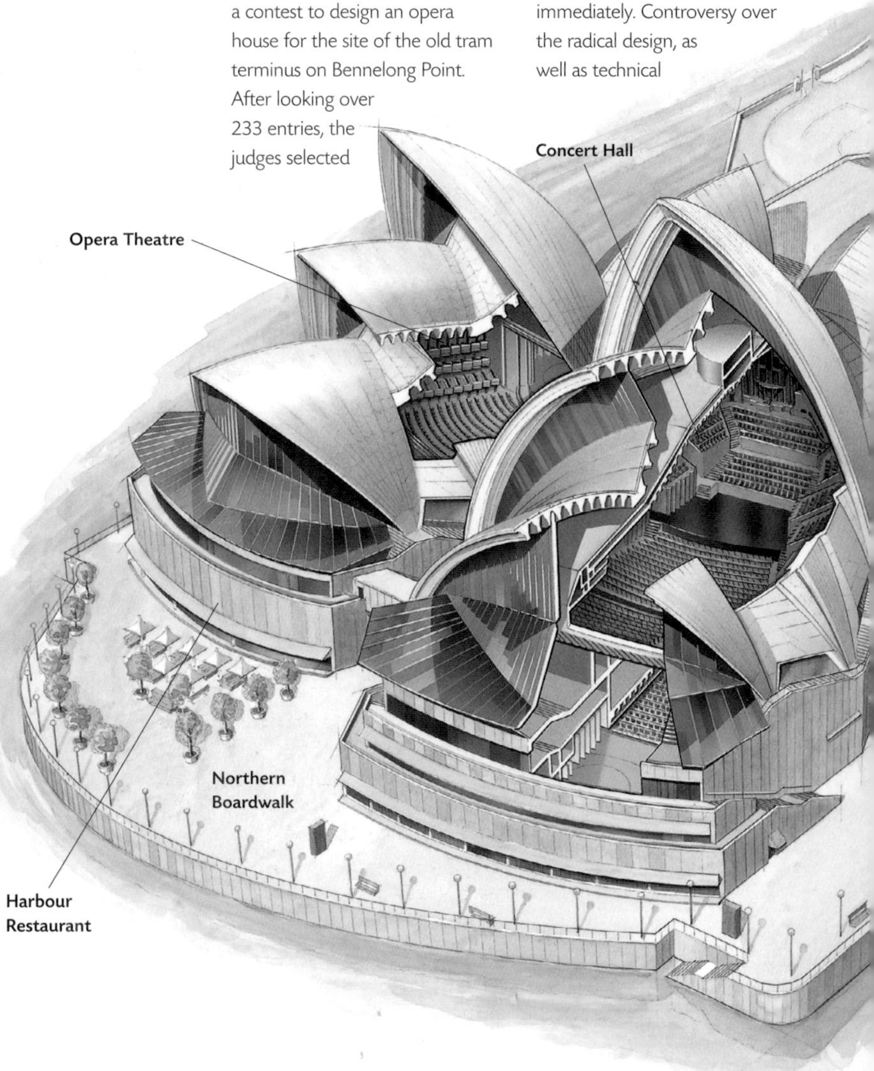

Concert Hall

Opera Theatre

Northern
Boardwalk

Harbour
Restaurant

problems with its construction, bogged down progress. Costs mounted, fueling the controversy. By 1966, Utzon had had enough. He withdrew from the project and returned to Denmark, bitter about what he saw as heavy-handed interference in his work.

The New South Wales government seemed glad to see Utzon go, turning the project over to a team of local architects. Costs continued to spiral. The state funded it with Opera House lotteries. By the time Queen Elizabeth II opened the building in 1973, Sydney's new landmark had cost more than ten times the original estimate, and it was ten years behind schedule. Its first production, appropriately enough, was Prokofiev's *War and Peace.*

Inside are the 1,507-seat **Opera Theatre,** the 2,679-seat **Concert Hall,** two smaller theaters, a cinema, an exhibition hall, and a restaurant. The second flock of sails, the "baby" opera house beside the main complex, contains **Guillaume at Bennelong,** one of Sydney's

**Monumental Steps**

**Guillaume at Bennelong**

**Playhouse**

**Western Boardwalk**

finest restaurants (see p. 368). Take a tour to see the complex.

Happily, more than 30 years after Utzon left Australia, the architect and the New South Wales government reached a rapprochement. In 1999, Utzon was appointed design consultant for remodeling the Opera House, and in 2003, the University of Sydney awarded him an honorary doctorate. Utzon died, aged 90, in 2008. ■

# Downtown Sydney

Once away from its dazzling waterfront, Sydney's concrete-and-glass canyons and traffic-clogged streets resemble those of cities the world over. Cranes on the skyline and construction pits between buildings speak of change. Nevertheless, a stroll through Sydney takes you shopping and sightseeing around a uniquely Australian downtown.

A good place to start is the almost ludicrously ornate Victorian-era **Sydney Town Hall** *(tel 1300 651301)*, on the corner of George and Druitt Streets (see map p. 83). Built of golden sandstone in 1874, it has an elaborate concert hall. Next

The Sydney Tower, built in 1981, is fast becoming an iconic landmark of the city.

to it is **St. Andrew's Cathedral** *(tel (02) 9265 1661)*, about the same age but simpler in style. This is the oldest cathedral in Australia, and at lunchtime on Fridays you can hear free recitals on the powerful pipe organ. The subway station of Town Hall lies beneath these two buildings.

Across Druitt Street is the beautiful **Queen Victoria Building,** built in 1898 for the city's fruit and vegetable markets. This extravagant three-story sandstone building stretches an entire city block along George Street and was carefully restored in the early 1980s, after having fallen into serious disrepair. The sculptured exterior is impressive, but the interior is even more opulent, with mosaics, stained-glass windows, and the elaborate one-ton Royal Clock, which is suspended from a central glass dome. The QVB, as it is known, houses more than 200 upscale boutiques and cafés and has some of the best shopping in Sydney. The cellar holds an inexpensive and varied food court. For something a bit more ostentatious, go across George Street, and in the **Strand Arcade** beneath the Hilton Hotel you'll find the exuberantly Victorian **Marble Bar.**

At the end of the QVB, turn right on Market Street. Two blocks will take you past the ornate **State**

## The Convict Barracks

Off Hyde Park's northern end stands Hyde Park Barracks, home to 800 convicts in Sydney's bad old days. Prisoners were marched out in chairs each morning, little more than slaves, to work on public projects or for one of the free settlers. After transportation to New South Wales ceased in 1848, the barracks became an immigration office and later a court building. The convict-architect Francis Greenway (see p. 61) designed this three-story structure in 1819 in a Grecian style. Today it is a museum on Sydney's social history. Aussies can check genealogical records here to see if any convicts are in their ancestral woodpiles.

---

Theatre *(49 Market St., tel 13 61 00)*, with its gilt decor, and on to the **Sydney Tower** *(100 Market St., tel (02) 9333 9222, $$$)*, on the corner of Pitt Street. Opened in 1981, the 960-foot-high (293 m) tower, with its gold minaret, is the tallest structure in the Southern Hemisphere. Few visitors pass up an opportunity to go to the observatory or one of the two revolving restaurants for sweeping views that stretch as far as the Blue Mountains (see pp. 104–105). If you're feeling daring, walk out onto the glass floor of the tower's **Sydney Skywalk** *($$$$$)*, nearly 900 feet (275 m) above the street.

## Hyde Park & North

Farther down Market Street is Hyde Park, with flower beds and fountains. This is Sydney's central park. Australia's first cricket match was played here in 1803, and on sunny days the park fills up with office workers having lunch. The art deco **Anzac War Memorial,** at the southern end of the park, was built in 1934 to commemorate the dead of World War I. A worthwhile detour here is the **Australian Museum,** on the southeast corner of Hyde Park. This massive sandstone structure houses the nation's largest natural history collection, as well as displays of Aboriginal artifacts.

North of the park, next to the Hyde Park Barracks (see sidebar above), is **The Mint** *(10 Macquarie St., tel (02) 9232 3488, $)*, which started out in 1814 as the Rum Hospital. After gold was discovered in the colonies, it became the Royal Mint, stamping out gold coins from 1854 until 1927. Today it is a museum of gold in Australia.

Beyond the mint is New South Wales's **State Parliament House** *(Macquarie St., tel (02) 9230 2111)*. The public gallery is open when parliament is sitting, and tours are available when it is not. Next door, the **State Library of New South Wales** houses historic records, including the ships' logs of Captains Cook and Bligh. The entryway floor has a mosaic of Capt. Abe Tasman's 17th-century chart of Australian waters.

Head past the **Museum of Sydney** and the Greenway-designed **Conservatorium of Music** *(tel (02) 9351 1263)*, with free lunchtime recitals on Wednesdays, to Circular Quay. ■

**Hyde Park Barracks**

✉ Queens Sq., Macquarie St.

☎ (02) 8239 2311

💲 $

**Australian Museum**

✉ 6 College St. (opposite Hyde Park)

☎ (02) 9360 6000

💲 $

**www.austmus.gov.au**

**State Library of New South Wales**

✉ Macquarie St.

☎ (02) 9273 1414

**Museum of Sydney**

✉ 37 Philip St.

☎ (02) 9251 5988

# Cricket

**Cricket is virtually a way of life for Australians in the summer. People play it in every park, on the beaches, and even in offices, where workers playfully bat at crumpled bits of paper with rolled up magazines around the water cooler. Even airline pilots have been known to make in-flight announcements when a vital wicket falls or a batsman makes his "century"—a landmark score of a hundred runs in a single innings (at-bat).**

**Lee Carseldine of the Queensland Bulls bats in a 2009 cricket match in Perth.**

This fascination with what appears to be one of the world's slowest games bemuses and puzzles most visitors—unless they come from South Africa, England, India, Pakistan, Sri Lanka, New Zealand, or the Caribbean. After all, this is a game that, in its "test match" version, takes five days to play, generally under a broiling sun, and as often as not results in a draw. All this time nobody ever seems to be doing much, except one bloke who keeps running across the field to hurl the ball at another well-padded bloke who slashes at it with a paddle-shaped bat. Maybe he'll hit it and run. Maybe he won't. Hours pass this way. "Baseball on Valium," is how some visiting Americans have dismissed it. But that is to miss all the game's drama and strategy.

The place to see a big-league cricket match in Sydney is the Sydney Cricket Ground (SCG), near Centennial Park in eastern Sydney. The ground holds a little more then 40,000 spectators. The nicest seating is in the elegant Members' Pavilion, built in 1886, but since this haven of politeness is open only to members and their guests, you will probably have to make do with one of the regular stands. The most atmospheric seating used to be the notorious Hill, a grassy patch opposite the Members' Pavilion, where shirtless spectators drank, brawled, and lazed away the scorching Australian afternoons, offering wittily obscene comments on the fielders. These days the Hill is gone, replaced with soulless but more comfortable seating.

There are several varieties of cricket, including the old-style, five-day-long test matches and the newer—and to traditionalists, more vulgar—one-day cricket. The game has become even more truncated with the very popular, almost frenetic, Twenty20 format, with each side bowling 20 overs in a game lasting just over three hours. The faster forms of cricket are becoming the game's money-spinners these days, and a big international match will have the most rousing atmosphere. If you want to get just a glimpse of the game, try going along to the Sydney Cricket Ground for a Sheffield Shield match—played between the states—late in the afternoon, when you can often get in for free to see the last hour's play.

## Rules of the Game

The rules are a little hard to explain, but if you ask an Aussie in the stands, he or she will undoubtedly be only too happy to give you a play-by-play rundown. Discerning Americans will be able to see several similarities to baseball. The game is played with a wide, flat bat made out of willow, and a red ball, slightly smaller but heavier than a baseball, with a single line of stitches around the middle. The playing area is an oval, generally much larger than a ballpark in the U.S. Each side has 11 players, and one team fields while the other bats.

Unlike baseball, cricket has two batsmen up at once, although only one at a time faces the pitcher (called a bowler). The batsman uses his bat to defend a wooden frame behind him, called "the stumps" or "wicket," upon which two pieces of wood, the bales, are balanced. If the bowler can get a ball past him and dislodge those bales, the batsman is out. To use cricket terminology, he's lost his wicket.

Bowlers hurl the ball stiff armed, making it bounce at the batter's feet. They use all manner of tricks to take a wicket, craftily putting spin on the ball so it bounces weirdly off the seam or simply relying on brute power and intimidation, racing in and hurling it at 100 miles an hour so that it rears up in the batsman's face. This can be a dangerous game. Strategically placed fielders wait with cupped hands to catch a nicked ball. As with baseball, anything caught on the fly is out. The fielder behind the wicket (the wicketkeeper) wears mitts, but nobody else does. It's a game for players with lightning-fast reflexes and tough, calloused hands, who don't mind the odd broken finger or three.

Batsmen have to try to hit the ball and score runs. The duel between batsman and bowler can go on for hours. A ball hit to the boundary is worth four runs. One hit over the fence, home-run style, is worth six. Otherwise the batsmen scamper back and forth between the stumps for single runs. Eventually somebody loses their wicket and a new batsman comes in. When a team loses ten wickets, its innings ends and the fielding side comes in to bat. In a test match, each side gets two innings.

Although professional cricket players are anything but choir boys—the beer drinking record of 56 cans on the flight from Sydney to London is held by a former Australian batsman—there are no American-style tantrums or umpire bullying displays on the field. The pride of nations rests on the decorum of their cricketers. Even outrageous umpiring decisions are accepted with tensely gritted teeth. Another note to globe-trotting American sports buffs: if the ball is hit into the stands, you must give it back.

## Sir Donald Bradman

When polls are run to nominate the greatest Australian of all time, the cricketer Sir Donald Bradman (1908–2001) regularly tops the list. The batting hero was not only the preeminent cricketer of his time, but Australians regard him as the greatest sportsman ever

Raised in Bowral, New South Wales, where he showed prodigious talent from an early age, the young Bradman first represented Australia against England in 1928 and quickly set about amassing record batting scores. By the time he toured England as captain for the last time in 1948, he had cemented his place as the greatest batter the game had ever seen. His career batting average of 99.94, just short of a freakish 100, remains almost double that of any cricketer before or since.

"The Don" retired to Adelaide, where he became a statesman of the game. Giving audiences to young cricketers and politicians alike, his name is often used to invoke the nationalist cause. The word Bradmanesque has entered the Australian lexicon and means succeeding far above all others.

# Darling Harbour

Once an eyesore of dilapidated wharves, Darling Harbour is now a humming tourism and leisure precinct on the waterfront. It opened in 1988, amid the fanfare of Australia's bicentennial, and the area has not looked back since. Skyscrapers have sprouted nearby, as have a convention-center-scale hotel and a glittering new casino, and businesses have shifted to the area. But Darling Harbour was designed for family-oriented entertainment—and it delivers.

Sydney's monorail links Darling Harbour with the Central Business District.

**Darling Harbour**
◭ 75 E2

**Visitor Information**
☎ (02) 9286 0111
🚝 Monorail from Market St. or Pitt St.; Sydney Explorer bus or ferry from Circular Quay

www.darlingharbour.com

The area's two biggest family attractions are the Powerhouse Museum and the Sydney Aquarium. Both are world class. The **Powerhouse Museum** is in an old electricity generating station that used to power Sydney's tramway system. Nominally a museum of applied industry (and it does have superb exhibits of working steam engines), it exuberantly exceeds its brief, offering imaginatively displayed collections on Australian music, costume jewelry, trains, and

more. The museum emphasizes hands-on fun and interactive displays and makes a particularly nice place to bring kids.

Darling Harbour's other blockbuster attraction is the **Sydney Aquarium** (the ferry stops here). Its transparent underwater tunnels allow visitors to stroll among the sharks, eels, and stingrays of its immensely popular "Open Ocean" exhibit. This is one of three oceanariums moored in the harbor in front of the aquarium building. Another is devoted to the harbor's own ecosystem, and the third to seals and sea lions. Inside the main building are coral displays, a Great Barrier Reef exhibit, and saltwater crocodiles. The aquarium's popularity is also its main drawback: The place can get very crowded on weekends. Nearby is the restored 1938 steam ferry, the S.S. *Steyne*. Star City, Sydney's glitzy casino-hotel complex, sprawls on the northeastern flank of Darling Harbour. Next to the aquarium, the small **Sydney Wildlife World** (*Aquarium Pier, tel (02) 9333 9288, $$$*) has wallabies, koalas, nocturnal marsupials, snakes, and birds.

## Around the Harbor

The aquarium is a good place to begin a looping walk around Darling Harbour. Start by walking across the **Pyrmont Bridge,** built

## INSIDER TIP:

**The Sydney Aquarium stays open until 10:00 every night—it's a great evening activity after dinner at one of Darling Harbour's many restaurants.**

—LARRY PORGES
*National Geographic editor*

in 1902 as the world's first electrically operated swing bridge to accommodate tall-masted ships. It is used only by pedestrians and the monorail today.

When you get across, the **Australian National Maritime Museum** is on the right. It tells

Australia's seagoing story from Aboriginal canoes and convict ships to 20th-century ocean liners. The broader story of Australia and the sea is also covered, from the age of exploration to surfing culture to the immigrants who have come by sea, both legally and illegally. A World War II destroyer, a Soviet sub, and a Vietnamese refugee boat are moored in the harbor in front.

On the left as you step off the Pyrmont Bridge is the enormous, glass-and-steel **Harbourside.** This tourist shopping mall has a multi-story food court, which developers hoped would make it the focal point for the Darling Harbour project. In fact, it is probably the least interesting feature of the precinct.

Half a mile west, the bustling **Sydney Fish Market** (*Bank Street, tel (02) 9004 1100*) on Blackwattle Bay is the city's main seafood market and a better spot for lunch. As well as weekly wholesale auctions, retail outlets sell fresh seafood and cheap sumptuous platters to eat inside or at tables outside.

A stroll along the harborside, past the **Sydney Exhibition Centre,** will bring you to the **Chinese Garden** (*Harbour Rd., tel (02) 9281 6863, $*) at the southern end of Darling Harbour. Effective at shutting out the hustle and bustle of the city, the walled enclave has a Lake of Brightness and Courtyard of Welcoming Fragrance. Chinese tea and cakes are available.

Get revved up again at the eight-story **IMAX Theatre** nestled in the freeway interchange nearby. Follow the waterfront back to Pyrmont Bridge, or catch the monorail as it slithers along the city streets. ∎

**Powerhouse Museum**
✉ 500 Harris St.
☎ (02) 9217 0111
$ $$
**www.powerhouse museum.com**

**Sydney Aquarium**
✉ Darling Harbour
☎ (02) 9262 2300
$ $$$
**www.sydneyaquarium .com.au**

**Australian National Maritime Museum**
✉ Darling Harbour
☎ (02) 9298 3777
$ $$
**www.anmm.gov.au**

**IMAX Theatre**
✉ Southern Promenade, Darling Harbour
☎ (02) 9281 3300

# Bohemian Sydney

In a city known the world over for its breezy, beachy indolence, bohemia (in shorts, thongs, and Bollé sunglasses) seems to be everywhere. Paddington and Darlinghurst, though, in the inner east, make a strong claim for primacy with their blend of seediness and sophistication. Oxford Street, the main thoroughfare, is a cavalcade of retro cafés, bookshops, nightclubs, strip joints, galleries dealing in ultracool kitsch, sex shops, and black leather.

The highlight of Sydney's Gay and Lesbian Mardi Gras is the spectacular parade down Oxford Street.

This spread-out strip has no particular social focus, although on Saturday mornings the bustling **Paddington Village Bazaar** comes close. One of the architectural features of Sydney's inner east is the elegantly restored Victorian-era row houses, their balconies trimmed with wrought iron that used to be known as "Paddington lace."

## Darlinghurst

Darlinghurst is a sort of trendy Little Italy, with its self-consciously cool sidewalk cafés. Stanley Street, which runs due east off Hyde Park, is the social scene here, and it is a good spot to linger over an espresso and the Sunday newspaper, soaking in the ambience and the sunshine.

**Kings Cross,** a few blocks farther north, is Sydney's red-light district—a weird blend of prostitution, crime, strip joints, nightclubs, fast food, and hard drugs, with a smattering of expensive restaurants and international hotels thrown in to confuse. The Cross, as it is known, was a popular R&R hangout for troops on leave during the Vietnam War, and it still attracts a lot of them, along with curious tourists,

## EXPERIENCE: Priscilla Tours

Stephan Elliott's 1994 film, The Adventures of Priscilla, Queen of the Desert, tells the tale of Sydney drag queens who take their show to the outback. An Academy Award winner for best costume design, the movie later inspired a musical. Today, it also provides the theme for flamboyant city tours by professional diva Portia

Turbo, who appeared in the movie. Fun bus tours (tel (02) 9310 0200, www .toursbydiva.com.au/), complete with champagne, take in the usual Sydney sights (Opera House, Harbour Bridge), as well as the gay haunts of the Oxford Strip, with opportunities to don a wig and perform.

runaways, derelicts, college students on a big night out, and bachelor parties (called Bucks' nights here). The El Alamein Fountain in Fitzroy Gardens is the area's focal point.

Just east, **Elizabeth Bay** rubs shoulders with the Cross, but it is decidedly quieter and infinitely more fashionable This was Sydney's fashionable bohemian quarter in the 1920s, and, with its stylish period apartment blocks, it is still popular with writers, entertainers, and journalists.

### Glebe & Balmain

The peninsular suburbs of Glebe and Balmain, in Sydney's inner west, used to be rough working-class neighborhoods for dockyard workers, but they have now been discovered and their houses carefully restored. Balmain is rich in Victorian-era waterfront pubs, while Glebe is a jumble of interesting hole-in-the-wall eateries, cafés, and bistros. (Balmain is accessible by ferry from Circular Quay or bus 442 from the Queen Victoria Building. To get to Glebe, take bus 431 or 433 along George St. and up Glebe Point Rd.)

### Newtown

Newtown (take the Liverpool-City rail line) is a funky melting pot of students, gays and lesbians, intellectuals, and artists, perched on the edge of Sydney University. Thirty years ago it was regarded as a grungy slum. Now it is fashionably chic, although it still has a strong underground feel to it. King

**INSIDER TIP:**

**Visit Jubilee Park at Glebe Point on Thursday nights to watch the weekly fire-twirling spectacle, then head over to Newtown for dinner or a cocktail to round out the evening.**

—BEN KEAR
National Geographic field researcher

Street, the main thoroughfare, has trendy cafés, ethnic restaurants, and secondhand bookshops. The hot, sweaty, and smoky pubs here are the focus of Sydney's dwindling live band scene. ∎

### Oxford Street

Bus 333 or 380 from Circular Quay runs the length of Oxford St.

### Paddington Village Bazaar

Corner of Oxford & Newcombe Sts.

### Kings Cross

Bus 324, 325, 326, or 327 from Circular Quay. Train station on Darlinghurst Rd.

# Beaches

There are more than 70 named beaches around Sydney, some of them on the harbor, others fringing the ocean. The closest ocean beach to downtown Sydney is Bondi Beach, which has become synonymous around the world with Aussie surf culture. On weekends this golden crescent of sand, located 5 miles (8 km) west of Sydney, becomes a coconut oil–scented kaleidoscope of thousands of beach towels, bronzed swimmers, surfers, and sunbathers.

Sydney's iconic Bondi Beach

### Bondi Beach

As a suburb, Bondi (pronounced Bond-EYE) calls to mind a fading seaside resort. Bondi's glory days would have been in the 1920s and '30s, judging by the art deco Bondi Hotel, the jumble of 1920s apartment blocks overlooking the beach,

and the gaudy Spanish-style Bondi Pavilion, which was built as deluxe changing rooms in 1928. In the 1990s, the town spent a lot of money to spruce up tired facades, landscape the foreshore, and improve Campbell Street—a traffic-clogged thoroughfare of ice cream parlors, surf shops, hostels, and flash cafés. Christmas on Bondi Beach was a family tradition, but drunken hooliganism has forced alcohol bans on the beach. Today, Bondi is crowded with local and visiting beach bums. It makes a great sunny, salty, breezy day out. A scenic 3-mile (5 km) walk wends around the cliff tops to the other beaches.

## Other Beaches

South of Bondi is **Tamarama Beach,** known as Glamarama because it is where Sydney's beautiful people hang out. A mile or so farther south are **Bronte** and **Coogee Beaches,** smaller versions of Bondi.

**Manly Beach,** north of the harbor, is probably Sydney's second best known crescent of sand. Manly (see p. 78) occupies a narrow spit of land that ends in the dramatic sandstone cliffs at the entrance to the

harbor. All these beaches are "outer beaches" facing the open Pacific.

The inner harbor has dozens of lovely beaches. One of the prettiest is **Balmoral,** on Hunters Bay. It has a genteel, Edwardian atmosphere, with palm trees and an old bandstand at the Bather's Pavilion, which is now home to an extremely classy restaurant. ■

**INSIDER TIP:**

Become a true local by signing up for surfing lessons at any of Sydney's popular beaches. Be prepared to be sore the next day—it's great exercise! The best surfing beaches are Bondi and Manly.

—FARNOUSH AFARINESH
*National Geographic*
*Channels International*

## Surf Lifesavers

Nothing evokes Sydney better than images of blue sky, golden sand, and the bronzed figures of its legendary surf lifesavers in their distinctive yellow and red caps. The world's first surf lifesaving club was formed at the Bondi Pavilion in 1906. The club was formed in response to a rising number of drownings, as increasing numbers of people began to pursue the new craze called bodysurfing. Few knew anything about riptides or surf conditions then, because until around 1900, the authorities discouraged daylight swimming as an affront to public decency.

Surf lifesaving clubs quickly sprang up all around Australia. There are now 305 of them, with 25,000 active members, who rescue about 11,000 swimmers each year. Surf lifesaving has also become a sport in its own right, with colorful surf carnivals.

Bondi's lifesavers, who guard Australia's busiest and most famous beach, have plucked more than 400,000 people out of the surf since 1906. To make sure you don't add to that tally, swim between the yellow-and-red lifesaving flags. If you do get caught in a riptide, do not try to fight it. Swim to the side to try to get out of it and raise your hand to attract a lifesaver.

# A Sydney-style New Year's

**If you are near Sydney over the Christmas–New Year's holiday, don't miss seeing the start of the great Sydney-to-Hobart yacht race on Boxing Day, the day after Christmas. The harbor fills with the sails of dozens of the world's fastest blue-water yachts, all jockeying for position ahead of the cannon fire that will start the annual 630-mile (1,014 km) race to Hobart, Tasmania, as well as those of thousands of spectator craft.**

The sight of Sydney Harbour in full flower is unforgettable—eclipsed only by the fireworks extravaganza that ushers in the New Year. This is the celebration seen worldwide, with hundreds of skyrockets zooming off the arch of Sydney's iconic bridge, the skies above alight with starbursts and the harbor filled with hundreds of yachts.

## Greeting the New Year

Australia is one of the first places in the world to greet the new year, and party-loving Sydneysiders really do it in style. Each year's celebrations follow a theme—2007, for example, marked the 75th birthday of the

INSIDER TIP:

**A New Year's resolution that's easy to keep is a late-night stop at historic Harry's Cafe de Wheels [*www.harryscafede wheels.com.au*] for one of the their famous "pies and peas."**

—CATHERINE PEARSON
*National Geographic contributor*

Harbour Bridge, while an earlier sparkling display for children at 9 p.m. had a Wizard of Oz theme, including dueling rainbow fireworks displays and a snazzy pair of giant pyrotechnic ruby slippers that popped into life on the bridge's ironwork.

In all, 6,500 pounds (3 tonnes) of explosives are used in these extravaganzas—more than

10,000 shells, 11,000 shooting comets, and 100,000 pyrotechnic effects in all. They are launched by computer from a series of barges anchored in the harbor, a complex arrangement involving more than 7,500 cues and taking months to plan and choreograph.

## Planning for Celebration

More than a million people will be thronging the vantage points along the waterfront, so having some idea in advance of where you want to be is a big help to having a nice time. Lists of venues and vantage points are available from tourist offices. Rules on alcohol consumption vary from place to place and vary from BYO to limited sales to none allowed at all. Glass is generally banned on safety grounds.

Access to some of the small but prime vantage points, such as Goat Island and Denison Island out on Sydney Harbour, are by ticket only, with the much-sought-after tickets going on sale late in November. Popular tickets include: Midnight at the Oasis, a night of high style at the Royal Botanic Gardens, gourmet meal and breathtaking views of the fireworks provided; and Lawn with a View, a picnic at Bennelong Lawn set against the grand Sydney skyline *(ticket details for both at www.rbgsyd.nsw.gov.au).* For a night of family fun, ring in the New Year at the Taronga Park Zoo with animal displays, live performances, and views of the harbor fireworks. Details about the zoo event and other New Year's Eve tickets can be found on Sydney's official website *(www.cityofsydney .nsw.gov.au/NYE).*

New Year's Eve fireworks explode off the Harbour Bridge.

# Zoos & Wildlife Parks

The warm breath of the bush is never far away in Sydney—long tentacles of bushland reach into the suburbs, possums come out to nibble rosebuds in backyard gardens, and, at night, hundreds of giant native fruit bats, or flying foxes, wheel in the corporate glow. However, your best chance of seeing Australia's unique wildlife up close is to visit one of the local zoos or wildlife parks.

Taronga Park Zoo has a lovely setting in Sydney Harbour.

### Taronga Park Zoo

🔺 75 E3

✉ Bradleys Head Rd., Mosman

☎ (02) 9969 2777

💲 $$$$

🚢 Ferry from Circular Quay

**Taronga Park Zoo** is the easiest to reach from Sydney. It sits on a leafy hill in Mosman, overlooking Sydney Harbour, just a 15-minute ferry trip from Circular Quay. Combination zoo-ferry tickets are available at the ferry landing.

The zoo has a world-class collection of wildlife, and the spacious enclosures resemble natural habitats. Nocturnal houses and low-light enclosures reduce the stress on night-loving animals, while allowing visitors to observe them. The gorilla rain forest and the chimpanzee park are always popular, but for visitors from outside Australia the enclosures where kangaroos, wombats, and other indigenous creatures are on display are must-sees. The koala one features a walkway that winds up to the creatures in the treetops.

Two major wildlife parks in Sydney's far western outskirts give closer, and perhaps more touristy, encounters with Australian fauna. **Featherdale Wildlife Park** *(217 Kildare Rd., Doonside, tel (02) 9622 1644, www.featherdale.com.au, $$$)* is the best for seeing koalas, kangaroos, wallabies, wombats, crocodiles, Tasmanian devils, kookaburras, and other birdlife. It's well worth a stop on the way to the Blue Mountains. The **Koala Park Sanctuary** *(84 Castle Hill Rd., West Pennant Hills, tel (02) 9484 3141, $$)* has a large resident population of cute koalas, with cuddling sessions, and up-close encounters with other marsupials and Australian birdlife.

On the other hand, the once rare flora that you can now touch is the Wollemi pine. In one of the most startling botanical discoveries of the 20th century, a stand of 37 of these Jurassic-era trees was found in an ancient gorge less than a hundred miles from downtown Sydney in 1994. A program to preserve the species proved so successful that in April 2006 the trees went on sale to the general public. (Visit *www.wollemipine .com* for more details.) ∎

Beyond glamorous Sydney, subtropical rain forests, high alpine grasslands, and dusty frontier outback

# New South Wales

Introduction & Map    102–103

Blue Mountains    104–105

Feature: Bushfires    106–107

Jenolan Caves    108

Tamworth    109

Hunter Valley    110–111

Along the South Coast    112–113

Snowy Mountains    114–115

Experience: Man from Snowy
River Rides    115

Broken Hill    116–117

Pacific Highway Drive    118–121

Experience: Houseboats on the
Hawkesbury    118

Outlying Territories    122–126

Experience: Wildlife Australia    125

Hotels & Restaurants    369–370

Alpine sunray, Kosciuszko National
Park, Snowy Mountains

# New South Wales

**New South Wales calls itself the Premier or First State, ostensibly because it was Australia's first colony but also because it tops the rest of Australia in just about everything these days, at least in the minds of the proudly parochial New South Welsh. Sydney is here, for one thing, and Sydney is the financial and arts capital of Australia, as well as the nation's biggest population center.**

In addition to Sydney, New South Wales has spectacular and diverse landscapes, from winter snowfields on the country's highest mountain (the 7,310-foot/2,228 m Mount Kosciuszko) to sultry banana plantations on the north coast and the outback to the west.

The mighty Murray River forms its southern boundary and nourishes the country's agricultural heartland. Broken Hill, one of the grand old Australian mining towns, is now an outback art colony, its clear, fragile light attracting painters and filmmakers.

For those on a time budget, this is the place to concentrate. Almost everything in Australia—rain forests, dusty outback landscapes, mountains, beaches—can be found here, including five World Heritage sites: an improbable mix of the Gondwana Rainforests; the lake beds of Willandra National Park, where Aborigines have lived for 40,000 years; Lord Howe Island,

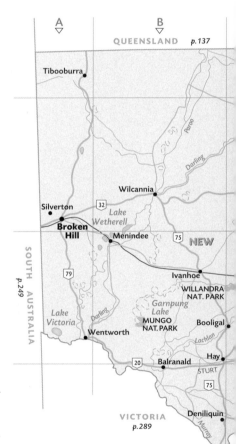

---

## NOT TO BE MISSED:

The spectacular panoramas from the Blue Mountains    104–105

Line dancing at the Tamworth Country Music Festival    109

Touring the wineries of the scenic Hunter Valley    110–111

A horse trek or alpine hike in the Snowy Mountains    114–115

Byron Bay, the funkiest resort along the north coast    121

Venturing offshore to lush, tropical Lord Howe Island    122–124

---

430 miles (692 km) off the central coast; the Blue Mountains just west of Sydney; and that grand architectural dame, the Sydney Opera House. New South Wales also has Tamworth, Australia's country music capital.

About an hour's drive north of Sydney, the Hunter Valley is Australia's oldest winemaking region and a popular weekend retreat. Cessnock, the main town in the valley, is surrounded by more than 120 wineries with ample opportunities to visit and taste. Follow the New England Highway through the valley to Scone, home to some of Australia's finest racehorse studs and glamorous polo tournaments. Farther north on the Pacific Highway are the World Heritage rain forests of Dorrigo National Park. ∎

Canberra

Area of map detail

# Blue Mountains

From a distance, the Blue Mountains resemble an old oil painting, with hazy blue hues that seem a trifle overdone. The blue haze is actually a fine mist of eucalyptus oil given off by dense forests. The droplets refract the sunlight, tinting the air and giving the horizon a painted-on effect. Although the Blue Mountains are only just over 3,000 feet high (915 m), they proved an impenetrable barrier for the first settlers.

It was not until 1813 that a trio of explorers—Lawson, Blaxland, and Wentworth—found a way through and opened up the wide, flat grazing country on the other side. In 1868, the railroad was built, opening up the mountains themselves. Suddenly it was possible for well-heeled Sydney-siders to escape the coastal heat

The Blue Mountains' scenic vistas are among the atmospheric area's many charms.

and take the air in the mountains. By 1900, Katoomba, Wentworth Falls, and Mount Victoria had become fashionable resorts, with high-toned restaurants and shops and graceful Victorian hotels to cater to those who didn't have the money to build a mountain retreat themselves. The high point was reached in the 1920s, with guesthouses catering to families, while the art deco Hydro Majestic in Medlow Bath drew society's high rollers.

New Englanders may find something nookish about these leafy old resort towns—with their antiques shops, cafés, and home-made fudge—that reminds them of home. The mountains have hiking trails and tourist marvels like the Scenic Railway, which plunges into a gorge in what is said to be the world's steepest railway. It even snows here, a little, in winter. In June, the region has a Yuletide Festival, with crackling fires, roast beef and Yorkshire pudding dinners, and hot spiced wine. Afternoon tea at the **Lilianfels Blue Mountains Hotel** (see p. 369) in Katoomba is a year-round tradition.

**Katoomba** is the main town in the Blue Mountains. It perches on the rim of the Jamison Valley, with spectacular outlooks over the wilderness below. This is the best place to base yourself if you decide against driving through the snarl of traffic in Sydney's western suburbs and take the train. Katoomba has hotels, inns, and B&Bs Almost everything is within walking distance of the station, and local buses serve the area as well. In fact, if you are short on time, the Blue Mountains can be a longish, but by no means unreasonable, day trip from Sydney. Bring a sweater because it will be cooler here than in Sydney.

A 20-minute walk down Katoomba Street takes you past antiques shops, galleries, and the sumptuous art deco **Paragon Café,** established in 1916 and famous since the 1920s for its fine handmade chocolates and confectionery, though it is noted more for its heritage value these days. Then you come to **Echo Point.** The view here is simply stunning. Off to the left are the **Three Sisters,** a formation of honey-colored sandstone nubs that take their name from an Aboriginal Dreamtime legend. One version tells of a tribal leader who turned his daughters to stone rather than risk their being carried away by raiding enemies. Unfortunately, he was killed in battle and could not reverse his spell.

Easy clifftop paths are marked along the edge of the valley. Or you can take the **Giant Staircase**—a steep set of steps cut into the rock—1,000 feet (300 m) down to the valley floor. From here you can take day hikes to popular features like the **Ruined Castle** rock formation, and longer treks as far as **Jenolan Caves,** 26 miles (42 km) away (see p. 108).

Or you can hike along the valley floor to **Orphan Rock** and then take the **Scenic Railway** back up to Katoomba *(tel (02) 4782 2699).* Nearby is the **Scenic Skyway** *(tel (02) 4782 2699),* a cable car that gives spectacular views of the valley.

**Leura,** smaller and prettier than Katoomba, lies about 2 miles (3.2 km) to the east. It has a quaint village atmosphere that evokes its 1920s origins. There are great cafés,

## INSIDER TIP:

**For a taste of tranquility, take a leisurely bushwalk in the Blue Mountains. Be sure not to miss the legendary sandstone Three Sisters rock formation.**

—DANIELLE WILLIAMS
*National Geographic Television*

art galleries, and antiques galleries. Scenic hiking paths lead to Leura Cascades, Bridal Veil Falls, and Gordon Falls. You can also hike along the clifftops to Katoomba.

Five miles (8 km) northwest of Katoomba is the old spa town of **Medlow Bath.** Because the eucalyptus-laden air was believed to have therapeutic powers, early 20th-century hoteliers hoped guests would come to take the waters as well. The **Hydro Majestic Hotel** *(tel (02) 4788 1002)* here still has its eye-catching art deco facade, and renovations promise to make it a top hotel again. Its dining room offers one of the best views of the valley. ∎

**Blue Mountains**
- Map p. 103
**Visitor Information**
- Great Western Hwy., Glenbrook
- 1-300 653 408

**Katoomba**
- 103 D3
**Visitor Information**
- Echo Point
- (02) 4739 6266

# Bushfires

On February 7, 2009, after prolonged drought and a severe heat wave, more than 400 bushfires broke out in the state of Victoria. Fanned by fierce winds, terrifying hundred-foot-high (30 m) flames roared through forests and towns claiming 173 lives, destroying 2,200 homes, and leaving 7,500 homeless.

**A bushfire rages near Alice Springs in Australia's Red Centre.**

Even to Australians, long used to bushfires, this tragedy—the country's worst natural disaster—was hard to believe. These were not isolated outback blazes but infernos that threatened the outskirts of Melbourne, Australia's second largest city. In the aftermath, the country tried to devise strategies to stop a recurrence, but this was not the first and will not be the last deadly bushfire. In 2005, for example, flames swept through the arid brushland of the Eyre Peninsula killing nine, and in 2003, the outskirts of Sydney and the suburbs of Canberra burned, killing four.

The journals of Australia's early explorers were filled with references to bushfires and a land shrouded by smoke. Many of the fires they encountered were caused by summer lightning strikes in the tinder-dry grass, but others were deliberately set by Aborigines, who used fire as a management tool to clear scrub, drive game, and help their ancient land to renew itself.

While scorched earth and the blackened ribs of a eucalyptus forest may not be pretty to look at, such periodic wiping out and starting over is vital for the health of the Australian bush. Many of its species, such as banksias, grass trees, and cycads are known as "fire climax" plants—those whose seeds are matured and released only by the intense heat of a bushfire. The eucalyptus even provides the tinder for its own eventual demise by continually shedding its crisp, paperlike bark. When fire comes, as it inevitably must, it sweeps away the forests' old, mature growth, allowing space for the next generation to sprout.

## History of Devastation

While this may be part of the natural order, it can have devastating human consequences, and not even the nation's most cosmopolitan neighborhoods are immune, as the residents of Melbourne were reminded in 2009, and Sydney and Canberra in 2003. In 1939, vast bushfires roared out of control throughout South Australia, Victoria, and New South Wales. And on Ash Wednesday in 1983, South Australians suffered one of the country's most devastating bushfires, as the Adelaide Hills went up in flames, with wildfires claiming dozens of lives and scores of fashionable homes.

## Risk & Renewal

Australians have had to learn to live with fire. Each day's fire danger is usually given with the weather report on the evening news. Homeowners prepare for the summer fire season by cutting away the bushy undergrowth from around their houses, clearing dead leaves and twigs from their guttering, and making sure their garden hoses are in good working order. Many join the volunteer fire brigade—known as the Country Fire Service (C.F.S.)—and devote weekends to training and practice. Town councils, working alongside the C.F.S. and meteorology bureau, often arrange controlled burn-offs to clean out the drying scrub, particularly if the winter has been rainy and the undergrowth has sprouted up thick and tall. The highest risk comes on hot, windy days, late in summer, when the bush is just so many square miles of crisp, dry tinder waiting for a spark. And that can literally be all it takes—a spark, or a carelessly discarded cigarette, to start a raging fire of biblical proportions.

There are few things more terrifying than an Australian bushfire, with its roaring walls of flame. Fueled by the flammable natural oils in the leaves and wood of the eucalyptus, which make each tree a potential torch, bushfires race from treetop to treetop, like chain lightning, sweeping down a hillside faster than a man can run or a horse can gallop—sometimes too fast even for a fleeing vehicle. There is a random quality to the destruction that Americans who live in the tornado belt of the Midwest would recognize: A car can be incinerated, while the one stranded immediately behind is untouched; one house can be razed, but its neighbor doesn't even get its gardens singed.

If the destructive power of its fires is awesome, the bushland's capacity for renewal seems nothing short of miraculous. Even with the blackened earth still warm and the air fragrant with eucalyptus smoke, there are dashes of green amid the ashes from the fire-resistant shrubs that survived the blaze. Within weeks, grasses are sprouting and the first shoots of the next generation of trees are peeking through.

Battling a 2006 blaze in Perth, Western Australia

# Jenolan Caves

The Jenolan Caves are a series of 300 limestone caverns in the hillsides about 50 miles (80 km) by road southwest from Katoomba. Back in the 1920s, this was the prime honeymoon spot for adventurous young Australians, who had to drive their jalopies over hairpin roads to get here.

**Jenolan Caves**

⊠ 103 D3

☎ (02) 6359 9311

$ $$–$$$$$

✉ Turnoff to the caves is marked 18 miles (28 km) W of Katoomba toward Lithgow on the Great Western Highway

**www.jenolancaves .org.au**

The walls of the old Jenolan Caves House Hotel, at the caves' entrance, are lined with faded black-and-white photos of picnickers and men in straw boaters rowing lady friends on subterranean lakes. Somehow the place has managed to retain a sense of that fresh innocence: It's touristy, but delightful at the same time.

**INSIDER TIP:**

**The final stretch of road from Katoomba into the Jenolan Valley is one-way (inbound) from 11:45 a.m.–1:45 p.m. There are alternate routes out of the valley, but plan ahead.**

—ROFF SMITH
*National Geographic author*

The caves are located on the edge of Kanagra-Boyd National Park. In the 1830s, they were a hideout for the bushranger James McKeown, an escaped convict who preyed on the coaches traveling through the mountains. After his capture, the caves became tourist attractions, but some of the farther reaches remain unexplored.

Eleven caves are open to the public, and the caverns and features have grandiose names such as **Temple of Baal, Pool of Cerberus,** and **Imperial Diamond.** Tours run every half hour, and the caves are graded in difficulty by how many steps they have. A "strenuous" cave may have as many as 1,575 steps, an easy one about 300. Adventure caving packages from two to six hours include abseiling and rock climbing. No experience is necessary, and overalls and a hat are provided.

Public transportation does not go to Jenolan Caves, but bus tours from Katoomba include the caves. This twisting drive through steep and dense forests is not for the faint-hearted, but the mountainside precipices give sweeping views over the pastoral country west of the ranges.

The areas has fine bushwalks, from the short, scenic Carlotta Arch Track to the three-day **Six Foot Track** all the way to Katoomba. Originally cleared as a bridle path in 1884, this track begins at the Explorers Tree on the highway in Katoomba (the Katoomba visitor center has walk maps) and stretches 28 miles (45 km). There are two campsites, and guided walks are available (*www.lifesanadventure.com.au*) with one night in an eco-lodge. ■

# Tamworth

**Tamworth is Australia's country music capital, a sort of antipodean Nashville. In case you didn't know this already, a 40-foot (12 m) Golden Guitar will clue you in as you drive into town. Pull into the Tamworth Country Centre beside the giant guitar, and meet some stars—at least in effigy: Chad Morgan, Slim Dusty, and Tex Morton, to name a few.**

If you have the radio on during the 250-mile (400 km) drive north from Sydney (on the Pacific and New England Highways), you will no doubt figure out that country music is big in Australia.

This love affair with country music started in 1965, when local radio station 2TM began its nightly *Hoedown* program and staged live shows at the Tamworth Town Hall. These shows attracted some of Australia's top country artists and drew large crowds from around the grazing districts.

In 1973, the inaugural Country Music Awards began and quickly snowballed into the annual **Tamworth Country Music Festival.** For ten days every January, up to 50,000 country music fans, musicians, impresarios, talent scouts, agents, and bush poets descend on Tamworth. Book well in advance if you plan to stay. The festival reaches its climax on Australia Day (January 26) weekend, when the Australasian country music awards—the Golden Guitars— are presented. Each year a new name is added to the **Roll of Renown,** near the Radio Centre. These days, the *Hoedown* radio program that started it all back in 1965 is still thriving,

Tamworth's music festival attracts rollicking bands, including the Pigs, whose high-energy performances earn raves.

broadcasting country music all night, every night.

The **Hands of Fame Cornerstone** on Kable Avenue has the concrete prints of more than 250 guitar-picking hands of country music stars. The **Winners Walkway** has bronze plaques set in the pavement, commemorating Golden Guitar winners since 1973.

Pick up a map at the visitor center and take a heritage walk around town, passing some fine old buildings. Out of festival time, you may not hear much country music as you make your way through Tamworth, but a recording studio can be visited by appointment. Ask at the visitor center for more information. ∎

**Tamworth**
103 E4
**Visitor Information**
Corner of Peel & Murray Sts.
(02) 6767 5300

# Hunter Valley

The Hunter Valley is an odd mix of coal-mining towns, racehorse country, and some of Australia's best known and oldest wineries. The first vines were planted here around 1830, and today there are more than 120 wineries in the valley. The region is only a three-hour drive from Sydney, so it has become a popular day trip or weekend getaway for city wine buffs and others.

The Hunter Valley produces some of Australia's most famous wines.

### Hunter Valley

🅰 103 E3

**Visitor Information**

✉ 455 Wine Country Dr., Pokolbin

☎ (02) 4990 0900

### Singleton

**Visitor Information**

✉ 39 George St.

☎ 1-800 449 888 (toll-free)

The old coal-mining town of **Cessnock** on Route 82 is the gateway to the **Lower Hunter Valley.** The heart of the winemaking region is around **Pokolbin,** about 6 miles (9.6 km) northwest of Cessnock on McDonalds Road.

Pokolbin is home to the Hunter Valley Wine Country visitor center, a great source of brochures and maps to guide you around the wineries of the region. Some of the labels on the maps will be familiar—Rosemount Estate and Lindemans, for example—but others will be mysteries worth exploring. Semillon and shiraz are the region's signature wines, but a number of varietals are grown. Several wineries also have restaurants.

Dozens of wineries, such as Lindemans and Tyrells, are concentrated within a few minutes' drive of each other. Almost all give free tastings. Some have barbecue and picnic facilities, and winemaking museums; others such as McWilliams, Tyrells, and Hunter Estate, give tours.

Wine, food, flowers, music, and art festivals pack a busy events calendar in the Hunter, with something happening every month of the year. Some highlights include **Hunter Semillon & Seafood** in April, and **Jazz in the Vines** and **Opera in the Vines,** both in October.

Although the wineries in the Lower Valley are well known, the scenery is rather flat and uninspiring. The **Upper Hunter Valley,** 50 miles (80 km) farther north, has only a dozen or so wineries but the scenery is better, and it is far less crowded on weekends.

The scenic country around **Scone** (Visitor information, tel (02) 6545 1526) is home to some of Australia's finest racehorse studs and wealthiest grazing families. You can tour some of the stud farms (ask at the visitor center), including the **Segenhoe Stud** (famous in the horse racing

world). It is best to visit in mid-May, during **Scone Horse Festival.**

About 10 miles (16 km) northeast of Scone is Gundy polo ground, where Australia's richest come to play. You can get a taste of this style of living at **Belltrees Station** (tel (02) 6546 1123), which was the family estate of author Patrick White. Guests stay in the farmhouse, self-contained cottages, or the mountain retreat, in the cool of the Great Dividing Range. To the east of Belltrees is **Barrington Tops National Park,** part of a World Heritage area (see p. 118). ■

**GETTING TO THE HUNTER VALLEY:** The New England Highway is the main access route for the Hunter Valley, although back-roads enthusiasts may want to try the old Putty Road, a tortuous byway that winds more than 100 miles (160 km) through the dense forests of the Great Dividing Range between Windsor, in Sydney's outer west, and Singleton.

## Top Australian Wine Regions

Australia, the world's fourth biggest exporter of wine, has more than 60 wine regions, concentrated mostly in South Australia (45% of all wine production), New South Wales (35%), Victoria (16%), and Western Australia (4%).

**South Australia:** Barossa Valley, one hour northeast of Adelaide, is the largest and most renowned wine region, and one of the oldest. Shiraz is its signature grape, but Cabernet Sauvignon, Grenache, Merlot, Riesling, Semillon, and Chardonnay all thrive here.

The McLaren Vale region, just 25 miles (40 km) south of Adelaide, produces excellent Shiraz and Cabernet Sauvignon, Merlot, Chardonnay, Sauvignon Blanc, and Riesling.

Located 80 miles (130 km) north of Adelaide, Clare Valley is the picturesque home of quality Riesling.

Coonawarra, 250 miles (400 km) southeast of Adelaide, is famous for its intensely flavored Cabernet Sauvignon, but it also produces Shiraz, Merlot, and Chardonnay.

**New South Wales:** Hunter Valley, 100 miles (160 km) north of Sydney, is Australia's oldest winery region and one of its largest, famous for its long-aging Semillon. Shiraz, Chardonnay, Verdelho, and others are also produced here.

**Victoria:** Yarra Valley, 30 miles (50 km) northeast of Melbourne, produces elegant cool-climate Pinot Noir and Chardonnay, and also Shiraz, Cabernet Sauvignon, Marsanne, Sauvignon Blanc, and Semillon.

**Western Australia:** Margaret River, a picturesque region 175 miles (280 km) south of Perth, grows a wide variety of premium grapes but is noted for Cabernet Sauvignon, Shiraz, Verdelho, and Australia's best Sauvignon Blanc.

**Tasmania:** A relative newcomer to Australia's wine scene, Tasmania produces aromatic wines unlike those of the warmer mainland. Some 60 wineries, including Pipers Brook and 9th Island in the Tamar Valley, produce Pinot Noir, Riesling, Pinot Grigio, and other varieties.

# Along the South Coast

Dropping south down the coast means taking it easy and escaping the rush of city life. The coast south of Sydney doesn't have the diverse scenery of the northbound Pacific Highway, but neither does it have its frantic pace. The Princes Highway rolls south through gentle farm country and placid little seaside towns.

The harbor at Wollongong, on the Illawarra Coast, south of Sydney

### Royal National Park
🏞 103 E3
**Visitor Information**
✉ Farnell Ave., Audley
☎ (02) 9542 0648

### Wollongong
🏞 103 E3
**Visitor Information**
✉ 93 Crown St.
☎ (02) 4227 5545 or 1-800 240 737 (toll free)

### Kiama
🏞 103 E2
**Visitor Information**
✉ Blowhole Point Rd.
☎ (02) 4232 3322

**Royal National Park,** about 20 miles (32 km) south of Sydney, was established in 1879, making it the second oldest national park in the world (behind Yellowstone in the U.S.). The park is immensely popular with Sydney bushwalkers and cross-country running clubs, but surprisingly few foreigners visit. That's a pity because it has some of New South Wales's finest cliff walks and wildflower displays, and bird-watchers can find as many as 200 species. Some excellent and easily accessible trails start at the railway stations of the small towns along the Princes Highway—**Engadine, Loftus, Heathcote, Otford,** and **Waterfall.** You can also rent canoes at the Audley boat shed *(tel (02) 9545 4967)* if you want to float the Hacking River.

Thirty miles (48 km) south of Audley on the Princes Highway is **Wollongong,** the third largest city in New South Wales, with a copper smelter, engineering plants, and coal mines. It suffers from its smokestack image, but it has good surf beaches and a pleasant feel. The harbor is particularly nice, with a fishing fleet, lighthouse, and seafood restaurants.

**Kiama,** 20 miles (32 km) farther, is a breezy seaside town. In 1797, explorer George Bass heard a "tremendous noise" coming from the cliffs above the bay. It occurs when big surf crashes through a rocky fissure known as the **Blowhole** and erupts as geysers up to 200 feet (61 m) tall. The sound and sight are awesome, but don't get too close; the waves can be deadly. Just west of town, a steep road leads up to the **Mount Saddleback Lookout** for sweeping views along the coast. **Jamberoo** is a pretty and historic village, 5 miles (8 km) inland.

Five miles (8 km) south of Kiama, take the turnoff to spectacular **Seven Mile Beach.** In 1933, aviator Charles Kingsford Smith took off from here on his pioneering flight across the Tasman Sea to New Zealand. The road hugs the coast for 16 miles (26 km) and joins the Princes Highway at Nowra. North of Nowra, a 15-mile (24 km) scenic detour on Route 79 goes north to the rustic **Kangaroo Valley,** which is popular with picnickers.

**Jervis Bay,** 20 miles (32 km) south from Nowra, has a fine sweep of coastline, white sandy beaches, and small hamlets such as Huskisson, the main center. Most of the territory is now the **Booderee National Park,** with rugged cliffs, sandy beaches, fine surf, walks, and botanic gardens.

South of Bermagui (see sidebar), the Princes Highway arcs inland to **Bega,** a cheesemaking town near the turnoff for the Snowy Mountains Highway. Come here in winter and you can surf in the morning and ski in the afternoon, if you make good time up the 100 miles (160 km) to the New South Wales snowfields.

Stay on the Princes Highway to reach the town of **Eden,**

established in 1818 as Australia's first whaling port. Whaling remained the town's major industry until the 1920s. The **Killer Whale Museum** (94 Imlay St., tel (02) 6496 2094, $) tells the story of those days, including the adventure of a Jonah-like whaler who was swallowed by a whale and regurgitated 15 hours later—still alive. Humpback and killer whales have returned to these waters and can be seen along the coast in spring.

Nearby **Ben Boyd National Park** (contact National Parks & Wildlife Service, tel (02) 6495 5000) contains magnificent expanses of temperate rain forest and fine coastal scenery. A 2-mile (3.2 km) trail up **Mount Imlay,** 19 miles (30 km) west of Eden, rewards hikers with fine views of the wilderness coastline. The highway bends inland and continues into the forests of Victoria's Gippsland and south Melbourne. ■

**Booderee National Park**
🏞 103 D2
Visitor Information
☎ (02) 4443 0977

**Bega**
🏞 103 D2
Visitor Information
✉ Lagoon St.
☎ (02) 6491 7645

**Eden**
🏞 103 D1
Visitor Information
✉ Corner of Mitchell & Imlay Sts.
☎ (02) 6496 1953

---

## Angling in Bermagui

**Bermagui** lies about 100 miles (160 km) south of Booderee National Park, off the highway south of Tilba. The town has been popular with big-game anglers since Zane Grey, author of westerns and a great marlin angler, began coming in the 1930s. Big-game fishing tournaments are held here, and operators run fishing trips. Catches include black marlin and yellow-fin tuna.

# Snowy Mountains

The Snowy Mountains are the highest mountains in the Great Dividing Range, an ancient spine that runs along Australia's eastern coast from northern Queensland south to the Grampian Ranges in central Victoria. They are modest by world standards—the loftiest is Mount Kosciuszko, 7,310 feet (2,228 m) high—and not really very snowy, but because of their vast area they have larger snowfields in the winter season than Switzerland.

**Cooma**

🏔 103 D2

**Visitor Information**

✉ 119 Sharp St.

☎ (02) 6455 1745
or 1-800 636
525 (toll-free)

On the New South Wales side of the mountains is the huge **Kosciuszko National Park,** more than 1.7 million acres (690,000 ha) of peaks, glacial lakes, meadows full of wildflowers, and deep forests. **Mount Kosciuszko** was climbed by Polish explorer Paul Edmund de Strzelecki in 1840, who named it in honor of the Polish freedom fighter Gen. Tadeusz Kosciuszko.

**Cooma,** about 250 miles (400 km) southwest of Sydney, is a good base for visiting the Snowy Mountains. Cooma was the construction headquarters for the Snowy Mountains Hydroelectric Scheme, one of Australia's great continent-taming public works projects, begun in 1949. More than 100,000 people worked on the complicated project, which included 16 major dams, seven power stations, and a vast engineering marvel of tunnels, lakes, and pipelines. When all of these were finished in 1974, the Tumut, Snowy, and Upper Murrumbidgee Rivers were providing 4 million kilowatts of electricity. The hydroelectric authority's **Snowy Information Centre** (Monaro Hwy., tel (02) 6450 5600) has films and displays about how the power scheme works.

The new resort town of **Jindabyne,** 40 miles (64 km) farther south, was built along a lake that formed when the Snowy River was dammed in the early 1960s. The original 140-year-old town of Jindabyne lies under the waters of the lake. The **Snowy Region Visitor Centre** in Jindabyne is the national park headquarters

Cross-country skiers wend their way along trails near Thredbo in the aptly named Snowy Mountains.

## EXPERIENCE: Man from Snowy River Rides

One of Australia's best loved poems, "The Man from Snowy River," written by Banjo Paterson in 1890, immortalizes the hard-riding stockmen of the high country. Though most of the cattlemen have gone, you can still ride "down by Kosciuszko . . . where air is clear as crystal, and the white stars fairly blaze."

**Jindabyne Equestrian Resort** (tel (02) 6456 7333, www.equestrianresort.com.au) in Jindabyne offers one- or two-hour rides, overnight camps, lessons, and a range of accommodations. Fishing holidays are also available.

**Reynella Kosciuszko Rides** (tel (02) 6454 2386, www.reynellarides.com.au) in Adaminaby, 30 miles (50 km) northwest of Cooma, offers multiday treks into the mountains of Kosciuszko National Park from October to April.

**Snowy River Horseback Adventure** (tel (02) 6457 8385, www.snowyriverhorse backadventure.com.au) in Jindabyne has two- to five-day horse treks though forest, meadow, and old stock routes from November to May.

and has maps and guides to Kosciuszko National Park.

### Skiing & Hiking

Between mid-June and early October, visitors to the Snowy Mountains enjoy a thriving ski season. However, while the Snowy Mountains do provide the best skiing in Australia, skiers from North America and Europe are likely to find the ski slopes rather gentle and the snow wet and slushy. Still, if you want to ski among the snow gum trees—a surreal sensation—make a reservation for lodging well in advance. **Thredbo,** 20 miles (32 km) southwest of Jindabyne, has the longest runs in Australia—almost 2 miles (3 km) with more than 2,200 feet (670 m) of vertical drop. Perisher Valley, Charlotte Pass, and Smiggin Holes are the other main downhill resort areas, all on Kosciuszko Road in the south-center of the park.

The popularity of cross-country skiing and snowshoeing has grown in recent years. But be careful, particularly if you're tempted to venture off the groomed tracks. While these mountains may be relatively low, the weather up here can be sudden, unpredictable, and savage.

For most visitors, spring and summer are more relaxed seasons in which to visit the Snowy Mountains. Hiking is fine—either day trips or extended walks—in the high country, the wildflowers are spectacular, and trout anglers have a big choice of crystal-clear lakes and mountain streams. Many ski lifts operate in the summer months, giving relatively easy access to the high country, and the ski resorts have accommodations. The summit of Mount Kosciuszko is accessible via Kosciuszko Road from Charlotte Pass (5.5 miles/9 km on foot, one way), or you can take the Kosciuszko Express Chairlift ($$ return, from Thredbo village to one of the high ridges, and from there do an 8-mile (12.9 km) walk to the summit and back. ∎

**Snowy Region Visitor Centre**

✉ Kosciuszko Rd., 10 miles (16 km) N of Jindabyne

☎ (02) 6450 5600

$ $ per car

**Australian Ski Areas Association**

☎ (02) 9326 4069

www.asaa.org.au

# Broken Hill

If you want a taste of outback life, this is the best place to come. Broken Hill, also known as the Silver City, is one of Australia's oldest outback mining towns. For more than a century, this town, about 750 miles (1,200 km) west of Sydney, has prospered from an ore body more than 5 miles (8 km) long, containing the world's richest known reserves of silver, lead, and zinc.

The old Silverton Hotel, a classic outback pub

**Broken Hill**

**A** 102 A4

**Visitor Information**

✉ Corner of Blende & Bromide Sts.

☎ (08) 8080 3560

**www.visitbrokenhill
.com.au**

Broken Hill is filled with grand architecture such as the hugely ornate **Trades Hall building** *(Sulphide St.),* built in 1898, with its pressed-iron ceilings and elaborate meeting hall. Built in 1891, the massive Italianate **Town Hall,** is on **Argent Street,** the city's main thoroughfare, which is lined with gracious two- and three-story hotels trimmed with iron lace.

All this opulence started in September 1883, when a boundary-riding cowboy named Charles Rasp came upon a huge boomerang-shaped ore body on a craggy rise known as the Broken Hill. Thinking the ore body was tin, he and some partners pegged it out. Only later did they learn that the 280-million-ton mass was

galena-sphalerite ore, unimaginably rich in silver, lead, and zinc. It was the grandest mother lode ever found—before or since—and it went on to spawn Australia's biggest mining houses: B.H.P., C.R.A., and North Broken Hill. By 1915, the boomtown that sprang up had grown to 35,000, with 61 pubs, hotels, and grog shops. It drew prospectors, miners, con men, prostitutes, and gamblers, and it became a honeypot for union radicals.

These days, "The Hill" is a considerably tamer town of about 20,000, and unlike most outback mining towns, it is easy for tourists to visit. Trains and buses have regular schedules, and daily flights arrive from the larger cities. The highways are good, even if the drive is a little tedious.

Filmmakers have discovered the area's beautiful light and average of 320 sunny days a year. *Priscilla, Queen of the Desert* was filmed here, as were videos for INXS and other rock groups. BMW, Pepsi, and Levi's have all shot commercials in the area.

But don't come expecting cosmopolitan dining, sophisticated nightlife, or luxury resorts. This is still a working mining town, even as the mines themselves run out of ore. A huge slag heap looms over the city, and streets have names such as Oxide, Sulphide, and Chloride. Broken Hill is where Australia's mining empires were born and where militant miners wrote the most bruising chapters of trade union history. On top of the slag heap, the moving **Miners Memorial** is lined with plaques honoring the hundreds of miners killed on the job.

While mining doesn't drive the town as it used to, recent rises in metal prices have seen some old mines reopen, including Delprats Mine, once the premier mine tour operator, now closed to visitors. You can tour **Day Dream Mine,** one of Broken Hill's oldest (1881), which is about 20 miles (32 km) north of town off the Silverton road *(book 1-hour tours at the visitor center, sturdy shoes essential).* Run by retired miner Kevin "Bushy" White, **White's Mineral Art Gallery & Mining Museum** *(1 Allendale St., tel (08) 8087 2878)* has a walk-in reconstruction of a mine and a vast collection of artworks created by Bushy himself using local minerals.

Twelve miles (19 km) north of Broken Hill is the ghost town of **Silverton,** where many commercials and movies, such as *Mad Max II,* have been filmed. The quaint old **Silverton Hotel** has often been renamed for movies and miniseries, and its walls are lined with photos and memorabilia.

Perhaps the most haunting place to visit, however, is the **Living Desert Sculptures**—a wind-swept hilltop just 4 miles (6.4 km) out of town, decorated with the enormous stone works of 14 sculptors from Australia and around the world *(take Kaolin St. out of town NW, then follow signposts).* Go there at sunset. It is magic.

Broken Hill is a good place to arrange tours farther into the outback and the desert (the tourist office lists operators). With your own vehicle, a good two-day loop is to head 80 miles (130 km) northeast of Broken Hill to **Mutawinji National Park,** with its red outcrops, swimming hole, and Aboriginal rock art. Then continue

## Outback Arts

Unlike other mining towns, Broken Hill has a flourishing arts community. The town attracted some of Australia's best known outback painters, including Hugh Schultz, John Pickup, Jack Absalom, and, most famous of all, the late Pro Hart, whose gallery *(108 Wyman St., tel (02) 8088 2992)* can be visited. Painters come like moths, lured by the desert light. There are murals, artwork in the pubs, and 28 art galleries around town.

on to **White Cliffs,** a fascinating opal mining town, where you can stay at the Underground Motel *(tel (08) 8091 6677)* before heading back to Broken Hill via crumbling, colonial **Wilcannia,** once the "Queen City of the West" on the Darling River. ∎

**Silverton**
🅰 102 A4

# Pacific Highway Drive

For deskbound Sydneysiders, the Pacific Highway is the road to adventure and sunshine, like an Australian Route 66. It meanders north along the coast toward the warmth of tropical Queensland, pausing at popular getaways such as Port Macquarie, Coffs Harbour, and Byron Bay. There is a little of everything—rain forest, empty beaches, seaside holiday towns, odd pockets of suburbia, hippie communes, and quiet farming villages.

Like the real Route 66—not the one of myth—the Pacific Highway can be narrow, heavily trafficked, tedious, potholed, and in some places downright dangerous. You may have to contend with the white-line fever of truckers making the run to Brisbane, eager families hurrying north to theme park holidays at Sea World or Movie Land on Queensland's Gold Coast, and convoys of retirees towing their campers north to softer, sunnier pastures in the tropics. Forget the sweeping interstates back home. Although

## NOT TO BE MISSED:

**Barrington Tops National Park • Bellingen • Dorrigo National Park • Byron Bay**

the highway is slowly being upgraded, only 40 percent is freeway, and the rest is road travel the old-fashioned way.

Directions are simple: Cross Sydney Harbour Bridge and keep driving north on Route 1 to the Queensland border, more than 500 miles (800 km) away. **Newcastle ❶** *(visitor information: 361 Hunter St., tel (02) 4974 2999)* is the first big town you come to, about 100 miles (160 km) out of Sydney. Once Australia's major steel producer, the city had to reinvent itself after the closure of the giant B.H.P. steel mills in 1999. The port still hums—it is the world's biggest coal port and export hub for the resource-rich Hunter Valley—but the state's second largest city has taken on cleaner and greener air. Newcastle has imposing heritage buildings, wide tree-lined streets, thriving arts and food scenes, good beaches, and a laid-back lifestyle. Turn off the highway here onto Route 15, the New England Highway, if you want to visit the **Hunter Valley ❷** wineries or explore the scenic horse country around Scone (see pp. 110–111).

The highway tends to run a few miles inland because the coast here has so many inlets and necks. Most of the interesting sights require a side trip. One of the most worthwhile is **Barrington Tops National Park ❸**, part of

## EXPERIENCE:
## Houseboats on the Hawkesbury

An idyllic way to see the Hawkesbury, and long a favorite holiday break with Sydneysiders, is to cruise the river on a fully equipped houseboat. Bookings are heavy, and prices soar during holiday periods, but are reasonable at other times, particularly midweek. Prices start at around A$500 for two nights on a 2–4 berth houseboat, A$1,000 for 8–10 berths. Operators include:

**Able Hawkesbury House Boats** *(River Rd., Wisemans Ferry, tel (02) 4566 4308, www.hawkesburyhouseboats.com.au)*

**Luxury Afloat Houseboats** *(Kangaroo Point Cruise Terminal, Pacific Hwy., Brooklyn, tel (02) 9985 7344, www.luxuryafloat.org).*

**Ripples Houseboat Holidays** *(87 Brooklyn Rd., Brooklyn, tel (02) 9985 5534, www.ripples.com.au)*

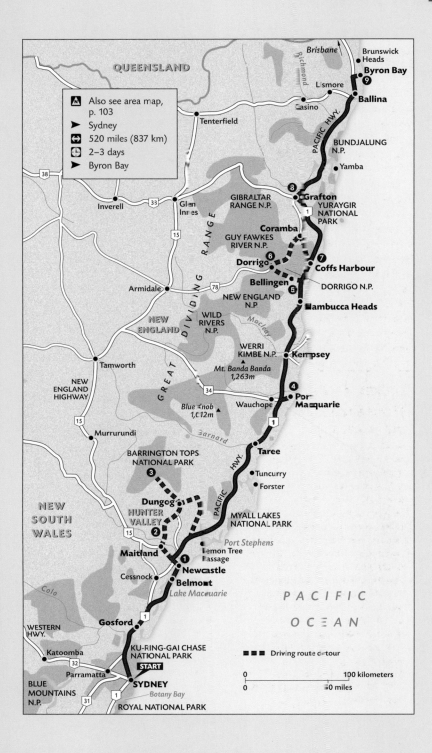

QUEENSLAND

*Brisbane*

Brunswick
Heads
**Byron Bay** ⑨

Lismore

Casino

**Ballina**

Also see area map,
p. 103
▶ Sydney
↔ 520 miles (837 km)
⌚ 2–3 days
▶ Byron Bay

Tenterfield

PACIFIC HWY.

BUNDJALUNG
N.P.

Yamba

38

Inverell    33    Glen
Innes

GIBRALTAR
RANGE N.P.

⑧ **Grafton**
YURAYGIR
NATIONAL
PARK

15

**Coramba**

GUY FAWKES
RIVER N.P.

**Dorrigo** ⑥    ⑦ **Coffs Harbour**

**Bellingen**    DORRIGO N.P.

Armidale    78

⑤

NEW ENGLAND
N.P.

**Nambucca Heads**

NEW
ENGLAND

WILD
RIVERS
N.P.

*Macleay*

DIVIDING  RANGE

Tamworth

WERRI
KIMBE N.P.

*Mt. Banda Banda
1,263m*

**Kempsey**

GREAT

NEW
ENGLAND
HIGHWAY

34

*Blue Knob
1,012m*

Wauchope

④ **Port Macquarie**

1

15

Murrurundi

*Barnard*

1

BARRINGTON TOPS
NATIONAL PARK

③

**Taree**

Tuncurry

Forster

**Dungog**
HUNTER
VALLEY
②

PACIFIC  HWY.

MYALL LAKES
NATIONAL PARK

15

NEW
SOUTH
WALES

**Maitland**

Cessnock

*Port Stephens*

Lemon Tree
Passage

①

**Newcastle**

**Belmont**

*Lake Macquarie*

PACIFIC

*Colo*

**Gosford**    1

OCEAN

WESTERN
HWY.

Katoomba

32

KU-RING-GAI CHASE
NATIONAL PARK

**START**

■ ■ ■  Driving route detour

Parramatta

BLUE
MOUNTAINS
N.P.

31

**SYDNEY**

*Botany Bay*

ROYAL NATIONAL PARK

0                100 kilometers

0                50 miles

the Gondwana Rainforests World Heritage Area *(tel (02) 4983 1031, turn north off the Pacific Hwy. to Gloucester, then take the Barrington Tops Rd.)*. The drive takes you through temperate rain forests and up onto mile-high windswept plateaus dotted with snow gums and covered with alpine bogs. This back road is not paved for much of its length, so do not attempt it in a conventional vehicle after heavy rains.

Back on the coast, you have a reasonable chance of seeing wild koalas in the bush around Lemon Tree Passage, near Port Stephens. Farther north is the **Koala Hospital** *(off Lord St.)*, in the touristic and thriving resort town of **Port Macquarie** ❹ *(visitor information: Clarence St., tel 1-300 303 155, toll free)*. The hospital is run by the Koala Preservation Society of New South Wales on the grounds of a historic homestead. About 200 sick and injured koalas are brought here each year for convalescence. You can visit them daily.

Ninety miles (145 km) north of Port Macquarie is the turnoff for **Bellingen** ❺ *(visitor information: tel (02) 6655 1522)*, 7 miles (11 km) off the highway via Route 78. This laid-back and picturesque village is tucked in the rain forest at the foot of a 1,000-foot-high (300 m) escarpment. Once a major timber town, it has long been a refuge for writers, craftspeople, and artists fleeing city life, and it is chock-full of galleries. Many of Bellingen's old buildings have

been classified by the Australian National Trust. The town has regular arts and music events, and there is a market in Bellingen Park on the third Saturday of every month.

The surrounding countryside is dotted with organic farms and communes. Australia doesn't have a lot of chocolate-box scenery, but there is some here. If you can spare the time, cross the Bellingen River, on the edge of town, and drive 10 miles (16 km) or so upstream through farm country to a picnic area by the river called the Promised Land. It is spellbinding.

Equally spellbinding, although tougher on the nerves, is the drive 20 miles (32 km) up the escarpment on Route 78, from Bellingen to **Dorrigo** ❻ *(visitor information: 36 Hickory St., tel (02) 6657 2486)*. Lookouts along the way give views of the Pacific Ocean. On top of the plateau are the World Heritage rain forests of **Dorrigo National Park.** This is one of the best thought-out parks in the nation, with a rain forest information center *(tel (02) 6657 2309)*, a skyline boardwalk through the rain forest canopy, and paths through the gloom on the forest floor. To get back to the Pacific Highway, you can either return through Bellingen or follow a gravel road to Coramba and then to Coffs Harbour.

By the time you reach **Coffs Harbour** ❼ *(visitor information: Pacific Hwy., tel (02) 6648 4990)*, you're far enough north to notice the

## Hippie Haven

**The main street of Nimbin, 45 miles (70 km) west of Byron Bay, wends though frontier wooden buildings adorned with psychedelia and Hindu iconography, past crystal shops, New Age healers, and hemp cafés. Welcome to Australia's hippie capital, a 1970s time warp of dreadlocks, bare feet, and tie-dye.**

**Nimbin was a sleepy dairy farming village hidden in the rain forest hills until the Aquarius Festival hit town in 1973. Organized by the Australian Union of**

**Students, thousands gathered for the ten-day counterculture experiment. Most returned to the "straight" world, but a few idealists decided to permanently turn on, tune in, and drop out by setting up nearby communes such as Tuntable Falls.**

**The experiment may not have gone exactly to plan; Nimbin is noted for periodic drug busts and its annual Mardi-grass hemp festival in May. But the town remains a magnet for spiritual seekers, artists, dropouts, and tourists alike.**

difference in climate. It's warm and sultry, and rain forests and banana plantations cling to the flanks of mountains that plunge right down to the coast. The motels are gaudier, too. Coffs is the home of the **Big Banana** *(1.5 miles, 2.5 km N of town on Rte. 1)*, a monumental piece of roadside kitsch designed to draw tourists and celebrate the banana industry. Australians have

North of Coffs Harbour, much of the coast is national park land, and side roads lead to quiet lengths of beach. **Grafton 8**, a genteel country town on the banks of the Clarence River, is kaleidoscopic in November (spring in Australia), when its jacaranda and flame trees are in full flower. You are starting to get into lush, tropical, sugar-growing country now, and

The Cape Byron lighthouse, built in 1901, protects Australia's easternmost point of land.

a peculiar penchant for building giant objects. More than 60 of them have been constructed around the country, and they are so breathtakingly awful and shamelessly touristy that they make you laugh and pull over, camera in hand. Which, of course, is precisely what they are meant to do. The Big Crayfish (Kingston, South Australia), the Big Merino (Goulburn, New South Wales), the Big Pineapple (Nambour, Queensland), and the Big Ned Kelly (Glenrowan, Victoria) are among the best known, along with the Big Banana, of course. Here at the Big Banana, you can tour a plantation, buy a banana smoothie, or browse in a souvenir shop whose entire theme is, you guessed it, exuberantly tacky bananas.

as you go farther north you'll see more houses built Queensland-style—elevated on stilts to let cooling air circulate and having wide wraparound verandas.

Not far south of the Queensland border, **Byron Bay 9** *(visitor information: 80 Jonson St., tel (02) 6680 8558)* is one of the prettiest places along the north coast. This used to be a blue-collar town whose main industry was the abattoir, but now it is the most popular resort town on the coast, filled with crafts, galleries, vegetarian cafés, folk music, and organic markets. You can watch humpback whales off the coast of nearby Cape Byron in June and July. The lighthouse has one of the most powerful lights in the Southern Hemisphere.

# Outlying Territories

Australia has a number of far-flung territories, a legacy of the British Empire when it managed, on London's behalf, a swag of colonial islands and dependencies. The easiest of these territories to visit are Norfolk Island, first occupied by an overspill of convicts from Sydney, and Lord Howe Island, an exclusive vacation destination for walkers, bird-watchers, and lovers of water sports. Accommodations are expensive, so many visitors come on a package deal.

Rising steeply from the sea, volcanic Lord Howe Island promises good snorkeling in the quiet lagoon on its western side.

**Lord Howe Island**
🅜   Map p. 123
**Visitor Information**
☎   (02) 6563 2114
**www.lordhoweisland
.info**

Other territories include Macquarie Island (regarded as part of Tasmania), in the subantarctic waters of the southern Indian Ocean, and Heard Island. Canberra claims nearly half of Antarctica as Australian territory, and it ruled Papua New Guinea until 1975.

## Lord Howe Island

About 500 miles (800 km) northeast of Sydney, the tiny volcanic speck of Lord Howe Island is a beautiful rain forest–clad, mountainous tropical idyll. It is part of New South Wales (and a very expensive part at that), so you do not need a passport to visit from mainland Australia. There are daily flights available, but most visitors come on package tours.

The crescent-shaped island, with a wide lagoon tucked within its arms, was sighted by Lt. Henry Lidgbird Ball in 1788, on the way from Sydney to Norfolk Island. The first settlers arrived in 1833, and for the next 50 years it was a watering point for U.S. and British whaling ships. Millions of years of isolation have given rise to a unique ecology on the island, and it was listed as a World Heritage site in 1982.

Lord Howe Island is now a popular destination for ecotourists from around the world. More than 120 bird species can be seen here, including the flightless Lord Howe woodhen, one of the rarest birds in the world.

**GETTING TO LORD HOWE ISLAND: Eastern Australia Airlines** (part of Qantas; *tel 131313*) has flights most days from Sydney, weekends from Brisbane, and from Port Macquarie, Feb.–June & Sept.–Dec.

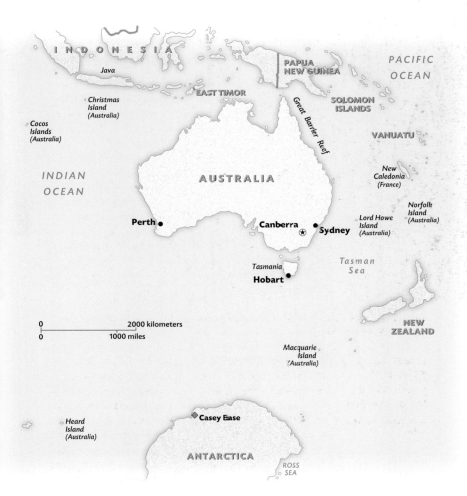

### Norfolk Island
▲ Map p. 123

**Visitor Information**

✉ Bicentennial Centre, Burnt Pine

☎ 6723 22147 or 1-800 214 603 (toll-free in Australia)

www.norfolkisland.com.au

**GETTING TO NORFOLK ISLAND:**
**Air New Zealand** *(Burnt Pine Travel, Taylors Rd., tel 6723 22195, www.airnewzealand.com.au)* flies every Saturday from Auckland.

**Norfolk Air** *(New Cascade Rd., tel 6723 24272 or 1-800 612 960, toll-free in Australia, www.norfolkair.com)* has three flights weekly from Brisbane & Sydney, one weekly from Melbourne & Newcastle (N.S.W.).

The waters around the island teem with fish and contain the world's southernmost coral reef, thanks to the tropical currents from Queensland's Great Barrier Reef. Diving and snorkeling are especially good. Hikers can scale dramatic **Mount Gower** (2,850 feet/866 m) for a stunning panorama of the island and the South Pacific. The slightly lower **Mount Lidgbird** is an extremely challenging, highly technical climb that is rarely attempted.

## Norfolk Island

Norfolk Island is a self-governing external territory of Australia, a tax haven about 1,000 miles (1,600 km) northeast of Sydney. It was sighted by Captain Cook in 1774. Its Norfolk pines (which could be made into masts) and wild flax (for linen sails) made it strategically important to the British Navy.

The island was settled as a penal colony shortly after the First Fleet arrived in Australia in 1788, but it was abandoned in 1814 for several years. Then a new penal colony was established to be "a place of the extremest punishment short of death." In this it was wildly successful. In the hands of the sadistic governor John Giles Price, Norfolk Island became synonymous with cruelty and terror.

The penal colony was shut down in 1855, and the following year the descendants of Fletcher Christian and other mutineers of H.M.S. *Bounty* were resettled here after outgrowing Pitcairn Island. Today about 40 percent of the island's 2,000 inhabitants are descendants of the mutineers.

The chief settlement on this tiny volcanic island is **Burnt Pine. Kingston** is the island's main attraction, a historic settlement built largely by convicts. The convict cemetery is especially poignant. **Norfolk Island National Park** has bushwalks and good fishing and diving. Getting here is an international flight—bring your passport and make sure you have a visa for Australia.

### Christmas Island & the Cocos Islands

Christmas Island and the Cocos lie in the Indian Ocean off the northwest coast of Western Australia. Regular flights leave from Perth, which is about 1,600 miles (2,560 km) from Christmas Island and 1,700 miles (2,720 km) from the Cocos. Christmas Island *(visitor information: tel (08) 9164 8382, www.christmas.net.au)* is covered

---

### 'Tis Mutiny, Mr. Lettuce Leaf

Thanks to the heritage of the mutineer descendants, Norfolk Island has a limited number of surnames, Christian being the most common. To help identify residents, the phone book includes an assortment of nicknames including: Lettuce Leaf, Dar Bizziebee, Moochie, Loppy, Smudge, Diddles, Tardy, Frenzy, Hose, Truck, and Rubber Duck, to name a few.

# EXPERIENCE: Wildlife Australia

Nothing beats the thrill of seeing animals in the wild. Some prime wildlife spotting destinations include Kakadu National Park (see pp. 188–191), particularly for crocodiles and wetland birdlife around the start of wet season in November. Other wildlife is numerous but less easy to spot, though nature tours offer a good chance.

At **Kangaroo Island** (see pp. 270–273) south of Adelaide, you'll spot more wildlife—seals, sea lions, penguins, and wallabies—than anywhere in Australia. It is your best chance of spotting koalas, whose numbers on the island have exploded since their introduction in the 1920s.

The koala conservation park on **Phillip Island** (see p. 307) in Victoria is another good place to see koalas, but the island is noted for the penguin colony that comes ashore every evening.

Australia's largest island, **Tasmania** (see pp. 330–354), has abundant wildlife such as wallabies, wombats, possums, and Tasmanian devils, but you'll have to go exploring in some of the national parks in order to find them.

**Monkey Mia** (see p. 229) in Western Australia is famous for dolphins that swim up to you in the shallows. Dolphins and other marine mammals thrive at **Rockingham** and **Bunbury** (see p. 226), south of Perth, and dolphin swim experiences are offered around the country. The **Eyre Peninsula** (see p. 246) in South Australia is a lesser-known area to sight dolphins, seals, and sea lions without the crowds, and you can even swim with white pointer sharks (in a

cage) off the coast from Port Lincoln. From June to October, whales can be sighted migrating along the southern coast, and **Hervey Bay** (see p. 148) in Queensland is the premier destination for humpback whale sightings. Then, of course, there's the marine wonderland of the **Great Barrier Reef** (see pp. 154–159), and lesser known **Ningaloo Reef** (see p. 231) in Western Australia, where you can swim with whale sharks from April to July.

## Wildlife Parks

If time is limited, wildlife parks across the country have all sorts of weird and wonderful marsupials, reptiles, and birdlife. Most big zoos also have natural walk-through

enclosures. Some of the most popular and accessible native wildlife parks include Steve Irwin's **Australia Zoo** on Queensland's Sunshine Coast (see pp. 146–147), **Currumbin Wildlife Sanctuary** on the Gold Coast (see pp. 144–145) for colorful birdlife, and **Lone Pine Koala Sanctuary** (see p. 143) in Brisbane. Sydney's **Featherdale Wildlife Park** (see p. 100) has a large selection of native wildlife, and the excellent **Taronga Zoo** (see p. 100) is just a ferry ride away from downtown. Melbourne also has a world-class zoo with native wildlife enclosures, and the renowned **Healesville Wildlife Sanctuary** (see p. 308) is one hour away in the Yarra Valley.

A koala, one of Australia's most recognizable inhabitants

**The forested slopes of Lord Howe Island offer excellent hiking.**

controversial facility and passed legislation excluding Christmas Island from Australia's migration zone, enabling it to detain refugees and deny them asylum.

An archipelago of 27 coral islands, the Cocos Islands are tranquil tropical destinations for fishing and diving. *(For information on visits, tel (08) 9162 6790, www .cocos-tourism.cc.)* Only two are inhabited—Home Island and West Island. A Scottish seaman, John Clunies-Ross, settled here in 1827 and began a coconut industry. For more than a century, this was the fiefdom of the Clunies-Ross family, which were granted the islands "in perpetuity" by Queen Victoria. During World War II, the Cocos Islands were an important flying-boat base. In 1955, the islands became an Australian external territory and in 1978, the Clunies-Ross family sold them for A$6.25 million (U.S. $4.75 million. In the 1980s, the 600 islanders voted for Australian citizenship rather than independence.

## Antarctica

If you just want to peek, Qantas (see p. 358) offers popular scenic flights over Antarctica during the Christmas holiday period; it is summer then, with 24 hours of daylight.

Actually getting to Australia's Antarctic Territories is more problematic and a lot more expensive. Tours from New Zealand (which may also touch base in Hobart) go into McMurdo Sound and visit Australia's Casey Base or Macquarie Island. *(For information, check out www.antarcticaflights.com.au.)* ∎

with tropical rain forest and surrounded by coral reefs. Almost two-thirds of the island is national park. Deep-sea fishing, diving, and hiking are the main activities here. Accommodations range from basic motels to the luxurious Sanctuary.

One of the biggest things on the island is the immigration detention center. The former Howard government built the

Smaller than some outback stations, home to Australia's National Gallery, the iconic War Memorial, and the seat of government

# Australian Capital Territory

Introduction & Map    128–129

Canberra    130–136

Feature: Anzac Day    134

Experience: Farm Stays    136

Hotels & Restaurants    370–371

Detail from outside the Canberra Civic Centre

# Australian Capital Territory

**After the six Australian colonies decided to form a nation in 1901, the next step was settling on a capital city—no easy task in a land notable for municipal jealousies, jump-and-bawl parochialism, and bickering politicians. Seven years of wrangling, two royal commissions, and numerous parliamentary debates followed as the various civic authorities put forth their arguments.**

The new constitution decreed that the capital was to be somewhere in New South Wales, but at least 100 miles (160 km) from Sydney. This distance was a sop to the intense rivalry between Sydney and Melbourne, which was the stand-in capital until a permanent site was chosen.

There was no shortage of candidates for the new capital. Even tiny Wentworth, in far western New South Wales, put in its oar, using

Canberra's sparkling centerpiece, Lake Burley Griffin was created with the damming of the Molonglo River in 1963.

a timeless argument that its position on the confluence of the Murray and Darling Rivers—two important steamboat routes—made it a natural capital.

In 1908, a parliamentary committee settled on a site diplomatically set between Sydney and Melbourne; as wits like to put it, the place was equally inconvenient to both cities. Although Limestone Plains, as the place was called, would never otherwise have had a city on it, the setting was certainly pretty enough. Surrounded by mountains about 200 miles (320 km) southwest of Sydney, it sits on a plateau about 2,000 feet (608 m) up, high enough to get cold crisp winters and, occasionally, snow.

Two years later, New South Wales ceded the 975-square-mile (2,526 sq km) parcel of land to the Commonwealth, and the Australian Capital Territory (A.C.T.) was formed. An annex at Jervis Bay on the New South Wales coast gave the A.C.T. a seaport. The same year, an international competition was launched to find a designer for the new capital city.

The winner was Walter Burley Griffin, a Chicago landscape architect who had been Frank Lloyd Wright's chief assistant. His vision was for a city radiating out from the Parliament building and having a man-made lake at its heart. The design was controversial, and although construction began in 1913, bureaucratic resistance and World War I prevented much progress being made.

Griffin finally resigned in 1920 and went on to design other towns: Griffith and Leeton in New South Wales, the Melbourne suburbs of Heidelberg and Eaglemont, and the Sydney suburb of Castlecrag.

The seat of government was shifted to the new city in 1927, but Canberra's growth continued to be slow. Twenty years later it was still a country town of only 15,000. After the National Capital Development Commission was established in 1958, the city began to grow. Griffin's original vision of an artificial lake as the city's centerpiece was finally realized in 1963, when the Molonglo River was dammed to form Lake Burley Griffin. Handsome public buildings sprouted up. Suburbs grew and spread, and by 1967, Canberra was a fully fledged city of 100,000.

Today about 350,000 people live here, in what is arguably Australia's greenest city, with extensive parks coursing throughout the suburbs, giving the 80-year-old purpose-built city a respectable, established air. ∎

## NOT TO BE MISSED:

Enjoying the expansive views from Black Mountain   130

Biking around Lake Burley Griffin   130–131

Taking in a free movie at the National Film & Sound Archive   132

Exploring Australian history at the National Museum   132

Parliament House, the nation's political heart   132–133

Browsing the art collection of the National Gallery   135

The Australian War Memorial, one of the great military museums in the world   135–136

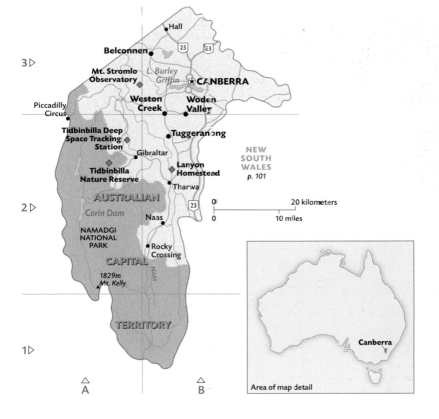

# Canberra

Canberra is young, smart, sporty, and generally prosperous, with plenty of restaurants, night-clubs, and a casino. It also has the National Gallery and the Parliament House, where you can watch Australia's politicians fling earthy abuse at each other—possibly the liveliest show in town. Some of Australia's best hiking and skiing are only a short drive away, and the bush wild-life is even closer. This is the only city in Australia where you might encounter a kangaroo.

Canberra City, viewed from the Mount Ainslie lookout

**Canberra**

🅜 129 B3

**Visitor Information**

✉ 330 Northbourne Ave.

☎ 1-300 554 144

**Australian Institute of Sport**

✉ Leverrier St., Bruce

☎ (02) 6214 1111

🕐 Tours 10 & 11:30 a.m., 1 & 2:30 p.m.

💲 $

🚌 Bus Nos. 7, 980

**Black Mountain** dominates the city center. Its futuristic communications tower has observation galleries and a revolving restaurant giving good views of the city. At the foot of the mountain are the **Australian National Botanic Gardens** (*Clunies Ross St., Acton, tel (02) 6250 9540, www.anbg.gov.au*), which closely follow Walter Burley Griffin's original vision for a native flora garden. Its 125 acres (51 ha) hold more than 6,000 species of native trees, ferns, shrubs, and flowers, including a rain forest and 600 varieties of eucalyptus. Bus No. 981 takes you to the gardens, the summit of Black

Mountain, and the **National Zoo & Aquarium** (*Lady Denman Dr., Weston Creek, tel (02) 6287 8400, www.nationalzoo.au, $$*). A walking trail winds up Black Mountain from Frith Street.

Just north of Black Mountain is the **Australian Institute of Sport.** This multimillion-dollar modernistic facility was built in 1981, at a low ebb in Australia's athletic history, to turn out world-class athletes. An interactive exhibition lets you measure your sporting fitness and aptitude. Some of Australia's top athletes lead daily tours.

Lake Burley Griffin sparkles at the center of Canberra, a bicycle-friendly city with more than 190 miles (300 km) of paths. Mr. Spokes Bicycle Hire *(near Acton Park ferry terminal, tel (02) 6257 1188),* on the north shore, rents bikes and pedal cars. Burley Griffin Boat Hire *(Acton Park ferry terminal, tel (02) 6249 6861)* rents canoes and pedal boats. Beside the north end of Commonwealth Avenue Bridge, the **Captain Cook Memorial Water Jet** spurts water 460 feet (140 m) into the air. Southeast around the lakefront on Aspen Island is the **Carillon,** with 55 bells in three towers.

Parkes Place, on the lake's south bank, has the neoclassical **National Library of Australia.** Among its 2.7 million books are the journals of the explorers Burke and Wills (see p. 44) and Captain Cook's log. The library displays Australian photography, art, and a model of Cook's *Endeavour.* It also has a café with free Internet access. Just across the road, **Questacon** *(Parkes Place, tel (02) 6270 2800, www.questacon.edu.au. $$)*–the National Science and Technology Centre–has more than 200 hands-on exhibits. The **High Court building** sits beside the lake, a little farther east along Parkes Place, and beside it is the **National Gallery of Australia** (see p 135).

The **Civic Centre,** around Vernon Circle on the north side of the lake, has shops, cinemas,

## National Library of Australia

- ✉ Parkes Place
- ☎ (02) 6262 1111
- 🕐 Tours Thurs. at 2:30 p.m.

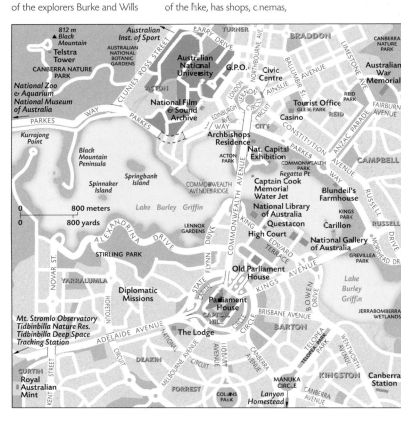

**National Film &
Sound Archive**

✉ McCoy Circuit
☎ (02) 6248 2000

www.nfsa.gov.au

**National
Museum of
Australia**

✉ Lawson
Crescent, Acton
☎ (02) 6208 5000

www.nma.gov.au

and restaurants, and the main post office. The casino is nearby, on Binara Street. The campus of the **Australian National University** (Balmain Ave., tel (02) 6125 5111, closed weekends, www.anu.edu.au) is just west of the city center, in the inner suburb of Acton.

**INSIDER TIP:**

## Walk or ride a bike around Lake Burley Griffin. The 3.75-mile (6 km) route around offers lots of fantastic photo ops.

—HOLLY SHALDERS
*National Geographic contributor*

Nearby is the **National Film & Sound Archive,** with interactive displays of Australian film and sound recordings dating back to footage from the 1896 Melbourne Cup. The **National Museum of Australia** offers a warts-and-all view of the nation's history, with eclectic exhibits, including a large collection of Aboriginal bark paintings and clothes worn by baby Azaria Chamberlain, notoriously killed by a dingo at Uluru in 1980.

### Canberra Outskirts

About 20 miles (32 km) southwest of Canberra on Paddy's River Road, **Tidbinbilla Nature Reserve** (tel (02) 6205 1233, $) has more than 15,000 acres (6,000 ha) of bushland with koalas, kangaroos, and birds, fine bushwalking trails, facilities for picnics and barbecues, and the Sanctuary, an impressive wetlands and wildlife enclosure. The **Tidbinbilla Deep Space Tracking Station** (tel (02) 6201 7880), a couple miles farther north, is one of the most sensitive listening posts in the world. It operates in conjunction with NASA, and its space center can be visited.

About 12 miles (19 km) south of the city and just off the Monaro Highway near Tharwa, the National Trust–listed **Lanyon Homestead** (tel (02) 6237 5136, closed Mon., $) has a museum with exhibitions on country life.

### Parliament House

Australia's billion-dollar Parliament House on Capital Hill, just south of Lake Burley Griffin, was opened in May 1988. Walter Burley Griffin's original vision for the city called for the parliament building to be sited on this hill, and he bitterly resented the decision of the authorities to situate the "temporary" seat of government lower down on King George Terrace.

The Old Parliament House, completed in 1927, was actually used for nearly 60 years. Now the **Museum of Australian Democracy** (King George Terrace, tel (02) 6720 8222), it is well worth a visit. The old chambers and prime minister's office, all leather and wood paneling, are just as the politicians left them in 1988.

The monumental new **Parliament House,** with its distinctive four-legged, 250-foot (76 m) flagpole, fits in beautifully with the city. Its design was the product of an international competition won in 1980 by Romaldo Giurgola from a New York firm. Parliament House took eight years to build, and naturally it was controversial.

Much of this beautiful building is open to the public. Outside the entrance is a mosaic called "Meeting Place," by Aboriginal

gallery above the Great Hall was created by 500 Australians. In the heart of the building, you can see one of only four known original copies of the Magna Carta, the document signed by King John of England in 1215 that restricted royal power. The grassy lawn (which sweeps back to cover the roof of the building) makes a lovely stroll.

**Parliament House**

- ☒ Capital Hill
- ☎ (02) 6277 5399
- 🚌 Bus Nos. 2, 3, 934

## Stolen Generations

From the 19th century to the 1970s, as many as 100,000 Aboriginal children were deliberately removed from their families by the state and by church missions. Known as the stolen generations, the children were placed in institutions or with white families, their language and culture denied. "Half-caste" children of mixed descent were particularly targeted.

Paternalistic laws gave state governments sweeping powers to seize indigenous children without legal recourse. The policy was ostensibly for their own protection and to ensure their education, although some Aboriginal Protection Boards expressed the belief that breeding out the race was a solution to the "Aboriginal problem."

Many white Australians were unaware of the policy until the 1997 release of

*Bringing Them Home,* a report commissioned by the government. It concluded that the policy was a gross violation of human rights and an "act of genocide, aimed at wiping out Indigenous families, communities and cultures."

Many saw the report as a milestone toward righting past injustices, but others balked, fearing compensation claims. Former Prime Minister John Howard rejected calls for a formal apology, saying Australia could not be held accountable for the actions of previous generations. Some conservatives denied it outright, claiming all the children were abandoned or given away willingly by their parents.

In 2007, new Prime Minister Kevin Rudd stood before parliament and offered an apology for the loss and suffering of the Aboriginal people.

artist Michael Tjakamarra Nelson. The foyer has marble staircases and green-gray marble columns that symbolize a eucalyptus forest. The floors are made of Australian native timbers, and the marquetry panels depict Australian flora. The **Great Hall** contains a 70-foot-long (21 m) tapestry based on a painting by Arthur Boyd. The 50-foot (15 m) tapestry in the

Most of the city's 60 diplomatic missions are in **Yarralumla,** about half a mile (0.8 km) west. The U.S. embassy is housed in a Williamsburg-style colonial building. The Thai embassy resembles a temple. Greece's evokes the Parthenon, and New Guinea's is similar to an ornate spirit house. In the neighboring suburb of

*(continued on p. 135)*

# Anzac Day

If you visit Australia around Anzac Day—April 25— you'll quickly notice that it is not just another holiday. On this day, Australians commemorate those who served and died in their country's wars. While many countries set aside a day to pay tribute to their fallen, few do it with such style and depth of emotion as Australia.

Thousands of names of the war dead etch the walls of the Australian War Memorial.

On April 25, 1915, 16,000 Australian soldiers of the Australia and New Zealand Army Corps (ANZAC) waded ashore on the Turkish coast near the town of Gallipoli. The landing was an ill-conceived part of Britain's campaign to capture the strategically important Dardanelles Strait, and by nightfall more than 2,000 Australians had died trying to capture a small bay flanked by cliffs and well-prepared Turkish soldiers. For the next eight months, the troops clung precariously to the beach without ever achieving a firm foothold. Thousands died before London issued the orders to withdraw.

The ANZAC lost 8,587 men in the fighting. What is not often mentioned is that the French lost just as many soldiers at Gallipoli, England lost three times as many, and the Turks had 86,000 dead. Those ancient nations had long

ago been bloodied in conflict; Australia and New Zealand hadn't, and so this battle took on deep mythological significance.

The first parade marking Anzac Day took place shortly after the end of World War I. Since then, the significance of this public memorial has steadily increased, and the parades have continued to grow larger as the children, grandchildren, and great-grandchildren put on the old campaign ribbons and step up to fill their ancestors' shoes, lest anyone forget. Ceremonies are held across the country and are open to spectators (see sidebar p. 50). The dawn service and parade are especially moving.

In 2003, the last known survivor of the Gallipoli campaign, from any army, died at age 102. Alec Campbell, an unassuming Tasmanian who had signed up for the war when he was barely 15, was given a state funeral.

**Deakin,** the Australian prime minister lives in his official residence, **the Lodge.** Some of the embassies have open days, when you can visit. Ask at the Canberra visitor center (see p. 130) for details.

## National Gallery of Australia

The National Gallery in Canberra stands on the south bank of Lake Burley Griffin below Capital Hill. It has works by European masters (Monet, Rodin, Picasso), American pop artists such as Andy Warhol, and African and Asian art. It also has the most comprehensive collection of Australian and Aboriginal art in the country.

Twelve galleries spread over three floors. The **Art of Aboriginal Australia and the Torres Strait Islands gallery,** near the entrance, is the most popular. The displays change every few months. Typical exhibits are bark paintings from Arnhem Land, burial poles of the Tiwi Islanders, and canvas paintings from central Australia and the Kimberley. One permanent feature is the **Aboriginal Memorial** (1988), which pays tribute to the Aborigines who suffered in the first 200 years of European settlement.

The upper level of the building contains the Australian art collection, including early colonial watercolors, the later 19th-century Romantics, and the nationalistic art of Tom Roberts, Arthur Streeton, Russell Drysdale, and Charles Conder. These artists were among the first to capture Australia's harsh landscapes and glaring light. Their paintings soon became some of Australia's best-loved icons.

Another display with iconic status is Sidney Nolan's series of 25 paintings of bushranger Ned Kelly, from the 1940s. There are also prints, photographs, ceramics, and textiles. A sculpture garden overlooks the lake.

## Australian War Memorial

The Australian War Memorial, with its heavy Byzantine lines and vaulted mosaic dome, is the most poignant monument in Canberra, attracting more visitors than any other building in the city. It sits at the foot of Mount Ainsley. Conceived in 1925 as a tribute to those who

**National Gallery of Australia**
- ✉ Parkes Place
- ☎ (02) 6240 6411

**Australian War Memorial**
- ✉ Treloar Crescent, Campbell
- ☎ (02) 6243 4211
- 🚌 Bus Nos. 10, 930

### War Memorials

Virtually every town and village in Australia has a war memorial. At first glance this seems a little out of place in such an isolated country. With the exception of a few bombing raids on Darwin and Broome in 1942, the continent itself has been largely untouched by the wars of the 20th century. But Australia has never been slow to answer the call of duty, sending soldiers to every major conflict in which Britain was involved since the late 19th century— and paying heavily. More than 102,000 Australians have been killed in these conflicts—catastrophic losses in a country with such a small population.

died in World War I, it was not completed until 1941. By then the nation was in the midst of an even greater conflict and threatened with invasion. The cloisters, reflection pools, and galleries pay tribute to the soldiers who died.

The memorial also houses one of the world's great military museums. It charts Australia's involvement in conflicts from the Sudan campaign and the Boer War in the late 19th century, through both World Wars, Korea, the Malaya and Borneo campaigns of the 1950s and '60s, Vietnam, Iraq, and Afghanistan. Displays include a Lancaster bomber, a Spitfire, and one of the two Japanese midget submarines that infiltrated Sydney Harbour in World War II.

More than a million visitors shuffle through the Hall of Memory every year. It houses Australia's Tomb of the Unknown Soldier—the remains of an unidentified Aussie killed in France in World War I and returned to Australia in 1993. The ceremony was attended by the few surviving veterans of that war and left few eyes dry when the bent old soldiers—100 years old or close to it—saluted their fallen mate.

Canberra's Anzac Day ceremonies (see p. 134) take place around the War Memorial. Tours of the War Memorial are free and quite frequent; call for details. The "Last Post" is played at closing. ∎

## EXPERIENCE: Farm Stays

Hundreds of farms all over Australia—from outback cattle stations to Tasmanian orchards—offer a great opportunity to experience rural life. Even though the country is overwhelmingly urban, ask Australians where to find the real Australia, and most likely they will say on the farm or in the outback.

Accommodations range from luxurious rooms in the homestead to something more basic in old shearers quarters. Most farms encourage visitors to join in the activities, and some offer excursions like canoeing, bushwalking, horseback riding, and fishing.

**Mowbray Park Farmstay** (tel (02) 4680 9243, www.farmstayholidays.com.au), an hour southwest of Sydney, has activities from milking cows to sheep shearing. **Aldville Station** (tel (07) 4655 4814, www.queenslandholidays.com.au) is an outback cattle and sheep station, 80 miles (125 km) northwest of Cunnamulla in Queensland. **Angorichina Station** (tel (08) 8354 4405, www.angorichinastation.com), in South Australia's Flinders Ranges, offers luxury farm stays and flights. In southeast Queensland, **Glassford Creek Farmstay**, (tel (07) 4974 1185, www.glassfordcreekfarmstay.com.au) is a cattle station with horseback riding. **Oxley Farm** (tel (08) 8522 3703, www.oxleyfarm.com.au) near Adelaide has family farm animal experiences.

Tourist offices list other farm stays. **Australian Farm Stay** (www.australianfarmstay.com.au) also has a good selection, and **Help Exchange** (www.helpx.net) has some free and pay-per-view listings. **WWOOF** (Willing Workers On Organic Farms, www.wwoof.com.au) lists organic farms that provide accommodations and meals.

A tropical paradise with heartland that is classic outback, from northern savanna to the grazing lands of "Waltzing Matilda"

# Queensland

Introduction & Map   138–139

Brisbane   140–143

**Experience: Brisbane from the Water**   143

Southeast Coast   144–149

**Experience: Turtle Treasures**   147

Tropic of Capricorn Drive   150–153

Great Barrier Reef   154–165

**Experience: Cruising the Great Barrier Reef**   160

**Experience: Sailing the Whitsundays**   162

Northern Queensland   166–180

**Experience: Sea Kayaking**   167

**Experience: Diving Australia**   168

Feature: National Parks   172–173

**Experience: Touring the Tip**   174

**Experience: Birdsville Races**   176

**Experience: Mount Isa Mine Tour**   178

Hotels & Restaurants   371–376

Sweetlips swim together above reef corals.

# Queensland

Queensland is where Australia goes on holiday, with thousands of miles of beaches, forest-clad mountains, and hundreds of tropical islands scattered along the Great Barrier Reef. In the south, the Gold Coast offers nightclubs and casinos, while the seaside towns and surfing beaches of the Sunshine Coast, north of Brisbane, bask in the world's "most perfect" climate.

Queensland began in 1824 as a penal colony, but by the 1840s, free settlers were streaming in, taking part in one of Australia's biggest land grabs. In 1859, Queensland became a colony in its own right and severed its ties with New South Wales. Gold, cattle, sheep, and sugar soon made it wealthy. From 1863, in one of the colony's grimmer chapters, Pacific islanders—the Kanakas—were conscripted to toil on the sugar plantations in conditions of virtual slavery. The practice, known as "blackbirding," was abolished in 1905.

For much of the 20th century, Queensland had a reputation as an antipodean Dixie. Blackbirding had stopped, but the harsh treatment of Aborigines continued, as did heavy-handed policing, machine politics, and a deeply conservative outlook—particularly during the 20-year reign of archconservative premier Sir Johannes Bjelke-Peterson. A former peanut farmer from Kingaroy, he kept Queensland in what the rest of Australia regarded as a time warp until he was voted out in 1989. A cathartic royal commission followed, as did a number of indictments, and these days Queensland is one of the most open and outward-looking parts of the nation, with an easy, down-home friendliness, even in the face of adversity: In March 2006, Tropical Cyclone Larry swept through northern Queensland, causing more than A$360 million (U.S. $320 million) in damage to property and crops. Happily, however, Queenslanders are highly resilient, and the tropical north has bounced back.

Queensland is a huge state, almost four times the size of California, with only 3.2 million people—about half of whom live in Brisbane.

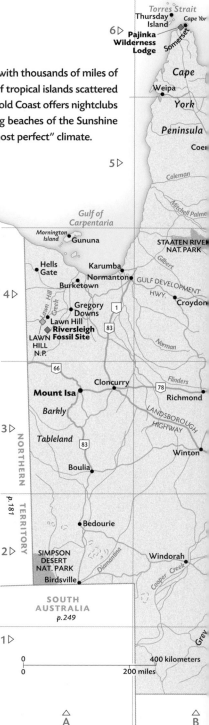

In addition to the southern beaches and the Great Barrier Reef, Queensland offers much more, including sweeping expanses of dusty outback in the north, the rugged wilderness of the Cape York Peninsula, the ancient rain forests of Cape Tribulation, the lush volcanic highlands of the Atherton Tablelands, mining towns, and frontier settlements along the Gulf of Carpentaria. ■

**NOT TO BE MISSED:**

The glitzy Gold Coast    144–145

Noosa Heads, the Sunshine Coast's classiest resort town    147

Fraser Island, where rain forest meets the beach    148–149

Cruising, diving, or snorkeling the Great Barrier Reef    154–165

A day sailing the tropical islands of the Whitsundays    162

Daintree National Park and its primeval rain forest    169

Lawn Hills National Park, an outback tropical surprise    178–180

Area of map detail

Canberra

QUEENSLAND

NEW SOUTH WALES
p.101

# Brisbane

With its parks and gardens, jogging and bike paths, perfect winter climate and cosmopolitan style, Brisbane—with a population of 1.9 million—has a pleasant, relaxed feel despite being Australia's third largest city. It sprawls around an elbow on the Brisbane River, about 20 miles (32 km) inland from the southeast Queensland coast, making it a good base for exploration.

Office towers back Brisbane's vibrant riverfront.

**Brisbane**

🅰 139 D1

**Visitor Information**

✉ Queen Street Mall (between Albert & Edward Sts.)

☎ (07) 3006 6290

**www.visitbrisbane .com.au**

By the early 1820s, Sydney had become civilized enough to want to forget its brutal roots. Sent north to scout out a new penal colony, John Oxley, surveyor-general for Gov. Sir Thomas Brisbane, settled on Moreton Bay (20 miles/32 km from the modern city). In 1824, a detachment of the 40th Regiment and a knot of Sydney's convicts arrived and set up camp near present-day Redcliffe. Unreliable water supplies and hostile Aborigines forced them to shift camp several times. They finally settled up the river where Brisbane is today.

With the exception of the Old Windmill on Wickham Terrace, built in 1828, there are very few reminders of those bad old days in modern Brisbane. A fire leveled the city in 1864, and most of its elegant buildings date from the 1880s, when gold, wool, sugar, and beef were building the state's fortunes.

Brisbane dozed away much of the 20th century, with the exception of the 1940s, when it became Gen. Douglas MacArthur's headquarters after the fall of the Philippines. It resumed its slumbers after the war, and as late as 1967 the tallest building in town was the clock tower of City Hall. The

Commonwealth Games in 1982 and the World Expo in 1988, which drew more than 18 million people, were Brisbane's coming-out parties. The city has hardly slept since.

By the early 1990s, when the rest of the nation was in recession, Brisbane's booming sunbelt economy lured thousands of job-seekers north from Sydney and Melbourne. Its suburbs were the fastest growing in Australia, with jobs and new businesses sprouting like bougainvillea after tropical rain. Even if you couldn't find a job here—and most people could—this comfortable city with a low cost of living and 300-plus days of sunshine every year was at the very least a great place to spend your idle time.

Brisbane sprawls, but visitors find it easy to get around because it has a very good public transport system of trains, river ferries, and

**TransLink (Brisbane Transportation)**

☎ 13 12 30

**www.translink.com.au**

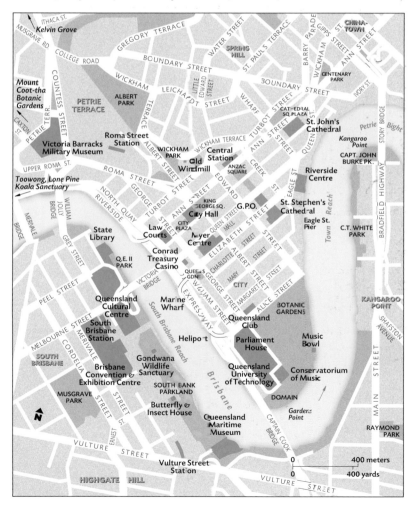

**Brisbane Botanic Gardens**

✉ Mt. Coot-tha Rd., Toowong

☎ (07) 3403 8888

**Sir Thomas Brisbane Planetarium**

☎ (07) 3403 2578

💲 $$

buses. The downtown hub sits on a neck of land formed by a loop in the river. This attractive city has the typical Australian blend of Victorian architecture and modern office blocks. Its unique touches include bougainvillea, palms, and (in the better suburbs) classic Queenslander houses—elevated wooden structures with verandas, designed to help air circulate.

behind the Gold Coast to the south, and the weird volcanic nubs of the Glass House Mountains to the north. Enjoy superb views from the restaurant and tearoom. There are also moderately strenuous bushwalking trails, the most popular being the hike to Slaughter Falls.

The **Brisbane Botanic Gardens,** at the foot of the

## South Brisbane

One of the liveliest parts of Brisbane is across Victoria Bridge. On weekends, crowds flock to the 40 acres (16 ha) of **South Bank Parklands** *(Stanley St. Plaza, tel (07) 3867 2051, www.visitsouthbank.com .au)* to drink caffè latte, in-line skate, watch street musicians, and stroll along the imported white sand of the artificial beach. There are also picnic and barbecue areas for public use. Another popular destination in the park is the **Queensland**

**Maritime Museum,** a two-level exhibition center featuring historic ship models as well as a 1900 pearling lugger and a World War II frigate. An outdoor market stretches for more than half a mile (1 km) on weekends. Nearby, along Grey Street, is the **Queensland Cultural Centre,** which includes the Queensland Art Gallery (mostly Australian artists), the Queensland Museum, the Performing Arts Complex, and the State Library.

## Brisbane Sights

Perhaps the best way to get a feel for Brisbane is to drive up **Mount Coot-tha,** about 5 miles (8 km) west of the city on the Western Freeway, and up the Mount Coot-tha Road. To get here via public transportation, take bus 471 from Ann Street, near King George Square. The hill is easily noticed from the city; it's the one bristling with TV towers. The view from its 800-foot (244 m) summit is spectacular—especially in the fine light just before dusk. The Brisbane River shimmers its way through suburbs spread out like a jeweled blanket. On a clear day you can see the mountains

mountain, have tropical plants in a postmodern dome, rain forests, a display of arid-zone flora, and a Japanese garden. Also in the botanic gardens is the **Sir Thomas Brisbane Planetarium.** It is the largest in Australia and an ideal way for Northern Hemisphere visitors to get acquainted with a sky full of new stars.

It is easy to explore downtown Brisbane on foot, and the City Council has free pamphlets of various heritage walking tours through the city. You can pick them up at City Hall. The commercial steel-and-glass heart of the city, and its historic districts, are in the blocks between Queen Street and the **City Botanic Gardens** at the tip of the peninsula. These parklands have 12,000 rosebushes, bamboo thickets, and poinciana trees. They are popular with in-line skaters, bicyclists, and office workers on their lunch hours. On summer evenings, classical music recitals are given on an open-air stage.

Much of Brisbane's dignified old architecture lines George, Queen, and Elizabeth Streets. The Treasury Building on Queen Street is a massive Renaissance-style edifice built in 1890. It now houses the **Conrad Treasury Casino.** At the southern end of George Street is Queensland's **Parliament House.** It was built in 1868 in French Renaissance style, with a few tropical touches, like shuttered windows, and a dome of Mount Isa copper. You can watch the political action from the visitors gallery when Parliament is in session. Just up the street is a row of Brisbane's most elegant Victorian mansions, trimmed with wrought-iron lace. They contain restaurants, bookshops, a National Trust gift shop, and a few professional offices.

For two blocks across the city center, Queen Street becomes an upscale pedestrian mall, with flower stalls and street musicians, all dominated by the huge five-story **Myer Centre** complex of department stores, boutiques, and cinemas. Two blocks north of the mall, on Albert Street, is Brisbane's opulent **City Hall,** arguably the biggest and grandest city hall in Australia. Constructed in rich Italianate style in the Depression years, it has a beautiful circular concert hall, a cathedral-quality pipe organ, and a 300-foot-high (91 m) clock tower that gives splendid views of the city.

The elegant **Story Bridge,** where the Bradfield Highway crosses the river, was designed by Dr. John Bradfield, architect of the Sydney Harbour Bridge. A climb to the top of the 1940s cantilevered icon is rewarded with sweeping views of the city. Story Bridge Adventure Climb *(170 Main St., Kangaroo Point, tel 1-300 254 627, www.storybridgeadventureclimb .com.au, $$$)* offers 2.5-hour climbs by day and night. ∎

**City Botanic Gardens**
✉ Alice St.
☎ (07) 3221 4528

**City Hall**
☎ (07) 3403 8888

---

## EXPERIENCE: Brisbane from the Water

The sluggish Brisbane River was once Brisbane's lifeline to the outer world. These days most of the old wharves are idle, and the river is more decorative than functional. **Kookaburra River Queens** *(tel (07) 3221 1300, www.kookaburrariver queens.com, $$$$–$$$$$)* offers afternoon excursions and evening dinner cruises on stylish Mississippi-style paddle steamers. Or buy a ticket for A$3 (U.S. $2.25) and ride through the heart of the city, from Bretts Wharf up to the University of Queensland, on one of the large blue commuter catamarans known as the **CityCat** *(www.translink.com.au).*

A popular day trip with visitors is to **Lone Pine Koala Sanctuary** *(708 Jesmond Rd., Fig Tree Pocket, tel (07) 3378 1366, www .koala.net, $$$),* with more than 130 koalas and other wildlife. Take the **M.V. Mirimar** *(tel 1-300 729 742, www.mirimar.com)* up-river to the sanctuary.

# Southeast Coast

The focus of southeast Queensland is the Gold Coast, Australia's answer to Miami, without the art deco and happily without the vice. But the region also includes the Sunshine Coast—a string of vacation villages, white sand beaches, and coastal mountains about an hour's drive north of Brisbane—as well as Fraser Island, a lush paradise of wildflowers, rain forests, colored sand cliffs, freshwater lakes, and a vast array of birdlife.

Surfers Paradise is a glitzy international tourist destination with high-rises crowding the beach.

## Gold Coast

   130 D1–E1

**Visitor Information**

✉ Cavill Ave. Mall, Surfers Paradise

☎ (07) 5538 4419

**www.goldcoast
tourism.com.au**

## Gold Coast

Stretching from South Stradbroke Island, about 35 miles (56 km) south of Brisbane, to Coolangatta on the New South Wales border, the Gold Coast is a relentless 25-mile (40 km) arc of surfing beaches, restaurants, motels, and developments. The glittering, brassy heart of it all is **Surfers Paradise,** where high-rise developments crowd the foreshore so closely that much of the beach is in shade in the afternoon. It doesn't seem to matter. Although warm sands and surf are still touted as

the Gold Coast's main attractions, these days they are really just backdrops for man-made amusements: nightclubs, theme parks, golf courses, boutiques, and an oversized casino.

The Gold Coast has been a vacation spot for Australians since 1884, when Cobb & Co. coaches made the trip down the coast from Brisbane to Coolangatta three times a week. The first high-rise beachfront apartments were built in the 1950s. These days more than 560,000 people live on this stretch of beach, and there are hotels, hostels, and campsites for another 100,000. More than a million overseas visitors come here every year, as well as several million Australians. Yet while the Gold Coast's population growth is three times the national average, a lot of locals are fleeing.

The Gold Coast is not for everybody. But if your tastes run to high-octane entertainment, you've found the antipodean distributor. Located 35 miles (56 km) south of Brisbane, **Dreamworld** *(tel (07) 5588 1111, www.dream world.com.au, $$$$$, )* is a theme park in Coomera where you can ride the Tower of Terror, reputedly one of the world's fastest and highest rides, play with a koala, and get jolted out of your seat at the IMAX theater. A mile down the road is **Warner Bros. Movie World** *(tel (07) 5573 8485, movie world.myfun.com.au, $$$$$).* Based on Hollywood movie sets, it has stunt and special-effects displays and a roller-coaster ride. Nearby is **Wet 'n' Wild Water Park** *(tel (07) 5556 1660, wetnwild .myfun.com.au, $$$$),* Australia's largest aquatic park. **Sea World,** at Main Beach *(tel (07) 5588 2205, seaworld.myfun.com.au, $$$$),* is the biggest marine park in the Southern Hemisphere. It has whales, sea lions, helicopter tours, and amusement park rides. Surfers Paradise has the **Ripley's Believe It or Not! Museum** *(tel (07) 5592 0040, www.ripleys.com.au, $$)* and the extravagant **Conrad Jupiter's Casino** *(tel (07) 5592 8100).*

## National Parks

The hinterlands away from the coast are a subtropical paradise of smallish national parks, with rich rain forests, hidden waterfalls, and panoramic lookout views.

**Burleigh Heads National Park** is just off the Gold Coast Highway. **Lamington National Park,** one of Queensland's most popular, is about an hour's drive southwest of Surfers Paradise. This park has 3,900-foot-high (1,190 m) mountains in the rugged MacPherson Range and densely forested valleys with lush subtropical vegetation. Two of the park's most popular sections, **Binna Burra** and **Green Mountains,** are both accessible from Canungra. More than 84 miles (136 km) of walking trails lace these wilderness areas. One fine hike stretches 13

**Queensland Parks & Wildlife Service**
✉ Burleigh Heads National Park
☎ 1-300 130 372

**Lamington National Park**
🅰 139 D1

**Binna Burra**
Visitor Information
☎ (07) 5533 3584

**Green Mountains**
Visitor Information
☎ (07) 5544 0634

### Crikey!

Steve Irwin (1962–2006) rose to prominence thanks to the television documentary series *Crocodile Hunter,* which aired globally. Raised around crocodiles on his parents' Queensland Reptile and Fauna Park, the young Steve had no fear of wildlife. Australia mourned when he was killed by a stingray barb that pierced his heart while filming on the Great Barrier Reef. He is survived by wife, Terri Irwin, and children, Bindi and Bob. His life's work continues at the popular **Australia Zoo** (see p. 147) and through the **Wildlife Warriors** foundation *(www.wildlife warrior.org.au).*

miles (21 km) between O'Reilly's Rainforest Retreat and the Binna Burra Mountain Lodge.

Another popular yet wild national park within an hour of the Gold Coast is **Springbrook National Park,** which has 3,000-year-old beech trees, gorges, and the 200-foot-high (60 m) Purling Brook Falls.

## Sunshine Coast

The Sunshine Coast starts at the Glass House Mountains and extends to the colored sands of Rainbow Beach 85 miles (140 km) farther north. Quieter than the Gold Coast, it has long been a vacation

One of the many lush coves within Noosa National Park

spot and is very popular with retirees from the cooler south. These days it is also a honeypot for families moving north from Sydney and Melbourne to enjoy Queensland's sunny promise.

Although it isn't as glitzy as the Gold Coast, the Sunshine Coast is still fairly heavily developed. It has

its share of exuberantly tasteless Aussie kitsch, too: the 50-foot-high (15 m) Big Pineapple near **Nambour,** the tacky Ettamogah Pub, and the enormous Big Shell at **Tewantin.** The fashionable end of the coast is Noosa Heads, a rather exclusive seaside town flanked by Noosa National Park and Cooloola National Park. You're better off leaving the beaches alone until you get close to Noosa. In the lower part of the Sunshine Coast, the hinterlands are far prettier, with their ginger, pineapple, and sugarcane plantations and rain forests.

Fifty miles (80 km) north from Brisbane on the Bruce Highway, the Glass House Mountains Road (Steve Irwin Way) rises into tropical farmlands in the **Glass House Mountains.** This dramatic range is a series of 16 volcanic necks, as much as 1,820 feet high (556 m), rising from sugarcane plantations. Captain Cook named them for the shape, which "very much resembles a glass house." Many of the peaks are protected by forest reserves and Glass House Mountains National Park, which has fine hiking trails to some spectacular lookouts. To get into the mountains, drive northwest of Beerburrum along a scenic, winding route to the **Glass House Mountains Lookout** for views of the coast. Farther north, and west of Glass House Mountains township, walks in the national park go to peaks such as Mt. Ngungun or the more demanding Mt. Tibrogargan and Mt. Beerwah (the highest).

The township of Beerwah is home to one of the Sunshine

Coast's main attractions, the **Australia Zoo** (*Steve Irwin Way, tel (07) 5436 2000, $$$$$*). Made famous by the Croc Hunter himself, this world-class zoo has acres of natural habitats, where you can have walk-through encounters with kangaroos and other Australian wildlife; the "Crocoseum," with its famous crocodile shows; and a growing collection of exotic animals from around the world.

The tranquil villages in the nearby **Blackall Range**—for example, Mapleton, Flaxton, and Montville—have a very 19th-century English feel. You will find arts-and-craft cottages, tearooms, antiques shops, and roadside fruit stalls, in addition to several small but stunning national parks.

The 17-mile (27 km) scenic drive from Maleny to Mapleton is arguably the most beautiful in Queensland. It includes waterfalls, rain forests, and panoramic views of the mountains. Follow the Glass House Mountains Road to Landsborough and head east on the Landsborough–Maleny Road. Six winding miles (9 km) later, the Montville Road on your right is the start of the drive, but it is worth detouring 2 miles (3 km) farther east to the pretty village of **Maleny** (*visitor information: 23 Maple St., tel (07) 5499 9033*). The lookout at **Mary Cairncross Park,** near the turnoff for the Montville Road, gives fine views of the Glass House Mountains. Once at Mapleton, the northern end of the drive, be sure also to stop at **Mapleton Falls National Park,** where a 400-foot (122 m) waterfall rushes into a deep,

---

## EXPERIENCE: Turtle Treasures

Visit the largest marine turtle nesting site on the east coast from late November to early March for an amazing experience. At Mon Repos, 8 miles (13 km) from Bundaberg, loggerhead and other turtles make the laborious journey up the beach to lay their eggs. The hatchlings emerge later in the season and head out to sea. **Queensland Parks & Wildlife Service** gives tours, which must be booked through the Bundaberg visitor center (*186 Bourbong St., tel (07) 4153 8888, www.bundabergregion.info*).

---

forest-cloaked valley. From Mapleton follow the Nambour Road 8 miles (13 km) west to the Pacific Highway and turn north for Noosa.

**Noosa Heads** has been a surfers' hangout since the 1960s but is now a chic international resort town. With admirable foresight, the local town planners have ruled that no buildings can be higher than the trees, so though Noosa has smart restaurants and luxury hotels, it still has a small-town feel.

Noosa is protected by the headlands of **Noosa National Park,** which has rain forest trails, beaches and views. Farther north are the beautiful colored sands of the **Cooloola National Park,** between Tewantin and Rainbow Beach. The park takes in a swath of hinterland, but it is the strikingly colored sandstone cliffs along 20 miles (32 km) of coast that catch the eye. You can see reds, ochers, yellows, and browns—more than 70 shades according to geologists, who estimate the age of the

---

**Noosa Heads**
**Visitor Information**
- ✉ Hastings St.
- ☎ (07) 5430 5000

**Noosa National Park**
- 🅰 139 D2

**Queensland Parks & Wildlife Service**
**Visitor Information Centre**
- ✉ Rainbow Beach
- ☎ (07) 5486 3160

## Fraser Island

⚓ 139 E2 & 155

**Visitor Information**

✉ Hervey Bay

☎ (07) 4124 8741

## Hervey Bay

**Visitor Information**

☎ (07) 4124 9855

**FERRIES: From Inskip Point:** *Rainbow Venture,* tel (07) 5486 3154; *Kingfisher Bay,* 1-800 072 555. **From River Heads, Hervey Bay:** *Fraser Venture,* tel (07) 4194 9222. **From Hervey Bay Boat Harbour:** *Fraser Dawn,* (07) 4194 9222.

cliffs at 40,000 years. Scientists debate whether oxides in the rock or decaying vegetable matter give these cliffs their color. Local Aborigines have a more romantic explanation: The cliffs were colored by a Rainbow Serpent who was killed by a boomerang when he came to the rescue of a young woman. Spectacular walking trails run along the coast. The visitor center, at the northern end of the park, has details on the park and on neighboring Fraser Island.

## Fraser Island

To describe Fraser Island as the world's largest sand island is accurate but misleading. Far from being just a big sandbar, this World Heritage site is, in fact, a tropical paradise dotted with crystalline lakes. The waters of this 80-mile-long (128 km) island teem with fish, and in winter, humpback whales shelter in Hervey Bay.

Located about 125 miles (200 km) north of Brisbane, Fraser Island is popular with bushwalkers, four-wheel-drive enthusiasts, and surfers. Despite the fact that up to 20,000 vehicles tour the island each year, it manages to retain its pristine wilderness feel. Ferries to the island go from **Inskip Point** *(8 miles/13 km N of Rainbow Beach)* and from **Hervey Bay,** a pleasant city of 55,000 reached by turning off the Pacific Highway at Maryborough.

Fraser Island was formed over many millions of years by currents washing sands up the coast, where they backed up against the edge of the continental shelf. Its lushness is a tribute to nature's remarkable powers of adaptation. Some trees store nutrients in their trunks, rather than rely on the sands, while others have above-ground roots capable of feeding off windblown nutrients. Still other plants obtain nitrogen from insects instead of the soil. The result is a remarkable and ancient growth of palms, ferns, and rain forest trees such as the satinay,

## A Dingo Stole My Baby

The 1988 film *A Cry in the Dark,* starring Meryl Streep, detailed one of Australia's most sensational criminal cases: the disappearance of baby Azaria Chamberlain from Uluru in 1980. Although Azaria's parents reported that a dingo had taken the baby from their tent, Lindy Chamberlain, Azaria's mother, was convicted of murder and jailed. She was exonerated eight years later. Tragedy stuck again in 2001, when dingoes killed a nine-year-old boy on Fraser Island.

Originally domesticated dogs brought from Asia 4,000 years ago, dingoes normally shy away from humans, but they become more brazen when accustomed to people in tourist areas. Attacks are rare, but dingoes will sometimes hunt in packs, making them a risk for children.

The dingo is conserved in some areas, notably Fraser Island, which has the purest breed. However, the world's longest fence runs 3,450 miles (5,600 km) across Queensland and South Australia and tries to keep dingoes out of southeastern Australia's farms. For the sake of the dingo and other visitors, do not feed them or encourage any interaction.

Sunlight filters through the rain forest canopy above a creek on Fraser Island.

which grows almost nowhere else and is highly sought after for its borer-resistant wood.

Fraser Island was first recorded by Captain Cook in 1770. It was named for Eliza Fraser, the wife of a sea captain whose ship foundered farther north in 1836. Aborigines killed some of the survivors—including Eliza Fraser's husband. Eliza was captured, but two months later, she was rescued by an unlikely alliance of escaped convicts and other Aborigines.

**Great Sandy National Park** covers all of Fraser Island and has rocky outcrops and magnificent dunes. Most of the island's 40 or so lakes—including the jewel-like and often crowded **Lake MacKenzie**—are concentrated in the south. The razor-sharp line of **Seventy-Five-Mile Beach,** along the eastern flank, has become a playground for four-wheel-drive adventurers. The forested central part of the island is comparatively untouched and offers tranquil bushwalking.

Plenty of organized tours of the island leave from Hervey Bay.

You can also visit Fraser Island on your own. If you want to drive on the island, you will need a four-wheel-drive vehicle and a permit *(obtainable at the River Heads store, just S of Hervey Bay, or at Marina Kiosk, Buccaneer Ave., Hervey Bay, tel (07, 4128 9800).*

A good place to start your exploration is **Central Station,** a former logging camp near the southern end of the island, where most of the tracks converge. You can get a taste of what's on the island by taking a short stroll along the astoundingly clear Wanggoolba Creek, through deep forests, prehistoric ferns, and enormous satinay trees. You are also likely to meet some of the island's other specialties—dingoes. Because of their island isolation, the dingoes of Fraser Island have never bred with dogs and are Australia's last genetically pure dingoes. Dogs are not permitted here lest they interbreed with the dingoes. In 2001, dingoes killed a nine-year-old boy here (see sidebar p. 148). Take care, watch your children, and do not feed the dingoes. ■

# Tropic of Capricorn Drive

Just the name Tropic of Capricorn conjures up the romance of faraway and exotic places. Otherwise known as the line of latitude at 23.5° south of the Equator, it slices through the northern third of Australia on maps. Here in Queensland, you can drive along the Tropic of Capricorn for almost 500 miles (800 km).

The Capricorn Highway goes from the sparkling seas at the southern end of the Great Barrier Reef into the heart of the dusty, sunburned outback at Longreach. It starts at **Rockhampton ❶**, about a third of the way north along the Queensland coast. The Tropic of Capricorn actually runs a mile or so south of town, but enterprising locals have quietly nudged it to a more convenient location just outside the Capricorn information center on the Bruce Highway, 2 miles (3 km) south of the town center *(tel (07) 4927 2055)*. A large and ornate brass sundial is out front, and at a brightly colored plaque you can stand with one foot in the Earth's southern temperate zone and the other in the torrid.

Rockhampton is a very pleasant, small tropical city of about 59,000, set along the Fitzroy River about 25 miles (40 km) inland from the coast. The **Riverside Information Centre,** on elegant Quay Street, is a source of advice on local sights *(tel (07) 4922 5339)*. Quay Street has ornate 19th-century architecture, thanks to the wealth that passed through here in the Mount Morgan gold rush of the 1880s and later when Rockhampton blossomed into the center for Queensland's cattle industry. The **Cattleman's Club** is particularly handsome.

Explore Aboriginal culture at the **Dreamtime Culture Centre,** on the Bruce Highway about 4 miles (6.4 km) north of town *(tel (07) 4936 1655, $$)*. To the south, acquaint yourself with the tropical plants of northern Queensland at the **Botanic Gardens** *(Spencer St.)*.

## NOT TO BE MISSED:

Australian Workers Heritage Centre • Australian Stockman's Hall of Fame • Qantas Founders Museum

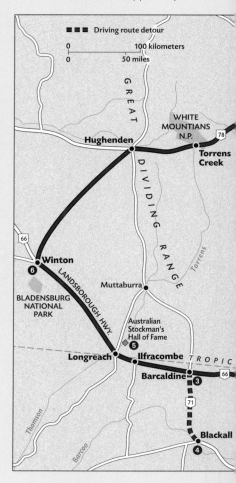

You should keep a couple of things in mind before you drive into the outback sunset on the Capricorn Highway. This is a genuine outback highway—paved but with long stretches of nothing between small settlements and towns. Keep an eye on the gas gauge, always carry extra drinking water, and be sure to have some cash, because banks and ATMs are scarce out here. Be prepared for the road trains—huge triple-rigged trucks of up to 170 tons (173 tonnes)—hauling supplies to lonely settlements and stations. They are nothing to be afraid of— the drivers are very skilled—but the first time one sweeps by can be a little unnerving.

The highway starts at a roundabout just south of Rockhampton and heads due west, past the sprawling cattleyards of big-time cattle country and over the Great Dividing Range. The road rolls through the timber mill town of Dingo, skirts Queensland's coalfields around Blackwater, then climbs over more ranges as it goes farther into outback Australia.

After 170 miles (274 km), you'll drive into **Emerald** *(visitor information: tel (07) 4982 4386)*, a pleasant town of fig-lined streets. The town's colonial railroad station has been listed by the National Trust. West of Emerald are what used to be the largest sapphire fields in the Southern

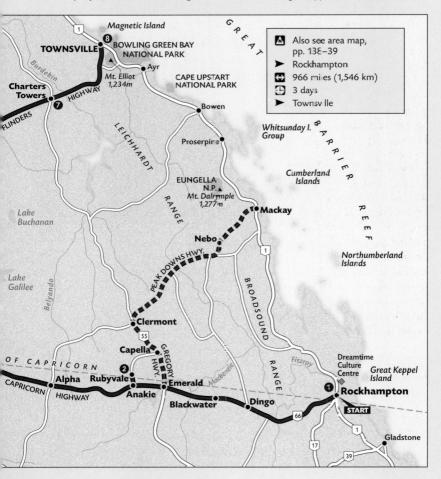

Hemisphere. The Star of Queensland, regarded as the finest black sapphire in the world, was found at Anakie and now resides in the Smithsonian Institution in the United States. You can visit two walk-in mines at **Rubyvale ❷**, and you can get a fossicking (prospecting) license if you want to try to find some gems yourself.

The highway runs from Anakie through 180 miles (290 km) of mostly empty outback before

information: Shamrock St., tel (07) 4657 4637), an hour south on the Matilda Highway. Blackall was home to one of Australia's legends, Big Jackie Howe, the greatest shearer of them all. In 1892, at nearby Alice Downs Station, Howe set a record by shearing 321 ewes in the union-prescribed workday of seven hours and forty minutes, using crude iron hand shears. A statue of Howe stands at the corner of

A quintessential outback image: saddles draped on a barn door near Winton

it reaches **Barcaldine ❸** (visitor information: Oak St., tel (07) 4651 1724). This town of 1,600 claims to be the birthplace of the Australian Labor Party. Striking shearers gathered here in the long hot months of 1891 to plan strategy in their bitter campaign against wealthy graziers. They met beneath a 150-year-old ghost gum that became known as the Tree of Knowledge. (The tree was destroyed in an act of vandalism in 2006; a memorial in its honor opened in 2009.) The **Australian Workers Heritage Centre** on Ash Street tells the story of the struggle.

You can make an interesting detour from Barcaldine to the town of **Blackall ❹** (visitor

Shamrock and Short Streets. On Thistle Street is another icon, a reproduction of the so-called Black Stump that surveyor Thomas Frazer used as his baseline for mapping the area in 1886. Anything beyond this marker was deemed to be "outback," and Australians today still sometimes refer to the remote parts of their country as "beyond the Black Stump."

Return to the Capricorn Highway at Barcaldine and go west to **Longreach** (visitor information: tel (07) 4658 4150), home to the superb **Australian Stockman's Hall of Fame ❺** (tel (07) 4658 2166, $$$). You'll see it from the highway about a mile before you get to

Longreach. It opened in 1988 with fanfare and some doubts that visitors would come this far to see it, but it has surpassed all expectations. It tells the story of Australia from the Dreamtime onward and focuses on the settlement of the outback. The excellent exhibits include photographs, videos, and slides of pioneer explorers, outback women, shearers, and cattlemen.

## INSIDER TIP:

**In Longreach, be sure to visit Banjo's Outback Theatre & Woolshed (www.outbacknow .com.au) for dinner and a show that includes songs, skits, and sheep shearing demonstrations.**

—STEPHANIE ROBICHAUX
*National Geographic contributor*

The Hall of Fame alone would be worth the drive out here, but Longreach has more. Qantas started operations here in 1921 as the Queensland and Northern Territory Air Service (it's the world's second oldest airline). The original hangar sits almost opposite the Stockman's Hall of Fame. Today it houses the **Qantas Founders Museum** (tel (07) 4658 3737, www.qfom.com.au, $$), which has displays of aviation history that include the airline's first plane, an Avro 504K, as well as one much more recent, a decommissioned 747; flown into Longreach in 2002, it presents a startling spectacle as you drive into town. The airline's original booking office, situated on the corner of Duck and Eagle Streets, is now Longreach's visitor information center.

The **School of Distance Education** is nearby; you can see how children who live on remote outback stations go to school by radio.

Longreach marks the end of the Capricorn Highway. From here the main highway veers north, away from the Tropic of Capricorn. Known as the Landsborough Highway, it runs 75 windswept miles (120 km) to the town of **Winton 6**. This is where Banjo Patterson reputedly wrote "Waltzing Matilda" (see sidebar below). The truth about the origin of the song is lost in time and municipal rivalry, but according to legend it was performed publicly for the first time in Winton's North Gregory Hotel (67 Elderslie St., tel (07) 4657 1375) in 1895. Visit the **Waltzing Matilda Centre** (tel (07) 4657 1466, $$), an engaging museum dedicated to Australia's most popular song. It offers recordings of many of the 500 different renditions of the song, as well as an excellent collection of outback history and lore—every bit as good, although not as large, as the Australian Stockman's Hall of Fame in Longreach.

From Winton you can loop back to the coast via Hughenden and then continue east on the Flinders Highway for 240 miles (386 km) to the colorful gold-mining town of **Charters Towers 7** and then on to **Townsville 8** (see p. 166) on the Coral Sea. If you don't go to Winton, you can vary the return journey by returning east from Longreach on the Capricorn Highway and turning north at Emerald to follow the Gregory and Peak Downs Highways to the coast at Mackay.

## Waltzing Matilda

**Written by bush poet Andrew B. "Banjo" Paterson, "Waltzing Matilda" seems an odd choice as Australia's unofficial national anthem. It tells the story of a swagman (hobo), who camps by a billabong (waterhole) and steals a jumbuck (sheep), only to jump into the river and drown escaping a trooper. Most likely based on the bitter shearers' strikes of the 1890s, when troops were sent in and shearers attacked sheep farms, the antiestablishment sentiment and use of colloquial language struck a deep chord with the Australian public.**

# Great Barrier Reef

Australia's crowning glory is the Great Barrier Reef, the chain of coral reefs and lush tropical islands that flanks the Queensland coast. No adjectives or glossy underwater photographs can adequately prepare you for that magical moment when you don a mask and poke your face into the warm tropical waters of this seductive dreamscape.

Loggerhead turtles can live for 50 years and grow to be five feet (1.5 m) long.

**Queensland Parks & Wildlife Service**

 Shoreline Close, Rosslyn Bay

☎ (07) 4933 6595

The Great Barrier Reef starts near **Lady Elliott Island** and stretches 1,300 miles (2,092 km) north to **Bramble Cay,** off the coast of Papua New Guinea. Although it is generally referred to as one reef, it is in fact a mosaic of more than 2,900 distinct reefs covering almost 90,000 square miles (233,100 sq km). The reefs change character along the way. In the south they form chains of sandy cays—coral outcrops that emerge above the water and have acquired a covering of vegetation. In the north, where the coral comes closest to the coast, it runs in long ribbons.

Throughout its length, the reef is a maze of sharp corals and shallow water, and it was a navigational nightmare for Australia's early explorers. In 1768, French explorer Louis Antoine de Bougainville might have put in a claim to mainland Australia had not the sound of waves washing against the corals put him off. Describing it in his log as the "voice of

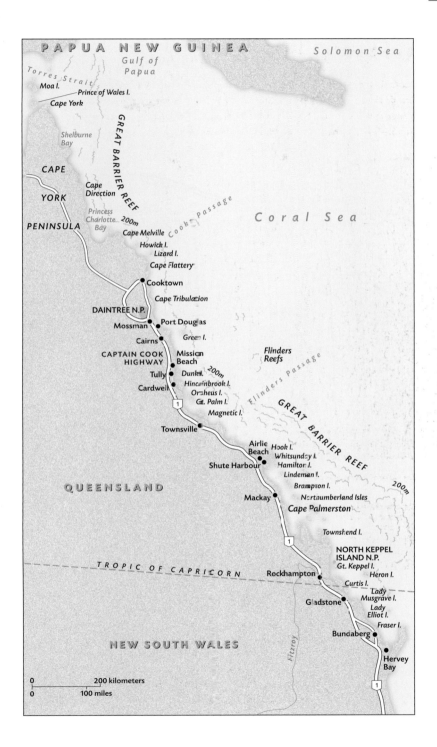

PAPUA NEW GUINEA
Gulf of Papua
Solomon Sea

*Torres Strait*
Moa I.
Prince of Wales I.
Cape York

CAPE

Shelburne Bay

YORK

Cape Direction

PENINSULA

Princess Charlotte Bay
200m
Cape Melville

Coral Sea

GREAT BARRIER REEF

Cook Passage

Howick I.
Lizard I.
Cape Flattery

Cooktown

Cape Tribulation

DAINTREE N.P.
Mossman        Port Douglas
Cairns         Green I.

CAPTAIN COOK
HIGHWAY        Mission
               Beach
Tully          Dunk I.
Cardwell       Hinchinbrook I.
               Orpheus I.
               Gt. Palm I.
               Magnetic I.

Flinders Reefs

200m

Flinders Passage

GREAT BARRIER REEF

Townsville

Airlie Beach
Shute Harbour

Hook I.
Whitsunday I.
Hamilton I.
Lindeman I.

QUEENSLAND

Mackay

Brampton I.
Northumberland Isles
Cape Palmerston

200m

Townshend I.

NORTH KEPPEL
ISLAND N.P.
Gt. Keppel I.
Heron I.

TROPIC OF CAPRICORN

Rockhampton

Curtis I.
Lady Musgrave I.
Lady Elliot I.
Fraser I.

Gladstone

NEW SOUTH WALES

*Fitzroy*

Bundaberg

Hervey Bay

0        200 kilometers
0        100 miles

## Reef Formation

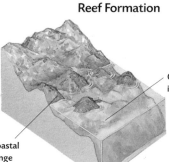

Coral growing in shallow water

Coastal range

As the last ice age ended and the Earth's climate warmed, Queensland's coast had a range of forested hills. Corals grew in the shallow waters of the continental shelf.

The water level rises and the coral begins to build upward.

Coral grows around submerged hills.

Glaciers and ice caps melted, raising the sea level slowly. As it rose, the coastal valleys filled, leaving islands. Coral grew upward on the old, dead coral below.

Inner reef of coral-fringed islands and coral cays

Outer reef of coral cays on the reef at the edge of the continental shelf

Coastal rain forest

Rising waters flooded farther inland. Fringing reefs grew around the inner reef islands; low coral cays developed on the spectacular reefs of the outer reef.

## Creatures of the Reef

Great white shark

Green turtle

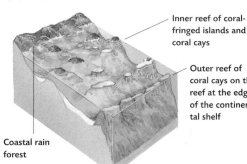

Coral polyp tentacles catch prey during the day, retract at night.

Coral cod

Featherstar

Blue sea star

Giant clam

God," he kept going. Thirty years later Matthew Flinders compared navigating the reef to threading a needle. Some couldn't do it. The reef contains more than 30 wrecks and continues to be occasionally bruised by keels and hulls today.

### Natural History of the Reef

A World Heritage site, the reef was built by a simple primitive organism, a marine polyp of the family Coelenterata. Billions of polyps huddle together in warm, salty, shallow water and grow toward the sunlight like brilliant

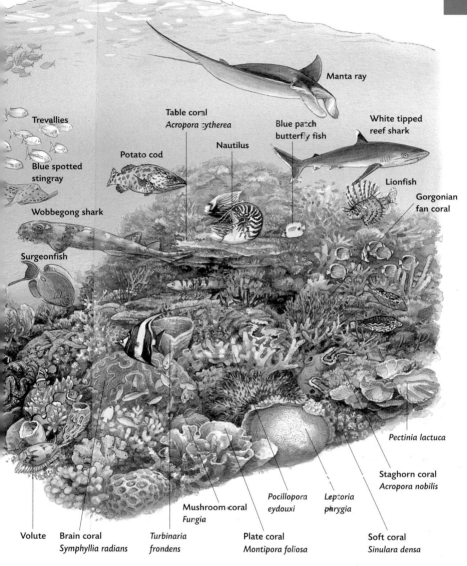

Manta ray

Trevallies

Table coral
*Acropora cytherea*

Blue patch
butterfly fish

White tipped
reef shark

Potato cod

Nautilus

Blue spotted
stingray

Lionfish

Gorgonian
fan coral

Wobbegong shark

Surgeonfish

Pectinia lactuca

Staghorn coral
*Acropora nobilis*

Pocillopora
eydouxi

Leptoria
phrygia

Mushroom coral
*Fungia*

Volute

Brain coral
*Symphyllia radians*

Turbinaria
frondens

Plate coral
*Montipora foliosa*

Soft coral
*Sinulara densa*

flowers. When one dies, a new
polyp grows on its skeleton.
They are known as hard corals,
for the skeletons they form.
Over millions of years, a vast
reef complex develops. Some
parts of the Great Barrier Reef
have been building for more
than 18 million years. Much of
the reef, however, dates from
the end of the last ice age,
about 15,000 years ago, when
sea levels started to rise.

## Reef Inhabitants

The reef is a world in itself, the
coral colonies providing food,
shelter, and hunting grounds
for billions of other creatures.
In addition to 400-odd species
of corals, the Great Barrier Reef
has more than 4,000 species

**Queensland Parks & Wildlife Service**

✉ Corner of Mandalay & Shute Harbour Rds., Airlie Beach

☎ (07) 4946 7022

**Great Barrier Reef Marine Parks Authority**

✉ P.O. Box 1379, Townsville

☎ 1-300 360 898

of mollusks, 350 species of echinoderms—sea urchins, sea stars, and sea cucumbers—and 4,000 varieties of sponges.

About 1,500 varieties of tropical fish swim around the reef, in almost every color imaginable. There are humpback whales, stingrays, giant turtles, and dugongs—the sea cows that gave rise to myths of mermaids. No place on land, not even the wildest rain forest, supports this kind of diversity. One of nature's most spectacular sights occurs here beneath a full moon on a few nights each spring: The corals spawn, releasing billions of eggs in a rainbow of colors.

## Exploring the Reef

Diving and snorkeling are the best ways to explore the reef. If you don't dive, or don't want to, it's no problem. Anyone can learn to snorkel in five minutes, and the only thing you'll miss out on is a longer period under the water. Most of the best displays are shallow anyway, and if you simply paddle face down along the surface, you'll be treated to vivid displays of tropical color and an eerie, dreamlike sensation of flying. You don't even have to get wet: many operators have glass-bottom boats through which you can view the reef.

If you do want to learn to dive, plenty of dive courses are available along the coast, particularly in tourist hubs like **Airlie Beach** and **Cairns** (see p. 167). They vary greatly in professionalism and price, so shop around. You can also do a single escorted dive with an instructor for about A$50 (U.S. $38).

## Great Barrier Reef Islands

More than 700 islands dot the lee side of the Great Barrier Reef. Many of them are uninhabited, tropical paradises.

Gorgonian fan coral and crinoids flourish in a gap in the reef where currents can bring nutrients.

Those that do have resorts offer varieties of paradise to suit every taste or budget. You can choose from family retreats, ecotourist lodges, some of the world's most exclusive resorts, or hard-partying college getaways.

**Southern Islands:** Most of the southern islands are clustered around the Capricorn Coast, between Bundaberg and Rockhampton. **Lady Elliott Island,** which marks the southern tip of the Great Barrier Reef,

## Threats to the Reef

The Great Barrier Reef has been a protected marine park since 1975. It is managed by the Great Barrier Reef Marine Parks Authority (GBRMPA), which tries to juggle the growing demands of tourism with the critical need to protect this ecosystem. One natural threat is the crown-of-thorns sea star, which eats coral and causes severe damage in its periodic outbreaks—but the damage that people do is far worse. Any dead or broken coral that you see has probably suffered from direct human attention or from tour-boat anchors. Consider this to be the world's greatest and most fragile china shop. Look, but don't touch.

Only a very few of the Great Barrier Reef islands are on the reef itself. The majority are continental islands, which means they are ancient coastal hilltops that became islands at the end of the last ice age about 15,000 years ago, when the sea level rose. Magnificent fringing coral reefs have grown around these islands, which are often wooded, with high mountains and spectacular views of the tropical seas and other islands nearby. Some are accessible by short ferry rides, others require a longer and more expensive journey. Three island resorts are actually coral cays themselves, and at low tide visitors can walk on the body of the reef. The islands are divided into three main groups: the southern islands (see below), the Whitsunday Islands in the center (see pp. 161–64), and the tropical northern islands (see pp. 164–65).

is a coral cay where divers stand a good chance of encountering loggerhead turtles and manta rays. In 1816 the seamen on the ship Lady Elliott made the first recorded sighting of the island, but it seems to have gone unsighted a little too often over the next 50 years. After an extraordinary number of shipwrecks, an elegant lighthouse was built here in 1866. It was a lonely place to be stationed, and several early lighthouse-keepers reputedly committed suicide. The lighthouse still stands but is much less lonely these days, with the Lady Elliott Resort (tel 1-800 072 200, toll-free), catering to 140 people and daily flights, including from Bundaberg and Hervey Bay.

Neighboring **Lady Musgrave Island,** about 25 miles (40 km) farther north, is a tiny uninhabited mote popular with yachtsmen

**Queensland Parks & Wildlife Service**

⊠ 136 Goondoon St., Gladstone

☎ (07) 4971 6055

for its pretty turquoise lagoon formed by sheltering coral. It is a low island covered with grasses, pandanus palms, pisonia, and casuarina trees. In the early 1900s, goats released on Lady Musgrave and Lady Elliott Islands devastated the landscape. A revegetation program that was started in the 1970s has been fairly successful. These days Lady Musgrave is one of the best islands in the southern reef on which to camp, although light sleepers may be disturbed by the colonies of terns and other raucous seabirds. *(Arrange permits through the Queensland Parks and Wildlife Service office in Gladstone. Only 40 campers are allowed on the island at a time.)* You can get there by boat or seaplane from Bundaberg. The M.V. *Lady Musgrave (tel (07) 5152 9011)* makes day trips to the island.

**Heron Island** is another of the coral islands. Located about 70 miles (112 km) from Gladstone, it is also one of the best-known islands on the reef—and with good reason. Its waters teem with coral and fish, making it a paradise for divers and snorkelers, and the island is a breeding ground for thousands of birds and turtles. Heron Island was first settled in the 1920s, when a turtle cannery was set up. In 1932, the cannery closed and a tourism

---

# EXPERIENCE: Cruising the Great Barrier Reef

Cairns/Port Douglas and the Whitsunday Islands are the most popular departure points for reef tours, but cruises can also be arranged in towns along the coast such as Mission Beach, Townsville, and Bundaberg. A mind-boggling array of sailing, diving, snorkeling, and overnight to one-week tours operate, but most visitors take a day cruise.

Most day companies have their own platforms on the outer reef, about 1.5–2 hours from Cairns, slightly longer than from farther south. All-day cruises include snorkeling and lunch, with extras such as undersea observatories, glass-bottom boats, and diving. Full-day cruises are A$130–230 (US$120–$210) per person. Main operators include:

### Cairns

**Great Adventures Cruises** *(Reef Fleet Terminal, 1 Spence St., www.great adventures.com.au):* Big

boats go to Green Island, a platform on the outer edge of the reef, or both. **Passions of Paradise** *(Reef Fleet Terminal, Cairns, www .passions.com.au):* Smaller sailing catamaran goes to Michaelmas Cay and Paradise Reef. **Sunlover** *(Reef Fleet Terminal, www.sunlover.com .au):* Fast catamarans go to Moore Reef and spend four hours.

### Port Douglas

**Quicksilver Connections**, *(Marina Mirage, tel (07) 4087 2100, www.quicksilver cruises.com.au):* Luxury

catamarans visit their outer reef platform and the closer Low Isles.

### Whitsundays

**Cruise Whitsundays** *(Abel Point Marina North, Airlie Beach, www.cruisewhitsun days.com):* Cruises from Airlie Beach sail to a pontoon at Knuckle Reef Lagoon, or those in a hurry can get a helicopter connection. **Fantasea** *(Shute Harbour Jetty, Shute Harbour, www .fantasea.com.au):* From Shute Harbour, Daydream, and Hamilton Islands, cruises take visitors to the Hardy Reef pontoon.

industry began to evolve. The island was declared a national park in 1943. Accommodations are at the Heron Island Resort *(tel (07) 4972 9055)*. The island is small enough to stroll around in an hour, but you have to stay as part of a package deal.

The party is at **Great Keppel Island,** with its white-sand beaches and nightlife. Great Keppel is the biggest of a chain of 19 islands that make up **Keppel Bay Islands National Park.** These hilly, eucalyptus woodland islands are remnants of the ancient Queensland coast. You can enjoy great diving, bushwalking, and camping here. Access is by boat from the Rosslyn Bay ferry terminal, northeast of Rockhampton *(tel (07) 4933 6744)*. Other Keppel Bay islands can be visited by water taxi from the Keppel Bay Marina *(tel (07) 4933 6244)*. Many of these islands are uninhabited, such as **Middle Island** and **Miall Island,** so campers have to take all supplies, including drinking water.

**Whitsunday Islands:** The Whitsunday Islands were named by Captain Cook, who sailed between the islands and the coast on Whitsunday in July 1770—or at least he thought he did. Although the devout captain kept meticulous logs, he had not allowed for the international dateline and was actually a day off.

The hundred or so Whitsunday Islands are perhaps the most gorgeous of Queensland's tropical paradises. These continental islands formed when the sea level

Whitehaven Beach on Whitsunday Island, one of the loveliest of the Great Barrier Reef beaches

rose after the last ice age, and they still resemble the mountaintops they once were. They are steep and lush, covered with dense pine forests. Although the islands are more than 30 miles (48 km) from the reef, they are fringed with coral. Many of them became national parks in the 1930s and now form a string of national parks, including the Whitsunday

**Whitsunday Islands**

139 D3 & 155

**Whitsunday Information Centre**

✉ Bruce Hwy, Proserpine

☎ 1-800 801 252

**www.whitsunday tourism.com**

# EXPERIENCE: Sailing the Whitsundays

Life doesn't get much better than sailing your yacht with friends and family around the tropical waters of the Whitsunday Islands. Cruise the calm waters sheltered by the Great Barrier Reef, drop anchor in sheltered coves, dive over the side to swim and snorkel, or cook up a seafood feast in the galley. Don't have a yacht? Never sailed? Never mind, the Whitsundays is the ideal place to go bareboating (DIY boating). A number of companies make it easy, renting fully equipped yachts, catamarans, and powerboats with from 2 to 12 berth.

Boating experience is preferred, but all new skippers are given three hours' instruction before sailing. If preferred,

a skipper is provided (at extra cost) for as long as necessary. Book ahead.
**Cumberland Charter Yachts** (Shop 2 Shingley Beach Rd., Abel Point Marina, Airlie Beach, tel (07) 4946 7500, www.ccy.com.au)
**Queensland Yacht Charters** (Abel Point Marina, Airlie Beach, tel (07) 4946 7400, www.yachtcharters.com.au)
**Sunsail Australia** (Front Street, Hamilton Island, tel (07) 4948 9509, www.sunsail .com.au)
**Whitsunday Private Yacht Charters** (18 Abel Point Marina, Airlie Beach, tel (07) 4946 6880, www.whitsunday-yacht.com.au)
**Whitsunday Rent A Yacht** (6 Bay Ter., Shute Harbour, tel (07) 4946 9232, www .rentayacht.com.au)

## Mackay
🅰 139 D3
**Visitor Information**
✉ Nebo Rd.
☎ (07) 4952 2677

Islands, Molle Island, Lindeman Island, and Repulse Islands. Although some of the islands have resorts on them, most are uninhabited, and on several you can camp next to pristine beaches. Day cruises through the Whitsunday Passage (between islands and coast) and the islands can be arranged in Airlie Beach, Shute Harbour, and Mackay.

**Brampton Island** is the southernmost of the Whitsundays, only 20 miles (32 km) northeast of **Mackay,** which is the departure point for ferries (tel (07) 4955 3066). Most of the island is parkland, with seven coral beaches and rain forests bright with rainbow lorikeets and butterflies, although tourist resorts have been here since 1933. You can hike to the summit of Brampton Peak (a one-hour hike, very steep; take water) for views of the surrounding island-dotted seas.

**INSIDER TIP:**

**Whitsunday's Whitehaven Beach, with its silica white sand, has a well-earned reputation as one of the region's finest beaches. Arrive early and stay late.**

—CATHERINE PEARSON
*National Geographic contributor*

**Whitsunday Island** is the largest of the islands—almost 30,000 acres (12,150 ha)—and probably looks much as it did when Captain Cook sailed past in 1770. The island has no resorts, just tropical forests, inlets, and unspoiled Whitehaven Beach—arguably the finest in the islands. If you want to go back to nature, this is one of the best places along the coast to do it. Cid Harbour, on the island's west coast, was an anchorage for part of the U.S. fleet just before the Battle of the Coral Sea (1943). Campsites run by the national parks service are there today. The Whitsunday Islands National Park office at Airlie Beach advises visitors on campsites and on what to bring.

**Hook Island,** directly north of Whitsunday, is the second largest in the group. It has an underwater observatory and a low-key private resort, the Hook Island Wilderness Resort *(tel (07) 4946 9470)*. A semisubmersible boat tours the island's spellbinding coral reefs.

**Lindeman Island** is another large member of the group—about 5,000 acres (2,025 ha)—and all is national park. The snorkeling is superb, as is the bird-watching in the island's forests. Butterfly Valley has rainbow lorikeets and spectacular blue tiger butterflies. You can see much of the Whitsunday chain from 700-foot-high (213 m) Mount Oldfield. Most visitors to the island stay at the Club Med Resort *(tel (07) 4946 9333)*.

**Hamilton, Daydream, and Hayman Islands** are the most developed of the Whitsundays. Hamilton, about 10 miles (16 km) south of Shute Harbour, is the most built-over of all, with a high-rise apartment tower, restaurants, marina, jetport, shopping boutiques, and sports complex *(tel 1 300 725 172, toll-free)*. The ferries to Hamilton Island leave from Shute Harbour, or you can fly direct from Sydney, Melbourne, or Brisbane.

Daydream Island is the smallest of the developed islands, lying only 3 miles (4.8 km) from Shute Harbour on the mainland

Nearly 5,000 species of mollusks inhabit the Great Barrier Reef, including the giant clam.

**North Barrier Reef National Parks information**

✉ Queensland Parks & Wildlife, Cardwell

☎ (07) 4066 8601 (for information on national parks on all the northern islands except Lizard Island)

The family-style Daydream Island Travelodge Resort *(tel 1-800 075 040, toll-free)* occupies the northern end of the island.

Hayman Island is the Whitsundays' most luxurious resort. People who know regard it as one of the finest resorts in the world. The stunning design incorporates reflection pools and tropical gardens, a seawater lagoon, and an opulent octagonal freshwater pool. Everything here projects luxury and style. This place is for guests only; don't even think about day trips *(tel 1-800 075 175, toll-free)*.

**Northern Islands:** In Far North Queensland—or FNQ for short—the reef veers closest to the coast, and the coral and fish life are the most colorful and diverse.

**Magnetic Island** was named by Captain Cook, who had some

problems with his compass when he sailed past in 1770 and decided the island must be magnetic. Nobody else's compass has ever been troubled by it, but the name remains. You can get to it from Townsville in as little as 20 minutes —it is only about 7 miles (11 km) away. As a result, Magnetic Island is increasingly becoming a suburb of Townsville. It has more than 2,500 residents, some of whom commute to jobs across the bay. The island is ringed with white-sand beaches, and more than half of it is national park, with excellent bushwalking tracks, fine lookouts, and koalas in the wild. If you miss the wild ones, you can visit a koala park or aquarium.

**Orpheus Island,** a small volcanic nub fringed by kaleidoscopic coral reefs, is 50 miles (80 km) farther northeast of Townsville. It is a national park, and its beaches have marvelous seashells.

Snorkelers glide across Watson's Bay at Lizard Island.

Farther up the coast looms the formidable tree-clad mass of **Hinchinbrook Island,** just across a narrow channel from Cardwell on the mainland. It is the largest island along this stretch of coast—about 250 square miles (648 sq km)—but was never settled, and today it is a nearly pristine wilderness of mangroves and white-sand beaches dominated by a line of steep, dark mountains rising to more than 3,000 feet (914 m). With the exception of the modest Cape Richards Resort *(tel (07) 4066 8585),* Hinchinbrook Island is still pretty much as it was two centuries ago. It can be visited on a day trip from Cardwell, but a better option if you have the time and energy is to walk the East Coast Trail or Thorsborne Trail (see sidebar right).

**Dunk Island** is just 3 miles (5 km) off the Queensland coast near Tully, about 125 miles north of Townsville. It is one of the most popular resort islands in northern Queensland, rich in birdlife, densely forested, and bright with tropical butterflies. You can fly there from Townsville or make a short crossing by ferry or water taxi from Mission Beach. Also in this group is little **Bedarra Island,** with a very exclusive resort *(tel (07) 4068 8233).*

**Green Island,** about 15 miles (24 km) from Cairns, is actually part of the reef. This coral island is less than half a mile (1 km) long, and Green Island Resort *(tel 1-800 673 366, toll-free)* takes up most of it.

**Lizard Island,** which is among the northernmost islands of the

## Thorsborne Trail

This difficult 20-mile (32 km) trek on tropical Hinchinbrook Island rewards with beaches, rain forest, waterfalls, and rich birdlife. Water taxis from Cardwell drop you off at the start of the walk and pick up from George Point at the end. The Rainforest & Reef Information Centre *(tel (07) 4066 8601)* in Cardwell has details. Taking 3 to 5 days, the hike is on a rough track, traversing hills, swamps, and creeks. Keep an eye out for crocs in coastal areas. Bring all food, tents, and cooking gear. Seven campsites are spaced along the trail, and camping permits must be reserved. Trails are limited to 40 people at a time, and the walk must be booked *(tel 13 13 0* or *www.epa.qld.gov .au)* well in advance (up to a year for school holidays).

Great Barrier Reef, has some of the finest coral reefs. It lies about 60 miles (96 km) north of Cooktown. Captain Cook landed here in 1770 and climbed Cook's Lookout (as it is now called) to plot a way through the reef ahead. He named the island for the large but harmless monitor lizards that still bask in the sun here. Lizard Island Resort *(tel (07) 4060 3999)* is luxurious and expensive. Or you could spend the night at the national park campground *(book at Queensland Parks & Wildlife in Cairns, see p. 167).* ∎

# Northern Queensland

Northern Queensland is home to Townsville, the region's industrial center and Australia's largest tropical city, and Cairns, the most useful base for visitors to the northern part of the Great Barrier Reef and a magnet for people who want adventurous activities—hang gliding, bungee jumping, white-water rafting, skydiving, and hot-air balloon rides. It also includes quiet resort beaches, exhilarating drives, and one of Australia's wildest corners, the Cape York Peninsula.

Cairns Harbour has long been a jumping-off point for excursions to the Great Barrier Reef.

**Townsville**
🅰 139 C4 & 155
**Visitor Information**
✉ Flinders Mall
☎ (07) 4721 3660

## Townsville

Two entrepreneurs—a Scot named Melton Black and a wealthy sea captain named Robert Towns—sowed the seeds of Townsville. In 1863, they built a wharf and a rendering plant here for cattlemen who couldn't reach the port at Bowen when the Burdekin River was in flood. Gold rushes at Cape River (1867), Ravenswood (1869), and Charters Towers (1871) helped the city prosper. During World War II, Townsville was a strategic base for U.S. and Australian forces, and it was bombed three times by the Japanese in 1942. Today it is one of Australia's biggest military towns and home to James Cook University.

Although Townsville is the administrative and commercial capital of northern Queensland, it struggles to hold the interest of tourists, who prefer more fashionable Cairns and Port Douglas farther north. Visitors who expect lush rain forest are surprised to see typical olive-gray Australian scrub.

The tropical heat and humidity are here, but the rain forests don't start for 100 miles (160 km) north along the Bruce Highway.

Townsville does have elegant tropical architecture and stately figs along the **Strand,** and the city has spent millions trying to entice tourists. A casino is now on the waterfront, along with the superb **Reef HQ Aquarium** (Flinders St. East, tel (07) 4750 0800, $$$), which has coral, anemones, and schools of colorful tropical fish.

Townsville is also a base for visits to the Great Barrier Reef, and it is the only access point to **Magnetic Island** (see p. 164). Even so, most tourists content themselves with a trip to the aquarium, a picnic on Magnetic Island, and a sunset view of the city lights from Castle Rock. Then they go on to Cairns and the north.

## Cairns

Beneath a range of rain forest mountains that rise steeply from the coast, this tropical city lives for the sea, and a recent refurbishment of the seafront esplanade has made it feel sunnier and breezier than ever.

Cairns started out in the 1860s as a camp for trepang fishermen, but a succession of gold and tin strikes in the Atherton Tablelands (see p. 170), just over the mountain range, lured settlers from farther south, and the town was established in 1876. In 1924, the railway from Brisbane made its northern terminus at Cairns.

Until the tourism boom in the 1980s, Cairns was a sleepy sugar town and laid-back seaside resort popular with marlin fishermen. Seemingly overnight it became a throbbing, fast-paced tourist spot. Yet while the development has made Cairns one of Australia's most popular destinations, it has virtually destroyed the tropical laziness that gave Cairns its charm. These days smaller Port Douglas, where the trains and the jumbo jets that descend on Cairns never came, has become the more fashionable vacation spot. The popular northern beaches just past the Cairns airport, such as Trinity Beach and upmarket Palm Cove, are quieter resort beaches close to Cairns.

Nevertheless, Cairns is a convenient base from which to explore the region. Visitors take day trips to the Great Barrier Reef, make excursions to the nearby islands, or charter deep-sea fishing boats. Or you can take a light aircraft 200 miles (322 km) into the vast Queensland outback for a stay at

### Cairns
🅜  139 C4 & 155
**Visitor Information**
✉  51 Esplanade
☎  (07) 4051 3588

**Queensland Parks & Wildlife Service**
✉  5B Sheridan St., Cairns
☎  (07) 4052 3096

---

## EXPERIENCE:
## Sea Kayaking

Between Townsville and Cairns lies popular Mission Beach, a burgeoning resort with fine beaches and offshore islands. A great way to explore the Coral Sea is to kayak out to rain forested **Dunk Island,** 3 miles (4.5 km) offshore. You can hire sea kayaks and do it yourself, possibly spotting dolphins or turtles on the way, then snorkel on the island's reefs or lunch at the chic Voyages Dunk Island resort. The easiest and best option for inexperienced kayakers is a guided day trip with **Coral Sea Kayaking** (tel (07) 4068 9154), which includes hotel pickup, lunch, and snorkeling gear.

# EXPERIENCE: Diving Australia

The Great Barrier Reef is Australia's unrivaled diving paradise, with myriad dive sites for the experienced and dive schools all along the coast for beginners looking to gain certification with a 4–5 day open-water course. Cairns, Port Douglas, Townsville, and Airlie Beach are the main dive centers, and prices are competitive.

From Cairns or Port Douglas, top dive destinations include **Lizard Island,** noted for its giant clams, and the **Cod Hole,** where you can hand-feed potato cod. **Osprey Reef** has magnificent soft corals and giant fish, including numerous reef sharks.

From Townsville, 56 miles (90 km) south, the **Yongala Wreck** teems with marine life, including sharks, manta rays, and turtles. Perfectly round **Wheeler Reef** on the edge of a drop-off also features spectacular large fish.

In the Whitsundays, teeming **Bait Reef** and **Hardy Reef** are top destinations. Farther south, **Heron Island** has superb snorkeling and diving, as does **Lady Elliot Island,** the southernmost island.

Australia's other standout dive destination is **Ningaloo Reef,** a lesser known but no less spectacular 160-mile (260 km) reef off the coast of Western Australia. Dive shops are in Exmouth and Coral Bay. Exmouth's Navy Pier at the end of the peninsula is one of the country's top shore dives.

Visit *www.scubaaustralia.com.au* for information on diving locations, operators, centers, and clubs all over Australia.

## Port Douglas

🗺 139 C4 & 155

**Visitor Information**

✉ 23 Macrossan St.

☎ (07) 4099 5599

## Quicksilver Catamarans: Cairns to Port Douglas

✉ Marina Mirage

☎ (07) 4087 2100
Offers fast catamaran service to Cairns, also day trips to the reef

the 1.5-million-acre (400,000 ha) **Wrotham Park Lodge** *(tel (02) 8296 8010, www.wrothampark.com.au),* a working cattle station that offers five-star accommodation and a privileged glimpse into a way of life that few visitors ever see.

## Port Douglas to Cape Tribulation

The chic resort town of Port Douglas is 40 miles (64 km) north of Cairns on the Captain Cook Highway. This is an idyllic road, one of the most beautiful and seductive in Australia, rolling past isolated beaches and lush tropical hills. If you have the time and energy, do the journey on a bicycle.

**Port Douglas,** 3 miles (5 km) off the highway, was a sleepy seaside fishing village until the

1980s, when it was discovered by tourists and resort developers looking for something new. Set in the rain forest beside the Coral Sea, the little village of 250 people seemed to be almost everyone's idea of a tropical hideaway. However, large-scale development has taken its toll, and the permanent population of 1,300 quadruples at peak tourist times.

Port Douglas is noted for five-star luxury resorts, such as the Sheraton Mirage *(Davidson St., tel (07) 4099 5888),* and for its golf course, marina, and upscale shopping complex. Although it seems geared to the top end of the market (Former U.S. President Bill Clinton has vacationed here), it has budget accommodations and eateries as well. Port Douglas is more relaxed than Cairns and has plenty for visitors to do: walking the Mossman Gorge, taking trips into the Daintree rain forest, or exploring the northern end of the Great Barrier Reef.

Still very much a small sugar town, **Mossman** is on the Captain Cook Highway around 9 miles (14 km) north of Port Douglas. Its major attraction is the lush, waterfall-laced **Mossman Gorge** about 3 miles (5 km) west. The Kuku Yulanji people, a local Aboriginal tribe, give guided tours, or you can follow a 2-mile (3 km) walking track on your own.

The quiet village of **Daintree,** 22 miles (35 km) farther up the highway, is set on the edge of the rain forests of the vast **Daintree National Park** stretching to the north. The village was established as a timber camp to cut the prized red cedars that grew here. These days, it is a base for cruises along the mighty **Daintree River—**a chance to putter through the tropical rain forest and spot saltwater crocodiles basking in the sun along the banks. One of the larger cruise operators is Daintree River Trains *(tel (07) 4090 7676, $$$)*.

**Cape Tribulation** is 22 miles (35 km) north of Daintree. To get there, take the ferry that crosses the Daintree River about 6 miles (10 km) south of Daintree. The ferries run every few minutes, from 6 a.m. to midnight *(tel (07) 4098 7788, A$20 return)*. The road beyond the ferry is paved all the way to Cape Tribulation.

The **Daintree Discovery Centre** *(tel (07) 4098 9171, $$$)*, about 5 miles (8 km) past the ferry, is a popular stop, with interpretive displays, a forest walkway, and a 75-foot (23 m) canopy tower lookout. Alternatively, turn off to the **Mount Alexandra Lookout** for sweeping (and free) views across the park to the coast. A number of excellent short walks in the park will get you out into

**Daintree**
🔺 139 C5 & 155
**Visitor Information**
✉ 5 Stewart St.
☎ (07) 4098 6133

Daintree National Park is one of the last strongholds of ancient Australian rain forests.

the rain forest and the mangroves. Don't miss the **Jindalba Boardwalk,** an easy loop through magnificent forest with a good chance of spotting cassowaries.

Cape Tribulation and nearby Mount Sorrow were named by Captain Cook when his ship grounded on a coral reef, forcing him to beach it near present-day Cooktown for repairs. For much of the next two centuries this lonely stretch of coastline was seldom visited. In the 1970s, a few hippies arrived, and the area began to be better known. It still has a remote feel, although in holiday periods you'll see plenty of tourists, and accommodations at Cape Tribulation often are full.

## INSIDER TIP:

**Dive with sea turtles and sea snakes at the wreck of the passenger ship S.S. *Yongala,* which sank near Townsville in 1911. This is one of the best dive sites in the Great Barrier Reef.**

—PETER FUNCH
*National Geographic field researcher*

The Cape Tribulation section of the Daintree National Park is a spectacular paradise of mist-shrouded mountains tumbling down to the Coral Sea. One of the wettest corners on Earth, the park has virgin tropical rain forest and coral reefs virtually side by side. It is the jewel of Queensland's 3,500 square miles (9,065 sq km) of wet tropics. Hidden in Cape Tribulation's dripping forests are primitive varieties of plants and flowers that are found nowhere else. Among them are species of angiosperms that are forerunners of all flowering plants. New species of ferns are frequently discovered. Crocodiles lurk in the mangroves and estuaries, and the forests have 120 bird species, from rainbow honey-eaters to the flightless cassowary, which stands more than 6 feet tall (2 m). Butterflies include the cobalt blue Ulysses and the huge Hercules moth, one of the largest in the world.

In the 1980s, conservationists and the timber industry fought a bitter campaign over the building of the **Bloomfield Track,** a four-wheel-drive road that connects Cape Tribulation with Cooktown, 100 miles (160 km) north. The conservationists lost that battle, but the attention focused on the rain forests led the federal government to nominate the forests for the World Heritage List. Today logging is banned in the area, and because ecotourism is now the dominant industry in far northern Queensland, rain forests are a vital part of the economy.

## Atherton Tablelands

Simply getting to this lush volcanic highland looming above Cairns can be as much fun as exploring it. The Kuranda Scenic Railway climbs the jungle-clad range that broods over Cairns to the cool moist heights of the Atherton Tablelands. One of the world's great short train journeys, the railway was built in 1891 to link the Herberton tin mines with the coast.

Pulled by a 125-year-old steam engine, the train skirts the coastline and then ascends the mountains in a series of switchbacks. It runs along a 600-foot (183 m) sheer precipice above the glories of the tablelands. Rain forest towns such as Atherton and Ravenshoe (pronounced RA-ENS-hoe) attract artists, back-to-nature types, and gypsies and have a friendly offbeat style. The little village of **Yungaburra,** about 8 miles (13 km) east of Atherton on the Gillies Highway, is a central

**Atherton Tablelands**

🗺 139 B4–C4

**Visitor Information**

✉ Silc Rd. & Main St., Atherton

☎ (07) 4091 4222

**Kuranda**

🗺 139 C4

**Visitor Information**

✉ Therwine St.

☎ (07) 4093 9311

**Kuranda Scenic Railway**

☎ (07) 4032 3964

The high, cool rain forests of the Atherton Tablelands shelter rare orchids, ferns, and brilliant tropical butterflies.

**Barron River Gorge** and through 15 tunnels cut into the stone. The 20-mile (32 km) ride ends at **Kuranda,** a rain forest town with a famous crafts market and an arty atmosphere. Crowds and trashy souvenirs in the market are lessening its charm, but it has gorgeous rain forest walks close by. A track from the picturesque colonial station takes you into the wilds of **Barron Gorge National Park.** Another way to reach Kuranda is on the **Skyrail Rainforest Cableway** (tel (07) 4038 1555), a 5-mile (8 km) cable car ride that leaves from Cairns's northern suburbs.

Having arrived by train, you need to rent a car to see the

spot from which to explore. Two of the loveliest crater lakes you'll ever see—**Lake Eacham** and **Lake Barrine**—are east off the Gillies Highway. Both are national parks, with swimming holes and bushwalks around their rims. A mile (1.5 km) or so south of Yungaburra, on the road to Malanda, is the **Curtain Fig Tree,** a massive, much photographed tangle of roots and vines.

A few miles south of Atherton, off the Kennedy Highway, is **Mount Hypipamee National Park.** More than 300 species of birds have been found in this forest. A path leads a quarter-mile (continued on p. 174)

# National Parks

Australia has more than 500 national parks and thousands of reserves, and they cover every kind of significant natural terrain in the country, including rain forests, deserts, islands, mountain ranges, and long stretches of haunting coastal dunes. Some are extremely remote, and visitors must travel across barren desert just to reach them, a journey that may be extremely dangerous for the inexperienced or the unprepared.

Not all of Australia's wild places require expedition planning. Some of the prettiest national parks are perched on the edge of cities. Royal National Park is on the coast just south of Sydney. In 1994, a bushfire in the Sydney suburbs destroyed about

Waterfalls pour over the escarpment in Kakadu National Park, Northern Territory.

90 percent of the park. Within a year, however, green shoots had appeared in the blackened soil, and the bush now is well on the way to recovery. Lush Dandenong Ranges National Park is only a suburban train ride from Melbourne.

A string of national parks protects 14 areas on the United Nations' World Heritage List. The Great Barrier Reef is among them. So is the Northern Territory's magnificent Kakadu National Park. This tropical wetland about three hours southeast of Darwin is the biggest tourist draw in the north. The main physical feature is the dramatic Arnhem Land escarpment, a 400-mile-long (640 km) line of massive sandstone cliffs. During the summer wet season, runoff from the monsoon rains spills over the cliffs in a series of spectacular waterfalls. In the dry season, the shrinking waterholes are raucous with thousands of migratory birds. Kakadu is on the World Heritage List for cultural reasons as well. Aboriginal culture here dates back more than 50,000 years, and thousands of rock-art murals decorate its gorges, rock shelters, and caves.

The haunting monoliths of Uluru–Kata Tjuta National Park (Ayers Rock and the Olgas) are also on the World Heritage list for both cultural and natural reasons. Australia's other World Heritage sites include Shark Bay in Western Australia, popular with tourists for its friendly dolphins but famous among paleo-botanists for the primitive blue-green algae matting the rocks on the edge of Hamelin Pool. These algae, called stromatolites, are living fossils dating back 3.5 billion years.

Some of Australia's other World Heritage sites are wilderness islands. Fraser Island, off

## 10 of the Best National Parks

**Cradle Mountain–Lake St. Clair NP:** In central Tasmania, the park features Australia's premier hike, the 40-mile (65 km) Overland Track, taking in snowy peaks and alpine meadows and lakes. See p. 346.

**Daintree NP:** Just 100 miles (160 km) north of Cairns, this park has ancient rain forest, mangroves, crocs, and white sand beaches at Cape Tribulation. See p. 169.

**Fraser Island (Great Sandy) NP:** The world's largest sand island off the Queensland coast near Hervey Bay has rain forest, dune lakes, dingoes, and miles of pristine beach. See p. 148.

**Freycinet NP:** Wineglass Bay is the jewel of this stunning park on Tasmania's sunny east coast, blessed with wonderful beaches and pink granite hills. See p. 350.

**Kakadu NP:** This World Heritage–listed park, 110 miles (170 km) from Darwin, has spectacular escarpments, waterfalls, rock art, and wetlands. See p. 188.

**Kosciuszko NP:** Skiing in winter, fine hiking in summer, and Australia's highest peak are highlights of this alpine wonderland in the Snowy Mountains of New South Wales. See p. 114.

**Nambung NP:** The Pinnacles, 155 miles (250 km) north of Perth, comprise hundreds of eerie limestone pillars jutting out of the desert. See p. 212.

**Port Campbell NP:** This park is home to the awe-inspiring Twelve Apostles, giant arches and islands carved by the sea from sandstone cliffs, 170 miles (280 km) from Melbourne. See p. 313.

**Purnululu NP:** In Western Australia's Kimberley region, the tiger-striped "Bungle Bungles" has spectacular sandstone domes, cliffs, and chasms. See p. 236.

**Uluru–Kata Tjuta NP:** The towering monolith of Uluru and nearby Kata Tjuta's strange rock domes lie 250 miles (400 km) southwest of Alice Springs. See p. 204.

the southeast coast of Queensland, is the world's largest sand island. It is forested with unique rain forest plants and trees, such as the satinay. Lord Howe Island is a tropical paradise about 430 miles (692 km) off the coast of New South Wales. The southwest corner of Tasmania, also on the World Heritage list, is cloaked by some of the world's last great stands of virgin temperate forest.

The Gondwana Rainforests of Australia is a group of 50 reserves covering about 570,000 acres (265,000 ha) in the coastal highlands of New South Wales and southeast Queensland. The Fossil Mammal sites are widely scattered: One is at Riversleigh in Queensland, and the other is more than 1,800 miles (2,896 km) away in the Narracoorte Caves of southeastern South Australia. As the name implies, these are treasure troves of fossil remains, revealing the history of Australia's unique fauna. The most obscure World Heritage site is Willandra

National Park, a sequence of dry Pleistocene lake beds that are located about 100 miles (160 km) northwest of Griffith in central New South Wales.

## Visiting National Parks

National parks are administered by the various states, and facilities vary. Some have resort accommodations inside or nearby, for example, the Flinders Ranges in South Australia and Watarrka (Kings Canyon) in Northern Territory. Other parks have pit toilets and picnic tables, and some have no facilities at all. Contact the park in advance if you want to stay, as some parks allow only a few visitors at a time, and you may have to reserve a camping spot or accommodations. You also need to find out what equipment to take. (The national parks agency in each state has details. For addresses and telephone numbers, see p. 366.)

**Cape York Peninsula**

🗺 138–139 B5–B6

Natures Powerhouse Visitor Information Centre

✉ Finch Bay Rd., Cooktown

☎ (07) 4069 6004

(400 m) along Dinner Creek to a rather sinister volcanic cavity that plunges a sheer 200 feet (61 m) into a dark, algae-covered pool. The 10-mile (16 km) "waterfall circuit" drive around nearby **Millaa Millaa** (south of Malanda) takes in the best of the area's waterfalls. Take the Theresa Creek Road off Palmerston Highway toward Millaa Millaa Falls, the first and most magnificent. Then drive through dense rain forests and farmland to Zillie, Mungali, and Elinja.

Thirty minutes from Millaa Millaa along the Palmerston Highway toward the coast, the **Mamu Rainforest Canopy Walkway** *(tel (07) 4064 5294, $$)* is a spectacular elevated, 1,100-foot-long

(350 m) walkway through the rain forest canopy to a cantilevered overhang and lookout tower.

## Cape York Peninsula

Driving up to the Tip, as Aussies call the Cape York Peninsula, is one of the great four-wheel-drive adventures on the continent, a challenging 500-mile (800 km) trek to mainland Australia's most northerly point.

This is most definitely not a trip for beginners or the ill-prepared. The roads and tracks are mostly dirt, and there are many river crossings. While it is possible under favorable conditions for a conventional vehicle to make it as far as the mining town of **Weipa,** about

---

## EXPERIENCE: Touring the Tip

Cape York Peninsula is the Holy Grail for four-wheel-drive adventurers. Plenty do the pilgrimage, but it is only for well-equipped vehicles, which usually travel in convoy. Depending on the route you take, you'll need a winch, chains, and plenty of experience fording rivers. Riverbanks can be steep and muddy, and crocodiles lurk in the water.

The main road—the Peninsula Development Road through Laura to Coen and Weipa—is unpaved but graded and easy going when dry. Serious off-roaders like to take tougher routes, such as the detour to Cape Melville. Past Weipa, a four-wheel-drive vehicle and experience using it are essential. Those after a challenge take the Old Telegraph Track. The alternative to doing it all yourself is to a take a driving tour, flight, cargo ship, or combination.

**Cape York by Four-wheel-drive:**
The following Cairns operators offer a variety of 4WD tours to Cape York, lasting from seven days to two weeks or more:

**Heritage Tours** *(tel (07) 4054 7750, www.heritagetours.com.au)*

**Oz Tour Safaris** *(tel 1-800 079 006, toll-free, www.oztours.com.au)*

**Wilderness Challenge** *(tel (07) 4035 4488, www .wilderness-challenge.com.au)*

**Cape York by Plane:**
**Qantaslink** *(tel 13 13 13)* has daily flights to Weipa from Cairns, while **Skytrans** *(tel 1-300 759 872)* flies from Cairns to Bamaga, Coen, Lockhart River, and Arukun.

**Cape York by Ferry:**
**M.V. Trinity Bay** *(tel (07) 4035 1234, www.seaswift .com.au)*, a working cargo ship, takes vehicles and up to 38 passengers in en suite cabins from Cairns up the coast to Cape York via Horn Island, Thursday Island, and Bamaga.

On Cape York Peninsula, rainless lightning storms may set the bush ablaze.

two-thirds of the way north, the final leg to the top is a very rough track, strictly for four-wheel-drive. During the summer monsoons, forget it. Happily enough, if you lack the experience or gear, you can take one of a number of four-wheel-drive tours to the Tip, or get there by air or barge from Cairns.

The launching pad for the cape is usually **Cooktown,** the northernmost town on the east coast. Lying on the croc-infested Endeavour River, it has a lazy frontier feel, but tourism is on the rise since the inland road from Cairns was paved in 2006. Most visitors, however, come up the more scenic Bloomfield Track from Cape Tribulation.

If air-conditioned travel to Cape York seems like roughing it, think how it was in 1848, when Edmund Kennedy led an ill-fated expedition to explore the peninsula. Of the 14 people who started, only three survived. Kennedy was speared by hostile Aborigines and died of his wounds. The only member of the party to reach the cape, where a ship was waiting, was the Aboriginal guide, Jacky Jacky.

In 1863, an adventurer named John Jardine established a pearling, coconut, and trading port called Somerset near the tip of the cape. His ambition was to make his little kingdom rival Singapore. In the following year, Jardine's sons Frank and Alexander drove a thousand head of cattle from Rockhampton all the way to the tip of the peninsula to help feed the struggling outpost. The remarkable venture opened up miles of new country, but in the end the termites and attacks by hostile Aborigines proved too much. In 1877, the Jardines gave up on Somerset and relocated the

## EXPERIENCE: Birdsville Races

Due south of Cape York in far southwest Queensland near the South Australia border, Birdsville is as remote as the Black Stump or mythical Woop Woop, synonymous with the outback in the Australian psyche. A mecca for four-wheel-drive adventurers, this settlement on the edge of the Simpson Desert comes alive in the first week of September, when more than 6,000 people flock to its infamous horse races (www.birdsville races.com) for drinking and partying in the dust. The town can be reached via the famed Birdsville Track in South Australia, or from Charleville in Queensland, both rugged routes for the well-equipped. Alternatively, **Skytrans** (tel 1-300 759 872, www.skytrans.com.au) flies to Birdsville on its Brisbane–Mount Isa run. The colorful **Birdsville Hotel** (tel (07) 4656 3244), right next to the airstrip, is the place to stay and swap yarns.

### Gulf of Carpentaria

🅼 Map pp. 138–139

**Visitor Information**

✉ Caroline St., Normanton

☎ (07) 4745 1065

**ROCK-ART TOURS:**
Trezise Bush Guide Service, tel (07) 4060 3236 (contact: Laura)

little community of 200 to nearby Thursday Island.

By then, all the action on the Cape York Peninsula was taking place much farther south, along the Palmer River, where a gold rush drew thousands of prospectors. The diggings were marked by racial strife between the Australian and Chinese prospectors, and the Aborigines who did not care for either in their territory.

**Laura,** about 200 miles (320 km) north of Cairns, was at the heart of the diggings, and 20,000 people a year passed through at the height of the boom. Laura is on the Peninsula Developmental Road, which you can join at **Mareeba,** west of Cairns on the Kennedy Highway. It is an easy drive, unless there has been heavy rain. There is not much to Laura itself, but it is the nearest township to the **Quinkan Reserve Aboriginal rock art galleries** near Split Rock, about 7 miles (11 km) south. The galleries are among the world's largest collections of rock art, with tens of thousands of paintings dating back more

than 13,000 years. Most haunting are the Quinkans—gaunt, angular, sinister figures with staring eyes, whom the Aborigines believe lurk in cracks in the rocks. Tours to the galleries can be arranged at the Quinkan Reserves Trust (tel (07) 4060 3214). The **Aboriginal Dance Festival,** held in Laura in June of odd-numbered years, is a riveting spectacle, worth arranging your itinerary around if you can be in Queensland then. The Ang-Gnarra Aboriginal Corporation in Laura (tel (07) 4060 3214) has information on local rock art and on the dance festival.

Many people are attracted to **Thursday Island,** off the tip of the cape, simply because this tiny spot in the Torres Strait is the end of the line. It is the most visited of the 60-odd Torres Straits Islands. Its residents are a multicultural swirl of Aborigines, Melanesians, Malay, Papuans, Chinese, and the descendants of Japanese pearl divers who worked here when the island was a pearling center. Today the clock with no hands in the local hotel says much about the present pace of life. Peddell's Ferry Service *(tel (07) 4069 1551)* makes the crossing from Seisia, at the tip of Cape York, to Thursday Island.

## Gulf of Carpentaria

The Gulf of Carpentaria and Queensland's rugged northwest are not for everyone. This is unvarnished outback, with mining towns, isolated ports, and rough pubs. The landscape is blindingly hot savanna, studded with termite mounds capable of breaking the axle of a four-wheel-drive vehicle. Crocodiles inhabit the rivers and mangroves along the edge of the gulf, and the lonely towns can be cut off for weeks when the monsoons hit in summer. Despite all that, the area has an odd frontier appeal that pulls you on.

It's about 450 miles (720 km) from Cairns to Normanton on the lonely and evocative **Gulf Developmental Highway,** which runs down the western flank of the Atherton Tablelands and into the savanna country. The tourist make-believe falls away; you're on a lonely highway into an outback barely changed from the days when explorers such as Burke

and Wills passed this way. About 150 miles (240 km) southwest of Cairns, the highway passes the **Undara Lava Tubes,** a vast series of hollow basalt chambers through which massive amounts of lava flowed in a volcanic eruption about 200,000 years ago. They are the largest such formation in the world and are well worth a visit.

---

**INSIDER TIP:**

**Consider a 4WD safari from Cairns to get the most out of little-known and remote Cape York and the Gulf of Carpentaria. [See sidebar p. 174.]**

—ROFF SMITH
*National Geographic author*

---

**Normanton** is a rough old river port that over the decades has served the local cattle stations, the 1880s goldfields around Croydon, and the silver mines in Cloncurry. The Norman River is rich with barramundi, tropical Australia's magnificent sweet-eating game fish. Catching their first barramundi is the goal of many Australian anglers heading to the tropics. If you'd like to try your hand, guided game-fishing trips can be arranged in town. If you decide to do a little fishing or boating, remember that these waters are home to some of the world's most dangerous saltwater crocodiles. Check out the 28-foot (8.5 m) plaster cast of what was reputedly the biggest of them

---

### Morning Glory

The atmospheric phenomenon called Morning Glory—a bizarre tubular cloud formation in the dawn skies in spring—is often visible over the Gulf of Carpentaria during the spring months, September to November.

---

**Undara Lava Tubes**

🗺 139 B4

**Lava Lodge Undara**

☎ Accommodations & tours of the lava tubes: (07) 4097 1900 or 1-800 990 992 (toll-free)

## Mount Isa

🗺 138 A3

**Visitor Information**

✉ Marian St.

☎ (07) 4749 1555

**www.mountisa.qld
.gov.au**

all—shot in the Norman River in 1957—near the town's garishly painted Purple Pub.

A 45-mile (72 km) side trip north from Normanton brings you to **Karumba,** a prawn-trawling port on the gulf. In the 1930s, it was a refueling stop for the Qantas Empire Flying Boats that flew between Britain and Australia. These days fishing enthusiasts flock here to try their luck at what is said to be the best light-tackle fishing in Australia. The gulf is filled with grunter, king salmon, blue salmon, and the famous barramundi. And, of course, saltwater crocodiles.

Except for the superb angling, you will find little else to do in Karumba. Sunsets over Karumba Point are gorgeous, as the blood red sun appears to melt into the gulf. The beach is gorgeous, too, but don't even think about a dip unless you are into wrestling with a crocodile.

A 150-mile (240 km) dirt track leads west from Normanton to

**Burketown,** population 230 and one of the loneliest towns in Australia, particularly during the wet season (Oct.–April), when it can be cut off for weeks. Although the road is bumpy, you normally do not need a four-wheel-drive vehicle in the dry season. The track runs through harsh spectacular country, past beautiful Leichhardt Falls.

If you are adventurous, you can drive to **Darwin** from Burketown along the **Gulf Track.** It is about 300 miles (480 km) of dirt track from Burketown to the next paved road, at Borroloola, and from there it is 600 miles (960 km) farther to Darwin. Attempt the Gulf Track only in the dry season. The less demanding **Wills Developmental Road,** another dirt track, goes 75 miles (120 km) south from Burketown to **Gregory Downs** cattle station. There you can turn off for Lawn Hill (Boodjamulla) National Park (see below) or take the Wills Highway 90 miles (145 km) southeast and turn south to Cloncurry.

The **Flinders Highway** runs east from Cloncurry to Townsville and the coast. West of Cloncurry, the highway runs 75 miles (120 km) to the sprawling mining town of **Mount Isa.** One of Australia's largest outback cities, with a population of 21,750 (marginally fewer than Alice Springs), Mount Isa claims to be the biggest city or municipal area in the world, covering almost 16,800 square miles (43,348 sq km). The main industry here is the giant silver-lead-zinc mine, also one of the biggest in the world. In August,

---

## EXPERIENCE:
## Mount Isa Mine Tour

The big attraction in Mount Isa is **Outback at Isa** *(19 Marian St., tel (07) 4749 1555, www.outbackatisa.com.au, $$$$)*, **featuring a multimedia gallery, outback park exhibiting Mount Isa's natural and indigenous heritage, and the fascinating Riversleigh Fossil Centre. The highlight, however, is undoubtedly the Hard Times Mine tours. Don overalls, hard hat, and lamp, and descend underground with experienced miners to learn how it's done and to try your hand with mine machinery on the rock face.**

Mount Isa is host to Australia's largest rodeo.

## Lawn Hill (Boodjamulla) National Park

Lawn Hill (Boodjamulla) National Park is one of Australia's jewels, an unexpected tropical oasis in the vast black

these ancient rain forests. They are lined with fan palms, fig trees, and ferns. The water attracts large numbers of mammals, birds, and reptiles such as water monitors, tortoises, and shy freshwater crocodiles. The Waanyi people have been here for 30,000 years, and the park is rich in rock art.

**Lawn Hill National Park**

🏕 138 A4
☎ (07) 4748 5572

Lawn Hill Gorge is a hidden tropical oasis of fan palms, parrots, and freshwater crocodiles.

soil plains of the gulf country. Locals and many visitors claim it is at least as spectacular as Kakadu (see pp. 188–191) and arguably more so, because its lushness is so surprising in the hot bleakness that surrounds it. It is a legacy of a time when all of northern Australia was covered with dense rain forests. When the climate grew warmer and drier, the forests retreated.

These gorges, which are watered by a series of springs in the limestone hills along the nearby Northern Territory border, are the last secluded pockets of

Trails and boardwalks lead hikers to the **Wild Dog Dreaming** and **Rainbow Dreaming** rock-art sites.

The park has about 15 miles (24 km) of walking tracks in all, but most visitors prefer to explore it by canoe or inner tube, floating in its clear, lime green waters looking up at the colored sandstone walls of the gorge rising 200 feet (60 m) above the pools. Although plenty of crocodiles live here, particularly in the lower parts of the gorge, these waters are safe for swimming. Freshwater crocodiles are smaller and much more timid than their saltwater cousins.

In the southern end of the park, the staggeringly rich limestone fossil beds of the World Heritage–listed **Riversleigh Fossil Site** tell the story of the past 20 million years. The fossils reveal that this was once a scary little jungle filled with carnivorous kangaroos, marsupial lions, rhinoceros-size wombats, and relatives of the now-extinct Tasmanian tiger. Also living here were birds, bats, and prehistoric pythons up to 25 feet (7.6 m) long. The fossil beds were actually a series of lakes where creatures came to drink. Fossilized remains have been extracted by blasting chunks out of the stubborn limestone beds. A roadside display contains some of the finds at the park. The fossil areas are a protected site.

## Cane Toad

**The large, warty, poisonous cane toad (Bufo marinus) was introduced into the sugarcane fields of northern Queensland in 1935 to combat the cane beetle. It has spread rapidly since then and now threatens biodiversity in a huge area from Kakadu National Park in the Northern Territory to Port Macquarie, near Sydney. Its poison sacs make the toad deadly to native amphibians, reptiles, and mammals, including freshwater crocodiles and quolls. Biological solutions are elusive, and community toad roundups remain the most effective control.**

In all, Lawn Hill is a hidden gem. Now comes the heartbreak part. There is a reason for the use of the adjective "hidden." This park is a long way from anywhere, and the final leg of the journey involves a long ride over a rough dirt track that is virtually impassable after heavy rains. A four-wheel-drive vehicle is recommended, although a conventional vehicle can make it through in dry weather, if the driver has experience on bush tracks. The park is about 250 miles (400 km) northwest of Mount Isa. The easiest drive there is to take the Burke Developmental Road north from Cloncurry to the Burke and Wills Roadhouse, and then go northwest on the Wills Highway. A 90-mile (145 km) drive will bring you to the Gregory Downs Hotel (tel (07) 4748 5566), an old outback pub. You can buy food and fuel here, and the pub also has accommodations.

Access to the park is on a track by the pub, and this final leg is a tough 70-mile (113 km) ride. It would be nice to say that the scenery along the track into the park is stunning—but it isn't. In fact, it is positively apocalyptic in its bleakness, which is what makes Lawn Hill itself such a delightful surprise. Six miles (9.6 km) east of the park entrance is Adel's Grove Kiosk (tel (07) 4748 5502), where you can buy supplies and rent canoes. A privately run campsite is here, with another in the park itself. Despite its remoteness, Lawn Hill is popular and the campsites are often booked. Check with the park office. ■

Colloquially known as the "Never Never" and home to two cherished icons: Uluru and the wild, monsoonal wetlands of Kakadu

# Northern Territory

Introduction & Map   182–183

Darwin   184–187

Kakadu National Park   188–191

Litchfield National Park   192–193

Nitmiluk National Park & Katherine   194–195

Arnhem Land & the Tiwi Islands   196–197

Alice Springs   198–201

Experience: Henley-on-Todd Regatta   199

Feature: Aboriginal Art   202–203

Experience: Buying Aboriginal Art   203

Uluru–Kata Tjuta National Park   204–208

Experience: Bushwalking   205

Experience: Aboriginal Australia   209

Watarrka National Park   210

Hotels & Restaurants   376–378

A traditional Aboriginal art dot pattern

# Northern Territory

**At 525,000 square miles (1,359,750 sq km), the Northern Territory is about the size of Alaska, but with only 220,000 inhabitants it is one of the least populated places in the world. About half of its residents live in Darwin, in the tropical north. Alice Springs, in the Red Centre, is the other main population hub. The rest of the population lives in Aboriginal communities, mining camps, or cattle stations.**

The first settlements in the territory were on Melville Island and the Coburg Peninsula in the 1820s, when the British hastened to claim the northern coastline ahead of the French and Dutch. Yet it wasn't until 1869, when Palmerston (later Darwin) was established, that Europeans took root.

The Northern Territory has the highest percentage of Aborigines in its population—about 31 percent—of any state in Australia. About 50 percent of the state is Aboriginal land. Much of it is remote, and visitors require a permit. But some Aboriginal communities are opening up, inviting responsible tourism operators onto their lands, or starting their own operations, both to create jobs and to share their ancient knowledge and arts.

Many people visit the territory just to see Uluru (Ayers Rock) and the wetlands in Kakadu, but the Northern Territory also has Kata Tjuta (the Olgas, near Uluru), the lost world of Watarrka, the MacDonnell Ranges near Alice Springs, and Nitmiluk Gorge near Katherine.

The tropical north has two seasons. The Wet runs through the summer, when heat, humidity, and monsoonal rain make life tolerable only to a special breed of frontier lovers. Bush tracks can be washed out for months, dry creek beds turn into cataracts, and wild tropical grasses grow as much as 30 feet (9 m) in a month. The Dry begins around April. The storms clear away, and for the next six months the country bakes beneath faultless skies. Daily high temperatures are in the high 80s°F (30°C). This is the best time to visit the north, or Top End. The buildup to the Wet starts again in October, with rising heat and humidity, and

---

**NOT TO BE MISSED:**

**Tropical Darwin   184–187**

**The wetlands marvel of Kakadu National Park   188–191**

**Swimming under waterfalls in Litchfield National Park   193**

**Experiencing indigenous culture in the Tiwi Islands   197**

**Walking through shady gorges in the MacDonnell Ranges   199–201**

**The sacred sites of Uluru–Kata Tjuta National Park   204–208**

---

dry thunderstorms that give no relief. In the central deserts, the weather is scorching during the summer and dry as parchment. Winters are cold and frosts are possible.

Visiting the Northern Territory requires planning because of the distances involved, but actually moving within it is fairly easy. The major highways are paved and even the gravel back roads are generally graded. Flights go to Alice Springs, Darwin, and Yulara (the resort near Uluru) from all parts of Australia. Alice Springs and Darwin are accessible by the Ghan train (see pp. 282–283).

Statehood—and the full right to determine its own affairs—continues to elude this last frontier. A referendum for full statehood was narrowly defeated in 1998, and although the territory is self-governing today, officially it remains answerable to the federal government in Canberra. ■

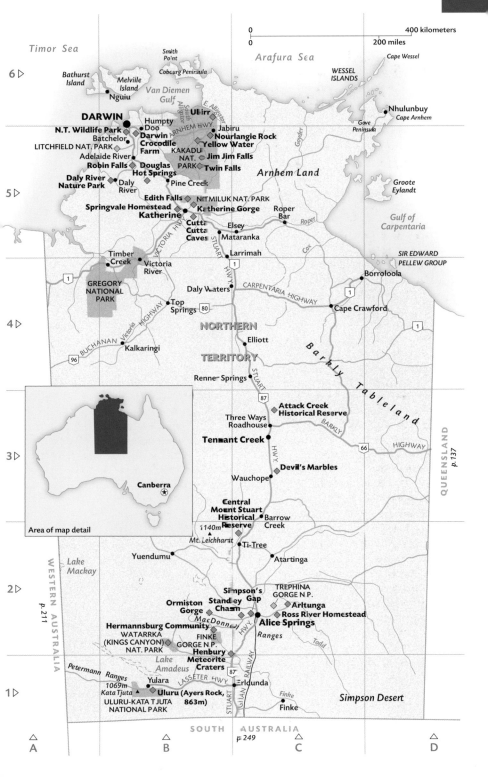

*Timor Sea*

*Arafura Sea*

WESSEL
ISLANDS

*Cape Wessel*

**6**▷

*Bathurst
Island*

Smith
Point

Cobourg Peninsula

*Melville
Island*

*Van Diemen
Gulf*

Nguiu

Ulirr

Nhulunbuy
*Cape Arnhem*

Gove
Peninsula

**DARWIN**

Humpty
Doo

Jabiru

**N.T. Wildlife Park**
Batchelor

**Darwin
Crocodile
Farm**

**Nourlangie Rock**
**Yellow Water**

**LITCHFIELD NAT. PARK**

KAKADU
NAT.
PARK

Adelaide River

**Jim Jim Falls**

**Robin Falls**
**Douglas
Hot Springs**

**Twin Falls**

*Arnhem Land*

*Groote
Eylandt*

**Daly River
Nature Park**
Daly
River

Pine Creek

**Edith Falls**

NITMILUK NAT. PARK

Roper
Bar

*Gulf of
Carpentaria*

**Springvale Homestead**
**Katherine**

**Katherine Gorge**

*Roper*

**Cutta
Cutta
Caves**

Elsey
Mataranka

SIR EDWARD
PELLEW GROUP

Larrimah

*Cox*

Timber
Creek

Victoria
River

**GREGORY
NATIONAL
PARK**

Daly Waters

CARPENTARIA HIGHWAY

Borroloola

Cape Crawford

**4**▷

*BUCHANAN*

Top
Springs

**NORTHERN**

*Victoria*

*HIGHWAY*

Kalkaringi

**TERRITORY**

Elliott

*Barkly Tableland*

QUEENSLAND
*p. 137*

Renner Springs

**3**▷

*WESTERN
AUSTRALIA
p. 211*

Canberra ✪

*Area of map detail*

Three Ways
Roadhouse

**Attack Creek
Historical Reserve**

*BARKLY*

*HIGHWAY*

**Tennant Creek**

**Devil's Marbles**

Wauchope

**Central
Mount Stuart
Historical
Reserve**

Barrow
Creek

1140m ▲
Mt. Leichhardt

Ti-Tree

Yuendumu

Atartinga

*Lake
Mackay*

**2**▷

**Simpson's
Gap**

TREPHINA
GORGE N.P.

**Ormiston
Gorge**

**Standley
Chasm**

**Arltunga**

**Ross River Homestead**

**Hermannsburg Community**

*MacDonnell*

**Alice Springs**

WATARRKA
(KINGS CANYON)
NAT. PARK

FINKE
GORGE N.P.

*Ranges*

**Henbury
Meteorite
Craters**

*Todd*

Petermann Ranges
1069m

*Lake
Amadeus*

*LASSETER HWY*

Yulara

**Uluru (Ayers Rock,
863m)**

Erldunda

*Simpson Desert*

*Kata Tjuta* ▲

ULURU-KATA TJUTA
NATIONAL PARK

*STUART*

*GHAN RAILWAY*

*Finke*

Finke

**1**▷

SOUTH    AUSTRALIA
*p. 249*

△
**A**

△
**B**

△
**C**

△
**D**

# Darwin

This prosperous modern city of 120,000 can come as quite a shock to first-time visitors who have come to the rugged tropical north expecting a brawling frontier settlement out of the movie *Crocodile Dundee*. Darwin is Australia's most suburban city, a white-collar enclave with a low-rise skyline and sprawl of neat suburban homes, shopping malls, cinemas, a casino, and fast-food chains.

The Northern Territory's Parliament building, Darwin

**Darwin**

[M] 183 B6

**Visitor Information**

[✉] Corner of Smith & Bennett Sts.

[☎] (08) 8936 2499

In its better neighborhoods, only the heat and the bright tropical flowers distinguish Darwin from a suburb of Melbourne. The elegant old-fashioned tropical-style houses, built of timber with sweeping verandas and elevated several feet off the ground in case of flooding, are mostly gone. In their place are brick ranch-style houses, less evocative but more resilient in a cyclone. Darwin is the world's lightning capital, and the frequent electric displays over the Arafura Sea beggar description.

This is a public service town at heart. Many of its citizens draw generous government paychecks, live in nice subsidized homes, and work in air-conditioned office blocks downtown. Nevertheless, Territorians cherish their rough-and-tumble, maverick image, and Darwin is genuinely a magnet for the adventurous, the restless, and the outcast (and the occasional wanted-by-police). It is a town of transients, and most residents are from somewhere else. Darwin is exceptionally ethnically diverse, with more than 50 nationalities represented here.

Darwin sometimes seems to be a parody of itself, self-consciously straining to maintain its frontier image. Tempers flare during the buildup to the wet season, when heat and humidity rise and the

## Cyclone Tracy

Cyclone Tracy almost obliterated the city of Darwin when it roared into town on Christmas Day in 1974, packing winds of more than 135 mph (215 kph). The city that was rebuilt from the wreckage is brighter and more cosmopolitan—and, one hopes, sturdier—than the ramshackle trading port that had grown up here.

police logs fill up with petty assaults. For some, Darwin's wet season is as depressing as the long Scandinavian winter; for others, it is an opportunity to see nature spring to life after the long dry season.

During the gold rushes of the 1880s, Darwin filled with fortune-seekers from all over Asia. The settlement was founded as Palmerston but renamed Port Darwin after the naturalist Charles Darwin, who passed through this harbor on the *Beagle* in 1839. In 1911, the name was simplified to Darwin. In the early days Darwin hoped to rival Singapore, but the harsh climate, sporadic tropical cyclones,

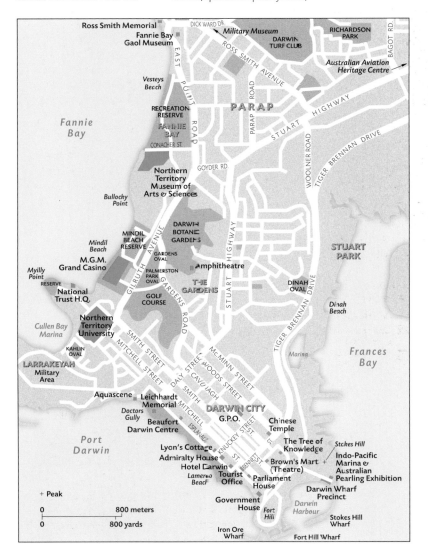

Ross Smith Memorial
Fannie Bay
Gaol Museum
DICK WARD DR.
Military Museum
DARWIN TURF CLUB
RICHARDSON PARK
BAGOT RD.
EAST POINT ROAD
ROSS SMITH AVENUE
Australian Aviation Heritage Centre
Vesteys Beach
RECREATION RESERVE
PARAP ROAD
STUART HIGHWAY
PARAP
Fannie Bay
FANNIE BAY
CONACHER ST.
ROAD
GOYDER RD.
WOOLNER ROAD
TIGER BRENNAN DRIVE
Northern Territory Museum of Arts & Sciences
Bullocky Point
DARWIN BOTANIC GARDENS
STUART PARK
Mindil Beach
MINDIL BEACH RESERVE
GARDENS OVAL
STUART HIGHWAY
Myilly Point
M.G.M. Grand Casino
GILRUTH AVENUE
PALMERSTON PARK OVAL
Amphitheatre
THE GARDENS
DINAH OVAL
TIGER BRENNAN DRIVE
Dinah Beach
RESERVE
National Trust H.Q.
GOLF COURSE
GARDENS ROAD
Cullen Bay Marina
Northern Territory University
KAHLIN OVAL
SMITH STREET
MITCHELL STREET
MCMINN STREET
Marina
Frances Bay
LARRAKEYAH Military Area
DALY STREET
SMITH
CAVENAGH
WOODS STREET
Aquascene
Leichhardt Memorial
Doctors Gully
MITCHELL
ESPLANADE
DARWIN CITY
G.P.O.
Chinese Temple
Beaufort Darwin Centre
KNUCKEY STREET
Port Darwin
Lyon's Cottage
Admiralty House
Hotel Darwin
Lameroo Beach
Tourist Office
BENNETT ST.
Parliament House
The Tree of Knowledge
Brown's Mart (Theatre)
Stokes Hill
Indo-Pacific Marina & Australian Pearling Exhibition
Darwin Wharf Precinct
Government House
Fort Hill
Darwin Harbour
Stokes Hill Wharf
+ Peak
0 — 800 meters
0 — 800 yards
Iron Ore Wharf
Fort Hill Wharf

**Northern Territory Museum of Arts & Sciences**

✉ Conacher St.

☎ (08) 8999 8201

and poor communications with the rest of the world were difficult obstacles to overcome.

In World War II, Darwin was a key base for Allied forces. Hastily built highways to Alice Springs and Mount Isa linked Darwin with the rest of Australia, and airstrips were bulldozed in the bush nearby. It was the only part of Australia of a peninsula jutting into the harbor. Although most of the early buildings were leveled, either by Japanese bombing or by Cyclone Tracy, some classic colonial tropical buildings still stand on the Esplanade—**Admiralty House** (now Char Restaurant) and **Lyon's Cottage** (both 1920s), and the restored **Government House**

---

## Bombing of Darwin

Following the attack on Pearl Harbor on December 7, 1941, Allied ships, planes, and troops were dispatched to Darwin, a key defensive port against the Japanese. Women and children were evacuated. On February 19, 1942, 188 Japanese planes attacked Darwin's harbor, sinking eight ships, damaging many more, and destroying the town before a second raid hit the military airfield. More than 240 people were killed; the remaining civilians fled, fearing invasion. Over the next year and a half, Japan raided Darwin 64 times but never invaded, its intent being to wipe out Allied military forces capable of countering its push into Southeast Asia.

---

subjected to sustained attack (see sidebar above). After the war, the city was rebuilt, but it reverted to its former torpor until Cyclone Tracy (see sidebar p. 184) leveled it again in 1974.

Today, it is an administration center, with government, mining, tourism, and the military as big local employers. With the arrival of the railroad in 2004 and vast new cargo-handling facilities at its port, it is casting itself as Australia's commercial gateway to Asia.

### Darwin Sights

Darwin is a base for expeditions to Kakadu, Katherine Gorge, or Litchfield National Park. There are also some worthwhile things to see while you are in town.

Downtown Darwin is a simple grid of wide streets at the end (built in 1870). The tourist office has information on other heritage buildings. The Esplanade runs along the edge of the ocean and makes a lovely evening stroll. A huge embroidered quilt, hanging in the nearby **Northern Territory Library** in Parliament House and crafted by people who lived here in the 1940s, tells the story of Darwin during World War II.

The **Northern Territory Museum of Arts & Sciences,** overlooking Fannie Bay about 2 miles (3 km) north of the city center, is one of the best cultural attractions in Darwin. Part of the massive rebuilding program after Cyclone Tracy, it houses a major collection of Aboriginal and Pacific Islander art. The national Aboriginal Art Award is held here every September. The museum also highlights the contribution of Southeast Asia to the development of Australia's tropical north. One of the most popular exhibits is the stuffed, late, and unlamented "Sweetheart," a 17-foot (5 m), 1,700-pound (770 kg) saltwater crocodile that terrorized local fishermen by attacking the outboard motors on their boats until he was captured in 1979.

Darwin has a number of very pretty beaches, but strong tides, crocodiles, and the presence of deadly box jellyfish six months of the year (Oct.–April, during which swimming is banned) have kept it from becoming much of a beach town. Nothing prevents you from rolling out your towel and catching some sun, but remember that you are in the tropics, so put on plenty of sunscreen.

**Mindil Beach** has a lively open-air market on winter evenings (May–Oct.). Scores of stands offer Asian food. Families set up elaborate picnics, kids play beach cricket, and crowds browse through racks of T-shirts, leather goods, bush hats, and all manner of other things. The nearby **Darwin Botanic Gardens** have one of Australia's finest collections of tropical plants—including more than 400 species of palms.

Across town, the old wharf area has become fashionable, with upscale eateries, outdoor cafés, and live entertainment on weekends in the old shed at the end of Stokes Hill Wharf. Living coral can be seen at the **Indo-Pacific Marine,** and the **Australian Pearling Exhibition** tells Darwin's story in the rough

days of Australia's pearling industry. At **Aquascene** you can feed the fish—milkfish, rays, and many others—that come in on the tide.

## Wartime Sites

Darwin holds special memories for veterans who spent time here during World War II. You can do a self-guided tour of the old oil storage tunnels near the wharf, which were dug into the rock beneath the city to protect vital fuel during air raids. The **Military Museum** tells the story of Darwin's World War II bombings. The **Australian Aviation Heritage Centre** has a Japanese Zero that was shot down over Darwin on the first raid, as well as a huge B-52 bomber on loan from the U.S. Air Force.

**INSIDER TIP:**

**Darwin Harbour's outdoor Deckchair Cinema is a great place to take in a movie (every night at 7:30 from mid-April to mid-November).**

—PETER TURNER
*National Geographic author*

The most poignant memories for those who served here may be triggered by driving south out of town to the abandoned airstrips. Signs by the side of the road point out which track to take. The strips are just clearings now, with rusting fuel drums scattered in the bush, eerily still except for the birds chirping in the treetops. ∎

**Darwin Botanic Gardens**
✉ Geranium St.
☎ (08) 8981 1958

**Australian Pearling Exhibition**
✉ Stokes Hill Wharf Rd.
💲 $

**Aquascene**
✉ 28 Doctors Gully Rd.
☎ (08) 8981 7837
🕐 Open for an hour around high tide; call for times
💲 $$

**Military Museum**
✉ East Point Reserve
☎ (08) 8981 9702

**Australian Aviation Heritage Centre**
✉ Stuart Hwy. (5 miles/8 km S of Darwin)
☎ (08) 8947 2145

**Deckchair Cinema**
✉ Darwin Harbour
☎ Program information: (08) 8981 0700
www.deckchair cinema.com

# Kakadu National Park

A wetlands marvel, Kakadu National Park stretches across nearly 8,000 square miles (20,000 sq km) of remote tropical wilderness, about 95 miles (153 km) southwest of Darwin. Australia's largest national park encloses the entire drainage basin of the South Alligator River—so named by Capt. Philip King, an early explorer who confused the area's many crocodiles with alligators when he surveyed Van Diemen Gulf (just to the north) in 1818.

Monsoon rains swamp Kakadu's wetlands and roads during the wet season, peaking January to March.

Kakadu contains more than 290 species of birds (about one-third of all known Australian bird species), 26 kinds of frogs, 74 species of reptiles, 68 species of mammals, and more than 10,000 varieties of insects. The list of Kakadu's flora and fauna is being lengthened all the time, and some species, such as the Oenpelli python (discovered only in 1977), are probably unique to the park. The wildlife provides some of the most enduring images of Kakadu: elegant Jabiru storks, thousands of galahs or magpie geese taking wing from a pool, and awesome giant saltwater crocodiles sunning themselves in the mud. Thousands of salties live in the park, and every tour guide seems to have an inexhaustible stock of macabre anecdotes about them. The park is not a great place for a dip.

Kakadu's human history dates back more than 20,000 years, and thousands of Aboriginal rock-art galleries can be found in the area's cliffs and rock shelters. More than 5,000 sites have been catalogued so far. Most are off-limits to visitors, either because they are too difficult to reach or because they have spiritual significance to the Gagadju people, who own the land and lease it to the government. Two accessible rock-art sites, however, are at **Ubirr** and **Nourlangie.**

## Mining

Controversy has raged over Kakadu's rich mineral resources for most of the park's history. Some of the world's richest uranium deposits are here, as well as gold, platinum, and palladium ore bodies in nearby Coronation Hill. The **Ranger Uranium Mine** has been in operation since 1979. The company, Energy Resources of Australia (ERA), is required to operate under strict environmental guidelines and set aside a trust fund for the eventual rehabilitation of the land when mining has stopped. Tours of the mine site include details of the environmental rehab program in addition to the company's (and some Aborigines') positive viewpoints on mining. Green groups have long been critical of the mine's performance and campaigned to no avail against expansion of the mine in 2007.

Four miles (6.5 km) west of the mine is the township of **Jabiru** (population about 1,800). It was built in 1981 to service the mining operation, but the growing popularity of Kakadu has made it something of a tourist center, complete with a luxury motel in the shape of a crocodile (see p. 376).

## Visiting Kakadu

Getting to the park is easy. Drive along the Stuart Highway south of Darwin and make a left turn onto the Arnhem Highway. This highway takes you past the colorful old pub at Humpty Do and through the heart of the park to Jabiru. Getting around this vast wilderness is something else. Four-wheel-drive vehicles or light aircraft are the best bets for reaching the most interesting and remote places. Excellent tours leave from Darwin, and the visitor center at the park headquarters has

**INSIDER TIP:**

**The swimming holes and waterfalls in Kakadu are fantastic, but remember to keep an eye out for signs telling you if crocodiles are present.**

—STEPHANIE ROBICHAUX
*National Geographic contributor*

helpful pamphlets, information on ranger-led walks, videos, and a visitor's guide to help you get the most out of your stay.

When to go is another matter. The Aborigines distinguish six different seasons in the Kakadu calendar, but choosing between the wet and dry seasons is complicated enough for most people. The dry season (May–Oct.) is by far the most popular, with heat and humidity at tolerable levels and the wildlife concentrated

**Kakadu National Park**

 183 B5

**Visitor Information**

✉ Kakadu Hwy., Jabiru

☎ (08) 8938 1120

**Freshwater crocodiles live along the tropical coastline.**

around a few shrinking water holes. To see Kakadu during the Wet, however, is to see it in all its glory, with booming monsoonal thunderstorms sweeping over the plains, cataracts spilling over the escarpment, and lush tropical grasses running riot. Against this you have to weigh the crushing heat and humidity, the fact that the wildlife will be dispersed throughout the park, and the flash floods that make much of Kakadu inaccessible. Go when the dry season has just begun, and you may get the best of both. There's no perfect time. It's a judgment call.

The most popular attractions in the park are Aboriginal rock-art sites at Nourlangie and Ubirr, the magnificent Jim Jim and Twin Falls, and Yellow Water, near the Gagadju Lodge, Cooinda, which is also the most convenient place to stay in Kakadu *(tel (08) 8979 0145).* There are no real long-distance trails in this park—something of a surprise and disappointment

to bushwalking visitors. Most of the trails are just short nature strolls, with the 7-mile (11 km) hike around Nourlangie being the most challenging.

**Nourlangie** is one of the easiest major sites to reach in Kakadu, only 20 miles (32 km) south of the park headquarters. It is a haunting deep-red sandstone formation, cloaked in forest, that falls away in steep cliffs with rock shelters clustered at its foot. A mile-long (1.6 km) walk takes you from the parking lot to **Anbangbang Shelter,** which has 20,000-year-old rock art. Nearby are sweeping views over the Arnhem Land Escarpment. If you want to hike, follow the 7-mile (11 km) Barrk Walk around Nourlangie. The park headquarters has a leaflet on this hike.

**Ubirr,** about 25 miles (40 km) north of the park headquarters on a paved road, depicts numerous animals, including tortoises, goannas, wallabies, and some that are long extinct, such as the thylacine, or Tasmanian tiger. You will also see depictions of the Rainbow Serpent—a powerful female character in the Aborigines' creation story and a frequent rock-art motif—and of mischievous Mimi spirits who dwell inside the rocks. Artistic styles vary, ranging from more than 20,000 years ago until the mid-20th century. A trail (about a mile/1.6 km round-trip) takes you from the parking lot to the rock-art galleries and includes a spectacular lookout over the East Alligator River and the rocky crags of Arnhem Land. A less frequented 4-mile (6.4 km) hike called **Sandstone and River Walk** runs along the river. **Guluyambi Cruises** *(tel 1-800 089 113, toll-free)* has a river trip with Aboriginal guides, from the start of the Sandstone and River Walk and upstream through dramatic scenery to the escarpment.

**Jim Jim** and **Twin Falls** are out of the way, about 70 miles (113 km) south of the park headquarters on a challenging four-wheel-drive track, but they are well worth a visit. They are best seen right at the beginning of the dry season, after the rains have stopped long enough for the road to be open and graded, but with enough water swelling Jim Jim Creek to make the falls an awesome sight. Water tumbles more than 700 feet (213 m) down the cliffs, including one unbroken 660-foot (200 m) fall,

into a large pool at the base. As the Dry takes hold, these falls can stop completely. Twin Falls is 6 miles (9.6 km) from Jim Jim, along an even trickier four-wheel-drive track and then a slippery climb up a forested gorge. The river cascades into an idyllic pool with a sandy beach. During the wet season, both of these spectacles are inaccessible.

For many people, **Yellow Water** is the highlight of their visit to Kakadu. It is a richly vegetated lagoon formed by Jim Jim Creek as it flows onto the floodplain about 30 miles (48 km) south of Jabiru. In the dry season, it teems with many species of waterfowl, and saltwater crocodiles bask in the mud. Sunrise and sunset are the best times to be on the lagoon. Regular boat cruises leave from nearby Cooinda Resort. ■

## Crocodiles

The world's largest reptiles, saltwater crocodiles *(Crocodylus porosus)*, or "salties," as they are affectionately known, average around 17 feet (5 m) and 1,000 pounds (450 kg), but can weigh double that and reach 23 feet (7 m). They inhabit the tropical coastal regions of Queensland, the Northern Territory, and Western Australia. Crocodiles prefer mangroves and river estuaries but can swim out to sea and across to islands. They can also be found in freshwater up to 62 miles (100 km) inland. Salties are not to be confused with "freshies," the smaller, less aggressive, and much less dangerous freshwater crocodiles *(Crocodylus johnstoni)*, also found in the north.

Saltwater crocodiles are very efficient killers. They lie hidden in the water until

prey approaches. Then they strike, exploding from the water, driven by their powerful tails. They grab their prey and drag them under, often employing the "death roll" to break necks and ensure drowning.

Salties can run quickly in short bursts, and the danger for humans is being snatched without warning. In crocodile areas, stay away from the water's edge, where they make be lurking just below the surface. Don't swim in the water—fresh or salt—unless you know it is safe.

At Kakadu you have a good chance of seeing crocodiles in the wild, or plenty of wildlife parks offer an easier option. The late Steve Irwin made crocodile shows famous at his Australia Zoo (see p. 147), where the "Crocoseum" is a popular attraction.

# Litchfield National Park

Only a two-hour drive from Darwin, Litchfield National Park is a beautiful collection of water-falls, sandstone formations, termite mounds, and crocodile-free swimming holes. Many people actually prefer this quieter and smaller park to the better known Kakadu, and it is a popular day trip for locals. As is usually the case in the Northern Territory, access is much easier during the dry season, from May to October.

Swimmers take a dip in the waters beneath Florence Falls.

Litchfield National Park is a 580-square-mile (1,500 sq km) parcel of rugged wilderness that takes in the Tabletop Range, a vast sandstone plateau covered by eucalyptus wood-lands. A series of spring-fed rivers spills over the rim of the plateau in spectacular waterfalls that plunge into rain forest valleys below.

The park's most popular attractions are Florence Falls, Wangi Falls, Tolmer Falls, and Tjaynera (Sandy Creek) Falls. There is no entry fee or visitor center in this park, although the national parks office in Batchelor has information on bushwalks, flora and fauna, the termite mounds, and the waterfalls.

## Driving to the Park

Plenty of organized tours of Litchfield National Park leave from Darwin, or you can drive there yourself, down the Stuart Highway and through the old mining town of Batchelor.

The park has two entrances. One is a gravel road from the north via the Berry Springs–Cox Peninsula Road. The other is a paved road from the east that starts in Batchelor. The two roads link up inside the park, so you can do Litchfield on a loop.

## The Lost City

The Lost City, Litchfield's freestanding sandstone formations, with its narrow alleyways and domes, may look like the work of a long lost civilization. But Mother Nature is to thank for these rock structures, carved out of wind and rain over the millennia. The sandstone is believed to be 500 million years old.

The **Territory Wildlife Park,** located about 30 miles (48 km) south of Darwin *(tel (08) 8988 7200, www.territorywildlifepark .com.au, $$),* is a worthwhile stop along the way, complete with an outstanding aquarium, aviaries, a reptile house, and nature trails. Day tours leave for the park from Darwin.

### Waterfalls

**Florence Falls:** If you enter Litchfield National Park through Batchelor, the 700-foot-high (212 m) Florence Falls is the first waterfall you'll come to, and the pool at the base is an excellent swimming hole. You can camp here or at the nearby Buley Rock Holes.

**Tolmer Falls:** You will find the turnoff to Tolmer Falls about 11 miles (17.7 km) past the turnoff for Florence Falls. In order to protect the nesting site of the rare orange horseshoe bat, visitors are forbidden to swim in the plunge pool here.

**Wangi Falls:** Another 4 miles (6.4 km) will bring you to Wangi Falls. The year-round waterfalls are certainly the most popular attraction in Litchfield National Park, with an idyllic tropical swimming hole and a rain forest boardwalk.

### The Lost City & Sandy Creek Falls

One of the other great attractions in the park is the **Lost City,** an eerie collection of weathered sandstone columns that resemble ancient ruins. The turnoff is about 4 miles (6.4 km) past the turnoff for Florence Falls. To get there, you bump another 5 miles

**INSIDER TIP:**

**Visit Litchfield with a cultural perspective and head out with Tess Atie, a local indigenous person. She'll fascinate you with stories of earlier times. Visit *www .ntindigenoustours.com.***

—MEREDITH BAXTER
*Territory Discoveries*

(8 km) along a steep, muddy four-wheel-drive track. The track will take you to **Tjaynera (Sandy Creek) Falls,** although it gets even more treacherous past the Lost City. It is easier to reach Sandy Creek Falls on a four-wheel-drive track leading directly off the main track through the park. ■

**Litchfield National Park**
183 B5
**Batchelor Office**
(08) 8976 0282

# Nitmiluk National Park & Katherine

Nitmiluk, or Katherine Gorge, is one of the three sights you should not miss in the Top End of the Northern Territory (along with Kakadu and Litchfield National Parks). It is a chain of 13 gorges carved out of the surrounding sandstone plateau by the mighty Katherine River during the past 25 million years or so. In addition to the towering orange cliffs, there are spectacular Aboriginal rock-art galleries that you can see while on a canoe trip or cruising on the river.

Canoeing is the most popular way to see Nitmiluk's ancient gorges.

## Katherine

Explorer John McDouall Stuart, who came this way in 1861, named the river after the daughter of one of his friends. Ten years later, a couple called Frank and Kate Knott set up a pub and general store. The town of Knotts Crossing (later Katherine) sprang up here. It was a rough-and-tumble outback settlement when a woman named Jeannie Gunn visited on her way to Elsey Station in 1902. Gunn wrote about Katherine's old pub, the Sportsman's Arms, in her classic novel about station life and Aborigines, *We of the Never Never*. For years, the presence of reliable water made Katherine a stopover point for drovers and prospectors crossing the desert.

By Northern Territory standards, Katherine is a bustling city of 8,500. The Tindal Air Force Base here is the main tactical fighter base for northern Australia, and the Royal Australian Air Force (R.A.A.F.) is the single biggest employer in town. The **School of the Air** on Giles Street gives tours of its facility so you can see how children in the outback are taught.

## Nitmiluk National Park

Nitmiluk National Park is about 20 miles (32 km) northeast of Katherine, at the end of a highway that runs from the town center. Most visitors come on a day trip during the dry season and go no farther than the second gorge. The river is flat, low, and calm at this time of year, and canoeists are impeded by piles of boulders that require portaging. Canoes can be hired from the park visitor center at the gorge, where you can also book boat tours to the second and third gorges (two and four hours) with Nitmiluk Tours (tel 1-300 146 743).

If you want to see all the gorges, plan on doing an overnight trek. The first legal campsite is **Smith's Rock,** in the fourth gorge. You can camp anywhere beyond here. The uppermost gorges are most easily seen by beaching the canoe after the fifth gorge and scrambling over the rocks for the last couple of miles.

During the wet season, however, the river becomes a formidable torrent. In 1998, Katherine was devastated by a one-in-500-year flood, as the river spectacularly burst its banks and turned the countryside into a vast lake.

Walking trails lead through the park's scenic bushland and down into the gorge. The longest and most challenging of these is the 50-mile (80 km) hike to **Leliyn (Edith) Falls.** You can also reach the falls by taking the Stuart Highway 28 miles (45 km) north of Katherine, then 12 miles (20 km) along the paved road to Leliyn, where there is a campground. The park visitor center has maps and guides. A bus shuttles between Katherine and the national park.

## INSIDER TIP:

Reserve in advance if you want to take the multiday hike to Edith Falls—the campsites only accommodate ten people at a time. Note that all hikes must begin before 1:00 p.m.

—LARRY PORGES
*National Geographic editor*

Five miles (8 km) southwest of Katherine, just off the Victoria Highway, **Springvale Homestead** is supposedly the oldest station in the Northern Territory. Built in 1879, it has accommodations and is open for tourist visits. Still farther south is the **Cutta Cutta Caves Nature Park,** which has 500-million-year-old limestone formations and caves that contain rare orange horseshoe bats. ■

**Katherine**
🗺 183 B5
**Visitor Information**
✉ Lindsay St. & Katherine Ter.
☎ (08) 8972 2650

**National Parks & Wildlife Service**
✉ 32 Giles St., Katherine
☎ (08) 8973 8888

**Nitmiluk National Park**
🗺 183 B5
**Visitor Information**
☎ (08) 8972 1886

# Arnhem Land & the Tiwi Islands

Aborigines hold big tracts of land in the Top End—the primeval wilderness of Arnhem Land, the Cobourg Peninsula, and Melville and Bathurst Islands. Much of this land is off-limits to individual tourists. Aborigines have lived in these remote places for more than 40,000 years, and for the most part they do not wish to be disturbed. They are responding to the growing interest in their culture, though, and there are a few unique opportunities for travel.

Cape Helvetius, on Bathurst Island, juts into the Timor Sea.

## Arnhem Land

The vast wilderness of Arnhem Land is slowly opening its doors to controlled tourism. The main settlement is the bauxite mining town of **Gove/Nhulunbuy** in the northeast corner. You don't need a permit to fly there, but this port has little appeal. Independent tourism outside it is virtually impossible. Travel permits take up to a year to be issued, and most go to game anglers heading up to Smith Point. If you want to try anyway, contact the Northern Land Council Office.

The Aboriginal-run **Bawaka Cultural Experiences** (tel (08) 8987 2304, e-mail: dhanbul@octa4 .net.au) has day and overnight trips to the Bawaka homeland on the unspoiled tropical beaches south of Nhulunbuy. The emphasis is on cultural experiences, from traditional fishing to art and craft to bush food appreciation. **Davidson's Arnhemland Safaris** (tel (08) 8927 5240, www.arnhemland-safaris.com) guides groups through Central Arnhem Land around Mt. Borradaile, home to sandstone hills, caves, and abundant Aboriginal art.

The most luxurious way to experience Aboriginal land is to visit **Seven Spirit Bay** (tel (08) 8979

## Deadly Stingers & Biters

Australia makes up for its lack of dangerous mammals with a host of creatures to keep a keen eye out for.

Common varieties of Australian snakes include the tiger snake (named for its stripes), brown snake, and red-bellied black snake. Deadliest but less common are the taipan and the suitably named death adder.

The only deadly spiders are the funnel web, found in suburban Sydney, and the red-back spider, widespread though only occasionally fatal.

Saltwater crocodiles, the world's largest reptiles, are found in far north Australia (see sidebar p. 191). Heed all signs announcing their presence. Smaller freshwater crocodiles can bite but impart no serious harm.

With all that coastline, Australia has many species of shark. Great white, tiger, bull, and whaler sharks all feed on large sea mammals. None specifically targets humans, though they might mistake you for a seal.

From November to March, look out in northern tropical waters for the box jellyfish, which can deliver multiple, potentially fatal stings from its trailing tentacles. Other dangers include the poisonous-spined stonefish and the pretty, but potentially fatal, blue ring octopus.

You are much more likely to be in a car accident than encounter any of these threats. Snakes are rarely sighted, and antivenins are widely available. Sharks strike only a handful of people—usually surfers and others in deep water.

---

0281), an ecotourism resort on the tip of the Cobourg Peninsula, about 130 miles (209 km) northeast of Darwin. It offers guided bushwalks and fishing trips and is reached only by light aircraft or four-wheel-drive vehicle.

## Tiwi Islands

**Bathurst Island** and **Melville Island**, about 50 miles (80 km) north of Darwin, are home to the Tiwi people. The Tiwi Land Council, which governs the islands, has opened them to small tour groups (not individuals). **Tiwi Tours** (tel (08) 8923 6523) is the only accredited operator. It does day trips from Darwin and camping in some of the most remote territory in Australia.

Tiwi language and culture developed independently of the rest of Aboriginal Australia. Features unique to this people include their *pukumani*, or burial poles, which are carved or painted with totems and motifs and set out around graves.

Tiwis have fiercely guarded their independence. The British established Fort Dundas on Melville Island in 1824, but it lasted less than five years. The Tiwis regained political control in 1978. Most Tiwis lead nontraditional lifestyles in the main settlement of Nguiu on Bathurst Island. Much of the islands remains a wilderness. Visitors can buy local artwork, meet with community leaders, and then head out to the bush. Overnight visits can include lessons in digging wild pumpkins, hunting goannas, and spearing fish. The packages are fairly expensive, but this is not an everyday trip. ■

**Northern Land Council Office**

✉ 45 Mitchell St., Darwin

☎ (08) 8920 5170

**www.nlc.org.au**

# Alice Springs

Alice Springs is an oasis town in the dramatic rocky walls of the MacDonnell Ranges. It is a good base from which to visit most of the attractions in Australia's Red Centre—notably Uluru (Ayers Rock) and Kata Tjuta (the Olgas).

The boisterous Camel Cup is held in Alice Springs each July.

## Alice Springs

🗺 183 C2

**Visitor Information**

✉ 60 Gregory Terrace

☎ (08) 8952 5800

**www.alicesprings .nt.gov.au**

## Northern Territory Parks & Wildlife Service

✉ South Stuart Hwy. (3 miles/ 4.5 km S of Alice Springs)

☎ (08) 8951 8211

The Alice, as it is known, was settled in 1871 as a relay station for the Overland Telegraph Line that stretched from Adelaide to Darwin. The old stone-built Telegraph Station, now a restored historical reserve a mile (1.6 km) north of town, was built near a permanent waterhole in the normally dry bed of the Todd River. The station was one of 12 built along the telegraph line, which hooked up in Darwin with the undersea cable from Java to connect Australia with the rest of the

world. You can walk to the station on a path by the riverbed. To drive there, take the Stuart Highway north and turn right at the sign about half a mile (1 km) out of town. The springs are a nice place for a cooling swim or a picnic.

The town was originally gazetted as Stuart, but the name was officially changed to Alice Springs in 1933. Nevil Shute's 1950 novel *A Town Like Alice* made it known across the world, but it wasn't until 1987 that you could drive here from Adelaide on a

paved road. The Alice today is a
modern little city of 22,000, laid
out on a five-street grid between
the bed of the Todd River and the
Stuart Highway.

Alice Springs has really lifted
its game in recent years on the
tourism front. Just west of town,
the **Alice Springs Desert Park**
is a superb botanic garden–style
attraction with imaginative
displays of the flora and fauna to
be found in the territory's various
ecosystems, and an entertaining
show, given by bird-handlers, of
the predatory desert birds.

Nearby, also on Larapinta
Drive, are the **Araluen Centre
for Arts & Entertainment,** with
its theater and art galleries; the
**Central Australian Aviation
Museum;** and the **Museum of
Central Australia.**

The **Royal Flying Doctor
Service** delivers medical services
to remote communities across
the country, and its Alice Springs
base has tours, an interesting
small museum, and a café, with
proceeds aiding this essential service. In a similar vein, visitors can
tour the **School of the Air,** the
"world's largest school," delivering
lessons to isolated students across

an area twice the size of Texas.
Once dependent on radio trans-
mission, students now rely mainly
on satellites and the internet.

There is a great lookout over
the city and the MacDonnell
Ranges from the top of Anzac Hill,
a steep but convenient rocky crag
near the top end of Todd Street.
You can drive up it.

South of the city, the **Frontier
Camel Farm** has camel rides and
a camel museum. Camels were
imported to Australia in the mid-
19th century to help open up the
country, and they were set free
after trains and roads had made
them obsolete. Now an estimated
15,000 camels trot around the
Red Centre, and thousands more
inhabit Western Australia. **Camels
Australia** (*Stuart Well, tel (08)
8956 0925*), about 55 miles
(88 km) south of Alice Springs,
does camel treks.

### MacDonnell Ranges

The Alice is the base for some
great day drives through the

**Alice Springs
Desert Park**
✉ Larapinta Dr.
☎ (08) 8951 8788
💲 $$
www.alicesprings
desertpark.com.au

**Royal Flying
Doctor Service**
✉ 8–10 Stuart Ter.
☎ (08) 8952 1129
💲 $
www.flyingdoctor.net

**School of the Air**
✉ 80 Head St.
☎ (08) 8951 6800
💲 $
www.assoa.nt.edu.au

**Frontier Camel
Farm**
☎ (08) 8950 3030

## Drought

Despite rain-drenched coasts and tropical wetlands, Australia is the driest continent and drought is an ever present threat. Prolonged drought, the worst on record, has affected parts of Australia since 1992. Much of the country has been placed on severe water restrictions. Western Australia and Victoria have been forced to build desalination plants, while southeast Queensland, one of the wetter parts of Australia, began recycling sewerage for drinking water in 2008, when dam levels fell to an alarming 20 percent of capacity.

The drought has since broken with a flood in Queensland and across the north, but southern Australia remains gripped by the prolonged dry that threatens farm incomes and has seen the Murray River, the countries longest, slow to a trickle, its wetlands and bird populations depleted in a growing ecological disaster.

Many blame global warming and point to Australia's energy consumption and carbon dioxide emissions, among the highest per capita in the world, much of it due to burning coal, Australia's biggest export. Poor management of inland waterways, over-irrigation, and the failure to build new dams despite a rapidly growing population have exacerbated the problem.

**Arltunga**

Visitor Information

☎ (08) 8956 9770

**INSIDER TIP:**

**The Western MacDonnells feature many picturesque waterholes to cool you off on a hot day. Try Ormiston or Glen Helen Gorges.**

—KELLIE HARPLEY
*NT Tourism*

deep, shady gorges and along the spectacular cliffs of the Eastern and Western MacDonnell Ranges. Unless you are part of a tour, you'll need your own transportation.

There are excellent walks in **Trephina Gorge National Park,** about 40 miles (64 km) northeast of Alice Springs on the Ross Highway, and around the nearby **Ross River Resort** *(tel 1-800 241 711, toll-free),* southeast of the highway a little farther on. Out here you'll have a fairly good chance of seeing a perentie—at

up to 7 feet long (2.1 m) the largest lizard in Australia and second in the world after its cousin, Indonesia's Komodo dragon. Be careful if you encounter one. They are astoundingly fast and have powerful razor-sharp claws. If frightened they will run up the highest thing they can see—even if it is you.

The ghost town of **Arltunga** is in the far Eastern MacDonnell Ranges, 65 miles (105 km) northeast of Alice Springs on the Ross Highway. It was settled in 1887, when gold was mined here, but abandoned in 1912, when the gold finally ran out. It has an excellent visitor center and guided tours on Sunday afternoons, May through September.

In the Western MacDonnell Ranges you will find **Simpson's Gap,** a deep cleft cut by tiny Roe Creek, about 12 miles (19 km) west of Alice Springs on Larapinta Drive. It was made famous by the paintings of Aborigine artist Albert Namatjira, one of Australia's best known outback painters and the first Aboriginal granted Australian citizenship. He died tragically of alcoholism in 1959.

Twenty miles (32 km) farther west, turn north off Larapinta Drive for about 6 miles (9 km) to reach **Standley Chasm,** an incredibly narrow gap whose near-vertical walls seem little more than shoulder-width apart, and where the sun shines only for an instant around noon. Three miles (5 km) west of the turnoff along Larapinta Drive, the road forks. The right (north) fork is Namatjira Drive. Appropriately enough for a road named after a great Aboriginal artist, it goes out to the **Ochre Pits,** about 40 miles (64 km) farther on, where ancient Aboriginal artists obtained their pigments. From there the road continues 10 miles (16 km) or so to rugged **Ormiston** and **Glen Helen Gorges.**

If you stay on Larapinta Drive for 50 miles (80 km), you reach **Hermannsburg Community.** This Aboriginal community was set up by South Australian Lutheran missionaries in 1877 and still has some of the original date palms they planted. The traditional German farmhouses have now been restored.

**Finke National Park** is 7 miles (11 km) on from Hermannsburg, and you need a four-wheel-drive vehicle to get there. In the park is **Palm Valley,** an isolated tropical pocket filled with Australian cabbage palms. The trees are unique to this gorge and have grown here since prehistoric times, when the climate was wetter.

Drive 60 miles (96 km) south or the Stuart Highway to reach the **Henbury Meteor Craters,** a few miles west off the highway on the Ernest Giles Road. The craters were formed several thousand years ago by the chunks of a meteor. The biggest crater is almost 600 feet (183 m) across. ∎

Standley Chasm in the Western MacDonnell Ranges glows red when the sun shines in briefly at midday.

# Aboriginal Art

Art has always played an important role in Aboriginal culture as a way of recording human events, honoring the land, and passing on to future generations the stories of creation and the deeds of supernatural beings. There are examples of paintings and rock engravings dating back at least 50,000 years, and the work of modern Aboriginal artists is increasingly in demand.

Aboriginal artist Kathleen Wallace with bush medicine and one of her paintings

## Rock Art

Aboriginal rock art gives a unique illustrated history of the continent over thousands of years. The earliest art in Kakadu, dated to the last ice age, shows an arid landscape in which hunters kill kangaroos with boomerangs. Later, trees and flowers begin to appear in the record as the ice age ended and sea levels began to rise. Hunters are shown using spears, which were more reliable than boomerangs in the newly dense scrub. One 6,000-year-old rock mural, in a remote corner of Kakadu, illustrates what some art historians believe to be the world's earliest battle scene. It shows 111 stick figures, apparently charging each other

and hurling spears. Eight have fallen, and blood is gushing from their spear wounds. Scientists speculate that conflicts such as the one depicted in the mural may have been caused by the slow rise of the sea, which over centuries forced coastal people to migrate inland and onto the higher territory of their neighbors. Aboriginal art of the 15th century represents the Macassar fishermen who arrived at that time from Indonesia, and art of the 18th and 19th centuries includes references to Europeans.

Art historians recognize several successive styles of rock art, starting with drawings of animals in what is known as the naturalist style. This was succeeded by the dynamic phase, in which motion, such as the trajectory of a spear, appears to be represented by scribbles, dashes, and dots. These paintings, the earliest of which are found in Kakadu and date from about 12,000 years ago, are the world's earliest forms of narrative art. Later came the curious "yam"-style paintings, in which humans and animals

## INSIDER TIP:

**Fancy a go at Aboriginal dot-painting? Try the three-hour Anangu Tour** (www.ananguwaai.com.au) **workshops at Uluru.**

—ROFF SMITH
*National Geographic author*

were represented with yam-shaped symbols. Next came the X-ray style, in which the skeletal frames of people and animals appear. It is a tribute to the remarkable longevity of Aboriginal culture that today's elders can often look at a piece of art created by an ancestor a hundred generations before and understand the story being told.

### Visiting Rock-art Galleries

Many rock-art sites remain inaccessible to tourists, in some cases because they are so remote but also because, after two centuries of disruption to their culture, Aborigines wish to keep the sacred sites private.

The richest area for rock art is in northern Australia: in Kakadu and Arnhem Land in the Northern Territory, and in the Kimberley region of Western Australia. Motifs include simple handprints, complex hunting scenes, and fabulous renditions of Rainbow Serpents—deities who played crucial roles in Dreamtime creation stories.

Some particularly magnificent galleries that are open to the public are Ubirr and Nourlangie in Kakadu (see p. 190), rock murals near the base of Uluru (see p. 207), and two of the Quinkan rock-art galleries near the town

of Laura in Queensland (see p. 176). Totally different from anything in Kakadu, Quinkan art contains paintings of the region's wildlife and illustrates the spiritual life of the Ang-Gnarra people. The spookiest images are those of the Quinkans, large and apparently malicious humanoid spirits who dwell in fissures in the rocks. Only two of the Quinkan galleries are open to the public, Split Rock and Guguyalangi.

### Modern Aboriginal Art

Many of today's Aboriginal artists continue to draw on the Dreamtime for inspiration, and centuries-old practices, such as painting on bark and mixing the same natural pigments as the ancestors, remain popular. Others have adopted nontraditional media, such as acrylic paints, and adapted Western artistic styles. The art they create comes in a variety of forms and includes everything from traditional dot paintings to exquisitely carved didgeridoos, decorated boomerangs, beautiful fabrics, and pottery.

## EXPERIENCE:
## Buying Aboriginal Art

Since the 1980s, Aboriginal art has enjoyed something of a boom. Indigenous artists have found creative new ways to express and preserve their culture and non-Aborigines have acquired a taste for Aboriginal art's unique and powerful style. **Arnhem Land**'s bark paintings and the abstract, dot-painted murals of central Australia are tremendously popular. Expect to pay good money for good art, but be wary of imitations. Non-Aborigines have been caught turning out "Aboriginal" art. Go to reputable dealers who know about the artists, and they will give you and the artists a better deal. For a list of Aboriginal-owned art galleries throughout Australia, see Travelwise, p. 384.

# Uluru–Kata Tjuta National Park

Uluru and Sydney Opera House share the distinction of being the best known landmarks in Australia. Uluru (also known as Ayers Rock) attracts more than half a million visitors each year. This haunting monolith in central Australia, one of the world's largest, rising almost 1,150 feet (350 m) from the flat scrub, is a remarkable spectacle. Understandably, Aborigines consider this a holy site.

A sunset view of Kata-Tjuta (the Olgas)

**Uluru–Kata Tjuta National Park**

⚠ 183 B1

**Visitor Information**

✉ Uluru National Park Entrance

☎ (08) 8956 1100

## Uluru (Ayers Rock)

The Rock lies about 200 miles (320 km) southwest of Alice Springs. It is the summit of a massive underground chunk of sandstone about 600 million years old. Geologists believe that only the top 10 percent of the rock is visible. Erosion over many millions of years has slowly exposed its mass, and weathering has revealed its characteristic red hue. Explorer Ernest Giles was the first European to set eyes on this wonder, back in 1872. The following year another adventurer, William Gosse, scaled the monolith with an Afghan camel driver and named it Ayers Rock after the premier of South Australia, Henry Ayers.

# EXPERIENCE: Bushwalking

From ten-minute riverside strolls to the 715-mile (1,144 km) Heysen Trail, thousands of walking trails cross the country. The best walks tend to be in national parks, where the trails are often well marked, but not always. Bushwalking in Australia tends to be a wilderness experience. The most popular trails get lots of traffic at peak times, but there are plenty of opportunities to have nature to yourself.

The best time to bushwalk in northern Australia is during the dry season (May–Sept.), while October–April is better for hiking in the southern states. The southern mountains can be snowed under in winter (June–Sept.) but are wonderful in summer (Dec.–Feb.), when temperatures can soar elsewhere. Spring and autumn are the overall best times to walk in much of the country.

Planning is required, especially for overnight hikes. Always check local conditions with park authorities and be fully equipped. Many bushwalks require some outdoors experience.

## Guided Walks

If you prefer guided walks, plenty of companies can transport your gear, cook your meals, set up your tent, or put you up in luxury accommodation. Tasmania has the pick of the luxury walks. Anthology (tel (03) 6392 2211, www.anthology .travel) operates **Cradle Mountain Huts Walk** and **Bay of Fires Walk** (see pp. 346 & 351), while **Maria Island Walk** (tel (03) 6234 2999, www.mariaislandwalk .com.au) is a wonderful four-day coastal walk staying in beach camps and a historic homestead. Good tour operators for guided walks throughout the country include: **Auswalk** (tel (03) 5356 4971, www.auswalk.com .au), **Parktrek** (tel (03) 9877 9540, www.parktrek.com), and **World Expeditions** (tel 1-300 720 000, www.world expeditions.com).

## INSIDER TIP:

On the Overland Track bushwalk, be sure to allow time to hike to Mount Oakley for some of Tasmania's most stunning views.

—JOHN & LYN DALY
Bushwalkers & authors of the
Take a Walk book series

Some of Australia's best bushwalks include:

**Australian Alps Walking Track.** A 406-mile (650 km) trek from Walhalla in Victoria to Tharwa near Canberra; or do just part, like Mount Bogong or Feathertop.

**Bondi-Bronte, Sydney.** A stunning 3-mile (5 km), one-hour stroll from Bondi Beach around the headlands.

**Cape to Cape Track, Western Australia.** See wild beaches, cliffs, and whales on this 85-mile (135 km), 7-day walk from Cape Naturaliste to Cape Leeuwin near Margaret River.

**Flinders Chase Coastal Trek, South Australia.** A 12-mile (19 km), day walk on Kangaroo Island with rugged coastal scenery, beaches, and abundant wildlife.

**Larapinta Track, Northern Territory.** Glorious gorges, chasms, and outback scenery along this 140-mile (223 km), 13-day trail west of Alice Springs.

**Mt. Kosciuszko Summit, New South Wales.** Take the chairlift in summer, then walk 4 miles (11 km), four hours, to the top of Australia's highest peak.

**Overland Track, Tasmania.** Australia's premier wilderness walk from Cradle Mountain to Lake St. Clair, 45 miles (73 km), 6–7 days, with huts along the way.

**Thorsborne Trail, Queensland.** Tropical wonders define this 20-mile (32 km) 3–4 day, walk on Hinchinbrook Island.

**Wineglass Bay Circuit, Tasmania.** A 7.5-mile (12 km), four-hour walk in Freycinet National Park to idyllic Wineglass Bay and Hazard Beach, then back around the coast.

In 1985, Ayers Rock was handed back to the Pitjantjatjara and Yankunytjatjara Aborigines, who promptly restored its ancient name of Uluru and then leased it back to the government for use as a national park. The local Aboriginal communities get 20 percent of the gate takings and a royalty of A$75,000 (U.S. $57,000) a year.

Tourism at the rock has boomed since the A$250-million (U.S. $190 million) Yulara resort complex opened in 1984. A local airstrip handles Qantas jets from Cairns, Sydney, and Perth. Philip Cox, creator of Sydney's Darling Harbour Exhibition Centre and a major force in the 2000 Olympic Games, designed the resort village, whose canopies resemble sails in the desert. Yulara has a wide range of accommodations, from the five-star opulence of Longitude 131 with its luxurious safari tents, down to plain old, do-it-yourself camping. The village is just outside the park boundaries, about 12 miles (19 km) from Uluru and a little more than 30 miles (48 km) from Kata Tjuta.

The excellent visitor center at the park entrance has displays about the fascinating geology, flora, and fauna in the park, and you can book tours with the operators licensed to run tours from Yulara. **Anangu Tours** *(tel (08) 8956 2123, www.ananguwaai .com.au)* is owned and operated by local Aborigines. Sunset, sunrise, dot-paintings, and walking tours are offered.

## To Climb or Not to Climb

For more than a century, tourists have clambered up the steep flank of Uluru without asking if the Aborigines minded people climbing on their sacred monolith. When somebody finally posed this fundamental question, the answer turned out to be yes.

Local Aborigines, who took possession of Uluru in 1985, have posted signs asking visitors not to climb the Rock, but almost one-third of its 350,000 annual visitors ignore the plea. The government is considering a proposal to ban the climb and impose other restrictions to protect the park from the crush of tourists.

The climb is not really all that wonderful—except perhaps as a way of burning off 1,500 calories in a sweaty, heart-thumping half-hour. The initial pitch is extremely steep and exposed—terrifying to anyone with a fear of heights—and the strain has induced some heart attacks.

Every year, on average, somebody dies on the Rock, either from heart failure or straying off the track. Now removed, crosses at the foot of the climb commemorated those who died and served as a warning. Ironically, they also served as a challenge for tourists, who posed for pictures by them before starting the climb.

The biggest trouble with climbing the Rock is that you lose sight of it. With its haunting mass under your feet, not before your eyes, you cannot experience its power and mystique. And, presumably, that is what drew you to the Rock in the first place. The gentle, 6-mile (9.7 km) walk around the base of Uluru (see p. 207) gives you a better sense of its size, shape, texture, and character as it rises up almost vertically from the desert floor. Best of all, you'll be respecting the wishes of the people who have loved and understood this marvel for many thousands of years.

**Seeing Uluru:** Everything here is about seeing Uluru. When all is said and done, you can do so in three ways. You can gaze up at it, climb it, or see it from the air with the flat red desert spreading out to the curve of the horizon. Helicopter flights over Uluru and Kata Tjuta are organized locally by Ayers Rock Helicopters *(tel (08) 8956 2077)*. The 7-mile (11 km) driving loop around the rock has a sunset viewing area on the west side

### INSIDER TIP:

**The swarming black flies at Uluru can be remarkably aggressive. Bring or buy a net face mask to help keep these pests at bay.**

—LARRY PORGES
*National Geographic editor*

and a good sunrise viewing spot on the northeast. About 30 percent of visitors attempt to climb Uluru despite requests not to (see sidebar p. 206).

A far better alternative to climbing Uluru is to take the pleasant and flat **Base Walk** that circles the rock. Walkers see some of the flora and fauna, and there is Aboriginal rock art in shelters near the base of the rock. A good place to begin the walk is at the Mala parking area, near the climbing trail up Uluru. The park visitor center

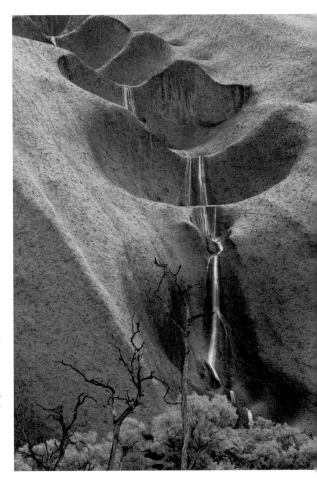

Water cascades from Uluru during a spring rainstorm.

supplies a brochure on this walk and on shorter hikes near the base. You can also join a walking tour *(Anangu Tours, $$$$$)* led by Aboriginal guides and learn about the ancient Aboriginal way of life and their uses for the various desert plants.

### Kata Tjuta (The Olgas)

Kata Tjuta, or the Olgas, is a collection of sandstone and

**Yulara Resort**
🅰 183 B1
☎ Reservations
1-800 809 622
(toll-free)

**Anangu Tours
Night Time Sky
Show**
☎ 1-800 803 174
(toll-free)
💲 $$, includes
transportation

arkose (sedimentary rock formed from granite sands) monoliths about 20 miles (32 km) west of Uluru on the Docker River Road. They form an eerie, hole-in-the-wall maze, and though they are not as well known as their world-famous neighbor, many visitors find them much more intriguing.

side of the formation remains off-limits to visitors—as well as to Aboriginal women, for it is a men's sacred site.

Because much of the park is sacred, there are only two hiking paths through Kata Tjuta. The main attraction is the **Valley of the Winds Walk,** a spectacular 4-mile (6.4 km) loop that winds

## The Dreamtime

Natural formations such as Uluru and Kata Tjuta often play key roles in Aboriginal stories of the Dreamtime. A central concept of Aboriginal spirituality, the Dreamtime is the time of creation, when the ancestral spirits rose up from the barren earth. Taking many supernatural forms, some part-human and some animal, the spirits traveled, hunted, and fought across the landscape, creating mountains, rivers, plants, the elements, animals, and eventually humans, who trace their ancestry back to different totemic spirits. The paths the spirits took are known as dreaming tracks, which link sacred sites. Ceremonies and songs often tell of the Dreamtime and provide the basis for Aboriginal law and custom.

In 1873, English-born explorer Ernest Giles (see p. 45) was the first European to see Kata Tjuta. He waxed lyrical about these "rounded minarets, giant cupolas and monstrous domes" and named them after Queen Olga of Württemburg. To the local Aborigines the rocks had always been Kata Tjuta, or "many heads," and they restored the ancient name once they regained possession of this site.

The largest of the many towering heads—there are 36 in all—is **Mount Olga**, which rises about 1,800 feet (549 m). Geologists believe the whole collection was once part of an enormous monolith ten times the size of Uluru. As with Uluru, the Aborigines regarded Kata Tjuta as a holy place, and the eastern

through ocher-red chasms, gorges, and cliffs. The way to the trailhead of this walk is clearly marked. For a shorter hike, there is a straight-forward, well-marked trail into the Olga Gorge.

### Taking Photos

Photographing Uluru or Kata Tjuta is fast becoming a thorny issue. Because Aborigines hold these places to be sacred, they believe that capturing images of them on film, other than at prescribed locations, is a form of desecration. Signs posted around the sites indicate where photography is permitted. Anyone planning to photograph the Rock for professional purposes must be approved by the local council, which often charges hefty fees. ■

# EXPERIENCE: Aboriginal Australia

Aboriginal culture is at its strongest in the outback, particularly the Northern Territory and
Western Australia. Parts of the Northern Territory did not have contact with Europeans until the
1940s, and some remote communities still live a semitraditional lifestyle. Permits are required
to enter Aboriginal lands, and the best way to experience indigenous culture is on a tour.

### Northern Territory

In the Northern Territory
at **Kakadu National Park,**
Kakadu Culture Camp *(tel
0428 792 048, www.kakadu
culturecamp.com)* offers bush
food tours, followed by a
traditional campfire dinner,
and night boat cruises. Or
get dropped into the **East
Alligator River** region by
helicopter (no roads) with a
guide and have this slice of
Arnhem Land to yourself.

In **East Arnhem Land,**
Bawaka Cultural Experiences
*(tel (08) 8987 2304, www
.yolngutourism.com)* has trips
to the Bawaka homeland
south of Nhulunbuy. The
emphasis is on cultural
experiences, from traditional
fishing to art and craft and
bush food appreciation.

At **Uluru–Kata Tjuta
National Park,** walk around
the Rock with the traditional
owners, the Anangu people
from Anangu Tours *(tel (08)
8956 2123, www.ananguwaai
.com.au).* Desert Tracks *(tel
(02) 6286 9033, www.desert
tracks.com.au)* has 1–5 day
tours of central Australia
with Pitjantjatjara guides.

### Western Australia

In Western Australia, Kepa
Kurl Discovery Tours *(tel (08)
9072 1688, www.kepakurl
.com.au)* has 4WD eco-
cultural tours along the
white beaches of **Esperance,**
explaining the Noongar's
relationship to the land.
**Broome** is a good place to
organize Aboriginal tours,
and 125 miles (200 km) north
on the superb beaches of
remote **Dampier Peninsula,**
an Aboriginal-owned wilderness camp, Kooljaman at
Cape Leveque *(tel (08) 9192
4970, www.kooljaman.com.au)*
has tents and cabin accommodation. Or stay at the
nearby Lombadina Commu-
nity *(tel (08) 9192 4936, www
.lombadina.com.au),* where
indigenous tours can also
be arranged. At **Wyndham,**
Wundagoodie Aboriginal
Safaris *(tel (08) 9161 1145,
e-mail: wuncargoordie2@big
pond.com)* has 4WD tours into
the remote north Kimberley
to rarely visited landscapes
and rock-art sites.

### South Australia

In South Australia,
Bookabee Tours *(tel (08)
8235 9954, www.bookabee
.com.au)* has 2- to 4-day
adventures in the **Flinders
Ranges,** taking in rock art
and regional indigenous history. Iga Warta *(tel (08) 8648
3737, www.igawarta.com),*
in the Northern Flinders
Ranges, has bush meals,
wildlife, and Adnyamathanha
cultural tours.

Many other tours oper-
ate around the country,
and many museums have
excellent indigenous galleries. Numerous Aboriginal
cultural centers—from the
Brambuk Cultural Centre
in Victoria's Grampians
National Park to the excellent
Tjupakai Aboriginal Cultural
Park in Cairns—offer interesting educational insights.

Australians of Aboriginal heritage

# Watarrka National Park

Watarrka National Park (formerly Kings Canyon) contains the deepest and most spectacular gorge in central Australia, with rocky pools, palms, and beehive-shaped outcrops that call to mind the Bungle Bungles (see pp. 236–237). The park has some superb walking trails, both around the rim of the canyon and up the gorge.

Visitors on the rim of the 310-foot-high (95 m) walls of Watarrka

**Watarrka
National Park**

🄰 183 B2

**Visitor Information**

✉ South Stuart
Hwy. (3 miles/
4.5 km S of Alice
Springs)

☎ (08) 8951 8211

This desert canyon has been virtually inaccessible until recent years, although it is only about 150 miles (240 km) southwest of Alice Springs. Even in the early 1990s getting here meant traveling a rough dirt track, and facilities were few. That changed with the building of the **Kings Canyon Resort** *(tel (08) 8296 8010)*. A paved highway now links Kings Canyon with Yulara Resort (see p. 206).

Two major walking trails both begin at the parking lot by the park entrance. The **Canyon Walk** is a three-hour hike that winds around the rim of the canyon, through a maze of rocky outcrops and the palm-filled Garden of Eden. Very different is the hour-long **Kings Creek Walk,** a scramble up the narrow gorge, with its boulders and ghost gums, to the idyllic pool and waterfall at its head. ■

Australia's wild west, a colorful blend of frontier styles and famous for its deep karri forests and shining capital city of Perth

# Western Australia

Introduction & Map   212–213

Perth   214–216

Experience: Day-tripping from
   Perth   216

Fremantle   217–218

Experience: Cooking Australia   218

New Norcia   219

Rottnest Island   220–221

Feature: Wildflowers   222–223

The Southwest   224–225

Margaret River   226–227

Shark Bay   228–229

Ningaloo Marine Park   230–231

Experience: Swim with Whale
   Sharks   231

Broome   232–233

Experience: Camel Treks   233

The Kimberley   234–235

Purnululu (Bungle Bungle)
   National Park   236–237

An Australian Bottlebrush wildflower

Gibb River Road Drive   238–239

Kalgoorlie-Boulder   240–241

Experience: Outback Australia   242

Eyre Highway & the Nullarbor
   Plain   243–248

Experience: For the Birds   245

Hotels & Restaurants   378–379

# Western Australia

The fortune-seeking Dutch navigators who sailed along Western Australia's coasts early in the 17th century did not suspect that behind a mask of low, flat, sunburned scrub lay one of the world's greatest mineralized zones. They merely mapped the coast and moved on. So, too, did English buccaneer William Dampier, when he visited in 1688 and 1699. It was almost a century before any European expressed interest in the place.

France laid claim to this dry, barren land in 1779, but interest wasn't high enough to establish a colony. By the mid-1820s, Britain had claimed the land and set up a colony near present-day Albany. However, because of its remoteness, vast size, and inhospitable deserts, Western Australia was the slowest of the colonies to develop. Not until the gold rushes of the 1880s and '90s did the colony begin to prosper. Even so, it retained its provincial, frontier atmosphere.

It is still a long, desolate hike across the continent to Perth, one of the world's most isolated cities. The enormous empty distances around the state mean that visitors to Western Australia have to give some thought and planning to where they want to go. This state covers almost a million square miles (2.6 million sq km)—one third of the entire continent—yet has only 10 percent of Australia's population.

The majority of Western Australia's 2.1 million inhabitants live within 50 miles (80 km) of Perth, the state's capital. Almost all the rest live along the coast. With its parks and gardens, dry, sunny Mediterranean climate, and yachtie Fremantle nearby, easygoing Perth is a bit like a nautical version of Adelaide.

The southwest corner of the state is a green jewel, with forests of majestic karri and jarrah trees, fabulous caves, and some of Australia's finest surfing beaches. The small but prestigious wine region around Margaret River, 150 miles (240 km) south of Perth, is rapidly gaining a following among connoisseurs. Albany, the oldest settlement in Western Australia, is a fine old whaling port lying close to the dramatic wildflower-covered peaks of the Stirling Range.

## NOT TO BE MISSED:

Historic Fremantle **217–218**

Spending time with the quokkas on sunny Rottnest Island **221**

The wineries of Margaret River **227**

The dolphins at Monkey Mia **229**

Swimming with the whale sharks on Ningaloo Reef **231**

Camel trekking on Cable Beach **233**

The stunning sandstone mounds of Purnululu National Park **236–237**

Driving through the Kimberley on the Gibb River Road **238–239**

A wheat belt surrounds Perth. Beyond it, to the east, are the goldfields and the brawling, redneck mining town of Kalgoorlie. Still farther out lies the empty, waterless waste known as the Nullarbor Plain, stretching more than 500 miles (800 km) to the South Australian border. It is crossed by the lonely Eyre Highway and the Indian-Pacific Railway.

The northern part of the state is rugged wilderness, leavened with scattered mining settlements, cattle stations, old pearling ports, and Aboriginal communities. Some of its most dramatic scenery—for example, the gorges in the Pilbara—is too remote for most visitors. Other places, such as the pearling port of Broome, the wilderness of the Kimberley, the otherworldly Purnululu (Bungle Bungle), and the beach at Monkey Mia have developed a must-see cachet despite their isolation. ■

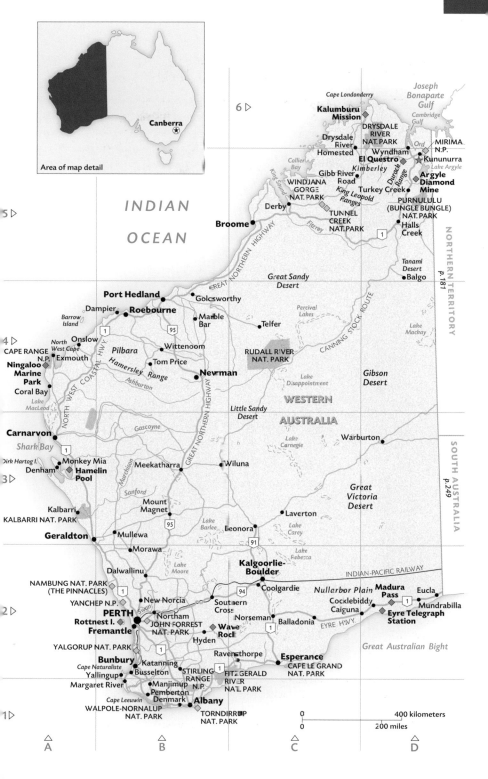

Area of map detail

Canberra

INDIAN

OCEAN

*Joseph*
*Bonaparte*
*Gulf*

6 ▷

*Cape Londonderry*    *Cambridge*
*Gulf*

**Kalumburu**
**Mission**

Drysdale
River
Homestead

DRYSDALE
RIVER
NAT. PARK

*Ord*    MIRIMA
N.P.

Wyndham    Kununurra

**El Questro**    *Kimberley*    *Lake Argyle*

*Collier*
*Bay*    Gibb River
Road    **Argyle**
**Diamond**
**Mine**

*King Sound*    WINDJANA    *King Leopold*    Turkey Creek
GORGE    *Ranges*
NAT. PARK

Derby    TUNNEL
CREEK
NAT. PARK    PURNULULU
(BUNGLE BUNGLE)
NAT. PARK

5 ▷    **Broome**    *Fitzroy*    Halls
Creek

*Tanami*
*Desert*

*Great Sandy*
*Desert*    •Balgo

Goldsworthy

**Port Hedland**    *Percival*
*Lakes*    *Lake*
*Mackay*

Dampier    **Roebourne**    Marble
Bar

*Barrow*
*Island*    Onslow    Wittenoom    •Telfer

4 ▷    *North*
CAPE RANGE    *West Cape*
N.P.    Exmouth    *Pilbara*    Tom Price    RUDALL RIVER
NAT. PARK    *Gibson*
*Desert*

**Ningaloo**
**Marine**
**Park**    *Hamersley*
*Range*    **Newman**    *Lake*
*Disappointment*

Coral Bay    *Ashburton*

*Lake*
*MacLeod*    WESTERN

**Carnarvon**    *Gascoyne*    AUSTRALIA

*Shark Bay*    *Little Sandy*
*Desert*    •Warburton

*Dirk Hartog I.*    Monkey Mia    *Lake*
*Carnegie*

Denham    **Hamelin**
**Pool**    Meekatharra    •Wiluna

3 ▷    *Murchison*    *Great*
*Victoria*
*Desert*

*Sanford*

Kalbarri    Mount
Magnet    •Laverton

KALBARRI NAT. PARK    *Lake*
*Barlee*    Leonora    *Lake*
*Carey*

**Geraldton**    •Mullewa    *Lake*
*Rebecca*

Morawa    INDIAN-PACIFIC RAILWAY

*Lake*
*Moore*    **Kalgoorlie-**
**Boulder**

Dalwallinu    Coolgardie    *Nullarbor Plain*    **Madura**
**Pass**    Eucla

NAMBUNG NAT. PARK
(THE PINNACLES)    New Norcia    Southern
Cross    Cocklebiddy    Mundrabilla

2 ▷    YANCHEP N.P.    Caiguna    **Eyre Telegraph**
**Station**

**PERTH**    Northam    Norseman    Balladonia

**Rottnest I.**    JOHN FORREST
**Fremantle**    NAT. PARK    **Wave**
**Rock**    *EYRE HWY*

YALGORUP NAT. PARK    Hyden    *Great Australian Bight*

Ravensthorpe

**Bunbury**    Katanning    **Esperance**

*Cape Naturaliste*    Busselton    STIRLING    FITZGERALD    CAPE LE GRAND
Yallingup    RANGE    RIVER    NAT. PARK

Margaret River    Manjimup    N.P.    NAT. PARK

Pemberton

*Cape Leeuwin*    Denmark    **Albany**

1 ▷    WALPOLE-NORNALUP
NAT. PARK    TORNDIRRUP
NAT. PARK

NORTHERN TERRITORY *p.181*

SOUTH AUSTRALIA *p.249*

0                    400 kilometers
0          200 miles

A          B          C          D

# Perth

In the 1980s, Perth was the base of high-rolling entrepreneurs whose dubious deals and shenanigans became known collectively as W. A. Inc. The music stopped after the stock market crash in 1987, but the city recovered to ride an even bigger boom, this time without the scandals, driven by massive mining exports to China and elsewhere. Today, mining dollars fund a perpetual building frenzy, the skyline eternally decked with cranes.

**Perth**

⚠ 213 B2

**Western Australia Tourist Centre**

✉ Corner of Wellington Place & Forrest Place

☎ 1-300 361 351

Perth is a city of 1.6 million inhabitants, with a futuristic skyline overlooking the Swan River and a Mediterranean lifestyle. It is frequently described as the loneliest city in the world. Adelaide, the nearest comparable Australian city, is almost 1,500 miles (2,400 km) away, and Canberra is more distant than the Indonesian capital of Jakarta. Perth's isolation has shaped the city's history and created a spirit

**INSIDER TIP:**

**Getting around Perth is easy with the free CAT buses, which run three routes around the city center. The tourist office carries maps.**

—PETER TURNER
*National Geographic author*

of independence among Western Australians, who occasionally talk of seceding from the rest of the country.

Perth was founded by Capt. James Stirling on August 12, 1829, as the Swan River Settlement. It had an inauspicious beginning. The idea was that the colony would be made up entirely of free

settlers, but when word passed around that the isolated settlement was surrounded by swamps and mudflats humming with mosquitoes, migration slowed

to a trickle. By 1850, a chronic labor shortage saw the colonists abandon their lofty ambitions and start importing convict laborers. Many of the city's grandest buildings—the **Town Hall, Supreme Court Buildings,** and **Government House**—were built by convict labor. In 1856, Perth was proclaimed a city. Gold strikes in the 1890s caused the population to jump 700 percent and sparked a construction boom. Unfortunately, most of Perth's grand Victorian buildings were demolished during the 1960s, '70s, and '80s to make way for the skyscrapers that dominate the city today.

Finding your way around Perth is fairly easy. The compact city is set out along the banks of the Swan River, which is its southern boundary. The **Perth Tram** (www.perthtram.com.au, $$$)—it's actually a bus—takes visitors to Perth's major attractions. The 90-minute tours depart from 565 Hay Street.

**Transperth (Perth transportation)**

✉ Plaza Arcade, off Hay St. Mall

☎ 13 62 13

🕒 Closed Sun.

**www.transperth.wa.gov.au**

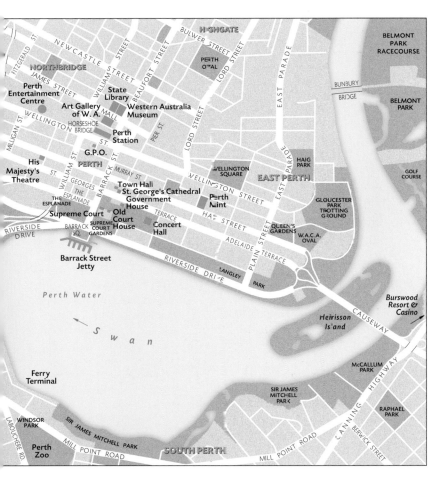

## Western Australian Museum

Francis St., Northbridge

(08) 9427 2700

www.museum.wa.gov.au

## Art Gallery of Western Australia

James St., Northbridge

(08) 9492 6622

www.artgallery.wa.gov.au

## Botanic Garden

Kings Park

(08) 9480 3634

Free guided tours

www.bgpa.gov.au

Perth's main shopping and tourist thoroughfares are the Hay Street and Murray Street pedestrian malls, which are linked by modern arcades and department stores. St. Georges Terrace is where the mining and oil companies have their headquarters. **Parliament House** is at the western end of this street, and you can tour the building when Parliament is not sitting.

Perth's railroad lines mark the northern boundary of the city. William Street arches over the downtown railway station via the Horseshoe Bridge and leads into raffish Northbridge, with its cafés, pubs, nightclubs, and bistros. The state art gallery and museum are on this side of the tracks as well. The **Western Australian Museum** includes displays on Aboriginal culture, the marine life of the Western Australian coast, and meteorites (many have been found in the outback). The **Art**

**Gallery of Western Australia** has collections of Australian, Pacific, and European art.

## Green Perth

In Perth's early days, steep Mount Eliza was regarded as a barrier to progress, and the city grew around it. As a result, Perth now has a beautiful 2,500-acre (1,013 ha) park on its western edge. This is **Kings Park,** one of Perth's most scenic attractions. Within it is the 40-acre (16 ha) **Botanic Garden** with more than 2,500 different Western Australian plants. The park's noisy flocks of birds and dazzling display of native wildflowers in spring are pleasing reminders that Perth is perched on the edge of the outback. Kings Park and much of the Swan River foreshore have excellent bicycle trails. Bikes can be rented in Kings Park at Koala Bicycle Hire (tel (08) 9321 3061).

The **Swan River** is the focus of the city, and it is set off by the green of Langley Park and the Esplanade. Although Perth is about 12 miles (19 km) inland, the river here is almost three-quarters of a mile (1.25 km) wide. Ferries from **Barrack Street jetty** (off the Esplanade) go to **Fremantle** (see pp. 217–18) and **Rottnest Island** (see pp. 220–21). The Narrows Bridge (and ferries from Barrack Street) cross to South Perth, where the **Perth Zoo** (20 Labouchere Road, tel (08) 9474 3551, $$) is set on well-landscaped grounds. A mile or so upstream, **Burswood Resort & Casino** (see p. 377) is a rollicking 1980s memento. ■

---

## EXPERIENCE: Day-tripping from Perth

Popular excursions from Perth and Fremantle include **Rottnest Island** (see pp. 220–221). Farther afield, but still an easy day trip, is **New Norcia** (see p. 219). The Pinnacles in **Nambung National Park** are 156 miles (251 km) north along the coast. Here, hundreds of limestone pillars, from a few inches to 15 feet (5 m) high, stick up from the desert floor. Once thought to be fossilized trees, they are now considered the result of wind erosion. **Wave Rock** (see p. 225) can be visited in a day (barely), but allow longer for the southwest (see pp. 224–225) and **Margaret River** (see pp. 226–227).

# Fremantle

A touch of Western Australia's colonial maritime flavor has survived in Fremantle, despite the extensive renovations associated with Australia's unsuccessful defense of the America's Cup in 1987. An old working-class dockyard city, it lies about 12 miles (19 km) west of Perth, where the Swan River enters the Indian Ocean.

Elegant colonial streetscapes make Fremantle one of Australia's most fascinating port cities.

Although engulfed by Perth's sprawl over the years, Fremantle has retained enough of its identity to keep it from becoming just another suburb. It was founded in 1829, a few weeks before Perth, and has more local color and sense of history, and a far more relaxed atmosphere, than its busier neighbor.

Fremantle was an almost useless port until 1890, when a brilliant engineer named Charles O'Conner blasted out a rocky bar and built an artificial harbor to accommodate larger trading vessels. Today a statue of O'Conner gazes out over his creation. Although known as a smart seaside town, Fremantle is still a working port with more than 2 miles (3 km) of docks.

This blue-collar city of 26,000 exudes a sort of raffishness—but that's nothing new. This is where Australia's only recorded formal duel took place, in 1832. But for the most part, Fremantle is a leisurely, sun-splashed town in which to stroll, take in the galleries and old buildings, sip cappuccino in the cafés on **South Terrace**, and unwind. On the weekends, **Fremantle Markets**, on South

**Fremantle**
🅰 213 B2
**Visitor Information**
✉ King Sq.
☎ (08) 9431 7878

# EXPERIENCE: Cooking Australia

Food has become a national obsession in Australia. The barbie might still be king, but the prawns are doused in wine, and all manner of Asian and Mediterranean flavors abound. Celebrity chefs are worshiped, reality TV cooking shows top the ratings, and cooking classes have popped up everywhere.

At **Faraway Bay** resort (tel (08) 9169 1214, www.farawaybay.com.au), in Western Australia's Kimberley region, cooking classes focus on local produce. In the Margaret River region, celeb chef Tony Howell runs cooking classes at the **Cape Lodge** hotel (tel (08) 9755 6311, www.capelodge.com.au).

In Sydney, the **Sydney Seafood School** (tel (02) 9004 1111, www.sydneyfish market.com.au) is a great place to try your hand at cooking Aussie-style.

**Simon Johnson** (tel (02) 9552 2522, www.simon johnson.com.au), a gourmet food store, has popular classes on food and wine.

In Queensland, the **Spirit House** (tel (07) 5446 8977, www.spirithouse .au) teaches Thai cooking in a lovely rain forest garden setting at Noosa. At **Mondo Organics** (tel (07) 3844 1132, www.mondo-organics.com.au), a Brisbane restaurant, courses emphasize healthy cooking.

In Melbourne, **Tony Tan** (tel (03) 9827 7347,

www.tonytan.com.au) emphasizes Asian food, but big-name guest chefs from around the country cover all styles. Teeming with fresh produce, **Queen Victoria Market** (tel (03) 9320 5822, www.qvm.com .au) has food and tasting tours as well as classes.

Wine leader South Australia also fancies itself a food capital. **Chapel Hill Winery Retreat** (tel (08) 8323 9182, www.chapel hillwine.com.au) combines cooking classes with wine at a McLaren Vale winery.

---

## Fremantle Prison

✉ 1 The Terrace
☎ (08) 9336 9200

**www.fremantle prison.com.au**

## Western Australian Maritime Museum

✉ Victoria Quay (Shipwreck Galleries on Cliff St.)
☎ (08) 9431 8444
🕐 Closed Wed.

**www.museum .wa.gov.au/ maritime/**

## Fremantle History Museum

✉ 11 Finnerty St.
☎ (08) 9430 7966

Terrace at the corner of Henderson Street, is a colorful, noisy bazaar where you can buy crafts, clothes, food, and other items. The town has a number of good restaurants and, as you might expect, the seafood is excellent. Sardines are a local specialty. The Fremantle Tram makes a 45-minute loop through the city from the Town Hall, near the intersection of High and Adelaide Streets.

City sights include the 12-sided **Round House** (High St.), built in 1831 and used as a jail. The imposing **Fremantle Prison** has gruesome reminders of its long history from early convict days until it was decommissioned in 1991. Visit the small museum and shop for free. Tours ($$) go on the half hour.

The **Western Australian Maritime Museum,** near the Round House, tells the story of seamanship along the Western Australian coast from the early days of the Dutch East India Company through the era of clipper ships and whalers. Pride of place goes to the remains of the *Batavia,* wrecked off the coast near Geraldton in 1629 (see p. 228).

The sturdy-looking **Fremantle History Museum,** which was originally designed as the colony's lunatic asylum, was built by convicts in the 1860s. It has a fine collection of early Western Australian art and displays about the Dutch East India Company's role in exploring "New Holland" in the 17th century. ■

# New Norcia

Established by Spanish monks in 1846, the Benedictine mission at New Norcia makes a fascinating—and unusual—day trip from Perth. Its blend of Byzantine, Gothic, and classical Spanish architecture is an exotic contrast to the miles of wheat fields and Australian scrub around it.

The mission's purpose was to convert Aborigines to Christianity, teach them European-style agriculture, and rescue them from persecution. The monastery's gentle approach worked well with the Aborigines, producing a harmonious agricultural community in the 19th century. The flour mill opened here in 1879 is still going, the oldest operating mill in Western Australia. By the turn of the century, the emphasis turned to education of European children. These days it is a meditative community, known for its museum and fine art gallery.

The monks have succeeded in balancing the needs of a contemplative religious community with those of a popular tourist attraction. Visitors can tour the **chapel,** take accommodations in old convent and college buildings, and browse in shops that sell olive oil pressed at the community. A more monastic-style retreat can be found at the **Benedictine Abbey Guesthouse.** The museum and art gallery have priceless collections of religious art and manuscripts. Many of the pieces were given by Spain's Queen Isabella II (r. 1833–1870). A signposted heritage walk goes through the grounds of the monastery, starting just outside the museum, or take a two-hour guided walk.

The 80-mile (129 km) drive to New Norcia on the Great Northern Highway is particularly rewarding in spring, when Western Australia's wildflowers are in bloom (see p. 222). The highway north of New Norcia rambles through the towns of Dalwallinu, Morawa, and Mullewa, all part of the **Wildflower Way,** which runs through a carpet of foxgloves, everlastings, and wattles. ■

**New Norcia**
A 213 B2
**Visitor Information**
☎ (08) 9654 8056
§ $$

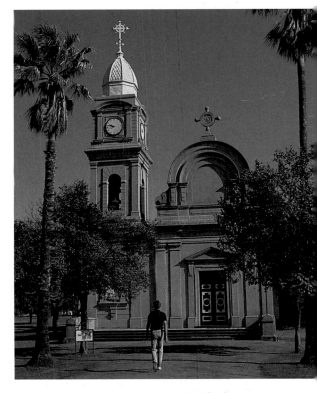

The architecture at New Norcia is a unique mix of styles.

# Rottnest Island

Although he described it as a terrestrial paradise, Dutch mariner Willem de Vlamingh clearly did not have tourism marketing in mind when he visited this little island just off the southern coast of New Holland in 1696 and named it Rottnest ("rat's nest," in Dutch). The "giant rats" he saw are actually quokkas, smallish cousins to wallabies—not rats at all. He pegged the scenery correctly, though.

Bathurst's lighthouse guards the coastline on Rottnest Island's northern flank.

**Rottnest Island**
🏕 213 B2
**Visitor Information**
✉ Ferry Landing, Thompson Bay
☎ (08) 9372 9732
**www.rottnestisland .com**

Rottnest Island is low and sandy, surrounded by turquoise waters with sparkling white beaches, and cooled by sea breezes. It has been a getaway for Perth's well-to-do population since the mid-19th century. Construction of Governor's Cottage, a summer retreat for the governor of Western Australia, was completed here in 1864. The building opened to tourists in 1917, and it was converted into the Rottnest Hotel in 1953.

The peaceful little island is about 10 miles (16 km) off the coast from Fremantle. Cars are not permitted, but wonderful bicycle and walking trails are available (you can rent bicycles on the

**INSIDER TIP:**

While the quokkas ambling around Rottnest Island's visitor center are friendly to the point of being brazen, you'll need to stay alert to spot them on the rest of the island, as they are much shyer in the wild.

—LARRY PORGES
*National Geographic editor*

island), and buses run around the island. Or you can take a tour. The island is only 7 miles (11 km) long and 3 miles (5 km) across at its widest. The main settlement is at **Thompson Bay.** The visitor center is here, next to the ferry landing. You can pick up brochures on the island's activities and arrange walking tours of the heritage buildings.

### Island Activities

Visitors come here to unwind, mostly on day trips from Perth, though the island has camping, cabins, houses to rent, and other accommodations. Sprawling on the beach is the single most popular activity, although snorkeling on some of the world's southernmost coral is also big. There are dive shops on the island, a dive and snorkeling trail on **Pocillopora Reef,** just south of the island, and glass-bottom tour boats. A historic train runs 5 miles (8 km) from Thompson Bay to the **Oliver Hill Battery,** in the center of the island, which was the site of gun emplacements in World War II. There are spectacular views from **Vlamingh's Lookout,** just south of the town.

### Getting to Rottnest Island

Regular ferries run from both Fremantle and Perth, or you can fly here on the Rottnest Air Taxi *(tel (08) 9292 5027)* from Perth's Jandakot airport. This is a hugely popular place—more than 400,000 people visit every year—and it can be very crowded on sunny weekends. Be sure to make a reservation if you plan to stay on the island. ∎

### Quokkas

Once found throughout the southwest of Western Australia, the quokka is now confined to a small protected colony on the mainland and on a few islands, notably Rottnest Island, which has the largest population of quokkas—around 10,000.

The size of a cat and somewhat similar in appearance to a wallaby, the cute quokka is the only member of the genus *Setonix.* Like other marsupials, it carries its young in its pouch.

Many quokkas show no fear of humans. You'll see plenty of them in Thompson Bay, often begging for food, but it is important not to feed them. Quokkas can fall very ill eating foods such as bread, potato chips, and meat.

# Wildflowers

Spring (Oct.–Nov.) is a magical time to visit Western Australia. More than 7,000 species of wildflowers burst into life, carpeting the deserts, plains, and mountains in a kaleidoscopic blaze of color. The rich golds of the feather flowers blend with the reds and pinks of boronias, and red-and-yellow clumps of blossoms glow on the banksia trees. Most of the species are unique to Western Australia, a legacy of the area's long periods of isolation.

**Blushing mountain bells,** *Darwinia lejostyla*

While you are still in Perth, you can get a taste of what lies over the horizon by viewing the brilliant displays of wildflowers in Kings Park between August and October. Then head into the deserts, the wheat belt, or the Stirling Range in the mountainous southwest. Out in these places, the flowering trees, bushes, and shrubs run riot. Jarrah forests, like those in John Forrest National Park, only 15 miles (24 km) east of the city, are particularly rich. Red and green kangaroo paws, blue leschenaultia, and pink calytrix are the most prominent, but there are hundreds of other varieties. Yanchep National Park, about 30 miles (48 km) north of Perth, is another good bet.

Or you can follow the Great Northern Highway 100 miles (160 km) northeast of Perth to the wheat-belt town of Dalwallinu, then drive along the Wildflower Way another 150 miles (240 km) to Mullewa. For much of

this drive, the roadside will be carpeted by wildflowers, particularly a type known as everlastings, whose petals endure after the flower itself has died. Farther north, Kalbarri National Park is vibrant with flowering banksia, grevillea, and melaleuca, and the forest floor is littered with flowering twine rushes and sedges. This beautiful coastal park, at the mouth of the ancient Murchison River, is famed for its magnificent gorges and sweeping coastal views—the spring wildflower display only gilds the lily, so to speak.

Some of the finest displays can be found in the southwest corner of the state. The jagged peaks of Stirling Range National Park are rich with pink, red, and gold flowers beautifully offset by bald granite. More than 50 species of orchid are found in the karri forests, and some of the *Dryandras* and species of *Darwinia* grow noplace else.

The heaths at Torndirrup National Park and Walpole-Nornalup National Park, near the windswept coast of Albany, become a carpet of flowers each spring and seem to illuminate nearby dunes and granite outcrops. Fitzgerald River National Park, between Albany and Esperance, harbors more than 2,000 species of flowering plants. Of these, about 80 or so species, including oddities such as the flame orange royal hakea and the delicate pink quaalup bell, are found nowhere else in the world. In 1978, this spectacular park was declared a World Biosphere Reserve by UNESCO.

The Western Australia Tourist Centre in Perth (see p. 214) has a pamphlet on the state's wildflower trails. Most bookstores have illustrated guides to the myriad species and varieties you can see in the state. Remember that,

**Mulla mullas among the dunes of the Great Sandy Desert**

tempting as it may be to pluck a few beauties, Western Australia's wildflowers are protected under the Native Flora Protection Act. Leave them for others to enjoy.

There are, however, increasing numbers of commercial wildflower farms around Australia—particularly Western Australia—as locals begin to capitalize on the growing international interest in Australian flowers. Australia now exports millions of dollars' worth of wildflowers, such as kangaroo paw and Geraldton wax flowers, each year.

# The Southwest

One of the most beautiful pockets of forest in Australia is in the southwest corner of Western Australia. This region has towering forests of karri and jarrah trees, gentle dairy country, rocky coasts, and the jagged expanse of the Stirling Range that riot with wildflowers every spring.

The Bicentennial Tree offers a spectacular view over the towering karri forests near Pemberton.

A nice tour of the area can be had by driving the 150 miles (240 km) along the coast south of Perth to the lovely Margaret River wine and surf region. Meander another 200 miles (320 km) farther through the forests to the historic whaling port of Albany.

**Nannup, Manjimup,** and **Pemberton** are pleasant old timber towns, surrounded by forests of karri and jarrah trees. The pale-barked karri are among the world's tallest trees and can reach more than 300 feet (90 m) in height. What you don't see when you drive through these ostensibly virgin forests is the clear-cutting that goes on out of sight. For more than a century, these ancient, majestic giants were subject to wholesale logging—a practice that largely came to an end in 2001 after a long and bitter public debate between industry forces and environmentalists, with a number of local celebrities becoming involved (such as the Booker Prize–winning author Tim Winton; see sidebar p. 225).

One of the most spectacular trees is the **Gloucester Tree,** north of Pemberton. If you have the nerve, you can make the exposed climb almost 200 feet (60 m) up its trunk into what is said to be the world's highest treetop fire lookout.

The truly scary climb follows 153 spiraling rungs around the trunk. Not many people try to reach the top, but the view is remarkable. The tree was 50 feet (15 m) higher until 1947, when the top was lopped off to make way for the platform. Pemberton claims the tallest karri tree ever felled: a 343-foot (105 m) titan brought down in the last century. South of Pemberton, you can also climb the **Bicentennial Tree,** even higher at 246 feet (75 m) but without the crowds.

Seventy miles (113 km) southeast of Pemberton is the **Valley of the Giants,** in Walpole National Forest, part of **Walpole-Nornalup National Park** near the town of **Denmark.** The forest is filled with karri trees. Several species of eucalyptus grow here and nowhere else, including rare red, yellow, and Rates tingle trees, and the red flowering gum. Walking trails here include the **Tree Top Walk,** a swaying wooden walkway (wheelchair accessible) through the canopy in the Valley of the Giants.

**Albany** is where the British laid claim to the western half of New Holland on Christmas Day in 1826. Soon this became a bustling whaling station, with French, American, and Australian whalers putting in here. Albany was Australia's last whaling port, ceasing operations in 1978. The old Whaling Station, about 15 miles (24 km) to the southeast, is now **Whale World** (*Frenchman's Bay Rd., tel (08) 9844 4021, www .whaleworld.org, $$*), a museum that gives an account of the days when around 850 whales were killed each season in these waters. Happily the whales have begun returning, and southern right whales are often seen from the cliffs along the shore.

Albany itself, a pretty town of 32,000, having a vaguely New England–like, nautical feel, is one of Western Australia's most popular holiday destinations. It has a rugged coast, and the dramatic **Stirling Range** rises abruptly about 40 miles (65 km) northeast.

Another popular sight is **Wave Rock,** which is located about 220 miles (350 km) east of Perth, near the wheat-farming town of Hyden. It is a block of granite, sculpted by three billion years of wind and rain to a perfect surfer's wave about 50 feet (15 m) high. ■

### Denmark
**▲** 213 B1

**Visitor Information**
- ✉ Strickland St.
- ☎ (08) 9848 2055

### Albany
**▲** 213 B1

**Visitor Information**
- ✉ Proudlove Parade
- ☎ (08) 9841 1088

---

## Tim Winton

One of Australia's best-loved authors, Tim Winton (1960– ), born in Perth and raised in Albany, celebrates Western Australian landscapes in his novels. The southwest features especially strongly in his works, which give a great sense of place if you are looking for a read while in the region.

Winton's latest novel, *Breath* (2008), is set in the fictional southwest logging town of Sawyer and is a 1970s coming-of-age tale, told through flashbacks, about teenage surfers who take increasing risks to escape their ordinary lives. *Shallows* (1984) is based in Angelus (read Albany), where whalers and conservationists confront each other. His best known book, *Cloudstreet* (1991), is a modern Australian classic chronicling the lives of working-class families in the suburbs of Perth.

# Margaret River

Margaret River is one of Western Australia's delights, an area of world-class wineries, karri forests, wildflowers, spectacular caves, and some of Australia's best surf beaches, only 150 miles (240 km) south of Perth. The region stretches about 60 miles (100 km) from Cape Naturaliste to Cape Leeuwin at the southwest tip of Australia, but skilled marketing has made the centrally located village of Margaret River the buzzword for the area.

**Margaret River**
🅰 213 B1
**Visitor Information**
✉ 100 Bussell Hwy.
☎ (08) 9780 5911

The past 30 years have seen this dairy-farming area discovered by successive waves of hippies, surfers, upscale winemakers, artists, and urbanites seeking an alternative lifestyle. Most recently it has become a weekend getaway for Perth's well-to-do. It is still a major surfing hangout, because the beaches between Cape Leeuwin and Cape Naturaliste have some of the most powerful breaks in Australia.

Surfing blurs the social lines here. In any one of the beach parking lots you may see late-model Mercedes parked beside impossibly battered 1960s-vintage Kombi vans. Everybody looks the same in a wetsuit. Basically two kinds of people live here: surfers and windsurfers. Those with boards go out first thing in the morning, and those with sails head out in the afternoon. Life's that simple and sunny.

The spectacular coast is a lovely drive. Just follow the Bussell Highway south out of Perth, 140 miles (225 km) or so through the beach towns of Mandurah, Bunbury, and Busselton, and from there onto the scenic Caves Road. On the way south, you might stop at **Bunbury** for a swim with dolphins. A pod usually swims into the harbor once a day (they are lured there with daily feedings). They seem happy to interact with swimmers. A leaflet from the Bunbury Information Centre explains the etiquette and ethics of contact with dolphins.

The turnoff to Caves Road is 5 miles (8 km) west of Busselton and takes you to the pleasant seaside town of **Dunsborough.**

Scenery along the coast near Yallingup is a pleasing mix of cliffs and sheltered bays.

A worthwhile detour from here is the 8-mile (13 km) excursion down the Cape Naturaliste Road to the historic **lighthouse** *(tel (08) 9755 3955, tours daily, $$)* on Cape Naturaliste and its sweeping views of the cape and Geographe Bay. In the winter, this is a good spot for seeing humpback and southern right whales.

Five miles (8 km) farther along, the Caves Road from Dunsborough brings you to **Yallingup,** where huge Indian Ocean surf crashes almost constantly onto the beach. Just before Yallingup, **Ngili Cave** is the area's most renowned cave, popular with tourists since 1899 and offering a range of expensive tours. The Caves House Hotel *(Caves Rd., tel (08) 9755 2131)* opened in 1905. The **Gunyulgup Galleries** represent a number of local craftspeople and sell fine pottery, paintings, and furniture made from prized jarrah wood.

## Wineries

Wineries can be found all along scenic Caves Road as it winds beside the coast. Although the wine region is generically called Margaret River, most of the wineries are actually concentrated in a knot about 10 miles (16 km) south of Yallingup. *The Margaret River Regional Vineyard Guide,* available at local visitor information offices, is your best guide.

The wines from Margaret River wineries tend to be fairly expensive compared with those of Australia's other premier wine districts, but there's no doubt about the quality. Names to look for include Cape Mentelle, Leeuwin Estate, Voyager, Vasse Felix, and Evans & Tate. Leeuwin Estate, which is just west of Margaret River, has particularly lovely grounds. Most of the wineries give free tastings. **Margaret River** is a funky village of artists, surfers, and aging hippies about 3 miles (5 km) off Caves Road.

## Caves

Because some of the most spectacular scenery south of Margaret River is underground, the scenic route through the region is called Caves Road. The limestone that helps make this a superb wine region is riddled with more than 150 caves The best is **Jewel Cave,** about 25 miles (40 km) south of Margaret River, with its baroque formations and needle-like helictites. Fossilized remains of Tasmanian tigers have been found in nearby **Moondyne Cave** *(-$)*, which is unlit. **Lake Cave,** about 15 miles (24 km) south of Margaret River, has a Tolkienesque entrance. Despite its name, **Mammoth Cave,** close to Lake Cave, is the least interesting. Guided tours are the only way to view these caves; obtain information from the **Cave Works Interpretive Centre** *(Lake Cave, Caves Rd., tel (08) 9757 7411).*

**Augusta** is an old timber port. If you continue south another 5 miles (8 km), you'll come to **Cape Leeuwin** lighthouse. Between May and September, the cape is good for whale-watching. It often feels like the last place on Earth, particularly when the sky is dark and threatening. ∎

**Bunbury**
🅰 213 B2
**Visitor Information**
✉ Carmody Place
☎ (08) 9792 7205

**Ngili Cave**
✉ Caves Rd.
☎ (08) 9755 2152
💲 $$–$$$$$

# Shark Bay

Sheltered by the Peron Peninsula and a chain of desolate islands, Shark Bay is a World Heritage site 450 lonely miles (725 km) north of Perth. It has ancient life-forms and some of Australia's oldest European history. The Dutch navigator Dirk Hartog landed here in 1616 on the island that now bears his name.

Winter mornings are generally the best time to encounter dolphins at Monkey Mia. As many as a dozen of these marine mammals have been recorded here at one time.

**Shark Bay**

🅰 213 A3

**Visitor Information**

✉ Knight Terrace, Denham

☎ (08) 9948 1590

Shark Bay is best known today for the bottlenose dolphins that swim in the shallows to play with humans. The drive from Perth, on the Northwest Coastal Highway through the seaport of **Geraldton,** is bleak and windy, and in summer searingly hot. The coastline north of Geraldton was the scene of several

Dutch shipwrecks in the 17th and 18th centuries, including the *Batavia* in 1629. The impressive **WA Museum Geraldton** has relics and other exhibits.

**Kalbarri National Park** is a worthwhile detour on the trek north. The turnoff is about 60 miles (96 km) north of Geraldton on the Northwest Coastal

Highway. The Murchison River runs through a spectacular series of deeply hewed gorges before it reaches the coast at Kalbarri, and the national park includes both gorges and coast. It is particularly beautiful in spring, when the wildflowers are in bloom.

## Visiting Shark Bay

The turnoff to Shark Bay is about 110 miles (177 km) farther north on the Northwest Coastal Highway. The scenery along Shark Bay itself is lovely in an arid, understated way.

The first turn off the road to Shark Bay goes 4 miles (6.4 km) to **Hamelin Pool.** The turquoise waters and the rocky coastline here are lovely, but what makes this place remarkable are the stromatolites, primitive blue-green algae that were one of the first lifeforms on Earth. These living fossils in Hamelin Pool are one of the most readily accessible populations of stromatolites in the world, and their presence was a big factor in giving Shark Bay its World Heritage listing. They thrive here because the sheltered waters are extremely clear and unusually saline. Fascinating as they undoubtedly are to paleontologists, the stromatolites look like blackened chunks of concrete matting. Information is available at the nearby historic **Telegraph Station** (tel (08) 9942 5905).

Past the turnoff to Hamelin Pool, the road runs to Denham along the spectacular **Shell Beach,** a unique 70-mile (112 km) coastline made up of countless shells

packed in some places almost 50 feet (15 m) deep. **Denham,** the most westerly town in Australia, was once a pearling port and has become the main tourist town on the peninsula.

## Monkey Mia

Fifteen miles (24 km) east of Denham is Monkey Mia and its famous beach where dolphins play. The interaction between humans and dolphins began in the early 1960s, when a small pod of dolphins allowed themselves to be petted. As a result of this early interaction, and apparent willingness on the part of the dolphins, a great deal of valuable marine research took place. Then a major tourism

**INSIDER TIP:**

**Although Monkey Mia is a long haul north from Perth, wading among the wild dolphins there is a magical experience most visitors never forget.**

—BARBARA A. NOE
*National Geographic editor*

industry developed. Dolphins are coaxed into the bay with regular feedings, appearing most mornings in the winter months—less frequently in summer—while staff try to keep tourists from doing anything too silly. Sometimes you'll see just a solitary dolphin, and other times you can see a dozen. ∎

**Geraldton**
🅰 213 A3
**Visitor Information**
✉ Corner of Bayly St. & Chapman Rd.
☎ (08) 9921 3999

**WA Museum Geraldton**
✉ Marine Terrace, Geraldton
☎ (08) 9921 5080
🕐 Closed Sun. a.m.

**Kalbarri**
🅰 213 A3
**Visitor Information**
✉ Grey St.
☎ (08) 9937 1104

# Ningaloo Marine Park

Ningaloo Reef is a spectacular, 160-mile (260 km) fringe to the rugged Northwest Cape, some 700 miles (1,125 km) north of Perth. Much shorter than the Great Barrier Reef, it is no less impressive. Unlike its better known cousin, it is easily accessible from shore—never more than 2 miles (3 km) out and in some places only a couple hundred yards. The reef has been designated a national marine park, and the dry hills of the cape form Cape Range National Park.

**Ningaloo Marine Park**
🅰 213 A4

**Coral Bay**
🅰 213 A4

**Visitor Information**
✉ Coral Bay Arcade, Robinson St.
☎ (08) 9942 5988

Getting to Ningaloo Reef from Perth is simple. Drive about 670 miles (1,080 km) north on the Northwest Coastal Highway to the isolated Minilya Roadhouse. From there a paved highway runs north, the length of the North West Cape, 50 miles (80 km) to pretty Coral Bay and another 90 miles (145 km) to Exmouth. Or you can take a Skywest plane *(tel (08) 9478 9999)* from Perth to Learmouth (near Exmouth).

The quiet seaside resort of **Coral Bay** is at the southern end of the reef. It has pretty white beaches and is popular with divers and snorkelers. Glass-bottom boat tours cater to nonswimmers.

## Ningaloo Reef

Ningaloo Reef is Australia's longest continuous fringing coral reef. It is one of only two reefs anywhere in the world on a western coast. Among its rare marine life are dugongs, humpback whales, manta rays, and greenback turtles. But perhaps the most impressive creatures are the whale sharks.

A whale shark and a scuba diver go for a swim along Ningaloo Reef.

The largest fish in the sea, these gentle plankton-eating giants grow up to 60 feet (18 m) long and weigh up to 15 tons. Swimming with the whale sharks and "flying" with the manta rays are becoming popular things for tourists to do.

The waters of **Ningaloo Marine Park** are divided into recreational, general, and sanctuary zones. The sanctuary zones are completely protected, allowing visitors to see these delicate reefs and the cycle of rare marine life. Manta rays are around the peninsula from May to November, and humpback whales pass through in June and July. Turtles lumber

## INSIDER TIP:

**For a real taste of the scorching Western Australian sun, visit Marble Bar, halfway between Ningaloo and Broome. On average, the town hits 100°F (37°C) more than 150 days per year.**

—PETER TURNER
*National Geographic author*

onto the beaches at night, in the summer between November and January, to lay their eggs.

Whale sharks can be observed here from April to the end of July, when the coral spawns and plankton bloom to give the behemoths a big feed. The best way to see them is with one of the specialist

### EXPERIENCE:
### Swim with Whale Sharks

Whale sharks (*Rhincodon typus*) are the world's largest fish, growing up to 60 feet (18 m) in length and weighing more than 15 tons (13.5 tonnes). Every year from April to July, large numbers of them arrive at Ningaloo Reef. Following regulations, snorkeling tours get to within 10 feet (3 m) for the reef's most amazing experience.

Full-day reef snorkeling tours, including lunch and gear, cost from A$365 (U.S. $332). If no whale sharks are sighted, you can go again free the next day, but no refunds are offered. The **Exmouth Visitor Center** handles reservations for Exmouth Dive Centre, King's Ningaloo Reef Tours, Ningaloo Blue Charters, Ningaloo Reef Dreaming, 3 Island Marine, Ningaloo Whaleshark-N-Dive, and Ocean Eco Adventures, all in Exmouth. Coral Bay Adventures, Ningaloo Experience, and Ningaloo Reef Dive operate out of Coral Bay.

charter operators, which send up spotting planes to find them. The experience is expensive but truly unforgettable.

## Exmouth

Exmouth, 90 miles (145 km) farther north up the peninsula, was built in 1967 to service the U.S. Navy's top-secret radio base, which communicated with American nuclear submarines patrolling the Indian Ocean. The Navy no longer operates the base, but the 13 huge transmitters that dominate the town are a charmless legacy of the Cold War. Today, tourism is the main industry, and Exmouth has its share of dive and snorkeling operators and charter boats. ∎

**Exmouth**
◪ 213 A4
**Visitor Information**
✉ Murat Rd.
☎ (08) 9949 1176
**www.exmouthwa
.com.au**

# Broome

Broome is a fascinating old pearling port on Western Australia's remote northwest coast. One of the classiest outback towns, it has a lifestyle as lazy as tropical sin. Its chief attraction is Cable Beach, regarded by aficionados as one of the world's most beautiful beaches. Imagine a 20-mile (32 km) stretch of golden sand almost half a mile (1 km) wide at low tide, offset against a warm, shimmering turquoise sea. All this only 2 miles (3.2 km) from the center of town.

Camel rides along Broome's shoreline are offered in the early morning and at sunset.

**Broome**

⚑ 213 C5

**Visitor Information**

✉ Corner of Broome Hwy. & Bagot Rd.

☎ (08) 9192 2222

**Pearl Luggers**

✉ 31 Dampier Ter.

☎ (08) 9192 2059

🕓 Closed Sun.

💲 $$

**www.pearlluggers .com.au**

English buccaneer William Dampier was the first European known to have landed here, when he was dodging a Spanish fleet in 1699. Almost 200 years passed before anyone realized what treasures lay on the shallow seabeds. The discovery of pearl shells sparked a pearl rush in the 1880s—the new coastal settlement was named for Frederick Broome, then governor of Western Australia.

By 1910, Broome was the world's pearling capital, accounting for more than 80 percent of the world's pearl shell (used to make buttons). The town itself was a brawling, bustling, multicultural mix of Malays, Chinese, Japanese, Filipinos, Timorese, Arabs, Aborigines, and Europeans, with a fleet of more than 400 pearling luggers. The best pearl divers came from Japan, and the 600 graves in the picturesque **Japanese cemetery** on Port Drive, at the edge of town, bear testimony to the dangers they faced. The pearling industry declined during the 1930s, but can be recalled thanks to **Pearl Luggers**—a historical exhibition of Broome's pearling past complete with a few original pearling luggers.

The Japanese bombed Broome in World War II, and the wrecks of a number of Dutch boats sunk in the harbor during the raids can be seen occasionally. One boat was supposedly carrying a secret diamond shipment from Java. Some of the diamonds were recovered, but most were never found. A beachcomber named Jack Palmer was found with some of the diamonds and arrested, but the charges were dropped. After the war, however, Palmer developed a taste for expensive cars. He died in 1958, taking his secret with him.

Modern Broome still has much of the flavor of the old days with its airy bungalows, palm-lined streets, and Chinese roofs. It went through a redevelopment phase in the early 1980s, thanks to Englishman Lord Alistair McAlpine, who built, among other things, the luxurious Cable Beach Club. Economic recession stalled McAlpine's plans, but Broome has bounced back with a tourism boom that sees the population of 14,500 treble in the peak winter tourist season. A host of tours, upmarket accommodations, and direct flights from the capital cities is transforming Broome into a chic resort.

The heart of downtown is so-called **Chinatown** (really only Carnarvon Street and Dampier Terrace), which has old-fashioned trading-post grocery stores, modern boutiques, and cafés. Here, in the hushed elegance of Paspaley's Pearls, you can buy a necklace of perfectly matched Broome pearls—for just A$200,000 (U.S. $177,000).

The quaint **Sun Pictures,** on Carnarvon Street, is reputedly the world's oldest outdoor movie theater. It was built by a pearling captain in 1916 and has barely changed since. You sit in old canvas sling chairs and take in the movie on a screen framed by palm fronds.

**Gantheaume Point,** about 2 miles (3.5 km) west of town on Gantheaume Point Road, has a red sandstone headland, lighthouse, and 130-million-year-old dinosaur tracks that are visible at very low tides. The **Broome Crocodile Park,** on Cable Beach Road, has hundreds of saltwater crocodiles.

## Cable Beach

But Broome's best attraction is still Cable Beach, the place where the first overseas telegraph cable was brought ashore in 1889, linking Australia with Java and London. The beach faces the Indian Ocean rather than the bay. A crowd usually assembles on the grassy knoll overlooking the beach to watch the incredible sunsets. Or you can go for gentle camel rides along the sands (see sidebar below). Don't be in a hurry to leave after the rim of the sun slices below the horizon—the most vibrant colors appear a few minutes later. If you are in Broome at full moon, you can see the Staircase to the Moon, an odd effect caused by reflected moonlight on the tidal flats. It resembles a golden staircase. ■

**Broome Crocodile Park**

⊠ Cable Beach Rd.
☎ (08) 9192 1489
🕐 Closed Nov.– March, & a.m. Sat. & Sun.
💲 $$$

---

**EXPERIENCE:**
# Camel Treks

The classic Broome photo shows a camel train walking along the sands of Cable Beach at sunset. Camel rides are now offered all over the outback—from Alice Springs and Uluru, in the Flinders Range, and at Silverton near Broken Hill—but the Cable Beach rides remain the most famous. **Broome Camel Safaris** (tel 0419 916 101), **Red Sun Camels** (tel (08) 9193 7423), and **Ships of the Desert** (tel 0419 954 022) all have sunset rides.

# The Kimberley

The Kimberley in Western Australia's wild northwest is generally regarded as Australia's last frontier. It is an ancient plateau, dissected by deep gorges, the craggy mountain strongholds of the Durack and King Leopold Ranges, and the bizarre sandstone formations of Purnululu (Bungle Bungle). The climate is savage, with violent storms during the summer monsoons. Lightning strikes in the dry season can spark awesome bushfires.

The giant Argyle Diamond Mine nestles in the southern edge of the Ragged Range.

**The Kimberley**
🅐 213 C5–D5
**Visitor Information**
✉ Coolibah Dr., Kununurra
☎ (08) 9168 1177

Few people live here permanently—about 38,000 in an area larger than California. Most residents have come up for a few years of adventure or good paychecks at one of the mines. The region has a few scattered settlements, some far-flung Aboriginal communities, and a sprinkling of lonely cattle stations that can be bigger than some U.S. states. Saltwater crocodiles live in the rivers and estuaries along this ragged and barely explored coast, and

bizarre boab trees dot the landscape. The Kimberley is hard to reach and challenging to explore, but is one of the world's truly wild places.

The frontier region's main road is the Great Northern Highway, which was paved only as recently as 1986. It links the Kimberley's three main towns—Kununurra, Derby (actually 20 miles/32 km off the highway), and Broome (see pp. 232–33)—with the cities of Perth and Darwin. The only other route through the Kimberley is the

Gibb River Road, which crosses 400 miles (645 km) of wilderness (see pp. 238–39).

## Kununurra

Kununurra—population 5,000— is the major town in the eastern part of the Kimberley and the best base for visiting the otherworldly Purnululu (see pp. 236–37) and the Argyle Diamond Mine. It is also a good jumping-off point for the Gibb River Road, which begins off the Great Northern Highway about 30 miles (48 km) west of town.

Kununurra is the area's newest town, built from scratch in 1961 to service the Ord River Irrigation Project that dammed the mighty Ord River. During the summer monsoon, the Ord was pouring more than 15 million gallons (59 million liters) of water into the sea every second. By holding back some of that water in the giant man-made Lake Argyle and using it to irrigate crops, the project has turned 29,000 acres (11,700 ha) of arid scrub into sugarcane and banana plantations, mango orchards, peanut and melon fields, and vegetable gardens.

One of the most spectacular and easily accessible hikes in the Kimberley is within walking distance of Kununurra. **Hidden Valley, in Mirima National Park,** is a miniature version of Purnululu, yet is only a mile from the center of town. Just follow Barringtonia Avenue to the edge of town and you will find it, a maze of tiger-striped sandstone formations.

The **Argyle Diamond Mine** (www.argylediamonds.com.au),

which is located about 100 miles (160 km) south of Kununurra, is the world's largest producer of diamonds. About 20 million carats a year, one-third of the world's production, comes out of this giant open-cut mine. Most of its output is industrial quality, but it also produces spectacular jewels. They come in a suite of brilliant colors: champagne and topaz hues, blues, greens, and, rarest of all, pinks, lilacs, and reds. The mine has no public access, but the Kununurra tourist office can arrange tours. ∎

### Australia: The Movie

Few Australians have visited the Kimberley, but the Baz Luhrmann film *Australia* (2008) has prompted a mini tourist rush to see the sweeping landscapes where much of the film was shot. Located 25 miles (40 km) off the Gibb River Road, **Diggers Rest Station** was a key filming location, particularly the boab trees on the property. The movie's Faraway Downs Homestead was a set built on the **Carlton Hill Station** (*not open to the public*), about 12 miles (20 km) west of Kununurra. The **Cockburn Range,** rising 2,000 feet (600 m) above the plains, features in the movie, which also used the **Home Valley Station,** at the base of the range, and **El Questro Wilderness Park** (see p. 239) for several filming locations.

# Purnululu (Bungle Bungle) National Park

It speaks volumes for the remoteness and inaccessibility of the Kimberley that these spectacular sandstone ranges were virtually unknown to non-Aboriginal Australians until the early 1980s, when a filmmaker who was doing a documentary for the Western Australian government shot some aerial footage of them at dusk. The haunting images seized the public's imagination, and Purnululu's striped formations are now a symbol of the Kimberley.

The striated sandstone formations at Purnululu's Piccaninny Creek

Aborigines have been coming into these eerie ranges for more than 20,000 years. The park's name, Purnululu, is the local Aborigine term for "sandstone"; the name Bungle Bungle may refer to a type of grass. In Australia these rock formations are almost as well recognized an outback icon as Uluru.

The first European to see the ranges was Alexander Forrest, who explored the Kimberley in 1879. As he was looking for prospective cattle-grazing land, he dismissed the spectacular ranges as useless wasteland and moved on. Over the next century, some of the big Kimberley pastoral leases included parts of the Bungle Bungle.

### Getting to the Park

Many people who see images of Purnululu resolve to go there, but getting into this remote 750,000-acre (304,000 ha) national park is no mean feat. It is accessible only during the dry season, and even then you need a four-wheel-drive vehicle or a helicopter and must carry your supplies. Scenic flights are easier. In 1997, about 40,000 tourists saw Purnululu, two-thirds of

Here you can either head north to **Echidna Chasm** (about 12 miles/19 km) or go south to **Piccaninny Creek** (about 20 miles/32 km). The Echidna Chasm area has tall, narrow gorges and dramatic cliffs, while at the Piccaninny

### INSIDER TIP:

**Camp at Kurrajong for Purnululu's northern attractions and at Walardi for those in the south.**

—STEPHANIE ROBICHAUX
*National Geographic contributor*

**Purnululu National Park**

 213 D5

**Visitor Information**

Department of Environment & Conservation, Kununurra

(08) 9168 4200

---

## Outback Driving

Remoteness and weather extremes in the outback require drivers to take extra precautions. Check local road and weather conditions, particularly in the wet season, and report your route to relatives or local authorities if heading off the main highways. Carry plenty of extra water, food, and fuel. If traveling off-road, consider renting a GPS and satellite phone or high-frequency radio. If you get lost or break down, stay with the vehicle. Stories abound of motorists who walked out for help and perished. It may take a day or two for someone to come along, but increasing tourism means the outback is not as isolated as it used to be.

---

them on sightseeing flights out of Kununurra, Turkey Creek, or Halls Creek. The tourist office in Kununurra has details of flights and tours into the park.

### Park Attractions

The vehicle turnoff to Purnululu is about 150 miles (240 km) south of Kununurra on the Great Northern Highway. From there you follow a rough, bouncing 35-mile (56 km) track to a point called Three Ways.

Creek area you will see the distinctive tiger-striped beehive-shaped sandstone formations for which the park is so famous. The tiger striping is the result of orange silica being interspersed with thin layers of black lichens. Climbing the ancient and fragile sandstone formations is forbidden in the park.

Once in the park, visitors can stay in Kurrajong Camp or Walardi Camp. Bungle Bungle is closed in the wet season (Jan.–March). ■

# Gibb River Road Drive

On a map of the Kimberley, the Gibb River Road looks like a handy shortcut between Kununurra and Derby, cutting 150 miles (240 km) off the Great Northern Highway route. But this rough track is emphatically not a shortcut; it is one of the great adventure drives on the continent. In the wet season *(Oct.–March)*, it is impassable.

Created in 1964 to bring cattle on the outlying stations to market, the Gibb River Road cuts 420 miles (676 km) through the heart of the Kimberley. It is still known as "the beef road" among locals, and travelers on it should keep an eye out for the massive road trains, loaded with cattle, booming along in a shower of gravel and dust. Also be wary of river crossings, for this is crocodile country.

A conventional vehicle can make it along the Gibb River Road, with care, but a four-wheel-drive vehicle is preferable. Food, fuel, and accommodations are available en route, but the distance between them can be great, so carry plenty of supplies, basic tools, and spares. If you don't want to drive yourself, you can join a four-wheel-drive safari from either end. Ask for information at the tourist office at Kununurra (see p. 234) or Derby *(tel (08) 9191 1426)*.

## Kununurra to El Questro

From **Kununurra ❶**, take the Great Northern Highway west for 25 miles (40 km) or so to the marked turnoff to the old seaport of **Wyndham ❷**. The Gibb River Road goes left off this road a couple of miles north of the turning, but before you take it, Wyndham is worth a visit. A quintessential Kimberley frontier town, Wyndham is surrounded by miles of shimmering tidal flats. It used to be known for bloodthirsty crocodiles that lurked in the marshes near the abattoir, waiting for offal. The meatworks closed in 1985, but Wyndham's tidal flats are still good for crocodile spotting.

One of the most spectacular views on Australia's wild north coast is from the **Five Rivers Lookout** on Mount Bastion, immediately

behind Wyndham. Drive up to the lookout 1,082 feet (330 m) above the tidal flats and see five major rivers—the Ord, Pentecost, Durack, Forrest, and King—empty sluggishly into Cambridge Gulf. The Shell service station *(tel (08) 9161 1281)* has local information. About 12 miles (19 km) west of town on the King River Road is the 2,000-year-old hollow boab tree that served as a prison in Wyndham's bad old frontier days.

The roughest stretch of the Gibb River Road is the first 150 miles (240 km). Some of the river crossings, such as the one through the Pentecost River, are potentially treacherous in the wet season until around May, but the countryside is magnificent.

Fifteen miles (24 km) west along the Gibb River Road is a turnoff for **El Questro**

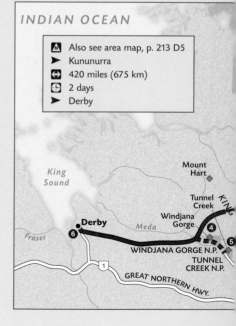

*INDIAN OCEAN*

| ⚠ | Also see area map, p. 213 D5 |
| ▶ | Kununurra |
| ⬌ | 420 miles (675 km) |
| ⏱ | 2 days |
| ▶ | Derby |

Wilderness Park ❸ *(tel (08) 9169 1777, open April–Oct., www.elquestro.com.au, $$)*, one million acres (400,000 ha) of cattle station turned massive tourist resort. Fishing trips, horseback rides, gorge cruises, Aboriginal rock art, and hiking tours are all offered to visitors. Accommodations range from high-priced homestead rooms cantilevered over Chamberlain Gorge, one of 50 gorges on the property, to upmarket tents at fern-filled Emma Gorge and budget camping sites at the Station Township. Another accommodation option for tourists is the nearby **Home Valley Station** *(tel (08) 9161 4322, www.homevalley.com.au)*.

## Onward to Mount Barnett

The next refueling point is the **Mount Barnett Roadhouse** *(tel (08) 9191 7007)*, which is 140 miles (225 km) farther on. Two stations on tracks off the road also have accommodations *(reserve in advance)*. **Imint i Store** *(tel (08) 9191 7471)* is located near the turnoff to the pretty, and very popular, Bell Creek Gorge. Farther still along the road is

---

**NOT TO BE MISSED:**

Wyndham • Five Rivers Lookout
• El Questro Wilderness Park
• Windjana Gorge National Park

---

the **Mount Hart Wilderness Lodge** *(tel (08) 9191 4645, www.mthart.com.au)*, which offers full-board accommodation.

## The Road to Derby

West of Mount Barnett Roadhouse, the road enters the dramatic King Leopold Ranges. A turnoff goes 20 miles (32 km) to the spectacular **Windjana Gorge National Park** ❹ and 25 miles (40 km) farther to **Tunnel Creek National Park** ❺. This was once part of a vast coral reef; over eons, the Lennard River cut its way through the rock to form gorges. Wade through Tunnel Creek to see flying foxes. The final 40 miles (64 km) of the road into **Derby** ❻ are paved.

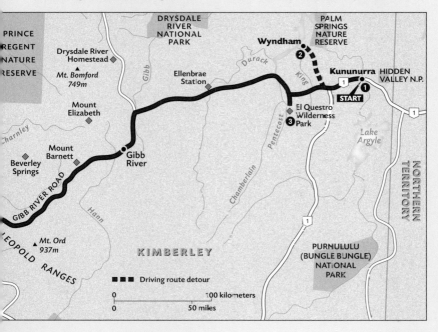

# Kalgoorlie-Boulder

Kalgoorlie sits on the Golden Mile, Australia's richest vein of gold-bearing ore. This frontier mining town is in the old outback tradition, with tattooed, shirtless miners, and "skimpies" (scantily clad barmaids) in its pubs. It is also a much-anticipated stop on the Indian Pacific train journey after the long westward trek across the Nullarbor Plain.

Kalgoorlie's main thoroughfare, Hannan Street, is lined with elaborate gold-rush architecture.

## Kalgoorlie

⚊ 213 C2

**Visitor Information**

✉ Corner of Hannan & Wilson Sts.

☎ (08) 9021 1966

The town got its start in 1893, when an Irish prospector named Paddy Hannan stumbled across nuggets lying on the ground beneath the tree where he had stopped with two of his mates to rest a lame horse. Having spent fruitless months at the gold diggings in nearby Coolgardie, the men could hardly believe their luck. They scooped up more than 100 ounces (2.8 kg) of gold in a few days and sparked the last of Australia's great gold rushes. Within a couple of months more than a thousand fortune-seekers came to the place known as Hannan's Find.

Later the fledgling town was given back its Aboriginal name, Kalgoorlie. By 1896, the town had a population of nearly 6,000 and a neatly arranged grid of tree-lined streets wide enough to allow camel trains to turn around. It was also providing the economic oomph to assure Western Australia's autonomy and eventual statehood. That year, authorities began building a 350-mile (560 km) pipeline from Mundaring Weir to bring clean water to this desperately dry desert town. The pipeline was completed in 1903, by which time Kalgoorlie had grown to a small city of

30,000, with more than forty hotels and eight breweries (it wasn't just water they thirsted for). The extended rail line to neighboring Boulder was the busiest in the state.

Kalgoorlie's luck as well as its ore has lasted longer than that of any of the early eastern gold towns. While it is very much alive today, Kalgoorlie had a brush with oblivion in the years after World War I, when rising costs and the falling price of gold depressed the outback community. A commodities boom in the 1970s, and new technology that enabled trace quantities of gold to be profitably extracted, gave Kalgoorlie a fresh lease on life. Today it is a bustling community of 30,000 (linked by a hyphen and municipal amalgamation to nearby **Boulder** in 1989). The town is Australia's largest gold producer and one of the richest sources of gold in the world.

## Kalgoorlie Sights

**Hannan Street** is lined with glorious gold-rush architecture, elegant old pubs, and the grandiose Town Hall. Kalgoorlie is very much a blue-collar town, although tourism is becoming important. The **WA Museum Kalgoorlie-Boulder** has excellent displays on the town's gold-rush heyday, Aboriginal history, and the region's days as a sandalwood supplier.

The underground tour of the **Mining Hall of Fame** (Goldfields Hwy., tel (08) 9026 2700, $$, www .mininghall.com) is one of the biggest draws in Kalgoorlie.

The **Super Pit** is the world's biggest open-cut gold mine—virtually a canyon. It is presently about 1,200 feet (370 m) deep and produces 800,000 ounces (22,676 kg) of gold each year. The mine is 2.2 miles (3.6 km) long by one mile (1.6 km) wide and growing by the day.

You can drive to the **Super Pit Lookout** on the Eastern Bypass Road just outside Boulder. For a sense of scale here, consider the fact that those "tiny" yellow dump trucks in that pit are actually the size of houses and carry more than 200 tons of ore. The lookout is usually open from 7 a.m. to 9 p.m., but is closed when blasting is being done in the mine. ∎

## Coolgardie

The area's first gold diggings began in 1892 in Coolgardie, about 25 miles (40 km) south of Kalgoorlie. Today, it's practically a ghost town—a sort of town-size mining museum, well worth a visit. The **Warden's Court Building**, the **Town Hall**, the **Post Office**, and the opulent **Marble Bar Hotel** attest to the prosperity this goldrush boomtown once enjoyed. The Old Courthouse on Bayley Street houses the **Goldfields Museum**, an interesting collection of early goldfield artifacts. The 1895 old mining warden's residence has been restored and listed by the National Trust.

**WA Museum Kalgoorlie-Boulder**

- ✉ 17 Hannan St.
- ☎ (08) 9021 8533
- 💲 Donation

**Coolgardie**

- ◩ 213 C2

**Visitor Information**

- ✉ Bayley St.
- ☎ (08) 9026 6090

# EXPERIENCE: Outback Australia

The outback is harsh and isolated, a vast region of desert and tropical wilderness, fascinating for its tales of human adaptation as much as the varied landscapes. There are many ways to explore and appreciate this unique part of the world, ranging from short flights to multiday camping excursions and four-wheel-drive adventures.

The easiest way to get into the outback is to fly to Alice Springs and Uluru, or drive through the Red Centre on the paved Stuart Highway. Alternatively, take the Ghan, the train named after the Afghan camel drivers who once plied this remote route (see pp. 282–283).

Adventure lies off the main highways. You can muster cattle (see p. 281), stay on an outback station (see sidebar p. 136), fly to impossibly remote pubs, or drive some of the old cattle tracks deep into the Never Never, as the outback is known in Australia.

## Driving the Outback

Though not to be undertaken lightly, nor in the blistering summer months, a four-wheel-drive adventure into the heart of Australia is an unforgettable experience. Classic routes include the **Oodnadatta Track,** following the old Ghan rail line north to Alice Springs, and the **Birdsville Track,** a famous stock route to the remote Queensland town of Birdsville. Both are now well-maintained gravel roads in the dry season, starting from Marree in South Australia. The nearby **Strzelecki Track** heads to Innamincka on Cooper Creek, where Burke and Wills died (carry plenty of food and water), and you can continue on to **Broken Hill,** another center for exploring the outback.

In the north, the **Gibb River Road** (see pp. 238–239) is one of the great adventure drives, and **Kakadu National Park** (see pp. 188–191) is an outback wonderland.

If you drive yourself, it is essential to plan ahead in detail. A great reference

## INSIDER TIP:

Be sure to read the fine print when researching outback tours. Accommodations and flights are not always included in the price.

—LARRY PORGES
*National Geographic editor*

is *www.exploroz.com*. Alice Springs, Darwin, and Broken Hill are good places to rent vehicles, and plenty of operators in these centers run outback tours.

## Tour Operators

In Alice Springs, **Ossies Outback 4WD Tours** (tel (08) 8952 2308, www .ossies.com.au) goes off-road through the MacDonnell Ranges to Uluru, across the Simpson Desert, and elsewhere. **Wayoutback Safaris** (tel (08) 8952 4324, www .wayoutback.com.au) heads to Uluru, Kings Canyon, and the MacDonnell Ranges.

In Darwin, **Venture North Australia** (tel (08) 8942 0971, www.northern australia.com) has tours to Kakadu, Arnhem Land, the remote Cobourg Peninsula, and the Kimberley. **Aussie Adventure** (tel (08) 8923 6523, www.aussieadventure .com.au) will take you on tours of the Red Centre, Kakadu, and the Tiwi Islands.

In Broken Hill, **Tri State Safaris** (tel (08) 8088 2389, www.tristate.com.au) has a great selection of trips right across the outback, while **Corner Country Adventure Tours** (tel 1-300 723 583, www.cornercountryadventure .com.au) goes to Birdsville and the desert regions.

## Sightseeing in the Air

Not a fan of dust? See the outback from the air. Take a day flight to the Birdsville pub for a burger and beer with **South West Air Service** (tel (07) 4654 3033, www.outbackairtours.com) or a 12-day luxury tour in a De Havilland Dash 8 with **Bill Peach Journeys** (tel 1-800 252 053 [toll-free], www .billpeachjourneys.com.au).

# Eyre Highway &
# the Nullarbor Plain

Driving the Eyre Highway along the edge of the Nullarbor Plain is the classic outback road trip—almost 1,500 miles (2,400 km) from Perth to Adelaide and most of it empty desert highway. Yet for all the barrenness of the landscape, you can enjoy remarkable views—the expanse of saltbush from Madura Pass, the Bunda Cliffs along the Great Australian Bight. But it is the steady humming of tires on pavement that brings home the awesome size of the continent.

In a cloud of steam and coal smoke, the first Transcontinental Express pulls into Kalgoorlie in 1917.

Strictly speaking, the Eyre Highway actually runs just south of the Nullarbor Plain (to cut directly across it you must take the train; see sidebar, p. 248), touching the plain itself only briefly in South Australia. Australia's first transcontinental automobile journey was made in 1912 following camel tracks across the desert. World War II and the threat of invasion inspired the authorities to build a highway linking Perth with the rest of Australia. Even into the 1960s, however, the road was still little more than a rough track, and anyone who made it

## Norseman

📍 213 C2

**Visitor Information**

✉ 68 Roberts St.

☎ (08) 9039 1071

across in a car was likely to get a mention in the Perth newspapers. In 1969, the Western Australian government paved the highway to the South Australia border, and the last parts were paved in 1976.

The first stage, if you are heading east from Perth, is the 400 miles (640 km) or so to the goldfields around Kalgoorlie. It is probably the least interesting part of the journey, a typical Australian highway through wheat fields and arid scrub with lengthening stretches between towns. To anyone coming from Europe or North America, it may even seem desolate. But this is the civilized part of the drive.

The adventure doesn't really start until you drive through **Norseman,** past the red warning sign that little or no water will be available for the next 800 miles (1,300 km), toward a heat-warped horizon. You need to have done

at least a bit of rudimentary preparation. Here the temperatures can soar to well over 120°F (49°C). Withering headwinds make your car work harder and chew up the gasoline, and the glare can be blinding. Be certain that your car is in good working order, that you have basic tools and spares, and above all, that you have brought extra water both for drinking and for the radiator. That said, the Eyre Highway is a reasonably well-used road that is paved and in good condition. It is the lifeline between

### INSIDER TIP:

**The Eyre Bird Observatory is an ornithologist's dream, but the last 7.5 miles (12 km) of the journey must be traveled by 4WD.**

—STEPHANIE ROBICHAUX
*National Geographic contributor*

Abandoned in 1929, the old telegraph station at Eucla has been slowly engulfed by sand.

Perth and the rest of the country, and if something went wrong you probably wouldn't have long to wait, but why take chances? Food and gasoline are expensive out here. Although the roadhouses can make electronic transactions, if the lines are down for any reason you will be stuck if you don't have some cash.

## Highway Roadhouses

Because no real towns are on the road between Norseman and the South Australian fishing port of **Ceduna,** 750 miles (1,200 km) away, you will find just a lonely archipelago of roadhouses, generally between 80 and 120 miles (130 and 195 km) apart. The first of these, **Balladonia,** was a telegraph station in the early days, and the ruins of the old stone buildings can be seen a few miles past the modern roadhouse complex. The early part of the drive from Norseman is surprisingly forested, but by the time you reach Balladonia you are well into the scrub. The nearby Balladonia sheep station is one of the oldest in this part of Western Australia, and it is still owned by the pioneering family that founded it. Balladonia's population is listed as nine, which gives you a hint of just how lonely the drive ahead is going to be.

Just past the old station, the road makes a beeline for the **Caiguna** roadhouse, motel, and campground *(tel (08) 9039 3459),* about 113 miles (182 km) away. This rigid straightaway at 90 miles (144 km) is the longest in

---

**EXPERIENCE:**
## For the Birds

Birders and committed conservationists will love the **Eyre Bird Observatory** *(PMB 32 Cocklebiddy via Norseman, tel (08) 9039 3450, www.eyrebirds.org).* This nonprofit research station attracts birders and scientists from around the world, and you can volunteer or undertake courses in bird banding and field techniques, mammal studies, dune conservation, and other activities. Courses are usually for a week, and accommodations are basic but comfortable, with meals provided. Reservations are essential.

---

Australia, and while that fact may interest you for the first 10 or 20 miles, you'll have a big sense of relief when you finally reach Caiguna. You could adjust your watch 45 minutes forward at this point to accommodate the local time zone, or just ignore it because you are passing through and time is rather meaningless out here.

**Cocklebiddy,** 40 miles (64 km) east of Caiguna roadhouse, is famous for the labyrinth of limestone caves beneath its flat, almost featureless plain. The system has some of the world's longest underwater caves. In 1983, a French team set what was then a world record for the world's deepest cave dive. Exploring these caves is difficult, dangerous, and best left to well-planned expeditions. What is easily accessible here is the **Eyre Bird Observatory** at the historic Eyre Telegraph Station *(tel (08) 9039 3450),* a few miles east of the Cocklebiddy roadhouse and down a track to

## Eyre Peninsula

An alternative to the Ceduna–Port Augusta leg of the Eyre Highway is to turn off at Ceduna and take the more scenic coast road around the Eyre Peninsula for wild beaches, cliffs, sheltered harbors, abundant seafood, and wildlife spotting.

Down the coast 55 miles (90 km) from Ceduna, **Streaky Bay** is noted for fishing, seafood, and fine beaches. Farther on, just off the highway, the otherworldly granite outcrop of **Murphy's Haystack** makes a good photo op, and the same road continues on to the **Point Labatt sealion colony,** viewed from the cliff top. To see these lumbering beasts up close, or to swim with the dolphins, arrange tours *(tel (08) 8626 5017)* at Baird Bay.

Detour off the highway for fine coastal scenery, empty beaches, and caves, before reaching the summer resort town of **Coffin Bay,** noted for its superb oysters and adjoining national park, with wild coastal scenery, birds, and other wildlife.

Similar is **Lincoln National Park,** 25 miles (40 km) away, just outside **Port Lincoln,** the thriving main town at the bottom of the peninsula. This attractive tuna-fishing port turned resort has plenty of tours for cruising, fishing, or swimming with the wildlife. The highway then heads north, skirting the quieter waters of Spencer Gulf, all the way to **Whyalla,** the state's second largest city and steel-producing port, and on to **Port Augusta.**

**INSIDER TIP:**

**Every October, the town of Ceduna** *(www .ceduna.net)* **hosts Oysterfest, three festive days of parades, food, and entertainment.**

—CAROLINE HICKEY
*National Geographic editor*

the cliff-lined coast on the Great Australian Bight (see sidebar p. 245).

**Madura Pass** is 340 miles (550 km) from Norseman. This is the most spectacular part of the drive, when the road suddenly starts down a steep, winding hill onto the **Mundrabilla Plains.** The views here are breathtaking and slam home the empty vastness of the country.

A few miles past the Mundrabilla roadhouse, the road starts

to climb again, winding its way toward Eucla Pass. If it is night, you'll be greeted by the sight of the illuminated Travellers Cross on top of the craggy pass.

**Eucla,** 103 miles (166 km) from Madura Pass, is worth a stop. The family-owned roadhouse and restaurant complex *(tel (08) 9039 3468)* is easily the best on the route and one of the few roadhouses in Australia where you can actually get a fresh salad. The owners are friendly and can direct you to some of the local sights and beaches, such as the picturesque ruins of the telegraph station, built in 1877 and now engulfed by dunes.

Beyond the haunting dunes around Eucla is the deep blue water of the **Great Australian Bight.** A weather observatory is also here—it recorded Western Australia's highest ever shade temperature (124°F/51°C) .

## Entering South Australia

East of Eucla the highway dog-legs around a meteor crater and 9 miles (14.5 km) later crosses the South Australian border at **Border Village.** If you are coming from South Australia, the agriculture check-point requires you to surrender any fresh fruits, vegetables, or honey you might have with you. If you are going east, the South Australian authorities will get you just outside of Ceduna.

Border Village is a monument to roadside tackiness. You'll see a 20-foot (6 m) fiberglass kangaroo, murals on the diner walls, and a cheery sign warning you to look out for UFOs, a reference to an incident a few years ago when a family claimed their car had been towed by aliens.

The highway clings to the Great Australian Bight for much of the next 100 miles (160 km) and has plenty of turnoffs to spectacular cliff-top lookouts. The banded Bunda Cliffs are up to 600 feet (180 m) high, and between June and October they make great viewing platforms for watching the annual migration of southern right whales.

The road veers inland to the Nullarbor Hotel/Motel *(tel (08) 8625 6271)* and the only stretch of the Eyre Highway that actually runs on the tree-less Nullarbor Plain. It skirts it for 20 miles (32 km) or so and then takes you back into saltbush scrub. A turnoff leads to the **Head of the Bight,** the best whale-watching viewpoint between June and October.

Ceduna is about 175 miles (280 km) ahead, through lightly forested country, and the line of white wheat silos along the port is a welcoming sight. This is the first town of consequence (population 3,570) after Norseman.

**Ceduna**
🗺 251 B3
**Visitor Information**
✉ 58 Poynton St.
☎ (08) 8625 2780

The Nullarbor Plain comes to an abrupt end at the 240-foot-high (73 m) Bunda Cliffs.

**Great Southern Rail**

✉ 422 King William St., Adelaide

☎ 13 21 47

**www.trainways .com.au**

From here the highway crosses the arid Eyre Peninsula, which is dotted with the ruins of stone cottages of settlers who tried to scratch a living on this soil in the 19th century.

Your drive along Eyre Highway eventually ends at **Port Augusta—** "Porta Gutta" in local-speak. Adelaide is located about 200 miles (320 km) south, through wheat and wine country.

In Adelaide, you can catch the Indian Pacific train (see sidebar below) back to Perth—your car can ride as well—to save you from having to re-cross the Nullarbor Plain. If you have developed a taste for outback driving and road-house hamburgers, you can make a left turn at Port Augusta and head along the lonely Stuart Highway (see pp. 284–288) toward the town of Alice Springs. ∎

## Rails Across the Nullarbor

The Indian Pacific train crosses the continent from Sydney to Perth. It winds its way through the Great Dividing Range and rolls across the western plains to the frontier silver mining town of Broken Hill. Then it goes on to Port Pirie and down to Adelaide, before heading westward across the Nullarbor Plain. Here the great train really hits its stride—crossing the vast and waterless expanse whose name is corrupt Latin for "no tree" *(nulla arbor)*.

For sheer size and scale, no place is like it—an 80,000-square-mile (207,000 sq km) limestone plateau, scoured by desert winds and scorched by temperatures that can easily exceed 120°F (49°C) beneath a pitiless summer sun. The plateau has no surface water at all, although an extensive system of flooded caves lies deep underground. Out here lies the world's longest stretch of straight railroad track—more than 300 miles (480 km).

The first European to cross the Nullarbor Plain was explorer Edward Eyre, who barely survived his harrowing journey into ceaseless winds and deadly heat in 1841. Afghan camel drivers and telegraph linesmen helped forge a trail across it later in the century. A railroad was begun in 1911—partly as an inducement to Western Australia to join the federation. Six years later, on October 23, 1917,

the nation's first transcontinental train rolled out of the South Australian town of Port Augusta.

Building the railroad was a logistical nightmare, akin to building a space station, because nothing there could sustain life. Everything had to be taken into the desert—food, housing, water, equipment, and building materials. Provisions were sent out weekly from either Kalgoorlie or Port Augusta on what became known as the Tea and Sugar Train. Until 1996 that train still ran weekly out of Port Augusta, servicing the tiny isolated camps and the few inhabitants. The train took three days to make the crossing, bringing tankers of fresh water, freight, mail, and news of the world.

The Indian Pacific runs at a brisker pace, taking a little more than two days to cross the continent. Despite its epic stature—and in part because of it—the train lost money for many years. A few years ago, it was given an expensive facelift in a bid to make it a sort of outback Orient Express. The result was more Aussie Nouveau, although the club cars and sleepers are quite comfortable. But the scenery can't be replicated anywhere else. Get more information about the train trip from Great Southern Railway *(tel 13 21 47, www.gsr.com.au).*

Australia's driest state, but a paradise of orchards, vineyards, and olive groves in the fertile southeast

# South Australia

Introduction & Map   250–251

Adelaide   252–258

Experience: Volunteering   255

Experience: Visiting Adelaide's Markets   256

Around Adelaide   259–279

Experience: Spotting the Elusive Platypus   261

Feature: Australian Wines   264–265

Experience: Wine Courses   265

Experience: Seasonal Work   267

Feature: Festival State   272–273

Experience: Festival Fever   273

Experience: Renting a Houseboat   275

Coober Pedy   280–281

Experience: Cattle Mustering   281

The Ghan   282–283

Experience: Great Train Journeys   283

Stuart Highway Drive   284–288

Experience: Flying over Lake Eyre   286

Hotels & Restaurants   379–382

Bottles in the Wine Museum, Yalumba Wines, Barossa Valley

# South Australia

**South Australia is a cornucopia of most of the finer things in life: great food, world-class wines, and a sunny cosmopolitan lifestyle. What makes this bounty all the more remarkable is that this is Australia's driest and most barren state. South Australia has a higher proportion of desert than any other state, with more than 80 percent of its surface receiving less than 10 inches (25 cm) of rain a year.**

The vast majority of South Australians live in the southeast corner of the state, a fertile pocket of land watered by the Murray River. Adelaide, perhaps Australia's most gracious capital city, is here, forming an island of elegant homes and high Victorian architecture surrounded by leafy parklands.

The climate here is Mediterranean, and the rural scenery is elegant, with stately red gums, broad vineyards, and old stone cottages. The Murray River runs through deep sandstone gorges teeming with birdlife, which you can see by steamboat. Victor Harbor, an hour or so south of Adelaide, is a popular seaside retreat, where southern right whales swim up to the coast during their winter migrations. Farther

Canberra ★

Area of map detail

south the haunting sweep of coastline known as the Coorong is a bird-watcher's paradise. Naracoorte Caves, in the far southeast, is a World Heritage–listed fossil site and home to almost half a million bats. Kangaroo Island still has unspoiled bush, old-fashioned villages, and almost tame wildlife only two hours by ferry from Adelaide's suburb of Glenelg.

Glenelg was where the first European settlers landed from the *Buffalo* in 1836. The following year Col. William Light pegged out the city of Adelaide in lines as crisp and straight as an accountant's left margin. The colony itself was the vision of entrepreneur Edward Wakefield, who wanted it to be a model settlement. Migrants purchased their land from the South Australia Company at two pounds an acre and brought along capital to invest in the colony. They were guaranteed religious and civic freedoms. No convicts here, thank you. This is the only state never to have been a penal colony.

Many early settlers came from the English gentry. By 1839, large numbers of Prussian and Silesian Lutherans had arrived, fleeing persecution, and, by 1842, were settling in the

## NOT TO BE MISSED:

**Sampling the arts in the gracious state capital of Adelaide   252–258**

**The cool retreat of the Adelaide Hills and Germanic Hahndorf   260–263**

**Touring the Old World wineries of the Barossa Valley   267–268**

**Kangaroo Island, a wildlife-spotting treasure trove   268–274**

**Cruising on a Murray River houseboat   276**

**Hiking the rugged Flinders Ranges, an oasis in the desert   277–279**

**The underground opal miners' homes in Coober Pedy   280–281**

**Driving though outback desert on the Stuart Highway   282–288**

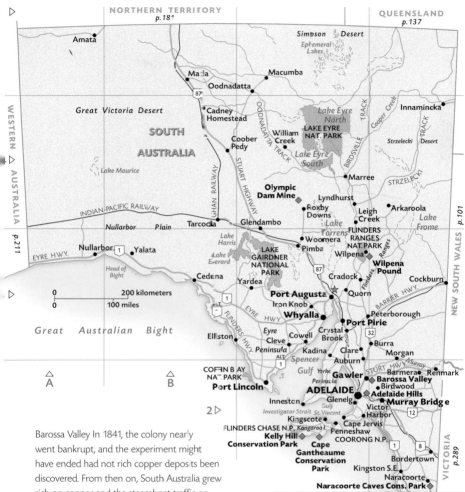

NORTHERN TERRITORY
p.181

QUEENSLAND
p.137

Amata

Simpson   Desert
Ephemeral
Lakes

Mada
Oodnadatta
Macumba

Great Victoria Desert

Cadney
Homestead

Lake Eyre
North
LAKE EYRE
NAT. PARK

Innamincka

SOUTH

Coober
Pedy

William
Creek

Lake Eyre
South

Strzelecki   Desert

AUSTRALIA

Lake Maurice

GHAN RAILWAY

STUART HIGHWAY

OODNADATTA TRACK

Marree

STRZELECKI

BIRDSVILLE TRACK

Cooper Creek

Olympic
Dam Mine

Lyndhurst

Leigh
Creek

Arkaroola

INDIAN-PACIFIC RAILWAY

Roxby
Downs

Lake
Frome

Nullarbor    Plain

Tarcoola

Glendambo

Lake
Harris

Lake
Torrens

Woomera

FLINDERS
RANGES
NAT. PARK

Pimba

Wilpena

Nullarbor

Yalata

Lake
Everard

LAKE
GAIRDNER
NATIONAL
PARK

Wilpena
Pound

EYRE HWY.

Head of
Bight

Cedena

Yardea

Cradock

Quorn

Cockburn

Port Augusta

Flinders Ranges

BARRIER HWY.

NEW SOUTH WALES
p.101

0        200 kilometers
0        100 miles

Iron Knob

Whyalla

Peterborough

Great   Australian   Bight

Elliston

Eyre

FLINDERS HWY.

EYRE
HWY

Port Pirie

32

Cleve

Cowell

Crystal
Brook

Burra

Peninsula

Kadina

Clare

Morgan

Spencer

Auburn

COFFIN BAY
NAT. PARK

Yorke

Gulf

Gawler

STURT HWY.

Barmera

Renmark

Murray

Port Lincoln

Peninsula

Birdwood

Barossa Valley

ADELAIDE

Adelaide Hills

Inneston

Glenelg

Victor
Harbor

Murray Bridge

Investigator Strait

St. Vincent

Kingscote

Gulf

Cape Jervis

12

FLINDERS CHASE N.P.

Kangaroo I.

Penneshaw

Kelly Hill
Conservation Park

Cape
Gantheaume
Conservation
Park

COORONG N.P.

1

8

Bordertown

VICTORIA
p.289

Kingston S.E.

Naracoorte

Naracoorte Caves Cons. Park

Coonawarra

Mount
Gambier

Penola

A    B    C    D

WESTERN   AUSTRALIA   p.211

**Barossa Valley** In 1841, the colony nearly went bankrupt, and the experiment might have ended had not rich copper deposits been discovered. From then on, South Australia grew rich on copper and the steamboat traffic on the Murray River, taking wheat and wool downstream and fortune-seekers upstream to the goldfields. South Australia held to its tradition of libertarianism. In 1894, women here became the first in the world to stand for Parliament and the second (after New Zealand) to be given the vote.

When you leave the state's southeast corner, the story changes, and South Australia quickly becomes one of the world's most inhospitable places—a scene of scrub, salt lakes, and arid mountain ranges. There are things to see here, though. The desert bursts into flower in spring, and the folded rock formations of

the Flinders Ranges have interesting wildlife. The Ghan train runs across the desert from Adelaide to Darwin in the Northern Territory. Or you can drive there on the Stuart Highway, through the opal-mining town of Coober Pedy, which has such savage desert heat that many residents live underground. Adventurous travelers can explore the Oodnadatta, Strzelecki, and Birdsville Tracks. To the west, the Nullarbor Plain stretches into Western Australia (see pp. 243–248). ■

# Adelaide

**Adelaide, also known as the City of Churches, was planned as a utopia when Col. William Light surveyed it in 1836. He laid out a simple grid, surrounded by parklands, on a pretty site with a chain of "enchanted hills" on its western flank.**

### Adelaide

🄰 251 C2

**Visitor Information**

✉ South Australian Visitor Information Centre, 18 King William St.

☎ (08) 8303 2249 or 1-300 655 276

The charming setting caused some initial controversy. Gov. John Hindmarsh had ordered Light to establish the city near the mouth of the recently explored Murray River, which authorities hoped would open the Australian continent just as the Mississippi River was opening North America. Light arrived only a few months before the first settlers were due and had to make his selection quickly.

**INSIDER TIP:**

**Be sure to take advantage of the expansive parklands surrounding central Adelaide, which give the city a "big country town" feel.**

—LAURA RUYKYS
*National Geographic field researcher*

After examining the frequently silted mouth of the Murray and the treacherous coastline nearby, he decided to locate the new city about 60 miles (96 km) away, farther up the Gulf of St. Vincent on an inland plain. This action infuriated Hindmarsh and sparked bitter arguments.

Nevertheless, Adelaide grew and prospered, while settlements along the exposed coastline were troubled by numerous shipwrecks. In 1878, a railway spur linked Adelaide with the bustling inland river port of Morgan, resolving the issue. However, it was too late for Colonel Light, who had died a broken man in 1839. "The reasons

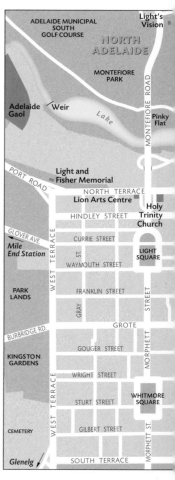

that led me to fix Adelaide where it is I do not expect to be generally understood or calmly judged at present," he wrote shortly before his death. "I leave it to posterity to decide whether I am entitled to praise or blame."

Posterity has come down firmly in Light's favor. The grateful city has erected a bronze statue of him on **Montefiore Hill,** a grassy knoll in North Adelaide, just above pretty Adelaide Cricket Ground and an ideal place to get a feel for the city. From here you can see the breathing space of parklands that surround the inner city, the twin spires of magnificent St. Peter's Cathedral, the graceful **Torrens River,** and the clean lines of the city skyline. The view is known as Light's Vision.

You can easily find your way around Adelaide, which is laid out in a grid. At the center is the grassy **Victoria Square,** where you can catch the tram to the beach at Glenelg (see

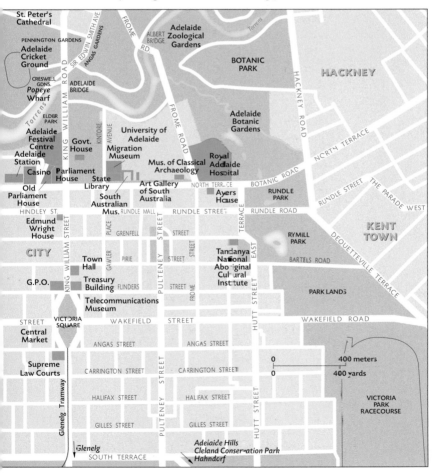

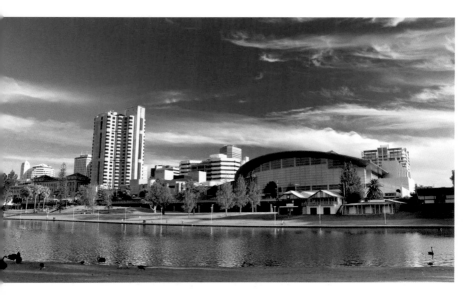

The Torrens River flows past central Adelaide and its many parks and gardens.

**Central Market**
- ✉ Gouger St.
- ☎ (08) 8203 7459
- 🕐 Closed Sun. & Mon.

pp. 259–260). There are plans to extend the popular old tram line into leafy North Adelaide as well. Tree-lined **North Terrace** is the cultural focus, with museums and fine colonial architecture. The main shopping precinct is along **Rundle Mall,** a sunny pedestrian way, bright with flower stalls and lively with street musicians and jugglers. **Hindley Street** is the town's red-light district, seedy in its way but very tame compared with Sydney's Kings Cross. On Gouger Street is one of Adelaide's gastronomic icons, **Central Market,** a paradise of local fruits and vegetables, cheeses, seafood, and meats. Gouger Street also boasts the highest concentration of restaurants in Adelaide. **Rundle Street** is the artsy café district, lined with winebars and bistros. This city is said to have more eateries per person than any other

in Australia. O'Connell and Melbourne Streets in North Adelaide are also well-known café strips.

Adelaide's character is hard to pin down. The city has a long-standing reputation for being conservative and even has a coterie of old, moneyed families known as "the Establishment." On the other hand, its Mediterranean climate, good food, and fine wine give it a hedonistic ambience. This is perhaps Australia's most vivacious city. The calendar is full of festivals, and the two professional Australian Rules football teams are cheered by crowds whose throaty parochialism would make a football-crazed Nebraskan blush.

## Adelaide Sights

On a map, downtown Adelaide resembles a lopsided hourglass set against a backdrop of green parklands. The larger portion is the commercial center, and the smaller section is North Adelaide, a leafy enclave set out by Colonel Light for the homes of the landed gentry. The elegant **Adelaide Bridge,** which spans the Torrens River, connects the two. This river, once just a seasonal trickle, has been dammed to form a long lake through this part of the city.

**South of the Bridge:** The best place to start exploring is south of the bridge, at the corner of King William Street and North Terrace. Virtually every major attraction is only a short stroll from here—the art gallery, festival center, South Australian Museum, Parliament House, Government House, casino, Botanic Gardens, and zoo. Most of them are on **North Terrace,** a grand tree-lined boulevard that showcases much of South Australia's solid colonial architecture.

Start on the west corner at the monumental **Parliament House,** with its massive marble Corinthian columns. Construction began in 1883 but took more than 50 years to complete because of a dispute about a dome (which was never built). The building is open to the public, and on days when Parliament is sitting, you can watch South Australia's representatives sort out state affairs. Beside it is the beautifully restored **Old Parliament House,** completed in 1855. Next door, farther west, is the grand old railroad station, built of honey-colored sandstone in 1929. Although its imposing neoclassic lines suggest great rail journeys, only suburban lines depart from here. The Indian Pacific (see p. 248), the Ghan (see pp. 282–283), and the Overlander (to Melbourne) all leave from the soulless Keswick terminal at Mile End, just off Burbridge Road, west of the city.

---

# EXPERIENCE: Volunteering

Most volunteer programs in Australia relate to conservation projects and offer great opportunities to work in the outdoors monitoring wildlife, collecting rain forest samples, planting trees, and other activities. Willingness is more important than experience. Lodging and transportation are usually provided, but volunteers must pick up the tab, which can sometimes be expensive.

**Conservation Volunteers** (tel (03) 5330 2600, www.conservationvolunteers .com.au) has projects such as tree planting, erosion and salinity control, seed collection, maintenance of walking tracks, and weed control throughout the country.

Day programs are free, and a small charge is made for overnight accommodations on longer projects.

**Earthwatch** (tel (03) 9682 6828, www .earthwatch.org.au) has wildlife monitoring expeditions to the Kimberley, Kangaroo Island, Ningaloo Reef, and other destinations, from 2 to 15 days (costing up to A$4,200/U.S. $3,850).

**Go Volunteer** (tel (03) 9820 4100, www.govolunteer.com.au) is a national volunteer recruiting body for community and other projects.

**WWF Australia** (tel 1-800 032 551, wwf.org.au) also lists conservation projects for volunteers.

## Adelaide Festival Centre

✉ King William Rd.
☎ 13 12 46

## South Australian Museum

✉ North Terrace
☎ (08) 8207 7500

## Art Gallery of South Australia

✉ North Terrace
☎ (08) 8207 7000

## Adelaide Botanic Gardens

✉ North Terrace
☎ (08) 8222 9311
💲 $ for Bicentennial Conservatory

The upper floors of the old railroad station were beautifully restored in the mid-1980s and turned into the elegant **Skycity Casino** *(open 24 hours).* Abutting the casino are the convention center and octagonal towers of the Hyatt Regency Adelaide, arguably the city's most luxurious hotel. Still farther west is the **Lion Arts Centre** *(Morphett St. at North Terrace),* where the Adelaide Fringe Festival is based. The center is a bright and airy building with exhibition galleries, theaters, bars, contemporary art galleries, and a cinema. The Jam Factory Craft and Design Centre in the Lion Arts Centre has high-quality glassware, pottery, and woodwork for sale.

The **Adelaide Festival Centre** is tucked behind Parliament House and the casino, on the banks of the Torrens River. This boxy version of the Sydney Opera House has better acoustics. Built in 1977, the modernistic complex contains a 2,000-seat theater, smaller 600- and 380-seat theaters, and an 800-seat recital

hall. Although the Adelaide Arts Festival runs only every other year, in February and March, the center itself is busy all year and is home to the South Australian Theatre Company, the experimental Space Theatre, and a small commercial art gallery. The sun-drenched plaza behind the complex, with its fountains and bright 1970-ish sculptures, is a popular place for office workers to bring a lunch. The manicured lawns that spill down to the riverbank are part of **Elder Park,** another popular picnic spot. There are brightly painted pedal-powered boats for rent along the bank, and a landing for the sightseeing boat *Popeye (tel (08) 8295 4747),* an Adelaide institution since 1935. On Sunday mornings, bands play in the lacy, cast-iron Victorian-era rotunda.

If you head east on North Terrace from your original starting point *(corner of King William St. & North Terrace),* you'll come first to **Government House**—or rather an iron gate through which you can glimpse neoclassical stonework and ornamental gardens dating from 1836. The elegant mansion is the home of the governor of South Australia—the official representative of the British crown in the state—and is not open to the public. Nearby are the hallowed portals of the very exclusive **Adelaide Club**—the bastion of the city's old boy network.

The place next door, however, does welcome visitors: the **State Library** *(tel (08) 8207 7250, www .slsa.sa.gov.au),* which houses a vast collection of books, maps, and historical material, as well as

---

## EXPERIENCE:
## Visiting Adelaide's Markets

If you are planning a picnic, or just enjoy the sight of wonderful produce, check out Adelaide's **Central Market** on Gouger Street. More than 250 stalls sell exotic fruit, sheep cheeses, German pastries, meats, fresh local produce, fish, and more. On Sundays from 9:00 a.m. to 4:00 p.m., the lively **Rundle Street Market** in the city's East End offers clothes, leather goods, jewelry, and crafts.

browsing sections well stocked with newspapers and free access to the Internet. It adjoins the **South Australian Museum,** easily distinguished by the full-size whale skeleton in its front gallery window. The museum has the world's largest collection of Aboriginal artifacts as well as an extensive Melanesian collection.

Next door is the **Art Gallery of South Australia,** which houses one of the nation's largest collections of Australian art. Excellent free audio guides are available at the front desk. Or you can join one of the free guided tours that meet at the entrance at 11 a.m. and 2 p.m. daily.

Tucked behind the library is the **Migration Museum** *(82 Kintore Ave, tel (08) 8207 7570),* a hidden gem with poignant displays about the lives of immigrants, who came to South Australia from a hundred nations. It is in the former Destitute Asylum, where homeless people of the last century were kept out of sight and out of mind. The grounds behind the museum are part of the University of Adelaide campus.

Continue along North Terrace (and across the street), and you'll come to **Ayers House** *(tel (08) 8223 1234, closed Mon., $),* which is said to be the finest example of Regency architecture in Australia. From 1855 to 1878, this 40-room bluestone mansion was the home of Henry Ayers, seven times premier of South Australia and the man for whom Ayers Rock (Uluru) was named. There is an elegant function center behind the house.

St. Peter's Cathedral's twin spires lord over Pennington Gardens in northern Adelaide.

The **Adelaide Botanic Gardens** are on the eastern end of North Terrace. Established in 1855, these formal gardens have been expanded to include a palm house and the Bicentennial Conservatory, holding a modest-size rain forest. From the Botanic Gardens, you can continue to the **Adelaide Zoological Gardens**—a pleasant, if small, zoo—then return to your starting point on the *Popeye,* along the Torrens River.

On Grenfell Street, **Tandanya** is the arts center and gallery space for the National Aboriginal

**Adelaide Zoological Gardens**
- ✉ Frome Rd.
- ☎ (08) 8267 3255
- 💲 $$$

**Tandanya**
- ✉ 253 Grenfell St.
- ☎ (08) 8224 3200
- 💲 $

**www.tandanya .com.au**

Cultural Institute, with rotating exhibitions, an arts shop (a great place to buy a didgeridoo), and cultural performances at noon every day except Monday.

**North Adelaide:** Colonel Light laid out the enclave of North Adelaide as the residential part of his utopian city, a small district surrounded by leafy parklands and within an easy stroll of downtown (just across the Torrens River). Some of the city's most gracious mansions are here, as are rows of old bluestone cottages and some of the city's trendiest cafés and restaurants. The broad Adelaide Bridge is an open invitation to explore this part of the city.

The wide swath of manicured lawn to your left, after you cross the bridge, is **Pennington Gardens,** which also has walkways, ornamental trees, and flower beds. Looming above it are the twin spires of **St. Peter's Cathedral.** One of Australia's finest neo-Gothic buildings, the cathedral was built between 1869 and 1904 and has a powerful, but mellow,

eight-bell carillon that is played on feast days. Up the hill, the road becomes **O'Connell Street,** the heart of North Adelaide's café scene. Alternatively, if you follow Sir Edwin Smith Avenue, to your right as you cross the bridge, you'll come to **Melbourne Street,** another cavalcade of restaurants, cafés, and bistros. Veer to the left in front of the cathedral and you'll reach the **Adelaide Cricket Ground,** regarded as one of the prettiest in the world. Even if you know nothing about the game, it is worth sauntering this way if a match is playing. In the main building, the small **Bradman Collection Museum** *(closed Sat. & Sun.)* displays memorabilia of Australia's greatest cricketer.

At the top of the hill behind the cricket ground is **Light's Vision** and the bronze statue of the city's founder. This is a great place to get a photograph of the city, especially at dusk when the first lights are flickering on. Colonel Light hadn't yet created Utopia when he first gazed on the floodplain below, but he could at least see where to put it. ■

## Pie Floaters

For all the elegant and innovative dining in Adelaide, one of the things Adelaideans love most is a "pie floater." Australians everywhere love their meat pies, consuming more than 260 million of them each year. Pies are generally served in a paper bag with a squirt of tomato sauce (ketchup, to Americans) and a napkin to catch the gravy as it drips down your chin. South Australians have developed their own peculiar variation on the national dish. They float the meat pie in a bowl of pea soup, then add the tomato sauce (appetizingly called "dead horse"). You may not understand the appeal, but almost every South Australian swears a "pie floater" is food fit for gods. Pie carts all over the city once served this ambrosia, but one by one the carts disappeared. Some cafés still serve this classic, however, and it shouldn't be missed. *Bon appétit.*

# Around Adelaide

Tucked between the sea and a range of hills, Adelaide offers plenty of options for a day out when the summer city begins to stifle. Take the tram for a half-hour ride to Glenelg, or drive up to the Mount Lofty hills for marvelous views and a fresh tang to the air.

The old tram, beachside amusements, and rambling hotels give Glenelg the air of an English resort.

## Glenelg & Beyond

For the quintessential Adelaide experience, take the restored 1929 tram from Victoria Square southwest to Glenelg, 6 miles (10 km) away. Fifty years ago this quaint old beach town was where Adelaide went on holiday, and even today it has the feel of an English seaside resort, despite rows of new apartment blocks.

South Australia's first settlers landed in Glenelg in 1836, and the gnarled gum tree where Gov. John Hindmarsh proclaimed it a new

colony still stands on McFarlane Street. A full-size reproduction of the settlers' ship, **H.M.S. Buffalo**, sits in the harbor, and on board is a popular seafood restaurant (tel (08) 8294 7000).

Glenelg has a bustling atmosphere during the week, but on the weekends it really hums. This beach is Adelaide's most popular and most accessible. Rent umbrellas, deck chairs, boogie boards, in-line skates, and bicycles along the waterfront. Trendy cafés and bookshops cram Jetty Road.

**Glenelg**
🔼 251 C2
**Visitor Information**
✉ Behind the Town Hall, Moseley Sq.
☎ (08) 8294 5833

### Adelaide Hills

 251 C2

**Visitor Information**

✉ 41 Main St., Hahndorf

☎ (08) 8388 1185 or 1-800 353 323 (toll-free)

Glenelg is one of a chain of beaches along the coast—running to the north are **West Beach, Henley Beach,** and **Grange Beach; Brighton** lies to the south. All have an old-fashioned air.

Northwest of the city, **Port Adelaide,** once a working-class suburb around the old wharves, has undergone gentrification, many of its fine historic buildings now fashionable cafés, pubs, and museums. Most interesting is the **Maritime Museum** (*126 Lipson St., tel (08) 8207 7570, $*), or just spend a few hours wandering around this fascinating area.

You won't see much surf along here because these beaches are on the sheltered **Gulf of St. Vincent.** Older locals, though, can tell you about the wild storm of 1948 that virtually destroyed Glenelg's jetty. The water comes up from the Southern Ocean, and it can be surprisingly brisk at times.

Occasionally sharks are spotted near the beach. Use caution, but don't let *Jaws* dissuade you from taking a refreshing dip. None of the locals do. Far more dangerous and ubiquitous are the deadly ultraviolet rays of the sun, which here in South Australia regularly register as "extreme" or higher.

## Adelaide Hills

A 20-minute drive southeast of the city on Glen Osmond Road and the Southeastern Freeway brings you to the Adelaide Hills. Called the "enchanted hills" by Colonel Light, they are leafy, green, and, on a hot day, as much as 15°F (8°C) cooler than Adelaide itself. As a consequence, they have been a retreat for Adelaide's gentility for more than a century, especially since the Southeastern Freeway has provided quick access to the city. Today, hill villages such as

Cleland Wildlife Park offers hands-on animal encounters within its 2,500-acre (1,000 ha) grounds.

## EXPERIENCE: Spotting the Elusive Platypus

Of all the strange animals in Australia, none is more curious than the platypus. This semi-aquatic, fur-covered mammal has a beak like a duck and a tail like a badger and lays eggs like a reptile. Males have poisonous spurs behind their webbed feet, the venom strong enough to kill a dog. When specimens first arrived in England, they were thought to be a hoax.

Platypuses inhabit rivers and streams on the east coast and throughout the Tasmanian wilderness. These mostly solitary, nocturnal animals dig burrows in riverbanks and dive to the bottom for small animals and insects, such as worms, crustaceans, and larvae.

Very few Australians have seen the shy platypus in its natural habitat. The best chance is with a guide. **Warrawong Wildlife Sanctuary** (Stock Road, Mylor, tel (08) 8370 9197, www.warrawong.com), in the Adelaide Hills, has a breeding program where platypuses live around a lake. To see them, book a guided night walk.

**Eungella National Park,** which is located 50 miles (80 km) west of Mackay in Queensland, is well known for platypus sightings on the Broken River. Patience and quiet are required. Dawn and dusk are the best times. **Rainforest Adventure Tours** (tel (07) 4959 8360) runs eco-tours from Mackay.

---

**Stirling** feel like genteel suburbs or hobby farm country.

For visitors, the Adelaide Hills offer beautiful hiking trails and conservation parks, wineries, historic villages, and numerous festivals. Consult the helpful visitor center in Hahndorf, just off the freeway about 20 miles (32 km) southeast of the city. Pick up a copy of the *Adelaide Hills Classic Country Drive* brochure for suggestions of great day trips.

Part of the **Mount Lofty Ranges,** the Adelaide Hills are dominated by the 2,362-foot (720 m) summit of Mount Lofty. (It's the tall one with the television antennas on it.) The Mount Lofty Ranges are believed to have originally been part of the Trans-Antarctic Mountains, which existed millions of years ago before the continents broke up and drifted apart. Mount Lofty's summit is easily accessible by car and gives sweeping views over the city, the coast, and the country inland. Take the Summit Road exit off the freeway, just before the town of Crafers (about 10 miles/16 km out of Adelaide), and follow it north for about 2 miles (3 km). On the right shortly after you leave the freeway, you'll pass the beautiful **Mount Lofty Botanic Gardens** (Summit Rd., tel (08) 8370 8370). The summit of Mount Lofty has a restaurant (tel (08) 8339 2600), and tourist office and gift shop (tel (08) 8370 1054).

Two hundred yards farther along the road, on your left, is the **Cleland Wildlife Park** (tel (08) 8339 2444, $$), a conservation park where you can cuddle a koala, hand-feed kangaroos and wallabies, or take a guided nighttime tour to see some of Australia's shy nocturnal wildlife.

Ten miles (16 km) farther east along the freeway is **Hahndorf,** the oldest German settlement in South Australia and one of the

### The Cedars

✉ Heysen Rd.,
Hahndorf

☎ (08) 8388 7277

🕐 Closed Mon.

### Capri Theatre

✉ 141 Goodwood
Rd., Goodwood

☎ (08) 8272 1177

www.capri.org.au

main attractions in the Adelaide Hills. Prussian and Silesian immigrants settled here in 1839, having come to Australia to escape religious persecution in their homelands. Today the village plays up its colorful German heritage, perhaps a little too enthusiastically for some tastes; it borders on the kitsch. It is a lively place, with German bakeries, tearooms, galleries, and craft shops. One of the town's most famous residents was the noted early 20th-century landscape painter Hans Heysen, who lived and worked in an elegant home called **The Cedars,** still owned by his descendants. About 300 of Heysen's paintings are on display in the house, located about

### INSIDER TIP:

**Step back in time and see a classic movie at the beautifully restored art deco Capri Theatre (*www.capri.org.au*) in the southern Adelaide suburb of Goodwood.**

—ROFF SMITH
*National Geographic author*

1.5 miles (2 km) north of town. In the center of town, the 1857 **Hahndorf Academy** (*68 Main St., tel (08) 8388 7250, www.hahndorf academy.org.au*) is an art and craft gallery with an interesting German migration museum and gallery of Heysen's drawings.

Rich with vineyards, the region has a long history of wine production (see pp. 263–266).

**Hiking:** The area has excellent hiking, from afternoon strolls through the bush to extended treks of a week or more in the Mount Lofty Ranges. One of Australia's finest and longest trails, the 715-mile-long (1,144 km) **Heysen Trail,** named after Hans Heysen, winds through the Adelaide Hills on its way north from the tip of the Fleurieu Peninsula to the heart of the Flinders Ranges, across some of South Australia's finest countryside. Most hikers do just short sections as a day trip, but a few hardy souls have done the entire length. Maps of the trail are available in many of Adelaide's camping shops (which are concentrated on Rundle Street). Huts and campsites are regularly spaced along the route, and the Youth Hostel Association (*135 Waymouth, Adelaide, tel (08) 8414 3000*) has small hostels at Mount Lofty and Mylor that groups can rent. The Heysen Trail is closed in summer because of potential bushfires.

**Going Farther:** The Adelaide Hills are a gateway north to the vineyards of the **Barossa Valley** (see pp. 267–268). To reach them, take the Onkaparinga Road exit from the freeway near Bridgewater, about 12 miles (19 km) out of Adelaide, and go north for about 30 miles (48 km) through the villages of Oakbank, Woodside, Birdwood, and Springton.

Or, to reach the **Fleurieu Peninsula** to the south, take the

Vineyards in the McLaren Vale weave a gentle pattern in the foothills of the Mount Lofty Ranges.

Mount Barker–Strathalbyn Road south from Stirling through the stunning hills and farmland of the Adelaide Hills to Macclesfield and Strathalbyn. From there it is an easy drive along the Goolwa Road to the pretty seaside towns of **Goolwa** and **Victor Harbor** (see pp. 274–276).

## Wine Districts

The Barossa Valley (see pp. 267–268) is the state's most important wine district. However, the Southern Vales, Coonawarra, the Clare Valley, and other regions are challenging its status, and new vineyards are being planted along the Murray River Valley, in the Adelaide Hills, and near Port Lincoln on the Eyre Peninsula.

The **Southern Vales,** on the Fleurieu Peninsula about 25 miles (40 km) south of Adelaide, is the state's oldest wine district. The first winery here started in 1838, and now more than 60 wineries

are in the area, which has gained a following for rich Shirazes and Cabernet Sauvignons. Chapel Hill, Hardy's Reynella, Hasle Grove, and Wirra Wirra are some of the better known labels. Most of the wineries are small, family concerns. The best time to visit is during the Sea & Vines Festival in June. There are tastings, feasts, and tours; special buses go around the wineries so visitors can drink and not worry about driving. The ideal base is the pretty little village of **McLaren Vale,** a rather trendy spot that has plenty of B&Bs, galleries, and craft shops. To get to the Southern Vales, follow Main South Road out of Adelaide to Old Noarlunga and from there follow the Victor Harbor Road another 3 miles (5 km) to the turnoff for McLaren Vale.

The **Adelaide Hills** (see pp. 260–262) also have a long history of winemaking and
(continued on p. 266)

**Wine District Visitor Information Centers:**

**Southern Vales**
✉ Main Rd., McLaren Vale
☎ (08) 8323 9944

**Adelaide Hills**
🅰 251 C2
✉ 41 Main St., Hahndorf
☎ (08) 8388 1185 or 1-800 353 323 (toll-free)

**Coonawarra**
🅰 251 D1
✉ 27 Arthur St., Penola
☎ (08) 8737 2855

**Clare Valley**
🅰 251 C3
✉ Main North Rd. & Spring Cully Rd., Clare
☎ (08) 8842 2131

**Renmark**
🅰 251 D2
✉ 84 Murray Ave.
☎ (08) 8586 6704

# Australian Wines

Since the 1980s, Australia has emerged as one of the world's great winemaking nations, internationally lauded for its use of innovative techniques to produce bold, fruity, and affordable wines. Connoisseurs around the world recognize regional Australian names such as Barossa Valley, Coonawarra, Margaret River, Clare, and Hunter Valley. Australian labels have consistently pulled down some of the world's most prestigious awards.

Brother John May tests the wine casks at the Seven Hills Winery in the Clare Valley.

Penfold's 1990 Grange Hermitage—Australia's premier red—was judged by the influential *Wine Spectator* magazine to be the international Wine of the Year when it was released in 1995. In 1999, the magazine rated the '55 Grange among the 12 finest wines of the 20th century, ranking it with such luminaries as the '21 Château d'Yquem and the Château Mouton-Rothschild '45. Although this success seemed to come suddenly, it was not a case of Aussie nouveau. Australian wines were winning international awards as long ago as the 1870s, and Victoria's Yerinberg winery took a gold medal at the Paris Exposition of 1889.

Viticulture in Australia dates back to 1788, when the First Fleet brought vine clippings from South Africa. By the 1830s, the Hunter Valley in New South Wales was producing wine, thanks largely to the efforts of a Scot, James Busby, who had studied viticulture in France and imported hundreds of clippings from France and Spain. Prussian and Silesian immigrants began growing wine grapes in South Australia's Barossa Valley in the 1840s, almost as soon as they arrived. Victoria's wine industry was kick-started in the 1850s with 10,000 clippings from Bordeaux's Château Lafite-Rothschild.

These bold beginnings were put on hold, however, in part by the outbreak of phylloxera that ravaged much of the world's vineyards in the late 19th century, and in part by fashion. Tastes moved on to fortified wines and away from table wine. It wasn't until the 1960s that Australians began making table wine in quantity again. (Australia's total 1959 crush for Cabernet Sauvignon was 69 tons/62 tonnes, compared with 315,000 tons/286,000 tonnes in 2010.)

### Australian Winemaking Today

Today, Australia is the world's fourth largest exporter of wine, after France, Italy, and Spain, with thousands of wineries, producing more than 330 million gallons (1.25 billion L) of wine every year, two-thirds of it for export.

Grapes are grown in every state—there is even a vineyard near Alice Springs. Boutique areas such as Margaret River (located in Western Australia) and the Yarra Valley (in Victoria) are on the cutting edge of fashion, but the lion's share of premium quality wine comes from South Australia. The Barossa and Clare Valleys, the McLaren Vale, and the Coonawarra region are the best known wine districts in the nation.

One of the main reasons for Australia's success is the willingness on the part of its winemakers to use the latest technologies to blend whatever regional varieties of grapes they need to produce bold fruity flavors. The result of these so-called New World techniques is a clean-tasting wine that evokes Australia's bright sunshine and costs far less than a European

**INSIDER TIP:**

**Penfold's Barossa winery goes beyond the usual wine tastings. You can don a lab coat, blend your own wine, and take home a bottle of your creation. [See sidebar below.]**

—JEANINE BARONE
*National Geographic writer*

vintage of comparable quality. Old World winemakers, on the other hand, have been bound by centuries-old traditions and prevented by law from taking such radical steps. But times are changing. These days Australian winemakers are in big demand in Europe, where they are helping some of the world's most famous houses develop their art into a science. In what would have seemed sacrilege only a few years ago, some European houses are now offering wines made "in the Australian style."

Penfold's Grange may be Australia's greatest red wine, but with a price tag of more than A$700 (U.S. $625) a bottle for the recent vintages (and into the thousands of dollars for some of the earlier ones), it is a little rich for most occasions. Even this outstanding red faces serious competition from other great Australian labels such as Henschke. The competition for best white wine is an open field, with runners from around the country.

---

## EXPERIENCE: Wine Courses

**Penfold's,** one of the country's great wineries, offers a unique wine experience at its Barossa Valley cellar *(Tanunda Road, Nuriootpa, tel (08) 8568 9408)*. In the winemakers' laboratory, guests can blend their own wines—from Grenache, Shiraz, and Mourvedre grapes—then bottle it to take home. Make Your Own Blend runs daily at 10 a.m. and 2 p.m.; reservations

are essential. Educate Your Palate is a series of wine education courses, lasting from two hours to two weeks, with tastings of local and world wines, at the **National Wine Centre of Australia** *(Botanic Rd., Adelaide, tel (08) 8222 9276, www.wineso.asn.au)*, an impressive complex near the city's Botanic Garden with wine-barrel-inspired architecture.

## Around Coonawarra

Located 25 miles (40 km) north of Coonawarra, **Naracoorte Caves Park**—which featured in David Attenborough's acclaimed BBC television series *Life on Earth*—has a huge population of bats. It is also a UNESCO World Heritage site, where an astounding collection of Pleistocene fossils have been discovered, including extinct marsupials like a giant kangaroo and a rhinoceros-size wombat.

Six miles (10 km) south of Coonawarra is the village of **Penola,** where Mother Mary MacKillop, a 19th-century Catholic nun, did much of her early work on behalf of the poor and disadvantaged. Her works and the subsequent reports of miracles prompted the Roman Catholic church to beatify her in 1995—the last step before her possibly becoming Australia's first saint.

**VISITING WINERIES:**
The Barossa Wine and Visitor Centre (see p. 267) and the South Australian Visitor Information Centre in Adelaide (see p. 252) can advise on tours and visits.

claim Australia's first known wine export—an 1845 hock from Echunga sent to England for Queen Victoria. These days, 33 wineries are in the hills, which are becoming known for their Chardonnay. Petaluma and Karl Seppelts Grand Cru Estate are two prominent local labels.

**Coonawarra,** about 250 miles (400 km) southeast of Adelaide, produces excellent reds. More than 20 wineries cram into this narrow region (12 miles/20 km long and a little more than a mile/2 km wide). Demand for Coonawarra's fabled *terra rossa* soil has pushed prices for land to absurd levels. Most of Australia's great Cabernet Sauvignons spring from this soil.

The **Clare Valley,** about 80 miles (128 km) north of Adelaide on Main North Road, has a lovely European feel to it and a lot less tourist hype than other districts. It was settled in the 1850s and named Clare by homesick Irish because its gentle landscape reminded them of County Clare. Winemaking in the valley began with Jesuit brothers, who grew grapes to make their own

communion wine. They named their monastery Seven Hills after the seven hills around Rome. Today, the Seven Hills winery, 6 miles (10 km) south of Clare, is still run by Jesuits, who continue their tradition of making sacramental wine but have diversified into table wines, port, and sherry. Tours of the winery and old stone cellars are available by appointment.

Seven Hills is one of 41 wineries in the region. They range from the small but highly regarded Grosset Wines, which is run out of an old butter factory in Auburn, to the giant, century-old Leasingham Wines near the town of Clare. The region is ideal for bicycling, with a number of bike trails, including the excellent 20-mile (30 km) Riesling Trail through the vineyards.

The **Murray River Valley** has long produced table grapes and cheap cask wine, but an increasing number of big-name wineries are planting vines here. The Kingston Estate winery, 140 miles (225 km) northeast of Adelaide near Barmera, is the pick of the region. Boston Bay Wineries and Delacolline Estate are the two major winemakers in Port Lincoln.

The sea view from the Boston Bay vineyard is stunning.

## Barossa Valley

The Barossa Valley is South Australia's premier wine area, producing almost one-fifth of the nation's wine and accounting for about 70 percent of its wine exports. It is home to some of Australia's most respected labels, such as Penfolds, Henschke, Peter Lehman, Orlando (Jacob's Creek), Wolf Blass, Yalumba, and Seppelts—the only winery in the world with an unbroken line of vintage ports dating back to 1878. The district also produces

cost of their passage. It was the first time in Australia's history that immigrants from somewhere other than England had been actively sought. In addition to their doughty work ethic, language, and culture, the newcomers brought their winemaking skills. Within a year, they had planted grapevines along Jacob's Creek, and by 1850, the valley had begun its long tradition of winemaking. The Barossa Valley's isolation protected it from the outbreak of phylloxera in the 1870s that ravaged the rest of the world's grapevines. As a result, some of the world's oldest Shiraz vines can be found here today.

### Barossa Valley

🗺 251 D2

**Visitor Information**

✉ Barossa Wine and Visitor Centre, 68 Murray St., Tanunda

☎ (08) 8563 0600

---

# EXPERIENCE: Seasonal Work

Good for one year, Working Holiday Visas enable young (18–30) travelers from Canada, the U.K., and the U.S. to undertake popular seasonal work (check *www.immi.gov.au* for details).

Hotels and restaurants, particularly in tourist areas, employ many overseas visitors during the high season. Picking fruit during harvest season is an easy way to help finance travels. Grape-picking work in wine areas such as the Hunter Valley, Barossa, and Mildura is hot but plentiful in February and March. Peaches

then apples, follow in the southern states, while mangoes (around Christmas in Atherton) and bananas are Queensland specialties. Prawn boats and fishing trawlers operate out of Cairns over the winter (May–Aug.). The ski resorts in the Australian Alps also have seasonal work over winter.

Websites with good information include: **Harvest Trail** (*jobsearch.gov.au/harvesttrail*), detailing harvest locations and times, and **Workabout Australia** (*www.workaboutaustralia.com.au*).

---

smoked meats, cheeses, and pickles that reflect its distinctive German heritage.

The valley was settled in 1842 by Prussian and Silesian Lutherans who were seeking religious freedom. They were persuaded to come to Australia by George Fife Angas, a wealthy and philanthropic South Australian landowner, who underwrote the

There is still a strong German feel to the valley. Old stone Lutheran churches dot the countryside, and the villages have German bakeries and butcher shops where goods are made according to family recipes. Old German names fill the phone books, and until recently some of the valley's older residents spoke an Australianized form of German

## Kangaroo Island

⛰ 251 C2

**Visitor Information**

✉ Gateway Visitor Information Centre, Howard Dr., Penneshaw

☎ (08) 8553 1185

## Barossa Valley Cheese Company

✉ 67b Murray St., Angaston

☎ (08) 8564 3636

**www.barossacheese .au.com**

known as Barossa-Deutsche.

The Barossa Valley is an easy 45-mile (72 km) drive north of Adelaide on Main North Road, with ample signs to the valley's main towns of Tanunda, Nuriootpa, and Angaston.

Of the three towns, centrally located **Tanunda** is the one most geared to tourists, with a pleasant

**INSIDER TIP:**

**Cheese lovers should follow the Barossa Valley cheese and wine trail. Start at the Barossa Valley Cheese Company in Angaston and pick up a trail map.**

—JEANINE BARONE
*National Geographic writer*

main street and a wide selection of craft galleries, cafés, and B&Bs. **Nuriootpa** is the valley's commercial hub. The small and quiet village of **Angaston,** to the east, is perhaps the prettiest. It was founded by George Fife Angas in the 1830s. His magnificent estate, Lindsey Park, is now one of Australia's top racing stables. It is not open to visitors, but you can visit his son's mansion, **Collingrove** *(6 miles/10 km via the road to Eden Valley southeast of Angaston),* now owned by the National Trust.

Most of the 60 cellars open to the public offer free tastings— although if you want to sample the priciest vintages and labels, you'll have to take out your wallet. Some, including **Seppelts** and

**Château Yaldara,** are open for tours. Seppelts is one of the best, and the drive from Nuriootpa is exceptionally scenic. The route runs along a 2-mile (3 km) avenue of ornamental date palms, with a Doric temple on the hillside (the temple is the Seppelt family mausoleum). A variety of tours is available to the wineries (you can travel by minivan, luxury Daimler, or restored 1935 Auburn convertible, among other vehicles), so everyone can partake in the tastings without violating Australia's strict drink-driving laws.

Food is also a big attraction, the most popular place being **Maggie Beer's Farm Shop** *(Pheasant Farm Rd., tel (08) 8562 4477).* This celebrity chef's gourmet outlet has local produce, food and wine tastings, and 2 p.m. cooking demonstrations.

The Barossa Vintage Festival— held over Easter week in odd-numbered years—draws thousands of visitors to the valley for a week of parades and shows. It is just one of the many festivals held here.

## Kangaroo Island

If Australia has been an ark for unique flora and fauna, Kangaroo Island (or K.I.) has been its lifeboat. This surprisingly large island, barely 10 miles (16 km) off the coast of South Australia, has remained an unspoiled haven for wildlife and offers a lazy, rural lifestyle only recently invaded by luxury retreats. The roads are mostly dirt, and drivers have to be careful not to dent their fenders on the high stone curbs in the villages. There are wallabies, kangaroos, koalas, platypuses, and echidnas on land, and the sea has seals, dolphins, sea lions, penguins, whales, and sharks; both have teeming birdlife.

The island has 24 national parks or conservation areas, covering about a third of its total area. The largest and best known is **Flinders Chase National Park,** which covers the western end of Kangaroo Island. The rest of the island has well-watered forests and rolling farmland, with a good reputation for such produce as sheep's milk cheeses, free-range chickens, freshwater crayfish, rock lobster, and King George whiting. Increasingly known for its honey, the island has the world's last pure strain of gentle Ligurian honeybees—brought here from Italy in the 1860s.

Australia's third largest island after Tasmania and the Northern Territory's Melville Island, Kangaroo Island, is about 90 miles (153 km) long and up to 30 miles (55 km) wide. It is sparsely populated, with only 4,400 inhabitants. The dramatic cliff-lined coasts and rocky shoals have claimed more than 40 ships since English navigator Matthew Flinders set eyes on the uninhabited island in 1802. Although Aboriginal artifacts dating back 30,000 years have been found here, archaeological evidence suggests the Aborigines left around 7,000 years ago. No one knows why.

Kangaroo Island was settled in 1806 by an assortment of escaped convicts and deserters from Yankee whaling ships. They camped near present-day American River, built a 34-ton (31 tonne) schooner out of local materials, and set about the wholesale slaughter of the seal population. They also

**FLYING TO KANGAROO ISLAND FROM ADELAIDE:**
**Air South** (08 ) 8234 4988
**Regional Express (Rex)** 13 17 13

**CAR RENTAL:** Rental companies do not usually permit their cars to be taken to Kangaroo Island. The island's car rental companies are located in Kingscote.

Stokes Bay, on the northern coast of Kangaroo Island, is one of scores of secluded nooks and bays.

raided Aboriginal camps on the mainland coast. By 1827, the island had acquired such an evil reputation that the colonial authorities sent in a military expedition and dragged almost the entire population away in chains.

An official attempt was made in 1836 to set up South Australia's first colony on the island (at Kingscote), but attention switched to Adelaide instead. Throughout much of the next century, Kangaroo Island remained undeveloped.

To remedy that, authorities gave free land to returned veterans from World War I and World War II. Many of the island's farmers are descendents of those soldiers.

Getting to the island is simple. You can fly daily to Kingscote from Adelaide Airport (see panel information, p. 269), but most visitors go by ferry. Kangaroo Island Sealink *(tel 13 13 01)* operates two vehicular ferries from Cape Jervis, about an hour south of Adelaide at the tip of the Fleurieu Peninsula.

## Kangaroo Island's Koalas

You are more likely to see a koala in the wild on Kangaroo Island than anywhere else. The koala population here has been estimated as high as 30,000—far outstripping the number of human residents on the island. The fact that the island has so many of these cuddly-looking marsupials is both a tribute to its qualities and a cautionary tale about well-meaning conservation.

Koalas are not native to the island. They were brought here in 1923, when it was obvious the species was in trouble. On the mainland, rapidly growing suburbs were gobbling up their habitat, and in Queensland they were being hunted as pests. More than three million koalas were killed after World War I, before they were finally protected in 1927. The seagirt wildlife stronghold of Kangaroo Island seemed a perfect place to relocate a few, and a group of 18 was released in Flinders Chase National Park.

The island was perfect for koalas because it had no diseases, no predators such as dingoes, and a seemingly unlimited supply of manna gums—one of their favorite foods. By 1996, however, the koala population had grown out of control, stripping the stately century-old

gum trees along the rivers and creating a potential environmental nightmare. The suggestion that 2,000 or so koalas would have to be shot provoked an international uproar. Letting them denude the forests until they starved seemed little better.

Relocation was not an easy option. Koalas are exceptionally finicky eaters. Their delicate stomachs can digest the leaves of only about a dozen of the 600-plus species of eucalyptuses. Those grow on well-watered soils along the coast—prime real estate for humans. Any small fragments of koala habitat that were left on the mainland were already fully populated by koalas. So it was decided to use fertility controls to keep the population in check. Some koalas were relocated to suitable homes. Despite these efforts, the number of koalas continues to rise.

One of the best places to see koalas is in Flinders Chase National Park. Or you can visit the Cygnet River on the eastern half of the island. They can be a little difficult to spot, nestled in the forks of gum trees, because their gray coats meld perfectly with the color of the bark. Look for an irregular bump when you run your eyes over a likely gum, and slowly a koala will appear.

The crossing takes 45 minutes and delivers you to Penneshaw. A bus service goes to Cape Jervis from Adelaide's hotels (*reservations necessary, call Sealink, tel 13 13 01*).

Kangaroo Island's growing popularity has transformed the local tourism industry, with options for visitors now ranging from good old-fashioned camping to exclusive luxury villas such as **Stone House** and the stunning **Southern Ocean Lodge** (*Hanson Bay, tel (02) 9918 4355, www .southernoceanlodge.com.au*), with prices to match the soaring clifftop location.

**Kangaroo's Wildlife and Parks:** The main reason people come to Kangaroo Island is to see wildlife and the island's national and conservation parks, for which you need a pass (see column information). One of the best ways to catch a glimpse of the often elusive native fauna is to go on a wildlife safari. One of the most personal is **Exceptional Kangaroo Island** (*tel (08) 8553 9119, www.exceptional kangarooisland.com*), a small firm owned and operated by expert local naturalists.

If you prefer to scout around independently, head first for **Cape Gantheaume Conservation Park** and the nearby **Seal Bay Conservation Park** to see sea lions—both about 30 miles (48 km) from Kingscote, Kangaroo Island's commercial center.

Farther to the west along the south coast are the pretty beaches at **Vivonne Bay,** the pure white dunes known as **Little Sahara,**

A koala perches in the fork of a gum tree at Flinders Chase.

and **Kelly Hill Conservation Park,** which has dunes and scrub underlaid by limestone caves (*tour bookings, tel (08) 8559 7231*). The caves were discovered in the 1880s by a stockman named Kelsey and his horse Kelly, which tumbled into them through a sinkhole. The National Parks and Wildlife Service runs caving tours.

**Flinders Chase National Park,** in the west, has a dramatic rocky coastline, picturesque old lighthouses, and eucalyptus forests filled with wildlife. The park headquarters is at Rocky River Homestead. On the northwestern

(continued on p. 274)

**VISITING KANGAROO ISLAND'S NATIONAL PARKS:** An Island Parks Pass (A$59/U.S. $53) is required for entry to the national parks on the island. It covers some camping fees and entitles you to "free" national parks tours. The pass can be purchased on arrival at the **Penneshaw Visitor Centre** or any Department of Environment & Heritage office.

# Festival State

South Australia's nickname is the Festival State. On its calendar are more than 400 festivals, carnivals, and sporting events ranging from the throaty high-octane roar of V-8 motor racing to the Festival of Ideas, from the Tour Down Under—the most prestigious cycling event in the Southern Hemisphere—to the Bohemian funkiness of the Fringe Festival.

Performers pose at WOMADelaide.

Depending on when you visit South Australia, you might take in events as varied as the **Barossa Valley Vintage Festival** (Easter in odd-numbered years), the **Australian Camel Cup** race in the outback town of Maree (July), and the **Schutzenfest** (January, with oompah bands). Oakbank's **Easter Racing Carnival** is Australia's greatest picnic-day horse race, and the **Bay to Birdwood Run** antique automobile rally attracts

more than 2,000 entries from Australia and around the world.

The most famous event is the **Adelaide Festival of the Arts.** For glamour, excitement, and size, it easily surpasses anything else of the sort in Australia. Held over three weeks in March in even-numbered years, it attracts major artists from Australia and around the world. The festival began modestly in 1960 with 51 shows, but has burgeoned into a feast of more than 300 plays, concerts, films,

**INSIDER TIP:**

Whether it's food, wine, music, arts, architecture, cycling, motoring, or writing that gives you a buzz, there's an associated festival for it in South Australia.

—LAURA RUYKYS
*National Geographic field researcher*

dance performances, and cabaret acts. Ticket prices are quite reasonable, and for those on a tight budget, there are free weekend concerts and fireworks displays on the banks of the Torrens River. The weather in Adelaide in March is generally perfect, with hot days and warm starry nights that make outdoor performances a treat.

Coinciding with the Festival of the Arts is the even more exuberant and sometimes very strange **Fringe Festival**. Originally staged by street artists as a protest to the perceived elitism of the arts festival, the Fringe Festival is now a power in its own right, an annual event drawing thousands of visitors to the city for a month of experimental theater, jugglers, comedians, offbeat entertainers, and film festivals. If the Festival of the Arts gives Adelaide a taste

of Manhattan, the Fringe Festival is more like New Orleans. Walk the café-lined streets on these summer evenings and you're likely to see anything. While all this is going on, Adelaide also hosts **Writers' Week,** during which well-known authors from Australia and overseas gather to discuss their works, launch books, and give readings. This event is free.

The annual World of Music, Arts, and Dance Festival in Adelaide—**WOMADelaide** —is also a big draw, attracting acts from around the world. Another major music event is the **Barossa Music Festival,** held each October in the Barossa Valley. The valley also hosts **Barossa Under the Stars,** at which international stars perform in an open-air concert near one of the big wineries. This annual festival usually takes place in late February or March. The **Country Music Festival** is celebrated each June in the town of Barmera (140 miles/225 km northeast of Adelaide).

Gourmet festivals are another tradition in South Australia. Every August, the Barossa Valley has a **Barossa Gourmet** weekend: Visitors travel around the wineries sampling wines with dishes created by some of South Australia's best restaurateurs. The South Australian Visitor Information Centre (see p. 252) has information about these and other festivals, or check *www.southaustralia.com.*

---

## EXPERIENCE: Festival Fever

Adelaide is abuzz from around mid-February to mid-March every year, when the **Adelaide Fringe Festival** *(www .adelaidefringe.com.au)* attracts nearly a million spectators to its performances. Featuring local and lesser-known artists, the festival was born in 1960 as an alternative to the prestigious Adelaide Festival of the Arts.

The **Adelaide Festival of the Arts** (www.adelaidefestival.com.au) has been held every other year since 1960, an era when the pubs closed at 6 p.m. and

censorship in the arts was rife. Queen Elizabeth was a festival patron then, and Dave Brubeck's jazz wowed audiences.

By the 1970s, South Australia was the most progressive state in the country, with a reform government keen to back the arts. The Adelaide Festival Centre was built, and the festivals went on to become the country's premier arts events.

Programs for both festivals are released around October. Many events are free, or you can buy tickets through Ticketek *(www.ticketek.com.au).*

corner of the island, about 65 miles (105 km) west of Kingscote on the island's main highway, is the square **Cape Borda Lighthouse,** built in 1858. The wild southwestern corner has the elegant **Cape de Couedic Lighthouse,** built along a line of sheer cliffs in 1906.

coastline was treacherous to shipping, and the fickle Murray River had a habit of silting up at the mouth. Visions of an antipodean New Orleans faded completely in 1878, when a rail spur linked the river town of Morgan, 150 miles (240 km) upstream, with the deepwater harbor at Port

The Victor Harbor coastline viewed from Rosetta Head

**Victor Harbor**

🄰 251 C2

**Visitor Information**

✉ The Causeway

☎ (08) 8551 0777

## Victor Harbor & Goolwa

The 1870s were the glory days of the Murray River, when steamboat traffic was at its height and civic boosters hoped that settlements such as Goolwa, Victor Harbor, and Port Elliott, near the river mouth, would one day rival New Orleans. Wool and grain from as far afield as Queensland was floated down the river to these ports, where clipper ships whisked them off to market in London.

Unfortunately, the exposed

Adelaide. The beachside villages found their métier instead as vacation resorts. A century later, these classic beach towns, about 60 miles (100 km) south of Adelaide, are still the getaway of choice among South Australians.

**Victor Harbor:** The biggest town on the Fleurieu Peninsula, this is a weekend destination for thousands of Adelaideans. Although Victor Harbor is only 50 miles (80 km) south of the city, it is generally about 10°F

(5°C) cooler. The drive from Adelaide, along Main South Road and Victor Harbor Road, takes you through the **McLaren Vale** wine country (see p. 263).

Victor Harbor sits on pretty **Encounter Bay,** where, in 1802, English navigator Matthew Flinders met his French counterpart Nicholas Baudin while both were exploring the South Australian coast. The town was founded in 1837 as a whaling station, and today the **South Australian Whale Centre** (Railway Terrace, tel (08) 8551 0750, $) is the place to learn about southern right whales (an endangered species) and whaling. Better still, come to Victor Harbor between June and October and see these magnificent leviathans. No longer hunted, they come into Encounter Bay on their annual migration and can be observed from the bluffs overlooking the bay. A large colony of fairy penguins lives on nearby Granite Island. You can walk out there along the causeway—a pleasant stroll—or take one of the trams pulled by Clydesdale horses.

**Goolwa:** With its beaches and rich beds of cockles, Goolwa became popular with homesick English migrants, who came down to gather cockles—just as they did on summer holidays back in the old country. The train bringing visitors came to be called the Cockle Train in the official railroad timetable. A restored version of the old steam-powered train still runs between Goolwa and Victor

Harbor on Wednesdays, Sundays, and school holidays.

The town has a strong nautical feel. Beams from the wreck of the *Mozambique* hold up the bar in the **Goolwa Hotel** *(30 Cadell St.),* and restored 19th-century steamboats do tours of the lower lengths of the Murray River. The **Goolwa Museum** *(11–13 Porter St., tel (08) 8555 2221)* covers Murray River ecology, 19th-century river trade, and the history of the Ngarrindjeri Aborigines, who have gathered cockles on these beaches for more than 10,000 years. Spirit Australia Cruises *(tel (08) 8555 2203)* runs Murray River tours leaving from the wharf near the massive bridge to Hindmarsh Island. Built in 2001 to service a marina real estate development on the island, the bridge sparked a national political battle after Ngarrindjeri women

**INSIDER TIP:**

**Visit Coorong National Park, two hours southeast of Adelaide, for hiking, fishing, bird-watching, and wetland boat tours.**

—MCKENZIE FUNK
*National Geographic writer*

objected to its construction, saying it violated sacred sites. The bridge was pushed through despite widespread opposition.

Goolwa is a good base for exploring the haunting sliver of sand dunes and coastal lagoons known as the **Coorong,** which

**Goolwa**

**Visitor Information**

✉ The Wharf

☎ (08) 8555 3810

**Mannum**

**Visitor Information**

✉ 6 Randell St.

☎ (08) 8569 1303

extends 100 miles (160 km) along South Australia's southeast coast. Home to more than 240 species of birds, it was the setting of the 1976 film *Storm Boy*, about an Aborigine who befriends a pelican.

## Lower Murray River

The Murray River is the longest and grandest river on the continent, and it is the only one that is navigable. It stretches 1,170 miles (1,883 km) from the Victorian high country to South Australia's windswept coastline. South Australia gets only the bottom 400 miles (640 km) of the river, but it gets the best scenery. The river here winds through sandstone gorges, past lagoons teeming with birdlife, and along riverbanks lined with stately Murray River gums.

By Mississippi or Amazon standards, the Murray is a trickle—barely a couple hundred yards wide. But on a continent as dry and dusty as Australia, it is life itself, accounting for more than half of the nation's fruit, vegetables, wine, meats, grains, cotton, and wool. In fact, the

quirky tasting drinking water for most of South Australia comes from the river. The river has also become the source of much debate in recent years, its waters severely depleted through over-irrigation and prolonged drought that threatens rural livelihoods and unique ecosystems alike.

The story of the Murray's steamboats began in South Australia. In 1853, a flour miller named William Randell put a crude steamboat, the *Mary Ann,* on the water near the river town of Mannum. Randell had never seen a steamboat before, but he could grasp the potential profit in being able to get his flour close to the Victorian goldfields, several hundred miles upstream. The *Mary Ann*'s makeshift boiler swelled like a football once pressure built up, causing the ship's engineer to run in terror. But these were robust times, and Randell simply bound the dodgy boiler with chain and kept on steaming up the river. A few days later, the *Mary Ann* was passed by another steamboat. The race was on. By the 1870s, more than 250 steamboats were on the river, and Randell's hometown of **Mannum** had become one of the nation's busiest inland ports, handling more than 20,000 bales of wool a year.

These days this quiet holiday town is a perfect place from which to get to know the river. It is an easy drive from Adelaide, following the Southeast Freeway 50 miles (80 km) to the old river port of **Murray Bridge** and then going 15 miles (24 km) north on the Mannum Road. A restored 1897

---

## EXPERIENCE:
## Renting a Houseboat

Houseboats can be rented at Murray Bridge, Mannum, and a number of villages along the Murray River. No license or special training is required, and river charts are provided. Information about rentals on the Murray can be obtained from visitor centers or from the **Houseboat Hirer's Association** (tel (08) 8395 0999, www.hsa.asn.au).

The paddle steamer *Melbourne* follows the Murray River near the town of Mildura.

steamboat, the **Marion,** is part of Mannum Dock Museum next to the visitor center and has short and overnight cruises. The grand Mississippi-style stern-wheeler **Murray Princess** ties up here between cruises *(Captain Cook Cruises, tel 1-800 804 84 [toll-free], www.captaincook.com.au).* It does three- to seven-night cruises along the river, running upstream through the sandstone gorges near Swan Reach. Another restored old steamer, the **Murray Expedition** offers five-day cruises *(tel (618) 8217 6100)* out of Murray Bridge. It is smaller and more intimate, and serves bush tucker, such as kangaroo. Both boats have air-conditioned cabins—important in summer when temperatures soar.

Murray Bridge is also home to the **Monarto Zoological Park** *(Princes Hwy., tel (08) 8534 4100),* a popular 2,500-acre (1,000 ha) big-game preserve.

The Murray is still a rural river, and the big steamboats simply tie up at a sandbar for the night. The stars are dazzling, and you wake up in the morning to a cacophony of galahs, cockatoos, and kookaburras. The crowds tend to be very Australian—the Murray River is a quintessentially Australian holiday spot.

If you want more independence, consider renting a houseboat (see sidebar p. 276). You'll get the same dramatic gorges, stars, and noisy birdlife, but you'll have even more of a sense of freedom. The houseboats are comfortable but fairly spartan—a bit like a floating camper van—with a kitchen, bunks, and a living room. Naturally, most include a barbecue.

## Flinders Ranges National Park

The Flinders Ranges make one of the most majestic national

## Flinders Ranges National Park

🗺 251 C3

**Visitor Information**

✉ Wilpena
☎ (08) 8648 0048

**Flinders Ranges Visitor Information Centre**

✉ 3 Seventh St., Quorn
☎ (08) 8648 6419

parks in Australia—an ancient folded landscape of craggy mountains and deep gorges, tinted purple and red in the clear desert light, and carpeted by wildflowers after the spring rains. With its vibrant hues, rich

**INSIDER TIP:**

Shy kangaroos are not always easy to spot, but at the Wilpena Pound campground in Flinders Ranges they come begging for food in the morning. Look but don't feed.

—PETER TURNER
*National Geographic author*

desert vegetation, and superb hiking trails, this spectacular outback wilderness has long been a favorite haunt of hikers, photographers, and painters.

Aboriginal artists and artisans have been coming into this rocky fastness for thousands of years to collect its rich ochers and workable stones. Matthew Flinders was the first European to see these mountains, when he sailed 200 miles (320 km) up Spencer Gulf in 1802. Within 40 years, the first graziers were staking claims in the southern portion of the ranges, and by the 1870s, farm towns and wheat fields could be found deep in the mountains. The newcomers hadn't reckoned on the fickleness of South Australia's outback, however, where a few seasons of gentle rains might be followed by

a decade of implacable drought. Today the ranges are dotted with crumbling ruins of stone farmhouses and ghost towns.

The Flinders Ranges are one of those all-too-rare instances in Australia where dramatic outback landscapes can be found a convenient distance from a capital city. A four-hour drive north of Adelaide on the Princes Highway brings you to **Port Augusta.** Six miles (10 km) before town, a marked turnoff on your right leads 25 miles (40 km) to Quorn and the solitary highway that leads another 70 miles (113 km) through Hawker and into the heart of **Flinders Ranges National Park.** A far more scenic (and not much longer) option is to drive north out of Adelaide on Main North Road, through the beautiful wine country around **Clare,** with scenic wheat fields and historic towns such as **Mintaro, Melrose,** and **Laura.** An additional 180 miles (290 km) brings you to Wilmington, where a sign directs you to Quorn and the Flinders Ranges. **Quorn** itself is an interesting outback town popular with vintage railroad buffs who come here to ride the Pichi Richi railroad *(tel 1-800 440 101, toll-free).* This restored train makes the 20-mile (32 km) run from the town to Pichi Richi Pass. Because of fire danger in this tinder-dry region, it operates only in the cooler, wetter months (March–Nov.).

The best known feature of the Flinders Ranges is **Wilpena Pound,** a vast amphitheater of red quartzite, purple shale, and cliffs that was formed by a dramatic upheaval of the Earth's crust about 450 million years ago. A quirk in the local climate gives the interior of Wilpena Pound considerably more rainfall than the surrounding desert. The floor of this lost world is covered with grasslands, native cypresses, casuarina trees, red gums, and, between September and November, a kaleidoscope of wildflowers. The pound is home to large numbers of wallabies, red kangaroos, and emus as well as huge flocks of rosellas, parrots, and galahs.

**Wilpena** comprises the Wilpena Pound Resort *(tel (08) 8648 0004)* as well as a store and a campsite. The resort visitor center has information on the walking trails inside Wilpena Pound itself.

Wilpena Pound is ringed by cliffs and is accessible only by foot through a narrow gorge at Sliding Rock. Hikes can be challenging. The best known trail here (or in South Australia, for that matter)

is the **Heysen Trail** (see p. 262). The most spectacular are the two steep trails that lead to the summit of **St. Mary's Peak,** which, at 3,822 feet (1,165 m), is the highest point in Wilpena Pound. Other trails climb up **Mount Ohlssen Bagge** and **Wangara Lookout.** Spring is by far the best time to do any hiking. In summer, the temperatures are scorching, with the bare rocks only magnifying the desert heat. No matter what time of year, bring a hat, put on sunscreen, and carry plenty of water. Four-wheel-drive tours and scenic flights over the ranges can be booked through the Wilpena Pound Resort.

The Flinders Ranges were significant to the Adnyamathanha ("hill people"), who lived here before Europeans arrived, and the dramatic rock formations inspired some Dreamtime legends. There are rock-art galleries at **Arkaroo** and **Sacred Canyon,** both a short drive from Wilpena. ■

Ancient coolibah trees line the valleys of the Flinders Ranges.

# Coober Pedy

The apocalyptic landscape around Coober Pedy looks like the work of a disturbed mind. For miles in every direction, the ground is covered by the sharp conical piles of clayish soil left by thousands of miners in their quest for opals. Australia produces 95 percent of the world's opals, and Coober Pedy is its richest field. The settlement's name comes from the corruption of a local Aboriginal phrase Kupa Piti, which means "white fellows in a hole."

Even the pub is underground at Coober Pedy.

**Coober Pedy**

◬ 251 B4

**Visitor Information**

✉ Hutchinson St.

☎ (08) 8672 5298 or 1-800 637 076 (toll-free)

Soon after opal was discovered here in 1915, this remote wasteland became a magnet for fortune seekers, adventurers, and drifters from around the globe. It still is, although tourism has become the main industry. Exactly how much opal is mined here is a matter of great speculation because lucrative finds are kept as secret as possible.

Located about 520 miles (850 km) north of Adelaide, the town is a rare stopover on the long, empty drive along the Stuart Highway to the Northern Territory. Although nobody would ever call this dusty place charming, it has a certain fascination. Shops sell opals and galleries offer pottery made from local clay.

Summer temperatures here routinely hit 120°F (49°C). Some of Coober Pedy's residents escape the unrelenting heat by living underground in hand-dug caves.

Far from crude holes, these cave houses can be very stylish, with all the modern conveniences, and the temperature inside them stays at a constant 72°F (22°C). The tourist office can arrange visits. Several motels in town are underground or offer underground rooms. Among them are **Radeka's Downunder Motel** *(tel (08) 8672 5223)* and the ironically named **Desert Cave Hotel** *(tel (08) 8672 3330, www.desertcave .com.au)*, the swankest place in town. It also has a good historic mining display, and a drink in the underground bar is de rigueur.

If you are feeling lucky, have a go at fossicking (the Australian term for "prospecting"). There is no particular logic for where opal might be. Just sink a hole and hope for the best, or pick through the mullock heaps (spoil heaps) and look for flashes of color others have missed. The best place to try your luck is at the safe **public noodling area** on Jewellers Shop Road. You can "noodle" (fossick) with out danger of tumbling into an old mine shaft, a real hazard that regularly claims lives in the mining areas outside town.

Other worthwhile attractions include mine tours such as the **Old Timers Mine** *(Crowders Gully Rd., tel (08) 8672 5555)*, an old opal mine hand dug in 1916. The **Serbian Orthodox Church** is the most photogenic of the underground churches.

The surreal **Breakaways,** 20 miles (33 km) north of Coober Pedy, are multihued mesa hills steeped in Aboriginal legend. A sunset visit is pure magic. ■

**OUTBACK MAIL RUN:** For a view of the real outback, off the main highway where few venture, tag along on the **Coober Pedy Mail Run** *(tel 1-800 069 911 [toll-free], www. mailruntour.com, Mon. & Thurs.).* Drive with the mailman on a 12-hour journey visiting outback stations, including the huge Anna Creek Station, on a loop across to Oodnadatta and William Creek. Bring a camera, sunscreen, and a big hat.

# EXPERIENCE: Cattle Mustering

The iconic outback stockman, cracking a whip astride his horse, is still a reality, although the Australian beef industry has changed markedly since its heyday in the 1970s. Motorbikes and helicopters are as much a part of mustering these days.

The old outback cattle tracks are now graded four-wheel-drive roads, but you can relive the thrill of a cattle drive on horseback with the **Great Australian Outback Cattle Drive** *(tel (08) 8463 4547, www.cattledrive.com .au)*, based at the huge Anna Creek Station outside William Creek in South Australia. Five-day tours include three days of droving and comfortable tented accommodations at the station.

The popular **Harry Redford Cattle Drive** *(tel (07) 4551 3311, www .harryredford.com.au)*, at Aramac in central Queensland, is a 19-day outback adventure driving 600 head of cattle 124 miles (200 km) along the Redford Track around May–June. All levels of horse-riding experience are catered for, and you can tag along for as many days as you like.

Cattle station farm stays (see sidebar p. 136) offer the chance to watch and sometimes join in. **Bullo River** *(tel (08) 8354 2719, www.bulloriver .com)*, at Timber Creek in the Northern Territory, encourages participation from May to October. If you like dairy cattle and green fields, try farm stays in Victoria or Tasmania. **Australian Muster Experience** *(Kingston Rd., Whyanbeel Valley, www .australianmusterexperience .com)*, near Cairns, puts on good mustering shows.

# The Ghan

Every Sunday afternoon (and Wednesday in winter), the train known as the Ghan pulls out of Adelaide's Keswick Railway Station northbound on a transcontinental journey that stretches 1,850 miles (2,979 km) through the harsh deserts in the center of the continent and arrives two days later in the palmy, tropical city of Darwin, on the Arafura Sea.

The sleek silver carriages of the Ghan rumble toward the desert city of Alice Springs.

**Great Southern Rail**

✉ 422 King William St., Adelaide

☎ 13 21 47

**www.gsr.com.au**

The Ghan was named to honor the Afghan camel drivers whose caravans had been a lifeline to the lonely desert town of Alice Springs before the eventual coming of the railroad in 1929. The railway made the camels superfluous, and thousands of them were let loose in the desert, where their descendants still run wild today.

The original Ghan went no farther north than Alice Springs, and although for decades there was much buoyant talk of one day extending the line all the way to Darwin, nothing much was done about it until 2001, when work

began on the final 880-mile (1,420 km) stretch of track. After more than a billion dollars was spent and 1.3 million tons (1.2 million tonnes) of steel tracks were laid, the new line opened in early 2004.

After departing Adelaide at 12:20 p.m. on Sunday, the Ghan heads north through the dry rolling wheat fields of South Australia's mid-north and then into **Port Augusta** before heading into the outback and central deserts. The train crosses the massive 15-span bridge over the **Finke River,** reputedly one of the world's oldest riverbeds, before pulling into **Alice Springs** around

2 p.m. the next day. After a four-hour stop—during which you can take a tour of the city—the Ghan continues on its way north to the tropics. An early morning stop is made at **Katherine**—during which you can tour the famous gorge—and the train pulls into **Darwin's** train station at 5:30 that afternoon.

The return journey leaves Darwin each Wednesday morning at 10:00, arriving back into Adelaide on Friday at 1:10 p.m.

The Ghan has first-class sleeping cars—Platinum and Gold Service—as well as holiday-class (Red Service) sleepers and budget-priced seats. Gold passengers have access to plush club cars, where predinner drinks are served, and dine on three-course meals served in the restaurant car. Red passengers can purchase meals in the diner and buffet car. The train also carries automobiles, so you can drive one way on the Stuart Highway (see pp. 284-88), and return by rail. ∎

**INSIDER TIP:**

Pack lightly for your Ghan train trip—you'll be charged extra if you exceed baggage weight and size limits. Visit *www.gsr.com.au* for info.

—STEPHANIE ROBICHAUX
*National Geographic contributor*

---

# EXPERIENCE: Great Train Journeys

Since the days when the railroad was king, many rail services have ended because of competition from cheap bus travel and discount flights, but those that remain offer the comfort, scenery, and romance that only rail travel can deliver.

Australia's two iconic train journeys are the **Indian Pacific** (see p. 248) and the legendary **Ghan** (see above). **Great Southern Rail** *(tel 13 21 47, www .gsr.com.au)* operates both, as well as the **Overlander** route from Adelaide to Melbourne.

New South Wales, Queensland, Victoria, and Western Australia also have regular passenger services. Some of the main ones include Sydney–Brisbane, Sydney–Melbourne, and Sydney–Canberra. The **Sunlander,** from Brisbane to Cairns, offers a leisurely journey along the coast; the **Tilt Train** is faster for shorter hops. **Queensland Rail** *(tel 1-300 131 722, www.travel train.com.au)* operates these services and some interesting trains into the outback, including the **Spirit of the Outback** (Brisbane–Longreach), the **Westlander** (Brisbane–Charleville), the **Inlander** (Townsville–Mt. Isa), and the **Savannahlander** (Cairns–Kuranda–Forsayth). Queensland's quirkiest train is the **Gulflander,** which travels from remote Normanton to Croydon.

Popular steam trains include **Puffing Billy,** through Melbourne's Dandenong Ranges; the **Great Zig Zag Railway,** with spectacular views of the Blue Mountains; the **Kuranda Scenic Railway,** from Cairns into the rain forest; and the coastal **Cockle Train,** from Goolwa to Victor Harbor.

A good website that shows all of Australia's rail services is *www.railmaps .com.au.*

# Stuart Highway Drive

The Stuart Highway runs through the outback from Port Augusta in South Australia to the Esplanade in Darwin—almost 1,700 miles (2,735 km) through the heart of the continent. It takes its name from the explorer John McDouall Stuart, who made an epic south-to-north crossing in 1861, and approximates his route and that of the Overland Telegraph Line, built in 1872.

The gas station, shop, café, and tourist office are all in one building in settlements like Oodnadatta.

The highway rolls through the desolate saltbush country and glaring white salt pans of South Australia's deserts, into the opal-mining town of Coober Pedy, across the Red Centre to Alice Springs, and on through a lonely archipelago of outback settlements in the Northern Territory.

## Port Augusta to Alice Springs

The paved, two-lane highway starts at **Port Augusta**, a truck-stop town (and the start of the Eyre Highway, see pp. 242–248). It is a good road, and unless you are venturing off onto one of the lonely bush tracks, you need no special equipment beyond spares and extra water for yourself and the car.

When Port Augusta slips beneath your rearview mirror, you are alone with your

---

### NOT TO BE MISSED:

**Coober Pedy • Alice Springs • Tennant Creek**

---

thoughts and miles of saltbush until you reach the scruffy little settlement called **Pimba,** 110 lonely miles (177 km) later. A turnoff here leads to **Woomera,** once a top-secret rocket-testing base during the Cold War of the 1950s and '60s. The Heritage Centre (corner of Dewrang & Banool Aves., tel (08) 8673 7042) has displays about Woomera's past and can arrange tours of the still-active rocket range. If you stay on the road to Woomera, another 45 miles (72 km) will take you to the massive **Olympic**

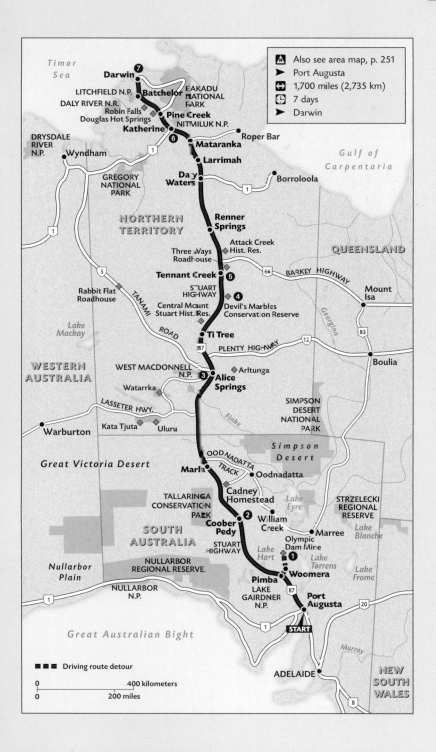

Timor Sea

Darwin **7**

LITCHFIELD N.P. Batchelor
DALY RIVER N.R.
Robin Falls KAKADU
Douglas Hot Springs NATIONAL PARK
Pine Creek
Katherine NITMILUK N.P.
**6**
Roper Bar

DRYSDALE
RIVER
N.P. Mataranka
Wyndham Larrimah

GREGORY
NATIONAL
PARK Daly
Waters Borroloola

Gulf of
Carpentaria

NORTHERN
TERRITORY Renner
Springs

Attack Creek
Hist. Res. QUEENSLAND
Three Ways
Roadhouse
Tennant Creek **5**
STUART
HIGHWAY **4**
Rabbit Flat Central Mount Devil's Marbles
Roadhouse Stuart Hist. Res. Conservation Reserve BARKLY HIGHWAY

Mount
Isa

Lake
Mackay Ti Tree
PLENTY HIGHWAY
83

WESTERN WEST MACDONNELL
AUSTRALIA N.P. **3** Arltunga
Alice Boulia
Watarrka Springs
LASSETER HWY. SIMPSON
Warburton DESERT
Kata Tjuta NATIONAL
Uluru PARK

Great Victoria Desert Simpson
Desert

OODNADATTA
TRACK
Marla Oodnadatta
Cadney STRZELECKI
TALLARINGA Homestead Lake REGIONAL
CONSERVATION Eyre RESERVE
PARK **2**
Coober William
Pedy Creek
Marree

SOUTH Olympic
AUSTRALIA Dam Mine **1**
NULLARBOR Woomera
REGIONAL RESERVE Lake
STUART Hart Lake
Nullarbor HIGHWAY Torrens Lake
Plain Frome
NULLARBOR Pimba
N.P. LAKE
GAIRDNER Port
N.P. Augusta
20
1
Great Australian Bight START
1

Murray

ADELAIDE NEW
SOUTH
WALES
8

■■■ Driving route detour

0            400 kilometers
0        200 miles

**Legend box:**
Also see area map, p. 251
Port Augusta
1,700 miles (2,735 km)
7 days
Darwin

**Dam copper-uranium mine** ❶. For information about this giant mining facility, and to
book a tour of it, contact the Olympic Dam
Tours Office *(tel (08) 8671 2001)*.

**Lake Gairdner National Park,** a vast
salt pan, sprawls off to the left as you drive
north of Pimba. In recent years, Lake Gairdner
has become a venue for land-speed record
attempts. More easily visited, however, is **Lake
Hart,** a blinding white salt pan just off the
highway to your right, about 30 miles (48 km)
northwest of Woomera.

The rough and tough opal-mining town
of **Coober Pedy** ❷ (see pp. 280–281) appears
on the horizon another 230 miles (370 km)
up the highway, over a weirdly desolate landscape. Be particularly careful if you are driving
this stretch of highway around dusk, because
scores of kangaroos are about. Most people,
whether they are going north or south on the
highway, find Coober Pedy a convenient place
to stop for the night. The town has plenty of
good motels and some reasonably decent places
to eat. (Outback Australia, as you'll quickly discover, is no gourmand's paradise. Anything more
original than meat pies, sausage rolls, greasy
chips, and spring rolls qualifies as haute cuisine.)

---

# EXPERIENCE:
## Flying over Lake Eyre

Lake Eyre, about 100 miles (160 km)
east of Coober Pedy, is Australia's
largest lake. For the most part it is a
shimmering white salt pan, but every 10
years or so, it floods and fills with water;
life sprouts and thousands of birds flock
to its shores. This last happened in 2009.
Although you can make the long drive
there with a 4WD vehicle, it's a long trip.
The best view is from the air, on a flight
from William Creek with **Wrightsair** *(tel
(08) 8670 7962)* or Marree with **TGS Air**
*(tel (08) 8675 8344)*. Both towns lie on
the Oodnadatta Track.

---

Coober Pedy is about 250 miles (400 km)
from the Northern Territory border, with
only the **Cadney Homestead** roadhouse
and the tiny hamlet of **Marla** to break the
scrubby monotony. The desert stretches of
South Australia, it must be said, are the least
interesting portions of the Stuart Highway.
Marla has the dubious distinction of frequently
being the hottest place in South Australia.
At both Cadney Homestead and Marla you
can take the rugged **Oodnadatta Track** into
even more hostile—albeit scenic—outback
to the lonely bush town of **Oodnadatta.**
Although a standard car in good condition can
do this excursion during the winter months,
it is a good idea to be well prepared, have
some bush experience, and let responsible
people know where you intend to go and
when you plan to return. Many other tracks,
leading to remote national parks such as **Lake
Eyre** or the **Simpson Desert,** are strictly for
four-wheel-drive vehicles. Seek advice before
venturing off the paved roads.

Fifty miles (80 km) after crossing the
Northern Territory border, the Stuart Highway
touches the Lasseter Highway, which heads
150 miles (240 km) west toward **Uluru** and
**Kata Tjuta** (see pp. 204–208). This paved
highway was named for prospector Harold
Lasseter, who supposedly found a fabulously
rich gold reef out in the desert in 1897 but
died trying to locate it again. The reef, if it
indeed exists, has never been rediscovered,
although not for want of trying. Also out this
highway is the spectacular **Watarrka** (Kings
Canyon, see p. 210).

Farther up the Stuart Highway, **Alice
Springs** ❸ (see pp. 198–201) is an oasis
town in the heart of the dramatic MacDonnell Ranges. You are now in Australia's Red
Centre, and are probably starting to feel as
though you've come a long way. The Alice (as
it is known) is an interesting town at the hub
of a lot of outback attractions and with scenic
hiking trails nearby—and it is worth spending
a few days here. If you want to return to

Adelaide without driving back through South Australia's northern deserts, you can load your car onto the Ghan train and ride back in style (see pp. 282–283).

## Alice Springs to Darwin

The Stuart Highway continues another 950 mostly empty miles (1,529 km) north of Alice Springs to the end of the line in Darwin. From Alice Springs the highway rolls

spectacle, particularly in the dusk or early morning light.

Three hundred miles (480 km) north of Alice Springs is **Tennant Creek ➎**. It was the site of a lonely telegraph relay station in the 1870s, and in the 1930s it was the focus of Australia's last gold rush. One of the major workings was found by a dog named Peko. Another was discovered by a one-eyed prospector named Jack Noble and his blind partner

Aborigines traditionally believe that the Devil's Marbles are the Rainbow Serpent's eggs.

north across the reddish, stony immensity of the Northern Territory outback, past the hamlet of **Ti Tree,** where Australia's first roadhouse was set up in the 1930s, and the **Central Mount Stuart Historical Reserve,** which marks the geographical center of Australia. Another 110 miles (177 km) brings you to the **Devil's Marbles Conservation Reserve ➍**. A campsite is here, and you can walk among the eerily rounded boulders. Geologists say they are the weathered remnants of a 1.5-billion-year-old granite formation. Aborigines believe the boulders are the eggs of the Rainbow Serpent. However you interpret them, they are a haunting

William Weaber, and it went on to become Australia's biggest open-cut mine until it closed in 1985. The **Telegraph Station** is open for visits; so is the old **Battery Hill Mining Centre,** where gold-bearing ore was crushed and treated. Legend has it that Tennant Creek itself was settled when a wagon, loaded with beer, broke down here in 1933. The teamsters couldn't be bothered to fix it and built a pub on the spot. Look around. If a story like that about Tennant Creek isn't true, it ought to be.

Fifteen miles (24 km) farther north, at the **Three Ways Roadhouse,** the Barkly Highway runs east off the Stuart Highway across flat, spinifex-covered tablelands to the lonely

Queensland border, about 280 miles (450 km) away. An additional 25 miles (40 km) up the Stuart Highway, a sign marks the **Attack Creek Historical Reserve.** In 1860, the explorer John McDouall Stuart came here on his first attempt to cross the continent, but he was attacked by Aborigines ("tall, powerful fellows") who objected to his trespassing on their land.

The little settlement of **Renner Springs** is generally regarded as the point where the dry desert climate of the center yields to the seasonal wet–dry of the Top End (the north of the Northern Territory). Although scrubby, the bush becomes greener and taller as you continue north.

**INSIDER TIP:**

Before starting out on the long drive north along the Stuart Highway, stop off at Port Augusta's Arid Lands Botanic Gardens (*www.australian-arid-lands-botanic-garden.org*) to learn about the beautiful and unique flora you're about to see.

—LAURA RUYKYS
*National Geographic field researcher*

**Daly Waters**—another 150 miles (240 km) north—was a vital refueling stop for early aviators such as Amy Johnson. During the 1930s, Qantas flights refueled here, and passengers were given a meal at the **Daly Waters Pub** (*tel (08) 8975 9927*), built in 1893 and said to be the oldest in the Northern Territory. It still serves good food and is filled with memorabilia from those early, seat-of-the-pants aviation days. The airfield (closed in the 1970s) and a restored World War II hangar are a legacy of its days as a staging post for Allied fighters and bombers en route to Darwin and the Dutch East Indies.

Reminders of World War II become more frequent as you close in on Darwin. Signs point to abandoned bush airstrips or ammo dumps. The town of **Larrimah,** 60 miles (96 km) north of Daly Waters, was a major military post during World War II and the terminus of the North Australia Railway. This narrow-gauge line had been intended to link Darwin with Alice Springs, but it had not gotten beyond Larrimah when World War II broke out. The line was abandoned after Cyclone Tracy struck in 1974, and the tracks have been torn up. Little is here now but a friendly old pub and a plain but interesting museum. It covers the town's war years and the history of road trains in the Northern Territory.

**Mataranka,** 50 miles (80 km) to the north, has thermal springs in a pocket of rain forest about 5 miles (8 km) east of town. The film *We of the Never Never* (1982) was made near here. The relaxing hot springs can get crowded. The **Mataranka Homestead Resort** (*tel (08) 8975 4544*) has accommodations and a restaurant.

**Katherine ❻** (see pp. 194–195) is the next town on the highway, and with a population of almost 10,000 it is easily the biggest metropolis you've seen since Alice Springs. The big attraction is **Nitmiluk National Park** (see pp. 194–195).

The last leg of the Stuart Highway—the 200 miles (320 km) to Darwin—crosses rolling bushland. At the old gold-mining town of Pine Creek, you can take a paved road into the heart of **Kakadu National Park** (see pp. 188–191). Ahead, turnoffs lead to scenic sites such as **Douglas Hot Springs,** the beautiful **Robin Falls,** and the **Daly River Nature Reserve.** Farther north, **Adelaide River** was a major WWII military post, and a large cemetery commemorates those killed in air raids. The Batchelor turnoff brings you to **Litchfield National Park** (see pp. 192–193). Keep going and you'll notice the houses and buildings are crowding closer together. Suddenly you are at the end of the line: **Darwin's ❼** palm-fringed Esplanade and the Timor Sea (see pp. 184–187).

Built on the wealth of the 1850s gold rushes and Australia's most diverse state—small, pretty, and prosperous

# Victoria

Introduction & Map   290–291

Melbourne   292–296

Experience: Colonial Tramcar Restaurant   293

Experience: Photo Walking Tours   296

Feature: Melbourne Cup   297

Melbourne Walks   298–303

St. Kilda   304

Main Yarra Trail   305

Experience: Biking Melbourne   305

Mornington Peninsula   306–307

Experience: Penguin Parade   307

Yarra Valley   308

The Dandenongs   309

Great Ocean Road Drive   310–315

Experience: Surfing   315

Victoria's Alpine Country   316–317

Feature: Australian Rules Football   318–319

Experience: Catch a Match   318

Inside Melbourne Central mall

Goldfields   320–321

Feature: Bushrangers   322–323

Murray River   324–325

Grampians National Park (Gariwerd)   326–327

Wilsons Promontory National Park   328

Hotels & Restaurants   382–384

# Victoria

Victoria is the smallest and greenest of Australia's mainland states and the only one without much "real" outback. A history of gentlemanly farming and of vast wealth from the 19th century's fabulous gold rushes have given the state, and especially its elegant capital Melbourne, a patrician, old-money air. The richest gold diggings were in Ballarat, Castlemaine, and Bendigo, but dozens of rich strikes were made around the state.

The 19th century's heady combination of boomtime wealth and civic pride gave Victoria magnificent public architecture and elegant colonial mansions. It is not unusual in this state to drive into a farm town and see an Italianate city hall as grand as a European opera house, probably set among ornamental palms and landscaped gardens. When you see one of these grand rural palaces, just start looking for the historical marker that tells the story of the local gold rush.

No large-scale gold mining goes on here now. Victoria today is a combination of breadbasket and industrial heartland, producing about a quarter of Australia's gross domestic product. The Murray River forms its border with New South Wales and irrigates vineyards, market gardens, and vast

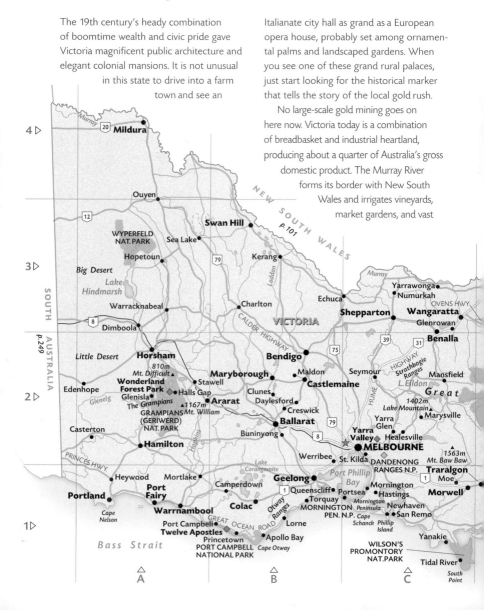

orchards. Victoria is known as the Garden State. Shepparton, in the north, is a sort of Cannery Row. The dry country in the west is golden with wheat and has some of Australia's best wool-producing regions. Dairies and cheese factories dot the state. The dense forests in Gippsland feed a timber industry, coal is mined in the La Trobe Valley, and beneath the waters of Bass Strait lurk Australia's second largest oil fields.

Victoria is Australia's smokestack industry hub, with car-manufacturing factories, chemical plants, and aluminum smelters, although, as manufacturing continues to shift offshore, the economy is dominated by service industries. Headquarters to Australia's biggest mining houses, Melbourne was for decades the nation's financial and banking center, a role it has partly conceded to Sydney.

For such a small state, Victoria has an astonishing variety of scenery, from temperate rain forests along the eastern coast to dusty outback scrub in the north to the sleek cafés of Melbourne's inner-city suburbs. Australia's best skiing is on the powdery slopes of the Victorian Alps, and some of its finest surf can be found

**NOT TO BE MISSED:**

Elegant Melbourne, a garden city of gracious architecture **292–296**

Touring the wineries and seeing native Yarra Valley wildlife **308**

Riding *Puffing Billy* through the cool, lush Dandenong Ranges **309**

Driving the Great Ocean Road to see the Twelve Apostles **310–315**

Hiking the Victorian Alps **316–317**

Seeing a fast and furious game of Australian Rules football **318**

Reliving the gold rush at Ballarat and other goldfield towns **320–321**

Taking a paddle steamer at the old river port of Echuca **325**

Hiking the Grampians and visiting its cultural center **326–327**

on the internationally famous Bells Beach. The Great Ocean Road, just west of Melbourne, is a fabulous coastal drive.

Melbourne itself—Australia's most European capital—has theaters, museums, and a sweeping range of cultures and cuisines. Unlike the rest of Australia, where interesting sights tend to be separated by hundreds of miles of dreary scrub, Victoria's attractions form a small, neat package. Everything is an easy scenic drive from Melbourne on excellent paved roads. ■

# Melbourne

For many years Melbourne was regarded as the patrician counterpoint to bold, brassy, nouveau riche Sydney, a vaguely stuffy, Old World sort of place where what mattered was who your family was and where you went to school. To some degree that stereotype still holds true, but recently Melburnians have been showing the world they also know how to kick up their heels.

Elegant, cosmopolitan Melbourne

## Melbourne

 290 C2

**Visitor Information**

✉ Victorian Tourism Visitor Information Centre, Federation Sq., corner of Swanston & Flinders Sts.

☎ (03) 9568 9658

**Information Booth**

✉ Bourke Street Mall

**www.thats melbourne.com.au**

For example, the city hosts a hugely successful Formula One Grand Prix race and has one of Australia's grandest and glitziest casinos; the once dreary south bank of the Yarra River has been transformed into a sleek cosmopolitan shopping precinct, while architectural marvels such as the huge new Federation Square complex have been popping up in the city center.

And yet the city has not lost touch with its patrician roots. This is still a city of elegant Victorian buildings, beautifully laid-out parks, and stately icons such as the Melbourne Club. Most of Australia's great mining houses are headquartered here, while the world's largest network of electric trams gives the city a pleasantly old-fashioned European flair.

Sports are big in Melbourne, which has nine professional Australian Rules football clubs. It hosts the Australian Open tennis tournament, as well as the Melbourne Cup—Australia's greatest horse race.

Melbourne has a vibrant mix of ethnic communities—particularly

Greek, Italian, and Asian—giving the city bustling markets, restaurants, delicatessens, and bakeries. Just choosing a restaurant in Melbourne means sifting through a United Nations of culinary styles. There is even a restaurant tram offering evening sightseeing tours around the city—a happy converging of several of Melbourne's strengths: excellent food, elegant architecture, and trams.

The city began in 1835 as a result of a dodgy land deal by two Tasmanian entrepreneurs, John Batman and John Pascoe Fawkner. They gave local Aborigines blankets, flour, axes, and trinkets in exchange for 500,000 acres (200,000 ha) of land around Port Phillip Bay. The unauthorized purchase annoyed the Colonial Office back in London, but they let it stand. Sixteen years later, fabulous goldfields were discovered around Ballarat, Bendigo, and Castlemaine, and the city's success was assured. Gold hunters flocked here—almost 2,000 a week at the boom's height—and, by 1861, gold-rush wealth had made Melbourne Australia's grandest city. You can see an audiovisual presentation on the gold-rush days in the gold vaults at the Old Treasury Building, on Spring Street.

These days, Melbourne comes a close second to archrival Sydney as the nation's financial capital and, with 4 million residents, is a bit smaller. But Melburnians still claim their city is the better place to live. Powerful voices support them: The Economist magazine regularly ranks Melbourne among the world's most livable cities.

Despite Sydneysiders' claim that Melbourne's climate is drizzly and bleak, the Victorian capital actually gets less rain than Sydney. In recent years, Melbourne has challenged its brash New South Wales rival on the glamour front as well, snaring such international events as the Australian **Formula One Grand Prix** and building Australia's largest and most glittering casino.

## Melbourne Sights

It is easy to get around Melbourne on its network of buses, trains, and trams. The Victoria government runs a free tram that loops through the downtown core. The free tram is cream and burgundy. Regular trams are green and gold.

Melbourne's Central Business District—CBD in local slang—is a pleasing mix of futuristic skyscrapers and Victorian-era sandstone facades. The city is set out on a grid, and you need only remember a few key streets. Excellent information booths can help you plan your explorations.

**Formula One Grand Prix**
☎ (03) 9258 7100
**www.grandprix .com.au**

---

### EXPERIENCE: Colonial Tramcar Restaurant

Trams are an icon of Melbourne and one of the best ways to tour the city. **Colonial Tramcar Restaurant** (tel (03) 9696 4000, www.tramrestaurant.com.au) goes one step further, offering two-hour lunch and dinner tours. Heritage trams depart from South Melbourne near Crown Casino and trundle through the city and around the leafy, Victorian-era suburbs to the south. Reservations are essential.

## Thinking Big

Australians love big things. On your travels in Victoria and the rest of Oz, keep an eye out for some of the weird, wonderful, and downright tacky oversized tourist totems that tower above the highway.

Many celebrate local farm produce, including: the Big Banana (Coffs Harbour, NSW), Big Barramundi (Daintree, QLD), Big Apple (Stanthorpe, QLD), Big Cheese (Bega, NSW), Big Lobster (Kingston, SA), Big Prawn (Ballina, NSW), Big Pineapple (Gympie, QLD), Big Ram (Wagin, WA), and Big Peanut (Atherton, QLD).

Others pay tribute to local wildlife: the Big Croc (Humpty Doo, NT), Big Tasmanian Devil (Mole Creek, TAS), Big Galah (Kimba, SA), Big Penguin (Penguin, TAS), and Big Pelican (Noosaville, QLD).

Some are just big for the heck of it: the Big Captain Cook (Cairns, QLD), Big Golden Guitar (Tamworth, NSW), Big Ned Kelly (Glenrowan, VIC), Big Stubbie (Tewantin, QLD), Big Milkshake (Warrnambool, VIC), and an all-time favorite, the Big Gumboot (Tully, QLD), awarded to the wettest town in Australia.

### Melbourne 360°

- 🗺 Map p. 300
- ✉ Rialto Towers, 525 Collins St.
- ☎ (03) 9629 8222
- 💲 $$

**www.melbournedeck .com.au**

### Queen Victoria Market

- 🗺 Map p. 300
- ✉ Victoria St., West Melbourne
- 🕐 Closed Mon. & Wed.

**www.qvm.com.au**

**Melbourne 360°,** the observation deck on the 55th floor of the Rialto Towers, gives a breathtaking view of the city. Nearby, the former **Commercial Bank of Australia** building *(333 Collins St.)*, with its high-domed banking chamber and massive vestibule, gives you an idea of the wealth that passed through this city in the glory days of the 19th-century gold rush and land boom. Bourke and Collins Streets are the city's main shopping thoroughfares, although La Trobe Street's glossy **Melbourne Central Mall** boasts the city's biggest concentration of stores in the city.

**Queen Victoria Market,** which opened in the 1870s, is a Melbourne institution and an exciting place to buy ingredients for a gourmet picnic. You will find fresh produce just off the farm, interesting cheeses, sausages, breads, meats, fish, nuts, and cakes. Shopping here is never dull or quiet. A multicultural mix of shopkeepers and stand holders shout, cajole, and banter to move their goods. If you get there late on Saturday afternoon, when they must either sell their produce or throw it away, you have a lot of latitude for bargaining. This cornucopia is on the north side of the city, only a few minutes by tram along Elizabeth Street from the city center. The market is in a series of decorative old iron sheds, with the cheeses, meats, small goods, and fish spread out in the delicatessen hall. The biggest sections sell clothes, shoes, leatherware, souvenirs, and all manner of good products at cheap prices. This is one of Melbourne's landmark buildings, distinctive for the livestock frieze above its portal. Tours of the market are available *(tel (03) 9320 5822)*.

Once you've bought your picnic ingredients—and you can even buy well-made baskets here—all you need is a convenient and elegantly landscaped park. A couple of good options are very close by. One is **Carlton Gardens** *(Victoria St.),* the grounds of the vast, high-domed Exhibition Buildings built for the Great Exhibition of 1880. Nearby is the enormous **Melbourne Museum,** opened in 2000, a postmodern architectural marvel that houses a number of huge collections and galleries—such as the **Bunjilaka Aboriginal Centre,** with its displays of Aboriginal culture;

## INSIDER TIP:

**For a great day trip and a close look at Australia's native wolf, visit the Dingo Discovery Center** (*www .dingodiscovery.net*), **about 25 miles (40 km) from Melbourne.**

—ARIAN WALLACH
*National Geographic field researcher*

the **Australia Gallery,** with its focus on the history of Melbourne and Victoria; and the **Children's Gallery,** with its hands-on multimedia exhibits. The Melbourne Museum spreads over six levels and includes a vast arboretum, containing more than 120 species of trees and plants, as well as IMAX Melbourne, with its huge 3-D movie screen.

Another picnic spot is the **Royal Melbourne Zoological Gardens,** established in 1862 and one of the oldest in the world, which is landscaped better than many cities' botanic gardens. It is about 2 miles (3 km) north of the market, in Royal Park, and you can reach it by tram No. 55 from William Street or an Upfield line train from Flinders Street Station. The Australian fauna enclosure has

a lake and bushland landscaping, where you walk among kangaroos and emus. The platypus house gives perhaps the best chance you'll have of seeing one of these elusive creatures, and the steamy tropical butterfly house is a delight. On certain summer weekend evenings, there are free jazz concerts, and the picnicker-friendly zoo even has a hamper-check, where you can leave your picnic basket while you stroll among the exhibits before you take it in to the concert.

**Crown Casino,** on the south bank of the Yarra River, is a star-studded entertainment and gambling complex that shook up this city when it opened in 1997. It is the country's largest casino, and also has flashy restaurants, bars, nightclubs, luxury boutiques, and the country's biggest hotel. It's

## Melbourne Museum

Map p. 300
✉ 11 Nicholson St.
☎ 13 11 22
💲 $

melbournemuseum
.vicgov.au

## Royal Melbourne Zoological Gardens

Map p. 300
✉ Elliott Ave., Parkville
☎ (03) 9285 9300
💲 $$$

## Crown Casino

Map p. 300
✉ Southbank
☎ (03) 9292 8888 or 1-800 818 088 (toll-free)
🕐 Open 24 hours

www.crownltd.com
.au

Picnickers near Melbourne's Yarra River

## Eureka Skydeck 88

▲ Map p. 300

✉ Eureka Tower,
7 Riverside Quay

☎ (03) 9693 8888

$ $$–$$$

**www.eurekaskydeck
.com.au**

the showpiece of the redeveloped **Southbank,** the city's bustling riverfront lined with fashionable restaurants, hotels, shops, street theater, and an excellent Sunday craft market. Overlooking it all, the Eureka Tower is the city's tallest skyscraper. On the 88th floor, **Eureka Skydeck 88** offers vertigo-inducing panoramas.

Like Southbank but less lively, **Docklands,** the old wharf area on the western edge of the city, now houses chic apartments, restaurants, and the **Southern Star** *(101 Waterfront Way, tel (03) 8688 9688, $$$),* a 394-foot-high (120 m) observation wheel with dramatic views.

To the east of the city, the **Melbourne Cricket Ground** *(www.mcg.org.au)* is the home of Australian Rules football. "The G," as the arena is called, also houses the **National Sports Museum** *(tel (03) 9657 8879, www.nsm .org.au, $$),* showcasing Australian sporting achievements. In January, this sports-mad city hosts the Australian Open tennis tournament at the nearby **Rod Laver Arena.**

Melbourne's warren of inner suburbs is notably diverse. Brunswick Street, in **Fitzroy,** is one of the city's seedier spots, but with its bohemian cafés, alternative bookstores, and grunge chic, also one of the most interesting places to have a cappuccino and people-watch on a Sunday afternoon.

Victoria Street in **Richmond** could pass for a back street in Hanoi, with its bewildering jumble of Vietnamese apothecaries, family-run grocery shops, fruit stalls, and carcasses hanging in butcher-shop windows. Signs are in Vietnamese, and scores of cramped eateries line the streets. Yet just a few blocks away, on Swan Street, is a small Greek enclave. Lygon Street, in **Carlton,** is Melbourne's Little Italy, full of Italian restaurants and gelaterias.

On the south side, **Prahran** is an upscale version of Fitzroy, its boulevards lined with jazzy-cool bistros, antique shops, and funky boutiques. Even farther south, the bayside suburb of **St. Kilda** (see p. 304) has a profusion of bakeries along Acland Street, in addition to a breezy foreshore promenade.

In general, the Yarra River forms the social divide in Melbourne. Real estate southeast of the river tends to be richer, greener, and hillier. **South Yarra** and **Toorak** are Melbourne's wealthiest and most exclusive enclaves, with leafy streets and luxurious mansions tucked away behind high walls. Land to the northwest of the Yarra is flat and dry, and it is largely filled with industry, airports, and a mass of blue-collar suburbs. ■

---

# EXPERIENCE:
## Photo Walking Tours

Photo walking tours take in famous Melbourne sights, while teaching you how to use all the functions on your camera. Expert advice shows you how to frame pictures, utilize light, and get the most out of your camera. Two-hour tours of the city center, Yarra River, or the beach suburb of St. Kilda run in the summer. Contact **Nebesky Images** *(tel (04) 3831 4499, www.nebeskyimages.com/phototours.html).*

# Melbourne Cup

**The Melbourne Cup is the horse race that stops a nation. This prestigious handicap event is run on Melbourne's Flemington racetrack on the first Tuesday of every November, and for three minutes life across Australia is held in suspense. City traffic is reduced to a trickle as the post time nears.**

All around Australia—even in the most remote corners of the outback—the pubs are full to bursting and latecomers stand on the sidewalk, craning their necks to see the TV screens over the crowd. Nothing beats being there at Flemington on race day, among hordes of partying racegoers, extravagant hats, and bookies surrounded by mobs of gamblers.

Run in 1861, the first Melbourne Cup was won by a horse named Archer, who won it again the next year. By 1888, the race was attracting crowds of more than 100,000.

The Melbourne Cup is the highlight of Melbourne's Spring Racing Carnival, which spreads over a couple of weeks and includes other top races such as the Caulfield Cup. It is a race for stayers. It started out as a 2-mile (3,218 m) event, but in deference to the metric system, the distance was shortened to 3,200 meters when Australia went metric in 1972.

The most famous Cup winner was Phar Lap, a New Zealand–born gelding who won in 1930. This phenomenal chestnut horse won 37 of his 51 starts and was taken to North America in 1932 to prove his mettle there. He died mysteriously after winning a single race in Mexico, and his death has been fertile ground for Australian conspiracy theorists ever since, with American gangsters the popular villains. In 1985, however, Phar Lap's trainer, Tommy Woodcock, reputedly made a deathbed confession that he feared he might have accidentally poisoned the horse with arsenic-based tonic. Today, Phar Lap's skeleton is in the National Museum of New Zealand; his hide is in the Museum of Victoria in Melbourne; and his huge heart rests in Canberra.

Jockey Glen Boss raises his arm in triumph after riding Makybe Diva to victory in the 2004 Melbourne Cup.

There may be some Australians who don't place a bet on the Melbourne Cup, but they are pretty rare. Even people who never normally follow horse racing, let alone place a bet, will have a flutter on The Cup. Most of those who place a bet enter the office sweepstakes, where everyone in the office kicks in a few dollars, and the horses are chosen at random. That way nobody has to study a complicated form sheet. They just kick back and wait for post time.

# Melbourne Walks

Flinders Street Railway Station is a great place to start your walking tours of Melbourne. Set on the bank of the Yarra, this spectacular Edwardian railroad station, built of honey-colored sandstone in 1907, is the hub of Melbourne's commuter train system. Above its main portal is a row of clocks, and generally a knot of people sits expectantly on the steps below. "Under the clocks" has been a traditional meeting place for generations.

Melbourne's Flinders Street Railway Station is still a focal point for the city.

Those steps look out on an interesting intersection. On the opposite corner is stately **St. Paul's Cathedral,** a neo-Gothic masterpiece completed in 1892 and the headquarters of Melbourne's Anglican Church. Across the street is the **Young & Jackson Hotel,** one of the oldest pubs in Melbourne and the home of "Chloe," a full-length nude painted in Paris in 1875 by Jules Lefèbvre. In 1880, "Chloe" was sent to the Melbourne Exposition, where judges ruled the picture obscene. The drinkers in the Young & Jackson Hotel hadn't any objections, and the painting has adorned the wall ever since. The pub is a bit rough, but it's worth going in to have a beer and see this Melbourne icon. She's on the second floor, in Chloe's Bar and Bistro. And facing the famous clocks, just across Swanston Street, is the huge, new Federation Square complex, an architectural marvel of zinc, glass, and sandstone panels. It houses, among other things, the **Melbourne Visitor Centre** (tel (03) 9658 9658); the **Australian Centre for the Moving Image** (tel (03) 8663 2200, www.acmi.net.au), a museum dedicated to film, television, video, and digital media; and the National Gallery of Victoria's Australian art collection at the **Ian Potter Centre: NGV Australia** (tel (61) 38662 1553, www.ngv.vic.gov.au).

There are two good walks from here (see map pp. 300–301). One walk takes you across the Yarra River to the cosmopolitan new Southgate shopping and café precinct, the botanic gardens, and some of Melbourne's oldest houses. The other explores the eclectic "real Melbourne," the downtown area north of the river.

## Walk One: Over the Yarra

Begin the first walk by exploring **Federation Square ❶**, taking in the magnificent architecture in the complex itself, the scenic glimpses of the river, and the vast collection of Australian art in the Ian Potter Centre. The ground floor is given over to indigenous art and displays of masks, totems, and bark paintings, as well as canvas paintings by Aboriginal artists. Upstairs, on the second floor, is the gallery's collection of paintings, sculptures, drawings, and photographs dating from the colonial era up to the 1980s.

Here you can see paintings by some of Australia's best known colonial artists, such as Conrad Martens and John Glover, as well as a collection of famously nationalistic paintings by a school of impressionists that emerged in Melbourne in the 1890s. They were known as the Heidelberg painters, after the little Yarra Valley village of that name in what was then the outskirts of Melbourne. Inspired by the French Impressionists of the day, they painted landscapes that celebrated the heat and dust and glare of Australia. A leading light of this school was Tom Roberts, whose 1890 painting "Shearing the Rams," capturing the camaraderie of the shearing shed, has become an Australian icon and is part of this gallery's collection.

From here, cross the river on the ornate old Princes Bridge. Ahead of you, the wide, tree-lined St. Kilda Road slopes gently upward to

the Shrine of Remembrance, a brooding gray Romanesque War Memorial.

On the right over the bridge, just past the towering spire of the Arts Centre, the National Gallery of Victoria's main installation is **NGV International** (180 St. Kilda Rd., tel (03) 8620 2222). It has a fine collection of European art from pre-Renaissance to contemporary, even though two of its most celebrated Rembrandt and Van Gogh paintings have recently proved to be fakes. The Asian, Oceanic, and decorative arts galleries are also well worth browsing, and big-name touring exhibitions show here.

Head back to the bridge and down the steps to the sun-drenched promenade that follows the south bank of the Yarra, past the Melbourne Concert Hall, to the classy river-bank development known as **Southgate ❷**. One of the finest views of the skyline is to be had from along here. This spot was industrial wasteland and its redevelopment in the 1990s was, surprisingly enough, the first real effort in the city's history to make use of the Yarra River as a scenic water feature. It was stunningly successful. Now the Yarra precinct known as Southbank, augmented by Federation Square, is the popular, fashionable focus of town, with five-star hotels, trendy boutiques, food courts and cafés, the Polly Woodside Maritime Museum, the Melbourne Aquarium (www. melbourneaquarium.com.au), and, of course, the huge Crown Casino complex (see p. 295).

Next, retrace your steps past Princes Bridge and follow the river upstream, on paths that meander through the parkland and gardens that run along the river—Alexandra Gardens, Queen Victoria Gardens, Kings Domain, and the Royal Botanic Gardens. They all meld together to form a delightful greenbelt flanking the river. The **Royal Botanic Gardens ❸** (www.rbgmelb.org.au), near the southern end of this green space, may be the finest botanic gardens in Australia and is rated amongst the best in the world. Dotted with century-old oaks and ornamental lakes, they

(continued on p. 302)

---

## NOT TO BE MISSED:

**Federation Square • Southgate • Royal Botanic Gardens**

---

# Central Melbourne

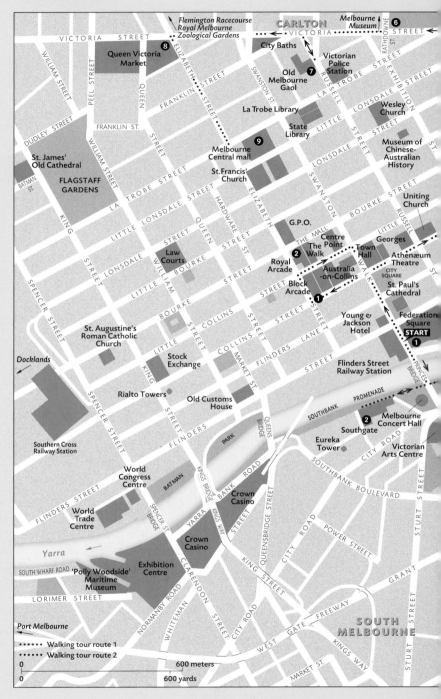

Flemington Racecourse
Royal Melbourne
Zoological Gardens

Melbourne
Museum **6**

CARLTON — VICTORIA —

VICTORIA STREET

WILLIAM STREET

PEEL STREET

Queen Victoria
Market **8**

ELIZABETH STREET

QUEEN STREET

City Baths

Old
Melbourne
Gaol **7**

Victorian
Police
Station

SWANSTON STREET

LA TROBE STREET

RUSSELL STREET

LITTLE LONSDALE STREET

EXHIBITION STREET

RATHDOWNE ST.

Wesley
Church

FRANKLIN STREET

FRANKLIN ST.

DUDLEY STREET

La Trobe Library

State
Library

Melbourne
Central mall **9**

St.Francis'
Church

Museum of
Chinese-
Australian
History

St. James'
Old Cathedral

FLAGSTAFF
GARDENS

BATMAN ST.

WILLIAM STREET

KING STREET

LA TROBE STREET

LONSDALE STREET

LITTLE LONSDALE STREET

QUEEN STREET

ELIZABETH STREET

G.P.O.

SWANSTON STREET

BOURKE STREET

LITTLE BOURKE STREET

RUSSELL STREET

Uniting
Church

Centre
Point

The
Point
Walk

THE MALL

Georges

Town
Hall

Athenæum
Theatre

CITY
SQUARE

Law
Courts

Royal
Arcade **2**

Australia
-on-Collins

Block
Arcade **1**

St. Paul's
Cathedral

SPENCER STREET

LONSDALE STREET

LITTLE BOURKE STREET

WILLIAM STREET

KING STREET

BOURKE STREET

LITTLE COLLINS STREET

QUEEN STREET

ELIZABETH STREET

MARKET ST.

SWANSTON STREET

RUSSELL STREET

Young &
Jackson
Hotel

Federation
Square

**START** **1**

PRINCES BRIDGE

St. Augustine's
Roman Catholic
Church

COLLINS STREET

FLINDERS LANE

Stock
Exchange

COLLINS STREET

FLINDERS STREET

Flinders Street
Railway Station

Docklands

Rialto Towers

Old Customs
House

FLINDERS STREET

PROMENADE

SOUTHBANK

Melbourne
Concert Hall

CITY ROAD

Southern Cross
Railway Station

QUEENS BRIDGE

PARK

**2**
Southgate

Eureka
Tower

Victorian
Arts Centre

World
Congress
Centre

BATMAN

KINGS BRIDGE

BANK STREET

KING STREET

QUEENSBRIDGE STREET

SOUTHBANK BOULEVARD

POWER STREET

STURT STREET

World
Trade
Centre

SPENCER ST BRIDGE

Crown
Casino

YARRA

CITY ROAD

GRANT STREET

FLINDERS STREET

Crown
Casino

Yarra

SOUTH WHARF ROAD

'Polly Woodside'
Maritime
Museum

Exhibition
Centre

NORMANBY ROAD

WHITEMAN STREET

CLARENDON STREET

CITY ROAD

KING STREET

WEST GATE FREEWAY

SOUTH
MELBOURNE

STURT STREET

LORIMER STREET

Port Melbourne

KINGS WAY

MARKET ST.

•••••• Walking tour route 1
•••••• Walking tour route 2

0 ————————————— 600 meters
0 ————————————— 600 yards

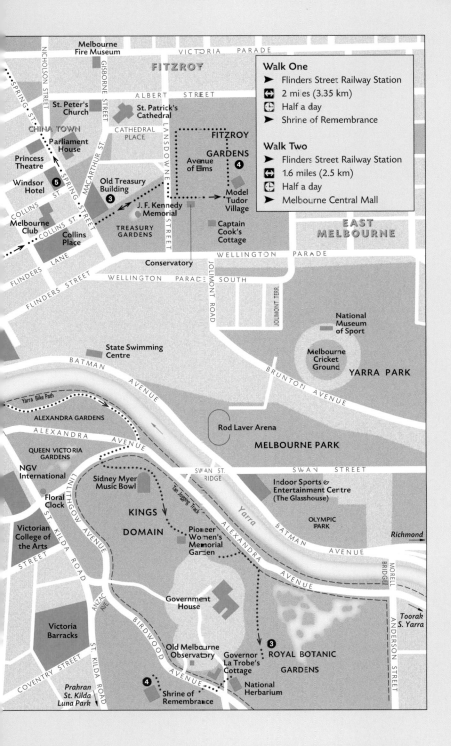

**Walk One**

▶ Flinders Street Railway Station
↔ 2 miles (3.35 km)
🕓 Half a day
▶ Shrine of Remembrance

**Walk Two**

▶ Flinders Street Railway Station
↔ 1.6 miles (2.5 km)
🕓 Half a day
▶ Melbourne Central Mall

Melbourne Fire Museum

FITZROY

VICTORIA PARADE

NICHOLSON STREET

ALBERT    STREET

GISBORNE ST.

St. Peter's Church

St. Patrick's Cathedral

CHINA TOWN

CATHEDRAL PLACE

LANSDOWNE ST.

FITZROY

GARDENS

Parliament House

Avenue of Elms

4

Princess Theatre

SPRING STREET

MACARTHUR ST.

Windsor Hotel    5

SPRING ST.

Old Treasury Building    3

Model Tudor Village

Collins St.

J. F. Kennedy Memorial

Melbourne Club

COLLINS ST.

TREASURY GARDENS

JOLIMONT STREET

Captain Cook's Cottage

EAST MELBOURNE

Collins Place

Conservatory

WELLINGTON    PARADE

FLINDERS LANE

FLINDERS STREET

WELLINGTON    PARADE    SOUTH

JOLIMONT ROAD

JOLIMONT TERR.

National Museum of Sport

State Swimming Centre

BATMAN    AVENUE

Melbourne Cricket Ground

YARRA PARK

Yarra Bike Path

BRUNTON    AVENUE

ALEXANDRA GARDENS

ALEXANDRA    AVENUE

Rod Laver Arena

MELBOURNE PARK

QUEEN VICTORIA GARDENS

SWAN ST. BRIDGE

SWAN    STREET

NGV International

Sidney Myer Music Bowl

Indoor Sports & Entertainment Centre (The Glasshouse)

Floral Clock

LINLITHGOW AVENUE

Tan Jogging Track

KINGS

DOMAIN

Yarra

ALEXANDRA

OLYMPIC PARK

Richmond

Victorian College of the Arts

ST. KILDA ROAD

Pioneer Women's Memorial Garden

BATMAN    AVENUE

AVENUE

MORELL BRIDGE

Government House

ANZAC AVE.

BIRDWOOD

Victoria Barracks

ST. KILDA ROAD

Old Melbourne Observatory

Governor La Trobe's Cottage

3    ROYAL BOTANIC

GARDENS

Toorak S. Yarra

ANDERSON STREET

COVENTRY STREET

AVENUE

National Herbarium

Prahran St. Kilda Luna Park

4

Shrine of Remembrance

form a lush landscape that spreads over 100 acres (40 ha) by the river. They were established in 1845, but it was the late 19th-century curators Baron Sir Ferdinand von Mueller and, later, W. R. Guilfoyle who created the present masterpiece. On summer nights (Dec.–March) plays are performed in the surrounding gardens and classic films shown on an outdoor screen. For more information check with the Moonlight Cinema *(www.moonlight.com.au)*.

You can explore the gardens on your own, run round them on a 3-mile (4.8 km) jogging track known as the Tan, or follow a self-guided walk. The elegant facade overlooking the gardens belongs to **Government House** *(for tours contact the National Trust, tel (03) 9656 9800)*, the residence of the British monarch's representative in Victoria. It is a copy of Queen Victoria's holiday palace on the Isle of Wight. **Governor La Trobe's Cottage** *(for tours contact the National Trust, tel (03) 9656 9800)* and the **National Herbarium** are located near the southern end of the Botanic Gardens. La Trobe's Cottage is a prefabricated dwelling sent over from England in 1840 to serve as the residence for the colony's first governor. The humble cottage is plainly furnished in period style, together with some of La Trobe's personal belongings.

A hundred yards (92 m) west of La Trobe's Cottage, near St. Kilda Road, is the **Shrine of Remembrance ❹**. It was built in 1934 to honor the fallen of World War I. Its eternal flame is now also a tribute to the dead of World War II, Korea, Vietnam, Malaya and Borneo, and the Gulf War. It was positioned and designed so that a sunbeam passes over the inner sanctum at 11 a.m. on November 11—the moment the armistice was signed in 1918 to end World War I. Galleries inside the shrine feature rotating exhibits. (Catch a tram on St. Kilda Road back to Flinders Street Station.)

Another option would be to take a cruise on the river itself—although keen walking enthusiasts might consider this cheating. The tour boats depart from Southbank and a landing near Princes Bridge, and tickets are available at a riverside kiosk or by calling Melbourne River Cruises *(tel (03) 8610 2600)*. Cruises go upriver past Melbourne's parks and gardens, or downriver past the city center to the docks. Alternatively, take a ferry cruise from Southgate down the river and out onto the bay to **Williamstown,** a picturesque Victorian-era seaside village, its main street lined with cafés. The trip takes 50 minutes, and you can get off to explore the suburb then take a later ferry back.

Melburnians enjoy a respite from city life at the Royal Botanic Gardens.

## Walk Two: The Real Melbourne

This inner-city stroll also begins beneath the clocks at Flinders Street Station. Cross Flinders Street and follow Swanston Walk into the heart of downtown. A few years ago Swanston Street was, in theory, closed to traffic to form a pedestrian mall, but taxis, buses, delivery vehicles, and 29.5-ton (27 tonne) trams are still allowed to use it, so you're safest on the sidewalks. A left turn and a short stroll down Collins Street takes you to the modernistic **Australia-on-Collins** shopping mall and the elegant **Block Arcade ❶**, built with gold-rush wealth in the 1880s and exquisitely restored in 1988. It has mosaic floors, an ornamental domed roof, and small shops. The **Hopetoun Tea Rooms** here also date from Victorian-era Melbourne. Nearby, the **Royal Arcade ❷**, on Little Collins Street, was built in 1869. It is guarded by statues of the mythical giants Gog and Magog.

Take Little Collins Street back to Swanston Walk and go right for one block to continue along Collins Street, then up a gentle hill to the grand **Old Treasury Building ❸**, on the far side of Spring Street. Built in 1857 to hold the fabulous wealth coming out of the goldfields, it houses the **City Museum** (tel (03) 9651 2233, $), with exhibits on Victoria's history from precolonial times to the present. The area around this upper end of Collins Street is known as the Paris End and has fashionable shops and galleries. The streetscape is particularly lovely at dusk, with fairy lights sparkling in the plane trees and shadows playing on the facades of the exclusive boutiques.

To the right of the Treasury Building as you face it are the beautiful **Treasury** and **Fitzroy Gardens ❹**, a favorite spot for office workers to eat lunch. On weekends, Fitzroy Gardens in particular is bright with picnickers and wedding parties having their photos taken among the flower beds or on the magnificent **Avenue of Elms.** This corridor of 130-year-old elms is one of the few in the world to have been spared

---

**NOT TO BE MISSED:**

**Fitzroy Gardens • Melbourne Museum • Queen Victoria Market**

---

Dutch elm disease. **Captain Cook's Cottage,** plucked from his native Yorkshire, was reassembled in the gardens in 1934 to help mark Melbourne's centenary—a rather odd tribute since Cook never set foot here.

Return to Spring Street and turn right to reach the **Windsor Hotel ❺**, opened in 1883. This old Melbourne icon has long been a favored haunt of royalty, prime ministers, visiting dignitaries, and old-money Australians. It is probably the last of Australia's grand hotels, and a lot of Australian history has taken place beneath these ornate ceilings, including the drafting of the nation's constitution in 1900. Afternoon tea at the Windsor is a Melbourne tradition that is well worth trying.

Continue along Spring Street, past the ornate 1886 **Princess Theatre,** and on for another three blocks to Victoria Street, where you'll find the old Exhibition Buildings, Carleton Gardens, and the huge new **Melbourne Museum ❻** complex (see p. 295).

Turn left down Victoria Street. A short side trip two blocks later, down Russell Street, will bring you to the **Old Melbourne Gaol ❼** (Russell St., tel (03) 9663 7228), where the notorious bushranger Ned Kelly (see pp. 322–323) met his fate on the gallows in 1881. Then continue a few blocks farther along Victoria Street to the bustling **Queen Victoria Market ❽**, a colorful Melbourne institution brimming with all the best in fruit, vegetables, meats, fishes, and cheeses Victoria has to offer, and where you can pick up the makings for a very classy picnic—right down to the basket (see p. 294).

Now walk down Elizabeth Street to the **Melbourne Central mall ❾** shopping center. From here, you can catch either a tram or the subway back to Flinders Street Station.

# St. Kilda

The suburb of St. Kilda is an old-fashioned seaside playground, with grand old hotels, a fading amusement park, and art deco apartments crowding a palm-lined esplanade and beach. Its seedy reputation has given way to cosmopolitan cool. It's also extremely popular and just a short tram ride from the city. Catch one of the trams (No. 16 or 96) clanging their way past Flinders Street Station, along St. Kilda Road, and 20 minutes later you're there.

St. Kilda's Acland Street is famous for its pastry shops, with their tempting windowfront displays.

**St. Kilda**
Ⓜ 290 C2

**Luna Park**
✉ Lower Esplanade, St. Kilda
☎ (03) 9525 5033
**www.lunapark.com.au**

**Fitzroy Street,** lined with watering holes and restaurants, is the main street heading down to the sea, where the **Esplanade** curves around the beach, past the pier and iconic music venues such as the Esplanade Hotel and the grand Palais Theatre. On Sundays, a lively craft market sets up here, and around the corner, crowds flock to **Acland Street,** famous for its cake shops, ethnic eateries, and bars.

Modeled after New York's Coney Island, **Luna Park** is a small and tacky but much-loved old fairground just off the Esplanade. The rides are tame and old-fashioned—the Scenic Railway roller coaster, bumper cars, and Ghost Train are the biggest hits.

The beach is good, with a comfortable holiday atmosphere. On summer weekends, professional beach volleyball tournaments or Iron Man competitions are occasionally held here. The pier, with the ornate kiosk at the end, attracts fishermen and Sunday strollers. It has a good view of the city skyline and the long curve of coastline of Melbourne's bayside suburbs. A bicycle path runs along this coast, from South Melbourne through St. Kilda and on to Brighton. ■

# Main Yarra Trail

Melbourne is a bicycle-friendly city, with an extensive network of flat bicycle paths to take an inquisitive cyclist through parklands, past gritty inner-city streetscapes, and along the breezy foreshore of Port Phillip Bay. One of the most popular cycleways is the Main Yarra Trail, which runs beside the tortuous Yarra River from the heart of the city into suburban parkland. This 22-mile (35 km) path is an ideal way to get to know Melbourne; half of it is described here.

On weekends the Main Yarra Trail is cheerfully busy with cyclists and picnickers, and the river and gum trees along the way make it astonishingly easy to forget you are in a city of three million. There are plenty of bike shops and bike rental businesses in Melbourne, including one right at the start of the path.

The trail starts beneath the ornate Princes Bridge, across the river from the Edwardian Flinders Street Station in the heart of the city. A nice prelude to the ride is cake and cappuccino —which you'll ride off anyway— in one of the sunny cafés at the nearby Southgate complex (see p. 299). Then head upstream as the river winds its way through **Alexandra Gardens.**

The riverside path goes south and east into some of Melbourne's most fashionable inner suburbs— parklike **South Yarra, Kew,** and **Hawthorn.** It elbows around a golf course in Hawthorn, then veers abruptly north into gritty working-class suburbs such as **Collingwood,** past some of the city's earliest industrial sites.

Follow the path through more parkland, looking back occasionally for striking views of the Melbourne skyline, and on toward the **Fairfield Park Boathouse.** Although

the path continues for a few more miles, this quaint old tearoom, which overlooks the river, is a good place to stop. You can get a nice lunch here, or rent a punt and row a little on the river. There really is a country feel to this little enclave, and it is quite a shock to walk only a couple hundred yards up a wooded path and step onto busy Heidelberg Road. Fairfield railroad station is a short ride away (across Heidelberg Road and up Station Street), and you can take the train to Flinders Street Station where you began. Another nice thing about cycling in Melbourne is that you can take your bike on the trains for free. ∎

## EXPERIENCE: Biking Melbourne

**Bicycle Victoria** (Level 10, 446 Collins St., North Melbourne, tel (03) 8638 8888, www .bv.com.au), a nonprofit dedicated to getting more people to pedal, sells excellent cycling maps to take you around the inner city, with roads color-coded to indicate which are safest for cyclists. Visit their website for a list of bike shops in the area; many places rent them out by the day.

The organization also has information on rides out of the city. If you don't have a car, double-check the rules about bringing your bike on public transportation.

# Mornington Peninsula

Two hours south of Melbourne are the fashionable beach towns of the Mornington Peninsula, where generations of Melburnians have gone to escape the rush of the city. A much-loved crescent of calm beach runs nearly 60 miles (96 km) along the inner rim of the bay. The open ocean side has a dramatic rocky coastline and good surf on the "back beaches." About 60 small but superb vineyards and winemakers dot the boot-shaped peninsula.

A volcanic monolith rises off the Mornington Peninsula's coast at Cape Schanck.

To get there, drive south on the Nepean Highway, along the bustling southeast flank of Port Phillip Bay, and past the suburbs of Mordialloc, Carrum, and Seaford. **Mount Eliza** marks the outermost commuter suburb. The fishing port of **Mornington,** a few miles farther south, has a scenic esplanade and the **Mornington Peninsula Art Gallery**—one of Victoria's best regional galleries. Every Wednesday there is a craft fair on Main Street.

The holiday feeling starts in **Dromana,** where the tourist office has brochures and maps for resorts down the peninsula. The bayside beaches from Dromana to Rye are bright with colored wooden shacks—bathing boxes. **Arthur's Seat State Park,** a 1,000-foot-high (300 m) granite outcrop, is nearby, with sweeping views of the bay and peninsula. In 1802, explorer Matthew Flinders climbed it to get his bearings (and learned from the view that he had sailed into the wrong bay).

**Cape Schanck,** a dramatic headland on the ocean side of the peninsula, is the site of an 1859 lighthouse. Excellent beach walks can be taken here, and the 16-mile (26 km) Two Bays Trail crosses the peninsula to Dromana.

**INSIDER TIP:**

Merricks General Wine Store, a cozy bistro and food shop, is a must-stop on your Mornington Peninsula wine tour.

—CATHERINE PEARSON
*National Geographic contributor*

On the bay side, **Sorrento** and **Portsea** are both fashionable little towns near the toe of the boot. Even the ice cream and fish-and-chips shops along the beach are upscale. The beaches are lovely, but take care for riptides, particularly on the open ocean beaches. In 1967, the Australian Prime Minister, Harold Holt, vanished while swimming in the surf here. Conspiracy theorists have had a ball with the incident, the most colorful theory being that he was taken aboard a Chinese submarine. The truth is that Holt, a powerful swimmer, disdained the rules and swam on unguarded beaches and was swept away by the ferocious riptides. Swim between the flags, and have a safe time!

At the tip of the peninsula, **Point Nepean National Park** has wonderful coastal scenery and the labyrinthine tunnels and crumbling fortifications of **Fort Nepean,** which was built in the 1880s to protect the narrow heads at the entrance to the bay. A trolley bus shuttles 4.5 miles (7 km) to the fort from the park visitor center *(tel (03) 5984 4276, $ entry, $$ trolley),* or you can drive halfway then get out and walk the trails.

From Sorrento you can take a ferry across the mouth of the bay to the pretty little seaside town of **Queenscliff.** The Peninsula Searoad Ferry *(tel (03) 5258 3244, www.sea road.com.au)* carries both passengers and vehicles.

**Phillip Island,** at the entrance to Westernport Bay, is another popular weekend destination. It is famed for the sunset parade of the fairy penguins that live on the island. This has become a highly commercialized tourist must in Victoria. A bridge crosses from San Remo on the mainland to the island town of **Newhaven,** where the visitor center is close to the bridge, and on to the main resort town of Cowes. The penguin parade takes place on Summerland Beach. Every evening the penguins—sometimes a few, sometimes dozens—emerge and waddle up the beach to their nests. ■

**Mornington Peninsula**

🅰 290 C1

**Visitor Information**

✉ Nepean Hwy., Dromana
☎ (03) 5987 3078

**Merricks General Wine Store**

✉ 3460 Frankston-Flinders Rd., Merricks
☎ (03) 5989 8088
**www.mgwinestore .com.au**

**Newhaven**

🅰 290 C1

**Visitor Information**

☎ (03) 5956 7447

---

**EXPERIENCE:**
# Penguin Parade

A large colony of 4,500 little penguins, the smallest of the species at just over a foot (30 cm) high, nests at **Summerland Beach** on Phillip Island. After sunset every evening, they return to their burrows to rest or feed their young in the breeding season (Aug.–March). The penguins are unfazed by the tour buses and packed stands, as first one animal emerges tentatively from the sea, then two, then a dozen, until a flood of cute penguins is waddling up the beach to the dunes. For details, contact **Phillip Island Nature Parks** *(tel (03) 5951 2835, www.penguins.org.au. $$$).*

# Yarra Valley

Melbourne's rural fringes—the Yarra Valley and the Dandenong Ranges—are well worth exploring. They have Victoria's best wineries, excellent bushwalking, and some beautiful drives through tall forests.

**Yarra Valley**
⚠ 290 C2
**Visitor Information**
✉ Old Courthouse, Harker St., Healesville
☎ (03) 5962 2600

The Yarra Valley, only an hour's drive northeast from Melbourne on the Maroondah Highway, is best explored by car. This region is one of Victoria's oldest wine producers. Vines were first planted here in the 1860s by Swiss immigrants Paul and Hubert de Castella. In 1889, the region earned gold medals at the Paris Exposition. Then came the dreaded phylloxera outbreak that ravaged the world's vines in the late 19th century and struck Victoria particularly hard. Later,

### INSIDER TIP:

**Rightfully known for its wines, the Yarra Valley has equally delectable olives. You can find both at Melbourne's Queen Victoria Market [see p. 294].**

—CATHERINE PEARSON
*National Geographic contributor*

Australia's palate shifted to fortified wines, and under these twin blows, winemaking in the valley seemed moribund. The last of the vines were pulled up in 1921.

These days the Yarra Valley is enjoying a renaissance, with more than 90 wineries in the region. One major presence is the French champagne-maker Moët et Chandon, whose **Domain Chandon winery,** near Coldstream, makes delectable sparkling wines. It has a delightfully airy tasting room with sweeping views of the vineyards. The **De Bortoli winery,** north of Yarra Glen on the Melba Highway, produces a dessert wine—called the Noble One—that is arguably Australia's best.

**Healesville,** about 12 miles (19 km) farther on the Maroondah Highway, has the **Healesville Wildlife Sanctuary** *(Badger Creek Rd., tel (03) 5957 2800. www.zoo.org .au, $$$),* established in the 1940s to care for injured or orphaned animals. Some are returned to the wild; others are used for breeding programs to help endangered species. There are more than 200 species of birds, mammals, and reptiles here.

Beyond Healesville, the Maroondah Highway twists its way up through the deep wet forests of the **Great Dividing Range.** The incredibly tall mountain ash throw the narrow road into cool green shade. The impression of driving through a cathedral would make you go at a stately pace even without the hairpin turns. Giant ferns, myrtle beech, manna gums, and small sparkling waterfalls catch your eye as you pass. There are pulling-off points where you can stop and admire the scenery. ∎

# The Dandenongs

Tinted blue by the mist of eucalyptus oil given off by the forests, the Dandenong Ranges are Melbourne's answer to Sydney's Blue Mountains (see pp. 104–105). Drive 20 miles (32 km) southeast of town on the Burwood Highway to Upper Ferntree Gully, and then turn north on the steep and winding Mount Dandenong Tourist Road into the forests.

*Puffing Billy* now hauls tourists instead of its original cargo of farm produce.

The mountains rise to more than 2,000 feet (610 m) and are cloaked with dense, lush growth. Some of the gullies are shaded by huge ferns, whose fronds form an overhead canopy, blocking out the sun and sheltering a rich growth of mosses, smaller ferns, and flowers, including more than 30 species of orchids. The ranges also have 100-odd species of birds but are especially known for lyrebirds. These skillful mimics can re-create almost any sound, including other birdcalls, the motorwind on a camera, and even a chainsaw.

Ferntree Gully National Park, Sherwood Forest, Doongalla Reserve, Olinda, and Mount Evelyn forests have been combined to form the **Dandenong Ranges National Park.** Popular with bushwalkers, the park has numerous short trails, many of them with city views. **Mount Dandenong** is the top day-trip destination, with a café and unrivaled views.

The restful villages up here have tearooms, craft galleries, B&Bs, and gracious old houses with beautiful gardens. At **Belgrave** you can catch an old steam train, *Puffing Billy (reservations, tel (03) 9757 0700, www.puffingbilly .com.au, $$$$$),* which was built in 1900 to haul farm produce and now winds along an 8-mile (13 km) track to Emerald Lake Park. ∎

**Dandenong Ranges National Park**

🗺 290 C2

**Visitor Information**

✉ 1211 Burwood Hwy., Upper Ferntree Gully

☎ (03) 9758 7522

**EXPLORING THE DANDENONGS:**
Hikers' guides to the Dandenongs, detailing paths and the flora and fauna you may see, are available in Melbourne. Belgrave can be reached by train out of Flinders Street Railway Station in Melbourne.

# Great Ocean Road Drive

Simply put, the Great Ocean Road is Australia's finest coastal drive. It starts at the seaside resort town of Torquay, about 60 miles (100 km) southwest of Melbourne, and hugs Victoria's spectacular, cliff-lined Shipwreck Coast for 150 miles (240 km) to the old whaling port of Warrnambool. From Melbourne, the direct route to Torquay is through Geelong, but the road down the Mornington Peninsula is more attractive.

On view is perhaps the most magnificent mix of scenery in Australia: hauntingly long sandy beaches, miles of rugged cliffs, wildflowers, and pretty fishing ports, set against the backdrop of the steep, rain forested Otway Ranges. The road's most famous landmarks are the Twelve Apostles, a series of dramatic rock pillars that rise from the sea near Port Campbell.

The road was built as a monument to the soldiers who had served in World War I. Construction began in 1918, and many of the 3,000

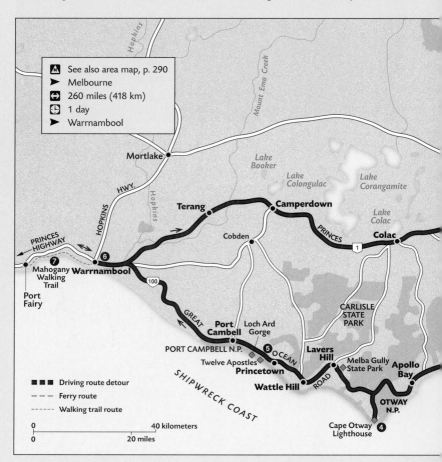

See also area map, p. 290
► Melbourne
↔ 260 miles (418 km)
⊕ 1 day
► Warrnambool

Driving route detour
Ferry route
Walking trail route

0        40 kilometers
0        20 miles

men who worked on it were themselves war veterans. It was completed in 1932, and since then it has been hugely popular with tourists and Victorians alike.

The Great Ocean Road *(www.greatocean road.org)* officially starts in the old vacation town of Torquay, 14 miles (23 km) south of Geelong. From Melbourne, you could cross the Westgate Bridge, follow the Princes Freeway 45 miles (72 km) to Geelong, and then take the Surfcoast Highway to Torquay. It's a quick drive, but not particularly scenic. Instead, detour on the Nepean Highway down the Mornington Peninsula (see pp. 306–307) to Sorrento or Portsea, and then take the ferry

## NOT TO BE MISSED:

Lorne • Cape Otway lighthouse
• The Twelve Apostles

across the mouth of Port Phillip Bay to the old maritime town of **Queenscliff ❶**. This pretty bayside town was founded in 1838 as a pilot boat station for ships entering the bay. Later it became a naval garrison town. The railway arrived from Geelong in 1879, and the town became a fashionable resort favored for its sea breezes, yachting, and grand hotels. Even

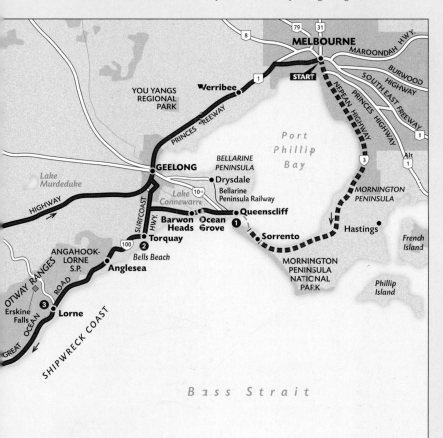

today the **Queenscliff Hotel** (see Travelwise, p. 384), built in 1887, and the **Vue Grand** (1884) on Hesse Street *(tel (03) 5258 1544)* are very elegant retreats. From Queenscliff, it is a 28-mile (44 km) drive via Ocean Grove and Barwon Heads to the Surfcoast Highway.

**Torquay ❷** *(visitor information: Surf City Plaza, Beach Rd., tel (03) 5261 4219)* has been a vacation spot since the late 19th century, but the surfing culture of the 1960s made it famous. Surf conditions along these beaches are close to perfect, and the Easter Surfing Classic, held on nearby **Bells Beach,** is a premier pro surfing event. In town, **Surf City Plaza** houses surf fashion outlets and board makers, including local companies Rip Curl and Quiksilver. Surf World surfing museum *(tel (03) 5261 4606, $)* is also in the plaza.

The road veers inland for about 10 miles (16 km) before coming down to the sea again at **Anglesea,** where kangaroos graze on the golf course, but from there it diligently winds its way along the rugged coast past miles of beaches, through the picturesque seaside town of **Lorne ❸** (about 25 miles/40 km from Torquay). Lorne has been a popular holiday resort since the 1860s, when coaches brought visitors over the Otway Ranges on muddy bush tracks. Today Lorne is one of the most fashionable retreats on the coast, popular with surfers and with bushwalkers, who can scramble up the ranges behind the town to see the delightful **Erskine Falls** or gain even more spectacular views of the coast. On a busy weekend, or around the Christmas holiday, its population can surge from 1,100 to more than 20,000. If you want to stay, avoid busy times or reserve well ahead. The Lorne Visitor Information Centre *(15 Mountjoy Parade, tel (03) 5289 1152)* has details of accommodations.

The narrow and twisting 25-mile (40 km) stretch from Lorne to **Apollo Bay** *(visitor information: tel (03) 5237 6529)* is one of the most dramatic sections of the Great Ocean Road. It hugs steep cliffs and winds around tight little inlets. The scenery is so beautiful that it can be hard to keep your eyes on the road—which is dangerous because the road is incredibly curvy as it picks its way along the cliffs. Happily, you can stop at plenty of lookouts.

After Apollo Bay, the road veers inland, climbing into the Otway Ranges and giving spectacular views of the ocean and rolling green hillsides spreading out behind. These steep

## Shipwreck Coast

If this coast is tough on drivers, it has been much more cruel to sailors. More than 80 vessels have come to grief along here, the most famous of which was the clipper *Loch Ard*. It went down on a cold, stormy night in June 1878, and of the 53 people on board, only two survived: an 18-year-old girl named Eva Carmichael and an apprentice seaman, Tom Pearce, also 18. They were washed into a long, narrow, high-walled gorge and sheltered in a cave until morning, when Pearce scaled the cliffs to summon help. The nation was stunned by the tragedy. Eva Carmichael lost both of her parents and five siblings in the disaster, and the popular hope was that she would strike up a romance with the young seaman who had saved her life. It wasn't to be, however. She came from a prosperous family in Ireland and returned there, while Pearce went back to sea, where he survived two more shipwrecks.

Today scenic trails loop around Loch Ard Gorge, and wooden steps lead down to the tiny beach and cave—Carmichael's Cave—where the two castaways spent their miserable night. The *Loch Ard's* anchor stands outside the visitor center in nearby Port Campbell, where the Loch Ard Shipwreck Museum tells the story of five other shipwrecks along the coast.

Despite their name, the powerful and impressive Twelve Apostles actually comprise eight sea stacks.

mountains, clad in temperate rain forests, are the wettest parts of Victoria, averaging more than 80 inches (2,000 mm) of rainfall a year.

If you've brought a stout pair of walking boots, Apollo Bay is the beginning of the **Great Ocean Walk,** a spectacular trail that hugs the coastline most of the way to the Twelve Apostles, 57 miles (91 km) away. The trail can be done as a whole or in stages, with maps and information on accommodations along the way available from Parks Victoria *(tel 13 19 63, www.parkweb.vic.gov.au).*

About 12 miles (19 km) after Apollo Bay, turn left (south) on a winding dirt track to **Cape Otway lighthouse ❹,** built out of local sandstone by convicts in 1848, in response to a series of shipwrecks on the reefs near the coast. The lighthouse is a paragon of reliability, never having broken down. There is no protection from bad luck or poor judgment, though. On the rocks below the cape, you can see the rusting anchor of *Eric the Red,* which foundered in 1880 with the loss of four lives.

The Great Ocean Road winds past the small but lovely **Melba Gully State Park,** with its luxuriant ferns, dense rain forests, and

eerie evening displays of glowworms, and on through the old timber town of **Lavers Hill.** The highway rejoins the coast at **Princetown** and follows it for several miles through **Port Campbell National Park,** a strip of spectacular coastline *(visitor information: tel (03) 5598 6089).* Storms over millions of years have eaten away at this coast, leaving the **Twelve Apostles ❺**—enormous rock pillars, more than 200 feet (60 m) tall—in the sea. To view these striking formations, park at the Twelve Apostles Centre and take the walkway under the highway to the cliff-top lookout points connected by a boardwalk. Early morning and late afternoon are best for spectacular pictures.

The Great Ocean Road ends where it joins the Princes Highway, east of the old whaling town of **Warrnambool ❻** *(visitor information: Flagstaff Hill, Merri St., tel (03) 5564 7838, www .warrnamboolinfo.com.au).* In winter months (June–Sept.), the southern right whales that use the shallows here as a nursery have become a popular attraction. Once hunted almost to extinction, their numbers are now slowly rebuilding, although there are still probably fewer than 7,000. Warrnambool's days as a

The Great Ocean Road threads between the sea and the Otway Ranges south of Lorne.

## EXPERIENCE: Surfing

Victoria's Bells Beach (see p. 312) is the home of Australian surfing, or at least the home of the Australian surf industry's major brands like Quiksilver and Rip Curl. The big swells at Bells are renowned, but good surf can also be found elsewhere along the Great Ocean Road, and on the Mornington Peninsula and Phillip Island.

**Sydney** lays claim to the country's most popular surf beaches. Bondi has decent surf, but the best waves are on the northern beaches stretching north from Manly.

For warmer water, head north. **Byron Bay** to **Surfers Paradise** is Australia's premier beach holiday stretch, with plenty of good surf spots. At the top is the **Gold Coast**'s Superbank, where theme parks proliferate. The council inadvertently made a theme park for surfers when it dredged the Tweed River to form this sand bank. On a good day, legend has it, you can catch a wave for more than a mile (2 km). The **Sunshine Coast** north of Brisbane also has good surf, but the Great Barrier Reef shelters most of the Queensland coastline.

In **Western Australia**, the coast from Cape Naturaliste to Cape Leeuwin has some of the biggest and most consistent surf in Australia. The westerlies here push huge swells along the Great Australian Bight to the **Eyre Peninsula**, which has noted waves at Streaky Bay, among others.

Surf lessons are offered almost anywhere a surf scene exists. Big-name beaches like Bondi and Noosa are most popular, but you might find smaller classes elsewhere.

See www.surfingaustralia.com or www.australia.com for more information.

---

whaling station are re-created at **Flagstaff Hill Maritime Village** *(tel (03) 5559 4600),* based around the lighthouse, lighthouse keeper's cottage, and fortifications built in 1887.

One of Australia's most intriguing shipwrecks is the "Mahogany Ship," reputedly buried in the sand between Warrnambool and Port Fairy. A couple of whalers first sighted it in 1836; upon examination, the Port Fairy harbormaster thought its design antiquated and its timbers unlike any he'd ever seen, "like mahogany." No record existed of such a ship being lost in the area, and local Aborigines said the wreck had always been there. Then, in 1880, a series of great storms obliterated the mysterious wreck, and they have never been seen since. Some historians believe it may have been a 16th-century caravel sent by the Portuguese government to secretly reconnoiter the south seas, in violation of a treaty with Spain. The ancient Dauphin Map, reputedly based on information from Portuguese archives, appears to show the south coast of Australia. The archives were destroyed in the Lisbon earthquake of 1755, so the question of which Europeans first saw Australia remains open.

The **Mahogany Walking Trail ⑦**, a 12-mile (19 km) coastal walk to Port Fairy, takes you past the area where the Mahogany Ship was last seen 120 years ago. Warrnambool's Visitor Information Centre has information on local walks and sights.

The historic seaside village of **Port Fairy** has picturesque streets lined with heritage buildings and stone cottages, many of them now B&Bs. This popular holiday spot also hosts the Port Fairy Folk Festival in March, one of the country's premier music events.

You can take the Princes Highway directly back to Melbourne, or continue on to Portland, Victoria's first town, and then along the coast to Adelaide.

# Victoria's Alpine Country

The high country of Victoria is great for hiking in summer and offers some of Australia's best skiing in winter. It stretches from Mansfield—about 100 miles (160 km) northeast of Melbourne—to the New South Wales border. Most of the state's ski resorts are in this area. Picturesque villages, wineries, and small farms nestle in the valleys at the foot of the 6,000-foot-high (1,800 m) mountains and make it a delightful place to tour.

Known as Australia's powder capital, Mount Hotham is one of Victoria's most popular ski resorts.

## Beechworth

🗺 291 D3

**Visitor Information**

✉ 103 Ford St.

☎ (03) 5728 8065

The heart of the alpine country is around the **Bogong High Plains,** a four-hour drive northeast of Melbourne on the Hume Highway. The route runs through Kelly Country, where bushranger Ned Kelly and his gang hid out (see pp. 322–323). In winter, you can see the snow-capped mountains from the town of **Glenrowan,** where they fought their last battle.

At **Wangaratta,** leave the Hume Highway and follow the Ovens Highway up the picturesque Ovens River Valley. As with much of Victoria, it was gold that opened up this neck of the woods. The town of **Beechworth** (*visitor information: Ford St., tel (03) 5728 3233 or 1-300 366 321, www.beechworth.com*)—north of the highway—was founded in 1852 on the heels of a big strike that produced more than 4 million ounces (113,400 kg) in the first 14 years alone. In its heyday, it was a town of 42,000 with 61 pubs, famous for its gaudy politics. Amid the brass bands, free drinks, mayhem, and vote-buying of the 1855 election, one candidate, Daniel Cameron, reputedly paraded to the polls on a horse shod with solid gold.

These days Beechworth is one of the prettiest and best-preserved of Victoria's gold towns, its wide streets lined with honey-colored buildings, classy restaurants, and museums. The **Burke Museum** (*Loch St.*)–named for explorer Robert Burke (see p. 43), who was the town's police commissioner–tells the story of the gold rush. The 3-mile-long (5 km) **Gorge Scenic Drive** is good to drive but even better on a bicycle. It takes you through old digging areas and past the Powder Magazine, now a museum. Beechworth is also on the **Murray to the Mountains Rail Trail,** from Wangaratta to Bright, the country's premier rail trail. The easy bitumen track runs past scenic wineries and farms.

## Into the Mountains

The mountains start just past Myrtleford, with the spectacular **Mount Buffalo National Park,** known for wildflowers and waterfalls. One waterfall, Crystal Brook, plummets almost 800 feet (243 m) in a single drop. There are nearly 90 miles (144 km) of hiking and cross-country ski trails on this mile-high (1.6 km) granite massif. You can drive to just below the summit of the Horn and walk to the top for a sweeping panorama.

The 20-mile (32 km) drive up the valley from Myrtleford to **Bright** is lined with small farms growing tobacco, peppermint, hops, and flowers. Bright has many European trees and in autumn is famous for its New England–like foliage. Bright's tourist information center has a leaflet on some of the lovely bushwalks in the area.

Beyond Bright the road forks. One branch leads to Mount Beauty and the ski resort of **Falls Creek.** The other winds its way to the 6,128-foot (1,862 m) summit of **Mount Hotham** and on to the village of Dinner Plain. Mount Hotham has perhaps the best powder skiing in Australia, while Falls Creek has the best cross-country skiing. It is the only ski village in Australia where everyone can ski directly from their lodges to the ski slopes.

In summer, there are magnificent hiking opportunities up here. **Mount Bogong** is a particularly nice–if somewhat steep–hike. Hikers with enough time and experience can tackle the 405-mile (650 km) **Alpine Walking Track,** which runs from Walhalla to the outskirts of Canberra. ∎

**Bright**
🗺 291 D2
**Visitor Information**
✉ 119 Gavan St.
☎ (03) 5755 2275

## Bogong High Plains

The Bogong High Plains in the Victorian Alps is wonderland for cross-country skiers in winter and hikers in summer, with huts scattered along the Alpine Walking Track and nearby walks to Mount Bogong and Mount Feathertop.

Easily accessed from the ski resorts of Falls Creek and Mount Hotham, the plains are home to some unique flora and fauna, including the rare mountain pygmy possum, thought to be extinct until one wandered into a ski hut in the 1960s. The Bogong moth also migrates here every year from November to March, when Aboriginal tribes once gathered to feast on the moths, which they called Bogong. Huge clouds of the large moths descend on Canberra and other southeast cities during their great summer migration away from the heat of the plains.

# Australian Rules Football

For seven months each year, suburban Melbourne becomes a patchwork of jealous footy fiefdoms—Collingwood, Essendon, North Melbourne, Carlton, and St. Kilda, to name a few. In all, this sports-mad city supports nine professional, big-league Aussie Rules football clubs—ten if you count neighboring Geelong—and just as many professional minor league ones. Some clubs date back to the 1850s, which makes them the world's oldest.

Club allegiances run in families, and after so many generations, team colors can form far sharper social distinctions than race, class, or money. During the footy season, about the only thing all these footy fanatics agree on is that it's sweet to see a Victorian team clobber one from interstate—especially one from South Australia.

There is no more quintessentially Melburnian activity than bundling up against the winter weather and heading down to the footy. If you're visiting Melbourne during the season, which runs roughly from March through September, go! This is the real Victoria: a bleacher seat, a meat pie, and bone-crunching action.

## EXPERIENCE: Catch a Match

Don't miss the chance to see a fast and furious Australian Rules game. The antics of the fanatical crowd are worth the entry ticket alone. Finals are sold out weeks before, but regular weekend and Friday night games from March to September are easy to catch. In Melbourne, head for the **M.C.G.** or **Etihad Stadium** at Docklands, near Southern Cross train station. Tickets can be booked at **Ticketmaster** (www .ticketmaster.com.au), advisable for one of the big games, but otherwise just line up at the stadium ticket window. Alternatively, the gates are opened for free entry in the last quarter (about two hours after the start time) if the stadium isn't full.

## The "Rules" of the Game

The plot can be a little hard for novices to follow, because there don't appear to be any rules in Aussie Rules, other than that each side has 18 players on the field.

In a nutshell the object is to kick, bounce, and punch the ball up the field until you are close enough to boot it between the goal posts for six points. When that happens, the goal post referee—who looks like he's wearing a lab coat—struts between the posts and quick-draws two imaginary pistols. The crowd goes wild. If the player misses the two narrowest uprights, but gets it between the two wider ones, he gets a point for almost.

## Nonstop Action & Athleticism

No doubt about it, this is one gutsy game. The players, who are built like basketball forwards with attitude, wear neither pads nor helmets, and they collide with reckless abandon—eyes only on the ball. They play at full tilt over four 20-minute quarters, leaping, kicking, chasing, wrestling, and tackling. Their athleticism is amazing. Imagine a bloke, maybe six feet eight (2 m) and 225 pounds (102 kg), leaping like a ballet dancer to snatch a football out of the air, then sprinting up the field, dodging tacklers, and booting the ball on a dead run 60 yards (55 m) for a goal. Injuries are common but the action never stops, not even when someone is being stretchered off.

## Weekly Clashes

The big game of the week is usually played at the Melbourne Cricket Ground (M.C.G.,

**Melbourne's Western Bulldogs take on the Sydney Swans in a 2008 Australian Football League match.**

see p. 296)—a sort of no-man's-land on the footy map, where both teams are visitors and 100,000-plus seats accommodate the crowd. Some of these clashes go down in footy history. The atmosphere is throbbing, blindly parochial, yet still quite friendly. There's none of the hooliganism that plagues English and European soccer. The physical contact stays on the field. Aussies generally conduct their footy feuds with barbed wisecracks—often hilariously funny, even to the recipient.

The season stretches into the last week of September and culminates with the Grand Final. If you are lucky enough to be here then and get a chance to go, or find yourself invited to a Grand Final party at a local's house—don't pass it up.

# Goldfields

A string of fabulous gold discoveries in the mid-19th century transformed Victoria's economy and created huge wealth in gold-rush towns such as Ballarat, Castlemaine, and Bendigo. The nouveau-riche towns flaunted their incredible wealth with elaborate gardens, bandstands, statuary, and grandly frivolous architecture. A tour of the cities and the Victorian goldfields makes a delightful three-day (or longer) drive from Melbourne.

Sovereign Hill at Ballarat is a living museum, re-creating life in gold-rush days.

**Ballarat**

🅐 290 B2

**Visitor Information**

✉ Corner of Eureka & Rodier Sts.

☎ (03) 5320 5741

**www.ballarat.com**

## Ballarat

Ballarat, the scene of the 1854 Eureka Stockade battle (see pp. 46–48), is only an hour or so west of Melbourne. Entering from the east, the ornamental trees, ornate buildings, and brilliant flowerbeds give a taste of the city's elegance and wealth. On the other side of town, the Western Highway runs along a 14-mile (22.5 km) Avenue of Honor, flanked with trees commemorating soldiers who died in World War I.

Gold was found at Ballarat in 1851, one of a series of strikes that sprang up like wildfires around central Victoria, and mining continued until 1918. Today, mining

companies are exploring the area again, armed with computer-age technology that could make this a gold town once again.

The center of town is rich with old buildings, among them the classical revival **Town Hall,** the **Mining Exchange** building (1888), and the **Art Gallery of Ballarat** (1884; *40 Lydiard St. N.*), which has an excellent collection of Heidelberg school and colonial paintings (see p. 64), and the original Eureka Stockade Flag. Heritage tours of the town center (and of Bendigo) are available *(London Bus Company, tel 1-500 544 169).*

Ballarat's main attraction is the living museum at **Sovereign Hill** *(Bradshaw St., tel (03) 5337 1100,* www.sovereignhill.com.au, $$$$). It re-creates the Ballarat of the gold-rush days, with coaches clattering down cobbled streets, old shops open for business, and gold diggings where you can try your luck. If you want to prospect further, the **Mining Exchange Gold Shop** (8A Lydiard St. N.) can supply maps, metal detectors, and the required Miners Right permit.

Follow the Midland Highway northeast to the gold-mining town of **Daylesford,** better known today as a spa town. Eighty percent of Australia's known mineral springs bubble up in this old volcanic area, and for more than a century, Victorians have come here to take the water. The town has organic eateries, alternative bookstores, and shops selling crystals and essential oils.

## Castlemaine

Castlemaine is farther north along the Midlands Highway. Reputed to have once had the richest shallow deposits of gold ever known, it is now one of Victoria's prettiest towns. Its streetscapes have not changed much since the 19th century.

Built in 1862, the superb neoclassic **Castlemaine Market** is topped by a statue of Ceres, the Roman goddess of the harvest. The restored building now houses the visitor center. An example of colonial architecture, **Buda** (corner of Urquhart and Hunter Sts., tel (03) 5472 1032) is now in the hands of the National Trust.

The nearby town of **Maldon** is considered to have the best-preserved architecture of

Victoria's goldfield towns. In 1966, the National Trust classified it as a "notable town" for its unspoiled and intact streetscapes.

## Bendigo

Bendigo is where the gold rush began in 1851. Its reputation for spectacular finds spread to China, and thousands of Chinese prospectors came to town in its boom days. After the initial alluvial strikes played out, gold continued to be mined in deep quartz reefs for more than a century. The last large mine closed in 1956, but mining companies hope new technology will lead to hidden bonanzas.

**INSIDER TIP:**

**A stroll though historic Maldon takes you back to 19th-century gold-rush days. Check out www.maldon.org.au for walk routes.**

—LARRY PORGES
*National Geographic editor*

Fabulous wealth and civic pride combined to make Bendigo an architectural jewel. One of the most elegant buildings is the **Shamrock Hotel,** built in 1897 on the corner of Pall Mall and Williamson Street, with a marble staircase, polished wood, and stained glass in its lobby.

For a taste of life in a mine, try the 200-foot-deep (60 m) **Central Deborah Mine** (76 Violet St., tel (03) 5443 8322, $$$). ∎

### Daylesford
🄰 290 B2
**Visitor Information**
✉ 96 Vincent St.
☎ (03) 5321 6123

### Castlemaine
🄰 290 B2
**Visitor Information**
✉ 44 Mostyn St
☎ (03) 5471 1795
**www.mount alexander.vic.gov.au**

### Maldon
🄰 290 B2
**Visitor Information**
✉ 93 High St.
☎ (03) 5475 2569
**www.maldoncastle maine.com**

### Bendigo
🄰 290 B2
**Visitor Information**
✉ Old Post Office building, 51–67 Pall Mall
☎ (03) 5444 4445
**www.bendigo tourism.com**

# Bushrangers

The gold-rush days were also the glory days of the bushrangers, or highway robbers. Whether recent immigrants or descendants of convicts who had been transported for political reasons, Irish people had little reason to love English authority. They frequently sheltered and supplied the bushrangers, kept them apprised of police movements, and built them into folk heroes. Many bushrangers were of Irish stock themselves.

Sidney Nolan did a series of Ned Kelly paintings, including "Death of Constable Scanlon" (1946).

Australia's first bushrangers were commonly known as "bolters," escaped convicts who took to the bush and lived by robbing passersby. By 1814, the dripping rain forests of Tasmania had come to shelter so many armed bolters that the government declared martial law, fearing that the outlaws would help the captive convicts to rebel and take over the island.

According to legend, the bushrangers were dapper gentleman-robbers, but in reality they were frequently violent and thuggish. In the setting of Australia's brutal penal colonies, however, any flouting of authority must have seemed heroic. Some bushrangers really did have a certain gallant style. When Tasmania's Matthew Brady learned that there was a reward on his head, he jauntily tacked up notices offering 20 gallons of rum for the capture of the colony's lieutenant-governor. Brady went to the gallows a hero in 1824, his cell filled with flowers, cakes, and letters from admirers. "Bold Jack" Donohoe was lionized by poorer Australians for his escapades. When he died in a shootout with New South Wales police in 1830, he became a martyr, remembered in ballads and in Bold Jack souvenir tobacco pipes sold by shopkeepers.

## Ned Kelly & His Gang

These heroes were eclipsed when Ned Kelly rode onto the scene. He was born in 1854 on a dirt-poor farm in northern Victoria, the son of an Irish convict. By the time he was 15, Ned had a conviction for assault. The next year he was sentenced to three years for horse theft, and in 1878 he gunned down three police officers who were coming to arrest him. With his brother Dan and two mates—Joe Byrne and Steve Hart—he fled into the Strathbogie Ranges. Over the next 18 months, the Kelly Gang conducted a series of dramatic raids. They once took over the town of Jerilderie, New South Wales, and held its citizens hostage. Here Ned dictated a rambling 10,000-word letter to the authorities justifying his actions, describing himself as an Irish Republican political activist. The authorities saw him as a murderous thief who had to be stopped.

In June 1880, the Victoria government dispatched a trainload of armed constables to track down the Kelly Gang. Tipped off that the law was coming, Ned and his cohorts took over the railroad town of Glenrowan and ordered workers to tear up the tracks. One of the hostages managed to get away and signal a warning to the troopers. A gun battle erupted between the lawmen and the Kelly Gang, who were holed up in the Glenrowan Hotel. The fighting lasted all night, and toward dawn the police torched the place. Ned tried to escape in the suit of armor he had made for himself, but he was wounded and captured. The rest of the gang perished in the flames, although popular myth has one (or more) of them escaping and living in quiet anonymity. Old men were still claiming to be Dan Kelly as late as the 1930s.

## Romantic Martyr

Ned Kelly was taken to Melbourne for trial, found guilty, and hanged at the Melbourne Gaol on November 11, 1880. His last words were either "Such is life" or "So it has come to this." The authorities soon learned that Ned was bigger and more romantic in martyrdom than he had ever been in life (see sidebar below). A writer in the *Bulletin* magazine noted: "These splendid bushrangers never came within a hundred yards of a woman without taking off their hats." In 1906 the Kelly Gang was the subject of the world's first feature film. It was so sympathetic to Ned and his friends that the Victorian authorities banned it in Kelly's old stomping grounds for fear that it would cause a riot.

## Ned Kelly's Legacy in Australian Pop Culture

Ned Kelly is as big in death as he ever was in life. He has been the subject of several movies since the 1906 *Story of the Kelly Gang*, as well as many books, songs, and paintings. Australian artist Sidney Nolan created an entire series of paintings in the 1940s on major Kelly gang events. Nolan's paintings can be viewed at the National Gallery of Australia in Canberra. *The True History of the Ned Kelly Gang*, a novel by Peter Carey, won the prestigious Booker Prize in 2001.

In spite of the fact that Kelly was a murderer, many remember him for embodying the rebellious qualities that are part of Australia's national character. A popular Aussie expression is to be "as game as Ned Kelly," or audaciously heroic.

# Murray River

The Murray River—with a colorful history of paddle steamers and bellicose steamboat captains—is Australia's longest river, running 1,170 miles (1,883 km) from Victoria's alpine country to South Australia's coastline, the Coorong. For much of its length it forms the border between New South Wales and Victoria. In 1824, explorers Hamilton Hume and William Hovell were the first Europeans to see the river, near the site of modern Albury-Wodonga.

Built 42 feet (12.7 m) above the river, Echuca's massive old wharf is still in business.

## Mildura

🅰 290 A4

**Visitor Information**

✉ 180–190 Deakin Ave.

☎ (03) 5018 8380 or 1-800 039 043 (toll-free)

**www.visitmildura .com**

By the 1860s, hard-riding cattlemen had claimed much of the land along the river's upper reaches. Among them was Jack Riley, the model for Banjo Paterson's *The Man from Snowy River*. Dozens of steamboats puttered up the river's lower reaches and along its major tributary, the Darling, bringing supplies to what had seemed useless land.

In 1887, George and William Chaffee were invited by the Victorian government to set up an irrigation system in northern Victoria. Since then, the Murray has become the life-blood for a good deal of Australia's agriculture.

Controlled by a series of locks and dams, its muddy waters support thousands of acres of orchards, vineyards, and cotton fields.

Although it is at most a couple of hundred yards wide, the red gums along its bank, its serpentine curves, and the bright sunshine have made the Murray River a classic vacation spot. Anytime but the staggeringly hot summer are good seasons to visit here.

## Mildura

Mildura, about a six-hour drive north from Melbourne on the Calder Highway, is the river town where the irrigation scheme began. It is an oasis, with ornamental palms along the waterfront, landscaped gardens, golf courses, and lawn tennis courts that Australia's Davis Cup players have compared favorably with Wimbledon. Lush orange orchards and vineyards surround the town, and it is easy to forget that beyond the green fringe lie miles of harsh outback mallee scrub and salt pan.

Several restored 19th-century paddle steamers offer cruises from Mildura, ranging from an hour to five days. A word to visitors expecting massive Mississippi-style steamboats: These are more like the *African Queen* in size (but better appointed) because of the confines of this shallow river. Hot-air balloon flights are also available.

## Echuca

Echuca is a colorful old Murray River port about three hours north of Melbourne on the Northern Highway, and it is the most interesting town on the river. An ex-convict named Henry Hopwood founded the town in 1853. He set a ferry crossing and, in 1859, built the Bridge Hotel. He shrewdly fixed his ferry schedule so that travelers had to wait for their crossing, and they generally waited in the pub, buying drinks. Hopwood prospered, and so did Echuca.

The gold rushes and the booming wheat trade made it one of Australia's biggest inland ports, with a massive wharf more than half a mile (800 m) long built out of red gum beams. When the railroads came, the river trade declined and Echuca faded, but it has found new life in tourism. The wharf has been restored and there are excellent restaurants and wood-carving galleries. A number of restored steamboats tie up at the old wharf for cruises along this pretty stretch of river, including one-hour excursions, lunch and dinner cruises, and overnight trips. Houseboats and canoe rentals are also available. ∎

### Echuca

⚑ 290 C3

**Visitor Information**

✉ Corner of Heygarth St. & Cobb Hwy.

☎ (03) 5480 7555 or 1-800 804 446 (toll-free)

**www.echucamoama.com**

## Mungo Man & the Walls of China

Mildura is a good base for visiting Mungo National Park, located about 70 miles (112 km) northeast in New South Wales. This significant World Heritage area has spectacular wind-sculpted dune formations known as the Walls of China, and is home to the earliest known human on the continent, Mungo Man. Found in 1974 at Lake Mungo, the fossilized remains, sprinkled in ochre and ritually cremated, date from at least 40,000 years ago.

Ancient, dried-up Lake Mungo once teemed with wildlife and attracted Aboriginal hunters, who camped on the shores. Rich fossil beds have also given palaeontologists a glimpse of the bizarre fauna that once roamed the lakeshores, including 10-foot-tall (3 m) kangaroos.

The dirt road to the park can be impassable when it rains *(contact the park office at tel (03) 5021 8900 in Buronga, just over the river from Mildura, for road conditions)*. Local Paakantyi Aboriginal guide Harry Nanya *(tel (03) 5027 2076, www.harrynanyatours.com.au)* runs very informative tours of the park.

# Grampians National Park (Gariwerd)

The Grampians—also known by their Aboriginal name, Gariwerd—are a formidable series of sandstone ridges that rise to more than 3,000 feet (900 m) in western Victoria. A national park of 500,000 acres (200,000 ha) incorporates the ranges, with cliffs, waterfalls, ancient rock shelters with Aboriginal art, and a kaleidoscope of wildflowers. The park offers scenic drives, bushwalking trails, great rock climbing, and the opportunity to see a lot of Australian fauna.

Wonderland Lookout offers a spectacular view.

It is an easy 150-mile (250 km) drive from Melbourne to Grampians National Park. The route passes through the goldfield town of Ballarat (see pp. 320–321) and the Great Western sparkling wine district, as well as the wheat and grazing country in western Victoria. **Halls**

**Gap** is the only town actually in the park. A picturesque spot, settled in 1840, it is a great place to base yourself while you explore the park. The national park visitor center has brochures, maps, and information about the Grampians' 400-million-year history.

The Grampians are actually a collection of mountain ranges bunched together, and a diversity of landscapes is found within the park: hot, arid mallee scrub in the north; deep forests of stringy bark and red gums in the south; lush, fern-filled gullies in the Wonderland Range; and even sub-alpine vegetation near the craggy summit of Mount William. Hiking trails vary from half-hour strolls to strenuous overnight hikes on the aptly named **Mount Difficult.**

The best known drives and trails in the park take in the **Wonderland Range,** close to Halls Gap. Many of the best viewpoints are accessible by car, with only a short hike to lookouts. The most popular viewpoint is the **Pinnacle,** hundreds of feet above the plains. It is a demanding 3.5-mile (5.5 km) circuit from the Wonderland car park and goes via the majestic Grand Canyon. Another heart-stopping lookout is called the Jaws of Death. **Mackenzie Falls,** off Mount Victory Road, is awesome, particularly when rains swell the river in winter months, .

## Rock Art

The ranges have the best Aboriginal rock-art galleries in Victoria. More than 4,000 motifs, painted in red and white, can be seen in rock shelters and caves throughout the park. Some are easily accessible. At **Gulgurn Manja,** in the northern tip of the park near Mount Zero, a short signposted hike from the roadside goes to a shelter with depictions of Kartuk, the carpet snake. In the

## Tug-of-War

The first European to explore these ranges (in 1836), Maj. Thomas Mitchell was also one of few early surveyors who tried to maintain Aboriginal place-names. However, he named these ranges after the Grampian Mountains in his native Scotland, presumably unaware that the Aborigines called them Gariwerd. The ranges have been the center of a name-based cultural tug-of-war. In 1991, the Victorian government formally revived the Aboriginal name, but a new administration changed it back to the Grampians, before both names were adopted.

west, along the Henty Highway near **Glenisla,** the Billimina and Wab Manja shelters have handprints and figures of fish and lizards. The **Brambuk Cultural Centre** *(tel (03) 5361 4000),* run by local Aboriginal communities, arranges tours of the rock-art sites. The park's visitor center is also here. The center has cultural displays and also a shop selling books and music.

The best time to visit the park is in the wet months of spring, when the waterfalls are flowing and the wildflowers are at their best. The park has more than a thousand species of ferns and wildflowers, and the Halls Gap Wildflower Exhibition is held here every September. ■

**Grampians National Park**
🄰 290 A2
**Visitor Information**
✉ Grampians Rd., Halls Gap
☎ 1-800 807 056 (toll-free)
**www.parkweb.vic .gov.au**

# Wilsons Promontory National Park

One of Victoria's most popular national parks, Wilsons Promontory lies about 150 miles (240 km) southeast of Melbourne on the South Gippsland Highway and draws thousands of hikers and nature lovers. It is the extreme southern tip of mainland Australia, jutting into Bass Strait and taking the full fury of its waters on the western flank while sheltering lovely beaches on the east. Much of the park was burned in the 2009 bushfires but is already regenerating.

**Wilsons Promontory National Park**

🄰  290 C1

**Visitor Information**

✉  Tidal River

☎  (03) 5680 9555 or 13 19 63

**www.parkweb.vic .gov.au**

Wilsons Promontory has an astonishing variety of landscapes for its relatively small size. It is also rich in wildlife, with kangaroos, wombats, wallabies, and koalas in plenty. It even has emus, which can often be seen feeding on the grasslands near the park entrance at Yanakie Isthmus, and many other birds—among them lorikeets, rosellas, and kookaburras.

**INSIDER TIP:**

Accommodations at Wilsons Promontory include cabins, lodges, and campsites. Space is limited, so be sure to reserve well in advance.

—STEPHANIE ROBICHAUX
*National Geographic contributor*

Bushwalking is the best way to see Wilsons Promontory. Those who do not have the time or energy for such pursuits can still get a taste of the place—one of the best views over Bass Strait and some of the tiny coastal islands is from **Sparkes Lookout,** just off the road to the town of **Tidal River.** The national park office is at Tidal River. Hiking possibilities range from half-hour strolls to overnight hikes down to the old lighthouse, built in 1859.

Three very popular shorter hikes from Tidal River are the **Squeaky Beach Nature Walk,** where half an hour of walking brings you to a beach of quartz sand so pure it squeaks under-foot. The **Lilly Pilly Gully Nature Walk** is a bit longer—about three hours round-trip—with rain forest, ferns, and gum-studded bushland where you may spot a koala.

Another popular hike is to the top of **Mount Oberon.** The enjoyable 4-mile (6.4 km) round-trip hike takes about two hours. From the Mount Oberon car park it is possible to hike out to the lighthouse at Southeast Point. It is a 12-mile (19 km) walk, so start early. You can overnight at the old lighthouse keepers' cottages, which have fully equipped kitchens. Bring food, water, and a sleeping bag. Spaces are limited; make reservations at the Tidal River visitor center. Reserve Tidal River campsites, huts, and cabins well in advance at holiday times. In January, the park is overrun with holiday makers. ■

An island state with two personalities: gentle English-style countryside and brooding Gothic mountains, cloaked in forests

# Tasmania

Introduction & Map   330–333

Hobart   334–337

Huon Valley Drive   338–339

Port Arthur   340–341

Southwest Wilderness   342–343

**Experience: Tasmanian Devil Conservation**   343

Feature: Tasmanian Greens   344

Franklin-Gordon Wild Rivers National Park   345

Cradle Mountain–Lake St. Clair National Park   346–347

**Experience: Overland Track**   347

Scenic Loop Drive   348–351

**Experience: Bay of Fires Walk**   349

Feature: Trout Fishing   352–353

**Experience: Fishing in Tasmania**   353

Bass Strait Islands   354

Hotels & Restaurants   384–385

The sturdy Tasmanian devil, a carnivore

# Tasmania

**Tasmania is one of those rare islands that really feels like an island. The cities and towns along its storm-lashed coasts all have a strongly maritime flavor and a history of whalers, sealers, clipper ships, and, often, tragedy. It is aloof, far beyond the 200 or so miles (320 km) that separate it from mainland Australia.**

After a few days here, it becomes apparent that this is an island with two distinct personalities. There is the dark and tragic Tasmania of brooding mountains, rainy forests, and sandstone ruins left from a violent colonial past. The other Tasmania, existing cheerily, if schizophrenically, beside it, is the one of gentle English villages with apple orchards and sheep grazing on the common, quiet lanes. Both are unlike anything you'll find elsewhere in Australia.

Dutch navigator Abel Tasman was the first European known to have sighted the island. He swept along its west coast in 1642, believing it to be a peninsula jutting out from mainland Australia, and named it Van Diemen's Land, after the governor of the Dutch East Indies. His tales of rainy coasts, forbidding mountains, and savages on the beaches did nothing to kindle any enthusiasm for the place among his masters, in Amsterdam and Java, and when his subsequent voyage in 1644 turned up pretty much the same things, the Dutch gave up on Australia altogether.

In 1803, the British decided to establish a penal colony on Van Diemen's Land, partly to forestall French interest in the place. Hobart Town was established the following year as a place to send convicts who had re-offended. Van Diemen's Land quickly became a byword for sadism and terror, rum and the lash, a reputation augmented by the barbaric prison camps established at Macquarie Harbour in 1821 and Port Arthur in 1832. By the time convicts ceased to be transported here in 1852, the island's reputation was so ghastly that its residents decided to change its name to the friendlier-sounding Tasmania.

Tasmania is a compact state, about the size of Scotland or Ireland. A third of its half-million residents live in Hobart. It is still very much an Anglo-Saxon community, with a deep social divide between the Greens and the predominantly blue-collar supporters of logging and mining. On the one hand, Tasmania has a higher percentage of its forests

## NOT TO BE MISSED:

The colonial-era buildings and scenic harbor of Hobart **334–337**

Driving through Huon Valley farmland to the tall trees **338–339**

Port Arthur, once a convict hell-hole now a scenic treasure **340–341**

The rain forests of Southwest National Park **342–343**

Cruising the wilderness of the Gordon River **345**

Cradle Mountain–Lake St. Clair and the Overland Track **346–347**

Taking a chairlift to the top of the Nut in historic Stanley **348–349**

Sweeping Wineglass Bay on the sunny east coast **350**

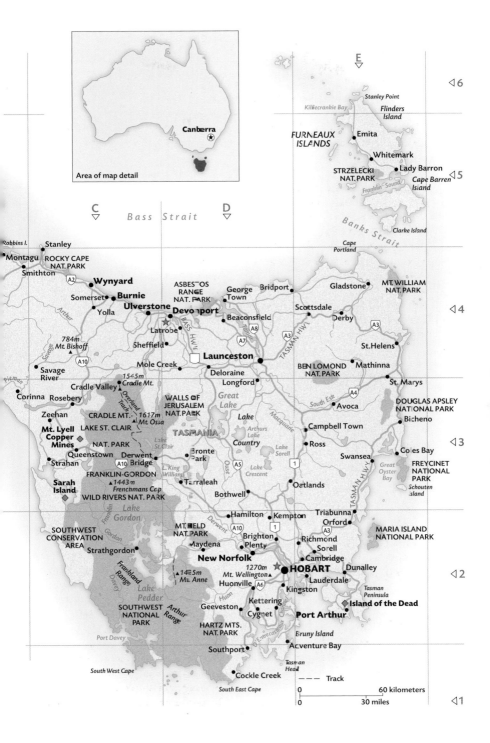

Area of map detail

Canberra

E

Bass Strait

C

D

Killiecrankie Bay

Stanley Point

Flinders Island

FURNEAUX ISLANDS

Emita

Whitemark

Lady Barron

STRZELECKI NAT. PARK

Cape Barren Island

Franklin Sound

Banks Strait

Clarke Island

6

5

Robbins I.

Stanley

Montagu

ROCKY CAPE NAT. PARK

Smithton

A2

Wynyard

Somerset

Burnie

Ulverstone

Yolla

Devonport

Latrobe

784m Mt Bishoff

Sheffield

Savage River

A10

Mole Creek

Cradle Valley

Corinna

Rosebery

1545m Cradle Mt.

Zeehan

CRADLE MT.

LAKE ST. CLAIR

Mt. Lyell Copper Mines

NAT. PARK

Queenstown

Derwent

Strahan

A10

Bridge

Sarah Island

FRANKLIN-GORDON

1443m Frenchmans Cap

WILD RIVERS NAT. PARK

Lake Gordon

SOUTHWEST CONSERVATION AREA

Strathgordon

Frankland Range

Davey

Gordon

Lake Pedder

SOUTHWEST NATIONAL PARK

Arthur Range

Port Davey

South West Cape

ASBESTOS RANGE NAT. PARK

George Town

Bridport

Beaconsfield

A8

A7

Launceston

Deloraine

Longford

WALLS OF JERUSALEM NAT. PARK

Great Lake

1617m Mt Ossa

TASMANIA

Lake St. Clair

Bronte Park

Derwent

King William

Tarraleah

A5

Bothwell

Hamilton

MT FIELD NAT. PARK

Maydena

A10

Brighton

Plenty

New Norfolk

1270m Mt. Wellington

1415m Mt. Anne

Huonville

A6

Geeveston

Kettering

Cygnet

HARTZ MTS. NAT. PARK

Southport

Cockle Creek

South East Cape

Scottsdale

A3

Derby

Tasman HWY

BEN LOMOND NAT. PARK

Mathinna

St.Helens

Gladstone

MT WILLIAM NAT. PARK

Cape Portland

4

A3

South Esk

Macquarie

A4

St. Marys

Avoca

Campbell Town

Ross

Lake Leake

Lake Sorell

Arthurs Lake

Lake Country

1

Oatlands

Kempton

Triabunna

Orford

A3

Richmond

Sorell

Cambridge

HOBART

Lauderdale

Kingston

Bruny Island

Adventure Bay

Tasman Head

DOUGLAS APSLEY NATIONAL PARK

Bicheno

Coles Bay

Swansea

Great Oyster Bay

FREYCINET NATIONAL PARK

Schouten Island

MARIA ISLAND NATIONAL PARK

Dunalley

Tasman Peninsula

Island of the Dead

Port Arthur

D'Entrecasteaux

Huon

3

2

- - - Track

0          60 kilometers
0      30 miles

1

devoted to national parks and conservation than any other Australian state, and it gave rise to the Wilderness Society, one of Australia's most left-leaning Green groups. On the other hand, it is also a lumberjack state that consistently produces world-champion axmen—300 pounds (135 kg) of hard red flesh and an awesome sight to see competing at the agricultural shows. Tensions continue to smolder.

Tasmania is small enough to drive across in a couple of hours, yet varied enough to hold your interest indefinitely. Hobart has gracious

pretty villages in the eastern half of the state evoke old Britain, with names like Swansea, Brighton, and Somerset, and have cream teas, antiques shops, and colonial B&Bs. The east coast has excellent surfing and the haunting ruins of Port Arthur.

## Tasmania's Aborigines

Some of the ugliest chapters of Australian history were written in Tasmania in the 19th century, when the settlers made a concerted and largely successful attempt at genocide.

**Grapevines climb a Tasmanian hillside in the Tamar River Valley near Launceston.**

Georgian architecture and a scent of the sea, and it lies just a short drive from the scenic Huon Valley, which spills along the coast. The southwest coast bears the brunt of the Roaring Forties gales and storms driven north from Antarctica. This is a vast World Heritage–listed wilderness, still barely explored. There is challenging bushwalking around Cradle Mountain and Lake St. Clair, and the central highlands have lakes filled with trophy-size trout. The

When the first Europeans arrived in 1803, an estimated 4,000 to 5,000 Aborigines were living on the island. These were the descendants of the original inhabitants who came here more than 11,000 years ago during the last ice age, when it was possible to walk across the shallow plain that is now Bass Strait. The Aborigines' early grudging distrust of the newcomers turned to outright hostility when they realized that these interlopers had not come to share their land but to seize it. They fought, and the settlers fought back—brutally.

By the 1820s, Aborigines were being shot on sight, poisoned with "gifts" of flour, or trapped like animals. Their children were used for forced labor. Aboriginal women were raped and killed. In 1830, the authorities formed the infamous Black Line of more than 2,000 armed citizens, who for three weeks beat the bush, shoulder to shoulder, driving out the Aborigines. The 150 Aborigines who survived were transported in 1834 to stormy Flinders Island on Bass Strait, where they were forced to become Christians and faded away in disease, grief, and malnutrition. The pitiful handful who survived were later allowed to return to Oyster Cove on Tasmania. The last of the full-blooded Tasmanian Aborigines—a woman named Truganini—died in 1856. For the next 120 years, her skeleton was in the Tasmanian Museum, until it was finally cremated and laid to rest on the waters of the D'Entrecasteaux Channel, off Oyster Cove, near where her people had lived.

## Tasmanian Ferry

You can fly to Tasmania, but the most dramatic way to approach this storm-tossed island is by sea. On the sea you get a feel for its rocky fastness and insularity, not to mention a taste of the Roaring Forties—the region of heavy westerly winds between latitudes 40° and 50° south, which old mariners wrote about and feared. The English navigator Matthew Flinders discovered the strait between Tasmania and Australia in 1798, when he circumnavigated the island and established that it was not a peninsula. He named the waters for the ship's surgeon, George Bass. The new, stormy passage cut the sailing time between Sydney and India, or Cape Town, by a week.

Every evening at six o'clock (and four mornings a week, Jan.–April) the *Spirit of Tasmania* slips away from Melbourne's Station Pier to make the 10-hour crossing over the Bass Strait

to Devonport, Tasmania. The ship can accommodate 1,140 passengers and 500 vehicles and has something of a cruise atmosphere with its pubs, restaurant, poker machines, and promenade decks. A Tasmanian tourism office is on board, along with cinemas, a games arcade, and an Internet kiosk. Reserve your ticket early, particularly during school vacations or if you want to take a vehicle (*tel 1-800 634 906 [toll-free], www.spiritoftasmania.com.au*).

**INSIDER TIP:**

**Fees apply for entry to Tasmania's national parks and can add up quickly. The best value is a Holiday Pass (A$60/U.S. $54 per vehicle), valid for all parks, which is available at park offices and visitor information centers.**

—PETER TURNER
*National Geographic author*

The ferry gives fine views of Port Phillip Bay, and if you are heading to Tasmania in autumn or winter, the lights of the receding Melbourne skyline are particularly pretty. The waters in the bay make smooth sailing, but this starts to change as the ship goes through the choppy seas out of the bay and into Bass Strait. If you are not a good sailor—or at least do not respond well to seasickness tablets—this voyage is not for you. The sea may be as smooth as a mill pond, but it can be rolling heavily, if not downright rough. Bass Strait has some of the world's stormiest seas because it acts as a funnel, compressing the full strength of the Roaring Forties gales.

The *Spirit of Tasmania* has a range of accommodations, from luxury suites to hostel-style bunks and reclining chairs. A buffet dinner and breakfast are included in the fare. Get up early the next morning to catch your first glimpse of Tasmania's rocky coastline and green hills ∎

# Hobart

Australia's second oldest city (after Sydney), Hobart looks far older because it has so many elegant, albeit convict-built, 19th-century buildings. Situated at the foot and lower flanks of Mount Wellington, it spreads out along both banks of the Derwent River, about 12 miles (19 km) from its mouth. Hobart's houses are mostly of timber, painted soft pastels, and call to mind places like Halifax, Nova Scotia, or St. John's, Newfoundland.

Hobart's skyline and harbor with cloud-shrouded Mount Wellington rising behind

**Hobart**

⚐ 331 D2

**Hobart Travel Centre**

✉ 20 Davey St.

☎ (03) 6238 4222

The city's focus is its harbor as well as the century-old stone warehouses and wharves that are located near Constitution Dock. Many of these buildings have been restored and converted into restaurants and pubs. This quarter of town becomes one of the most boisterous spots in Australia over the Christmas–New Year's holiday, when the Sydney–Hobart Yacht Race enters the dock (*information at Tourism Tasmania, www. discovertasmania.com.au; or at Hobart Travel Centre*).

Hobart was founded in 1804 after an earlier attempt to settle at Risdon Cove, on the eastern side of the harbor, had failed. The new town, built on Sullivans Cove, was named Hobart Town after Lord Hobart, then Britain's colonial secretary. The name was streamlined in 1881. Although its founder, Lt. Col. David Collins, had a poet's eye when it came to selecting a lovely setting for the city, he had a laissez-faire attitude to town planning. When Lachlan Macquarie, the public works–minded governor of New South

Wales, visited in 1811, he lamented the town's chaos and ordered that a simple grid of streets be laid out. Thanks to him, Hobart is today a very easy city to get about, with its downtown streets arranged in a grid around Elizabeth Street Mall. Noplace in the center is more than a few minutes' walk from the waterfront.

Sullivans Cove and the bustling Franklin Wharf have been the town's commercial heart since the 1830s, when Hobart was one of the world's whaling capitals. Fortunes were made in whale

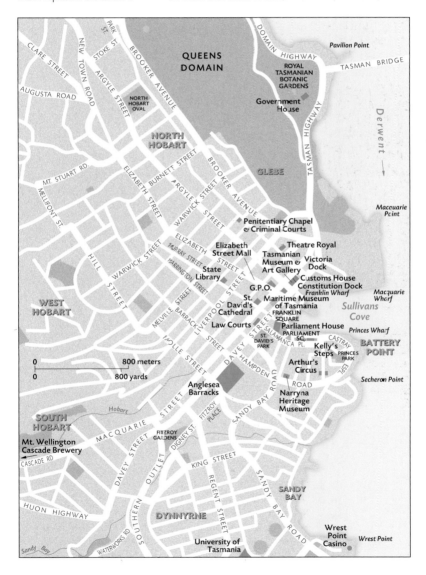

**Tasmanian Museum & Art Gallery**

🗺 Map p. 335

✉ 40 Macquarie St.

☎ (03) 6211 4177

**www.tmag.tas .gov.au**

**Narryna Heritage Museum**

🗺 Map p. 335

✉ 103 Hampden Rd.

☎ (03) 6234 2791

🕐 Closed Sat.–Mon.

💲 $

**www.narryna.com.au**

**Maritime Museum of Tasmania**

🗺 Map p. 335

✉ Corner of Davey & Argyle Sts.

☎ (03) 6234 1427

💲 $

**www.maritimetas .org**

oil, shipbuilding, and trading in wool, meat, and flour. Between 1835 and 1860, as the town grew wealthier, a new line of handsome sandstone warehouses was erected on Salamanca Place. These beautiful old buildings have been sensitively restored and converted into craft galleries, cafés, fruit and vegetable markets, and gourmet shops.

**INSIDER TIP:**

**Take a Saturday stroll around Hobart's Salamanca Place market for its vast array of food, arts and crafts, and entertainment.**

—DANIELLE WILLIAMS
*National Geographic Television*

On Saturday mornings, on the plaza in front of **Salamanca Place,** a crowded market sells anything from healing crystals to velvet paintings of Elvis. If the shopping doesn't sate your taste for the bizarre, you can always nurse a cappuccino at one of the sidewalk tables at the Retro Café and watch the Tasmanians.

A narrow stairway, known as **Kelly's Steps,** leads between two of the warehouses on Salamanca Place up to **Battery Point.** Named for the cannon that were set up in 1818 to protect the city's harbor, Battery Point became a blue-collar neighborhood for mariners, shipwrights, sailmakers, coopers, and longshoremen. Later, as Hobart continued to

prosper, wealthy merchants began building in this area as well. Hobart in general, and Battery Point in particular, has escaped the wrecking-ball of development. As you wander these 150-year-old tangled alleyways, with their stone churches, corner shops, and jumble of workers' cottages, it is easy to imagine yourself back in the days of whaling.

More than 90 of Hobart's public buildings have been listed by the National Trust. About 60 of these buildings, including some of Australia's finest examples of Georgian architecture, are along Macquarie and Davey Streets, which have almost unspoiled 19th-century streetscapes. Hobart's earliest surviving building is the Commissariat Store, built by convict labor in 1808. Now it houses the **Tasmanian Museum & Art Gallery**. The gallery has fine displays on Tasmania's Aborigines and a good collection of colonial art.

The **Narryna Heritage Museum** is an elegant 1836 Georgian mansion in Battery Point with an extensive collection of 19th-century items. The **Maritime Museum of Tasmania,** in the historic Carnegie Building, is near Constitution Dock, the maritime heart of the city.

The visitor center has heritage building brochures, and the National Trust *(tel (03) 6223 7570)* has heritage walking tours, as does Hobart Historic Tours *(tel (03) 6230 8233),* which also has pub and dinner walking tours. Or try the Historic Churches Walking Tour *(tel (03) 6231 4033, Wed. only).*

## Mount Wellington

The best overview of Hobart is from the top of Mount Wellington, which looms more than 4,000 feet (1,270 m) above the city to the west and is sometimes covered with snow. This mountain dominates the city and draws visitors like a magnet, one of the most famous to climb it being Charles Darwin, who scaled it in 1836.

There are walking trails to the summit (it's about a two-hour climb), or you can drive up the winding auto road that turns off the Huon Highway. Just head inland, southwest of Hobart, along Cascade Road.

On the way you'll pass Cascade Gardens and the **Cascade Brewery**, which looks like a grand French château nestled in the foothills. This is Australia's oldest brewery—and its best, according to a sizeable proportion of beer lovers. It began in 1832 and still makes beer in a traditional way, using the cold clear water that cascades down the mountainside. You might notice some childhood photos of actor Errol Flynn in the brewery museum. He grew up around here.

The stone **Pinnacle Observatory Shelter** on the craggy summit of Mount Wellington gives a stunning view of the city, out to the mouth of the Derwent River and over the wild countryside stretching out for miles in every direction.

The first European to climb this peak was explorer George Bass, who stopped here in 1798 (and gave his name to the Bass Strait; see p. 333). The road to the summit was opened in 1937. The view is particularly dramatic when the valleys below are in broken mists or rain, as they often are. No matter what the weather, bring a jacket or sweater, even if it seems warm down in Hobart. ■

### Cascade Brewery

✉ 140 Cascade Rd.
☎ (03) 6224 1117
$ $$$

**www.cascade brewery.com.au**

English novelist Anthony Trollope once dismissed Mount Wellington as "just enough of a mountain to give excitement to ladies and gentlemen in middle life."

# Huon Valley Drive

This is the heart of Tasmania's picturesque apple orchard district and where the valuable Huon pines were first discovered. You'll find fishing villages, dairies, tranquil island beaches, and the savage wilderness strongholds of the Hartz Mountains. You can see the valley on a pleasant day trip or over several days, depending on your pace and time.

To begin, follow Davey Street south out of the city, where it becomes the Huon Highway, for a hilly and scenic drive down into the valley.

The first apple orchard was planted in the Huon Valley in 1841, and within ten years apples were being exported to New Zealand and India. By the 1920s, nearly 30,000 acres (12,150 ha) of orchards were growing more than 500 varieties of apples. These days the valley has diversified into wine, salmon, and tourism, although apples and cider mills are still big. (Only eight varieties are grown these days, with Red Delicious the mainstay.) The valley is also Tasmania's cherry-growing center. At Grove, 20 miles (32 km) out of Hobart, you can visit **Huon Apple & Heritage Museum** ❶ *(tel (03) 6266 4345 in Grove)*.

The town of **Huonville** ❷, 5 miles (8 km) farther south on the highway, is the valley's commercial center. Timber became a big industry here when settlers discovered the Huon pines—"green gold," in the eyes of pioneers. This slow-growing softwood, unique to Tasmania, is nearly rot proof and quickly became popular with 19th-century shipbuilders. Thousand-year-old trees are hard to replace, and few Huon pines are left in the valley today. You can arrange an exhilarating jet boat ride through the falls on the Huon River with Huon River Jet Boats *(tel (03) 6264 1838)*, which doubles as the tourist information center.

Another 15 miles (24 km) south on the Huon Highway brings you to **Geeveston,** an old timber town and the gateway to the Hartz Mountain wilderness. The **Forest and Heritage Centre** *(Church St., tel (03) 6297 1836, www .forestandheritagecentre.com.au)* has displays on the timber industry and walking guides to **Tahune Forest Reserve,** where you can see magnificent stands of ancient Huon pines. The reserve is about 15 miles (24 km) west of Geeveston on

---

**NOT TO BE MISSED:**

**Huon Apple & Heritage Museum**
• **Waratah Lookout** • **Adventure Bay**

---

a partially paved, marked road. By the road are picnic grounds, walking trails, and several good viewpoints. The popular new **Tahune Forest Airwalk and Visitor Centre** *(tel (03) 6297 0084, www.forestrytas.com.au, $$$)* offers spectacular walks through the old-growth Huon pine forest at canopy height, on a 2,000-foot (600 m) treetop walkway that offers stunning views over the rivers and to the Hartz Mountains. A scenic off-road detour leads to the **Arve Valley** and some of the world's largest hardwood trees, eucalyptuses that rise nearly 300 feet (91 m).

Described by Sir Edmund Hillary as some of the wildest country he'd ever seen, the magnificent Hartz Mountains loom just to the west. Part of Tasmania's World Heritage area, **Hartz Mountains National Park** ❸ has dense rain forests, snow-covered dolerite peaks, and rugged alpine moors. The spectacular **Waratah Lookout,** about 15 miles (24 km) from Geeveston, is reached by a rough track off the road to the Tahune Forest Reserve. The park's trails are challenging but recommended, especially a six-hour (round-trip) hike to the 4,117-foot (1,255 m) summit of Hartz Peak. If you decide to hike, be prepared for sudden and extreme changes of weather, and carry warm, waterproof clothing no matter how nice the day appears when you leave Hobart. For information on trails, contact the Forest and Heritage Centre in Geeveston.

Retrace your route as far as Huonville and then take the Channel Highway. It runs along

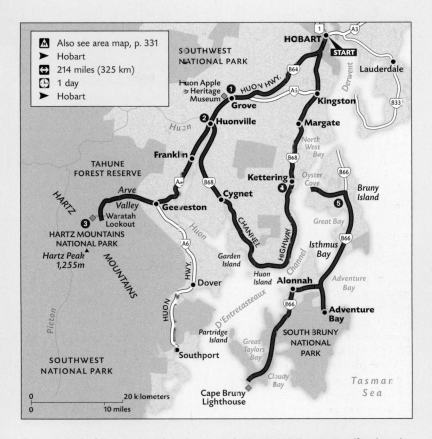

- Also see area map, p. 331
- Hobart
- 214 miles (325 km)
- 1 day
- Hobart

SOUTHWEST NATIONAL PARK

HOBART

START

Lauderdale

Huon Apple & Heritage Museum

Grove

HUON HWY

Kingston

Margate

Huonville

Huon

North West Bay

Franklin

TAHUNE FOREST RESERVE

Kettering

Oyster Cove

Bruny Island

Arve Valley

Waratah Lookout

Geeveston

Cygnet

HARTZ MOUNTAINS NATIONAL PARK

Hartz Peak 1,255m

Great Bay

Garden Island

Isthmus Bay

HIGHWAY

HUON

HWY

Dover

Huon Island

Alonnah

Adventure Bay

MOUNTAINS

Picton

D'Entrecasteaux

Partridge Island

Adventure Bay

SOUTHWEST NATIONAL PARK

SOUTH BRUNY NATIONAL PARK

Southport

Great Taylors Bay

Cloudy Bay

Tasman Sea

Cape Bruny Lighthouse

20 kilometers
10 miles

the eastern bank of the Huon River, through the orchard town of **Cygnet,** which has black swans and old timber cottages, and along the D'Entrecasteaux Channel to **Kettering ❹,** about a 40-mile (64 km) drive from Huonville. Orchards and fields of strawberries and raspberries surround this old fishing port. The waters of **Oyster Cove,** 3 miles (5 km) northeast of Kettering, supported generations of Aborigines, and it was here that the last few Tasmanian Aborigines were allowed to return.

From Kettering, regular ferries make the short hop to **Bruny Island ❺.** Buy tickets at the Bruny D'Entrecasteaux Visitors Centre *(tel (03) 6267 4494),* next to the ferry terminal. Sighted by Abel Tasman in 1642, this island was a veritable crossroads for 18th-century explorers: James Cook, Captain Bligh, Matthew Flinders,

John Cox, Bruni D'Entrecasteaux (for whom the island is named), and Nicholas Baudin visited here. A botanist on one of Bligh's expeditions is believed to have planted the first of Tasmania's apple trees. Later, the island was a base for whalers. Today it is tranquil, with rain forests, guesthouses, and seafood restaurants. The island is about 30 miles (48 km) long, and most accommodations are at **Adventure Bay,** in the southern half, which also has the best scenery. Built in 1836, the **Cape Bruny Lighthouse,** at the southwest tip reached via road B66 through Alonnah, is the second oldest in Australia.

From Kettering drive back to Hobart through Margate and **Kingston,** where the Australian Antarctic Division headquarters *(Channel Hwy.)* has displays on early expeditions, as well as the latest information.

# Port Arthur

"It was all out of keeping with the place, a sort of bringing together of heaven and hell," wrote American novelist Mark Twain when he visited Port Arthur on a world tour in the 1890s. Certainly it is hard to reconcile the gentle beauty of the countryside with the brutal past of the prison camp on this peninsula, 59 miles (94 km) southwest of Hobart.

The old Gothic-style church adds a touch of gentle melancholy to the ruins of Port Arthur.

**Port Arthur**
🗺 331 E2
**Visitor Information**
✉ Port Arthur Historic Site
☎ (03) 6251 2371
💲 $$$–$$$$$

From 1832 until it was closed in 1877, Port Arthur was the final stop for many of the colony's most dangerous offenders. Its founder, George Arthur, decreed that "the most unceasing labour is to be extracted from the convicts, and the most harassing vigilance over them is to be observed." More than 12,000 passed through. Escape was almost impossible. The peninsula is linked to the mainland by a narrow isthmus barely 100 yards (92 m) wide, which was patrolled by guards and lined with savage dogs. The frigid waters that crash at the foot of these dolorite cliffs were believed to be filled with sharks.

Things got even worse in 1852, with the construction of the Model Prison based on a new concept of punishment devised in Britain: total sensory deprivation. Prisoners who had previously had the comfort of casting their eyes on soft green hills were now kept in tiny isolation cells for 23 hours a day. They were never permitted to speak, and during their solitary hour of exercise they were forced to wear hoods and shuffle around the yard in chains. Not surprisingly, many of the men went insane. No matter—the prison opened its own mental ward. The decision finally to close the prison is said to have been influenced by the dreadful publicity it received from Marcus Clarke's novel *For the Term of His Natural Life* (1874).

## Visiting Port Arthur

When fires swept through the place in the 1890s, there were few regrets, and locals hoped the flames would wipe the memories off the map completely. The major restoration effort begun in the 1970s has preserved much of Port Arthur, and 250,000 visitors come here each year. It is Tasmania's biggest tourist attraction. More than 60 buildings are scattered around the site, including the **Lunatic Asylum,** which now holds a collection of chains, cat-o'-nine-tails, and crude convict uniforms. Some of the buildings have been fully restored, but others have been left as ruins amid the gardenlike setting. Visitors can wander around the penal colony at will; the entry fee gives access to all buildings in the complex.

Even in daylight, Port Arthur can be a haunting place for a stroll, but things get eerie after dark, with ghostly apparitions and phenomena recorded since the 1870s. Guides carrying lanterns lead nightly ghost tours of the buildings and ruins. They are surprisingly spooky. Boat tours go from the main part of the prison

to the **Island of the Dead,** where 1,769 convicts were buried. A solitary convict used to live on the island to dig the graves. "Australia has many parking lots but few ruins," wrote Robert Hughes in *The Fatal Shore.* "Port Arthur is our Paestum and our Dachau, rolled into one."

A terrible—and hopefully final—postscript to the prison's brutal history was written one Sunday afternoon in April 1996, when a lone gunman named Martin Bryant killed 35 people (see sidebar below). Port Arthur's Broad Arrow Café, where he murdered 20 victims, was gutted and its ruins built into a memorial garden to those who died. Bryant is now serving a life sentence in Hobart's Risdon Prison, without possibility of parole. ■

## 1996 Tragedy

Every Australian remembers April 28, 1996, when a 28-year-old Hobart man entered the Broad Arrow Café at Port Arthur and began firing a rifle into the Sunday lunchtime crowd. By the time the killing spree was over, 35 were dead and 21 injured. The country was horrified. Since the 1980s, Australia had witnessed a number of indiscriminate killings by disturbed men armed with semiautomatic weapons. The government decided to act and introduced some of the world's strictest gun laws. No such mass killings have occurred since.

# Southwest Wilderness

Tasmania's southwest wilderness is one of the world's few remaining untouched places, with vast tracts of virgin temperate rain forests, swamp gums more than 300 feet (91 m) high, rare ferns and lichens, and wild rivers boiling through the gorges. Rain falls on more than 200 days a year. The gloomy, storm-lashed coastline of the southwest cape has remained virtually unchanged since Abel Tasman swept past these rocks in 1642.

Cushion plants on the north ridge of Mount Anne in the southwest wilderness

These days Tasmania's southwest wilderness is protected as **Southwest National Park** and the adjacent **Southwest Conservation Area**—which together compose a 2.5-million-acre (1 million ha) wilderness stronghold with some of the most challenging and remote hikes on the planet. But these hikes should be attempted only by experienced bushwalkers who are well equipped for sudden savage turns in the weather. This area is noted for violent storms, mists, and cold rain, even in summer.

The hiking trails themselves scramble up steep muddy slopes, over rocky quartzite crags that may require ropes, and across miles of swampy buttongrass marshes infested by leeches. You'll have to carry everything with you, although you can arrange an airdrop of extra supplies if you are planning an extended hike.

The reward for all this hardship is immersing yourself in the solitude and isolation of a primeval world so fresh and new it seems to have the first dew still on it. If this sounds like something you are interested in, consider tackling the **South Coast Track,** a 55-mile (88 km) trail that stretches from Cockle Creek to Port Davey. This moderate-to-difficult route is maintained and generally takes about a week to ten days to traverse. Most hikers fly into Malaleuca airstrip and hike east, back to Cockle Creek. Other, even more imposing challenges include the **Port Davey Track,** the **Western Arthurs Traverse,** and the **Mount Anne Circuit.** Some of these trails can be linked up for an expedition-length trek.

## INSIDER TIP:

**Hiking in the south-west wilderness is amazing but isn't for casual day-trippers. Be prepared for rough conditions and terrain.**

—BARBARA A. NOE
*National Geographic editor*

Unless you are flying in or starting your walk at Cockle Creek, you'll reach the park via the Strathgordon Road and the rough sidetrack to Scotts Peak, where the trails begin. Always register your intentions with the park ranger at Mount Field or with the police, and ask about conditions before heading out. Specialist hiking maps and guidebooks for this wilderness are on sale in outdoors shops in Hobart. Two airlines *(Par Avion: tel (03) 6248 5390, www.paravion .com.au; and Tas Air: tel (03) 6248 5088, www.tasair.com)* fly hikers in and out of the park.

Scenic flights are a less strenuous way of enjoying this magnificent wilderness. Par Avion also operates a wilderness camp and runs a tour boat on the Davey River that goes into the heart of the national park. ■

**Southwest National Park**
◮ 331 C2–D1

**Parks & Wildlife Service**
✉ 134 Macquarie St., Hobart
☎ 1-300 135 313
**www.parks.tas .gov.au**

**Forest & Heritage Centre (Visitor Information)**
✉ Church St., Geeveston
☎ (03) 6297 1836

---

## EXPERIENCE: Tasmanian Devil Conservation

The Tasmanian devil is a carnivorous marsupial found only in Tasmania, although it once inhabited the mainland. Primarily a carrion eater, it has the most powerful jaws of any mammal and uses them to crush bones. It has a squat body about the size of a small dog and emits a ferocious snarling when feeding or threatened. Although not the cutest of Australia's marsupials, it bears only passing resemblance to the crazed, whirling Looney Tunes cartoon character that gave it such a bad reputation.

Seen as a threat to livestock, devils were hunted by Tasmanian farmers until they were protected in 1941. Since then, a new threat has killed up to 50 percent of the population—devil facial tumor

disease. DFTD is an extremely rare and transmittable cancer that causes tumors and swelling on the face, usually resulting in death within a year. No cure has been discovered. As insurance, devils are being bred in quarantine areas and sent to the mainland to ensure survival of the species.

The **Tasmanian Devil Conservation Park** *(tel (03) 6250 3230, www.tasmanian devilpark.com),* in Taranna on the highway to Port Arthur, is a wildlife park where you can see plenty of Tasmanian devils, as well as other native wildlife. In a disease-free area, they are also helping to ensure devil survival. You can aid by becoming a "Friend of the Devil" as a donor or volunteer.

# Tasmanian Greens

When you look at a map of Tasmania, the first thing you notice is the huge swath of green covering the lower left quarter of the state. Tasmania has a higher percentage of its land set aside for conservation and national parks, much of it World Heritage listed, than any other state in Australia—and a legacy of bitter environmental protests.

Protestors take to the water in 1982 to demonstrate against the Franklin River dam.

Tasmania's strident environmental movement began at Lake Pedder, which sprawls along the edge of the southwest wilderness. Before 1972, this tiny jewel was accessible only by light plane. But then the Tasmanian Hydro Electric Commission dammed the nearby Gordon River, flooding the lake and surrounding valleys to create Australia's largest inland freshwater catchment. Conservationists, who had lost their battle to stop the dam, formed the Wilderness Society in 1976 to better organize for the next confrontation. They didn't have to wait long.

The Hydro Electric Commission's next plan was to dam the Franklin River, the last major wild river in Tasmania. This sparked a bitter and divisive campaign in Tasmania, which snowballed into international protest when the Tasmanian government continued with its proposal even after the river and surrounding

wilderness received World Heritage listing in December 1982. Protesters came from around Australia and overseas to throw up a human blockade to the bulldozers. Hundreds were arrested. The new Labor government that came to power in Canberra in March 1983 stopped the building of the dam.

Tasmania's environmental movement has elected two Green Party senators to the federal parliament, including Greens leader Bob Brown. Pulp mills and wood chipping are the biggest Green topics in Tasmania these days, but calls are growing for Lake Pedder to be drained and returned to its natural state—a cause championed by the Wilderness Society. Although this did not happen by the hoped-for year of 2000, the group continues the fight. The Tasmanian Environmental Centre (91 Mary St., Hobart, tel (03) 6234 5566, www.tasmanianenvironmentcentre .org.au) has information on current issues.

# Franklin-Gordon Wild Rivers National Park

Franklin-Gordon Wild Rivers National Park exists pretty much for itself. Many of its million acres (400,000 ha) are covered by dense rain forest and rugged mountains, and they are virtually inaccessible on foot. Boats or scenic flights are really the only way to see the park.

## Gordon River

Scenic cruises go out of **Strahan,** a remote town of 600 on the central west coast near Macquarie Harbour. Most visit **Sarah Island** and the ruins of its notorious prison camp, then putter up the tannin-rich waters of the Gordon River another 20 miles (32 km) or so. The Gordon is Tasmania's largest river, and reflections of ancient Huon pines on its mirror-smooth surface make evocative photographs. Seaplane tours of the park and of Southwest National Park leave from Strahan on Wilderness Air *(tel (03) 6471 7280).* The Strahan Wharf Centre *(tel (03) 6471 7488)* can help with information on the park.

## Franklin River

More adventurous visitors may wish to raft the wild Franklin River. The full trip takes up to 14 days, through some of the world's most challenging and most remote white water. It starts on the Collingwood River, about 30 miles (48 km) west of Derwent Bridge, and ends at Heritage Landing, where a seaplane retrieves you.

This is emphatically not a trip to attempt independently, unless everyone in your party is extremely experienced. A number of outfits run river trips (see right) that do not require experience. Those on a time budget can do an eight-day trip.

## Hiking

The trail up the spectacular, 4,734-foot-high (1,443 m) Frenchmans Cap gives some breathtaking views. The southeast face is a sheer 1,500-foot (457 m) cliff of white quartzite, and the mountain is prone to mists and violent storms. The hike is for experienced bushwalkers only. It starts at the Lyell Highway, 19 miles (30 km) west of Derwent Bridge. The 29-mile (46 km) round-trip hike takes three to five days. ∎

### Franklin-Gordon Wild Rivers National Park
🅼 331 C3

**RAFTING:** Tour operators offering rafting packages on the Franklin include: **Rafting Tasmania,** P.O. Box 403, Sandy Bay, (03) 6239 1080, www.raftingtasmania.com; **Water by Nature (Tasmania),** 1-800 111 142 (toll-free), www.franklinrivertasmania.com; and **World Expeditions,** 1-300-720 000, www.worldexpeditions.com.

The Franklin River draws adventurers from around the globe.

# Cradle Mountain–Lake St. Clair National Park

Cradle Mountain–Lake St. Clair National Park is Tasmania's most popular wilderness park. Its deep gorges, mountain peaks, glacier lakes, and broad expanses of alpine moorland are challenging enough to excite any bushwalker, yet it is still (at least by Tasmanian wilderness standards) fairly accessible. Its southern end is only a two-hour drive north from Hobart on the Lyell Highway, and its northern one is about 50 miles (80 km) from Devonport.

**Cradle Mountain–Lake St. Clair National Park**

🗺 331 C3

The first person to begin campaigning for the area's preservation was an Austrian naturalist, who built himself a chalet in the Cradle Valley in 1912. He lived long enough to see 130,000 acres (52,650 ha) of the valley set aside as a scenic reserve in 1927. The World Heritage–listed park has since grown to 400,000 acres (162,000 ha). It contains 5,305-foot (1,617 m) **Mount Ossa,** Tasmania's highest peak, and beautiful **Lake St. Clair,** Australia's deepest freshwater lake (600 feet/183 m deep).

Many exciting trails cross through these mountains, but the **Overland Track** is the biggest draw. Hundreds of bushwalkers flock here each summer to trek the 40 miles (65 km) from Cradle Mountain in the north to the southern tip of Lake St. Clair. It is a stunning trail, through wildflower-dotted high-country meadows, buttongrass marshes, and deep forests of beech, Tasmanian myrtle, and pandanus. It typically takes six days and is a satisfying challenge for experienced and well-equipped hikers. Side trips—up Mount Ossa, for example—can easily double your time in the wilderness. You're limited only by the amount of supplies you can carry. Half a dozen main huts along the trail provide accommodations, but it's essential to bring a tent because bad weather or fatigue may force an unscheduled stop.

The weather here is notoriously fickle, and sudden storms on these exposed ridges can easily trap the unwary or the foolish. Snow is possible even in summer. Rain, mud, and leeches are near certainties at

Cradle Mountain rises 5,069 feet (1,545 m) above sea level.

# EXPERIENCE: Overland Track

The Overland Track—Australia's most famous hike—normally takes six days and boasts stunning scenery. You must carry food, a fuel stove, tent, and sleeping bag with you, and be prepared for freezing conditions, even in summer. Alternatively, Anthology (tel (03) 6392 2211, www.anthology.travel) provides all gear on guided trips staying in exclusive huts.

**Permits & Bookings:** The hike requires a Parks Pass and payment of a hiking fee. From Nov. to April, you must hike from north to south. Only 34 places are available, so book well in advance (www.overland track.com.au), especially during Dec. and Jan.

**Accessing the Trailheads:** In summer, **Tassielink** (1-300 300 520, www .tassielink.com.au) has buses to the northern end of the trail and a connection at the southern end. **Maxwell Coaches** (tel (03) 6492 1431, www. maxwell-coaches.com.au) has year-round shuttles from Cynthia Bay to Derwent Bridge (with buses to Hobart), and between Devonport and Cradle Mountain.

**Walking the Track:** A typical itinerary includes: **Day 1**, Ronny Creek (or Waldheim Hut) to Waterfall Valley Hut, 6.2 miles (10 km), 6 hours (sidetrip: Cradle Mountain). **Day 2**, to Lake Windermere Hut, 4.6 miles (7.5 km), 3 hours (sidetrip: Lake Will & Innes Falls, or Barn Bluff). **Day 3**, to Pelion Hut, 10.2 miles (16.5 km), 6 hours. **Day 4**, to Kia-Ora Hut, 5.5 miles (9 km), 3 hours (sidetrip: Mount Ossa). **Day 5**, to Bert Nichols Hut 6.2 miles (10 km), 4 hours, (sidetrips: D'Alton and Fergusson Waterfalls, or Hartnett Falls). **Day 6**, to Narcissus Hut, 5.5 miles (9 km), 3 hours, then take the boat to Cynthia Bay or walk (9.3 miles/15 km, 5 hours, along the lake).

all times. However, the scenery and sheer exhilaration of being in this wilderness is well worth any hardships. Late summer is the best time to go, although some exceptionally experienced hikers have enjoyed the challenge of winter traverses.

Most hikers start at the northern end of the park and go south to Lake St. Clair. If you want to avoid the last day's hike around the lake, you can arrange to have a launch (tel (03) 6289 1137) pick you up at Narcissus Hut and take you to the trailhead at Cynthia Bay.

The stunning lake cruise is also a great way to get a taste of the Tasmanian wilderness. Or you can do a day trip on the Overland Track by taking the boat to the northern end of the lake and hiking back—a very scenic six-hour walk. **Cynthia Bay**, at the southern entrance, has a ranger station, restaurant, and lodge with luxury and budget accommodations.

At the northern end of the park, daily buses run between Launceston, Devonport, and Burnie to the entrance in Cradle Valley (in winter, the schedule is reduced to three days a week). This end of the park has excellent ways to savor the wilderness. The spectacular half-mile (800 m) **Visitor Centre Rainforest Walk** is wheelchair-accessible. Scenic flights are flown by Cradle Mountain Helicopters (tel (03) 6492 1132). Information on shorter day and half-day hikes is available at the interpretive center. ∎

**Cradle Mountain Northern Entrance**

**Visitor Information**

- ✉ Cradle Valley
- ☎ (03) 6492 1110; ranger station: (03) 6492 1133, hut reservations: (03) 6289 1137

**Southern Entrance**

**Interpretive Center**

- ✉ Cynthia Bay, Lake St. Clair
- ☎ (03) 6289 1172

# Scenic Loop Drive

Tasmania's compactness, the fact that it is an island, and the scenic loop of highway that stands out on the map make circling the island by car the most obvious and rewarding way of getting to know the place. The scenic loop is about 600 miles (960 km) in all, although with side trips to the Huon Valley, Port Arthur, and Macquarie Harbour on the rugged west coast, you'll likely add a bit more.

Secluded Wineglass Bay in Freycinet National Park is accessible by foot or by boat.

The drive takes in primeval rain forests and brooding mountain ranges, wild rivers, towering trees, and lakes filled with trout. There are mining ghost towns, ruined penal colonies, and the maritime charm of Hobart. Along the north and in the midlands, gentle landscapes with old stone churches and cottages call to mind England.

## North & West Coasts

You could begin this tour almost anywhere in Tasmania—Hobart, Launceston, or straight off the ferry at Devonport, if you brought a car. This description starts in **Devonport ❶**, a bustling port and tourist town, and goes counter clockwise.

Follow the coastal highway northwest out of town to the logging and paper milling port of **Burnie,** named after William Burnie, a director of the Van Diemen's Land Company, an enterprise founded in London in 1825, with a million pounds (U.S. $1.6 million) in capital and a grant of about 300,000 acres (121,500 ha) in northwest Tasmania.

The company got off to a rocky start. Prized sheep, horses, and cattle died, European agricultural equipment—imported at great cost—proved unsuitable, and the Aborigines fought bitterly to keep their land. In its first 32 years, the company paid only two small dividends. While shareholders lost money, the company's exploration of the rugged wilderness opened up the northwest. The discovery of tin at nearby Mount Bischoff sparked a rush to the northwest, and the deepwater seaport at Burnie flourished. Unfortunately, Burnie itself is a dreary smokestack city despite its beautiful pastoral surrounds. Better to skate through the old port and onto **Wynyard** (visitor information: 8 Exhibition Link, tel (03) 6442 8330), a pleasant seaside community just 12 miles (19 km) farther along the highway. This dairy town is a good place to catch a flight to King Island (see p. 354) or visit **Rocky Cape National Park ❷**, with its profusion of wildflowers, including rare native orchids, and white sandy beaches. The place has a long human history. For more than 8,000 years Aborigines sheltered in caves in these quartzite hills. Two major caves—**North** and **South Caves**—contain huge shell middens, bones, and tools. There are plenty of trails in the park, but no toilets or water supplies.

Take a detour by following the Bass Highway northwest for about 40 miles (64 km) to reach **Stanley,** a picturesque fishing village at the foot of a dramatic volcanic neck known as the **Nut.**

The Van Diemen's Land Company set up its headquarters here in 1826, and built its slate-roofed store in 1844. The restored building is now open to the public. The **Nut Chairlift** (Browns Rd., tel (03) 6458 1286) gives access to the top of the Nut. The view is spectacular.

The loop drive goes south on the Murchison Highway, which leaves the Bass Highway between Wynyard and Burnie. After about 30 miles (48 km) you will reach the **Hellyer Gorge State Reserve ❸**, with its deep rain forest of sassafras, giant myrtle, and huge ferns. Forests such as these used to be the haunts of the Tasmanian tiger. At one time, many of these striped, carnivorous marsupials roamed the wilderness. The Van Diemen's Land Company placed a bounty on them and they were hunted to extinction, with the last supposedly dying in a Hobart zoo in 1936. But there have been persistent reportings of Tasmanian tigers, so just maybe a few still live in the wilder corners of the northwest. If so, one likely spot is the almost untouched **Arthur-Pieman Conservation Area,** a rain forest wilderness on the west coast. It is accessible by a 45-mile (72 km) detour each way off the highway to the nearly deserted gold mining town of **Corinna ❹**, where you can take wilderness cruises (Pieman River Cruises, tel (03) 6446 1170) through the spectacular deep gorges on the Pieman River.

The Murchison Highway becomes the Zeehan Highway 50 miles (80 km) farther south of the turning to Corinna. A turnoff at this point leads to the colorful old mining town of **Zeehan** (visitor information: Main St., tel (03) 6472 6800). This was a boomtown mining silver, lead, and zinc around the turn of the 20th century, with enough money for the local Gaiety Theatre to draw the likes of Enrico Caruso and Harry Houdini. Today it is a quiet village of 900. You can continue through Zeehan to **Macquarie Harbour** and **Strahan ❺**, the only town on the west coast and the base for visiting the remains of the penal colony on **Sarah Island** and the Gordon River (see p. 345).

The Zeehan Highway continues 20 miles (32 km) south to **Queenstown ❻**, a mining center built up around the **Mount Lyell Copper Mine.** The apocalyptic moonscape left by its busy mining and smelting industry has

---

## EXPERIENCE: Bay of Fires Walk

When the Bay of Fires topped a world's hottest travel destination list, locals objected, saying they didn't want the attention. That sums up this remote, pristine part of Tasmania's east coast, where virgin forest and turquoise seas bound dazzling white sand beaches.

The area is protected by **Mount William National Park** (St. Helens office: tel (03) 6376 1550). Hikers can walk along the beach and stay at basic campsites, but the big attraction is the guided **Bay of Fires Walk** with **Anthology** (tel (03) 6392 2211, www.bayoffires.com.au).

The walk begins at **Boulder Point,** a three-hour bus ride from Launceston. The **Bass Strait Islands** lie on the horizon, and the 6-mile (9 km), 4-hour walk along the beach passes layers of shells from thousands of years of Aboriginal feasts. Capt. Tobias Furneaux gave the bay its name in 1773 for the string of Aboriginal fires spread out along the beach.

The first night's stay is in twin-share tented accommodations at the **Forester Beach Camp,** where hikers enjoy dinner served with Tasmanian wine.

The next day, you will explore beach and sand dunes on a 9-mile (14 km), 7-hour walk to the **Bay of Fires Lodge,** the highlight of the trip. This award-winning lodge is a masterpiece of understated eco-elegance. Hikers spend two nights at the lodge, with an option of kayaking the next day before the walk out and transportation back on the fourth day.

## NOT TO BE MISSED:

Rocky Cape National Park • Hellyer
Gorge State Reserve • Lake St. Clair
•Richmond • Freycinet National Park

become an attraction in its own right: bare hills
tinted pink, gold, gray, and purple.

From Queenstown the highway winds a
tortuous 50 miles (80 km) through mountains
to Derwent Bridge. A very short—3-mile (4.8
km)—detour here will bring you to the jewel-like
**Lake St. Clair 7**. A lodge has accommodations
and meals, and the launch trip across the lake
gives some breathtaking glimpses of Tasmania's
pristine wilderness.

The highway continues to **Hobart 8** (see
pp. 334–336) through the hop-growing center
around **New Norfolk,** settled in 1808 and
now a very English-style town. Take the Tasman
Highway out of Hobart. A very worthwhile
short detour (8 miles/13 km, north from
Lindisfarne) goes to **Richmond 9** (visitor
information: 48 Bridge St., tel (03) 6260 2132), a
well-preserved colonial village, with Georgian
cottages and old stores. The four-span stone
bridge, built by convicts between 1823 and
1825, is the oldest in Australia. A short drive
back to the highway leads to **Sorell,** a historic
village founded just after Hobart in 1805.

### East Coast

A drive along Tasmania's east coast is nothing
like a drive through the west. The eastern
countryside is gentle, with a mild climate and
seaside villages around secluded beaches.
Forty miles (65 km) north of Sorell on the
Tasman Highway is **Orford,** a pleasant seaside town and the jumping-off point for the
ferry (Triabunna Bookings, tel 0419 746 668) to
**Maria Island National Park 10**—an 1820s'
penal colony but today a wildlife reserve
popular with bird-watchers (ranger's office: tel
(03) 6257 1420, www.parks.tas.gov.au).

The highlight of the east coast is **Freycinet
National Park 11** (visitor information: tel (03)
6256 7000), which includes Schouten Island
and the Friendly Beaches. To get there you
follow the highway 50 miles (80 km) past
Orford, through Swansea, to a turnoff on your
right to Coles Bay, the headquarters for the
park. Cape Freycinet has hiking, birdlife, and
camping on **Schouten Island.** Sheltered **Wineglass Bay,** with shimmering beaches of white
quartzite sand, is about a two-hour hike from
the parking lot on a well-marked trail.

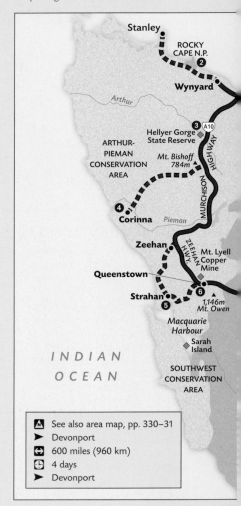

Going north, the highway hugs the coast for 40 miles (64 km), then veers through an old whaling town, **St. Helens,** and inland through farmland, dairies, and rain forests. After 100 miles (160 km) you reach **Launceston ⑫,** Tasmania's second city, with a population of about 70,000 *(visitor information: Cornwall Sq., 12–16 St. John St., tel (03) 6336 3133, www.launceston .tas.gov.au).* It sits near the confluence of the North Esk, South Esk, and Tamar Rivers. **Cataract Gorge,** where the South Esk tumbles into the Tamar, is ten minutes out of town.

Although it is almost as old as Hobart, Launceston (founded 1805) is a high-Victorian town—a legacy of its glory days when prospectors came to Tasmania in the hopes that its forests hid gold. For information on the town's architecture, go to the **Old Umbrella Shop** *(60 George St., tel (03) 6331 9248),* now a National Trust center, built in the 1860s and lined with rare Tasmanian blackwood.

From Launceston the highway circles back toward Devonport, about 70 miles (112 km) west, and closes the scenic loop of Tasmania.

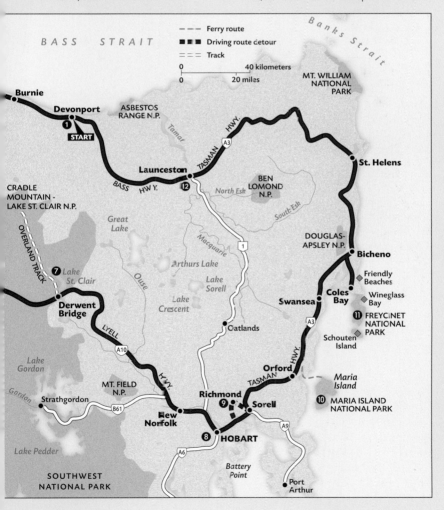

# Trout Fishing

Thanks to the persistence of the 19th-century amateur naturalists who brought brown and rainbow trout eggs from England, Tasmania is today an excellent trout-fishing destination. Its highland lakes host world fly-fishing championships.

Cold, clear waters and hard gravel riverbeds made Tasmania the perfect place to introduce trout.

Trout are not native to Australia. Amateur naturalists of the 19th century, with a Victorian-era notion that a bit of England could improve any landscape, began trying to import trout and trout eggs in the early 1860s, but they were defeated by the long sea journey. In 1864, however, a man named James Youl succeeded in getting a batch of eggs out from England in an ice chest. The eggs survived a remarkable 91-day relay of clipper ship, steamer, riverboat, and finally horseback, to be released in a few ponds near the Tasmanian town of Plenty. Youl was later knighted—in part, for his efforts in bringing this gentleman's gamefish to Tasmania. (Later, the descendants of these fish stocked New Zealand as well.) The town of Plenty, about 30 miles (48 km) northwest of Hobart, has a fishing museum (Salmon Ponds, tel (03) 6261 5663) set on English-style grounds.

Trout occupy an unusual niche in Australia's ecology mindset. Introduced species have been almost invariably a disaster for local wildlife. The introduction of rabbits for sport shooting in 1859 and European carp into the rivers in 1872 are the most famous and catastrophic environmental blunders in the continent's history. These days a more environmentally aware Australia spends millions trying to eradicate nonnative species such as rabbits, foxes, carp, blackberry vines, and cane toads, which were introduced with harmless intention. But trout have a certain élan, and although they are believed responsible for putting heavy competitive pressure on already threatened native species, they nevertheless enjoy a sort of honorary "native" status. They are seen as genteel, they don't muddy the rivers and lakes they swim in, and they make a significant contribution to the Tasmanian economy. Thousands of anglers flock to the state from all over the world, where their patience can be rewarded with trophy-size brown, rainbow, and lake trout.

There are a lot of good fishing holes and a number of professional guides around the state to help you find them. Back in the early 1970s, more than 350,000 brown trout fingerlings were released into Lake Pedder, and another 500,000 rainbow trout were put into Lake Gordon (both are on the edge of the southeast wilderness area). They flourished in the nutrient-rich waters, and there are (possibly apocryphal) tales of anglers catching 45-pound (20 kg) brown trout out of Lake Pedder. Whatever the truth of those boasts, the average size for brown trout in this lake is a very respectable 10 pounds (4.5 kg).

The midlands of Tasmania have trophy fishing lakes and spectacular scenery. Great Lake, Arthurs Lake, Lake Sorell, and Lake Crescent are some of the most productive, although the area has numerous smaller lakes and fishing holes. Trout were released here not long after they arrived from England, and by 1868, trout weighing nearly 10 pounds (4.5 kg) were being caught in Arthurs Lake. To get an idea of what is in those waters, stop in at the old Castle Hotel in Bothwell. While you'll no doubt hear a lot of fisherman's lies, the stuffed and mounted 25-pound (11 kg) trout over the bar offers its own mute testimony.

Tasmania's trout season opens early in August, although a few rainbow trout waters do not open until early October. The season lasts until April. The Inland Fisheries Service (*17 Back River Rd., New Norfolk, tel (03) 6261 8050, www.ifs.tcs.gov.au*) has information on bag limits, licenses, and minimum-size regulations.

---

## EXPERIENCE: Fishing in Tasmania

Tasmania has thousands of waters for trout fishing, particularly in the Central Highland lake country south of Deloraine. At altitudes of more than 3,300 feet (1,000 m), the area is dotted with lakes within easy access of each other and the rest of the island.

Top spots include **Arthurs Lake,** renowned for its brown trout, and **Great Lake,** teeming with rainbow and brown trout. As well as these dammed hydro lakes, smaller **Penstock Lagoon** has excellent fly-fishing while **Nineteen Lagoons** offers a wide range of fishing environments.

In the northern midlands, **Brumbys Creek's** crystal waters are excellent for sight-fishing and **Macquarie River** is good for flood-fishing in spring. Also popular are the Meander River, South Esk River, and Lake Trevallyn near Launceston, and the Derwent and Huon Rivers near Hobart.

These outfits can put together packages, including accommodations:
**Fish Wild Tasmania** (*Sandy Bay, tel (03) 6223 8917, www.fishwild tasmania.com*)
**Hayes on Brumbys** (*Cressy, tel (03) 6397 5073, www.flyfishtasmania .com.au*)
**Ken Orr's Tasmanian Trout Expeditions** (*Brady's Lake, Wayatinah, tel (03) 6289 1191, www .orrsometassietrout.com.au*)
**Rainbow Lodge** (*Miena, tel (03) 6259 8090,* www.rainbowlodgetas mania.com.au)
**Red Tag Trout Tours** (*Kingston, tel (03) 6229 5896, www.redtagtrout .com*)
**Rod & Fly Tasmania** (*Mountain River, tel (03) 6266 4480, www.rodandfly .com.au*)
**Tasmanian Escape** (*Youngtown, tel (03) 6344 1206, www.tasmanian escape.com*)
**Trout & Adventure Tasmania** (*Bronte Park, tel (03) 6289 1009, www .tarraleah.com*)
**Trout Territory** (*Cressy, tel (03) 6397 5001, www .troutterritory.com.au*)

# Bass Strait Islands

Tasmania includes two outer island groups in the violent waters of Bass Strait—the Hunter Islands off the northwest coast and the Furneaux Islands off the northeast. They are well off the usual tourist routes.

FLIGHTS TO THE ISLANDS: To Launceston via Flinders Island: Airlines of Tasmania, 1-800 144 460 (toll-free) or (03) 6359 2312. To King Island from Burnie and Devonport: Tasair, (03) 6248 5088 or (03) 6462 1070, www.tasair.com.au

King Island Tourism
☎ 1-800 645 014 (toll-free)

www.kingisland .org.au

## Hunter Islands

King Island is the largest of the Hunter Islands. This low, 40-mile-long (64 km) island is blessed with lush pasture grasses found nowhere else in Australia. It produces incredibly rich hand-made cheeses and thick double creams. Legend has it the grasses came from seeds in the straw-filled mattresses washed ashore from shipwrecks, of which the island has had more than any other part of Australia. The worst was when an immigrant

**INSIDER TIP:**

Don't miss a visit to King Island Dairy *(www .kidairy.com.au)*. Yes, it's a long way to come for cheese . . . but it sure is delicious cheese.

—LARRY PORGES
*National Geographic editor*

ship, the *Catarqui,* foundered in 1845 with the loss of 399 lives. Today the island has four lighthouses. **Cape Wickham** in the north is the tallest in the Southern Hemisphere and gives a splendid view of the island.

The island's biggest attraction, the **King Island Dairy,** on North Road about 5 miles (8 km) north of Currie, gives tours and free

tastings. The island has no public transportation. Rent a car from Howell's Auto Rent *(tel (03) 6462 1282)* or Cheapa Island Car Rentals *(tel (03) 6462 1282).*

## Furneaux Islands

The 52 Furneaux islands are at the eastern end of Bass Strait. In 1798, Matthew Flinders charted the biggest, **Flinders Island,** which became a base for sealers, who virtually wiped out the local seal population. In 1834, the 135 Tasmanian Aborigines who survived the Black Line were sent here (see p. 333).

Flinders Island has granite mountains, secluded beaches, and excellent fishing, scuba diving, and rock climbing. There are numerous bushwalking trails in **Strzelecki National Park,** including a hike to the wind-scoured summit of Mount Strzelecki. You can look for Killiecrankie "diamonds"—actually a form of local topaz—on the beach at Killiecrankie Bay.

Like King Island, Flinders is noted for its farm produce, but also for handmade chocolates and fine woolens. The main settlements are **Whitemark** on the west coast and **Lady Barron** on the south. The **Emita Museum,** about 12 miles (19 km) north of Whitemark, tells the story of the Aborigines' time on the island. For car rental, contact Flinders Island Car Rentals *(tel (03) 6359 2168).* ∎

# Travelwise

Planning Your Trip   356–358

How to Get to Australia   358–359

Getting Around   359–361

Practical Advice   361–364

Emergencies   364–365

Information Offices   365–366

Hotels & Restaurants   367–385

Shopping   386–387

Activities   388–389

A four-wheel-drive is favored outback transportation.

# TRAVELWISE

## PLANNING YOUR TRIP

### When to Go

Australia is good for vacations year-round. For a short trip without a fixed itinerary, spring and autumn give the most flexibility. The wildflowers in the west are particularly beautiful in the spring.

### Climate

The Australian spring runs from September through November, summer from December until March, autumn from March through May, and winter from June until September. Seasonal weather varies widely in the different parts of Australia.

The best summer weather occurs in the southern states, where everyone seems to live outdoors and take to the balmy seas. The center is scorchingly hot in summer, and the flies are at their worst. In the far north, temperatures may be slightly cooler, but the tropical humidity and monsoon downpours can be depressing, while poisonous box jellyfish make the sea too dangerous for swimming. On the other hand, some choose to head north during the summer in order to escape the crowds and the cities, and to see the Top End luxuriantly green and in full flood. The electrical storms are fantastic that time of year, and the barramundi fishing is superb.

In winter the southern states have snow, and some tourists come for the skiing. In the north the humidity and water levels drop. Travel is simpler, and wildlife is easier to spot, as it clusters around the remaining watering holes. This is the best time of year to see crocodiles.

## Calendar of Events

See also Holidays, p. 363

### January

**Perth Cup** (*Perth; Jan. 1*) A popular horse-racing event
**Cygnet Folk Festival** (*Cygnet, Tasmania; second weekend*) Features folk and world music, including local performers
**Sydney Festival** (*Sydney*) Three full weeks of arts, music, food, and dance
**Tamworth Country Music Festival** (*Tamworth, New South Wales; weekend nearest to Australia Day, Jan. 26*)
**Australian Open Tennis Championships** (*Melbourne*) International grand slam event
**Australia Day** (*Jan. 26*) Festivities nationwide, with music concerts in Sydney, Canberra, and Brisbane

### February

**Perth International Arts Festival** (*Perth*) Three weeks of opera, theater, dance, music, and art
**Royal Hobart Regatta** (*Hobart, Tasmania*)
**Tropfest** (*Nationwide*) World's largest short-film festival, screening in the capital cities
**Sydney Gay and Lesbian Mardi Gras** (*Sydney*)

### March

**Adelaide Festival of Arts** (*Adelaide; biennially, occurring in even-numbered years*) Three-week festival of the arts
**Moomba Waterfest** (*Melbourne*) Weeklong festival ending with a street parade
**Port Fairy Folk Festival** (*Port Fairy, Victoria*) Four-day celebration of music, with concerts and classes
**Formula 1 Australian Grand Prix** (*Melbourne*) Australia's premier motor-sport event

### April

**Melbourne International Comedy Festival** (*Melbourne*) Three-week event
**Sydney Royal Easter Show** (*Sydney*) Two-week festival with livestock, sideshows, and rodeos
**The Rip Curl Pro** (*Bells Beach, southwest of Melbourne*) Famous competition featuring the world's top surfers

### May

**Outback Muster & Drovers' Reunion** (*Longreach, Queensland*) Two-day festival with events related to droving

### June

**The Dreaming** (*Woodford, near Brisbane*) Three-day indigenous arts festival

### July

**Melbourne International Film Festival** (*Melbourne*)
**Northern Territory Royal Shows** Agricultural shows at Darwin, Katherine, Tennant Creek, and Alice Springs
**Camel Cup** (*Darwin*) Camel races and carnival atmosphere

### August

**Beer Can Regatta** (*Darwin*) Boats made entirely out of beer cans
**City2Surf** (*Sydney*) 8.75-mile (14 km) fun run between Hyde Park and Bondi Beach
**Darwin Rodeo** (*Darwin; held on third weekend*)
**Henley-on-Todd Regatta** (*Alice Springs, Northern Territory*) Held in dry riverbed, using leg-powered bottomless boats (see p. 199)

### September

**Shinju Matsuri (Festival of the Pearl)** (*Broome, Western Australia*)

**Royal Melbourne Show**
*(Melbourne)* Livestock, sideshows, and rides
**Royal Adelaide Show** *(Adelaide)*
Weeklong agricultural and horti-cultural show
**Perth Royal Show** *(Perth)* Live-stock, sideshows, and rides
**Australian Rules Football League (AFL) Grand Final** *(Melbourne)*
**Birdsville Races** *(Birdsville, Queens-land)* Weekend of horse-racing, in aid of the Royal Flying Doctor Service (see p. 18)

### October

**Melbourne Fringe Festival**
*(Melbourne)* Three-week alterna-tive celebration of the arts
**Queen's Birthday** *(nearest Mon-day to Sept. 30)* State holiday in Western Australia
**Melbourne International Arts Festival** *(Melbourne)* Music, theater, dance
**Bathurst 1000 Touring Car Race** *(Bathurst, New South Wales)*
Mount Panorama circuit
**Royal Shows** *(Hobart & Launces-ton, Tasmania)* Agricultural and horticultural shows
**Australian Motorcycle Grand Prix** *(Phillip Island, Victoria)*

### November

**Melbourne Cup First Tuesday**
*(Flemington, Melbourne)* Australia's premier horse race

### December

**Sydney to Hobart Yacht Race**
*(leaves Sydney on December 26, Boxing Day)* Australia's leading ocean race

## Travel Insurance

Always take out adequate insurance when you travel, especially for medical needs. Costs for ambulance or helicopter rescue, emergency surgery, or travel home can be exorbitant. Ensure that the policy covers all of the activities that you are likely to undertake.

## Entry Formalities
### Visas

Many travelers may now obtain authority to enter Australia through the Electronic Travel Authority (ETA) system, which replaces the need for an Austra-lian visa. The tourist ETA is valid for multiple entries into Australia (each entry to a maximum of three months) over a period of one year and costs A$20 (U.S $15.50). The similar eVisi-tor system applies to European passport holders and is free for tourist and business visits. A busi-ness ETA allows multiple entries into Australia for the life of your passport. Restrictions apply. ETAs can be obtained through your travel agent (who may charge a fee), from your airline, or online at *www.immi.gov.au*. Apply at least two weeks before departure.

Travelers not eligible for an ETA or eVisitor, and those wishing to stay for longer than three months or to work, must obtain a visa. Further advice and application forms may be obtained from your travel agent or from the Austra-lian embassy, high commission, or consular office.

### Customs

Items brought in for personal use, for example cameras, laptops, radios, and film, are exempt from duty. If you take a laptop, it is a good idea to register it with your own customs officials before leav-ing for Australia. You should also be prepared to "boot up" the lap-top on request. Travelers over the age of 18 may bring 2.25 liters (0.6 gl) of alcohol into Australia, 250 cigarettes, or 250 grams (9 oz) of tobacco, and gifts to the value of A$900 (U.S. $800) duty free. Travelers under 18 may bring gifts to the value of A$450 (U.S. $400) without attracting duty.

There are no restrictions on the amount of Australian or foreign currency you can import or export, although sums exceeding A$10,000 (U.S. $7,700), or its equivalent, should be declared on the appropri-ate inbound customs forms.

For detailed information on customs controls and restrictions, contact the relevant Australian high commission, embassy, or consular office listed on p. 358, or visit *www.customs.gov.au*.

### Quarantine

Australia has very strict quaran-tine laws designed to keep out pests and diseases. Planes are routinely fumigated by the cabin staff. Do not attempt to bring any fruit, seeds, vegetables, foodstuffs, or animal or plant products into the country. (Simi-lar border controls are also in place between Australian states.) If you inadvertently carry any such item into the control zone, place it in one of the many clearly labeled disposal bins. Do not attempt to take it through cus-toms, and if in doubt, declare it. Sniffer dogs check for foodstuffs as well as drugs. If you have hiking boots, expect to produce them for inspection. Any soil adhering to the soles must be cleaned off. Also expect items such as straw hats and wooden clogs to be scrutinized.

### Drugs & Narcotics

Sniffer dogs check for drugs and narcotics. Such checks are com-monplace and penalties for carry-ing illegal substances are severe. Medicines for personal use should be clearly labeled. Obtain a state-ment from your doctor if you are importing a large number of pharmaceuticals or if they are of a restricted type.

## Australian Embassies Abroad

### United States
1601 Massachusetts Ave., N.W.
Washington, D.C., 20036
Tel 202/797-3000
Fax 202/797-3168
*www.usa.embassy.gov.au*
Offices also in Atlanta, Chicago,
Denver, Honolulu, Houston,
Los Angeles, New York, &
San Francisco

### Canada
50 O'Connor St., Suite 710,
Ottawa, Ontario, K1P 6L2
Tel 613/236-0841
Fax 613/236-4376
*www.ahc-ottawa.org*
Also in Toronto & Vancouver

### United Kingdom
Australia House
The Strand, London, WC2B 4LA
Tel 020-7379 4334
Visa information 0906 550 8900
*www.australia.org.uk*
Also in Edinburgh

### Australian Dept. of Foreign Affairs & Trade
*www.dfat.gov.au*

# HOW TO GET TO AUSTRALIA

## Choosing a Ticket
Australia is so far away from
just about anywhere else in the
world that most people arrange
in advance to go there rather
than making it an optional part
of an itinerary. It is not a cheap
destination, but you can save
money by shopping around for
your ticket, going out of season,
and planning ahead. At the minimum, you should investigate the
savings available through advance
purchase ticketing, such as Apex.
Major carriers include:

### Qantas
Within Australia:
Tel: 13 13 13 (Reservations)
*www.qantas.com.au*
Within United States:
Tom Bradley Intl. Terminal
380 World Way
Room 4124
Los Angeles, CA 90045
Tel 800/227-4500
*www.qantas.com*

Within United Kingdom:
395 King St.,
London W6 9NJ
Tel 08457 747 767
*www.qantas.co.uk*

### Air New Zealand
United States: 800/262-1234
United Kingdom: 0800 028 4149
*www.airnewzealand.com*

### British Airways
United Kingdom: 0844 493 0787
*www.britishairways.com*

### Cathay Pacific
United States: 800/233-2742
*www.cathaypacific.com*

### Singapore Airlines
United States: 800/742-3333
United Kingdom: 0844 800 2380
*www.singaporeair.com*

### United Airlines
United States: 800/864-8331
*www.united.com*

### V Australia (Virgin)
United States: 800/444-0260
*www.vaustralia.com*

The options for ticketing are
practically endless. You may
want to travel at a set time or
for a limited period, or fly with a
certain carrier, or go direct. There
are free stopovers along certain
routes, for example, Hawaii or
New Zealand out of Los Angeles;
Singapore or Bangkok out of
London. You have to decide

what comforts you will and won't
compromise on, and what you
can and can't afford in time and
money. You may also wish to
buy air and bus discount passes
before you go (see Getting
Around, below.) Check with your
travel agent, and don't forget
the consolidators, who often
offer the best bargains. Always
check for package conditions and
restrictions, and be prepared
to negotiate.

## Package Tours
There are three main options
for package tours (and endless
variations within them). The first
is to fly independently but spend
your time with a tour company,
for example:

### AAT Kings
*www.aatkings.com*
U.S.: 801 East Katella Ave., 3rd
Floor, Anaheim, CA 92805, tel
714/456-0505
Australia: Bondi Junction, New
South Wales 2022, tel 1-300
556 100

### Australian Pacific Touring
*www.aptouring.com.au*
U.S.: 4605 Lankershim Blvd., Suite
712, North Hollywood, CA 91602,
tel 800/290-8687
Australia: 475 Hampton St., Victoria 3181, tel (03) 9277 8555

Second, you can buy a package that includes flights, hotels,
and rental cars or sightseeing,
with **Qantas, British Airways,**
or **United Vacations** *(in U.S., tel
888/854-3899)*, for example.

Third, there are customized
package vacations. Check the
newspapers, ask your travel agent,
or contact companies such as:

### Fishing International
*www.fishinginternational.com*
U.S.: 5510 Skylane Blvd., Suite

200, Santa Rosa, CA 95403, tel
800/950-4242

**ITC Golf Tours**
*www.itcgolftours.com*
U.S.: 2428 Lewis Ave., Signal Hill,
CA 90755, tel 562/595-6905.

## Airports

Most visitors arrive in Sydney,
though international flights
also arrive at Perth, Melbourne,
Brisbane, Adelaide, Cairns, and
Darwin airports.

Sydney International Airport,
Kingford Smith, is 7 miles (11 km)
south of the city and can be
reached by bus, rail, and taxi.
International and domestic flights
have separate terminals. Shuttle
buses and trains link the terminals
to each other and to the Central
Railroad Station, Town Hall, and
Circular Quay. Many city hotels
operate their own shuttle buses. A
taxi to the city center costs around
A$50 (U.S. $45) and takes about 30
minutes. Rail services go to Central
Station. *Note:* A departure tax is
assessed. This is usually prepaid as
part of your air ticket.

## GETTING AROUND
## By Air

Australia has an excellent
network of domestic air services,
and vigorous competition
between Qantas and Virgin Blue
and budget airlines Jetstar and
Tiger means that you can get
some very good deals, particularly
if you shop via the internet and
are prepared to be flexible in
your travel plans. Carriers offer
substantial savings through
e-tickets and website specials,
and these deals are often
advertised in newspapers as well.
International travelers may also
be able to purchase an airpass
through Qantas, which will
entitle them to a set number
of discounted domestic flights

while they are in the country.
The passes must be purchased
before arrival in Australia. Prices
vary according to the number
of flights requested. Details are
available on the Qantas website.
Virgin Blue also has air passes.

**Jetstar**
Reservation line: 13 15 38
*www.jetstar.com*
**Qantas**
Reservation line: 13 13 13
*www.qantas.com.au*
**Tiger Airways**
Reservation line: (03) 9335 3033
*www.tigerairways.com*
**Virgin Blue**
Reservation line: 13 67 89
*www.virginblue.com.au*

## By Car

Drive on the left and pass on
the right. Remember to yield to
traffic coming from the right at
traffic circles. (Pedestrians should
remember to look right for traffic
when crossing a road.) Roads are
generally well kept. You need to
take special care if driving long
distances, though, especially if
you use outback dirt tracks. (See
Driving Safely, below.)

### Renting a Car

Rental costs vary according to
season, demand, availability, and
the size and type of car required.
Check whether the cost covers
unlimited mileage. Certain
companies add an additional
charge for miles traveled over
a stated limit. Prices start at
around A$40 (U.S. $35) a day or
A$250 (U.S. $220) a week for a
manual-gearshift, economy car.
There may also be local or airport
surcharges. Always check the condition of the car before you drive
away and report any concerns
immediately. Normally you must
return the car to the place from
which it was rented. Occasionally

cars may be dropped elsewhere
(for a fee).

You may get a cheaper rate if
you reserve the car before you
leave home. Most major agencies,
for example, Avis, Hertz, and
Budget, have an international
booking section. They give advice
on rates, restrictions, and availability
at your chosen destination and, if
you choose, will reserve a car for
your arrival.

**Avis,** 1-800 225 533
**Hertz,** 13 30 39
**Budget,** 1-300 362 848 or
(03) 9853 9399

### Rental Conditions

In order to be allowed to drive
in Australia, you must have a
valid driver's license and be at
least 21 years of age (a premium
may be charged for any driver
under 25). Third-party insurance
and collision damage waiver are
compulsory and are included in
the cost of the rental. Comprehensive coverage and personal
accident insurance are available at
extra cost, but check the coverage
provided by your home car and
travel insurance policies. Nearly
all companies will insist that you
pay for the rental with a major
international credit or charge
card. You may well find additional
insurance protection on the card
you use for payment.

### Four-wheel-drive Vehicles

A four-wheel-drive (4WD)
vehicle is essential for outback
travel. The rental and insurance
costs are higher than for an
ordinary car. Damage to the
vehicle caused by the driver is
not covered by insurance.

### Motorhomes & Camper Vans

Motorhomes and campers may
be rented locally in all states. The
minimum rental period is usually
one week, and good reductions

may be obtained for longer periods. Rates are highest in the main holiday season of December and January. Motorcycles can also be rented.

### Driving Regulations

The use of seat belts is compulsory in Australia. Drivers must ensure that passengers wear them—failure to do so results in a fine. Fines may follow you home because car rental companies will supply customer address details to the authorities.

### Road Signs

Signs are easy to understand. Speeds and distances are given in kilometers. Speed limits vary from 50 kph (31 mph) in residential areas to 110 kph (68 mph) on the highways. Speed limits are strictly enforced.

### Fuel

Fuel (unleaded or diesel) is sold by the liter. Expect to pay around A$1.30 a liter (U.S. $4 a U.S. gallon) in the city and around A$1.70 a liter (U.S. $5 a U.S. gallon) in the outback.

### Alcohol

Permitted blood alcohol limits are low, and it is wise to avoid all alcoholic drinks when in charge of a vehicle. Police checks are frequent and the penalties severe.

### Driving Safely

Long-distance driving has its own hazards in Australia. Although the main highways are well maintained, they can be very tiring. Always build sufficient rest periods into any journey time, and do not underestimate the draining power of the sun and its glare. Always carry a good supply of water and snacks.

If planning to use dirt tracks, ensure that the vehicle is suitable and that you are prepared for emergencies. Check the weather forecast and road conditions with the local police before setting out. Deep, fine "bulldust" can prove hazardous for even an experienced four-wheel-driver. Flash floods and dust storms are common in season (which varies from area to area; check with local police offices for information). Be wary of animals on the road, particularly at dawn and dusk.

The need for care cannot be overemphasized. Know where you are on your maps. Breakdown or other assistance may not be easy to attract. As well as water and snack foods to sustain you in case of emergency or delay, take warm blankets. A flashlight (with spare batteries) will help if you are stranded overnight. Use common sense and have a healthy respect for an unforgiving environment. Carry a good first-aid kit, spare fuel, and adequate tools to make basic repairs to your vehicle.

If you are planning to visit a remote national park, find out from locals and police at your starting point about road conditions, what gear to take, and what to do if things go wrong. Listen to advice, and always leave word with a responsible person or the local police about where you are going and when you expect to return.

### Automobile Associations

Australian automobile associations provide services to members of most foreign motoring organizations. You need to have a valid membership card from your own organization if requesting a service. Breakdown assistance may also be available.

**A.A.A. (Automobile Association of Australia)**
216 Northbourne Ave.
Canberra
ACT 2601
Tel (06) 6247 7311

**NRMA Motoring & Services**
74–76 King St.
Sydney
Tel 13 11 22

### What to Do in an Accident

Take the names and addresses of any witnesses, the driver of the other vehicle, and the owner if different. Note the make, model, and registration number of the other vehicle. Exchange insurance information and contact details. Make a note of damage to the vehicle and any injuries to yourself and other persons. Record details of the scene—visibility, traffic flow, road details, and surface conditions. Record details of the collision, including speed of travel and point of impact.

All accidents, unless they are minor scrapes, must be reported to the police. Cooperate with the police officer. Make a note of the officer's name, number, and where he or she may be contacted. Draw a sketch of the accident showing the layout of the road and the position and movement of the vehicles involved. Keep all of these details for the insurance report.

### Buying a Vehicle

Before you buy a motor vehicle in Australia, check that it has a current annual Roadworthiness Certificate (RWC), in addition to making the obvious safety checks. When you want to resell a car, it is advisable to return to the state in which you bought it.

## By Bus

### Long-Distance Bus Routes

If money is a constraint, or if you have the time and want to get a feel for the immense size and geography of the country, go by bus. Traveling the long-distance bus routes is usually the cheapest way of getting around Australia. All the major cities and highways are serviced by large express companies that link up with regional operators serving smaller communities. All the major carriers have comfortable buses with onboard sanitary facilities. Air-conditioning is the norm, and drivers often run videos on overhead monitors.

The main interstate busline in Australia is Greyhound. A series of passes, with varying duration and with varying degrees of flexibility, are offered. Travelers to Tasmania can use the local Tassie Link bus pass (www.tigerline.com.au), which offers circuits of the island in 7-, 10-, 14-, or 21-day periods.

## Greyhound
United States: 800/633-3403
Australia: 13 14 99 or 13 20 30,
www.greyhound.com.au

## Bus Tours
Many Australian travel operators run bus, or coach, tours. These range from a few days in luxury, air-conditioned buses and hotels, to several weeks camping out of a beaten-up jalopy. The former provides interesting narration, a minimum of physical activity, and every creature comfort. For the latter, everyone is expected to lend a hand and enjoy a sleep under the stars. Some of the most popular tours run out of Darwin and Adelaide to Alice Springs and Uluru (Ayers Rock). Other popular routes are Cairns–Brisbane and Brisbane–Sydney. Check with your travel agent or with Tourism Australia for further information.

## By Train
### Long-Distance Train Routes
The Indian Pacific runs twice a week from Sydney to Perth (and vice versa) via the Nullarbor Plain, with a running time of 65 hours (see p. 248). The Ghan train runs once a week (twice in winter) from Adelaide to Darwin (via

Alice Springs) through the outback (see pp. 282–283), and once a week to Alice Springs alone. The Sunlander runs daily from Brisbane to Cairns (and vice versa) and takes 32 hours. All these services have luxury packages that include sleeper accommodations and meals.

Service in the Ghan or Indian Pacific comes in two main classes: The Gold Service—an essential first-class sleeper, with en suite cabin and all meals in the dining car—and the less expensive Red Service—a standard sleeper service and a café car where you can purchase meals. A still cheaper option is the day-nighter seats, with meals and snacks available for purchase.

You can make reservations at the main rail stations in Alice Springs, Darwin, Katherine, Melbourne, Perth, and Adelaide's Parkland Terminal in Keswick. The main office of Great Southern Railway (Ground floor, 422 King William St., Adelaide) also takes reservations, or book online at www.gsr.com.au.

Great Southern Railway also operates the Overlander, a weekly overnight service from Adelaide to Melbourne and return.

## By Boat
The only regular maritime service in Australia is the Spirit of Tasmania car ferry that sails between Melbourne and Devonport, Tasmania (see p. 333). The sailing takes around 10 hours and is often cursed by rough seas.

Some international cruise lines, for example Holland America Lines, P&O, and Princess Cruises, sail around Australia. Typically they dock at Sydney and continue along the coastline stopping at Brisbane and Cairns to the east, Melbourne, Adelaide, and Hobart to the south, or Fremantle in the west.

Numerous pleasure boats, catamarans, and yachts operate out of the mainland towns along the east coast and islands on the Great Barrier Reef, and out of Exmouth on the west coast for Ningaloo Reef. Some give a day's island hopping, with dolphin-watching and whale-watching, snorkeling, and scuba diving. Others go for up to a week of diving and sailing out at sea.

There are river cruises along the Murray River in South Australia (see pp. 276–277) and Victoria (see pp. 324–325), Myall Lakes in New South Wales, and the Hawkesbury River north of Sydney.

## PRACTICAL ADVICE
### Children
Most hotels allow children under a certain age to stay in their parents' room for free or at a discounted rate. The cutoff age varies considerably (the average is 12). A few hotels still charge for children as if they were adults. The Australian suburbs have a large number of family restaurants, with special menus for children, high chairs, and booster seats.

### Communications
#### Mail
Stamps may be purchased from post offices, hotels, and many shops. The rate for domestic letters is 55 Australian cents (45 U.S. cents). Standard rates for postcards and letters up to 1.7 ounces (50 g) is A$1.45 (U.S. $1.25) to Asia/Pacific and A$2.10 (U.S. $1.80) to the rest of the world, including North America. Parcels up to 44 pounds (20 kg) can be sent by air or sea through post offices.

#### Poste Restante
Larger offices have a free poste restante (general delivery) service (as do some outback offices).

Take proof of identity, such as a passport or driver's license, when collecting.

## Telephones

Australia has an excellent telephone system and modern exchange. There are numerous public telephones that take both coins and phone cards. Many city telephones also accept credit cards. Phone cards are readily available and are sold in 5, 10, 20, and 50 Australian dollar units. Local calls from public phones cost 50 cents for an unlimited amount of time. The same call from a private phone costs around 30 cents.

Long-distance calls can be made from public telephones but are expensive. Calls to the U.S. cost about A$4.50 (U.S. $4) per minute, about half that to the U.K. Rates are slightly cheaper on weekends. Far cheaper are the international calling cards sold by many convenience stores and newsagents. From any telephone, you dial a local or toll-free number then enter your PIN and the overseas number.

Toll-free numbers in Australia have the prefix 1-800. Six-digit numbers starting with 13 are charged at local rates, regardless of where the answering office might be.

Telstra and Optus operate the two main mobile phone networks, and a number of other companies, such as Vodaphone and Virgin, use these two networks. Telstra has slightly better coverage, but both networks cover almost all the populated areas. Cell phones are of minimal use in the unpopulated outback. Prepaid SIM cards are readily purchased. Local calls are generally expensive, about 80 cents per minute. International rates, however, are cheaper than public phones, about A$1 (U.S. $0.90) per minute to the U.S., slightly more to the U.K.

To call from Australia to the U.S. or Canada use the prefix the number with 00 11 1. To call from Australia to the U.K. use 00 11 44.

## Fax

Faxes can be sent from any hotel business center or post office, where rates are A$4 (U.S. $3.50) for the first page and A$1 (U.S. $0.90) for each subsequent page.

## E-mail & Online Services

All the big cities have online services at Internet cafés. These allow you to use the internet and send e-mail at a half-hour or hourly rate (around A$10/U.S. $7.75 an hour). If you have a laptop, check with your local provider before leaving for Australia. Several larger service providers, such as AOL, have local Australian numbers that you can access from your hotel. Many hotels offer Internet access at lobby terminals, or in-room with wireless or LAN connections for your laptop, but rates are usually high. Some cafés offer free wireless Internet. Mobile phone companies also offer prepaid broadband wireless through the mobile networks along with a USB modem.

## Conversions

Australia uses the metric system. Useful conversions are:

## Weights & Measures

1 mile = 1.61 kilometers
1 kilometer = 0.62 mile
1 pint = 0.47 liters
1 liter = 2.12 pints
1 U.S. gallon = 3.78 liters
1 pound = 0.37 kilos
1 kilo = 2.20 pounds
1 ounce = 31 grams
1 foot = 0.30 meters
1 meter = 39.37 inches

## Clothing

*Women's clothing*

| | | | | | |
|---|---|---|---|---|---|
| American | 8 | 10 | 12 | 14 | 16 | 18 |
| Australian | 10 | 12 | 14 | 16 | 18 | 20 |

*Men's clothing*

| | | | | | |
|---|---|---|---|---|---|
| American | 36 | 38 | 40 | 42 | 44 | 46 |
| Australian | 92 | 97 | 102 | 107 | 112 | 117 |

*Men's shirts*

| | | | | |
|---|---|---|---|---|
| American | 15 | 15.5 | 16 | 16.5 | 17 |
| Australian | 38 | 39 | 41 | 42 | 43 |

*Women's shoes*

| | | | | |
|---|---|---|---|---|
| American | 6 | 6.5 | 7 | 7.5 | 8 | 8.5 |
| Australian | 6.5 | 7 | 7.5 | 8 | 8.5 | 9 |

*Men's shoes*

| | | | | |
|---|---|---|---|---|
| American | 8 | 8.5 | 9.5 | 10.5 | 11.5 | 12 |
| Australian | 7 | 7.5 | 8.5 | 9.5 | 10.5 | 11 |

## Electricity

Australian electrical appliances have plugs with three flat pins. Electrical voltage is 240 AC, 50 cycles. Most visitors need to use an adapter.

## Gay & Lesbian Travelers

Gay and Lesbian Tourism Australia (*www.galta.com.au*) promotes gay and lesbian travel within Australia and is an excellent source of help and information.

## Liquor Laws

It is against the law for anyone under the age of 18 to buy alcohol or consume alcohol in public. Serving hours for public bars are usually 10 a.m.–10 p.m., Monday through Saturday, Sunday hours vary. Restaurants, clubs, and hotel lounges have more flexible hours. Alcohol is sold at liquor stores, hotels, and other licensed premises (not on supermarket shelves).

Many restaurants are licensed to sell alcohol, but some may only be able to sell it to you if you are having it with a meal. Others are BYO (bring your own). Most restaurants will allow you to BYO; they may charge a small corkage fee for opening the bottle and serving it to you.

## Media

### Newspapers
News Corporation's *The Australian* is the only newspaper available countrywide. Otherwise, each state has its own daily paper: the *Sydney Morning Herald* and *The Age,* from Melbourne, are the best known quality papers.

### TV Channels
There are three commercial networks (Seven, Nine, and Ten), plus the government-owned but substantially independent Australian Broadcasting Corporation channel (Channel Two) and the similarly established multicultural channel, SBS. Cable is provided by the dominant network, Foxtel, which feature sports channels, movie channels, and news channels such as CNN.

### Radio
There are numerous radio channels on the AM and FM bands. In Sydney, 2GB and 702ABC have news and talkback programs; 2WS, 2-DAY-FM, and MMM play popular music; jjj is the youth station; and ABC-FM and 2MBS are devoted to classical music.

## Money
The unit of currency is the Australian dollar, which consists of 100 cents. Coins are available in 5, 10, 20, and 50 cents, and 1 and 2 dollars. Bills are in 5, 10, 20, 50, and 100 dollar denominations. Different colors and sizes make them easy to identify.

Traveler's checks are a straightforward and secure way to carry money. You may change traveler's checks at almost any bank or licensed money changer, using your passport and/or driver's license as proof of identity. Fees vary from bank to bank, as do commission charges, but are around A$5–10 per transaction.

The major international credit cards are widely accepted throughout Australia, and even small towns seem to have an ATM allowing Mastercard or Visa cash withdrawals, or through overseas savings accounts linked to the Cirrus or Plus networks. Major charge cards, such as American Express, are also widely accepted. You should carry cash or long journeys in the outback. In all cases, it is sensible to carry a mixture of traveler's checks, credit cards, and cash.

## Holidays
January 1 (New Year's Day)
January 26 (Australia Day)
March/April (Good Friday, Easter Saturday, Easter Sunday, and Easter Monday)
April 25 (Anzac Day)
Second Monday in June (Queen's Birthday, national holiday except Western Australia)
December 25 and 26 (Christmas Day and Boxing Day)

## National Trust
The National Trust *(www.nationaltrust.org.au)* is dedicated to the preservation of historic buildings throughout Australia, many of which are open to the public.

Membership gives you free entry to any National Trust property. Helpful leaflets on historic buildings and walks around many towns and cities are available at National Trust offices:

**Australian Capital Territory**
Old Parliament House Shop
King George Terrace, Canberra
Tel (02) 6273 4744

**New South Wales**
Watson Rd., Sydney
Tel (02) 9258 0123

**Northern Territory**
4 Burnett Place, Darwin
Tel (08) 8910 0165

**Queensland**
95 William St., Brisbane
Tel (07) 3223 6666

**South Australia**
Ayers House
288 North Terrace, Adelaide
Tel (08) 8212 1133

**Tasmania**
Brisbane & Campbell Sts., Hobart
Tel (03) 6231 0911

**Victoria**
Tasma Terrace
4 Parliament Place, Melbourne
Tel (03) 9656 9800

**Western Australia**
Old Observatory, 4 Havelock St.
West Perth
Tel (08) 9321 6088

## Opening Hours
**Shop** hours vary from state to state, but the core opening hours are Monday to Friday 9 a.m. to 5 p.m. and Saturday 9 a.m. to 1 p.m. Many towns have late-night shopping Thursday and/or Friday to 9 p.m. Shops in many tourist areas, and shopping malls in the cities, also open on Sunday. **Banks** are open Monday to Thursday 9:30 a.m. to 4 p.m., and Friday 9:30 a.m. to 5 p.m. In some states banks are also open on Saturday mornings. **Post offices** are open Monday to Friday 9 a.m. to 5 p.m. Many post offices open on Saturday mornings as well.

## Photography & Video
Quality film and processing are available throughout Australia. Take extra care in the tropical heat, which may affect the life and quality of your film and batteries. The intense glare from the sun and its reflection on the water may bleach your photographs of color. The best

light for photography generally occurs in the early morning and late afternoon.

## Senior Travelers

There are various discounts for senior citizens in Australia, but senior citizens visiting from abroad cannot claim them. However, it is always worth asking about discounts or promotional rates, particularly at hotels, with tour operators, and at car rental agencies.

## Swimming & Beaches

Australia has some very fine beaches and swimming holes. As always when swimming off unfamiliar beaches, take notice of tides, currents, and forecast weather conditions. It is advisable to swim only on beaches that have lifeguard support or supervision. A red-and-yellow flag indicates that it is safe to swim. A red flag warns that you should stay out of the water because of strong currents, rough seas, or less obvious dangers such as sharks, blue-ringed octopuses, or scorpion fish.

Between October and May, the seas of the tropical north may contain poisonous box jellyfish (stingers). All year round, the saltwater crocodile poses a serious danger to swimmers. Always heed signs warning of crocodiles. If you are camping, keep at least 50 yards (46 m) back from the water's edge, and don't follow the same route when going to fetch your water.

## Time Differences

Australia has three time zones. **Eastern Standard Time** East coast states—Tasmania, Queensland, Victoria, & New South Wales: 10 hours ahead of Greenwich Mean Time (GMT) and 15 hours ahead of U.S. Eastern standard time.

**Central Standard Time** South Australia & Northern Territory: 9.5 hours ahead of GMT. **Western Standard Time** Western Australia: 8 hours ahead of GMT.

During the summer most states observe Daylight Savings Time, moving the clock forward by one hour. If used, Daylight Savings Time begins in October and ends in March or April, depending on the state.

## Tipping

Tipping is not an Australian tradition. It is a matter of choice. A waiter at a quality restaurant, however, would anticipate a gratuity of up to 10 percent of the total bill if you have been satisfied with the service.

## Travelers with Disabilities

The Australian Tourist Commission has Consumer Helplines around the world and provides a fact sheet, called "Travel in Australia for People with Disabilities," with the addresses of helpful organizations in each state or territory.

**N.I.C.A.N.,** National Information Communications Network (48 Brookes St., Mitchell, ACT, tel (02) 6241 1220 or 1-800 806 769 [toll-free], www.nican.com.au), provides an Australia-wide directory of accessible accommodations and sporting and recreational facilities.

**A.C.R.O.D.,** Australian Council for the Rehabilitation of the Disabled (33 Thesiger Ct., Deakin, ACT, tel (02) 6283 3200, www.nds.org.au), offers advice on state-based help organizations, accommodations and specialist tour operators.

**Air travel** All of Australia's airports have facilities for travelers with disabilities. Certain Qantas jets carry skychairs and have an accessible toilet on board.

**Trains** Facilities vary. The Indian Pacific (Sydney–Perth) line, for example, has cabins with wheelchair access. A skychair is used for boarding and movement between carriages. Conditions may not suit everyone. For further information, contact Great Southern Railway (tel (08) 8213 4592).

**Car rental** Avis and Hertz have cars with hand controls. They must be reserved in advance but can be collected from major airports at no extra charge.

**Parking & public toilets** Major city councils can provide mobility maps to visitors.

**Ferry** The Spirit of Tasmania (see p. 333) has four wheelchair-accessible cabins and provides access to the public areas on the ship.

## Volunteer Vacations

**Conservation Volunteers** (tel (03) 5330 2600, www.conserva tionvolunteers.com.au) organizes practical conservation projects for volunteers and, on longer projects, organizes food and accommodations for a reasonable contribution towards costs. For details on their programs and other organizations offering volunteer opportunities, see "Volunteering" p. 255.

# EMERGENCIES

## Emergency Telephone Number

Throughout Australia, the toll-free emergency services number for fire, ambulance, or police is **000**.

## Embassies & Consulates

Most countries have an embassy or high commission within Canberra and a consular office in the major cities. Visa applications are generally handled in Canberra. For consulates, consult the local telephone directory.

**United States**
21 Moonah Place

Yarralumla
Canberra
ACT 2600
Tel (02) 6270 5000

**Canada**
Commonwealth Ave.
Yarralumla
Canberra
ACT 2600
Tel (02) 6273 3844

**United Kingdom**
Commonwealth Ave.
Yarralumla
Canberra
ACT 2600
Tel (02) 6270 6666

## Health
Medical care in Australia is excellent and not expensive. A doctor's appointment typically costs around A$40 (U.S. $35). The U.K., New Zealand, Sweden, the Netherlands, and a few other countries have reciprocal health care arrangements with Australia, and residents from these countries are entitled to free or heavily subsidized medical treatment at public hospitals and certain clinics.

### Inoculations
None are essential. Cholera, malaria, and yellow fever are unknown, though tropical diseases such as dengue fever are a problem (see Insects, below). It is sensible to be vaccinated against tetanus and hepatitis (A and B)—but that is true whether you are traveling or not.

### Spiders & Snakes
Thirteen of the most poisonous snakes and spiders in the world live in Australia. Snakes live in the water as well as on the land, but both prefer to stay out of your way and usually go before you've had a chance to spot them. If you are bitten by a snake, try to remember what it looked like (but never pursue it), and go straight to the hospital for antivenin. Most snake venom needs a few hours to take hold, but the shock of the bite can be as dangerous as the bite itself.

The most dangerous spiders in Australia are the red back and funnel web. The latter is most common and most poisonous in the suburbs of Sydney. Again, if bitten, try to remember the features of the spider and go straight to the hospital.

### Sunburn
Do not underestimate the power of the sun. Australia has the highest incidence of skin cancer in the world. The hole in the ozone layer is directly above Australia, and the country's clear blue skies offer very little protection from the sun's burning and dangerous ultraviolet radiation. Try to stay out of the sun at its peak strength, between 11 a.m. and 3 p.m. Always wear properly applied, high-factor suntan lotion and a hat. Keep your neck and arms well covered. Protect your eyes with quality sunglasses that fit well.

### Insects
Flies can be a horrific nuisance in the outback, where they will settle on you by the hundred, seeking moisture from your ears, eyes, and nose.

Mosquitoes can also be a real problem in Australia, not just for the irritation of their bites but also because they may be carrying the Ross River virus or dengue fever. These can be as debilitating as malaria, or worse.

Ask advice locally and use an effective insect repellent or fly net when necessary.

## INFORMATION OFFICES
Tourism Australia is the main national tourism body, with a good website for visitor information (*www.tourism.australia.com*) and offices in many countries.

**United States**
6100 Center Drive
Suite 1150
Los Angeles, CA 90045
Tel: 310/695-3200

**United Kingdom**
Australia Centre, Australia House
6th Floor
Melbourne Place/Strand
London WC2B 4LG
Tel: 020-7438 4601

### Internet Information
For online versions of local newspapers try:

*www.theage.com.au* (Melbourne)
*www.smh.com.au* (Sydney)
*www.news.com.au* (all of Australia)

For up-to-date weather reports, visit the Bureau of Meteorology's website at *www.bom.gov.au*.

Telephone numbers for the whole of Australia can be checked out at *www.telstra.com*.

### State Tourism Offices
Local tourist information centers are listed throughout this book. Staff know their region and can make reservations. In addition, many offices have their own websites with extensive listings of accommodations and tours. Some offices produce plenty of good handouts, others just stock advertising brochures and act primarily as booking agencies.

Every state in Australia has its own tourism body that oversees marketing and planning and coordinates visitor information centers across the state. State tourism bodies produce some very useful glossy brochures, but as a general rule, they do not service visitors. However, they do have websites that you will find useful:

**Australian Capital Tourism**
*www.visitcanberra.com.au*

**Tourism New South Wales**
*www.visitnsw.com*

**Northern Territory**
*www.travelnt.com*

**Tourism Queensland**
*www.queenslandholidays.com.au*

**South Australian Tourism Commission**
*www.southaustralia.com*

**Tourism Tasmania**
*www.discovertasmania.com*

**Tourism Victoria**
*www.visitvictoria.com*

**Western Australia Tourist Commission**
*www.westernaustralia.com*

## National Parks Offices

Every state also has offices for the departments in charge of the national parks, the environment, natural resources, and heritage. These are variously named, but all offer information and advice on visiting national parks, heritage sites, and nature reserves. The larger national parks have their own information offices. Details of those are given on the relevant pages.

Increasingly, national park services charge for entry into parks and also levy camping and other fees. Entry into most parks in Queensland, Victoria, and Northern Territory is free, for now. Fees and park passes are listed on state park authority websites, along with useful information on camping, hiking, and other activities. Parks Australia, a national body, controls a handful of national parks, notably Kakadu and Uluru–Kata Tjuta.

**New South Wales**
National Parks & Wildlife Service
59–61 Goulburn St.
Sydney
Tel (02) 9995 5000 or
1-300 361 967
*www.environment.nsw.gov.au*

**Northern Territory**
Parks & Wildlife Service
Goyder Centre
35 Chung Wah Terrace
Palmerston
Tel (08) 8999 4555
*www.nt.gov.au/nreta*

**Parks Australia**
Level 4
5 Farrell Place
Canberra
Tel (02) 6274 1111
www.environment.gov.au

**Queensland**
Environmental Protection Agency
160 Ann St.
Brisbane
Tel (07) 3227 8185 or 1-300
130 372
*www.epa.qld.gov.au*

**South Australia**
Department for Environment and Heritage
77 Grenfell St.
Adelaide
Tel (08) 8204 1910
*www.environment.gov.au*

**Tasmania**
Parks & Wildlife Service
134 Macquarie St.
Hobart
Tel 1-300 135 513
*www.parks.tas.gov.au*

**Victoria**
Parks Victoria
Level 10/535 Bourke St.
Melbourne
Tel (03) 8627 4699 or 13 19 63

**Western Australia**
Department of Environment and Conservation
The Atrium
168 St. Georges Terrace
Perth
Tel (08) 6467 5000
*http://dec.wa.gov.au*

# Hotels & Restaurants

Cities have a wide variety of hotels and restaurants. In the country, except in tourist areas, accommodations and food are much more limited. An Australian specialty is the backpackers hostel, offering cheap but clean beds, sometimes in a dormitory. Aimed at traveling students, they also accommodate many older visitors on a budget. It might be worth checking hotel websites for special offers, but generally online booking agencies, such as www.wotif.com, offer the best prices, often much cheaper than walk-in or phone rates, particularly at top-end hotels.

## ACCOMMODATIONS
### Hotels

All the state capitals in Australia have luxury hotels belonging to international chains. Hotel groups providing high-quality accommodations are easily accessible to travelers. Rooms may usually be booked through the hotels' international network. In both town and country areas throughout Australia, more modest hotel accommodations are also available. In the outback, the only hotel is the local pub. The mainland coasts and the islands of the Great Barrier Reef have resort hotels, with a wide range of recreational activities available to guests.

### Hotel Rates

The ranges of prices given for hotels are based on the standard full price for a double room. Off season, many hotels are prepared to offer guests special rates. It is always worth asking if any such arrangements are available during the time you plan to visit.

### Motels

Travelers on a budget find these establishments good value. They offer comfortable bedrooms, sometimes with small kitchenettes and often with a single as well as a double bed. Most are located on main roads on the outskirts of towns and cities, but some can be found in city centers. Prices range from A$40–100 (U.S. $30–75) per night per room.

### Guesthouses & Homestays

These accommodations range from a simple bedroom in a family home to a fully converted barn or a romantic country house. Prices start at A$60 (U.S. $53) a night, per double room, with breakfast, but can be more than A$200 (U.S. $178) a night in boutique places. Good websites to check include www.australian becandbreakfast.com.au, www .bbbook.com.au, and www.ozbed crdbreakfast.com.

### Hostels

Australia has an extensive and competitive network of hostels. The **Australian Youth Hostels Association** (www.yha.com.au) has hostels nationwide. Standards vary considerably, from the rustic cabin with water drawn from a creek to the 500-bed modern building, with air-conditioning, swimming pool, sauna, launderette, and state-of-the-art kitchen facilities. Top-end prices hover at A$40 (U.S. $36) per night, for a bunk in a dorm. Hostels are aimed at young, independent travelers, although no age restrictions apply. Guests tend to be members of one or more hosteling organizations. Membership privileges include reservations, discounts on travel, activities, and basic supplies. Further details of membership and travel centers may be obtained from the website above. Other hostel networks include **VIP Backpackers** (www .vipbackpackers.com), **Nomad**

Backpackers (www.nomadsworld .com), and **Base Backpackers** (www.basebackpackers.com).

### Farm Stays

Visitors can watch the everyday work on a farm, explore the surroundings, and enjoy hearty farm cooking (see sidebar p. 136). Holders of a visitor's visa are not officially permitted to take paid work on a farm, but voluntary work is possible (see sidebar p. 364).

### Camping, RVs, & Motorhomes

The majority of parks are well equipped with power hookups, hot and cold water, toilets, showers, waste disposal, and coin-operated laundry facilities. Many also have public telephones, television and recreation rooms, a swimming pool, and convenience stores. Occasionally it may be possible to rent bed linen. Site-owned RVs or cabins, often with private sanitary facilities, may also be rented. Automobile associations (see p. 360) publish annual guides to Australian camping and RV parks.

## RESTAURANTS

Major cities have a huge variety of eating places: hamburger joints, vegetarian cafés, ethnic restaurants from a bewildering number of countries, and elegant, celebrity chef–owned restaurants. Small towns, particularly outback ones, will not be able to offer much more than basic eateries.

Closings for holidays may vary from year to year. It is advisable to check and to reserve a table.

## Abbreviations

L = lunch
D = dinner
AE=American Express, DC=Diners Club, MC=Mastercard, V=Visa.

In the following selection, hotels are listed under each location by price, then in alphabetical order, followed by restaurants also by price and alphabetical order.

## ■ SYDNEY

### 🏨 THE OBSERVATORY
**$$$$$**
89–113 KENT ST., THE ROCKS
TEL (02) 9256 2222
FAX (02) 9256 2233
www.observatoryhotel
.com.au
Located a few minutes from downtown, this hotel has a star-ceilinged indoor pool and deep spa baths. Sumptuous guest rooms have marble bathrooms and balconies.
🛈 100 🅿 🚈 Wynard 🖨 🕲
🕲 🖀 🎦 🕲 All major cards

### 🏨 PARK HYATT SYDNEY
**$$$$$**
7 HICKSON RD., THE ROCKS
TEL (02) 9241 1234
FAX (02) 9256 1555
http://sydney.park.hyatt.com
One of the most luxurious hotels in Sydney, with good views of the Opera House. Spacious, comfortable rooms have marble bathrooms and walk-in closets.
🛈 158 🅿 🚈 Circular Quay
🖨 🕲 🕲 🖀 🎦
🕲 All major cards

### 🏨 RUSSELL
**$$$–$$$$**
143A GEORGE ST., THE ROCKS
TEL (02) 9241 3543
FAX (02) 9252 1652

www.therussell.com.au
Rooms and rates vary considerably at this small, friendly hotel. A pleasant roof garden has harbor views.
🛈 30 🅿 🚈 Circular Quay
🕲 All major cards

### 🏨 HOTEL ALTAMONT
**$$–$$$**
207 DARLINGHURST RD.,
DARLINGHURST
TEL (02) 9360 6000
FAX (02) 9360 7096
www.altamont.com.au
Great value with bright, spacious rooms, this funky hotel is in a lively area and a 20-minute walk from the city center. It also has apartments a few doors down.
🛈 76 🕲 🕲
🕲 All major cards

### 🏨 HUGHENDEN BOUTIQUE
**$$–$$$**
14 QUEEN ST., WOOLLAHRA
TEL (02) 9363 4863
FAX (02) 9362 0398
www.thehughenden.com.au
This heritage hotel is close to Sydney's main concentration of antique shops and art dealers. A cooked breakfast is included in the basic rate.
🛈 36 🅿 16 🕲 🕲
🕲 All major cards

### 🍴 CLAUDES
**$$$$$**
10 OXFORD ST., WOOLLAHRA
TEL (02) 9331 2325
http://claudes.com.au
Relaxed, elegant dining, and the best French cuisine in Sydney. Business attire. Reservations essential.
🛎 40 🕒 Closed L & Sun.–
Mon. 🕲 🕲 🕲 All major cards

## SOMETHING SPECIAL

### 🍴 GUILLAUME'S AT BENNELONG
**$$$$$**

SYDNEY OPERA HOUSE,
BENNELONG POINT
TEL (02) 9241 1999
www.guillaumeatbennelong
.com.au
For a special experience, dine under the iconic sails of the Sydney Opera House. The restaurant, with its stunning views of the city and harbor, is under the stewardship of acclaimed chef Guillaume Brahimi and has already claimed a swag of international awards. Contact: enquiries@guillaumeatbennelong.com.au
🛎 80 🅿 🚈 Circular Quay
🕒 Closed D Sun., L Sat.–Wed.
🕲 🕲 🕲 All major cards

---

### 🍴 BATHER'S PAVILION
**$$$$–$$$$$**
THE ESPLANADE,
BALMORAL BEACH
TEL (02) 9968 1133
www.batherspavilion.com.au
A restored turn-of-last-century beach house, converted to a

restaurant, the Bather's Pavilion serves up tasty seafood in a delightful setting. It also has a more casual café section.

85 🚫 🕃
🗃 All major cards

## 🍴 BANJO PATERSON COTTAGE RESTAURANT
$$$$
PUNT RD., GLADESVILLE
TEL (02) 9816 3611
www.banjopaterson.com
A delightful waterfront restaurant set in an 1830s sandstone cottage that was the childhood home of Australia's best-loved poet, Banjo Paterson.
🕐 Closed L Mon.–Thurs. & Sat., D Sun.–Mon.
🗃 All major cards

## 🍴 SAILOR'S THAI
$$$–$$$$
106 GEORGE ST., THE ROCKS
TEL (02) 9251 2466
www.sailorsthai.com.au
Housed in the old Sailor's Home (1864), the restaurant downstairs serves modern Thai food with style. Or squeeze in at long tables in the cheaper canteen upstairs.
80 🚫 🕃 🗃 All major cards

## 🍴 LORD NELSON BREWERY
$$$
CORNER OF ARGYLL & KENT STS., THE ROCKS
TEL (02) 9251 4044
www.lordnelsonbrewery.com
This is one of Sydney's oldest pubs—licensed since 1841—and beside the meals in its brasserie, serves up an interesting blend of beers brewed on the premises, some of them surprisingly potent. If the brasserie's closed, you can still get snacks at the bar.
80 🕐 Closed L Sat.–Wed., D Sun.–Mon. 🚫 🕃
🗃 All major cards

## 🍴 RIPPLES AT SYDNEY WHARF
$$$
56 PIRRAMA RD., PYRMONT
TEL (02) 9571 1999
www.ripplescafe.com.au
Near the Maritime Museum at Darling Harbour, fabulous water and city views complement modern dishes with an emphasis on local produce. A sister restaurant is at Milsons Point underneath the Bridge.
🕐 60 🚫 🗃 All major cards

## 🍴 GOLDEN CENTURY
$$–$$$
393–9 SUSSEX ST.
TEL (02) 9212 3901
www.goldencentury.com.au
Top-notch Cantonese-style cooking. Take your pick of seafood from the huge surrounding tanks.
600 🚇 Central Town Hall
🚫 🕃 🗃 All major cards

## 🍴 ZUSHI
$$–$$$
239 VICTORIA ST.
DARLINGHURST
TEL (02) 9357 3533
This very popular little place has great sushi and box sets at reasonable prices. No reservations, but this restaurant strip, a five-minute walk south of Kings Cross station, has plenty of other options if full.
45 🚇 Kings Cross
🕐 Closed L Sun. 🚫 🕃
🗃 All major cards

## ■ NEW SOUTH WALES

### BLUE MOUNTAINS

### SOMETHING SPECIAL

## 🏨 LILIANFELS BLUE
## 🍴 MOUNTAINS
$$$$$
LILIANFELS AVE., ECHO POINT, KATOOMBA
TEL (02) 4780 1200

FAX (02) 4780 1300
www.lilianfels.com.au
Small, sumptuous resort in a turn-of-the-century guesthouse. In the heart of the Blue Mountains with wonderful valley views. Elegant dining at Darley's Restaurant. Afternoon tea here is an institution. Reservations essential.
🕐 85 🅿 🚫 🕃 🗃 📶 📺
🗃 All major cards

## 🏨 ECHOES BOUTIQUE HOTEL
$$$$–$$$$$
3 LILIANFELS AVE., KATOOMBA
TEL (02) 4782 1966
www.echoeshotel.com.au
Magnificent mountain views, stylish rooms, fine dining, and quiet seclusion make this a wonderful boutique retreat or honeymoon indulgence.
🕐 14 🅿 🚫 🕃 🗃
🗃 All major cards

## 🍴 CAFÉ BON TON
$$–$$$
192 THE MALL, LEURA
TEL (02) 4782 4377
www.bonton.com.au
The restaurant and its menu have Italian influences. Nice atmosphere and good food.
100 🅿 6 🚫
🗃 All major cards

## 🍴 PARAGON CAFÉ
$$
65 KATOOMBA ST., KATOOMBA
TEL (02) 4782 2928
Delightful café serving satisfying, home-cocked, comfort foods and great coffee. It also sells delicious chocolates.
50 🕐 Closed L & D Sun.–Mon. 🚫 🗃 AE, MC, V

### HUNTER VALLEY

## 🏨 PEPPERS GUEST HOUSE
## 🍴 HUNTER VALLEY & RESTAURANT
$$$$

EKERTS RD., POKOLBIN
TEL (02) 4993 8999
FAX (02) 4998 7739
www.peppers.com.au
Guesthouse set in extensive gardens, with comfortable, unfussy accommodations. The in-house restaurant ($$$) has a reputation for fine wines and serves good Asian/Mediterranean-style cuisine.
🛏 47 + homestead 🅿 17
🔲 🈺 🔲 All major cards

### 🏨 OLD GEORGE &
### 🍴 DRAGON INN
### $$$–$$$$
48 MELBOURNE ST.,
EAST MAITLAND
TEL (02) 4933 7272
FAX (02) 4934 1481
www.oldgeorgeanddragon
.com.au
The inn at this former convict settlement exudes old wealth and Victorian charm. Regarded as one of the best restaurants outside Sydney, the **Old George & Dragon Restaurant**, in a separate building, serves Classic Anglo-French dishes like sautéed kidneys with mustard sauce or gamey venison, accompanied by Hunter Valley's best wines.
🛏 5 🅿 14 🔲 🔲
🔲 All major cards

### 🏨 CONVENT AT
### 🍴 PEPPER TREE
### $$$
HALLS RD., POKOLBIN
TEL (02) 4998 7764
FAX (02) 4998 7323
www.peppers.com.au
This converted Roman Catholic convent is about 100 years old and has a pretty vineyard setting. Charmingly old-fashioned rooms, each with a porch. The complex also contains **Robert's Restaurant** ($$$$), recommended for its excellent innovative menu. The basic rate includes breakfast.
🛏 17 🅿 17 🔲 🔲 🈺
🔲 All major cards

## COAST: NORTH
## OF SYDNEY

### 🏨 BYRON BLISSHOUSE
### $$$$$
23 CHILDE ST., BYRON BAY
TEL (07) 4124 9943
www.byronblisshouse.com.au
From Balinese-inspired villas at Belongil Beach to a Victorian cottage in town, some of the coast's most luxurious and stylish accommodations are offered. A day spa is part of the package.
🛏 7 🅿 🔲 🔲
🔲 All major cards

### 🏨 OPAL COVE RESORT
### $$–$$$$
PACIFIC HWY. NORTH,
COFFS HARBOUR
TEL (02) 6651 0510
www.opalcove.com.au
On the beach near town with a big pool, the smaller hotel rooms are good value; suites and villas are more luxurious.
🛏 173 🅿 🔲 🔲
🔲 All major cards

### 🍴 FIG TREE, BYRON BAY
### $$
4 SUNRISE LANE, EWINGSDALE
TEL (02) 6684 7273
www.figtreerestaurant.com.au
Impressive old farmhouse serving Mediterranean-style cuisine. A few miles out of Byron Bay, but worth the drive.
🍴 80 🅿 30 🕐 Closed L Sun.–Thurs. & D Sun.–Wed.
🔲 🔲 All major cards

## SNOWY MOUNTAINS

## SOMETHING SPECIAL

### 🏨 COCHRAN HORSE
### TREKS
### $$$$$
"YAOUK," ADAMINABY, NSW
TEL (02) 6454 2336
www.cochranhorsetreks
.com.au
Run by Peter Cochran, a fifth-generation Snowy River

cattleman whose ancestor, Lachie Cochran, was one of the legendary horsemen who inspired Banjo Paterson's poem "The Man from Snowy River." The three- to seven-day treks run through the rugged, awe-inspiring Snowy River countryside. Meals included. See also p. 114.
🛏 Guests stay in tents
🔲 MC, V

### 🏨 BERNTI'S MOUNTAIN
### 🍴 INN & RESTAURANT
### $$$–$$$$$
MOWAMBA PL., THREDBO
TEL (02) 6457 6332
FAX (02) 6457 6348
www.berntis.com.au
This friendly inn with sauna and spa offers delightful mountain views. Also open during school summer holidays when it is cheaper.
🛏 30 🅿 15 🕐 Open ski season & school holidays
🔲 🔲 All major cards

### 🏨 PERISHER VALLEY
### 🍴 $$$–$$$$$
MOUNT KOSCIUSZKO RD.,
PERISHER VALLEY
TEL (02) 6459 4455
FAX (02) 6457 5177
www.perisher.com.au
This luxury hotel has sumptuous suites, fabulous food, sauna, and spa. Rates include breakfast, dinner, and transfers to the hotel. **Snowgums Restaurant** for excellent dining.
🛏 31 🕐 Open ski season only
🔲 🔲 All major cards

## ■ AUSTRALIAN
## CAPITAL
## TERRITORY

## CANBERRA

### 🏨 HYATT HOTEL
### CANBERRA
### $$$$–$$$$$
COMMONWEALTH AVE.,
YARRALUMLA

---

🏨 Hotel  🍴 Restaurant  🛏 No. of Guest Rooms  🍴 No. of Seats  🅿 Parking  🚉 Rail Station  🕐 Closed  🛗 Elevator

TEL (02) 6270 1234
FAX (02) 6281 5998
www.canberra.park.hyatt.com
Within the Parliamentary Tri-
angle, this beautifully restored
hotel is an elegant example of
Australian art deco. Extensive
landscaped gardens.
🛈 249 🅿 🖨 🅢 🅒 🌊 🛡
🅒 All major cards

### 🏨 CROWNE PLAZA CANBERRA
$$$–$$$$$
1 BINARA ST.
TEL (02) 6247 8999
FAX (02) 6257 4903
www.crowneplaza.com
Renovations have restored this
hotel to among Canberra's
best, and the central location
is unbeatable.
🛈 295 🅿 🖨 🅢 🅒 🌊 🛡
🅒 All major cards

## SOMETHING SPECIAL

### 🏨 OLIMS CANBERRA
$–$$
AINSLIE & LIMESTONE AVES.,
BRADDON
TEL (02) 6248 5511 OR
1-800 020 016 (TOLL-FREE)
FAX (02) 6247 0864
www.olimshotel.com.au
Heritage-listed, split-level
executive apartments around
a landscaped central courtyard.
Cheaper rates on the weekend. E-mail: reservations@
olimshotel.com
🛈 126 🅿 50 🖨 🅢 🅒
🅒 All major cards

### 🍽 WATERS EDGE RESTAURANT
$$$$
40 PARKES PLACE, PARKES
TEL (02) 6273 5066
www.courgette.com.au
Fine-dining delight with French
influences in a wonderful
lakeside locale make this one
of Canberra's best.
🍴 76 🕐 Closed Mon.–Tues.
🅢 🅒 🅒 All major cards

### 🍽 THE CHAIRMAN & YIP
$$$
108 BUNDA ST., CANBERRA
TEL (02) 6248 7109
www.thechairmanandyip.com
Innovative Chinese food is
fused with Western influences
in this stylish restaurant.
🍴 150 🕐 Closed L Sat.–
Mon. & D Sun. 🅢 🅒
🅒 All major cards

### 🍽 PROMENADE CAFÉ
$$$
HYATT HOTEL CANBERRA,
COMMONWEALTH AVE.,
YARRALUMLA
TEL (02) 6269 8810
http://canberra.park.hyatt
.com
The elegant dining room of
the Hyatt Hotel Canberra
complements the Hyatt's art
deco style. The à la carte menu
shows flair, but the buffets are
most popular.
🍴 130 🅿 🕐 Closed D Sun.–
Mon. 🅢 🅒 🅒 All major cards

## OUTSIDE CANBERRA

### 🏨 BRINDABELLA STATION
$$$
BRINDABELLA VALLEY,
BRINDABELLA
TEL (02) 6236 2121
FAX (02) 6236 2128
www.brindabellastation
.com.au
This historic farm in a classic
bush setting offers farm-stay
experience in two-bedroom,
self-contained cottages.
🛈 2 cottages 🅿 🕐 Closed
Dec. 25 🅢 🅒 MC, V

## ▪ QUEENSLAND

## BRISBANE

### 🏨 EMPORIUM HOTEL
$$$$$
1000 ANN ST.,
FORTITUDE VALLEY
TEL (07) 3253 6999
FAX (07) 3253 6966

www.emporiumhotel.com.au
This boutique newcomer has
superb rooms and an attention
to detail that make it Bris-
bane's finest luxury hotel.
🛈 106 🅿 🅢 🅒 🌊 🛡
🅒 All major cards

### 🏨 BEAUFORT HERITAGE
### 🍽 $$$$–$$$$$
BOTANIC GARDENS, EDWARD ST.
TEL (07) 3221 1999
FAX (07) 3221 6895
www.stamford.com.au
In the downtown district by
the botanic gardens, this is one
of Brisbane's top luxury hotel.
All of the elegant guest rooms
overlook the river. **Siggi's Res-
taurant** is one of Brisbane's
most popular eating places.
🛈 252 🅿 250 🖨 🅢 🅒 🌊
🛡 🅒 All major cards

### 🏨 CONRAD TREASURY HOTEL & CASINO
$$$$–$$$$$
WILLIAM ST.
TEL (07) 3306 8888
FAX (07) 3306 8880
www.conradtreasury.com.au
A fine example of Edwardian
baroque. Suites are individually
decorated, and rooms have
antique furnishings.
🛈 130 🅿 🖨 🅢 🅒 🛡
🅒 All major cards

### 🏨 SEBEL KING GEORGE SQUARE
$$$–$$$$$
KING GEORGE SQ.
TEL (07) 3229 9111
FAX (07) 3229 9518
www.mirvachotels.com
This twin-towered luxury hotel
is opposite City Hall and has
good discounts.
🛈 438 🅿 🖨 🅢 🅒 🌊 🛡
🅒 All major cards

### 🏨 WATERMARK HOTEL
$$–$$$
551 WICKHAM TERRACE
TEL (07) 3831 3111
FAX (07) 3832 1290

www.watermarkhotel
brisbane.com.au
Just a short walk from the city
center with park views. Excellent service and value.

🛏 95 🅿 50 ⊟ 🔳 🔲 ⛱
🔳 All major cards

🏨 **BELLEVUE HOTEL**
**$$**

103 GEORGE ST.
TEL (07) 3221 6044
FAX (07) 3238 2288
www.marquehotels.com
Good-value accommodations
right in the heart of town
(opposite the casino).

🛏 99 🅿 30 ⊟ 🔳 🔲 ⛱ 🔳
🔳 All major cards

🏨 **DORCHESTER INN**
**$–$$**

484 UPPER EDWARD ST.
TEL (07) 3831 2967
FAX (07) 3832 2932
www.dorchesterinn.com.au
Faded but comfortable motel-
style rooms with kitchen, near
the train station, offer real
budget value.

🛏 10 🔳 🔲 🔳 MC, V

🍴 **URBANE**
**$$$$–$$$$$**

179 MARY ST.
TEL (07) 3229 2271
www.urbanerestaurant.com
Wonderful fine-dining restau-
rant regularly tops award lists.
Reservations essential.

🪑 60 🅿 🕐 Closed Sun.–
Mon. & L Sat. 🔳 🔲
🔳 All major cards

🍴 **ECCO BISTRO**
**$$$–$$$$**

CORNER OF BOUNDARY &
ADELAIDE STS.
TEL (07) 3831 8344
www.eccobistro.com
Once an old tea warehouse,
now a stylish bistro with
innovative cuisine. Bug (a local
crustacean) is popular on the
changing menu.

🪑 85 🕐 Closed Sun.–Mon. &
L Sat. 🔳 🔲 🔳 All major cards

🍴 **LIBERTINE
RESTAURANT & BAR**
**$$$**

THE BARRACKS,
61 PETRIE TERRACE,
PADDINGTON
TEL (07) 3367 3353
www.libertine.net.au
Interesting Vietnamese-French
cuisine and stunning decor in
renovated heritage buildings is
great for intimate dining or a
drink and snack at the bar.

🪑 100 🅿 🕐 Closed Mon.
& L Tues.–Thurs. 🔳 🔲
🔳 All major cards

🍴 **CHA CHA CHAR**
**$$–$$$**

SHOP 3, PLAZA LEVEL,
EAGLE ST. PIER
TEL (07) 3211 9944
www.chachachar.com.au
Stylish grill restaurant over-
looks the river in the fashion-
able Eagle St. Pier precinct.
Specializes in steaks.

🪑 90 🔳 🔲 🔳 All major cards

🍴 **CROSSTOWN EATING
HOUSE**
**$$**

23 LOGAN RD.,
WOOLLOONGABBA
TEL (07) 3162 3839
http://thecrosstown.com.au
Popular café offering informal
dining in a renovated ware-
house. Simple, well-prepared
dishes won't shred the wallet.

🪑 80 🕐 Closed Sun.–
Mon. & L Tues. 🔳 🔲
🔳 All major cards

🍴 **KIM THANH**
**$$**

93 HARDGRAVE RD., WEST END
TEL (07) 3844 4954
www.kimthanhrestaurant
.com.au
A variety of delicious Chinese
and Vietnamese dishes at very
reasonable prices.

🪑 110 🔳 🔲 🔳 All major cards

---

## PRICES

**HOTELS**
An indication of the cost of
a double room in the high
season is given by $ signs.

| | |
|---|---|
| $$$$$ | Over $280 |
| $$$$ | $200–$280 |
| $$$ | $120–$200 |
| $$ | $80–$120 |
| $ | Under $80 |

**RESTAURANTS**
An indication of the cost of
a three-course meal without
drinks is given by $ signs.

| | |
|---|---|
| $$$$$ | Over $90 |
| $$$$ | $70–$90 |
| $$$ | $50–$70 |
| $$ | $30–$50 |
| $ | Under $30 |

---

🍴 **GOVINDA'S**
**$**

UPSTAIRS AT 99 ELIZABETH ST.
TEL (07) 3210 0255
www.brisbanegovindas
.com.au
Cheap, filling vegetarian meals.

🪑 100 🕐 Closed D Mon.–
Thurs. & L Sun. 🔳 🔲 No cards

## GOLD COAST

🏨 **HYATT REGENCY
SANCTUARY COVE**
**$$$$$**

MANOR CIRCLE, CASEY RD.,
HOPE ISLAND
TEL (07) 5530 1234
FAX (07) 5577 8234
www.sanctuarycove
.hyatt.com
This huge, but exclusive, resort
has a large number of facilities,
including two golf courses.

🛏 243 🅿 ⊟ 🔳 🔲 ⛱ 🔳
🔳 All major cards

---

### 🏨 SHERATON MIRAGE
### 🍴 GOLD COAST
**$$$$–$$$$$**
SEA WORLD DR.,
BROADWATER SPIT, MAIN BEACH
TEL (07) 5591 1488
FAX (07) 5591 2299
www.starwoodhotels.com
Set among beautiful gardens,
this luxury development has
its own secluded beach and
a number of fine restaurants.
The Marina Mirage, a luxury
shopping complex, is nearby.
ⓘ 293 🅿 🚭 🅢 🅒 🌊 🍸
🅒 All major cards

### 🏨 O'REILLY'S RAINFOREST
### GUESTHOUSE
**$$$–$$$$$**
LAMINGTON NATIONAL,
PARK RD.
TEL (07) 5502 4911
www.oreillys.com.au
Elegant family-run guesthouse
dating back to the 1920s and
situated in the cool heights,
3,000 feet (915 m) up in the
Lamington National Forest
with stunning views.
ⓘ 65 rooms, 38 villas
🅒 All major cards

### 🏨 SURF PARADE RESORT
**$$–$$$**
210–218 SURF PARADE,
SURFERS PARADISE
TEL (07) 5538 8863
FAX (07) 5598 8862
www.surf-parade-resort
.com.au
Tower-block apartments in
Surfers Paradise offer great
value, and this is one of the
best. One-bedroom apart-
ments have kitchen, spa bath,
and balconies.
ⓘ 96 🅿 🚭 🅢 🅒 🌊 🍸
🅒 All major cards

### 🍴 OSKAR'S ON BURLEIGH
**$$$**
43 GOODWIN TERRACE,
BURLEIGH HEADS
TEL (07) 5576 3722
www.oskars.com.au

A well-known restaurant that
overlooks the beach. Good
wine and delicious seafood.
🍴 50 🅿 🚭 🅒
🅒 All major cards

### 🍴 SHOGUN, SURFERS
### PARADISE
**$$$**
90 BUNDELL RD.
TEL (07) 5538 2872
Classic Japanese dishes served
with flair. Teppanyaki and à la
carte are offered.
🍴 100 🕐 Closed L
🚭 🅒 🅒 All major cards

## SUNSHINE COAST
## & FRASER ISLAND

### 🏨 HYATT REGENCY
### COOLUM
**$$$$–$$$$$**
WARREN RD., COOLUM
TEL (07) 5446 1234 OR
1-800 637 876 (TOLL-FREE)
FAX (07) 5446 2957
http://coolum.regency
.hyatt.com
Private Mediterranean-style
villas and rooms near the
beautiful Coolum beach.
ⓘ 324 🅿 200 🚭 🅒 🌊 🅒
🍸 🅒 All major cards

### 🏨 NOOSA SHERATON
### RESORT
**$$$$**
HASTINGS ST., NOOSA HEADS
TEL (07) 5449 4888
FAX (07) 5449 2230
www.starwoodhotels.com
Everything you expect from a
luxury hotel, plus a number of
suites and poolside villas.
ⓘ 221 🚭 🅢 🅒 🌊 🍸
🅒 All major cards

### 🏨 KINGFISHER BAY
### RESORT
**$$$**
FRASER ISLAND
TEL 1-800 072 555
www.kingfisherbay.com
The only luxury accommoda-

tions on this World Heritage
island, with modern buildings,
built of timber and finished in
natural colors, strung along a
pretty bay on the west coast.
ⓘ 261 🅿 🚭 🅒 🅒 🌊
🅒 All major cards

### 🍴 BISTRO C
**$$$**
49 HASTINGS ST., NOOSA HEADS
TEL (07) 5447 2855
www.bistroc.com.au
In a town of variable dining
standards, Bistro C has
consistently good food and a
wonderful beachside aspect.
🍴 70 🅒 🅒
🅒 All major cards

## GREAT BARRIER REEF:
## SOUTHERN

### 🏨 VOYAGES HERON
### ISLAND
**$$$$$**
TEL (07) 4972 9055
www.voyages.com.au
Right on the reef, this island
is a diver's paradise and ideal
for snorkeling, with the clear-
est waters in June and July.
Accommodations range from
standard rooms to comfort-
able suites. One beach house
is also available. Meals are
included in the basic price.
ⓘ 116 🌊 🅒 All major cards

### 🏨 LADY ELLIOT ISLAND
### ECO RESORT
**$$$–$$$$**
TEL (07) 4156 4444
www.ladyelliot.com.au
Accommodations are in
simple, waterfront cabins on
this 100-acre coral cay with
good diving and white coral
beaches. Sea turtles visit Oct.–
March. Breakfast and dinner
are included in the basic price.
ⓘ 49 🌊 🅒 All major cards

### 🏨 GREAT KEPPEL ISLAND
### HOLIDAY VILLAGE
**$–$$$**

TEL (07) 4939 8655
www.gkiholidayvillage.com.au
Great Keppel has a big faded
resort, or stay at this modest
place and sample all the
island's beauty at a fraction
of the cost. Basic rooms, tents
on wooden platforms, cabins,
cottages, and water-based
activities are offered.
🛈 17 🚫 All major cards

## GREAT BARRIER REEF: WHITSUNDAY ISLANDS

### 🏨 HAYMAN ISLAND RESORT
$$$$$
GREAT BARRIER REEF
TEL (07) 4940 1234
FAX (07) 4940 1567
www.hayman.com.au
An unbelievably luxurious
resort. The very stylish, three-
level complex includes tropical
gardens, huge salt- and
freshwater pools, and lagoons.
Children welcome. The basic
price includes breakfast; full-
board packages are available.
🛈 214 🖨 🚫 🔞 🏊 📺
🚫 All major cards

### 🏨 VOYAGES DUNK ISLAND
$$$$$
DUNK ISLAND, PMB 28,
VIA TOWNSVILLE
TEL (07) 4047 4740
FAX (07) 4068 8528
www.voyages.com.au
Dunk is one of only three rain
forest islands on the reef. The
popular resort has four levels
of accommodations: bayview
rooms and suites, and slightly
cheaper garden rooms. Full-
board packages and childcare
facilities are available.
🛈 148 🔞 🏊 📺
🚫 All major cards

### 🏨 ELANDRA MISSION BEACH
$$$$
THE POINT, MITCHELL ST.,

SOUTH MISSION BEACH
TEL (07) 4068 8154 OR
1-800 079 090 (TOLL-FREE)
FAX (07) 4068 8596
www.elandraresorts.com
A stylish resort in a rain forest
with private beach. Overlooks
Dunk and Bedarra islands.
🛈 55 🅿 🚫 🔞 🏊
🚫 All major cards

### 🏨 HAMILTON ISLAND RESORT
$$$–$$$$$
PMB
HAMILTON ISLAND
TEL (07) 4946 9999
FAX (07) 4946 8888
www.hamiltonisland.com.au
Accommodations range from
exclusive Qualia pavilions to
rooms in high-rise towers.
Plenty of activities and out-
standing sports facilities. The
basic price is for room only.
🛈 680 🖨 🚫 🔞 🏊 📺
🚫 All major cards

## GREAT BARRIER REEF: NORTHERN

### 🏨 GREEN ISLAND RESORT
$$$$$
P.O. BOX 898, CAIRNS
TEL (07) 4031 3300
FAX (07) 4052 1511
www.greenislandresort.com.au
This coral cay and its sur-
rounding reef are a national
park. The luxury resort houses
92 guests and is reached by
catamaran out of Cairns.
The only drawback is the big
number of day-trippers on the
island until 4 p.m.
🛈 46 🔞 🏊 🚫 All major cards

### 🏨 LIZARD ISLAND RESORT
$$$$$
PMB 40, CAIRNS
TEL (07) 4060 3999
www.lizardisland.com.au
This has everything that you
might expect at an exclusive
resort. The rock-star rates

include all meals and the use
of all facilities, which include
tennis courts, windsurfers, din-
ghies, and fishing equipment.
🛈 40 🔞 🏊 🚫 All major cards

## TOWNSVILLE & MAGNETIC ISLAND

### 🏨 JUPITERS 🍴 TOWNSVILLE HOTEL & CASINO
$$$–$$$$
BOX 1223, SIR LESLIE THIESS DR.,
TOWNSVILLE
TEL (07) 4722 2333 OR
1-800 079 210 (TOLL-FREE)
FAX (07) 4772 4741
www.jupiterstownsville.com.au
This busy waterfront hotel has
spacious and surprisingly quiet
rooms and a good restaurant.
Views to Magnetic Island.
🛈 192 🅿 300 🖨 🚫 🔞 🏊
📺 🚫 All major cards

### 🏨 ISLAND LEISURE RESORT
$$–$$$
4 KELLY ST., NELLY BAY,
MAGNETIC ISLAND
TEL (07) 4778 5000
FAX (07) 4778 5042
www.islandleisure.com.au
A resort with self-contained
cabins set in tropical gardens.
🛈 17 cabins 🅿 9 🚫 🔞 🏊
📺 🚫 All major cards

### 🏨 ALL SEASONS MAGNETIC ISLAND
$$
MANDALAY AVE., NELLY BAY,
MAGNETIC ISLAND
TEL (07) 4778 5200 OR
1-800 079 902 (TOLL-FREE)
www.magneticresort.com
An 11-acre (4.5 ha) garden
resort just over a mile (2 km)
from the beach.
🛈 96 🅿 20 🚫 🔞 🏊
📺 🚫 All major cards

## 🏨 WATERS EDGE THE STRAND
**$$**

63 THE STRAND
TEL (07) 4721 1777 OR
1-800 804 812 (TOLL-FREE)
www.watersedgethestrand
.com
A pleasant seafront hotel with
good service. The ocean view
rooms are worth the extra.
🛏 45 🅿 50 🔄 🚭 🔆 🏊
📺 🔆 All major cards

## CAIRNS

## 🏨 PULLMAN REEF HOTEL CASINO
**$$$$–$$$$$**

CORNER OF SPENCE &
WHARF STS.
TEL (07) 4030 8888
FAX (07) 4030 8788
www.reefcasino.com.au
Well-located near the
waterfront cruise terminal, this
lavish hotel has good rooms,
luxury suites, four restaurants,
and a host of bars.
🛏 128 suites 🅿 🔄 🚭 🔆 🏊
📺 🔆 All major cards

## 🏨 REEF HOUSE
**$$$–$$$$$**

99 WILLIAMS ESPLANADE,
PALM COVE
TEL (07) 4055 3633
FAX (07) 4055 3305
www.reefhouse.com.au
This delightful beachfront
resort sits behind a grove
of paperbark trees. Veranda
rooms have cane furniture,
while Brigadier rooms have a
nostalgic military ambience.
🛏 70 🅿 🔄 🚭 🏊
🔆 All major cards

## 🏨 ROYDON BEACHFRONT HOLIDAY APARTMENTS
**$$$–$$$$**

83–87 VASEY ESPLANADE,
TRINITY BEACH
TEL (07) 4057 6512
FAX (07) 4055 6883
www.roydon.com.au

Past the airport, the good
northern beaches, such as
Trinity Beach and Palm Cove,
are close to the city but
quieter and not as developed
as Port Douglas. Apartment
complexes offer great value,
such as this one opposite
Trinity Beach with spacious
one- to three-bedroom, fully
self-contained apartments.
🛏 20 🅿 🔄 🚭 🔆 🏊
🔆 All major cards

## 🏨 PACIFIC INTERNATIONAL
**$$$**

ESPLANADE & SPENCE STS.
TEL (07) 4051 7888 OR
1-800 079 001 (TOLL-FREE)
FAX (07) 4031 1445
www.pacifichotelcairns.com
This former top hotel is a little
dated but offers great value
and location. Guest rooms in
are on the seafront.
🛏 174 🅿 40 🔄 🚭 🔆
🏊 🔆 All major cards

## 🍽 COOLUMS ON THE BEACH
**$$$**

CORNER OF HIBISCUS LN. &
OLEANDER ST.,
HOLLOWAYS BEACH
TEL (07) 4055 9200
www.coolumsonthebeach
.com.au
Fine food is served in a roman-
tic location right on the beach,
a 15-minute drive north of the
city. Weekend breakfasts are
also popular.
🍴 80 🕐 Closed Mon. & L
Tues.–Fri. 🚭 🔆 All major cards

## 🍽 MONDO CAFÉ BAR & GRILL
**$$**

HILTON INTERNATIONAL HOTEL,
WHARF ST.
TEL (07) 4052 6782
This casual dining café (order
at the bar) has cheap grills,
Asian fare, and wonderful al

fresco dining, with tables on
the waterfront.
🍴 160 🅿 100 🕐 Closed L
🚭 🔆 All major cards

## PORT DOUGLAS & CAPE TRIBULATION

## 🏨 SHERATON MIRAGE
## 🍽 **$$$$$**

PORT DOUGLAS RD.,
PORT DOUGLAS
TEL (07) 4099 5888
FAX (07) 4099 5398
www.starwoodhotels.com
This opulent resort has every
luxury. There are acres of blue
lagoons and pools, and the
grounds reach down to Four
Mile Beach. The **Zai** Japanese
restaurant is part of the hotel.
🛏 294 + 105 villas 🅿 🔄 🚭
🔆 🏊 📺 🔆 All major cards

## 🏨 PINK FLAMINGO
**$$$**

115 DAVIDSON ST.,
PORT DOUGLAS
TEL (07) 4099 6622
FAX (07) 4099 4571
www.pinkflamingo.com.au
Stylish studios and one-
bedroom villas are set in a
delightful tropical garden at
this small resort. No children.
🛏 12 🅿 🚭 🔆 🏊
🔆 All major cards

## 🍽 CATALINA
**$$$**

32 WHARF ST., PORT DOUGLAS
TEL (07) 4099 5287
A great place to head for a
sophisticated dinner after
a day on the reef. It is justly
famed for its seafood, and the
setting is delightful.
🍴 40 🕐 Closed L & Mon.
🚭 🔆 All major cards

## DAINTREE/ CAPE TRIBULATION

## 🏨 BLOOMFIELD WILDERNESS LODGE
**$$$$$**

P.O. BOX 966, CAIRNS

TEL (07) 4035 9166
FAX (07) 4035 9180
www.bloomfieldlodge.com.au
Isolated resort with fan-cooled wooden cabins set in the remote and beautiful Daintree rain forest along the Bloomfield River. Four-night minimum stay. Packages include gourmet meals and air transfers from Cairns.
🛈 17 🖼 🏧 All major cards

### 🏨 DAINTREE ECO LODGE & SPA
$$$$$
DAINTREE RD., DAINTREE
TEL (07) 4098 6100
FAX (07) 4098 6200
www.daintree-ecolodge.com.au
Tree-house chalets set above the rain forest canopy near the Daintree River, with a range of spa treatments.
🛈 30 🅿 30 🏊 🖼 🏧
🏧 All major cards

## SOMETHING SPECIAL

### 🏨 SILKY OAKS LODGE
### 🍴 & RESTAURANT
$$$$$
FINLAY VALE RD.,
MOSSMAN GORGE
TEL (07) 4098 1666
FAX (07) 4098 1983
www.silkyoakslodge.com.au
Air-conditioned colonial-style cabins sit on stilts looking onto the rain forest or the lodge's natural rock swimming pool. Excellent **Treetop Restaurant** and a good selection of Australian wine.
🛈 60 🅿 50 🏊 🏧 🖼
🏧 All major cards

### 🏨 CAPE TRIBULATION RESORT & SPA
$$$$
CAPE TRIBULATION RD.,
CAPE TRIBULATION
TEL (07) 4098 0033 OR
1-800 816 525 (TOLL-FREE)

FAX (07) 4098 0047
www.capetribulationresort.com.au
The resort villas are built of native woods and have lovely views. There is a very pretty beach and easy access to both the Great Barrier Reef and the rain forest of Cape Tribulation.
🛈 40 villas + 27 units 🅿 30
🏊 🖼 All major cards

### 🏨 DAINTREE HERITAGE LODGE & SPA
$$$–$$$$$
TURPENTINE RD.,
COOPER CREEK, DAINTREE
TEL (07) 4098 9138
FAX (07) 4098 9004
www.heritagelodge.net.au
Cabin resort surrounded by rain forest adjoining Cape Tribulation National Park.
🛈 20 🅿 20 🏊 🖼
🏧 All major cards

### 🏨 RED MILL HOUSE
$$$
11 STEWART ST.,
DAINTREE VILLAGE
TEL (07) 4098 6233
www.redmillhouse.com.au
There are excellent bird-watching opportunities at this enjoyable B&B in an old Queenslander house.
🛈 6 🅿 6 🖼 🏧 MC, V

## ◼ NORTHERN TERRITORY

## DARWIN

### 🏨 CROWNE PLAZA
$$$$
32 MITCHELL ST.
TEL (08) 8982 0000
FAX (08) 8981 1765
www.ichotelsgroup.com
Darwin's top hotel in a great location. Good value.
🛈 233 🅿 10 🍴 🏊 🏧 🖼
🏧 All major cards

### 🏨 HOLIDAY INN ESPLANADE
$$$–$$$$$
116 THE ESPLANADE
TEL (08) 8980 0800
FAX (08) 8980 0888
www.holidayinn.com
Striking five-floor, waterfront hotel, set on tropical parkland.
🛈 197 🅿 100 🍴 🏊 🏧 🖼
🖼 🏧 All major cards

### 🏨 NOVOTEL ATRIUM DARWIN
$$$
CORNER OF PEEL ST.
& THE ESPLANADE
TEL (08) 8941 0755
FAX (08) 8981 9025
www.novotel.com
Hotel set in tropical gardens right on the Esplanade. Each of the spacious guest rooms has its own small kitchen.
🛈 138 🅿 80 🍴 🏊 🏧 🖼
🏧 All major cards

---

🏨 Hotel  🍴 Restaurant  🛈 No. of Guest Rooms  🎫 No. of Seats  🅿 Parking  🚉 Rail Station  🕐 Closed  🛗 Elevator

## 🍽 CHAR RESTAURANT

$$$
THE ESPLANADE (CORNER OF
KNUCKEY ST.)
TEL (08) 8981 4544
www.charadmiralty.com.au
In the heritage-listed Admiralty
House, this stylish steak restaurant also serves vegetarian and
seafood dishes. Try the croc
and crab lasagna. The shade
garden is a magic place to dine
on a balmy evening.
🍴 300 🗠 All major cards

## ALICE SPRINGS

## 🏨 CROWNE PLAZA
## 🍽 ALICE SPRINGS

$$$–$$$$$
82 BARRETT DR.
TEL (08) 8950 8000
FAX (08) 8952 3822
www.ichotelsgroup.com
Set on landscaped lawns
beside the Todd River, with
the MacDonnell Ranges as a
backdrop, this is the best hotel
in Alice Springs. Its **Hanuman**
restaurant is a local favorite.
🛏 236 🅿 100 🗠 🗠 🗠
🗠 All major cards

## 🏨 LASSETERS HOTEL
## CASINO

$$$–$$$$
BARRETT DR.
TEL (08) 8950 7777 OR
1-800 808 975 (TOLL-FREE)
www.lassetershotelcasino
.com.au
A sleek modern hotel just out
of town that houses a casino.
🛏 76 🅿 20 🗠 🗠
🗠 🗠 All major cards

## 🏨 DIPLOMAT MOTEL

$$–$$$
CORNER OF GREGORY TERRACE
& HARTLEY ST.
TEL (08) 8952 8977
FAX (08) 8953 0225
http://diplomatmotel.com.au
A central location, friendly
staff, and comfortable rooms.
🛏 81 🅿 80 🗠 🗠 🗠
🗠 All major cards

## 🍽 OVERLANDER
## STEAKHOUSE

$$$
72 HARTLEY ST.
TEL (08) 8952 2159
www.overlanders.com.au
This landmark restaurant
is a carnivore's delight and
is strong on native meats,
including crocodile, kangaroo,
and camel.
🍴 170 🅿 15 🕐 Closed L
🗠 🗠 All major cards

## COBOURG PENINSULA

## 🏨 PEPPERS SEVEN SPIRIT
## BAY

$$$$$
TEL (08) 8979 0281
www.peppers.com.au
"Seven-star" luxury in the
heart of Arnhem Land,
Australia's most spectacularly
remote region. Cottage-style
"habitats"—with fine dining
and the opportunity to visit
rare Aboriginal rock-art galleries. Air access only—flights and
visitor's permits arranged by
the lodge.
🛏 23 🗠 All major cards

## KAKADU
## NATIONAL PARK

## SOMETHING SPECIAL

## 🏨 GAGUDJU CROCODILE

$$$$
FLINDERS ST., JABIRU
TEL (08) 8979 9000
FAX (08) 8979 9098
www.holidayinn.com
This famous deluxe hotel at
Kakadu is shaped like a giant
crocodile. Rooms follow the
curve of the croc's body and
have French windows that
overlook the swimming pool
in its stomach. The reception is
through its mouth.
🛏 110 🅿 60 🗠 🗠
🗠 All major cards

## YULARA (AYERS
## ROCK RESORT)

## 🏨 DESERT GARDENS
## 🍽 $$$$$

YULARA DR.
TEL (08) 8296 8010
FAX (02) 9299 2103
www.ayersrockresort.com.au
Set among extensive gardens
with ghost gums and flowering native shrubs, this hotel
offers friendly service and
secluded modern rooms.
**Whitegums** and the smaller
**Bunya Bar** serve fresh, healthy
fare in a relaxed atmosphere.
🛏 160 🅿 🗠 Some
🗠 🗠 🗠 All major cards

## 🏨 SAILS IN THE
## 🍽 DESERT & KUNIYA
## RESTAURANT

$$$$$
YULARA DR.
TEL (08) 8296 8010
FAX (02) 9299 2103
www.ayersrockresort.com.au
Giant sails shade this airy
three-story hotel. Luxurious
rooms have balconies or
verandas overlooking the
garden. A tower offers views
of Uluru. There are also spa
rooms and deluxe suites.
🛏 231 🅿 20 🗠 🗠 Some
🗠 🗠 🗠 All major cards

## WATARRKA
## NATIONAL PARK

## 🏨 KINGS CANYON
## RESORT

$$$–$$$$$
ERNEST GILES RD.
TEL (08) 8956 7442
FAX (08) 8956 7410
www.kingscanyonresort
.com.au
The hotel has well-equipped,
air-conditioned rooms overlooking the desert. There
are also budget rooms and a
campsite. The resort offers a
choice of buffet, à la carte, and
barbecue meals. It is expensive

for the standards but is the only option at the canyon.

[i] 96 [P] 100 [S] [≈]
[S] All major cards

# ■ WESTERN AUSTRALIA

## PERTH

### [H] INTERCONTINENTAL BURSWOOD & CASINO
**$$$$$**

GREAT EASTERN HWY.,
VICTORIA PARK, BENTLEY
TEL (08) 9362 7777
FAX (08) 9470 2553
www.burswood.com.au
The guest rooms are opulent, the golf course is well groomed, and the house casino is open 24 hours.

[i] 405 [P] 1,000 [≡] [S] [S] [≈]
[≈] [Y] [S] All major cards

### [H] RICHARDSON HOTEL
### [¶] $$$$$

32 RICHARDSON ST.,
WEST PERTH
TEL (08) 9217 8888
FAX (08) 9214 3931
www.therichardson.com.au
Perth's finest hotel, and one of Australia's best small luxury hotels, has spacious rooms, exceptional service, and the excellent **Opus Restaurant.**

[i] 74 [P] [≡] [S] [S] [≈] [Y]
[S] All major cards

### [H] HYATT REGENCY PERTH
**$$$-$$$$**

99 ADELAIDE TERRACE
TEL (08) 9225 1234
FAX (08) 9325 8899
http://perth.regency.hyatt
.com
All you would expect from a luxury hotel, and in a delightful river setting. Two floors are dedicated to the Regency Club. A little dated but look out for great deals.

[i] 367 [P] [≡] [S] [S] [≈]
[Y] [S] All major cards

### [H] NEW ESPLANADE
**$$$**

18 THE ESPLANADE
TEL (08) 9325 2000
FAX (08) 8221 2190
www.newesplanade.com.au
Comfortable three-star rooms in a great location. Outstanding views of the Swan River. Look for online deals to avoid the high rack rates.

[i] 66 [P] 151 [≡] [S] [S]
[S] All major cards

### [¶] 1907
**$$$$**

26 QUEEN ST.
TEL (08) 9436 0233
www.1907.com.au
Housed in a century-old building, fine dining in sumptuous, classic decor. Down an alleyway, this Perth hot spot also has a very popular bar.

[≡] 60 [⊕] Closed L Sat.–Mon. & D Sun.–Mon. [S] [S]
[S] All major cards

### [¶] FRASER'S
**$$$**

FRASER AVE., KINGS PARK
TEL (08) 9481 7100
www.frasersrestaurant.com.au
The menu changes daily in this popular Australian eatery. Always good preparations of native meats and seafood. Reservations essential.

[≡] 160 [P] [S] [S]
[S] All major cards

### [¶] PERUGINO
**$$$**

77 OUTRAM ST., WEST PERTH
TEL (08) 9321 5420
www.perugino.com.au
Italian restaurant with a reputation for fine food and exemplary service. The imaginative menu takes advantage of fresh seasonal produce. Reservations essential.

[≡] 110 [P] 25 [⊕] Closed L Sat. & all Sun. [S] [S]
[S] All major cards

### [¶] LITTLE CREATURES
**$$-$$$**

40 MEWS RD., FREMANTLE
TEL (08) 9430 5555
www.littlecreatures.com.au
Great pizzas, chilli mussels, and a range of more elaborate meals are offered at this landmark Fremantle boutique brewery down by the fishing docks. Reserve a table in the sun at lunchtime.

[≡] 500 [S] [S]
[S] All major cards

## BROOME

### [H] CABLE BEACH CLUB RESORT
**$$$$$**

CABLE BEACH RD.
TEL (08) 9192 0400
FAX (08) 9192 2249
www.cablebeachclub.com
Asian-themed luxury hotel set in landscaped oriental gardens, with rooms, bungalows, and suites, plus an elegant restaurant. Stunning views over Cable Beach.

[i] 263 [P] [S] On request
[S] [≈] [S] All major cards

## THE KIMBERLEY

## SOMETHING SPECIAL

### [H] KIMBERLEY CRUISE CENTRE
**$$$$$**

TEL (02) 9527 3630
www.kimberleycruises.com.au
Cruise along the north Kimberley coast aboard *True North*, a luxury vessel equipped with helicopters for sightseeing access to the rugged plateaus. Six-day trips, meals included.

[i] 18 cabin rooms [S]
[S] All major cards

## SOMETHING SPECIAL

### [H] WILDERNESS CHALLENGE
**$$$$**

TEL (07) 4035 4488
www.wilderness-challenge
.com.au
This company offers 6-, 9-,
and 16-day overland 4WD
camping (tent) safaris through
the heart of the Kimberley.
A 15-day option with stays
in a variety of accommo-
dations—cattle stations, bush
pubs, etc.—is also available.
⊙ each 4WD holds a max of
13 people 🚭 🔥 MC, V

### 🏨 EL QUESTRO
**$–$$$$$**
TEL (08) 9169 1777
www.elquestro.com.au &
www.elquestrohomestead
.com.au
A remote million-acre
(400,000 ha) cattle station in
the eastern Kimberley offering
everything from camping to
five-star luxury and a wide
variety of activities—from
fishing, swimming, and wildlife
viewing to helicopter picnics
at your own private billabong.
Transfers arranged from
Kununurra.
⊙ 78 🚭 🔥 🏊 🔥 All major cards

## NINGALOO REEF

### 🏨 SAL SALIS NINGALOO REEF
**$$$$**
P.O. BOX 471
EXMOUTH
TEL (08) 9949 1776
www.salsalis.com.au
Award-winning, tented eco
camp only a stone's throw
from one of Australia's spectacular but least viewed coral
reefs. Meals, snorkeling, and
sea kayaking included.
⊙ tents 🔥 MC, V

## ROTTNEST ISLAND

### 🏨 HOTEL ROTTNEST
**$$$**
THOMPSON BAY SETTLEMENT

TEL (08) 9292 5011
www.hotelrottnest.com.au
Elegant colonial mansion, built
in 1864, and now a stylish
hotel and restaurant. Rates
include breakfast.
⊙ 18 🚭 🔥 All major cards

## SOUTHWEST

### 🏨 CAPE LODGE
**$$$–$$$$$**
CAVES RD., YALLINGUP,
MARGARET RIVER
TEL (08) 9755 6311
FAX ( 08) 9755 6322
http://capelodge.com.au
Country retreat in the heart
of a plantation. Overlooking
a private lake, the mansion
house has 18 luxurious guest
rooms, a fine-dining restaurant, and cooking classes.
The basic rate includes a
wonderful breakfast.
Children discouraged.
⊙ 18 🅿 20 🚭 🔥
🔥 All major cards

### 🏨 FLINDERS PARK LODGE
**$$$**
CORNER OF LOWER KING &
HARBOUR RDS., ALBANY
TEL (08) 9844 7062
FAX (08) 9844 8044
www.parklodge.com.au
Beautifully styled rooms in
this B&B hotel have a classical
bent. Sumptuous breakfasts
are included in the price.
⊙ 8 🔥 🔥 All major cards

### 🍽 VOYAGER ESTATE
**$$$–$$$$**
STEVENS RD., MARGARET RIVER
TEL (08) 9757 6354
www.voyagerestate.com.au
While touring the wineries,
lunch at this fine winery res-
taurant. Innovative entrees and
mains, or the platters, offer a
number of taste treats.
🍴 95 🕐 Closed D 🚭 🔥
🔥 All major cards

## SOUTH AUSTRALIA

### ADELAIDE

### 🏨 INTERCONTINENTAL
**$$$$–$$$$$**
NORTH TERRACE
TEL (08) 8231 1234
FAX (08) 8231 1120
www.intercontinental.com
Luxury hotel in the heart of
town, beside the Adelaide
Festival Centre.
⊙ 367 🅿 ➰ 🚭 🔥 🏊 🔥
🔥 All major cards

### 🏨 FIRE STATION INN
**$$$$**
80 TYNTE ST., NORTH ADELAIDE
TEL (08) 8272 1355
North Adelaide's original fire
station, built in 1866 and now
a small and funky hotel. An
immaculately restored 1942
fire truck decorates one of the
suites. Breakfast included.
⊙ 3 suites 🅿 Prepaid
parking permit 🚭 🔥

### 🏨 STAMFORD GRAND
**$$$$**
MOSELEY SQ., GLENELG
TEL (08) 8376 1222
FAX (08) 8376 1111
www.stamford.com.au
A high-rise resort on Glenelg
Beach with superb sea views.
⊙ 240 🚭 🔥 🏊 🔥
🔥 All major cards

### 🏨 HILTON
### 🍽 INTERNATIONAL
**$$$–$$$$$**
BOX 1871, 233 VICTORIA SQ.
TEL (08) 8217 2000
FAX (08) 8217 2001
www1.hilton.com
Luxury hotel in the city center.
Excellent restaurant, the
**Grange** (see p. 380).
⊙ 380 🅿 30 ➰ 🚭 🔥 🏊 🔥
🔥 All major cards

---

🚭 Nonsmoking   🔥 Air-conditioning   ➰ Indoor Pool   🏊 Outdoor Pool   🔥 Health Club   🔥 Credit Cards

## ⊞ HOTEL RICHMOND
**$$$**

128 RUNDLE MALL
TEL (08) 8223 4044
www.hotelrichmond.com.au
Small, chic art deco hotel,
built in 1929 and elegantly
refurbished, in the heart of
the city.
ⓘ 30 🅵 ⊠ AE, MC, V

## 🍴 GRANGE RESTAURANT
**$$$$$**

HILTON INTERNATIONAL,
233 VICTORIA SQ.
TEL (08) 8237 0737
www.thegrangerestaurant
.com.au
Not so much a restaurant
as a "dining experience,"
eight-course set menus with
wine are served by one of
Australia's most celebrated
chefs, Cheong Liew, a master
of Asian-European fusion.
🪑 70 🕐 Closed L & D Sun.–
Tues. 🅵 🅵 ⊠ All major cards

## 🍴 CHLOE'S
**$$$$**

36 COLLEGE RD., KENT TOWN
TEL (08) 8362 2574
www.chloes.com.au
A glamorous restaurant with
a modern French menu and
a 20,000-bottle wine cellar
housing some of Australia's
finest wines.
🪑 100 🅿 40 🕐 Closed
L Sat. & all Sun. 🅵 🅵
⊠ All major cards

## 🍴 GAUCHOS
## ARGENTINIAN
## RESTAURANT
**$$$$**

91–93 GOUGER ST.
TEL (08) 8231 2299
www.gauchos.com.au
Famed for its steaks, although
seafood lovers and vegetarians
are catered to as well.
🪑 210 🕐 Closed L Sat.–Sun.
🅵 🅵 ⊠ All major cards

## SOMETHING SPECIAL

## 🍴 THE MANSE
**$$$$**

142 TYNTE ST., NORTH ADELAIDE
TEL (08) 8267 4636
www.themanserestaurant
.com.au
Elegant, innovative cooking
makes this one of Adelaide's
fine-dining gems. The Mon-
day-night degustation menu
showcases the chef's skills.
🪑 60 🕐 Closed L Sat.–Thurs.
& D Sun. 🅵 🅵
⊠ All major cards

## 🍴 JOLLEYS BOATHOUSE
**$$$–$$$$$**

1 JOLLEYS LANE
TEL (08) 8223 2891
www.jolleysboathouse.com
Victorian-era boathouse on
the banks of the Torrens River
serves up trendy contemp-
orary fare in a bright airy
conservatory setting.
🪑 120 🕐 Closed Sun.
🅵 ⊠ All major cards

## 🍴 UNIVERSAL WINE BAR
**$$$**

285 RUNDLE ST.
TEL (08) 8232 5000
www.universalwinebar.com.au
This longtime favorite with
Adelaide's café society always
has some imaginative tasty
treats on the menu and an
interesting wine list.
🪑 80 🕐 Closed Sun.
🅵 🅵 ⊠ All major cards

## 🍴 APOTHECARY 1878
**$$–$$$**

118 HINDLEY STREET
TEL (08) 8212 9099
www.theapothecary1878.
com.au
Elegantly restored 19th-
century pharmacy now houses
the city's best wine bar and an
upmarket Italian restaurant.

🅵 🅵 ⊠ All major cards

---

## PRICES

**HOTELS**
An indication of the cost of
a double room in the high
season is given by **$** signs.

| | |
|---|---|
| **$$$$$** | Over $280 |
| **$$$$** | $200–$280 |
| **$$$** | $120–$200 |
| **$$** | $80–$120 |
| **$** | Under $80 |

**RESTAURANTS**
An indication of the cost of
a three-course meal without
drinks is given by **$** signs.

| | |
|---|---|
| **$$$$$** | Over $90 |
| **$$$$** | $70–$90 |
| **$$$** | $50–$70 |
| **$$** | $30–$50 |
| **$** | Under $30 |

---

## 🍴 SPARROW KITCHEN
## & BAR
**$$–$$$**

10 O'CONNELL ST.,
NORTH ADELAIDE
TEL (08) 8267 2444
The stylish, always popular
café in one of Adelaide's
most popular restaurant
strips has a long menu of
tapas, pizza, pasta, and
good Italian-inspired mains.
Also a favorite for breakfast
on weekends.
🪑 100 🅵 🅵
⊠ All major cards

## 🍴 YING CHOW
**$–$$**

114 GOUGER ST.
TEL (08) 8211 7998
Gouger Street has plenty of
Asian cheap eats. This no-frills
institution is always popular
for good food at low prices.
🪑 60 🅵 ⊠ MC, V

---

⊞ Hotel  🍴 Restaurant  ⓘ No. of Guest Rooms  🪑 No. of Seats  🅿 Parking  🚉 Rail Station  🕐 Closed  🚻 Elevator

## OUTSIDE ADELAIDE: ADELAIDE HILLS

### 🏨 THORNGROVE MANOR
$$$$$
GLENSIDE LANE, STIRLING
TEL (08) 8339 6748
FAX (08) 8370 9950
www.slh.com
Gothic turrets and gables
outside, and an interior to
match, with comfortable, well-
appointed rooms. Adelaide is
20 minutes away by car.
🛈 6 🅿 12 🚭 ❄
🚾 All major cards

### 🏨 ADELAIDE HILLS COUNTRY COTTAGES
$$$$–$$$$$
BOX 100, OAKBANK
TEL (08) 8388 4193
www.ahcc.com.au
Attractive cottages with
antique furnishings, in rolling
countryside. Adelaide is a 40-
minute drive away.
🛈 3 🅿 🚭 ❄ 🚾 MC, V

### 🏨 GRAND MERCURE, 🍴 MOUNT LOFTY COUNTRY ESTATE
$$$–$$$$
74 SUMMIT RD., CRAFERS,
MOUNT LOFTY
TEL (08) 8339 6777
FAX (08) 8339 5656
www.mtloftyhouse.com.au
Sumptuous and elegant
country house in a gorgeous
setting. **Piccadilly Restaurant**
($$$) has a varied menu and
some of Australia's finest
wines. Stunning views over
the valley.
🛈 29 🅿 50 🍴 🚭 ❄ 🏊
🚾 All major cards

## SOMETHING SPECIAL

### 🍴 BRIDGEWATER MILL RESTAURANT
$$$$
MOUNT BARKER RD.,
BRIDGEWATER
TEL (08) 8339 9200
www.bridgewatermill.com.au
This converted mill houses a
stylish lunchtime restaurant
that is said to be one of the
best in the state. Contemporary Australian menu.
🍴 50 🅿 30 🕐 Closed
D & Tues.–Wed. 🚭
🚾 All major cards

## BAROSSA VALLEY

### 🏨 THE LOUISE & 🍴 APPELLATION
$$$$$
CORNER OF SEPPELTSFIELD &
STONEWELL RDS., MARANANGA
TEL (08) 8562 2722
www.thelouise.com.au
One of the Barossa's top
luxury lodges, with sweeping
views over the valleys and hills.
The attached **Appellation** restaurant (reservations essential; tel
(08) 8562 4144, $$$$–$$$$$) is
one of the finest in the valley,
if not the state.
🛈 35 🅿 20 🕐 Closed L
Mon.–Sat. 🚭
🚾 All major cards

### 🏨 COLLINGROVE HOMESTEAD
$$$$
EDEN VALLEY RD., ANGASTON
TEL/FAX (08) 8564 2061
www.collingrovehomestead
.com.au
Peaceful retreat in a beautiful
English-style garden setting.
🛈 5 🅿 6 🚭 ❄
🚾 All major cards

### 🏨 ALMOND HILL
$$$
61 NORTH ST.
ANGASTON
TEL (08) 8564 3451
www.almondhill.com.au
A stylish and friendly B&B,
with spectacular views over
the vine-carpeted valley.
🛈 1 🅿 🚭 ❄
🚾 All major cards

### 🍴 1918 BISTRO & GRILL
$$$
94 MURRAY ST., TANUNDA
TEL (08) 8563 0405
www.1918.com.au
Housed in a restored villa,
this delightful restaurant uses
regional produce and has an
outstanding wine list.
🍴 80 🚭 ❄ 🚾 All major cards

### 🍴 VINTNERS BAR & GRILL
$$$
NURIOOTPA RD., ANGASTON
TEL (08) 8564 2488
www.vintners.com.au
Contemporary restaurant in a
beautiful vineyard setting, with
exquisite service, imaginative
fare, and an excellent wine list.
One of the best in the valley.
🍴 85 🅿 200 🕐 Closed Sun.
🚭 ❄ 🚾 All major cards

### 🍴 BLOND COFFEE
$$
60 MURRAY ST., ANGASTON
TEL (08) 8564 3444
www.blondcoffee.com.au
Breakfast and lunch are served
in this stylish, and extremely
popular, coffee shop.
🍴 50 🕐 Closed D 🚭 ❄
🚾 MC, V

## CLARE VALLEY

### 🏨 CHAFF MILL VILLAGE HOLIDAY APARTMENTS
$$$
310 MAIN NORTH RD., CLARE
TEL (08) 8842 1111
FAX (08) 8842 1303
These luxury, self-contained
apartments in the heart of the
Clare Valley, are just a stroll
from shops and restaurants.
🛈 6 🅿 🚭 ❄
🚾 All major cards

## FLEURIEU PENINSULA

### 🏨 MCLAREN VALE STUDIO APARTMENTS
$$$$

---

🚭 Nonsmoking  ❄ Air-conditioning  🏊 Indoor Pool  🏊 Outdoor Pool  💪 Health Club  🚾 Credit Cards

222 MAIN RD., MCLAREN VALE
TEL (08) 8323 9536
www.mvsa.com.au
Modern one-bedroom apartments with all amenities, fully equipped kitchens, and private verandas with barbecue.
⚊ 6 🅿 ⚊ ⚊
⚊ All major cards

### 🏨 CAPE JERVIS TAVERN
**$$**
CAPE JERVIS
TEL. (08) 8598 0276
Simple but adequate rooms. Counter meals are available.
⚊ 7 🅿 ⚊ ⚊ AE, MC, V

## COOBER PEDY

### 🏨 DESERT CAVE
**$$$–$$$$**
HUTCHISON ST.
TEL (08) 8672 5688 OR
1-800 988 521 (TOLL-FREE)
FAX (08) 8672 5198
www.desertcave.com.au
A quality hotel—with some rooms underground, typical of this opal-mining community.
⚊ 50 🅿 50 ⚊ ⚊ ⚊ ⚊
⚊ All major cards

## FLINDERS RANGES

### 🏨 RAWNSLEY PARK STATION
**$–$$$$$**
WILPENA RD., VIA HAWKER
TEL (08) 8648 0030
FAX (08) 8648 0013
www.raawnsleypark.com.au
This outback station offers a range of tours and accommodations, from camping and simple cabins to self-contained holiday units. The real standouts are the luxury eco villas on private, secluded sites with amazing mountain views.
⚊ 27 🅿 ⚊ ⚊
⚊ All major cards

### 🏨 WILPENA POUND RESORT
**$–$$$$**
WILPENA POUND
TEL (08) 8648 0004
FAX (08) 8648 0028
www.wilpenapound.com.au
Wilpena Pound township is this resort, which runs the campground, shop, visitor center, restaurant, and motel-style rooms in the main building. Rooms are expensive, but the scenic position is unbeatable.
⚊ 60 🅿 60 ⚊ ⚊ ⚊
⚊ All major cards

## KANGAROO ISLAND

## SOMETHING SPECIAL

### 🏨 SOUTHERN OCEAN LODGE
**$$$$$**
HANSON BAY
TEL (08) 8559 7347
FAX (08) 8559 7350
www.southernoceanlodge.com.au
Breathtaking ocean views matched by stunning contemporary architecture at one of Australia's great lodges. Luxury suites are strung out along the cliff top, and the dining and lounge areas have panoramas.
⚊ 21 🅿 ⚊ ⚊ ⚊
⚊ All major cards

### 🏨 KANGAROO ISLAND SEAFRONT RESORT
**$$$–$$$$**
49 NORTH TERRACE, PENNESHAW
TEL (08) 8553 1028
FAX (08) 8553 1024
www.seafront.com.au
The resort overlooks a beach that has a colony of fairy penguins. Rooms, villas, and cottages available.
⚊ 25 🅿 60 ⚊ ⚊
⚊ All major cards

## MURRAY RIVER

### 🏨 RENMARK HOTEL/MOTEL
**$$–$$$**
MURRAY AVE., RENMARK
TEL (08) 8586 6755
www.renmarkhotel.com.au
Carefully renovated three-story art deco hotel on the river. Counter meals, a good bistro ($$), and a dining room.
⚊ 68 🅿 50 ⚊ ⚊ ⚊ ⚊
⚊ All major cards

### 🏨 LOXTON
### 🍴 HOTEL/MOTEL
**$$**
45 EAST TERRACE, LOXTON
TEL (08) 8584 7266
www.loxtonhotel.com.au
Basic rooms in the pub plus motel units. The bistro ($$) is very good.
⚊ 55 🅿 30 ⚊ ⚊ ⚊
⚊ All major cards

## ◼ VICTORIA

## MELBOURNE: DOWNTOWN

### 🏨 GRAND HYATT
**$$$$$**
123 COLLINS ST.
TEL (03) 9657 1234
FAX (03) 9650 3491
http://www.melbourne.grand.hyatt.com
Luxury hotel fitted out in flamboyant style. Four floors form the even more opulent Grand Club. All rooms have marble bathrooms and king-size beds. Excellent service.
⚊ 547 🅿 ⚊ ⚊ ⚊ ⚊
⚊ ⚊ All major cards

### 🏨 THE ADELPHI
**$$$$–$$$$$**
187 FLINDERS LANE
TEL (03) 8080 8888
FAX (03) 8080 8080
www.adelphi.com.au
This central hotel has a cool, almost clinical style but is nonetheless very comfortable. The top floor has an unusual lap pool.
⚊ 34 🅿 ⚊ ⚊ ⚊ ⚊ ⚊
⚊ All major cards

---

🏨 Hotel  🍴 Restaurant  ⚊ No. of Guest Rooms  ⚊ No. of Seats  🅿 Parking  🚉 Rail Station  🕐 Closed  ⚊ Elevator

## 🏨 MELBOURNE MARRIOTT

**$$$$–$$$$$**

CORNER OF EXHIBITION
& LONSDALE STS.
TEL (03) 9662 3900 OR
1-800 331 118 (TOLL-FREE)
FAX (03) 9663 4297
www.marriott.com
Luxury boutique hotel in the
heart of Melbourne. Spacious
rooms and suites, and lots of
pampering for guests.

🛈 185 🅿 😊 😊 😊 🔲 🎽
😊 All major cards

## SOMETHING SPECIAL

## 🏨 THE WINDSOR

**$$$$**

103 SPRING ST.
TEL (03) 9633 6000
FAX (03) 9633 6001
www.thehotelwindsor.com.au
Built in 1883, this elegant
National Trust property is
an Australian landmark. The
nation's constitution was
drafted in one of its upstairs
suites. The hotel has exemplary Old World service with
modern charm. Afternoon tea
here is a special treat.

🛈 180 🅿 😊 😊 😊 🎽
😊 All major cards

## 🏨 ALTO HOTEL ON BOURKE

**$$$–$$$$**

636 BOURKE ST.
TEL (03) 8608 5500
FAX (03) 9606 0766
www.altohotel.com.au
Near Southern Cross Station
in a refurbished heritage
building, this eco-friendly
hotel has a range of smart
accommodations, from small
hotel rooms to three-bedroom
apartments. Check online
booking sites for best rates.

🛈 142 🅿 😊 😊 😊 🎽
😊 All major cards

## 🍴 TAXI DINING ROOM

**$$$$$**

LEVEL 2, TRANSPORT HOTEL,
FEDERATION SQUARE,
CORNER OF PRINCES BRIDGE &
NORTHBANK ST.
TEL (03) 9654 8808
www.transporthotel.com.au
Not a cab driver's diner,
but a slick urban restaurant
serving innovative modern
fare with a dash of Japanese.
Head upstairs away from the
frenetic bar.

🔲 115 😊 😊 All major cards

## 🍴 FLOWER DRUM

**$$$$–$$$$$**

17 MARKET LANE
TEL (03) 9662 3655
www.flower-drum.com
Elegant surroundings,
wonderful Cantonese food,
and a well-selected wine list.
Reservations essential.

🔲 175 🕐 Closed L Sun.
😊 😊 😊 All major cards

## 🍴 GROSSI FLORENTINO

**$$$–$$$$$**

80 BOURKE ST.
TEL (03) 9662 1811
www.grossiflorentino.com
This Melbourne institution,
established for more than 100
years, serves wonderful Italian
cuisine. The downstairs grill
dishes up homemade pastas
and good Italian coffee, while
those seeking more elaborate
fare can head upstairs to the
formal restaurant.

🔲 150 🕐 Closed Sun. & L Sat.
😊 😊 All major cards

## 🍴 CODA BAR & RESTAURANT

**$$$–$$$$**

141 FLINDERS LN. (CORNER OF
OLIVER LN.)
TEL (03) 9650 3155
www.codarestaurant.com.au
A happening basement bar
with tapas-style taste treats
and more substantial mains.

🔲 80 🕐 Closed Mon. & L
Tues. 😊 😊 All major cards

## MELBOURNE SUBURBS

## 🏨 HOTEL URBAN ST. KILDA

**$$$–$$$$**

35–37 FITZROY ST., ST. KILDA
TEL (03) 8530 8888
FAX (03) 8530 8800
www.hotelurban.com.au
Stylish modern rooms close
to the action in St. Kilda make
this boutique hotel a favorite
stay outside the city center.

🛈 80 🅿 😊 😊 😊 🎽
😊 All major cards

## 🏨 SEASONS HERITAGE MELBOURNE

**$$–$$$$**

572 ST. KILDA RD., MELBOURNE
TEL (03) 8506 8888
FAX (03) 8506 8899
www.seasonsheritage
melbourne.com.au
Halfway between the city
center and St. Kilda, with a
tram out front. Value rooms
range from small studios to
two-bedroom apartments.
The old building has three
premium heritage suites.

🛈 142 🅿 😊 😊 😊 🎽
😊 All major cards

## 🍴 STOKEHOUSE

**$$$–$$$$$**

30 JACKA BLVD.
ST. KILDA
TEL (03) 9525 5555
www.stokehouse.com.au
Set in a stunning location
with excellent bay views, this
popular establishment has
a less expensive downstairs
cove specializing in wood-fired
pizzas and a pricier Italian
restaurant upstairs.

🔲 170 😊 All major cards

## 🍴 CAFFÉ E CUCINA

**$$$**

581 CHAPEL ST., SOUTH YARRA
TEL (03) 9827 4139
www.caffeecucina.com.au
It can be hard to get a table
at this split-level Italian café,

---

😊 Nonsmoking 😊 Air-conditioning 🖼 Indoor Pool 🏊 Outdoor Pool 🎽 Health Club 😊 Credit Cards

which is renowned for its food.
Reservations essential upstairs.
🏮 45 🕓 Closed Sun. 🌀
🌀 All major cards

### 🍴 CHINTA RIA JAZZ
$$
176 COMMERCIAL RD., PRAHRAN
TEL (03) 9510 6520
This is a lively blend of
Malaysian cuisine and jazz,
in the heart of Prahran's
restaurant district. It's very
reasonably priced, too.
🏮 50 🌀 🌀 🌀 All major cards

### 🍴 BRUNETTI CARLTON
$–$$
194–204 FARADAY ST., CARLTON
TEL (03) 9347 2801
FAX (03) 9347 9152
www.brunetti.com.au
Just off Lygon St. (Mel-
bourne's Little Italy), this
famous Italian cake shop
offers all manner of sweet
delights, great coffee, and a
few pasta and other dishes.
🛈 200 🌀 🌀 All major cards

### OUTSIDE MELBOURNE: GREAT OCEAN ROAD

### 🏨 QUEENSCLIFF HOTEL
### 🍴 $$$
16 GELLIBRAND STREET,
QUEENSCLIFF
TEL (03) 5258 1066
www.queenscliffhotel.com.au
Grand old Victorian hotel,
built in opulent style in 1887
with wide sweeping verandas
and ornamental iron lacework,
located in a historic seaport,
not far from the start of the
Great Ocean Road. Award-
winning dining.
🛈 15 🅿 🌀 🌀 All major cards

### 🏨 CLAERWEN RETREAT
$$–$$$$$
480 TUXION ROAD,
APOLLO BAY
TEL (03) 5237 7064
www.claerwen.com.au
An attractive and tasteful

place near the famed Twelve
Apostles on the Great Ocean
Road and the pleasant seaside
town of Apollo Bay.
🛈 4 suites, 2 3-bedroom
cottages, & 2 studios 🅿 🏊
🌀 AE, MC, V

## BALLARAT

### 🏨 QUALITY INN HERITAGE
### 🍴 ON LYDIARD
$$$–$$$$$
15 LYDIARD ST. NORTH,
BALLARAT
TEL (03) 5327 2777
www.heritageonlydiard
.com.au
Delightful rooms and suites in
a superbly restored gold rush-
era bank building. The wine
bar serves great tapas.
🛈 13 🅿 ⧓ 🌀 🌀 🌀
🌀 All major cards

## ECHUCA

### 🏨 RIVER GALLERY INN
$$$
578 HIGH ST.
TEL (03) 5480 6902
www.rivergalleryinn.com
This renovated 19th-century
building has spacious, comfort-
able B&B rooms decorated
with antique flair.
🛈 8 🅿 8 🌀 🌀
🌀 All major cards

### 🍴 OSCAR W'S
$–$$$
OLD ECHUCA WHARF
TEL (03) 5482 5133
www.oscarws.com.au
This elegant restaurant is
wonderfully situated on the
town's historic wharf, overlooking a majestic gum-lined
bend of the Murray River. The
food is marvelous, the wine list
superb, and, for a bit of fun, in
the afternoons the kookaburras come down from their
trees to be fed.
🏮 100 🌀 🌀
🌀 All major cards

## MILDURA

### 🏨 STEFANO'S
$$$$
GRAND HOTEL RESORT, 7TH ST.
TEL (03) 5023 0511
www.stefano.com.au
Superb Italian cuisine and a
fantastic wine list are offered
up in the century-old hotel's
wine cellar. The set menu
makes the very best of fresh,
local produce.
🏮 60 🕓 Closed L & Sun.
🌀 🌀 🌀 All major cards

## ■ TASMANIA

## HOBART

### 🏨 ISLINGTON PRIVATE HOTEL
$$$$$
321 DAVEY ST.
TEL (03) 6223 3900
FAX (03) 6234 9053
www.islingtonhotel.com
There are just suites at this
converted 19th-century mansion. Beautiful gardens with a
fine view of Mount Wellington. Breakfast included.
🛈 8 🅿 8 🌀 🏊
🌀 All major cards

### 🏨 GRAND CHANCELLOR HOTEL
$$$$–$$$$$
1 DAVEY ST.
TEL (03) 6235 4535 OR
1-800 625 138 (TOLL-FREE)
www.ghihotels.com
Luxury hotel on the wharf,
with well-appointed, spacious
guest rooms. Great water
views and competitive rates.
🛈 234 🅿 150 ⧓ 🌀
🌀 🏊 🛗 🌀 All major cards

## SOMETHING SPECIAL

### 🏨 HENRY JONES ART HOTEL
$$$$–$$$$$

25 HUNTER ST.
TEL (03) 6210 7700
FAX (03) 6210 7755
www.thehenryjones.com
Once a jam factory, this unique hotel on the waterfront has won numerous tourism and architecture awards for its stunning makeover. Superb suite rooms, unusual artworks, and unrivaled character.
🛈 56 🅿 ⬍ 🚭 🔆
🔆 All major cards

### 🏨 LENNA OF HOBART
### $$$–$$$$
20 RUNNYMEDE ST.,
BATTERY POINT
TEL (03) 6232 3900
www.lenna.com.au
A 19th-century building with Old World charm and a reputation for excellent cuisine at **Alexander's** restaurant (see below).
🛈 50 🅿 50 ⬍ 🚭
🔆 All major cards

### 🏨 COLVILLE COTTAGE
### $$$
32 MONA ST.
TEL (03) 6223 6968
FAX (03) 6224 0500
www.colvillecottage.com
This pretty cottage with a white-picket fence has six comfortable private rooms.
🛈 6 🅿 3 🚭 🔆 🔆 MC, V

### 🍴 ALEXANDER'S
### $$$
LENNA OF HOBART HOTEL,
20 RUNNYMEDE ST.,
BATTERY POINT
TEL (03) 6232 3900
www.alexandersrestaurant
.com.au
Beautifully presented dishes, perhaps the best cooking on the island, from an international menu. Business attire. Reservations essential.
🍴 50 🅿 🕐 Closed L
🚭 🔆 All major cards

### 🍴 MURES UPPER DECK RESTAURANT
### $$
VICTORIA DOCK
TEL (03) 6231 1999
www.muresupperdeck.com.au
Excellent seafood in a great waterfront location.
🍴 50 🅿 40 🚭
🔆 All major cards

## LAUNCESTON

### 🏨 COUNTRY CLUB
### 🍴 TASMANIA
### $$$–$$$$$
COUNTRY CLUB AVE.,
PROSPECT VALE
TEL (03) 6335 5777 OR
1-800 030 211 (TOLL-FREE)
FAX (03) 6343 1880
www.countryclubtasmania
.com.au
Set in manicured gardens, this luxury club and casino has lots of amenities, including one of the best golf courses in Australia. The club is home to the formal **Terrace Restaurant.**
🛈 104 🅿 ⬍ 🚭 🔆 🏊 🛟
🔆 All major cards

### 🏨 CITY PARK GRAND
### $$–$$$
TAMAR & WILLIAM STS.
TEL (03) 6331 7633
www.cityparkgrand.com.au
The comfortable guest rooms have furnishings to match the inn's opulent Victorian style.
🛈 22 🅿 18 🚭 🔆 Some
🔆 All major cards

### 🍴 STILLWATER RIVER CAFÉ RESTAURANT
### $$$–$$$$
RITCHIES MILL, PATERSON ST.
TEL (03) 6331 4153
www.stillwater.net.au
On the Tamar River, casual by day, at night a formal restaurant offering adventurous modern Australian cooking, with à la carte and set menus.
🍴 60 🕐 Closed D Sun. 🚭
🔆 All major cards

## REST OF TASMANIA:

### 🏨 BAY OF FIRES LODGE
### $$$$$
BAY OF FIRES
TEL (03) 6392 2211
www.bayoffires.com.au
Remote, eco-friendly lodge in Mt. William National Park, overlooking a stunning isolated beach. Guests hike into the lodge as part of a four-day package. Outside the walking season (May–Sept.), guests can book accommodations only.
🛈 22 🅿 18 🚭 🔆 Some
🔆 MC, V

### 🏨 FREYCINET LODGE
### 🍴 $$$$–$$$$$
COLES BAY
TEL (03) 6257 0101
www.freycinetlodge.com.au
Environmentally sensitive resort of private cabins (with one or two bedrooms) overlooking Great Oyster Bay in Freycinet National Park. Basic rate includes breakfast. Dine on the premises at the **Freycinet Restaurant,** with fine views and seafood.
🛈 60 🅿 60 🚭
🔆 All major cards

### 🏨 CRADLE MOUNTAIN
### 🍴 LODGE
### $$$–$$$$
CRADLE MOUNTAIN NATIONAL PARK
TEL (03) 6492 2103
www.cradlemountainlodge
.com.au
Inviting timber cabins, some with fireplaces, stand among the forest on the edge of Cradle Mountain National Park. The lodge offers a wide range of activities. The **Highland Restaurant** is wonderful.
🛈 96 🚭 🔆 All major cards

---

🚭 Nonsmoking 🔆 Air-conditioning 🏊 Indoor Pool 🏖 Outdoor Pool 🛟 Health Club 🔆 Credit Cards

# Shopping

There is never any shortage of kitsch offerings for tourists in Australia. Everything from stuffed koalas, made-in-Taiwan boomerangs, insulated beer-can holders (usually adorned with off-color blokey jokes), plastic kangaroos, coasters, and tacky T-shirts can be found in garish little shops from coast to coast. Most Aussie souvenirs—even the little Australian flags waved on Anzac Day—tend to be made somewhere in Asia. Happily, finding something a bit more tasteful, memorable, and authentic to take back home is fairly easy.

## Aboriginal Art

Powerful and unique, Aboriginal art has become a highly prized commodity in the art world, with prices for significant works by top artists stretching into the tens of thousands of dollars. Sadly, big money and the fact that few laymen have a good understanding of Aboriginal art have drawn a lot of hucksters into the business. Consequently, buying Aboriginal art can be tricky. Your best bet is to stick to Aboriginal-owned and -operated galleries or to buy directly from the artists themselves.

The kinds of pieces offered vary from bark paintings to boomerangs, wood carvings, textiles, pottery, and didgeridoos. Good pieces will not be cheap, but then fine art never is. Expect to pay in the neighborhood of A$200 (U.S. $178) (and up!) for a nice didgeridoo, for example. Some Aboriginal-owned galleries include:

### Darwin
**Raintree Aboriginal Art Gallery**
5/20 Knuckey St.
Tel (08) 8941 9933

### Uluru
**Maruku Arts and Crafts**
Uluru–Kata Tjuta Cultural Centre
Tel (08) 8956 2153
*www.maruku.com.au*

### Kakadu
**Injalak Arts and Crafts**
Oenpelli
Tel (08) 8979 0190
*www.injalak.com*

### Alice Springs
**DesArt**
11/54 Todd St. Mall
Tel (08) 8953 4736
*www.desart.com.au*
DesArt represents a number of other Aboriginal-owned galleries in central Australia and can help you contact reputable dealers.

If you are not going into the outback and still want to purchase Aboriginal art, try:

### Sydney
**Aboriginal and Tribal Art Centre**
117 George St., The Rocks
Tel (02) 9247 9625

### Melbourne
**Aboriginal Gallery of Dreamings**
73–77 Bourke St.
Tel (03) 9650 3277
*www.aboriginalgalleryofdreamings.com*

There are other reputable dealers, so it is worth asking around.

## Arts & Crafts

Australia is rich in artistic talent, and visitors can find interesting galleries and craft shops across the continent.

One of Australia's most commercially successful artists is Ken Done, who has marketed his bright, color-splashed paintings into a very popular line of merchandise with a chain of galleries in Sydney and along the Queensland coast. Disdained by Australia's serious art community, Done is revered abroad, particularly in Japan, where exhibitions of his work draw huge crowds. Some of his galleries are:

### The Ken Done Gallery
1–5 Hickson Rd., The Rocks
Sydney
Tel (02) 8274 4500
*www.kendone.com*

### Done Art & Design
4 Spence St.
Cairns
Tel (07) 4031 5592

In Adelaide, the **Jam Factory Contemporary Art & Design** *(19 Morphett St., tel (08) 8231 0005 and 94 Gawler Place, tel (08) 8223 6809, www.jamfactory.com .au)* offers glass, ceramics, wood, textiles, and jewelry made by some of Australia's finest artisans:

## Clothing

Australia has some stylish outback clothing outfitters, and although they are starting to make their mark overseas, their roots are still firmly in the outback, making reliable gear for stockmen, farmers, and stationhands as they have for generations. If you want authenticity, as well as excellent clothes, start with a pair of R. M. Williams boots or the Tasmanian-made Blundstone boots.

The South Australian-based **R. M. Williams** has been making boots and saddlery equipment for outback stockmen and riders since the 1930s. Their kangaroo leather boots are incredibly soft and fit like a glove. The company is also justly famous for its tough moleskin trousers and fashionable outdoor clothing. Its gear is readily available in all cities.

In Sydney, the main store is at 389 George St., tel (02) 9262 2228; in Melbourne, it's at the Shot Tower, Shop 229 Melbourne Central, 300 Lonsdale St., tel (03) 9663 7126. Visit www.rmwilliams .com.au for details on outlets around Australia (and overseas).

Blundstone boots have been a working-class icon since they were first produced in 1870, but lately have been getting a worldwide cachet, popping up as fashion musts on the streets of London and New York. For information on stores, contact the company's Hobart office (tel (03) 6721 2222, www.blundstone .com).

Although Australia is reckoned the world's driest inhabited continent, some of the world's best wet-weather gear is produced here. Both R. M. Williams and Thomas Cook (http://thomascookclothing. com.au), another long-established outfitter, make excellent oilskins, but the old classic stockman's oilskin is made by the Queensland-based Driza-Bone, which has been making them for more than a century. They are widely available around Australia. Information on retailers can be reached by telephone at (03) 9425 2222, by e-mail at drizagpo@drizabone.com.au, or at www.drizabone.com.au.

To round off the Man from Snowy River look and to ward off the fierce Australian sun, slap on an Akubra hat. Ruggedly made out of rabbit fur felt, these hats are beloved by generations of bushmen, who use them for everything from carrying water to picking up a hot billy can out of a campfire. They even wear them on their heads. These, too, are widely available. Consult the company's website at www.akubra.com.au.

Other quintessentially Australian labels are Explorer socks, Stubby shorts, Holeproof underwear, and Chesty Bonds T-shirts and singlets. These can be found in most department stores.

## Opals

Australia has 95 percent of the world's supplies of opal. Most of it is found in outback South Australia, near the town of Coober Pedy, with the New South Wales town of Lightning Ridge and the South Australian town of Andamooka accounting for much of the rest.

Almost every jeweler and souvenir shop in Australia seems to offer opals in one form or another, with special tax-free prices for tourists.

As with any precious stone, there are a number of factors that go into determining the value of an opal, such as clarity, color, and pattern. The first criterion is the base color of the stone. A black opal is the most valuable, followed by a crystal (or almost transparent) opal, with milky opals bringing up the rear. The next thing to look for is the dominant color. Red-fire opal is the most valuable, followed by green, then blue. The pattern of colors on the stone is also important in determining its value. Harlequin opal, in which the colors are in large defined patches, is the most sought after. Pinfire opal, with its thousands of tiny specks of color, is generally less valuable.

The stones themselves come in three grades. The most valuable is solid opal, followed by doublets (a two-part stone consisting of precious opal glued to another, less valuable opal), then triplets (a three-part stone with a core of precious opal, a backing of a less valuable stone and a transparent top piece). Accurately assessing opal is a job for experts. Stick to reputable jewelers, shop around, and compare prices.

In Sydney, the following shops offer more than most:

National Opal Collection
60 Pitt St.
Tel (02) 9251 1599
www.nationalopal.com
Stocks opal jewelry and loose opals. They are unusual in mining and cutting their own stones, and have a shopfront museum with opalized fossils, a recreated opal mine, and more.

Opal Fields
190 George St., The Rocks
Tel (02) 9247 6800
Australian opal stones and jewelry featuring the collections of seven designers. Also a museum of opal fossils and specimens.

## Wine

Australia is justifiably famous for its bold, fruity, and well-crafted wines, but with more than 2,300 different winemakers around the country, navigating so many unknown labels can be a little confusing for visitors. A number of useful guides are on the market, two of the best being the Penguin Good Australian Wine Guide and James Halliday's Australian Wine Companion, which are available in most bookstores.

The major wine districts have helpful visitor centers:
Hunter Valley (see pp. 110–111)
Margaret River (see pp. 226–227)
Barossa Valley (see pp 266–267)
McClaren Vale, Clare Valley, and Coonawarra (see pp. 264–265)

# Activities

Australia's sunny climate and open-air lifestyle lend themselves to a huge range of activities for visitors. Plan your holiday carefully and book ahead if you are specific about what you want to do. Otherwise, find help at a visitor information center. They will be able to tell you of the local possibilities and can probably book you a suitable option on the spot.

## Camel Trekking

Experience outback Australia as the original explorers did: from the back of a dromedary. You can camel-trek in Broome (see p. 239), Silverton (see p. 117), and many other places around the country, but the Northern Territory has the biggest concentration of camel-trek operators. In Alice Springs, **Pyndan Camel Tracks** *(Jane Road, tel 04 1617 0164, www .cameltracks.com)* does short treks around the desert, and **Camels Australia** *(Stuarts Well, Stuart Highway, tel (08) 8956 0925, www.camels-australia.com .au)* has overnight camping treks to High River, Renners Rock, Doctors Stones, and Homestead. **Uluru Camel Tours** *(tel (08) 8950 3030, http://ulurucameltours .ananguwaai.com.au)* at Yulara will take you around the Rock.

For a real camel adventure, check out **Outback Camel Company** *(tel (07) 3850 7600, www.cameltreks.com.au)*, which runs treks and expeditions around the country, including a 28-day crossing of the Simpson Desert..

## Cruising

Queensland's idyllic Whitsunday Islands are one of the world's most beautiful places for yachts and cruising. For those visitors to Australia who like to do it themselves, charter boats can be arranged on the Whitsundays (see p. 162).

Tour operators offer daylong and multiday sailing cruises, some on well-known racing yachts of the past. Among them are:

*Maxi Ragamuffin*
Tel (07) 4946 7777
*Apollo* (of Sydney–Hobart Yacht Race fame)
Tel 1-800 635 334

## Diving

Exploring the Great Barrier Reef is a highlight of a visit to tropical Queensland, and if you do not know how to dive, there are numerous diving schools all along the Queensland coast eager to teach you, and some of the world's finest coral reefs in which to learn. As with anything, it is wise to shop around and be wary of cut-rate operators. Expect to pay in the neighborhood of A$400 (U.S. $355) for a five-day open-water certification course.

Cairns has a reputation for being the reef's diving capital, as well as typically being the first port-of-call for Great Barrier Reef visitors. A list of a few long-standing operators includes: **Deep Sea Divers Den** *(tel (07) 4046 7333, www.diversden.com.au)*, **Pro Dive** *(tel (07) 4031 5255, www.prodivecairns. com)*, **Tusa Dive** *(tel (07) 4031 1028, www.tusadive.com)*. Airlie Beach and Townsville are other popular dive-school locations.

If you are already a certified diver or simply want to do some snorkeling on the reef, finding a boat to take out to the reef is about as difficult as finding a casino in Las Vegas. They come in all shapes and sizes, from gleaming catamarans to yachts to powerboats, and cater to all budgets. Trips last from a day to several days.

**Falla**, *(tel (07) 4041 2001, www .fallacruises.com.au)* and the above-mentioned Tusa Dive are two

well-established operators in Cairns, but there are many others.

Good diving can be found in other locations, of course, from Ningaloo Reef in Western Australia to the wrecks scattered around Tasmania's King Island. Consult local tourist authorities for advice and recommendations (see also sidebar p. 168).

## Four-wheel-drive Safaris

The Cape York Peninsula, the Northern Territory, and Western Australia's rugged and remote Kimberley offer some of Australia's best outback adventuring. Four-wheel-drive vehicles are necessary to get into the wildest and most interesting regions, and if you don't care to risk the driving yourself, numerous outfitters from Cairns to Darwin, Alice Springs, and Broome will take you. Standards vary, so shop around and consult local tourist authorities. One well-established outfitter is Cairns-based **Wilderness Challenge** *(tel (07) 4035 4488, e-mail: info@wilderness-challenge.com.au, www.wilderness-challenge.com.au)*, which leads treks to the tip of Cape York and through the heart of the Kimberley. (See also sidebar p. 242.)

## Surfing

Right from the moment Hawaiian surfer Duke Kahanomoku brought surfing to Australia (at Sydney's Freshwater Beach) in 1915, riding the breakers that roll into the island continent's 24,000 miles (39,000 km) of coastline has been an Australian passion.

If you do not know how to surf but would like to learn, there are plenty of surfing schools to teach you. Enquire at the local tourist information office or at surf and dive shops.

**New South Wales:** One of the best known beaches is Bondi (see pp. 96–97), but Manly and Sydney's other northern beaches offer good surf, too. South of Sydney, probably the best is at Cronulla. Byron Bay, on the NSW north coast, is another very popular surfing hangout.

**Southern Queensland:** A string of surfing beaches stretches along the Gold Coast. As well as Surfers Paradise, try Burleigh Heads or Kirra. The Sunshine Coast also has good surfing right up to Noosa Heads.

**Western Australia:** You'll find some great surf around Margaret River, about 140 miles (224 km) south of Perth.

**South Australia:** The best known surfing beach in South Australia is far-flung Cactus Beach, west of Ceduna. There are more convenient places on both the east and west sides of the Fleurieu Peninsula, though.

**Victoria:** The Bells Easter Classic competition is held on Bells Beach, near Torquay on the spectacular Great Ocean Road, about 100 miles (160 km) southwest of Melbourne. Wilsons Promontory and the ocean side of the Mornington Peninsula also offer good surfing.

**Tasmania:** There is good surf around Marrawah on the west coast, and the beaches near St. Helens are just some of the surfing locations on the east coast, but the water around the island is cold.

## White-water Rafting

Australia may be the world's driest inhabited continent, but when the rivers run here, they really run, with Tasmania, the

Snowy Mountains, and the jungle-clad mountains near Cairns offering exhilarating wild water. Two of the better known wilderness operators are:

**World Expeditions**
Sydney Office
Level 5, 71 York St., Sydney
Tel (02) 8270 8400 or
1-300 720 000
www.worldexpeditions.com

**Peregrine Adventure**
Head Office
Level 3, 380 Lonsdale St.,
Melbourne
Tel 1-300 143 119
www.peregrineadventures.com

By far the most remote and wildest rafting option is on Tasmania's Franklin River, a challenging two-week-long trek through some of the most remote wilderness on the planet. Both of the above operators run expeditions on the Franklin.

## Further Information

Below is a list of organizations to contact for information about specific activities.

**Bird-watching**
Birding Australia
Suite 2-05, 60 Leicester St.,
Carlton, VIC 3053
Tel (03) 9347 0757
www.birdsaustralia.com.au

**Canoeing**
Australian Canoeing Inc.
1st Floor, Sports House,
6 Figtree Drive,
Sydney Olympic Park,
Homebush Bay, NSW
Tel (02) 8116 9727
www.canoe.org.au

**Cycling**
Cycling Australia
Level 2, 280 Coward St.,
Mascot, NSW 2020

Tel (02) 9339 5800
www.cycling.org.au

**Ecotourism**
Ecotourism Australia
Suite 4, Plumridge House,
36 Agnes St.,
Fortitude Valley, QLD 4006
Tel (07) 3252 1530
www.ecotourism.org.au

**Fishing**
Recfish Australia
P.O. Box 187
Grange, QLD 4051
Tel (02) 3356 1111
www.recfish.com.au

**Golf**
Golf Australia
Level 3, 95 Coventry St.,
South Melbourne, VIC 3205
Tel (03) 9626 5050
www.golfaustralia.org.au

**Sailing**
Yachting Australia
Level 1, 22 Atchison St.,
St. Leonards,
Sydney, NSW 2065
Tel (02) 8424 7400
www.yachting.org.au

**Surfing**
Surfing Australia
P.O. Box 1613,
Kingscliff, NSW 2487
Tel (02) 6674 9888
www.surfingaustralia.com

**Tennis**
Tennis Australia
Batman Ave.
Melbourne, VIC 3000
Tel (03) 9626 5050
www.tennis.com.au

# INDEX

**Bold** page numbers
indicate illustrations.
CAPS indicates
thematic categories.

**A**
Aboriginal culture **22, 209**
    art **181, 202,** 202–203,
        257–258, 386
    dance 176
    Dreamtime 208
    history 20–23, 133, 332–333
    literature 56
    music **57,** 59
    place names 327
    rock art **32–33,** 176, 179,
        188–189, 190, 202–203, 327
    sacred places 206, 208
    tourist experiences **11,**
        196–197, 209
Activities 388–389
Adelaide 252–258
    Adelaide Botanic Gardens 257
    Adelaide Cricket Ground 258
    Adelaide Festival Centre 256
    Art Gallery of South Australia
        257
    Ayers House 257
    Elder Park 256
    festivals **272,** 272–273
    Government House 256
    hotels and restaurants 379–381
    Light's Vision 258
    Lion Arts Centre 256
    map 252–253
    Migration Museum 257
    North Adelaide 258
    North Terrace 254, 255
    Parliament House 255
    St. Peter's Cathedral **257,** 258
    shopping 256, 386
    South Australian Museum 257
    State Library 256–257
    Tandanya 257–258
Adelaide area 259–263, 266–271,
    274–279
    Adelaide Hills 260–263, 266,
        381
    Angaston 268
    Barossa Valley **249,** 262, 263,
        265, 267–268, 273
    Clare Valley **264,** 266, 381
    Cleland Wildlife Park **260,** 261
    Coonawarra 266
    Coorong 275–276
    Encounter Bay 275
    Fleurieu Peninsula 262–263,
        381–382
    Flinders Ranges NP 209,
        277–279, **279,** 382
    Glenelg **259,** 259–260
    Goolwa 275–276
    Hahndorf 261–262
    Heysen Trail 262, 279

Kangaroo Island 125, 205,
    268–271, **269, 271,**
    274, 382
Lower Murray River 276–277,
    **277**
Mannum 276–277
McLaren Vale 263, **263**
Mount Lofty Ranges 261, **263**
Murray River Valley 266
Naracoorte Caves Park 266
Penola 266
Port Adelaide 260
Quorn 278
Southern Vales 263
Victor Harbor **274,** 274–275
Wilpena Pound 278–279
wine regions 263, **263,**
    266–268
Adelaide Hills 260–263, 266, 381
Air travel 358, 359
Albany 225
Alice Springs **198,** 198–201, 286,
    377, 386
Alice Springs Desert Park, Alice
    Springs 199
Alien species 72, 352
Alpine country, Victoria 316–317
Amusement parks 145, 304
Angaston 268
Antarctica 126
Anzac Day 50, 134
Aquariums 92–93, 130, 167
Architecture **63,** 63–64, 121, 294
Argyle Diamond Mine **234,** 235
Arltunga 200
Arnhem Land **32–33,** 196–197, 209
Art galleries *see* Museums
Art Gallery of Ballarat 320
Art Gallery of New South Wales,
    Sydney 82, **82**
Art Gallery of South Australia,
    Adelaide 257
Arthur's Seat SP 306
Arts 56–65
    Aboriginal **181, 202,** 202–203,
        257–258, 386
    architecture **63,** 63–64, 121,
        294
    cinema 60–61, 95, 132, 145,
        233, 235
    dance 59, 176
    festivals 272–273
    literature 56, 58–59, 225
    music **57,** 59–60, **60,** 109,
        **109,** 356
    painting 64–65, **65,** 117
    rock art **32–33,** 176, 179, 188–
        189, 190, 202–203, 327
    television 61–63, 363
    theater 59, 256
Atherton Tablelands 170–171, **171**
*Australia* (movie) 235
Australia Zoo, Sunshine Coast
    125, 147
Australian Capital Territory
    Canberra 65, 127–136,
        370–371
    hotels and restaurants 370–371
    map 129
    National Trust 363
    tourism website 366

Australian Institute of Sport,
    Canberra 130
Australian Museum, Sydney 89
Australian National Botanic Gardens,
    Canberra 130
Australian National Maritime
    Museum, Sydney 93
Australian Rules football 318–319,
    **319,** 357
Australian Stockman's Hall of Fame,
    Longreach 152–153
Australian War Memorial, Canberra
    **134,** 135–136
Ayers House, Adelaide 257
Ayers Rock *see* Uluru

**B**
Balladonia 245
Ballarat **63, 320,** 320–321, 384
Balmain, Sydney 95
Balmoral, Sydney 97
Bank hours 363
Barcaldine 152
Barossa Valley **249,** 262, 263, 265,
    267–268, 273, 381
Barrington Tops NP 118, 120
Bass Strait Islands 354
Bathurst Island **196,** 197
Battery Point, Hobart 336
Bawaka Cultural Experiences 196
Bay of Fires 349
Beechworth 316–317
Bega 113
Bellingen 120
Belltrees Station 111
Ben Boyd NP 113
Bendigo 321
Benedictine Abbey Guesthouse,
    New Norcia 219
Bermagui 113
Bicentennial Tree **224,** 225
Bicycle Victoria 305
Bicycling 77, 216, 305, 389
Birding 68–69, 245–246, 389
Birdsville 176
Black Mountain, Canberra 130
Blackall 152
Blackall Range 147
Block Arcade, Melbourne 303
Blue Mountains **104,** 104–105, 369
Boat trips 361, 388, 389
    Brisbane River 143
    Coral Sea 167
    Franklin-Gordon Wild Rivers NP
        345, **345**
    Great Barrier Reef 160
    Hawkesbury River 118
    Murray River 276–277, 325
    Nitmiluk NP 195
    Sydney Harbour 79
    Tasmania 333
    Whitsunday Islands 162
    Yarra River 302
Bogong High Plains 316, 317
Bondi Beach, Sydney 77, **96,** 96–97
Boomerangs 23
Border Village 247
Botanic Garden, Perth 216

Boulder 241
Bradman, Sir Donald 91
Brampton Island 162
Bright 317
Brisbane **42–43, 140,** 140–143,
    371–372
    map 141
Brisbane Botanic Gardens,
    Brisbane 142
Broken Hill **116,** 116–117
Broome **232,** 232–233, 378
Bruny Island 339
Bunbury 125, 226
Bunda Cliffs 247, **247**
Bungle Bungle NP 173, **236,**
    236–237
Burke and Wills expedition 44–45
Burketown 178
Burley Griffin, Lake, Canberra **128,**
    130–131
Burnie 348
Bus travel 360–361
Bushfires **106,** 106–107, **107**
Bushrangers **322,** 322–323
Bushwalking see Hiking
Byron Bay 121, **121**

C

Cable Beach, Broome 232, **232,** 233
Cabramatta, Sydney 77
Caiguna 245
Cairns 160, **166,** 167–168, 375, 386
Camels **198,** 199, **232,** 233, 388
Camping 367
Canberra 127–136
    Australian Institute of Sport 130
    Australian National Botanic
        Gardens 130
    Australian War Memorial **134,**
        135–136
    Black Mountain 130
    Civic Centre **127,** 131–132
    hotels and restaurants 370–371
    Lake Burley Griffin **128,**
        130–131
    map 131
    Museum of Australian
        Democracy 132
    National Film & Sound Archive
        132
    National Gallery of Australia
        65, 135
    National Library of Australia
        131
    National Museum of Australia
        132
    Parliament House 132–133
Cane toads 180
Canoe trips 195, 389
Canopy walkways 174, 225, 338
Cape York Peninsula 174–177, **175**
Capricorn, Tropic of 150–153
Car rentals 359–360
Carpentaria, Gulf of 177–179
Carseldine, Lee **90**
Cascade Brewery 337
Castlemaine 321
Caves 108, 227, 245, 280–281

Cellular phones 362
Central Mall Melbourne **289**
Central Station, Fraser Island 149
Children, traveling with 361
Chinatown, Broome 233
Chinese Garden, Sydney 93
Christmas Island 124, 126
CHURCHES
    St. Andrew's Cathedral, Sydney
        86
    St. Peter's Cathedral, Adelaide
        **257,** 258
Cinema 60–61, 95, 132, 145, 233,
    255
Circular Quay, Sydney 74, 76, 84, **85**
City Botanic Gardens, Brisbane
    142–143
City Hall, Brisbane 143
Civic Centre, Canberra **127,** 131–132
Clare Valley **264,** 266, 381
Cleland Wildlife Park **260,** 261
Climate 10, 26–27, 356
Clothing 362, 386–387
Cocklebiddy 245
Cocos Islands 124, 126
Coffs Harbour 120–121
Colonial Tramcar Restaurant,
    Melbourne 293
Conversions 362
Convict colonies see Prisons
    and prisoners
Coober Pedy **280,** 280–281,
    286, 382
Cook, James 36, **37,** 38–39
Cooking lessons 218
Cooktown 175
Coolgardie 241
Cooloola NP 147–148
Cooma 114
Coonawarra 266
Coorong 275–276
Coot-tha, Mount, Brisbane 142
Cradle Mountain–Lake St. Clair NP
    173, **346,** 346–347
Cricket **38–39, 90,** 90–91, 258
Crocodiles 70, **190,** 191, 197
Crown Casino, Melbourne 295–296
Currency 11, 363
Customs (border control) 357
Cycling see Bicycling
Cyclone Tracy 184

D

Daintree NP **30, 169,** 169–170, 173,
    375–376
Daly Waters 288
Dance 59, 176
Dandenong Ranges NP 309
Darling Harbour, Sydney 77, 92–93
Darlinghurst, Sydney 77, 94–95
Darwin **184,** 184–187, 376–377, 386
    map 185
Day Dream Mine 117
Daydream Island 163–164
Daylesford 321
Devil's Marbles Conservation
    Reserve 287, **287**
Diamond mines **234,** 235

Dingoes 148, 149
Disabilities, travelers with 364
Diving **71,** 153, 168, 221, 388
Dolphins 226, **228,** 229
Dorrigo NP 120
Dreamtime 208
DRIVES
    Gibb River Road, Western
        Australia 238–239
    Great Ocean Road, Victoria
        310–315
    Huon Valley, Tasmania
        338–339
    Pacific Highway, New South
        Wales 118–121, **121**
    scenic loop drive, Tasmania
        348–351
    Stuart Highway, South Australia
        284–288
    Tropic of Capricorn,
        Queensland 150–153
Driving 237, 359–360
Drought 200
Drugs 357
Dunk Island 165, 167

E

Echuca **324,** 325, 384
Ecotourism 389
Eden 113
El Questro Wilderness Park
    238–239
Elder Park, Adelaide 255
Electricity 362
Elizabeth Bay, Sydney 95
Elizabeth Farm 64
E-mail 362
Embassies and consulates 358,
    364–365
Emerald 151
Emergencies 364
Encounter Bay 275
Environmental concerns 344, **344**
Esplanade, St. Kilda 304
Eucla **244,** 246
Eureka Stockade 46–48
Exmouth 231
EXPERIENCES
    Aboriginal Australia 209
    Adelaide festivals 273
    Adelaide markets 256
    Anzac Day 50
    Australian English language 19
    Australian Rules football 318
    Bay of Fires walk 349
    Biking Melbourne 305
    Birdsville horse races 176
    Brisbane boat trips 143
    bushwalking 205
    buying Aboriginal art 203
    buying opals 31
    camel treks 233
    Cape York Peninsula four-
        wheel-drive trip 174
    cattle mustering 281
    Colonial Tramcar Restaurant,
        Melbourne 293
    cooking lessons 218

Eyre Bird Observatory
bird-watching 245
farm stays 136
Great Barrier Reef cruises 160
Great Barrier Reef diving 168
Hawkesbury River houseboats
118
Henley-on-Todd regatta,
Alice Springs 199
Lake Eyre fly-over 286
Melbourne photo walking
tours 296
Mount Isa mine tour 178
Murray River houseboats 276
outback Australia 242
Overland Track, Tasmania 347
penguin viewing 307
Perth excursions 216
platypus sightings 261
Priscilla tours 95
sea kayaking 167
seasonal work 267
Snowy River horseback
riding 115
surfing 315
swimming with whale sharks 231
Sydney Harbour cruises 79
Tasmania fishing 353
Tasmanian devil conserva-
tion 343
train journeys 283
turtle nesting 147
Vegemite 25
volunteering 255
Whitsunday Islands sailing
trips 162
wildlife 125
wine courses 265
Exploration and discovery 33–39,
43–45
maps 34–35, 40
Eyre, Lake 286
Eyre Bird Observatory 245–246
Eyre Highway 243–248
Eyre Peninsula 125, 246

**F**
Fairfield Park Boathouse 305
Fairy penguins 307
Family vacations 361
Farm stays 136
Featherdale Wildlife Park, Sydney
100, 125
Ferry trips 79, 333
Festivals 98, **99,** 176, **272,** 272–273,
356–357
Finke NP 201
Fires **106,** 106–107, **107**
Fishing 113, 177, 178, **352,** 352–353,
358, 389
Fitzgerald River NP 222
Fitzroy, Melbourne 296
Fitzroy Gardens, Melbourne 303
Five Rivers Lookout 238
Fleurieu Peninsula 262–263,
381–382
Flinders Chase NP 205, 269, 270,
271, **271**
Flinders Island 354

Flinders Ranges NP 209, 277–279,
**279,** 382
Flinders Street Railway Station,
Melbourne 298, **298**
Flora **66,** 70–72, **211, 222,** 222–
223, **223**
Florence Falls **192,** 193
Food and drink **24,** 24–25, 218, 258,
265, 357, 362
Football 318–319, **319,** 357
Fossils 173, 179–180
Four-wheel-drive trips 174, 242,
**355,** 359, 388
Franklin-Gordon Wild Rivers NP
345, **345**
Franklin River 344, 345, **345**
Fraser Island 148–149, **149,**
172–173, 373
Fremantle **217,** 217–218
Freycinet NP 173, **348,** 350
Frontier Camel Farm, Alice Springs
199
Furneaux Islands 354

**G**
Gallipoli, Turkey **48, 49**–50
Gantheaume Point 233
GARDENS
Adelaide 257
Alice Springs 199
Brisbane 142–143
Canberra 130
Melbourne 294, **295,** 299, 302,
**302,** 303
Perth 216
Sydney 78, 84, 93, 98
Gay and lesbian travelers 362
Geeveston 338
Geography 26–31
Geraldton 228
Ghan (train) **282,** 282–283
Gibb River Road, Western Australia
235, 238–239
Glass House Mountains 146
Glebe, Sydney 95
Glenelg **259,** 259–260
Gloucester Tree 224–225
Gold Coast **144,** 144–145, 315,
372–373
Gold mining 28, **46–47,** 46–48,
240–241, 320–321
Golf 359, 389
Goolwa 275–276
Gordon River 345
Gorge Scenic Drive, Beechworth 317
Government House, Adelaide 256
Government House, Melbourne
302
Government House, Sydney 84
Governor La Trobe's Cottage,
Melbourne 302
Grafton 121
Grampians NP **326,** 326–327
Great Barrier Reef 154–165
cruises 160
diving and snorkeling 158, 168
hotels and restaurants 373–374
islands 158–165

map 155
reef formation **156,** 156–157
threats 159
wildlife 70, 125, **154, 156–157,**
157–158, **158, 163**
Great Dividing Range 308
Great Keppel Island 161
Great Northern Highway 222, 234
Great Ocean Road, Victoria 310–
315, **314,** 384
map 310–311
Great Ocean Walk 313
Great Sandy NP 149
Green Island 165
Gulf Developmental Highway 177
Gulf of Carpentaria 177–179
Gulf Track 178

**H**
Hahndorf 261–262
Hamelin Pool 229
Hamilton Island 163
Hartz Mountains NP 338
Hawkesbury River 118
Hayman Island 164
Healesville Wildlife Sanctuary
125, 308
Health see Medicine and health
Henley-on-Todd regatta, Alice
Springs 199, 356
Hellyer Gorge State Reserve 349
Henbury Meteor Craters 201
Hermannsburg community 201
Heron Island 160–161
Heysen Trail 262, 279
HIKING
New South Wales 105, 115,
205
Queensland 145–146, 165, 205
South Australia 262, 279
Sydney 77, 205
Tasmania 205, 342–343, 345,
346–347, 349
trails 205
Victoria 205, 313, 316–317,
328
Western Australia 205
Hinchinbrook Island 165
Hippies 120
History 32–55
convicts 39–42
exploration and discovery
33–39, 43–45
gold rushes 28, **46–47,** 46–48,
240–241, 320–321
government and politics 48–49,
54–55
immigration **51,** 52–53
prehistory 32–33
settlement 42–43
World War I **48,** 49–50
World War II 50–52, 186, 187
Hobart **334,** 334–337, 384–385
map 335
Holidays 50, 134, 356–357, 363
Hook Island 163
Horse racing 111, 176, 297, **297**
Horseback riding 115

Hotels and restaurants
  accommodations 367
  farm stays 136
  restaurant variety 25, 367
  tipping 10, 364
  underground lodging 281
  Australian Capital Territory
    370–371
  Melbourne 293
  New South Wales 105,
    369–370
  Northern Territory 376–378
  Queensland 371–376
  South Australia 281, 379–382
  Sydney 368–369
  Tasmania 384–385
  Victoria 293, 303, 312,
    382–384
  Western Australia 239,
    245–246, 378–379
Hotham, Mount **316,** 317
Houseboats 118, 276
Hunter Islands 354
Hunter Valley **110,** 110–111,
  369–370
Huon Valley, Tasmania 338–339
  map 339
Hyde Park, Sydney **76,** 89
Hydro Majestic Hotel, Medlow
  Bath 105

**I**

Ian Potter Centre: NGV Australia,
  Melbourne 298, 299
Immigration **51,** 52–53
Indian Pacific train 248
Inoculations 365
Insects 365
Insurance 357
Internet 362, 366
Introduced species 72, 352
Irwin, Steve 145

**J**

Jabiru 189
Jellyfish 69, 197
Jenolan Caves 108
Jewel Cave 227
Jim Jim Falls 191
Jindabyne 114–115

**K**

Kakadu NP 172, **172,** 173, **188,**
  183–191, **190,** 209
  hotels and restaurants 377
  shopping 386
Kalbarri NP 222, 228–229
Kalgoorlie **240,** 240–241, **243**
Kangaroo Island 125, 268–271, **269,**
  271, 274, 332
  Flinders Chase NP 205, 269,
    270, 271, **271**
Kangaroos 66–67, 67–68, **68**
Karumba 178
Kata-Tjuta **204,** 207–208
Katherine 194–195, 283, 288
Katoomba 104–105

Kayaking 167
Kelly, Ned **322,** 323
Keppel Bay Islands NP 161
Kiama 112–113
Killer Whale Museum, Eden 113
Kimberley region **66,** 218, **234,**
  234–235, 378–379
King Island 354
Kings Cross, Sydney 77, 94–95
Kings Park, Perth 216
Koalas **&** 67–68, **125**
  sanctuaries 100, 125, 143
  viewing 9, 68, 120, 125, 270,
    **271**
Kosciuszko NP **101,** 114–115, 173,
  205
Kununurra 235
Kuranda 171
Kuranda Scenic Railway 170–171

**L**

Lady Elliott Island 159, 168
Lady Musgrave Island 159–160
Lake Gairdner NP 286
Lamington NP 145–146
Language 19, 54
Larrimah 288
Launceston 351, 385
Laura 176
Lava tubes 177
Lawn Hill NP 178–180, **179**
Leeuwin, Cape 227
Lesbian and gay travelers 362
Leura 105
Light, William 252–253
Light's Vision, Adelaide 253
Lindeman Island 163
Lion Arts Centre, Adelaide 256
Liquor laws 362
Litchfield NP **192,** 192–193
Literature 56, 58–59, 225
Living Desert Sculptures 177
Lizard Island **154,** 165, 168
Lizards 69
Lofty, Mount 261, **263**
Loggerhead turtles 154, **154**
Longreach 152–153
Lord Howe Island 122–124, **126,**
  173
Lorne 312
Lost City 193
Luna Park, St. Kilda 304

**M**

MacDonnell Ranges 199–201, **201**
MacKillop, Mother Mary 256
Magnetic Island 164, 167, 374–375
Mail service 281, 361, 363
Main Yarra Trail, Victoria 305
Maldon 321
Mamu Rainforest Canopy Walkway
  174
Manly 78
Manly Beach, Sydney 97
Mannum 276–277
Maps
  Adelaide 252–253
  Australian Capital Territory 129

Brisbane 141
Canberra 131
Darwin 185
exploration 34–35, 40
Gibb River Road 238–239
Great Barrier Reef 155
Great Ocean Road, Victoria
  310–311
Hobart 335
Huon Valley, Tasmania 339
Melbourne 300–301
New South Wales 102–103,
  119
Northern Territory 183
outlying territories 123
Perth 214–215
Queensland 138–139, 150–151
scenic loop drive, Tasmania
  350–351
South Australia 251, 285
Stuart Highway 285
Sydney 74–75
Sydney Harbour, Sydney 83
Tasmania 330–331, 339,
  350–351
Tropic of Capricorn 150–151
Victoria 290–291, 310–311
Western Australia 213,
  238–239
Margaret River **226,** 226–227
Markets 256, 294, 303
Mataranka 288
McLaren Vale 263, **263**
Meat pies 258
Medicine and health 20, 77, 199,
  365
Medlow Bath 105
Melbourne **4, 292,** 292–303
  bicycling 305
  Block Arcade 303
  boat trips 302
  Central Mall **289**
  cooking lessons 218
  Crown Casino 295–296
  festivals 356, 357
  Fitzroy 296
  Fitzroy Gardens 303
  Flinders Street Railway Station
    298, **298**
  Government House 302
  Governor La Trobe's Cottage
    302
  horse racing 297, **297**
  hotels and restaurants 293, 303,
    382–384
  Ian Potter Centre: NGV
    Australia 298, 299
  Main Yarra Trail 305
  map 300–301
  Melbourne Museum 295
  NGV International 298, 299
  Old Treasury Building 303
  Prahran 296
  Queen Victoria Market 294,
    303
  Richmond 296
  Royal Botanic Gardens **295,**
    299, 302, **302**
  Royal Melbourne Zoological
    Gardens 295

shopping 303, 386, 387
Shrine of Remembrance 302
Southgate 299, 305
walks 296, 298–303
Williamstown 302
Young & Jackson Hotel 298
Melbourne Cup 297, **297**
Melville Island 197
Meteors 201
Migration Museum, Adelaide 257
Mildura 324–325, 384
Mindil Beach, Darwin 187
Mines and mining 28–31
    Argyle Diamond Mine **234,** 235
    Battery Hill Mining Centre 287
    Broken Hill 116–117
    gold mining **46–47,** 46–48,
       240–241, 320–321
    Mount Isa 178
    Olympic Dam mine 284, 286
    opals 280–281
    Ranger Uranium Mine 189
    sapphires 151–152
Mint, Sydney 89
Mirima NP 235
Mobile phones 362
Monasteries 219
Money 11, 363
Monkey Mia 125, **228,** 229
Morning Glory phenomenon 177
Mornington Peninsula **306,**
   306–307
Mossman Gorge 169
Mount Buffalo NP 317
Mount Hypipamee NP 171
Mount Isa 178
Mount Lofty Ranges 261, **263**
Mount William NP 349
Movies *see* Cinema
Mrs. Macquarie's Point, Sydney
   82, 84
Mungo NP **29,** 325
Murray Bridge 276–277
Murray River 276–277, **277, 324,**
   324–325, 382
Murray River Valley 266
Museum of Australian Democracy,
   Canberra 132
MUSEUMS
   Art Gallery of Ballarat 320
   Art Gallery of New South
     Wales, Sydney 82, **82**
   Art Gallery of South Australia,
     Adelaide 257
   Australian Museum, Sydney 89
   Australian National Maritime
     Museum, Sydney 93
   Australian Stockman's Hall of
     Fame, Longreach 152–153
   Fremantle History Museum,
     Fremantle 218
   Goolwa Museum, Goolwa 275
   Ian Potter Centre: NGV
     Australia, Melbourne 298,
     299
   Killer Whale Museum, Eden 113
   Melbourne Museum,
     Melbourne 295
   Migration Museum, Adelaide
     257

Mint, Sydney 89
Museum of Australian
   Democracy, Canberra 132
National Film & Sound Archive,
   Canberra 132
National Gallery of Australia,
   Canberra 65, 135
National Museum of Australia,
   Canberra 132
NGV International, Melbourne
   298, 299
Northern Territory Museum
   of Arts & Sciences, Darwin
   186–187
Powerhouse Museum, Sydney
   92
Qantas Founders Museum,
   Longreach 153
Queensland Maritime Museum,
   Brisbane 142
South Australian Museum,
   Adelaide 257
Sovereign Hill, Ballarat **320,**
   320–321
Waltzing Matilda Centre,
   Winton 153
Western Australian Maritime
   Museum, Fremantle 218
Whale World, Albany 225
White's Mineral Art Gallery
   & Mining Museum, Broken
   Hill 117
Music **57,** 59–60, **60,** 109, **109**
Mutawinji NP 117


**N**

Nambung NP 173, 216
Naracoorte Caves Park 266
Narcotics 357
National Film & Sound Archive,
   Canberra 132
National Gallery of Australia,
   Canberra 65, 135
National Library of Australia,
   Canberra 131
National Museum of Australia,
   Canberra 132
National Trust 363
New Norcia 219, **219**
New South Wales 101–126
   Blue Mountains **104,** 104–105,
     369
   Broken Hill **116,** 116–117
   drive 118–121
   hiking 105, 205
   hotels and restaurants 105,
     369–370
   Hunter Valley **110,** 110–111,
     369–370
   Jenolan Caves 108
   Kosciuszko NP **101,** 114–115,
     173, 205
   maps 102–103, 119
   national parks office 366
   National Trust 363
   Pacific Highway drive 118–121,
     **121**
   Snowy Mountains **101, 114,**
     114–115, 370

south coast **112,** 112–113, 370
surfing 389
Tamworth 109, **109**
tourism website 366
wine regions 111
*see also* Sydney
New Year's Eve 98, **99**
Newcastle 118
Newspapers 363
Newtown, Sydney 77, 95
NGV International, Melbourne
   298, 299
Nimbin 120
Ningaloo Marine Park 125, 168,
   **230,** 230–231, 379
Nitmiluk NP 194, **194,** 195
Noosa Heads 147
Noosa NP **146,** 147
Norfolk Island 124
Normanton 177
North Adelaide, Adelaide 258
North Terrace, Adelaide 254, 255
Northern Queensland 166–171,
   174–180
   Atherton Tablelands 170–171,
     **171**
   Cairns 160, **166,** 167–168,
     375, 386
   Cape Tribulation 169–170,
     375–376
   Cape York Peninsula 174–177,
     **175**
   Gulf of Carpentaria 177–179
   Lawn Hill NP 178–180, **179**
   Port Douglas 160, 168–169,
     375
   Townsville 166–167, 374–375
Northern Territory 181–210
   Alice Springs **198,** 198–201,
     286
   Arnhem Land **32–33,** 196–197,
     209
   Darwin 184–187
   hiking 205
   hotels and restaurants 376–378
   Kakadu NP 172, **172,** 173, **188,**
     188–191, **190,** 209, 377, 386
   Katherine 194–195, 283, 288
   Litchfield NP **192,** 192–193
   map 183
   national parks office 366
   National Trust 363
   Nitmiluk NP 194, **194,** 195
   shopping 386
   Tiwi Islands 197
   tourism website 366
   Uluru–Kata Tjuta NP 173, 204,
     **204,** 206–208, **207**
   Watarrka NP 210, **210,**
     377–378
Northern Territory Museum of Arts
   & Sciences, Darwin 186–187
Nourlangie 190
Nullarbor Plain 243–248


**O**

Old Treasury Building, Melbourne
   303
Olgas *see* Kata-Tjuta
Olympic Dam mine 284, 286

Online services 362, 366
Opals 31, 280–281, 387
Orpheus Island 164
Otway, Cape 313
Outback 18–20, 237, 242, **355**
  schools 20, 153, 195, 199
Overland Track, Tasmania 205,
  346–347

**P**
Pacific Highway 118–121, **121**
Package tours 358–359
Paddington, Sydney 77, 94
Painting 64–65, **65**, 117
PARKS
  national parks 172–173, 366
  Arthur's Seat SP 306
  Barrington Tops NP 118, 120
  Ben Boyd NP 113
  City Botanic Gardens, Brisbane
    142–143
  Cleland Wildlife Park **260**, 261
  Cooloola NP 147–148
  Cradle Mountain–Lake St. Clair
    NP 173, **346**, 346–347
  Daintree NP **30, 169**, 169–170,
    173, 375–376
  Dandenong Ranges NP 309
  Dorrigo NP 120
  El Questro Wilderness Park
    238–239
  Elder Park, Adelaide 256
  Finke NP 201
  Fitzgerald River NP 222
  Flinders Chase NP 205, 269,
    270, 271, **271**
  Flinders Ranges NP 209,
    277–279, **279**, 382
  Fossil Mammal sites 173,
    179–180
  Franklin-Gordon Wild Rivers NP
    345, **345**
  Fraser Island 148–149, **149,**
    172–173, 373
  Freycinet NP 173, **348**, 350
  Grampians NP **326**, 326–327
  Great Sandy NP 149
  Hartz Mountains NP 338
  Hellyer Gorge State Reserve
    349
  Kakadu NP 172, **172**, 173, **188**,
    188–191, **190**, 209, 377, 386
  Kalbarri NP 222, 228–229
  Keppel Bay Islands NP 151
  Kings Park, Perth 216
  Kosciuszko NP **101**, 114–115,
    173, 205
  Lake Gairdner NP 286
  Lamington NP 145–146
  Lawn Hill NP 178–180, **179**
  Litchfield NP **192**, 192–193
  Lord Howe Island 122–124,
    **126**, 173
  Mirima NP 235
  Mount Buffalo NP 317
  Mount Hypipamee NP 171
  Mount William NP 349
  Mungo NP **29**, 325

Mutawinji NP 117
Nambung NP 173, 216
Naracoorte Caves Park 266
Ningaloo Marine Park 125, 168,
  **230**, 230–231, 379
Nitmiluk NP 194, **194**, 195
Noosa NP **146**, 147
Point Nepean NP 307
Port Campbell NP 173
Purnululu NP 173, **236**,
  236–237
Rocky Cape NP 348
Royal NP 112, 172
Shark Bay NP 172
Southern Queensland national
  parks 145–146
Southwest NP **342**, 342–343
Springbrook NP 146
Tunnel Creek NP 239
Uluru-Kata Tjuta NP 173, 204,
  **204**, 206–208, **207**, 209
Walpole-Nornalup NP 222, 225
Watarrka NP 210, **210**,
  377–378
Wilsons Promontory NP 328
  see also Zoos and wildlife parks
Parliament House, Adelaide 255
Parliament House, Brisbane 143
Parliament House, Canberra
  132–133
Passports 357
Paterson, A. B. "Banjo" 16, 56, **58,**
  115, 153
Pearling industry 232
Pemberton 224–225
Penal colonies see Prisons and
  prisoners
Penguins 307
Penola 266
Perth **107**, 214–216, 378
  map 214–215
Phillip Island 125, 307
Photography 208, 296, 363
Pichi Pichi railroad, Quorn 278
Pie floaters 258
Plants see Flora
Platypuses 261
Point Nepean NP 307
Poisonous animals 69, 197, 365
Pokolbin 110
Poms (British) 54
Port Adelaide 260
Port Arthur **38–39, 340**, 340–341
Port Campbell NP 173
Port Douglas 160, 168–169, 375
Port Fairy 315, 356
Port Lincoln 246
Port Macquarie 120
Post offices 287, 351, 363
Powerhouse Museum, Sydney 92
Prahran, Melbourne 296
Prehistory 32–33
Prisons and prisoners 39–42, 124,
  218, 340–341
*Puffing Billy* (train) 309, **309**
Purnululu NP 173, **236**, 236–237

**Q**
Qantas Founders Museum,
  Longreach 153
Queen Victoria Building, Sydney 88
Queen Victoria Market, Melbourne
  294, 303
Queenscliff 311–312
Queensland 137–180
  Brisbane **42–43**, 140–143,
    371–372
  cooking lessons 218
  Great Barrier Reef 70, 125,
    154–165, 168, 373–374
  hiking 205
  hotels and restaurants 371–376
  maps 138–139, 150–151
  national parks office 366
  National Trust 363
  Northern Queensland 160,
    166–171, 174–180,
    375–376, 386
  Southeast Queensland 144–149
  surfing 389
  Tropic of Capricorn drive
    150–153
Queensland Maritime Museum,
  Brisbane 142
Queenstown 349–350
Quinkan Reserve Aboriginal rock
  art galleries 176
Quokkas 221
Quorn 278

**R**
Rabbits 72
Radio 363
Ranger Uranium Mine 189
Restaurants see Hotels and
  restaurants
Richmond, Melbourne 296
Richmond, Tasmania 350
Right whales 275, 313
Riversleigh Fossil Site 179–180
Rock art **32–33**, 176, 179, 188–189,
  190, 202–203, 327
Rockhampton 150
Rocks area, Sydney **73**, 76, 84–85
Rocky Cape NP 348
Rottnest Island **220**, 220–221, 379
Royal Botanic Gardens, Melbourne
  **295**, 299, 302, **302**
Royal Botanic Gardens, Sydney 78,
  84, 98
Royal Flying Doctor Service 20, 199
Royal Melbourne Zoological
  Gardens, Melbourne 295
Royal NP 112, 172

**S**
Sailing 389
St. Andrew's Cathedral, Sydney 88
St. Clair, Lake 350
St. Kilda 296, 304, **304**
St. Peter's Cathedral, Adelaide
  **257**, 258
Salamanca Place, Hobart 336
Salt pans 286
Saltwater crocodiles 191, 197

Sandy Creek Falls 193
Sapphires 151–152
Scenic loop drive, Tasmania
    348–351
    map 350–351
Schanck, Cape 306, **306**
Schools, outback 20, 153, 195, 199
Scone 111
Scuba diving **71**, 158, 168, 221, 388
Sea kayaking 167
Seaplanes 79
Senior travelers 364
Seven Hiills Winery, Clare Valley
    **264**, 266
Seven Mile Beach 113
Seven Spirit Bay 196–197
Shark Bay 172, **228**, 228–229
Sharks 70, **71**, 197, **230**, 230–231
Shipwrecks 312, 315
Shopping 386–387
    Aboriginal art 203, 386
    markets 256, 294, 303
    opals 31, 387
    opening hours 363
Shrine of Remembrance,
    Melbourne 302
Silverton **116**, 117
Simpson's Gap 200–201
Six Foot Track 108
Skiing **114**, 115, 316, **316**, 317
Skin cancer 77
Snakes 69, 197, 365
Snorkeling 158, **164**, 221, 231
Snowy Mountains **101**, **114**,
    114–115, 370
Snowy River 115
South Australia
    Aboriginal experiences 209
    Adelaide 252–258, 272–273,
        356, 357, 379–381, 386
    Adelaide area 125, 205, 209,
        **249**, 259–263, 266–271,
        274–279, 381–382
    Coober Pedy **280**, 280–281,
        286, 382
    cooking lessons 218
    entry from Western Australia
        247–248
    festivals **272**, 272–273, 356,
        357
    Ghan (train) **282**, 282–283
    hiking 205
    hotels and restaurants 281,
        379–382
    maps 251, 285
    national parks office 366
    National Trust 363
    Stuart Highway drive 284–288
    surfing 389
    tourism website 366
    wine regions 111, 263, **263**,
        266–268
South Australian Museum, Adelaide
    257
South coast, New South Wales **112**,
    112–113, 370
South Coast Track, Tasmania
    342–343

Southeast Queensland 144–149
    Fraser Island 148–149, **149**,
        172–173, 373
    Gold Coast **144**, 144–145, 315,
        372–373
    national parks 145–146
    Sunshine Coast 146–148, 373
Southern Vales 263
Southgate, Melbourne 299, 305
Southwest, Western Australia **224**,
    224–225, 379
Southwest wilderness, Tasmania
    **342**, 342–343
Sovereign Hill, Ballarat **320**,
    320–321
Spiders 69, 197, 365
Springbrook NP 146
Standley Chasm 201, **201**
Stanley 348–349
State Library, Adelaide 256–257
State Library of New South Wales,
    Sydney 89
State Parliament House, Sydney 89
Stations 18–20, **20–21**, 153, 195,
    281
Steamboats 276–277, **277**, 325
Story Bridge, Brisbane 143
Stuart Highway 284–288
    map 285
Sun Pictures, Broome 233
Sunburn 365
Sunshine Coast 146–148, 373
Super Pit, Kalgoorlie 241
Surf rescue **52–53**, 97
Surfers Paradise 144, **144**, 145
Surfing **15**, 226, 312, 315, 388–389
Swimming 69, 97, 226, 231, 364
Sydney 73–100
    airport 359
    Art Gallery of New South Wales
        82, **82**
    Asian culture 77
    Australian Museum 89
    Australian National Maritime
        Museum 93
    Balmain 95
    Balmoral 97
    biking 77
    boat trips 78, 79
    bohemian Sydney 94–95
    Bondi Beach 77, **96**, 96–97
    Cabramatta 77
    Chinese Garden 93
    Circular Quay 74, 76, 84, **85**
    cooking lessons 218
    Darling Harbour 77, 92–93
    Darlinghurst 77, 94–95
    downtown Sydney **88**, 88–89
    Elizabeth Bay 95
    Featherdale Wildlife Park 100
    gay and lesbian life **94**, 94–95
    Glebe 95
    Government House 84
    hiking 77, 205
    hotels and restaurants 368–369
    Hyde Park **76**, 89
    Hyde Park Barracks 89
    Kings Cross 77, 94–95

Koala Park Sanctuary 100
Manly Beach 97
maps 74–75, 83
Mint 89
monorail **92**
Mrs. Macquarie's Point 82, 84
New Year's Eve 98, **99**
Newtown 77, 95
Paddington 77, 94
Powerhouse Museum 92
Priscilla tours 95
Queen Victoria Building 88
Rocks area **73**, 76, 84–85
Royal Botanic Gardens 78,
    84, 98
St. Andrew's Cathedral 88
shopping 386, 387
State Library of New South
    Wales 89
State Parliament House 89
surfing 315
Sydney Aquarium 92–93
Sydney Fish Market 93
Sydney Harbour **16–17**, **78**,
    78–87, 98
Sydney Harbour Bridge 64, **78**,
    **80–81**, 81, 85
Sydney Opera House **60**, 84,
    86–87, **86–87**
Sydney Tower **88**, 89
Sydney Town Hall 88
Taronga Park Zoo 98, 100, **100**
transportation 77
walks 79, 82–85

**T**
Tahune Forest Reserve 338
Tamworth 109, **109**
Tandanya, Adelaide 257–258
Taronga Park Zoo, Sydney 98,
    100, **100**
Tasmania 329–354
    Aborigines 332–333
    Bass Strait Islands 354
    Cradle Mountain-Lake St. Clair
        NP 173, **346**, 346–347
    environmentalism 344, **344**
    ferry 333
    Franklin-Gordon Wild Rivers NP
        345, **345**
    hiking 205
    Hobart **334**, 334–337,
        384–385
    hotels and restaurants 384–385
    Huon Valley drive 338–339
    maps 330–331, 339, 350–351
    Mount Wellington 337, **337**
    national parks office 366
    National Trust 363
    Port Arthur **38–39**, **340**,
        340–341
    scenic loop drive 348–351
    Southwest wilderness **342**,
        342–343
    surfing 389
    tourism website 366
    trout fishing **352**, 352–353
    wildlife viewing 125
    wine regions 111

Tasmanian devils **329**, 343
Tasmanian tigers 349
Taxis 10
Telephones 362
Television 61–63, 363
Tennant Creek 287
Tennis 389
Territory Wildlife Park 193
Theater 59, 256
Theme parks 145, 304
Thorsborne Trail 165, 205
Three Sisters 105
Thursday Island 176
Tidbinbilla Deep Space Tracking
    Station 132
Tidbinbilla Nature Reserve 132
Time zones 364
Tipping 10, 364
Tiwi people 197
Tjaynera Falls 193
Toads 180
Tolmer Falls 193
Torquay 312
Torres Straits Islands 176
Tourism offices 365–366
Townsville 166–167, 374–375
Trains 283, 361
    Ghan **282**, 282–283
    Indian Pacific train 248
    Kuranda Scenic Railway
      170–171
    Pichi Pichi railroad, Quorn 278
    *Puffing Billy* (train) 309, **309**
Trams 293
Transportation 358–361
    *see also* Boat trips; Trains
Travel insurance 357
Tree climbing 224–225
Tribulation, Cape 169–170, 375–376
Tropic of Capricorn drive 150–153
    map 150–151
Trout fishing **352**, 352–353
Tunnel Creek NP 239
Turtles 147, **154**
Twelve Apostles 313, **313**
Twin Falls 191

**U**
Ubirr 190–191
Uluru **26–27**, 204, 206–207, **207**,
    386
Uluru–Kata Tjuta NP 173, 204, **204**,
    206–208, **207**, 209
Undara Lava Tubes 177

**V**
Vegemite 25
Vegetation *see* Flora
Victor Harbor **274**, 274–275
Victoria 289–328
    alpine country 316–317
    bicycling 305
    bushfires 106
    Dandenong Ranges NP 309
    goldfields 320–321
    Grampians NP **326**, 326–327
    Great Ocean Road 310–315,
      384

hotels and restaurants 293, 303,
    312, 382–384
Main Yarra Trail 305
maps 290–291, 310–311
Melbourne **4**, 218, **289**,
    292–303, 305, 356, 357,
    382–384, 386, 387
Mornington Peninsula **306**,
    306–307
Murray River **324**, 324–325
national parks office 366
National Trust 363
St. Kilda 296, 304, **304**
surfing 389
Wilsons Promontory NP 328
wine regions 111, 308
Yarra Valley 308
Video 363
Vineyards *see* Wines and wineries
Visas 357
Volunteer opportunities 255, 364

**W**
**WALKS**
    Melbourne 296, 298–303
    Sydney 79, 82–85
Wallace, Kathleen **202**
Walpole-Nornalup NP 222, 225
Waltzing Matilda Centre, Winton
    153
Wangi Falls 193
War memorials **134**, 135–136, 302
Warrnambool 313, 315
Watarrka NP 210, **210**, 377–378
Wave Rock 225
Weather 10, 26–27, 356
Websites, informational 366
Wellington, Mount 337, **337**
Western Australia 211–248
    Aboriginal experiences 209
    Boulder 241
    Broome **232**, 232–233, 378
    cooking lessons 218
    drives 238–239
    Eyre Highway 243–248
    Fremantle **217**, 217–218
    Gibb River Road 235, 238–239
    hiking 205
    hotels and restaurants 239,
      245–246, 378–379
    Kalgoorlie **240**, 240–241, **243**
    Kimberley region **66**, 218, **234**,
      234–235, 378–379
    maps 213, 238–239
    Margaret River **226**, 226–227
    national parks office 366
    National Trust 363
    New Norcia 219, **219**
    Ningaloo Marine Park 125, 168,
      **230**, 230–231, 379
    Nullarbor Plain 243–248
    Perth **107**, 214–216, 378
    Purnululu NP 173, **236**,
      236–237
    roadhouses 245–246
    Rottnest Island **220**, 220–221,
      379
    Shark Bay 172, **228**, 228–229

    Southwest **224**, 224–225, 379
    surfing 315, 389
    tourism website 366
    wildflowers **222**, 222–223, **223**
    wine regions 111, 227
Western Australian Maritime
    Museum, Fremantle 218
Whale sharks **230**, 230–231
Whale World, Albany 225
Whales 227, 275, 313, 315
White Cliffs 117
White-water rafting 389
White's Mineral Art Gallery &
    Mining Museum, Broken
    Hill' 117
Whitsunday Islands 161–164
Wildflowers *see* Flora
Wildlife 66–72
    dangerous 69–70, 197, 365
    threats to 72, 180, 352
    *see also* Zoos and wildlife parks;
      specific animals
Williamstown, Melbourne 302
Wilpena Pound 278–279
Wilsons Promontory NP 328
Windsor Hotel, Melbourne 303
Wines and wineries 111, **264**,
    264–265, 387
    Adelaide area 263, **263**,
      266–268
    Hunter Valley **110**, 110–111
    Margaret River 227
    Victoria 111, 308
Winton **152**, 153
Winton, Tim 225
Wollongong 112, **112**
Woomera 225
World War I **48**, 49–50
World War II 50–52, 186, 187
Wyndham 209, 238
Wynyard 348

**Y**
Yallingup 227
Yarra Valley 308
Yellow Water 191
Young & Jackson Hotel,
    Melbourne 298

**Z**
Zeehan 349
Zoos and wildlife parks
    Brisbane 125, 143
    Cleland Wildlife Park **260**, 261
    Healesville Wildlife Sanctuary
      125, 308
    Melbourne 295
    Sunshine Coast 125, 147
    Sydney 93, 98, 100, **100**, 125
    Territory Wildlife Park 193
    Tidbinbilla Nature Reserve 132

# ILLUSTRATIONS CREDITS

2-3, Roger Ressmeyer/Corbis; 4, Dave G. Houser/
Corbis; 8, Eric Isselée/Shutterstock; 11, Craig
Lamotte/Corbis; 12, Debra James/Dreamstime.com;
13, Laviana/Shutterstock; 15, ASP/Pierre Tostee/
Reuters/Corbis; 16-17, SuperStock; 20-21, Sorrel
Wilby/Australian Geographic Images; 22, Carolyn
Johns/Wildlight; 24, Bjorn Austraat/iStockphoto.
com; 26-27, Gary Bell/Oceanwidelmages.com;
29, Jiri Lochman/Lochman Transparencies; 30,
Sam Abell/NGS Image Collection; 32-33, Penny
Tweedie/Corbis; 37, Coo-ee Picture Library; 38-39,
John Carnemolla/Corbis; 42-43, "South Brisbane
from the North Shore, Moreton Bay, Australia,"
1868, Baines, Thomas (1820-75)/© National Library
of Australia, Canberra, Australia/The Bridgeman Art
Library; 46-47, "Australian Gold Diggings," c.1855,
Stocqueler, Edwin (1829-c.1880)/© National Library
of Australia, Canberra, Australia/The Bridgeman Art
Library; 48, Hulton Archive/Getty Images; 51, David
Moore/Wildlight; 52-53, Annie Griffiths Belt/NGS
Image Collection; 55, Medford Taylor/NGS Image
Collection; 57, Lorrie Graham/Wildlight; 58, Coo-ee
Picture Library; 60, Australian Tourist Commission;
63, A. Baker/AA Photo Library; 65, Charles Meere,
"Australian beach pattern," 1940, oil on canvas,
91.5x122cm, The Art Gallery of New South Wales,
© Margaret Stephenson-Meere, reproduced with
permission. Photo: Jenni Carter for AGNSW; 66-67,
Sam Abell/NGS Image Collection; 68, Jean-Paul Fer-
rero/Getty Images; 71, Jeffrey L. Rotman/Corbis; 73,
Chee-Onn Leong/Shutterstock; 76, weareadventur-
ers/iStockphoto.com; 78, Paul Souders/WorldFoto;
82, Philip Quirk/Wildlight; 85, P. Kenward/AA
Photo Library; 88, Phillip Minnis/Shutterstock; 90,
Paul Kane/Getty Images; 92, Sergio Pitamitz/Corbis;
94, Tom Keating/Wildlight; 96, Danielle Williams;
99, Mick Tsikas/epa/Corbis; 100, Steve Day/AA
Photo Library; 101, Andres Ello/Shutterstock; 104,
Chee-Onn Leong/Shutterstock; 106, Sam D'cruz/
Dreamstime.com; 107, Negativea_digital_photog-
raphy/Dreamstime.com; 109, Ross Beckley; 110,
Jonathan Marks/Corbis; 112, Jonathan Marks/
Corbis; 114, Sin Tong Chong/Dreamstime.com; 116,
Spectrum Colour Library; 121, Jonathan Marks/
Corbis; 122, Lord Howe Island Tourism Associa-
tion; 125, Iain Curry/Dreamstime.com; 126, Paul
Wright/Corbis; 127, Simona Dumitru/Dreamstime.
com; 128, Jonathan Marks/Corbis; 130, Jose Fuste
Raga/Corbis; 134, Paul Souders/WorldFoto; 137,
David Doubilet/NGS Image Collection; 140, Patrick
Oberem/iStockphoto.com; 144, Richard Eastwood/
Corbis; 146, Nick Rains/Corbis; 149, Mark Lang/
Wildlight; 152, Craig Lamotte/Corbis; 154, Gary
Bell/Oceanwidelmages.com; 158, Gary Bell/Ocean-
widelmages.com; 161, Greg Hard/Wildlight; 163,
Gary Bell/Oceanwidelmages.com; 164, Robert Hol-
mes/Corbis; 166, Nick Rains/Corbis; 169, George
Grall/NGS Image Collection; 171, Ian Courtney/

Australian Butterfly Sanctuary; 172, Leo Meier/
Corbis; 175, Sam Abell/NGS Image Collection; 179,
Peter Jarver Gallery; 181, Ralph A. Clevenger/Corbis;
184, George Clerk/iStockphoto.com; 188, Mogens
Trolle/Shutterstock; 189, Paul A. Souders/Corbis;
192, Dennis Sarson/Lochman Transparencies; 194,
Dennis Sarson/Lochman Transparencies; 196, Col
Roberts/Lochman Transparencies; 198, Philip Quirk/
Wildlight; 201, James Davis/Eye Ubiquitous; 202,
John Van Hasselt/Corbis; 204, Andrea Paggiaro/
Dreamstime.com; 207, Paul Souders/WorldFoto;
209, Anne Clark/iStockphoto.com; 210, Dennis Sar-
son/Lochman Transparencies; 211, Kitch Bain/Shut-
terstock; 217, Coo-ee Picture Library; 219, Tourism
Western Australia; 220, Johnny Lye/Dreamstime.
com; 222, Marie Lochman/Lochman Transparen-
cies; 223, Marie Lochman/Lochman Transparencies;
224, Jiri Lochman/Lochman Transparencies; 226,
Paul Morton/iStockphoto.com; 228, Bill Belsen/
Lochman Transparencies; 230, Mike Kelly/Getty
Images; 232, John Carnemolla/Corbis; 234, John
Carnemolla/Corbis; 236, Greg Perry/Shutterstock;
240, Jiri Lochman/Lochman Transparencies; 243,
Mitchell Library, State Library of New South Wales;
244, Ron Ryan/Coo-ee Picture Library; 247, John
Carnemolla/Corbis; 249, Milton Wordley/Wildlight;
254, Benjamin Goode/iStockphoto.com; 257, Stuart
Elflett/Shutterstock; 259, Ron Ryan/ Coo-ee Picture
Library; 260, Courtesy Cleland Wildlife Park; 263,
Milton Wordley/Wildlight; 264, R. Ian Lloyd; 269,
Milton Wordley/Wildlight; 271, John Carnemolla/
Corbis; 272, South Australia Tourism Commission;
274, Matthew Weinel/Dreamstime.com; 277, John
Carnemolla/Corbis; 279, SuperStock; 280, Grahame
McConnell/Australian Geographic Images; 282, Ron
Ryan/Coo-ee Picture Library; 284, Grenville Turner/
Wildlight; 287, Sue Passmore/Eye Ubiquitous; 289,
Neale Cousland/Shutterstock; 292, Ilya Genken/
Shutterstock; 295, Coo-ee Picture Library; 297, AAP
Image/Martin Philby; 298, SuperStock; 302, John
W. Banagan/Getty Images; 304, Ron Ryan/Coo-ee
Picture Library; 306, Kirrily Stewart/Dreamstime.
com; 309, Philip Quirk/Wildlight; 313, Robyn
Mackenzie/Shutterstock; 314, John Baker/Corbis;
316, Mark Lang/Wildlight; 319, Neale Cousland/
Shutterstock; 320, James Davis/Eye Ubiquitous;
322, National Gallery of Australia; 324, Ron Ryan/
Coo-ee Picture Library; 326, Coo-ee Picture Library;
329, Sean Davey/Corbis; 332, Sam Abell/NGS
Image Collection; 334, James Davis/Eye Ubiquitous;
337, Len Stewart/Lochman Transparencies; 340,
Len Stewart/Lochman Transparencies; 342, Tour-
ism Tasmania/Geoff Murray; 344, Coo-ee Picture
Library; 345, Matthew Newton; 346, Gerd Ludwig/
NGS Image Collection; 348, S. Wilby & C. Ciantar/
Lochman Transparencies; 352, Tourism Tasmania/
Dennis Harding; 355, Dennis Sarson/Lochman
Transparencies.

National Geographic

TRAVELER

# Australia

**Published by the National Geographic Society**

John M. Fahey, Jr., *President and Chief Executive Officer*

Gilbert M. Grosvenor, *Chairman of the Board*

Tim T. Kelly, *President, Global Media Group*

John Q. Griffin, *Executive Vice President; President, Publishing*

Nina D. Hoffman, *Executive Vice President; President, Book Publishing Group*

**Prepared by the Book Division**

Barbara Brownell Grogan, *Vice President and Editor in Chief*

Marianne R. Koszorus, *Director of Design*

Barbara A. Noe, *Senior Editor*

Carl Mehler, *Director of Maps*

R. Gary Colbert, *Production Director*

Jennifer A. Thornton, *Managing Editor*

Meredith Wilcox, *Administrative Director, Illustrations*

Cinda Rose, *Series Art Director*

**Staff for this Book**

Lawrence M. Porges, *Project Editor*

Kay Kobor Hankins, *Art Director*

Linda Makarov, *Designer*

Mary Stephanos, *Text Editor*

Connie D. Binder, *Indexer*

Michael McNey, Nicholas P. Rosenbach, and Mapping Specialists, *Map Production*

Stephanie Robichaux, *Editorial Assistant*

Jack Brostrom, Bridget A. English, Maura Walsh, *Contributors*

Al Morrow, *Design Assistant*

**Manufacturing and Quality Management**

Christopher A. Liedel, *Chief Financial Officer*

Phillip L. Schlosser, *Vice President*

Chris Brown, *Technical Director*

Nicole Elliott, *Manager*

Rachel Faulise, *Manager*

**National Geographic Traveler: Australia (Fourth Edition)**

**ISBN: 978-1-4262-0596-5**

First edition: Edited and designed by AA Publishing (a trading name of Automobile Association Developments Limited, whose registered office is Norfolk House, Priestley Road, Basingstoke, Hampshire, England RG24 9NY. Registered number: 1878835).

Drive maps drawn by Chris Orr Associates, Southampton, England

Cutaway illustrations drawn by Malings Partnership, Derby, England

Founded in 1888, the National Geographic Society is one of the largest nonprofit scientific and educational organizations in the world. It reaches more than 285 million people worldwide each month through its official journal, *National Geographic,* and its four other magazines; the National Geographic Channel; television documentaries; radio programs; films; books; videos and DVDs; maps; and interactive media. National Geographic has funded more than 8,000 scientific research projects and supports an education program combating geographic illiteracy.

For more information, please call 1-800-NGS LINE (647-5463) or write to the following address:

National Geographic Society
1145 17th Street N.W.
Washington, D.C. 20036-4688 U.S.A.

Visit us online at www.nationalgeographic.com

For information about special discounts for bulk purchases, please contact National Geographic Books Special Sales: ngspecsales@ngs.org

For rights or permissions inquiries, please contact National Geographic Books Subsidiary Rights: ngbookrights@ngs.org

Printed in China

The Library of Congress has cataloged the first edition as follows:

Smith, Roff Martin.
    National Geographic Traveler. Australia
            p    cm
        Includes index.
        ISBN 0-7922-7431-8 (alk. paper)
        1. Australia—Guidebooks.
        1. National Geographic Society (U.S.)
    11. Title: Australia
    DC16.N37  1999
    914.404'839—dc21            98-54974
                                CIP

The information in this book has been carefully checked and to the best of our knowledge is accurate. However, details are subject to change, and the National Geographic Society cannot be responsible for such changes, or for errors or omissions. Assessments of sites, hotels, and restaurants are based on the author's subjective opinions, which do not necessarily reflect the publisher's opinion.

10/PPS/1

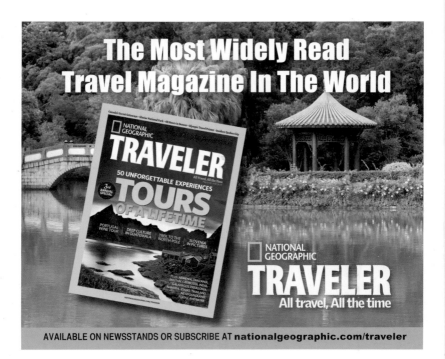